I0130964

PSYCHOLOGY
AND SOCIAL POLICY

PSYCHOLOGY AND SOCIAL POLICY

Edited by

Peter Suedfeld, PhD
University of British Columbia
Vancouver, British Columbia, Canada

Philip E. Tetlock, PhD
University of California
Berkeley, California, USA

Routledge
Taylor & Francis Group

LONDON AND NEW YORK

PSYCHOLOGY AND SOCIAL POLICY

First published 1992 by Hemisphere Publishing Corporation.

Published 2018 by Routledge
2 Park Square, Milton Park, Abingdon, Oxon OX14 4RN
52 Vanderbilt Avenue, New York, NY 10017

First issued in paperback 2018

Routledge is an imprint of the Taylor & Francis Group, an informa business

Copyright © 1992 by Taylor & Francis

All rights reserved. No part of this book may be reprinted or reproduced or utilised in any form or by any electronic, mechanical, or other means, now known or hereafter invented, including photocopying and recording, or in any information storage or retrieval system, without permission in writing from the publishers.

Notice:
Product or corporate names may be trademarks or registered trademarks, and are used only for identification and explanation without intent to infringe.

This book was set in Times Roman by Hemisphere Publishing Corporation. The editors were Nancy Niemann and Carolyn V. Ormes. The production supervisor was Peggy M. Rote; the typesetter was Wayne Hutchins. Cover design by Debra Eubanks Riffe.

A CIP catalog record for this book is available from the British Library.

Library of Congress Cataloging-in-Publication Data

Psychology and social policy / edited by Peter Suedfeld and Philip E. Tetlock.
    p. cm.
    Includes bibliographical references and index.

    1. Policy sciences—Psychological aspects.   2. Social policy—Psychological aspects.   I. Suedfeld, Peter, date.
II. Tetlock, Philip.
H97.P775   1991
361.6′1′019—dc20   91-18349
ISBN 1-56032-063-X   CIP

ISBN 13: 978-1-138-98407-3 (pbk)
ISBN 13: 978-1-56032-063-0 (hbk)

The editors dedicate this book to the people who will have to live with the social policies developed, for better or worse, with influential contributions from our fellow psychologists—in particular, to:

Paul C. Tetlock   Michael T. Suedfeld
Joanne R. Suedfeld Robinson
David L. Suedfeld

Contents

II
DOMESTIC POLICY

III
THE CRIMINAL JUSTICE SYSTEM

Contributors

JOSEPH B. ADELSON, University of Michigan, Ann Arbor, USA
KATHERINE BECKETT, University of California, Los Angeles, USA
WILLIAM R. BEER, Brooklyn College of the City University of New York, USA
LEONARD BERKOWITZ, University of Wisconsin, Madison, USA
JAMES G. BLIGHT, Brown University, Providence, Rhode Island, USA
JAMES BONTA, Ministry Secretariat, Solicitor General of Canada, Ottawa, Ontario,
    Canada
STEVEN CHAFFEE, Stanford University, Stanford, California, USA
MARY T. DZINDOLET, University of Texas, Arlington, USA
ROGERS ELLIOTT, Dartmouth College, Hanover, New Hampshire, USA
LEONARD D. ERON, University of Illinois, Chicago, USA
JONATHAN L. FREEDMAN, University of Toronto, Ontario, Canada
PAUL GENDREAU, University of New Brunswick, St. John, Canada
JANE GOODMAN, University of Washington, Seattle, USA
HUGH JORDAN HARRINGTON, Hughes Aircraft Company, Los Angeles, California,
    USA
L. ROWELL HUESMANN, University of Illinois, Chicago, USA
IRVING L. JANIS, Yale University, New Haven, Connecticut, and University of
    California, Berkeley, USA (Deceased)
JOHN C. KIRCHER, University of Utah, Salt Lake City, USA
JACQUES-PHILIPPE LEYENS, Catholic University of Louvain, Louvain–la Neuve,
    Belgium
DANIEL LINZ, University of California, Santa Barbara, USA
ALAN J. LIZOTTE, State University of New York, Albany, USA
ELIZABETH F. LOFTUS, University of Washington, Seattle, USA
DAVID T. LYKKEN, University of Minnesota, Minneapolis, USA
NEIL M. MALAMUTH, University of California, Los Angeles, USA
LEON MANN, University of Melbourne, Carlton, Victoria, Australia
ROBERT MAURO, University of Oregon, Eugene, USA
LAKE McCLENNEY, Professional School of Psychology, San Francisco, California, USA
MICHAEL E. McCLOSKEY, Johns Hopkins University, Baltimore, Maryland, USA
JUDITH McKENNA, Weinberg & Green, Baltimore, Maryland, USA

NORMAN MILLER, University of Southern California, Los Angeles, USA
PAUL B. PAULUS, University of Texas, Arlington, USA
DAVID C. RASKIN, University of Utah, Salt Lake City, USA
PETER SUEDFELD, University of British Columbia, Vancouver, Canada
PHILIP E. TETLOCK, University of California, Berkeley, USA
HANS TOCH, State University of New York, Albany, USA
MOLLY TREADWAY, Johns Hopkins University, Baltimore, Maryland, USA
CHARLES W. TURNER, University of Utah, Salt Lake City, USA
RALPH K. WHITE, George Washington University, Washington, DC, USA
DOLF ZILLMANN, University of Alabama, Tuscaloosa, USA

Preface

Controversies over social policy are a dominant feature of modern life. Policies must now be developed to deal with many issues that have previously been left to fate or to individual choice. The need for planning continues to grow as the world economy and polity become more interdependent, communication and transportation become more rapid, spheres of decision become more subject to societal and governmental shaping, and possible courses of action are expanded by the progress of science and technology. This book is an examination of the participation of psychology as a science of profession, and psychologists as scientists and professionals, in debates about the policies that might serve as the best means to desired ends.

Such debates increasingly involve appeals to scientific expertise. By now, very few are ever carried on for long without one side or another—usually both—calling on science to buttress a position. Sometimes this is quite appropriate: The best solution to a problem may hinge on scientific knowledge or on the use of the scientific method to gather the knowledge needed. But not all social questions hinge on such data, nor are such data always accessible. Nevertheless, appeals are made to science even when science cannot or should not answer.

Here, we face the phenomenon of inappropriately transferred credibility; for examples, when television stars who appeared in a show fictionalizing a social problem are asked to testify before Congressional committees trying to draft legislation dealing with that problem, or when athletes and popular musicians assume and are granted authoritative roles in disagreements about economics, race relations, education, or foreign policy. The misuse of science is perhaps a less blatant example. Protagonists may offer supposedly fact-based answers when the questions are not factual, as in the argument over the point at which a developing organism should be regarded as a human being. Some debaters may magnify small anomalies in an attempt to discredit a massive data base, as in the "creation science" controversy. One position may be emphasized and others ignored, giving a false picture of consensus even though scientists vigorously disagree, as in the case of global warming. Debaters may extrapolate from minimal evidence to produce monumental speculations, as in the detailed descriptions of "nuclear winter."

The culprits are not only politicians, activists, the media, or the public: Scientists themselves get caught up in the same game. Many people whose professional lives have been dedicated to the careful collection and balanced evaluation of evidence have been known to throw all this overboard when the opportunity arises to use their scientific credibility in the service of some personally important cause. The heat of verbal battle may sweep aside the qualifications that usually characterize conclusions presented in scientific publications.

The social sciences are obviously relevant to many social dilemmas, and people who choose such disciplines may have strong feelings about social issues. Not surprisingly, then, social scientists have enthusiastically drawn upon their training, methods, and status in advocating particular policies. Our own discipline, psychology, has been highly visible in this regard. The introductory chapter presents a tiny sample of *ex cathedra* statements of this sort, issuing from the most prominent psychological societies. Most readers will already know that these organizations have made many such advocacy statements and that a much larger number have been issued by other groups and by individual professionals in psychology, economics, sociology, anthropology, and political science. In fact, almost any newspaper will provide new examples each day.

The purpose of this book is to examine this involvement. The first chapter offers a general analysis of the kinds of issues in which psychology has taken an active role and examines the propriety and possible consequences of advocacy. It also presents some cautionary notes on the role(s) of psychologists, and particularly of their professional associations, in policy debates.

The rest of the book is divided into three major areas: international issues, domestic policies, and criminal justice. Several topics in each area are covered. Each topic is discussed in two chapters. The chapter authors are scientific experts who have well-known positions on the particular topic. We asked each contributor to prepare an independent review of the social science data relevant to policy development on the topic and of the policy positions that had been advocated by social scientists and then to evaluate the adequacy and appropriateness of the recommendations in light of the data.

Each pair of authors was selected on the basis that in the past one had taken an activist stance—that is, made or supported policy recommendations on the basis of existing data—while the other had been less confident that the data would justify recommendations. Neither author saw the contribution of the other prior to writing: We wanted to avoid the danger that personal confrontation might affect the assessment of the scientific evidence. Of course, because both participants were already prominent in the controversy, in a few cases one contributor guessed the identify of the other contributor and targeted the resultant chapter accordingly.

Both we and the contributing authors had some surprises. Some of the controversies we wanted to include—for example, the nature of racism in U.S. society and what to do about it—had to be dropped because no willing spokesperson appeared for one side or the other. In other cases, potential contributors were tired of the controversy or did not wish to re-engage adversaries with whom they had contended in the past. Some of the papers turned out to be uncharacteristically ambivalent, compared with previous writings of the author. Perhaps the knowledge that the chapter would appear in immediate proximity to a critique made the writer less forthright or motivated a new and more cautious set of conclusions. One author who had been recruited to represent a particular side of a controversy was persuaded by his review of the literature that it was the wrong side and wound up in the role opposite to his intended one. We can fairly say that putting this book together was a learning experience, both for ourselves and for at least some of our contributors.

The chapters should be read for their own specific contributions to individual policy debates. The literature reviews and evaluations will be useful in understanding the strengths and weaknesses of the relevant psychological evidence. Beyond that, however, we hope that the paired chapters dealing with each topic will serve as case studies of scientific involvement in policy advocacy, from which appropriate principles and procedures may be derived and generalized.

Peter Suedfeld
Philip E. Tetlock

1

Psychologists as Policy Advocates: The Roots of Controversy

Peter Suedfeld and Philip E. Tetlock

At first glance, the chapters in this book appear to have very little to do with one another. The authors cover an enormous range of intellectual and policy areas: from nuclear deterrence to pornography, from affirmative action to the accuracy of eyewitness testimony. On closer inspection, however, the common theme becomes obvious. In each policy domain, the authors are grappling with the same fundamental question, but often they reach radically different answers. The question is whether behavioral and social scientists, either as individuals or through their professional organizations, have enough evidence to justify their taking sides on controversial political issues, and if so, under what conditions, on what grounds, and in what way.

Looking at the scholarly community at large, it is clear that this question has already been answered, usually in the affirmative. Advocacy positions taken by psychologists, both as individuals and as groups, share the same problems and characteristics, although those taken by groups involve additional issues of consensus, delegation, and legitimacy. But notwithstanding these difficulties, psychologists have expressed themselves freely on a wide range of policy issues.

Many policy-related statements and recommendations have been made by psychologists and by psychology organizations. Among the shared characteristics are a clear stand on one side of a controversial, or at least debatable, issue and the implication that this stand is based on a foundation of knowledge to which psychologists have special access by virtue of their professional training and experience. Consider the following selection of proclamations issued during the past 50 years:

- We, as psychologists, protest most emphatically against the common belief that wars are necessary results of human nature. This opinion is without scientific foundation.—Society for the Psychological Study of Social Issues Council, 1937, quoted in Kimmel (1986).
- [The American Psychological Association (APA) Council of Representatives] urges all members of the APA . . . to work toward the readmission of Israel to full participation in UNESCO [United Nations Educational, Scientific, and Cultural Organization]. . . .—APA Council, 1976.
- [The Council] recognizes officially and makes suitable promulgation of the fact that it is scientifically and psychologically baseless, as well as in violation of

human rights, to discriminate against men because of their sex [in child custody, adoption, child-care occupations, and parental leave].—APA Council, 1977.

• . . . we call upon [the U.S. and the U.S.S.R.] to adopt an immediate mutual freeze on all further testing, production, and deployment of all nuclear warheads, missiles and delivery systems; and . . . upon the Administration and the Congress to transfer the funds saved to civilian use.—APA Council, 1983.

• The American Psychological Association is opposed to any attempts to require by statute or other means the inclusion of "creationism" within the science curriculum of the public schools.—APA Council, 1983.

• The American Psychological Association (1) encourages parents to monitor and to control television viewing by children; (2) requests industry representatives to take a responsible attitude in reducing direct imitable violence . . . and in providing more programming for children designed to mitigate possible effects of television violence, consistent with the guarantees of the First Amendment. . . . —APA Council, 1985.

• Be it resolved that the American Psychological Association: encourage the elimination of both amateur and professional boxing . . . communicate its opposition to boxing to appropriate regulating bodies; assist state psychological societies to work with their state legislatures to enact laws to eliminate boxing. . . .—APA Council, 1986.

ADVOCACY: A CONTROVERSIAL ROLE

Statements of this sort can be viewed in at least two alternate ways. One is that the people making them are exercising their rights as citizens in a democracy in trying to influence public policies; the other is that they are speaking on the basis of knowledge that they have because of their special training and expertise in behavioral science, which is unavailable to the average citizen. In the former case, positions can be based on political ideology, moral codes, or self-interest (see Rudmin, 1986). But the latter viewpoint gives these comments an *ex cathedra* quality. To use a social psychological label, the implication is that the source has "expert knowledge" (French & Raven, 1959) that calls for more than just routine attention to what is said.

Our purpose is to consider this claim. First, we should dispose of the possibility that the claim is not being made. If it were not (that is, if these colleagues were speaking merely in their role as citizens), we would expect such arguments to appear in general-circulation magazines and newspapers, rather than in professional and scientific books and journals (and most prominently in *American Psychologist*, surely the most widely read psychology journal in the world). The authors' professional qualifications and affiliations would be irrelevant and therefore omitted (cf. Rapoport, 1984). At most, the affiliations might be appended (perhaps disingenuously) "for identification only." References in the text to psychological data or theories would be muted or absent. And, of course, we would not have such statements issued as the official positions of the committees and governing councils of professional organizations or of those organizations themselves.

If we accept that involvement in advocacy is based on at least self-perceived special knowledge, what are the main points of the debate? One set of arguments revolves around pragmatic consequences for psychology; another, about the appropriate role of organized psychology in advocacy; and a third, the extent to which the self-perception of relevant expertise is correct. To what extent are the psychological and cognate databases adequate for the justification of advocacy positions? Related to this issue, and to the value of psychological advice on policy, is a concern about the extent to which facts discovered through scientific research can and should be separated from value judgments based on the ideology of the organization or individual.

THE PRAGMATIC ASPECTS OF ADVOCACY

Policy involvement by psychologists has had a long history. In the past century, psychologists in their role as citizens have taken stands on a wide range of controversial issues; and in their role as scientists they have enjoyed a string of successes in developing a knowledge base for improvements in applied practices and principles. In the early part of this century, several leaders of the profession were confident enough about these contributions to believe that large-scale social planning and design should be based on behavioral science research. Skinner's *Walden Two* (1948) is the best-known, but by no means the first, example of this genre (see Morawski, 1982).

Psychologists as citizens have been politically active for as long as psychology has been an identifiable discipline. Our colleagues and our profession have a record of taking positions on controversial issues. We can look back to Hugo Münsterberg's vociferous and generally anathemized opposition to United States' participation in World War I; John Dewey's part in the examination of Stalinist oppression in the 1930s; Wolfgang Köhler's emigration from Germany at least in part because of the Nazi persecution of Jews; the wide-ranging involvement of social psychologists and several of their organizations in criticizing various sociopolitical trends in the United States in the 1940s and 1950s (Harris, Unger, & Stagner, 1986). Also there has been E. C. Tolman's resignation from the University of California over the loyalty oath issue and the more recent support of Soviet dissidents and oppressed Chileans by APA Council resolutions.

It should be emphasized in the context of this book that the cases mentioned above did not directly cite the *imprimatur* of psychological knowledge. While the participants were clearly identified as psychologists, they generally acted from explicitly moral or political positions rather than from any claimed scientific expertise. One may argue that this is one place where science is not value-free, that an open society is a crucial prerequisite for the self-correcting process of generating knowledge, and that this rule applies to knowledge about human behavior (i.e., about the professional field of the scientific psychologist).

In Support of Advocacy

Psychologists devote their professional lives to the study of circumstances, many of which are directly or indirectly related to the state of society and the health and well-being of individuals. One of the officially stated purposes of the American Psychological Association is "to advance psychology . . . as a means of promoting human welfare" (American Psychological Association, 1984). Thus, both our area of concentration and the goal of our profession are consistent with the idea that we have an ethical basis for speaking out on policy issues. It would, in fact, be a violation of APA's purpose and of our ethical obligations as both citizens and professionals not to speak out.

It follows from this position that if psychologists hold themselves aloof from policy debates, there may be serious costs. Not only could they be perceived as uncaring or as self-admittedly irrelevant (Task Force on Psychology and Public Policy, 1986), but useful psychological data and theories could be prevented from reaching a wide public audience. Politics abhors a vacuum; if the research community refrains from involvement in public controversies, someone else—perhaps much less principled and informed—simply will fill the void.

Proponents of advocacy have argued that psychologists are indeed uniquely qualified to investigate the causes of and potential solutions to many social problems. Among these are the concomitants of poverty and discrimination, criminal justice, issues of war and peace, child-rearing, facilities for physically and mentally handicapped people, and so on. Scientific studies in child development, social psychology, cognition, perception, learning, motivation, and physiological psychology can and have shed light on the implications of past and current policies related to these social issues. Perhaps more important, psychological research may help us to anticipate the effects of future policies or, conversely, to design future policies to reach desired effects (see, e.g., Kimmel, 1985). The latter role, that of conducting studies related to possible alternate policies (as opposed to merely evaluating current ones), has been supported even by colleagues generally cautious about psychology's advocacy role (Cook, 1985). The question of legitimate expertise, which is at the heart of the debate, will be considered at length later in this chapter.

Prominent psychologists have strongly supported involvement in policy issues, not only on the substantive grounds of being able to make useful contributions (e.g., Cook, 1984; Deutsch, 1969), but also because such action would increase public support for the profession (DeLeon, 1986; Pallak & Kilburg, 1986; Task Force on Psychology and Public Policy, 1986). In the case of the APA, the degree of support for specific positions is difficult to ascertain, although in at least some instances a majority of members has been shown to favor Council resolutions. Even there, a warning is clear: As survey researchers are well aware, the result will depend on how the question is worded (see Schumann & Presser, 1981, on the sometimes dramatic differences resulting from different ways of putting the same substantive question on surveys). For example, two surveys concerning the nuclear freeze resolution cited in this chapter showed that support for the APA Council's action ranged from under 60% to 76% of the respondents (McConnell et al., 1986; Polyson, Stein, & Sholley, 1986; see also Schumann & Presser, 1981).

Arguments Against Advocacy

Pragmatic arguments opposing advocacy have highlighted a number of hazards. These include the danger of degrading the level of psychological discourse, the infringement of the ethics of scientific/professional roles, and possible negative repercussions for psychology itself if its practitioners get too embroiled in policy debates.

Modes of Discourse

Ethical and moral constraints differ greatly when one speaks as a politically involved partisan as opposed to a presumably disinterested scientist. Types and levels of deception, omission or distortion of opposing points of view, and *ad hominem* attacks are routine in political argument. They are expected and probably discounted by audiences, at least to some degree.

Scientists, on the other hand, are bound by both codified and implicit rules to present and evaluate information and arguments fully and dispassionately. The point is not whether this ideal is achievable in reality; it is that the scientist is supposed to strive toward it and that audiences imbued with respect for this goal may respond with less skepticism than they would in the more usual arenas of policy discourse. Scientists themselves, caught up in the debate, may come to shed more heat than light. Judge David L. Bazelon, in our opinion one of the most sophisticated and open-minded of American jurists in regard to the social sciences, has criticized psychologists' failure to disclose all the facts underlying their conclusions both in the courtroom and in the public arena (Bazelon, 1982). Psychologists who have served as expert witnesses can testify to the temptation to exaggerate one's database in the heat of cross-examination.

The dangers of blurring the line have another unintended effect: the growing suspicion by scientists themselves that their colleagues may not be fully honest and disinterested when they get involved in advocacy issues (Hammond & Adelman, 1976). The proposed science court, with an explicitly adversarial relationship between scientific proponents and opponents of alternative policies, would have institutionalized this suspicion. The image of scientists hunting for the advantage of whichever side hired them (or engaged their emotions) was chilling to many people, and the idea of the science court seems to have been abandoned. A better piece of advice may be derived from Harold T. Shapiro's (1984) editorial in *Science* on the appropriateness for universities of taking general policy positions, a closely analogous matter. Shapiro reminds academicians of the traditional ideal that their institutions are neutral sources of knowledge and points out the dangers—both pragmatic and ethical—of abandoning this stance.

Exploiting Irrelevant Status

Another problem is whether it is ethically appropriate to use professional status in political argument. As we have seen all too frequently in the case of popular entertainers, sports figures, and celebrities of many sorts, media prominence in one role appears to increase the individual's credibility (or at least attention-getting ability) in many other roles, even those that are completely unrelated to one's original basis of eminence (cf. McGuire's 1985 discussion of the persuasion-facilitating effects of irrelevant source characteristics).

In professional matters, psychology's code of ethics explicitly prohibits offering services in areas outside the individual's specialization. Is it then ethical for scientists to claim professional expertise in a context where such expertise is substantively irrelevant or at least dubious, but where they know it will lend their arguments additional weight? Should we not expect our colleagues to follow stricter standards in such situations than we expect from movie stars or the authors of best-selling fiction?

Effects on Psychology

We must also raise the question of the effects that policy advocacy can have on the profession. Specific criticisms have been leveled not only at organizational pronouncements, but at a number of individual initiatives. One notorious example was Kenneth B. Clark's APA presidential address (1971), which suggested that mental health professionals monitor the psychological stability of governmental leaders and administer medication to ensure that power was used "positively." The subsequent arguments covered all bases, from the tenuousness of the factual foundation for such a role, through the rejection of behavioral scientists taking on the role of a supra-government, to the anti-democratic elitism of the recommendation (Tetlock, Mitchell, & McGuire, 1991).

More recently, a major arena has been nuclear disarmament. Some of the more controversial comments have included Lifton's (1982) hypothesis of "psychic numbing." The hypothesis posits that someone who voices a fear of nuclear war is afraid of nuclear war; people who do not voice fear have merely repressed their fear because it is so overwhelming. Although this psychological catch-22 has been attacked, it has become so popular in some circles that an attempt was made in the late 1980s to incorporate nuclear numbing as a diagnostic category in the psychiatric *Diagnostic and Statistical Manual*.

One paper proposing that patients in psychotherapy should be subjected to awareness-raising concerning the dangers of nuclear war includes a disclaimer that "I do not propose that we diagnose and incarcerate politicians or scientists for their nuclear madness" (Nelson, 1986, p. 551). This statement appears one page after the remark that "We need to see things as they actually are. This is perhaps our greatest psychological challenge." In a critique, Flanagan and Sommers (1986) raised a number of ethical objections to this approach, arguing for the need for therapists to be committed to the patient's freedom to make his or her own choices.

Let us move to another topic. Herbert Kelman (1983) has argued that the United States government should take steps toward legitimizing a formal Palestine Liberation Organization role in talks with Israel. Again, the position is obviously controversial, but, although the proposal was based upon psychological expertise (Kelman assessed Yasser Arafat's cognitive style as manifested in conversation, an assessment that played a key role in the formulation of his recommendation), the scientific justification for it is less than overwhelming. Questions can be asked about the validity and reliability of Kelman's estimate of overt cognitive complexity (flexibility, willingness to compromise, understanding the other side's point of view, and openness to new information, ideas, and policy proposals) from the particular database. Also questionable are the relationship between overt (i.e., verbally expressed) and covert complexity; the relationship of either of these complexities to Arafat's willingness to accept a cooperative solution to the Israeli-Palestinian conflict; the relationship between any hypothetical willingness and actual behavior, given that the latter is constrained by Arafat's dependence on other Palestinian, non-Palestinian Arab, and non-Arab groups and leaders; and whether in view of political realities such a solution is feasible, regardless of Arafat's personal stance or cognitive characteristics.

Similar complications can be adduced for the Israeli and American responses to any proposal such as Kelman's. Rebuttals (Kendler, 1983; Mansdorf, 1983) argued that there is neither empirical evidence nor theoretical justification to support the policy proposal. One title sums up the issue: "Scientific conclusions or political advocacy?"

An equally vexing matter is the possible rebound effect outside the ranks of psychologists. How does the general public and smaller groups within it, such as government officials or elected office-holders, react to statements by groups of psychologists on nuclear strategy or public funding of daycare centers? Like psychologists themselves, they may be unaware that a position has even been taken, but many, and particularly those who have official and/or professional involvement in the issue, will probably be better informed. They may think the statements right or wrong. They may also consider the making of such statements, irrespective of their own political stance, legitimate or illegitimate (Bazelon, 1982; De Leon, 1986; Fishman & Neigher, 1982; Hatch, 1982).

These judgments may have significant consequences for the discipline and its practitioners in the future. Statements such as "The myth of 'value-free' psychologists pursuing 'truths' about human behavior is no longer a functional ideology for our profession" (Task Force on Psychology and Public Policy, 1986, p. 914) would certainly not encourage decision makers or the public to perceive our recommendations as disinterested.

As another example, Haan (1982, p. 1097) has suggested that "The Reagan administration's attack on social research may reflect its intuitive apprehension that social science often 'bootlegs' moral values that run counter to conservative ideologies." The history of the involvement of psychology in policy debates validates this apprehension empirically, not just intuitively, but even if we ignore ideological bias, we may ask ourselves whether it is appropriate for us to "bootleg" any moral value under the cover of social science (see also Hatch, 1982).

Advocacy by Organized Psychology

Aside from psychological organizations that were established specifically to influence social policy [e.g., the Society for the Psychological Study of Social Issues, the Psychologists' League, or Psychologists for Social Responsibility (see Harris et al., 1986)], official advocacy positions have been under fire. The American Psychological Association, the world's largest organization of psychologists, may serve as an example. As we indicated previously, there has been membership support for various resolutions of the APA Council of Representatives; on the other hand, there has been vocal dissent from specific position statements as well as from the whole idea of making such statements outside a narrowly defined area (e.g., Miller, 1969). This area covers issues directly related to psychology as a discipline and profession. Examples are funding levels for behavioral science, the regulation of animal research, or hospital privileges for clinical psychologists. Even in cases such as these, one may argue about the self-aggrandizing positions of a supposedly scientific body (particularly when the statements are cast in terms of "evidence").

In view of the dual nature of APA as a professional guild and a scientific society, the latter criticisms are probably unreasonable. Nor is this kind of advocacy unique to APA. Many scientific organizations have lobbied intensely for support of "big science" enterprises such as the human genome project and the Superconducting Super Collider. But the disaffection and defection of many colleagues from APA is a demonstrable fact (Mangan, 1987), and even aside from personal communications by a number of our friends and acquaintances, there is evidence that disagreement over advocacy positions is at least a contributory cause (e.g., Bergin, 1982). In 1975, two thoughtful observers (Rappoport & Kren, 1975) suggested a moratorium on APA advocacy while several difficult aspects of the issue were examined. This pause did not occur, and the problem continued to get worse. Recent proposals that would have drastically restructured the APA, while primarily reflecting a scientist-professional split, were designed partly to alleviate conflict about advocacy.

A 1969 survey (Policy and Planning Board, 1970) already disclosed strongly divergent views on the part of APA members. Cautionary remarks have been made by leading psychologists, some of them the very people who have been effective researchers in policy-related areas (Hartsough & Savitsky, 1984; Kendler, 1983; Miller, 1969; Sarason, 1984, 1986). Miller's comments are particularly interesting because they refer to the human welfare clause of the APA bylaws, so highly valued by the proponents of advocacy: "Let us by all means do everything we can to promote human welfare, but let us not forget that our real strength in that cause will come from our scientific knowledge, not from our national Association" (p. 1065). It has also been suggested that our expertise be turned toward designing good tests of possible social policy rather than toward making recommendations about it (Campbell, 1969; Cook, 1985).

There are probably few, if any, psychologists who would propose that our organizations *never* take a policy stand. It is the range of issues on which such positions have been taken that fuels the flames. For example, the Council of Representatives has put APA on record for taking policy stands against the United Nations resolution that Zionism is a form of racism, in favor of U.S. participation in UNESCO, against corporal punishment of children, for the Equal Rights Amendment, supporting gun control laws, opposing the required teaching of "creation science" in public schools, and condemning torture.

One result of this scattergun approach has been a continuing major dispute about the circumstances that legitimize official pronouncements on social and political matters. What issues should come within our purview? What kinds of statements should we feel free to make? What kind of review and authorization process should be required before a statement is promulgated? These are all controversial topics that affect the leaders, administrators, and members of the organization.

The confusion, whether inadvertent or not, between our roles as citizens and as scientists has played a major role in the heated debate over official advocacy. In almost every instance when scientific organizations have sponsored such pronouncements, various members have objected on at least two grounds. First, no one has a right to speak for the society unless all members have had a chance to register their position (or, given the diversity of psychology, perhaps those members who are experts in the specific field). This leads to the question, supposing that such a referendum were held, what outcome would justify the organization in voicing an opinion? Total unanimity on important social issues is most unlikely but anything less seems to ignore the perspectives of those members who disagree with the official stance. A report of precise distributions would be less contentious within the organization, but would hardly make for the clarion call that seems to be the point of taking positions in the first place.

Second, members join a professional society for professional purposes, and not for general political ones. When they want to express their judgment as citizens, they should do so through organizations established for that purpose, in the voting booth, and in other contexts not tied to their professional identity. Thus, the professional organization has no business expressing a formal position on such issues, even in the unlikely case that every single member agreed on that position.

A third criticism is the danger that the organization's official voice will violate its own ethical precepts. For example, the Ethical Principles of Psychologists, promulgated by APA, includes the following (Principle 4, Section g): "Psychologists present the science of psychology . . . fairly and accurately, avoiding misrepresentation through sensationalism, exaggeration, or superficiality. Psychologists are guided by the primary obligation to aid the public in developing informed judgments, opinions, and choices" (APA *Directory*, 1985, p. xxix). Yet APA itself has been accused of misrepresenting available data on homosexuality in a Supreme Court brief (Cameron & Cameron, 1988). To quote these authors, ". . . in violation of standards for scientific reporting, [a finding] was pulled out of context so that it favored the APA position, and the studies the APA cited in this section of the brief were either contrary to, nonsupportive of, or did not bear upon the APA's contentions" (p. 255). Cameron and Cameron cite another article of the Ethical Principles, 1a: "[Psychologists] provide thorough discussions of the limitations of their data . . . and they acknowledge the existence of alternative hypotheses and explanations of their findings." They conclude, "Ostensibly an association of psychologists should perform according to its standards when attempting to influence public policy. The American Psychological Association does not appear to have fulfilled this obligation in its *amicus curiae* brief to the Supreme Court" (p. 269).

A similar criticism was voiced concerning APA's *amicus curiae* briefs on whether adolescents seeking abortions should have to obtain their parents' consent. The APA argued against such a requirement, on the basis that the research literature shows that "minors 14 years of age and older generally possess the . . . demonstrated capacity for rational decision making, to a degree that is not measurably different from that of adults." According to the critics, "The briefs overstated what is known about the development of decision-making skills" (both quotes from Gardner, Scherer, & Tester, 1989, p. 897).

Even more disturbing is a comparison between the adolescent abortion rights issue and another APA *amicus curiae* brief, this time on whether an adolescent should be subject to the death penalty. Here, although the jury had decided that "the crime was especially heinous, atrocious and cruel," the APA argued against the death penalty on the grounds that the scientific literature "shows differences between adolescents and adults in ability to plan and control behavior. In addition, the research literature shows that adolescents are more vulnerable than adults and do not take into account, as adults are able to, the consequences of their behavior" (both quotes from Sandler, 1988, p. 2).

Obviously, one can argue about the validity of these criticisms. The point is that there is at least a clear possibility that those speaking for the APA, in their zeal to advance certain social policy positions and combat others, may ignore or misinterpret the evidence and even contradict themselves from one instance to the next. Such actions bring the organization into disrepute among its own members and the entire field of psychology into disrepute among jurists and ordinary citizens.

Self-contradiction stemming from an official position can result in more concrete injury as well. In 1986, the APA Council of Representatives adopted a resolution attacking apartheid in South Africa, one of whose clauses stated that the

APA "urge[s] American psychologists to refuse to collaborate in projects sponsored by the South African government until human rights reforms are instituted." Shortly thereafter, APA received an appeal for help from a South African psychologist who wanted to establish a training program for Black health service workers to treat head- and brain-injured patients (an appreciable proportion of whom would probably have been the victims of police violence). Because the project was getting some funding from the South African government, the Council of Representatives decided to stick to the letter of its resolution and denied any assistance. To most observers, this decision appeared to be directly contrary to the spirit of the anti-apartheid motion (and, it should be said, overruled a positive recommendation from the APA Committee on International Relations in Psychology).

Our View on Advocacy

In harmony with our feeling that any advocacy role requires disclosure, the authors of this chapter want to make clear where we stand. We do not pretend to be neutral on these issues. Even if playing by scientific rules—full disclosure of all evidence, even that adverse to one's own cause, as well as of the weaknesses of the evidence in favor of that cause—handicaps scientists in the political arena, in our view the ethics of the profession require such adherence. Modes of discourse inappropriate to science remain inappropriate, no matter what political questions are involved or how fervent a scientist's feelings are. If he or she wishes to abandon these rules, the scientific role and any associated status or claim to expertise must be abjured.

Our own position is one of cautious involvement. We are comfortable with psychology taking on the role of compiling and disseminating information. Given the complexity of social issues and the nature of social science data, we are much less comfortable with the idea that the discipline should act as a policy advocate (cf. Weiss & Weiss, 1981) except under limited circumstances and in limited ways.

THE ISSUE OF EXPERTISE

How right psychologists are to claim special knowledge is one of the primary sources of tension in this book. In general, proponents of advocacy assume or assert that psychologists do in fact have professional knowledge that can and should be applied to social problems (see Argyris, 1975). Just how it should be applied is a topic of disagreement. Should the psychologist be an advocate for particular ideologies or positions (Bramel & Friend, 1981) or a neutral expert making knowledge and judgment available to any comer (Münsterberg, 1913; Weiss & Weiss, 1981)? Should the application be open and nonmanipulative (Argyris, 1975), or should it be pursued covertly, without letting members of the target audience know that they are in effect serving as subjects (Abelson & Zimbardo, 1970; Ball-Rokeach, Rokeach, & Grube, 1984; Varela, 1971; Zimbardo, 1972)?

Equally knowledgeable psychologists disagree about when the database of our discipline justifies taking policy positions. The opposing judgments rest on different epistemological baselines for assessing the minimal amount and quality of scientific evidence that would justify advocacy on given topics. This is one of the major issues that this book addresses. We argue that there are different thresholds of acceptability for disseminating informatión relevant to a policy and for taking a scientific position on that policy. We do not expect to resolve this conflict; indeed, it has been thoughtfully argued that the philosophical tensions attendant to the diversity of professional activities and outlooks of psychologists make it impossible to resolve (Hillerbrand, 1987). We do hope, however, to shed additional light on the matter.

It can be argued that even at their worst, research data are better than the kind of anecdotal evidence so frequently used to develop or to justify policy positions even where research data exist (Nisbett & Ross, 1980, in Chapter 3). A few well-publicized examples of welfare fraud or of violent crime by parolees may have more impact on welfare or parole policy than many carefully conducted statistical studies. The law of small numbers applies: Each such example is inferred to stand for vast numbers of as yet undiscovered counterparts. Observers who are impressed even by the low quality of the evidentiary base in key policy issues may be willing to set a low threshold of data requirements for psychology's involvement in policy debates.

Conversely, being better than abysmally bad is not necessarily the same as being good enough. Before making a public commitment, psychologists and their organizations should insist on standards of scientific rigor and quality of evidence comparable to those by which we would judge a manuscript submitted to one of our better journals. From this standpoint, a research literature consisting of a few studies, some perhaps with flawed designs, limited ecological validity, or inconsistent findings, does not warrant a scientific or organizational position. We must demand a higher threshold of proof.

One possibly useful guideline for judging advocacy is to look at history. What types of problems are particularly amenable to social science–based interventions?

Empirical Focus

Expertise rather than morality plays the major role in successful translations from psychological research data to real world applications. Behavior modification, based on evidence from laboratory studies of conditioning and arousal, does not claim particular moral insights as opposed to those of psychoanalysis; but its results, in certain specifiable situations, show it to be more powerful in eliminating a range of agonizing, life-restricting behavior patterns (Wolpe, 1981). Equipment and environments designed to fit human limitations and capacities, as measured by human factors researchers, can facilitate performance and satisfaction while reducing accidental injuries and deaths. They are not superior in some abstract moral sense, but they work better.

We obviously do not mean that empirical advances are unrelated to morality or values. One can argue that a relatively mechanistic treatment procedure is less humane and therefore morally inferior to one that leads to greater self-insight, regardless of their relative effects on a particular symptom. Others can maintain, just as easily, that relieving a patient of distressing symptoms or reducing discomfort, stress, and inefficiency at work are both pragmatically and ethically desirable. That, in fact, is the point: The argument over values can go in directions not determined by the bare facts.

Compatibility of Scale

Another aspect of successful data-based applications is that they tend to move from evidence collected under limited, small-scale research conditions to comparably limited, small-scale problems. Let us look, for example, at ways to increase intergroup cooperation. A relevant line of psychological theorizing is Allport's (1954) analysis of how prejudice may be reduced through interracial contact under specified conditions. Basic research (Sherif, 1958) had demonstrated that the existence of superordinate goals (where a solution is important to both groups, and neither group can solve the problem alone) leads to increasing collaboration and diminishing intergroup hostility. Aronson and Osherow (1980) integrated these points in developing a program to increase interracial harmony in primary school classrooms. Each child is given one component of a body of knowledge, and the group task can only be solved if all of the components are considered. This "jigsaw" procedure sets up superordinate goals in such a way as to ensure that pupils from all ethnic backgrounds have crucial parts of the solution. This and similar methods of "cooperative learning" have resulted in increased cross-ethnic friendships within the classroom and, in a few studies, outside it as well (Slavin, 1985).

Moving to Social Policy

Building on a history of active involvement in political issues and a history of successful small-scale applications (note that we posit two separate histories here), psychologists individually and collectively have moved toward using their research data to justify public policy positions. But neither of the two distinct streams of tradition necessarily makes a joining of this sort either morally or pragmatically appropriate.

In general, the shift from micro- to macro-level applications runs into obstacles that do not hinder within-level transfer out of the laboratory. Many of these problems find psychologists unprepared (and sometimes unaware).

Complications of Complexity

Among other problems, macro-level applications can lead to a potentially enormous range of unanticipated and frequently undesired side effects. These result from adding a great range of alternate considerations and uncontrolled variables. Relatively simple causal chains observed in the laboratory and then in small-scale applications are transplanted to social systems with large numbers of interacting moderator variables and complex causal feedback loops. These complicate both the factual and moral aspects of the situation far beyond anything sensed in the original research. As a result, techniques that have proven efficacious and morally uncontroversial can lose both virtues when blown out of their proper proportion.

For example, token economies may translate reinforcement theory into helpful procedures for training handicapped patients in some aspects of health care. But when the approach is advocated as a societal blueprint, it runs into enormous empirical problems of individual differences, reactance, and intrinsic motivation. It also activates fundamental moral issues such as the trade-offs between freedom and social control, what to do with deviant citizens, and the most fundamental dilemma of political and constitutional theory: Who controls the controllers (Dahl, 1989; Meehl, 1975)?

Let's look again at the cooperative learning example cited earlier. The data indicate that this procedure often has the desired effect on interracial friendships. But how should it be operationalized as a social policy? And even if it could be so operationalized, what would the impact of such a policy be on the development of autonomous information seeking, on self-reliance, on the level of aspiration and striving among the best (as well as among average) performers, and on the consequent levels of achievement, economic efficiency, and societal innovation? A recent reviewer concludes that "The practical implications of the research . . . are unambiguous" (Slavin, 1985, p. 60). Perhaps, but they are certainly grossly incomplete; for example, the review does not at all address the issue of academic achievement.

Incompatible Philosophies

Another serious difficulty is a possible mismatch between our world view and the topics to which we address ourselves. Some assumptions that are common in psychology may not be appropriate in other contexts. Among relevant examples are the applications of the underlying philosophy of clinical psychology and psychiatry to issues of criminology (Menninger, 1968; Szasz, 1961) and international crisis management (Blight, 1986; Garfinkle, 1986). In the latter context, psychologists may be unsuccessful in applying well-supported theoretical generalizations because they misjudge the tractability of the conflict of interest between the two states. Various other misperceptions may also prove to be obstacles (e.g., Goodwin, 1971).

Opportunity Costs and Trade-Offs

Pursuing one desirable outcome may preclude or impair the pursuit of other equally desirable goals. For example, channeling educational resources into programs promoting interracial harmony may reduce the amount of money available for promoting exceptional talent in mathematics and science. A variant of this dilemma is that policies designed to reach desired ends may also involve harmful side effects.

Problems Related to Research Design

One set of problems in this category concerns all of the familiar issues related to the external or ecological validity of research evidence. Real-world policies involve many more causal variables than researchers can manipulate, randomize, hold constant, or simply be aware of, even in the most rigorous and meticulous research program. At a minimum, great caution is advised. Research experience in a remarkably broad range of the subareas of psychology—cognitive, social, environmental, educational, health, personality, and industrial/organizational— indicates that the main effects of today frequently become the first- and higher-order interaction effects of tomorrow (cf. Cronbach & Snow, 1977; Gergen & Davis, 1985; McGuire, 1983; Meehl, 1978). The literature abounds in references to interactions between personality and situational variables, aptitudes and treatments, and contexts and tasks.

There is also an inherent bias in psychological research that hampers its generalization on the large scale. The goal in most studies is to maximize between-group variance. As a result, experimental treatments are designed to be as distinct from each other as possible without compromising internal validity. But in real policy making, a politically acceptable solution may call for integrative policy mixes, that is, for taking selected components from each of various alternatives. The effects of such policy mixes do not always fall between the effects of the component policies.

SEPARATING FACTS FROM VALUES

We believe that the conceptual and methodological problems involved in generalizing from the psychology laboratory to large-scale social policy are daunting, more so than one might infer from the confident assertions of committed activists (e.g., Bevan, 1982; Task Force on Psychology and Public Policy, 1986). But there is also an entirely different set of objections stemming from a separate set of concerns. These concerns and objections are based on the familiar debate concerning the proper relationship between empirical facts and moral values. The history of the scientific enterprise reveals an evolution of perspective on this relationship that ranges from the view that science reveals the designs of God (or historical inevitability) and is thus, essentially, the handmaiden of religion (or the class struggle) to Hume's position that one cannot validly argue from descriptive, factual premises to prescriptive conclusions (see, e.g., Graham, 1981). Some recent statements on the topic have asserted that the separation of the two realms is not merely undesirable, but by the nature of human beings and of science (and particularly of psychology) even theoretically impossible (Howard, 1985; Manicas & Secord, 1983).

This debate has attracted many psychologists, perhaps more so as the profession becomes more involved in making normative statements outside its obvious spheres of special knowledge. Some behavioral scientists (e.g., Bramel & Friend, 1981; Fox, 1986; Larsen, 1986) argue that the most appropriate function of the field is to criticize and offer alternatives to currently dominant social assumptions, policies, and groups. This argument has perhaps made more headway in the strictly social sciences than in psychology (cf. Ginsburg, 1987; Kolata, 1987). These writers usually conclude that very little effort has been made in this direction. Others (e.g., Robinson, 1984) equally firmly hold that the task is to develop empirically grounded and rigorously testable theories of human behavior and to avoid becoming entangled in nonscientific debates about value-defined policies. These observers usually conclude that we are failing to live up to these standards and are embroiling ourselves in controversies in which we have no business meddling.

We have already referred to the disturbing possibility that fervent advocacy may impair the scientist's openness about the limitations of data relevant to a debate. The temptation is to note only the strengths of the evidential basis for one's own position and only the weaknesses of that supporting the opposition. There is a possibly even more dangerous implication, that scientists may actually suppress data that support the "wrong" side (i.e., not merely ignore or belittle them in policy debates, but actually work to keep them from becoming publicly known). As an ominous example, not long ago a group of psychologists (Pollack, Crain, Borbely, Naimark, & Rabinowitz, 1983) criticized the *American Psychologist* for publishing an article on the solidly established abuse of psychiatry in suppressing political dissent in the Soviet Union (Faraone, 1982). While the critique addressed itself partly to the substance of the article (which was later thoroughly supported by public statements of the Soviet government), its self-admitted major objection was that such publications might impair U.S.–Soviet detente and exacerbate international tension.

It is bad enough that the repercussions of some social movements affect scholarship and stifle inquiry (Mednick, 1989) by making it difficult to obtain financial, moral, and professional support for dissident lines of research and theorizing. Some colleagues have gone further, even so far as to propose that lines of research be abandoned if they could lead to socially undesirable outcomes. Sarason (1984) takes this position about research on racial differences in intelligence, which he feels should not be supported or encouraged (for dissenting views on that article, see "Comments on Sarason," 1985). It is only one step from there to withholding publication. Will we have to live with a code according to which a true believer can ethically shred data that contradict his or her view of the ultimate good? *Can science live with such a code?*

For our part, we feel that suppressing facts assumes too much omniscience on the part of the scientist. In other words:

> *Knowledge is supposed to belong to the storehouse of human information, not to some preferred person or subgroup. By the same token, of course, uses of which some researchers might approve would be disliked by other scientists. There is no justification for assuming that researchers are uniquely qualified to dictate or control the possible uses of knowledge that they produce. Scientific expertise does not ensure civic virtue, morality, or wisdom. (Suedfeld, 1980, p. 421)*

As with freedom of speech in general, we hold with John Stuart Mill that the free marketplace of ideas is the proper forum for debates not only about data but about their implications, and that the suppression of evidence for political reasons is a violation of scientific ethics (see also Mahoney, 1985).

We agree with those who claim that there is no value-free science. The tenet that science should be value-free is itself valued-based. "Value freeness" is also obviously limited to sets of values that lie outside science *per se*. No advocate of the scientific method for generating knowledge would suggest that as scientists we should compromise those values on which science itself is philosophically based: empiricism, free inquiry, public verifiability, and so on, even though scientists may not see completely eye to eye on what all of these terms mean in a given context (see Howard, 1985; Krasner & Houts, 1984). In a particular situation, the scientist's role and its ethical concomitants may have to be subordinated to other roles (parent, citizen, ideologue), but that is a separate, although not always easily separable, issue.

The Goal of Differentiation

We agree that one cannot easily divorce facts from values. Getting involved in policy arguments reflects one set of values; so does opposition to such involvement; and so does saying nothing at all. But the proposition we advance is that a clear recognition of value implications is crucial to the scientist's participation in such disputes. When behavioral researchers append their professional credentials to a policy position, they are at least implicitly promising to adhere to the value system of the scientist, not the polemicist. That means they are under special obligation to present all of the facts as far as known, describe the limitations of the empirical base, acknowledge inconsistent or contradictory facts and theories, and clearly separate speculations, guesses, and personal preferences from the findings and explanations derived from the research.

Further, we contend that this role differentiation is crucial if social science is to be at all credible in its contributions to policy debates, particularly in view of the obstacles to generalization mentioned earlier. Knowledgeable segments of the political audience are aware, in broad outline if not in detail, of the limitations of our data and theories. For us to take strong positions without acknowledging those limitations is, in effect, to mislead our audience, and we will lose credibility when a significant portion of the listeners can detect the deception (cf. Bazelon, 1982). Given the dynamic, continuous nature of the research process, it is also true that anything we don't know today we may know tomorrow. Conversely, anything we think we know today may turn out tomorrow to have been wrong. Unqualified extrapolations are thus triply inappropriate.

The Value Bias of Psychologists

There is one more point concerning past involvement in policy disputes. Earlier in this chapter, we mentioned some of the previous occasions on which psychologists and their organizations have taken public stands. Without having conducted a systematic content analysis, we nevertheless consider it safe to assert that the positions taken by our colleagues have typically been on the liberal side of such arguments. The dominant values expressed have been on the side of reduction of military forces, negotiated compromise of international disagreements, "reducing social class inequalities and redistributing power" in society (Albee, 1986), preferential treatment for disadvantaged groups, emphasizing the rights of defendants in criminal trials, and so on (e.g., American Psychological Association, 1987).

It should be noted that, as the accepted liberal position has changed on some issues, so has the dominant voice within psychology. Support for the war effort in the 1940s has been replaced by an emphasis on arms control and peace studies; the drive for equal opportunity in education and employment has given way to advocating affirmative action. There is pressure by accreditation committees toward meeting statistical goals of representativeness among the faculty and students of academic departments of psychology, and within the APA itself, slates based on demographics for governance bodies. Also, early support for the fight against censorship has been succeeded by opposition to the free dissemination of violent and pornographic material (see Harris et al., 1986; Huesmann & Malamuth, 1986).

Among the dangers of advocacy is formal or informal punishment for colleagues whose interpretation of the data goes against the conventional wisdom of the day (Chesler, Sanders, & Kalmuss, 1989; Lineberry, 1988; Stein, 1988). The persecution of Eysenck and Jensen for their positions on the heritability of personality and intelligence comes easily to mind. At the time of this writing, a similar situation exists for Philippe Rushton, a Canadian psychologist who interprets his and others' data as showing genetically determined racial differences on a wide range of characteristics, from sexual behavior and child-rearing to intelligence. Although during the 1988–1989 period he held a Guggenheim Fellowship and published several articles (not all on race) in peer-reviewed journals, his department has judged his performance to be below minimum acceptable standards and has admitted to using a more rigorous method of evaluation than usual.

Like all major policy issues, the ones on which our profession has taken positions involve value trade-offs. Decision makers must choose between the advantages and disadvantages of competing policy options. No realistic policy option has only advantages or only disadvantages, a consideration that too often disappears in the writing of position statements.

A general question frequently raised in this context concerns the relationship between one's interpretation of the facts and one's own value preferences (see, e.g., Albee, 1983; Eysenck, 1982). Historical observation (Jervis, 1976) and social psychological theory (e.g., Festinger, 1957; Heider, 1958) both suggest that the relationship between these two classes of variables is likely to be substantial. Granted that it is hard to separate the causal direction of the two components (i.e., the degree to which factual assessments shape value judgments or vice versa), it is reasonably clear that policy advocates often align assessments and preferences in highly consistent and predictable configurations. An analyst's affirmation of egalitarian objectives, for example, typically coincides with the ascription of poverty and criminality to external, societal causes such as discrimination or class oppression. Low acceptance of egalitarianism as a value usually goes with the tendency to make largely internal attributions such as to lack of ability, laziness, impulsivity, and unwillingness to delay need gratification.

A Hypothetical Study

One way to disentangle the relative importance of factual and value disagreements as determinants of policy preferences would be through a thought (but potentially actual) experiment. Experts can be asked to assume that there is agreement on, for example, the relative contribution of continuing research on space weapons systems to defense against nuclear attack on the one hand and to destabilization of the nuclear balance of power on the other. Should we implement a defense system that raises the percentage of incoming enemy missiles destroyed in flight from 10% to 75% if such implementation would also raise the probability of an enemy first strike by a factor of 3? If in such "as if" situations the respondents still disagree on policy issues, then the disagreement is based on value differences. Of course, the interpretation can be made only if all relevant data questions are included in the hypothetically accepted set of established facts. The other side of this experiment would be a direct measurement of the experts' judgment about facts.

Some Real Studies

The factual and value components of policy disagreements are notoriously confounded (cf. Gowans, 1987). Because disentangling them is so difficult, some social scientists have concluded that the effort should be abandoned, and that psychologists should accept a moral responsibility to support particular sides in these controversies (e.g., Haan, 1982; Larsen, 1986). Other colleagues, however, have made valiant efforts to tease apart the relative importance of factual and value disagreements, and have carefully avoided becoming partisans of one side or another in situations calling for their professional expertise.

There is, for instance, an impressive social science literature on assessing the risks of technological innovation (Fischhoff, Lichtenstein, Slovic, Derby, & Keeney, 1981). This work explores different procedures for deciding how much gain (in, for example, energy efficiency, agricultural productivity, accessibility of a nutritious and varied diet, or industrial efficiency) is worth how much risk (here, as a result of the use of nuclear power generators, recombinant DNA, food additives, and fossil fuels).

The authors present a series of guidelines that we find very persuasive. They emphasize the complex, situation-specific nature of the problems and the very low probability of finding a single all-purpose solution; the limitations of the knowledge base and the concomitant importance of political and value considerations; and the crucial role of problem definition in the process of seeking solutions. They also show the need to monitor and improve the decision-making process and the requirement of being explicit and honest about all of the above (see also Slovic, 1987). Our own view of the wide range of social advocacy issues is that psychologists would do well to follow these recommendations regardless of topic.

An exemplary study by Hammond and Adelman (1976) tried to isolate the factual and value components of a policy controversy. The debate was the choice of appropriate ammunition to be used by the Denver Police Department; it involved a seemingly hopeless tangle of facts and values. In helping to resolve the controversy, Hammond and Adelman succeeded in separating technical issues such as the relative characteristics and probable effects of various types of ammunition on shooting outcomes from the importance of these outcomes. The outcomes were factual issues such as the bullet's ability immediately to incapacitate its target versus the likelihood that it might pass through the target and ricochet or hit a bystander. These factors were differentiated from value judgments about, for example, the relative importance of immediate stopping power versus risk to bystanders.

Technical (ballistics) experts were asked to evaluate the technical issues. Community leaders were considered to be the relevant experts on the social values attached to the issue by their own constituencies and were given the task of assessing the value components. Both groups worked in the absence of information from the other.

The result was a generally acceptable solution, the choice of a bullet that represented the best combination of high stopping ability with low secondary risk. Significantly, the researchers themselves made neither technical nor value judgments. Their role was to operationalize the judgments of the two groups of experts.

This kind of disaggregating procedure is rare in social science research, and the success of Hammond and Adelman may well be difficult to replicate in highly polarized political environments. For example, the Colorado decision makers were willing to give equal weight to the different values involved. As Hammond and Adelman recognized, this was a prerequisite for a consensual solution and is probably not universally generalizable. We doubt, for example, that Likud (the present governing political party of Israel) and PLO participants in Kelman and Bloom's (1973) Middle East conflict resolution workshops would agree to give equal weight to the issues of secure borders for Israel and the right to a Palestinian homeland. Similarly, in Colorado, agreement was obtained on what constituted technical expertise in ballistics and on a list of acceptable expert consultants, a prerequisite for separating the factual and value issues. We doubt that the Middle

East workshop participants would so easily agree on the composition of a consultant group on military and strategic issues. Trying to imagine Palestinian guerilla
leader Abu Nidal and former Israeli defense minister Ariel Sharon coming to such
an agreement illustrates the magnitude of the problem.

Factual Controversies and Value Controversies

In the sections that follow, we have selected a number of currently controversial
social issues. Each case has engaged the attention of psychologists to a greater or
lesser degree. In each case, prominent behavioral scientists have read the existing
database as strongly implying the preferability of a particular policy decision that,
if adopted, would have far-reaching, important effects. In each case, there are also
colleagues who disagree with the view that any particular policy can be firmly
based on the available scientific knowledge.

Disputes focus on both the acceptability of the available data as a foundation of
policy and the value judgments made by colleagues in using those data as an
advocacy tool. Although both types of disagreements probably exist in just about
every policy debate, in some cases the value conflict is the center and crux of the
disagreement. A particular policy can exalt some values as more important than
others and sacrifice or at least compromise the latter to promote the former. In
other areas, factual disagreements are paramount: whether the data being cited in
support of particular policies are strong enough to be so used and further whether,
regardless of their strength, they indeed imply the policy they are used to justify.

Going through the topics one by one, we find a distribution from debates in
which the two sides generally agree on the facts but not on their policy implications (that is, where value conflicts define the opposing positions) to those where
the two disagree about the facts (data conflicts). But traces of both appear in each
case, and our own reading of the arguments identifies the following major themes
and contradictions.

International Relations

1. The relative merits of simple and complex decision-making strategies is
primarily a factual issue, with both psychological and political components. On the
psychological level, complex information processing can exact costs that strongly
affect its efficiency and probable success (Suedfeld, 1983, 1988; Suedfeld &
Tetlock, 1990; Tetlock, 1986, 1989). On the political side, the debate is about
whether decisions reached through complex cognitive processes are necessarily
more adaptive than those derived from simple cognitive strategies, or, rather,
under what circumstances is either of these more adaptive. Analysts may disagree
as to the complexity of the environment and, as a consequence, disagree as to how
critical complexity of thought is to making effective policy decisions. For example, an analyst who subscribed to a unified, rational-actor model of Soviet foreign
policy might have viewed the invasion of Afghanistan as only one in a series of
planned gradual expansions of Soviet hegemony over neighboring countries. This
interpretation calls for much less of a multidimensional assessment of the invasion
of Afghanistan than would an analysis of Soviet behavior as the product of compet-

ing institutional political factions. Such disagreements derive not from psychological theory but from divergent factual assessments of the international scene.

Although value trade-offs can emerge in assessing the pros and cons of simple and complex decision-making procedures (e.g., the comparative hazards of exaggerating and underestimating pluralistic influences in Soviet foreign policy at different times in history), value disagreements are less salient. Decision-analysis technology often appears value-neutral, its function being to resolve a problem, not to judge moral appropriateness. Nonetheless, decision analysis clearly does raise moral issues. These are related to whether the decision analyst is a "hired gun" who would not have discriminated between advising the Nazi government on how best to maximize its territorial expansion in Europe without war prior to 1939 and advising the Kennedy administration on how to achieve the right mix of influence tactics to induce the Soviets to withdraw their missiles from Cuba in 1962.

2. A fairly evenly mixed case is that of nuclear deterrence. Factual concerns include the conditions under which, according to available data, threats or reassurances constitute the more effective way of influencing a competitor's behavior. Nonpsychological technical and political debates also abound, primarily about issues such as the nature of Soviet geopolitical intentions (Hough, 1985; Pipes, 1984), the possibility of limited nuclear war, the verifiability of arms control agreements (Policy Forum, 1987), the effects of particular weapons systems on international stability (Tetlock et al., 1991), and the extent and severity of a hypothetical "nuclear winter" (e.g., Marshall, 1987; Sagan, 1983/1984; Seitz, 1986).

There are two value questions. The more abstract of these concerns is whether nuclear deterrence can be ethical regardless of circumstances or outcomes. The other revolves around the acceptability of an error in one of two directions. One is failing to communicate adequate resolve to a potential aggressor, thus increasing the likelihood of being victimized by aggression; the other is failing to reassure an insecure adversary of one's own peaceful intentions, thus increasing the likelihood of a conflict spiral and an unnecessary and perhaps dangerous arms race. One frequently expressed value position is that, given the power of nuclear weapons, no increase in the latter risk is acceptable, regardless of effects on the former.

3. The extent of fear of nuclear war among children represents a mainly factual debate. One group of observers asserts that according to acceptable scientific evidence such fear is widespread, intense, and psychologically injurious among contemporary American youth; opponents argue that the evidence fails to demonstrate the validity of this claim.

Assuming that the traumatization of a generation of young citizens is highly undesirable, there are value implications. For example, if the pervasive fear of nuclear war were in fact reliably established, what weight should it be given in policy debates as opposed to the weight given to considerations of national security? What nuclear strategies (e.g., building an even stronger deterrent force, developing an effective technological defense by intensifying work on the Strategic Defense Initiative, negotiating arms control, or instituting immediate nuclear disarmament) would serve to reduce this fear? Or, in the absence of such a direct solution becoming immediately feasible, what educational policies (e.g., "peace" or "strength" curricula in the schools) should be developed (see, e.g., Dalby, 1986)?

Domestic Policy Issues

4. The affirmative action issue engages both kinds of argument, and very similar points are raised concerning these policies. The major factual disputes center around several topics. One is the current pervasiveness of racial and gender discrimination in the United States, specifically in the area of employment. Another is the degree to which underrepresentation of a particular demographic group in a particular occupational niche reflects past or current discrimination as opposed to the working of impersonal market forces and different patterns of preferences and aptitudes across groups.

Another set of factual questions is more complex. There is some doubt as to how much affirmative action programs as currently structured actually benefit those who need them. It has been charged, for instance, that affirmative action helps mostly people who are well educated, middle-class, and well adjusted to society. Members of this group who also happen to belong to protected categories benefit from the program; disadvantaged individuals, whether or not they belong to identified minorities (adolescent drop-outs in the inner city, the rural poor), may be too far out of the mainstream to gain much.

A more psychologically focused issue is the effect of such programs on their beneficiaries. Is there possible damage to self-esteem and aspiration level among individuals who are selected for employment, promotion, education, etc., on the basis of race or gender? Do they feel that they are "tokens" whose colleagues view them with resentment? What happens to those who, because of insufficient preparation or ability, are incapable of performing at the required level? What is the effect of all of this on people outside the protected groups in terms of racial or gender backlash?

Value arguments include the relative importance of the right of every person to obtain rewards in accordance with his or her merit, implying that no preference be given on any other criterion, versus the need to remedy past or current injustices to groups defined by extraneous characteristics and the importance of maximizing efficiency and productivity in a highly competitive international environment, a goal that could be endangered by affirmative action. Such interference may or may not lead to a possible loss in general economic well-being and progress (Schmidt & Hunter, 1981). Given that such a loss could in turn impair the domestic economy, leading to particularly severe impacts on the very same groups purportedly served by affirmative action policies, what probability of each outcome justifies any particular decision on the issue?

5. Arguments about censorship of pornography and of violent television shows are also fundamentally both factual and value arguments. Researchers in both areas disagree as to whether the investigations conducted to date have sufficient ecological validity to justify policy recommendations. The value debate is, first, whether a potential decrease in crimes against women (or in general social violence) justifies the infringement of First Amendment guarantees and, second, whether even a firmly established increase in the probability that a small percentage of viewers may commit such acts would justify the denial of access to the material for all potential users.

6. Gun control is primarily a factual issue: what, if any, laws concerning the possession of firearms would lead to a reduction in social violence? Disagreements are based on the different statistics cited, the rationalizations offered for findings

that are incongruent with the author's position, the choice of examples for argument by analogy, the "real" meaning of the Second Amendment to the Constitution, and the like. Only beyond this level do we get the weighing of trade-offs between individual freedoms and social dangers.

Criminal Justice

7. The death qualification of jurors may or may not lead reliably to increased probability of conviction, a factual question. How it is answered raises questions of value. To what extent should society be more averse to releasing the guilty than to convicting the innocent, given the many safeguards against the latter eventuality that are already built into the system? Thus, either answer to the factual question leads directly to the moral issue about the desirability of increasing (or decreasing) the conviction rate, with concomitant implications for the rights of the accused versus the rights of actual and potential victims.

8. In the use of the polygraph, the crucial question is consensually accepted to be the factual one: What proportions of false positives and false negatives are found when lie detectors are used? The value conflicts are the acceptability of various answers to the empirical question, the right of the individual to privacy and against self-incrimination, and the appropriateness of mechanical intrusions into what has traditionally been a human decision-making process.

9. Although the use of machinery is not involved in the case of eyewitness testimony, there is an analog in the debate over populist versus technocratic approaches to legal judgment. Historically, representative members of the community—jurors—are the triers of fact and decide for themselves the degree to which any evidence (including the testimony of an eyewitness) is credible. Whether psychological evidence on this issue should be allowed to influence the decision (especially given the authority of an expert witness) is a fundamental value question. Another is, again, society's willingness to accept incorrect convictions or incorrect acquittals. This is particularly relevant here, since psychologists giving direct (as opposed to rebuttal) evidence on eyewitness accuracy tend to question the validity of witness identifications. Thus, to the extent that their testimony is believed by the jury, it tends to increase the chances of acquittal. The empirical question, as to the ecological validity and general status of eyewitness accuracy research, seems to be less controversial as a body of convincingly rigorous studies emerges, but how applicable that literature is to a specific criminal case can certainly be argued.

10. Factual issues are at the heart of disagreements about the effects of long-term incarceration. The disputants address the extent to which life in prison is psychologically debilitating, either in extent (what proportion of prisoners is so affected?) or in degree (how badly debilitated are they?). Second, there is a debate about whether good (trouble-free) adjustment to the institution is a negative predictor of adjustment to life after release. Third, there is a vigorous dispute about the efficacy of programs designed to rehabilitate convicts and prepare them for life as law-abiding, productive citizens upon their discharge from prison. There are some value implications, although most people consider them secondary: If prison is debilitating, does the state have the right to use it anyway, to protect the rest of society? Does the state have the right to meddle with the convict's personality in

rehabilitation programs, or is confinement the only legitimate purpose of a prison sentence?

This completes the rapid overview of the policy controversies covered in this book. The reader will see the various arguments presented, in much more detail, in the various position papers.

ANOTHER LOOK AT THE SPSSI/APA RESOLUTIONS

Before going on, it might be interesting to take another look at the resolutions excerpted at the head of this chapter. Where do they fall along the distributions identified above? In addition to identifying factual and value issues, we will also consider a factor particularly germane to this class of statement: the relevance of the issue to psychology as a science and profession.

1. There is no scientific basis for the opinion that war is inevitable.

Although this is clearly a factual claim, it is a dubious one. There are, and there were at the time of the statement, competent and even eminent colleagues (including Sigmund Freud) who interpreted the evidence differently. Further, the evidence against the proposition is certainly no better than the evidence for it. Thus, the SPSSI resolution is at best one-sided (telling some of the truth, but not all of it), and presumably heavily motivated by the value system of its promulgators.

2. Readmission of Israel to UNESCO.

This is completely value-based, and with tenuous relevance to any central interest of APA.

3. Discrimination against men in the context of child-rearing is scientifically baseless.

The theoretical and empirical issues in gender-related child-rearing merit more consideration than the APA's cursory dismissal gives them. Leaving aside the values obviously supported by the statement, a more balanced commentary on the scientific aspects would have been appropriate.

4. Urging a nuclear freeze.

Psychologists can hardly claim expertise on this extremely broad issue, which involves a complex mixture of geopolitical, military, technological, economic, and ideological factors. The resolution is a simplistic value statement in an area where the professional standing of psychologists is at best debatable.

5. Creationism should not be required in the public school curriculum.

Although the data for rejecting creationism as a scientific theory is overwhelming, it is only marginally psychological. We disagree between ourselves on this resolution. Suedfeld, favoring stricter limits on advocacy involvement by scientific organizations, feels that it is only remotely relevant to APA and that our Council should have left it alone, whereas Tetlock argues that it directly affects science and therefore psychology. Tetlock further maintains that cases of religion masquerading as science are just as deserving of condemnation as instances of politics masquerading as science; Suedfeld does not have a strong objection to that argument, but thinks that the APA is not in a very strong position for issuing censures against the first kind of masquerade given its own predilection for the second.

6. Careful monitoring of television programming.

The data on this one seem fairly persuasive, the resolution gives due acknowledgment of Constitutional rights, and the statement seems both better grounded and better balanced than many.

7. Making boxing illegal.

The conclusion, based upon the neurological damage that can be incurred by boxers, is reasonable and well-founded in data, However, since boxers engage in the sport voluntarily, taking a paternalistic stand in favor of legal prohibition introduces a political (nonempirical) complication.

So as not to criticize only the major U.S. organizations, let us now add a resolution endorsed by the Annual General Meeting of the Canadian Psychological Association ("AGM votes . . . ," 1987):

> Whereas: *use of the death penalty is against our professional, ethical, and scientific values;* and whereas: *in our scientific judgment studies of the effects of capital punishment on homicide rates have shown no evidence whatsoever for deterrence;* be it resolved that: *the membership of the Canadian Psychological Association opposes the reinstatement of the death penalty in Canada.*

This resolution, which passed by a vote of 139:7:7, is certainly as egregious an example as any above. It fails our criteria on just about every count. In short, the resolution fails to spell out its own value bases, eliminates by fiat a real controversy in the scientific literature, and sets up only a "straw man" as the opposing viewpoint.

To begin with, approximately 4.6% of the membership voted against the resolution, which was then promulgated in the name of the Association.

Even if we overlook the failure to specify the professional and ethical values violated by the death penalty, what, one wonders, are the relevant scientific values? A quotation from some handbook of the three types of values might have clarified the issue.

It is doubtful that each of the 139 pro-resolution members had read the scientific literature carefully enough to have a scientific judgment on the issue. To say that there is "no evidence whatsoever" favoring deterrence is simply untrue. Although not dominant, such evidence could indeed be found in the literature (cf. Ehrlich, 1982; Forst, 1983).

Even if we accept the assertion, is deterrence the only argument that needs to be considered? In fact, one could argue that to execute some people in order to deter others would itself violate professional and ethical values, if not scientific ones. The resolution ignores a range of arguments, both factual (e.g., capital punishment would protect potential future victims by executing people who have already shown themselves capable of murder or other heinous crimes) and value-based (e.g., many religious and moral codes support the view that at least under some circumstances the unlawful taking of a human life can be expiated only by losing one's own).

We have tried hard not to allow our agreement or disagreement with the resolutions to bias our judgments of their empirical or moral foundations and appropriateness. In fact, although each of us disagrees with some of the resolutions (not necessarily the same ones), we tend to have high agreement on the extent to which databases and value systems are prominent in the pedigree of each.

It appears that the APA has become somewhat more cautious or selective about the public positions that it is willing to take in political and social controversies, perhaps because of the internal problems caused by its earlier liberties. The urgings of some groups or individuals within the Association that certain statements be made (e.g., on political situations in other countries, on the causal roots of violent behavior) have been declined. We applaud this change, regardless of whether we agree with the positions being (or not being) taken.

CONCLUSIONS

Before going on to the chapters reviewing the various advocacy disputes in detail, we once again state our conclusions and recommendations:

Psychologists should be scrupulously careful to differentiate their participation in policy debates as interested citizens or advocates from participation as behavioral scientists. We agree with Fischhoff et al. (1981), who maintain that careful differentiation here is an integral part of good mental hygiene.

The normative guidelines for these two roles differ significantly. Participation as a behavioral scientist calls for making explicit the distinction between facts and values; for stating one's values clearly; and, when discussing the facts, for presenting all of the relevant evidence (including its limits, gaps, and contradictions).

These are themselves policy-advocating suggestions. Further, our position is controversial among social scientists, resting (as do other such positions) on both factual claims and moral (value) assumptions. Adopting George Kelly's recommendation of reflexivity, let us analyze the recommendation in the same way we analyze the policy controversies that follow. Let us look separately at factual and value issues.

One factual question is the extent to which policies derived from psychological data are likely to be "better" than those developed without reference, or even in contradiction, to such data. This is a crucial question. Given the limitations of psychological knowledge and the even greater problems, already discussed, of extrapolating from such knowledge to macro-level policies, we cannot give a simple answer. However, although we feel it wise to move cautiously, we certainly do not dismiss the view that psychological data can contribute, to a greater or lesser degree depending on the issue, to the development of good policies. The qualifications in that statement identify important areas for research.

Second, even if we posit that the influence of psychologists on policy decisions is generally desirable, is that influence likely to be maximized by the cautious stance we recommend for behavioral scientists acting in role, or rather by a more unqualified advocacy position? The literature on one-sided versus two-sided arguments, and other research on communications and persuasion, may be relevant here.

Third, what is the effect of the two approaches likely to be, in the short and long term, internally (i.e., the reactions of our colleagues and members of our professional organizations) and externally (on the general public and its various segments)? There are no data available on this issue aside from anecdotal comments.

The value questions include whether scientists have a special obligation to be open and self-critical about their own positions in policy debates, even if this reduces their influence. We think that the ethics of psychology, both as explicitly written and as implicitly handed down across generations of scientists, dictate an affirmative answer. Is complete disclosure a basic and general ideal of science? We think so. Our position, obviously, is that due admission of uncertainty is definitely more honest and probably more persuasive in the long term. Such an approach is also less likely to invite hostility from those who may at some point discover that policies based on our advice were not satisfactory.

Last, these and the previous questions pose the critical one: How much of their integrity as scientists are psychologists, individually and collectively, willing to trade off to increase their immediate influence as policy advocates?

REFERENCES

Abelson, R. P., & Zimbardo, P. G. (1970). *Canvassing for peace.* Ann Arbor, MI: Society for the Psychological Study of Social Issues.
"AGM votes to oppose capital punishment." (1987, Summer). Canadian Psychological Association *Highlights,* p. 11E.
Albee, G. W. (1983). Political ideology and science: A reply to Eysenck. *American Psychologist, 38,* 965–966. (Comment.)
Albee, G. W. (1986). Toward a just society: Lessons from observations on the primary prevention of psychopathology. *American Psychologist, 41,* 891–898.
Allport, G. (1954). *The nature of prejudice.* Cambridge, MA: Addison-Wesley.
American Psychological Association. (1984). *Amended Bylaws,* Article I: Washington, DC: Author.
American Psychological Association. (1985). *Directory of the American Psychological Association.* Washington, DC: Author.
American Psychological Association. (1987). In the Supreme Court of the United States: Lockhart v. McCree. Amicus curiae brief. *American Psychologist, 42,* 59–68.
American Psychological Association Council. (1976). Proceedings of the American Psychological Association, Incorporated, for the year 1975. *American Psychologist, 31,* 406–434.
American Psychological Association Council. (1977). Proceedings of the American Psychological Association, Incorporated, for the year 1976. *American Psychologist, 32,* 408–438.
American Psychological Association Council. (1983). Proceedings of the American Psychological Association, Incorporated, for the year 1982. *American Psychologist, 38,* 649–682.
American Psychological Association Council. (1985). Proceedings of the American Psychological Association, Incorporated, for the year 1984. *American Psychologist, 39,* 621–653.
American Psychological Association Council. (1986). Proceedings of the American Psychological Association, Incorporated, for the year 1985. *American Psychologist, 40,* 633–663.
Argyris, C. (1975). Dangers in applying results from experimental social psychology. *American Psychologist, 30,* 469–485.
Aronson, E., & Osherow, N. (1980). Cooperation, prosocial behavior, and academic performance:

Experiments in the desegregated classroom. In L. Brickman (Ed.), *Applied social psychology annual* (Vol. 1, pp. 163–196). Beverly Hills, CA: Sage.

Ball-Rokeach, S. J., Rokeach, M., & Grube, J. W. (1984). *The great American values test: Influencing behavior and belief through television.* New York: Free Press.

Bazelon, D. L. (1982). Veils, values, and social responsibility. *American Psychologist, 37,* 115–121.

Bergin, A. E. (1982) On Garfield, Hatch, and psychology's values. *American Psychologist, 38,* 958–959. (Comment.)

Bevan, W. (1982). A sermon of sorts in three plus parts. *American Psychologist, 37,* 1303–1322.

Blight, J. G. (1986). How might psychology contribute to reducing the risk of nuclear war? *Political Psychology, 7,* 617–660.

Bramel, D., & Friend, R. (1981). Hawthorne, the myth of the docile worker, and class bias in psychology. *American Psychologist, 36,* 867–878.

Cameron, P., & Cameron, K. (1988). Did the American Psychological Association misrepresent scientific material to the U.S. Supreme Court? *Psychological Reports, 63,* 255–270.

Campbell, D. T. (1969). Reforms as experiments. *American Psychologist, 24,* 1409–1429.

Chesler, M. A., Sanders, J., & Kalmuss, D. S. (1989). *Social science in court: Mobilizing experts in the school desegregation cases.* Madison: University of Wisconsin Press.

Clark, K. B. (1971). The pathos of power: A psychological perspective. *American Psychologist, 26,* 1047–1057.

Comments on Sarason. (1985). *American Psychologist, 40,* 965–968.

Cook, S. W. (1984). The 1954 social science statement and school desegregation. *American Psychologist, 39,* 819–832.

Cook, S. W. (1985). Experimenting on social issues: The case of school desegregation. *American Psychologist, 40,* 452–460.

Cronbach, L. J., & Snow, R. E. (1977). *Aptitudes and instructional methods: A handbook for research on interactions.* New York: Irvington.

Dahl, R. A. (1989). *Democracy and its critics.* New Haven, CT: Yale University Press.

Dalby, S. (Guest Ed.). (1986, July). On teaching peace. *Issues in Education and Culture,* No. 2.

DeLeon, P. H. (1986). Increasing the societal contribution of organized psychology. *American Psychologist, 41,* 466–474.

Deutsch, M. (1969). Socially relevant science: Reflections on some studies of interpersonal conflict. *American Psychologist, 24,* 1076–1092.

Ehrlich, I. (1982). On positive methodology, ethics, and polemics in deterrence research. *British Journal of Criminology, 22,* 124–139.

Eysenck, H. J. (1982). Political ideology and science. *American Psychologist, 37,* 1288–1299. (Comment.)

Faraone, S. V. (1982). Psychiatry and political repression in the Soviet Union. *American Psychologist, 37,* 1105–1112.

Festinger, L. (1957). *A theory of cognitive dissonance.* Evanston, IL: Row, Peterson.

Fischhoff, B., Lichtenstein, S., Slovic, P., Derby, S. L., & Keeney, R. L. (1981). *Acceptable risk.* New York: Cambridge University Press.

Fishman, E. B., & Neigher, W. D. (1982). American psychology in the eighties. *American Psychologist, 37,* 533–546.

Flanagan, R., & Sommers, J. (1986). Ethical considerations for the peace activist psychotherapist. *American Psychologist, 41,* 723–724. (Comment.)

Forst, B. (1983). Capital punishment and deterrence: Conflicting evidence? *Journal of Criminal Law and Criminology, 74,* 927–942.

Fox, D. R. (1986). Beyond individualism and centralization. *American Psychologist, 41,* 231–232.

French, J. R. P. Jr., & Raven, B. H. (1959). The bases of social power. In D. Cartwright (Ed.), *Studies in social power* (pp. 150–167). Ann Arbor: University of Michigan Press.

Gardner, W., Scherer, D., & Tester, M. (1989). Asserting scientific authority: Cognitive development and adolescent legal rights. *American Psychologist, 44,* 895–902.

Garfinkle, A. M. (1986, Spring). Crisis decision making: The banality of theory. *Orbis,* pp. 13–41.

Gergen, K., & Davis, K. E. (1985). *The social construction of the person.* New York: Springer-Verlag.

Ginsburg, M. B. (1987). Contradictions in the role of professor as activist. *Sociological Focus, 20,* 111–122.

Goodwin, L. (1971). On making social research relevant to public policy and national problem solving. *American Psychologist, 26,* 431–442.

Gowans, C. W. (1987). *Moral dilemmas.* Oxford: Oxford University Press.

Graham, L. R. (1981). *Between science and values.* New York: Columbia University Press.

Haan, N. (1982). Can research on morality be "scientific"? *American Psychologist, 37,* 1096–1104.

Hammond, K. R., & Adelman, L. (1976). Science, values, and human judgment. *Science, 194,* 389–396.

Harris, B., Unger, R. K., & Stagner, R. (Issue Eds.). (1986). 50 years of psychology and social issues. *Journal of Social Issues, 42,* No. 1.

Hartsough, D. M., & Savitsky, J. C. (1984). Three Mile Island. *American Psychologist, 39,* 1113–1122.

Hatch, O. G. (1982). Psychology, society, and politics. *American Psychologist, 37,* 1031–1037.

Heider, F. (1958). *The psychology of interpersonal relations.* New York: Wiley.

Hillerbrand, E. (1987). Philosophical tensions influencing psychology and social action. *American Psychologist, 42,* 111–118.

Hough, J. (1985). Gorbachev's strategy. *Foreign Affairs, 64,* 33–55.

Howard, G. S. (1985). The role of values in the science of psychology. *American Psychologist, 40,* 255–265.

Huesmann, L. R., & Malamuth, N. M. (Issue Eds.). (1986). Media violence and antisocial behavior. *Journal of Social Issues, 42,* No. 3.

Jervis, R. (1976). *Perception and misperception in international politics.* Princeton, NJ: Princeton University Press.

Kelman, H. C. (1983). Conversations with Arafat: A social-psychological assessment of the prospects for Israeli-Palestinian peace. *American Psychologist, 38,* 203–216.

Kelman, H. C., & Bloom, A. H. (1973). Assumptive frameworks in international politics. In J. Knutson (Ed.), *Handbook of political psychology* (pp. 261–295). San Francisco: Jossey-Bass.

Kendler, H. H. (1983). Scientific conclusions or political advocacy? *American Psychologist, 41,* 1122–1127.

Kimmel, P. R. (1985). Learning about peace. *American Psychologist, 40,* 536–541.

Kimmel, P. R. (1986). The SPSSI investigation, or Special Prosecutors for Stopping Soviet Infiltration. *Journal of Social Issues, 42,* 115–143.

Kolata, G. (1987). Anthropologists turn advocates for the Brazilian Indians. *Science, 236,* 1183–1187.

Krasner, L., & Houts, A. C. (1984). A study of the "value" systems of behavioral scientists. *American Psychologist, 39,* 840–850.

Larsen, K. S. (Ed.). (1986). *Dialectics and ideology in psychology.* Norwood, NJ: Ablex.

Lifton, R. J. (1982). Beyond psychic numbing: A call to awareness. *American Journal of Orthopsychiatry, 52,* 619–629.

Lineberry, R. L. (1988, 18 July). This week's citation classic. *Current Contents: Social and Behavioral Sciences, 20*(29), 14.

Mahoney, M. J. (1985). Open exchange and epistemic progress. *American Psychologist, 40,* 29–39.

Mangan, K. S. (1987, 29 April). Academic psychologists are dropping out of association in discord with practitioners. *Chronicle of Higher Education, 33*(33), 12 & 14.

Manicas, P. T., & Secord, P. F. (1983). Implications for psychology of the new philosophy of science. *American Psychologist, 38,* 399–413.

Mansdorf, I. J. (1983). On Kelman's "Conversations with Arafat." *American Psychologist, 38,* 1122–1123. (Comment.)

Marshall, E. (1987). Nuclear winter debate heats up. *Science, 235,* 271–273

McConnell, S. C., Brown, S. D., Ruffing, J. N., Strupp, J. K., Duncan, B. L., & Kurdek, L. A. (1986). Psychologists' attitudes and activities regarding nuclear arms. *American Psychologist, 41,* 725–727.

McGuire, W. J. (1983). A contextualist theory of knowledge: Its implications for innovation and reform in psychological research. In L. Berkowitz (Ed.), *Advances in experimental social psychology* (pp. 2–47). New York: Academic Press.

McGuire, W. J. (1985). Attitudes and attitude change. In E. Aronson & G. Lindzey (Eds.), *Handbook of social psychology* (pp. 233–346). New York: Random House.

Mednick, M. T. (1989). On the politics of psychological constructs: Stop the bandwagon, I want to get off. *American Psychologist, 44,* 1118–1123.

Meehl, P. (1975). Comments in control and countercontrol: A panel discussion. In T. Thompson & W. S. Dockens, III (Eds.), *Applications of behavior modification* (p. 511). New York: Academic Press.

Meehl, P. (1978). Theoretical risks and tabular asterisks: Sir Karl, Sir Ronald, and the slow progress of soft psychology. *Journal of Consulting and Clinical Psychology, 46,* 806–834.

Menninger, K. (1968). *The crime of punishment.* New York: Viking.

Miller, G. A. (1969). Psychology as a means of promoting human welfare. *American Psychologist, 24,* 1063–1075.

Morawski, J. G. (1982). Assessing psychology's moral heritage through our neglected utopias. *American Psychologist, 37,* 1082–1095.

Münsterberg, H. (1913). *Psychology and industrial efficiency.* Boston: Houghton Mifflin.

Nelson, A. (1986). Psychological equivalence. *American Psychologist, 40,* 549–556.

Nisbett, R., & Ross, L. (1980). *Human inference: Strategies and shortcomings of social judgment.* Englewood Cliffs, NJ: Prentice-Hall.

Pallak, M. S., & Kilburg, R. R. (1986). Psychology, public affairs, and public policy. *American Psychologist, 41,* 933–940.

Pipes, R. (1984). *Survival is not enough: Soviet realities and America's future.* New York: Free Press.

Policy and Planning Board (APA). (1970). APA and public policy: A survey of member views. *American Psychologist, 30,* 496–502.

Policy Forum. (1987). Verification and arms control. *Science, 235,* 406–414.

Pollack, C., Crain, I. J., Borbely, A., Naimark, H., & Rabinowitz, C. (1983). Soviet psychiatry. *American Psychologist, 38,* 1401–1402.

Polyson, J., Stein, D., & Sholley, B. (1986). Psychologists and nuclear war: A national survey. *American Psychologist, 41,* 724–725. (Comment.)

Rapoport, A. (1984). Preparation for nuclear war: The final madness. *American Journal of Orthopsychiatry, 54,* 524–529.

Rappoport, L., & Kren, G. (1975). What is a social issue? *American Psychologist, 30,* 838–841.

Robinson, D. N. (1984). Ethics and advocacy. *American Psychologist, 39,* 787–793.

Rudmin, F. (1986). History of peace psychology: Comment on Morawski and Goldstein. *American Psychologist, 41,* 586–588. (Comment.)

Sagan, C. (1983/1984, Winter). Nuclear war and climatic catastrophe. *Foreign Affairs, 62,* 257–292.

Sandler, D. (1988, June). What proof? *APA Monitor, 19*(6), 2. (Letter.)

Sarason, S. B. (1984). If it can be studied or developed, should it be? *American Psychologist, 39,* 477–485.

Sarason, S. B. (1986). And what is the public interest? *American Psychologist, 41,* 899–905.

Schmidt, F. L., & Hunter, J. E. (1981). Employment testing: Old themes and new research findings. *American Psychologist, 36,* 1128–1137.

Schumann, H., & Presser, S. (1981). *Questions and answers in attitude surveys: Experiments on question form, wording, and context.* New York: Academic Press.

Seitz, R. (1986, Fall). In from the cold: Nuclear winter melts down. *The National Interest,* pp. 3–17.

Shapiro, H. T. (1984). Is taking sides a good idea for universities? *Science, 225,* 9. (Editorial.)

Sherif, M. (1958). Superordinate goals in the reduction of intergroup conflicts. *American Journal of Sociology, 63,* 349–356.

Skinner, B. F. (1948). *Walden Two.* New York: Macmillan.

Slavin, R. E. (1985). Cooperative learning: Applying contact theory in desegregated schools. *Journal of Social Issues, 41*(3), 45–62.

Slovic, P. (1987). Perception of risk. *Science, 236,* 280–285.

Stein, G. J. (1988, January-February). Biological science and the roots of Nazism. *American Scientist, 76*(1), 50–58.

Suedfeld, P. (1980). *Restricted environmental stimulation: Research and clinical applications.* New York: Wiley.

Suedfeld, P. (1983). Authoritarian leadership: A cognitive-interactionist view. In J. Held (Ed.), *The cult of power: Dictators in the twentieth century* (pp. 1–22). Boulder, CO: East European Monographs.

Suedfeld, P. (1988, July/August). Authoritarian thinking, groupthink, and decision-making under stress: Are simple decisions always worse? *Transaction/Society, 25*(5), 25–27.

Suedfeld, P., & Tetlock, P. E. (1990). *Integrative complexity: Theory and research.* Unpubl. manuscript, University of British Columbia and University of California, Berkeley.

Szasz, T. (1961). *The myth of mental illness: Foundations of a theory of personal conduct.* New York: Dell.

Task Force on Psychology and Public Policy. (1986). Psychology and public policy. *American Psychologist, 41,* 914–921.

Tetlock, P. E. (1986). Psychological advice on foreign policy. *American Psychologist, 41,* 557–567.

Tetlock, P. E. (1989). Structure and function in political belief systems. In A. Protkanis, S. Breckler, & A. Greenwald (Eds.), *Attitude structure and function* (pp. 129–151). Hillsdale, NJ: Erlbaum.

Tetlock, P. E., Mitchell, G., & McGuire, C. (1991). Psychological perspectives on nuclear deterrence. *Annual Review of Psychology, 42,* 239–276.

Varela, J. A. (1971). *Psychological solutions to social problems.* New York: Academic Press.

Weiss, J. A., & Weiss, C. H. (1981). Social scientists and decision makers look at the usefulness of mental health research. *American Psychologist, 36,* 837–847.

Wolpe, J. (1981). Behavior therapy versus psychoanalysis. *American Psychologist, 36,* 159–164.

Zimbardo, P. G. (1972). The tactics and ethics of persuasion. In B. T. King & E. McGinnies (Eds.), *Attitudes, conflict, and social change* (pp. 81–99). New York: Academic Press.

I

INTERNATIONAL RELATIONS AND FOREIGN POLICY

2

Cognitive Complexity in International Decision Making

Irving L. Janis† and Leon Mann

DECISION MAKING: SIMPLE VERSUS COMPLEX

It is necessary to clarify the nature of the debate regarding the merits of complexity and simplicity of decision-making procedures in international affairs. A contrast has been drawn between scholars who favor complexity in national and international decision making (e.g., Janis & Mann, 1977) and those who emphasize the role of simple solution strategies in dealing with international problems (e.g., Suedfeld, 1988). In this debate the two sides are seen as differing in the entrenchment of their respective positions. The procomplexity camp comprises stalwarts of an uncompromising position whose motto could be: "complex approaches for all complex decisions." The prosimplicity camp contains advocates of a flexible position that approves of simple decision rules for solving major international crises.

We maintain that this is a false characterization of the opposing views. Drawing a stark contrast between "simple" and "complex" decision-making processes is not particularly useful for evaluating the effectiveness of different procedural strategies for making major policy decisions. More specifically, we do not expect a variable that can range from very simple to very complex will prove to be linearly related to achieving the policy makers' objectives. Rather, what we do expect is that one particular procedural strategy that is *moderately* complex will prove to yield better outcomes on the average than strategies that are either less complex or more complex. The moderately complex set of procedures is designated as *vigilant problem solving* (Janis, 1989; Janis & Mann, 1977). In this chapter we compare this procedural strategy with a number of other strategies, some much simpler and others much more complicated.

SHORTCOMINGS OF SIMPLE DECISION RULES

Harassed and constrained policy makers often rely on simple decision rules for solving different problems. Sole reliance on those decision rules in major interna-

---

†Irving L. Janis died on 15 November 1990. This chapter, submitted to the editors in 1989, was one of Janis' last works.

tional crises is likely to lead to failure (Janis, 1989). Three types of simple decision rules can be identified: cognitive decision rules (e.g., availability, "satisficing," analogizing); affiliative decision rules (e.g., avoid punishment from other
power holders, rig acceptance) and egocentric decision rules (e.g., "satisfy self-
aggrandizing motives," "retaliate when humiliated").

Simple decision rules all have the advantage of providing shortcuts that enable
the decision maker to cope with time limitations, lack of knowledge, social pressures, and emotional stress, which interfere with high quality decision making
(Janis, 1989, p. 28). Simple decision rules enable the decision maker to by-pass
large amounts of information otherwise involved in a crucial decision. They include highly selective search strategies, protective codes to ensure survival in case
the decision turns out to be a disaster, and single-principle rules of thumb for
choosing a course of action.

An example of a simple search rule is embodied in the "satisficing" approach
described by Herbert Simon (1976), which is a strategy for searching only a
fraction of the information relating to the problem. It involves the decision maker
in examining alternatives sequentially until one is found that is good enough because it meets the minimum requirements. There is no consideration of the likelihood that other, unexamined alternatives could be vastly superior.

An example of a simple choice rule is the "historical precedents" principle.
This rule directs the decision maker to "do what we did last time if it worked and
the opposite if it didn't" (cf. Jervis, 1976; May, 1973). An example of an affiliative rule that provides protection is the "protect your interests" rule, practiced
particularly by astute middle-level executives who find out what the power holders
really want before advocating a position.

Common to all simple decision rules is their application in what is sometimes
called quick-and-easy decision making and sometimes called seat-of-the-pants decision making.

We assume that simple decision rules can be useful as supplementary aids in
high quality policy making (for example, to screen or reduce the set of alternatives
under consideration). Our basic postulate, however, is that exclusive reliance on
such rules for processing information or for selecting policy alternatives is highly
dangerous when vital interests are at stake.

When a crucial policy decision is required, one of the shortcomings of relying
on simple decision rules is that they lead to a choice from among a potentially
narrow set of alternatives. They direct the decision maker to be selective in consideration of alternatives. They do not provide adequate guidance to the decision
maker on the prior question: How is the set of eligible alternatives to be identified
in the first place? Simple decision rules have the additional drawback of inducing
premature choice, based only on one or two selection criteria, such as historical
precedent, retribution, or acceptability to the majority (cf. George, 1974).

Decision makers who rely on a few simple decision rules practice a simplistic
strategy. This is the unjustifiable simplification of a decision problem in
cases that require a more complex strategy to avoid serious errors (Janis, 1989, p.
27ff). We do not oppose simple decision rules, as such. They have their place,
but not as a substitute for the careful information search, deliberation, and planning that is essential for major policy decisions at the national and international
levels.

HIGHLY COMPLEX PROCEDURES
AND THEIR SHORTCOMINGS

Complexity in decision making refers to procedures that entail extensive processing of information as well as intensive group deliberations and reliance on sophisticated technical and statistical processes. The latter processes usually require the assistance of expert decision analysts using computer systems to structure or interpret the problem and to recommend the best available choice. Among the most complex procedural strategies are those proposed by professional policy analysts, who attempt to make use of expected utility theory, systems analysis, computer modeling, or decision-tree analysis (see Abelson & Levi, 1985; Hogarth, 1980).

Complex decision rules involve a thorough search through all information pertaining to alternatives and application of a choice rule that purports to provide an optimal solution to the problem. Examples of complex decision rules are the equal weights rule and the weighted additive rule. Both rules require the decision maker to examine all alternatives and take into account the value (or weighted value) of each attribute for every alternative before choosing the best one (cf. Payne, Bettman, & Johnson, 1988).

In general, complex decision rules are more costly in time and effort than simple decision rules. Sometimes they are more accurate, sometimes they are not (see Tetlock, 1989). Complex procedures often generate mountains of computer printouts of all the data bearing on the problem and this in turn generates calls for assistance from professional analysts to make sense of the data. As Zeleny (1981, p. 359) points out, "more information does not necessarily imply better decisions."

Should political decision makers collaborate with decision analysts to apply the highly complex procedures of interactive computer-based decision aids to help solve policy problems? Examples of decision technology include problem-structuring aids for formalizing the structure of a problem, bootstrapping aids for automating the entire sequence of decision making, and recomposition aids for integrating and examining the contents of the problem structure (cf. Wisudha, 1985). These aids are usually based on very complicated rules. They include decision-tree analysis based on expected-utility principles (Ulvila & Brown, 1982), and multiple-attribute utility decomposition, known as MAUD (Humphreys & McFadden, 1980).

MAUD is a sophisticated computer-based decision aid that is designed to enable the decision maker to take account of compensatory trade-offs and to select the alternative that attains the best overall utility score across all attributes. Although MAUD appears straightforward, it involves the decision maker in specifying a set of alternatives and the requisite attributes, determining the weight for each attribute, awarding a scale score (or utility) on each attribute for each alternative, and then summing the scores to obtain a preference. These complex procedures assume but cannot provide a high degree of comparability of attributes and a high degree of precision and reliability in assigning utility scores to attributes. Moreover, it may often be unwarranted to assume that the best alternative will emerge from adding up utility scores.

Humphreys and McFadden (1980) conclude that the MAUD decision aid is more useful in raising general decision-making capability than in solving immediate decision problems. Nevertheless, procedures involving complex decision rules and complex decision technology may prove effective in certain types of decisions, such as environmental decisions involving the siting of pumped storage facilities, liquefied natural gas terminals, or toxic waste releases (Van der Pligt, 1988). But we, along with many other social scientists, expect that for most policy decisions involving international relations, domestic political issues, and public welfare issues, decision analysis involving these highly complex procedures will prove ineffective and could even be counterproductive (see Slovic, Fischhoff, & Lichtenstein, 1977).

When overloaded with extraneous information, people may actually be hindered from getting to the core of a problem. Information overload tends to produce confusion. It may also produce a dilution effect in which the full impact of relevant and useful information is attenuated by masses of irrelevant information (cf. Nisbett, Zukier, & Lemley, 1981). When only one or two pieces of information are critical for sizing up a problematic situation, having additional, often confusing or unnecessary information can have adverse effects (Tetlock, 1989; Tetlock & Boettger, 1989).

What we propose as an alternative to simplistic seat-of-the-pants procedures and highly complex decision analysis procedures is the procedural strategy of vigilant problem solving (Janis, 1989; Janis & Mann, 1977). We believe that for most important political decisions, this moderately complex set of procedures will yield better outcomes than either less complex procedures that rely on simple decision rules or highly complex decision-analysis procedures like the ones we have just discussed. Whether this assumption is correct remains to be settled by empirical evidence from future research. There is already at hand, however, some preliminary evidence suggesting our assumption is plausible, which we shall summarize after we describe the essential procedures.

NATURE OF VIGILANT PROBLEM SOLVING

Vigilant problem solving consists of procedures that meet the criteria for relatively high quality policy decisions. What are the criteria? The following seven procedural criteria have been extracted by Janis and Mann (1977) from the extensive research on effective decision making by individual executives and by members of policy-making groups in government, business corporations, and public welfare organizations. To the best of his or her ability, the decision maker:

1. Surveys a wide range of objectives to be fulfilled, taking account of the multiplicity of values that are at stake;
2. Canvasses a wide range of alternative courses of action;
3. Intensively searches for new information relevant to evaluating the alternatives;
4. Correctly assimilates and takes account of new information or expert judgments, even if the information or judgment does not support the course of action initially preferred;
5. Reconsiders the positive and negative consequences of alternatives originally regarded as unacceptable, before making a final choice;
6. Carefully examines the costs and risks of negative consequences, as well as the positive consequences, that could flow from the chosen alternative;

7. Makes detailed provisions for implementing and monitoring the chosen course of action, with special attention to contingency plans for dealing with problems that could materialize.

For purposes of investigating the quality of policy decision making, each of the seven criteria should be conceptualized as a continuum on which the decision maker can be given a low, medium, or high rating. At the lower end of each continuum are instances of executives who introduce a new policy without doing much to meet each criterion, for example, practically no surveying of objectives, canvassing of alternatives, or search for new relevant information. Any gross failure to meet one of the criteria, when dealing with a vital policy issue, can be regarded as a symptom of defective policy making. An important feature of vigilant problem solving is that all the essential steps are carried out sufficiently well that none of the seven symptoms is displayed.

In the case of routine and minor decisions, failures to meet the criteria are not necessarily symptoms of defective decision making, because for such decisions simple procedures are cost effective, even though they can lead to errors that were avoidable. When there is little at stake, avoidable errors are generally tolerable. It is not worth the time and effort to go through the steps of vigilant problem solving. The term *defective decision making* is reserved for decisions about policy issues that have serious consequences for vital interests of the organization or nation.

One reason for using the lower end of each continuum for our theoretical analyses and research is that there are ambiguities about the upper end. When has more than enough been done already? This question often cannot be answered. For major policy decisions, the amount of information that is potentially relevant concerning possible consequences of the options under consideration is far greater than anyone would ever be able or willing to collect. And, of course, it is difficult to judge when the point is reached where it is no longer worth the costs of procuring and processing more information. A very high rating can itself be misleading, because sometimes policy makers become preoccupied with meeting one or another of the criteria, regardless of the triviality of the problem and the cost in organizational time and resources.

There are fewer ambiguities to contend with when judging whether policy makers have done so little that they have failed to meet a criterion. Accordingly, it seems preferable to assess the quality of the procedures used by policy makers with reference to the lower end of the continuum for each of the seven criteria, that is, to determine the number of gross symptoms of defective policy making.

The essential steps of vigilant problem solving are represented in Figure 2.1, which summarizes the main components described by social scientists who have studied policy making. Figure 2.1 is not intended as an ideal model for the making of policy decisions. It is a realistic descriptive model of what most executives demonstrate they are capable of doing when they try to do the best job of decision making under the circumstances. The model describes what executives can do despite the constraints of limited capacity to process information, incomplete knowledge, and unresolvable uncertainties. Among the additional constraints that are often present are social pressures from other power holders and the need to cope with the psychological stress generated by decision conflicts.

The hallmark of high quality decision making is that by the time the policy makers arrive at their final choice and move toward closure, they have carried out

Challenge:
Threat or opportunity (e.g., crisis posing threat to vital interests)

Step 1
Formulating the problem:
Q.1 What requirements should be met:
• Dangers to be averted
• Gains to be attained
• Costs to be kept to tolerable levels?
Q.2 What seems to be best direction of solution? (top-of-the-head survey of alternatives)

Step 2
Using informational resources:
Q.3 What prior information can be recalled or retrieved?
Q.4 What new information should be obtained:
• Expert's forecasts
• Intelligence reports, etc.?

Step 3
Analyzing and reformulating:
Q.5 Any additions to or changes in the requirements?
Q.6 Any additional alternatives?
Q.7 What additional information might reduce uncertainties?

Step 4
Evaluating and selecting:
Q.8 What are the pros and cons for each alternative?
Q.9 Which alternative appears to be best?
Q.10 Any requirements unmet? (If so, can they be relaxed or changed? If not, might a modification be better?)
Q.11 How can potential costs and risks be minimized?
Q.12 What additional plans are needed for implementation, monitoring, and contingencies?

Deciding after adequate search, appraisal, and planning—manifested by absence of the following defects in decisionmaking procedures:
1. Gross omissions in survey of objectives.
2. Gross omissions in survey of alternatives.
3. Poor information search.
4. Selective bias in processing information at hand.
5. Failure to reconsider originally rejected alternatives.
6. Failure to examine some major costs and risks of preferred choice.
7. Failure to work out detailed implementation, monitoring, and contingency plans.

CLOSURE
Internal consolidation of the choice:
• Bolstering it by playing up the advantages and playing down the disadvantages.
• Soliciting supportive information.
• Refuting unwelcome information about drawbacks.

+

Social commitment to the choice:
• Announcing it to interested parties.
• Promoting it, especially among implementers and policy evaluators who are unenthusiastic.

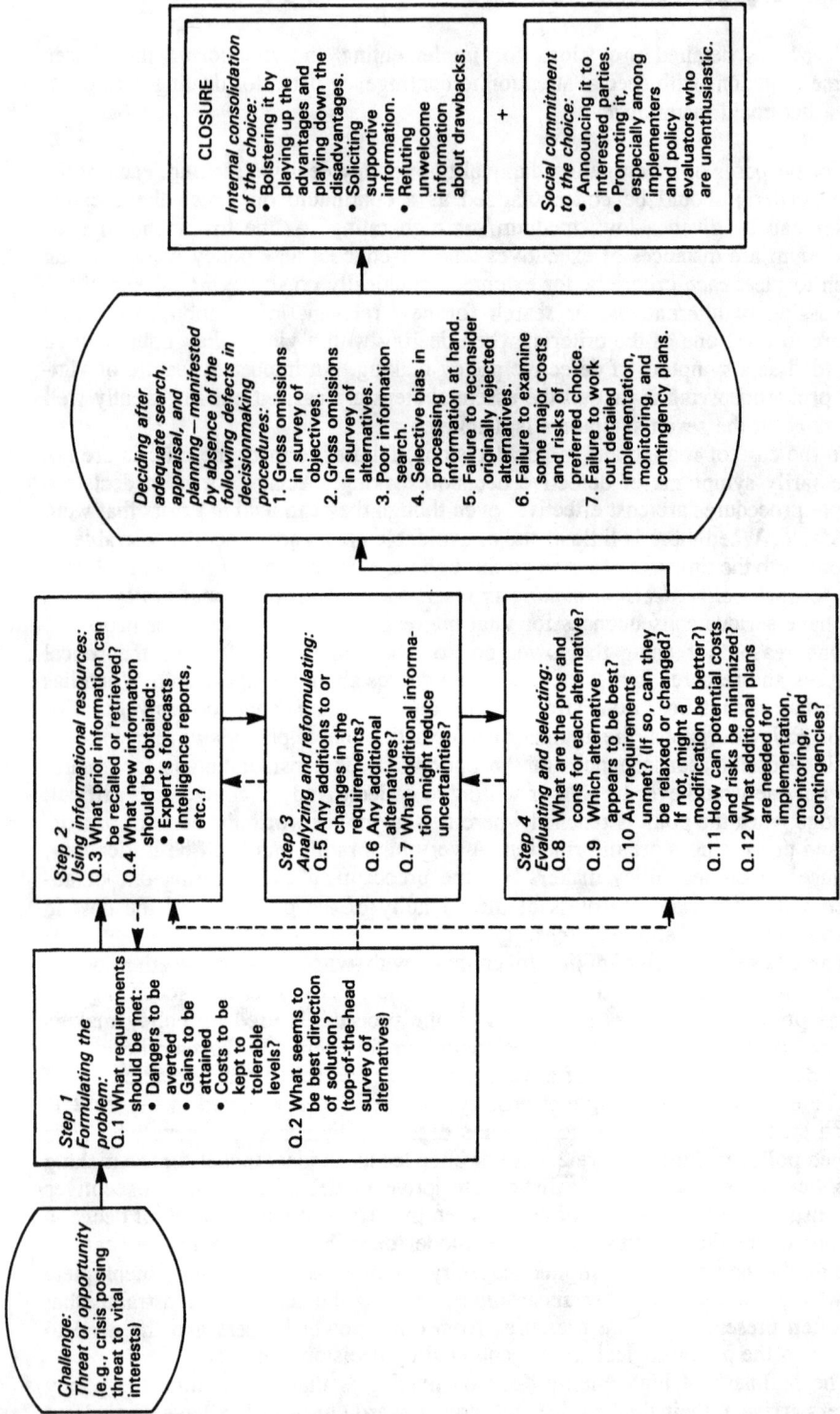

Figure 2.1 Main steps characterizing a vigilant problem-solving approach to decision making. (Reprinted from *Crucial decisions: Leadership in policy making and crisis management* by Irving L. Janis. Copyright © 1989 by The Free Press, a division of Macmillan, Inc.)

the essential steps of vigilant problem solving. That is to say, they answer all the key questions listed in Figure 2.1 sufficiently well so that there are no remaining symptoms of defective decision making at the time they commit themselves to a chosen course of action. Obviously, it would be much less costly, in terms of time and effort, to use a simplistic strategy based on one or two simple decision rules than to carry out all the steps of the vigilant problem-solving strategy shown in Figure 2.1. But the outcome may prove to be much more costly in terms of the policy makers' main objective.

RELATIONSHIP OF VIGILANT PROBLEM SOLVING TO OUTCOMES

We expect that the relatively high quality procedures of vigilant problem solving will be positively related to successful outcomes, but we cannot expect more than a modest correlation because many other factors also contribute to outcomes. Even a well-designed policy can fail because of uncontrollable actions by competitors. Or unforeseeable internal obstacles and chance events can prevent the organization from implementing a policy the way it was intended. Also, unsuccessful policy outcomes stemming from the leaders' oversimplified beliefs and ideological stereotypes can give rise to faulty assumptions about the requirements for a good solution or about the consequences of the choice. Other variables also moderate the relationship between the quality of the decision making process and the outcome (e.g., time constraints and the signal-to-noise ratio of whatever information is available). Even when policy makers are open-minded and conscientious about obtaining factual information pertinent to the issue, the evidence available may be erroneous or too ambiguous to indicate that their initial presumptions are wrong. Nevertheless, the quality of the procedures used to arrive at decisions is often a major determinant of successful outcomes.

When policy makers do a poor job of collecting relevant information, appraising consequences, and making contingency plans, the outcome of their policy decision could, nevertheless, turn out to be success. The net effect of chance and uncontrollable factors occasionally provides them with good luck. But we expect the likelihood of success to be considerably greater when sound procedures for information search, appraisal, and planning are used.

We now turn to an examination of research evidence bearing on our central assumption, that failure to engage in vigilant problem solving substantially increases the likelihood of unfavorable outcomes of consequential decisions.

There is indirect evidence that decision makers who take account of the requirements for satisfying their objectives and values, as assumed by expected utility theorists, sometimes choose good solutions (Abelson & Levi, 1985). This implies that the policy makers have gone through at least a few of the essential steps of vigilant problem solving. The evidence is equivocal because the investigators did not make any observations of the decision-making process and the findings could be interpreted in other ways.

More direct evidence of the effectiveness of a vigilant problem-solving approach is provided by the systematic study by Herek, Janis, and Huth (1987). The main purpose of this study was to investigate the relationship between quality of decision-making processes used and outcome of the policy decisions made by the

U.S. government in 19 major international crises. For each crisis, detailed ratings were made of the presence or absence of each of the seven symptoms of defective policy making listed in the fourth column of Figure 2.1 (see p. 38).

Examination of the "Total Symptoms" column in Table 2.1 reveals that the U.S. crisis managers in the White House used fairly high-quality procedures in making a substantial proportion of their decisions. For 8 of the 19 crises (42%), there were either no symptoms at all or only one symptom of defective decision making, which indicates that the crisis managers used a vigilant problem-solving approach about as well as could be expected under crisis conditions. But in the other 11 cases, the crisis managers evidently did not do so. The policy-making process in 4 crises (21%) was of medium quality (two or three symptoms), and in 7 crises (37%) it was of low quality (four or more symptoms).

One of the implications of the observed variability in number of symptoms displayed by the crisis managers is that policy makers who demonstrate that they have the capability for vigilant decision making do not always use it. For example, the crisis managers in the Nixon administration displayed only one defective decision making symptom in the Yom Kippur War crisis in 1973, whereas they displayed all seven symptoms in the Indo-Pakistani War crisis in 1971.

There are marked variations, perhaps arising from differences in decision-making capabilities or skills, among the different groups of crisis managers in

Table 2.1 Processes and outcome scores for 19 major international crises (Herek, Janis, & Huth, 1987)

Crisis	Quality of process (Total symptoms of defective policy making)		International conflict	U.S. interests
			Outcome score	
Indochina (1954)	0		+1	+1
Quemoy-Matsu II (1958)	0	16%	+1	+1
Laos (1961)	0		+1	0
Greek Civil War (1947)	1		−1	+1
Quemoy-Matsu I (1954–1955)	1		+1	+1
Berlin Wall (1961)	1	26%	0	0
Cuban Missile Crisis (1962)	1		+1	+1
Yom Kippur War (1973)	1		+1	+1
Invasion of South Korea (1950)	2		0	+1
Suez War (1956)	2	16%	+1	−1
Jordan Civil War (1970)	2		+1	+1
Berlin blockade (1948–1949)	3	5%	−1	+1
Tonkin Gulf incidents (1964)	4	10%	−1	0
Vietnam Ground War (1965)	4		−1	−1
Vietnam Air War (1964–1965)	5		0	−1
Arab-Israeli War (1967)	5	16%	0	0
Cambodian incursions (1970)	5		0	−1
Korean War escalation (1950)	6	5%	−1	−1
Indo-Pakistani War (1971)	7	5%	0	0

Note. The cases are ordered according to total number of symptoms of defective decision making displayed by the President and other top-level leaders of the United States government. Outcome scores of −1 indicate that both outside experts agreed that the crisis outcome was unfavorable, +1 indicates agreement that the outcome was favorable, and 0 indicates disagreement. Table 3 in Herek, Janis, and Huth (1987) is the source for the outcome ratings shown in this table, but as published in the December 1987 issue of the Journal of Conflict Resolution (Volume 31, page 672) under the heading of Erratum.

different presidential administrations. For example, crisis managers in the Eisenhower and Kennedy administrations displayed fewer symptoms than those in the Truman, Johnson, and Nixon administrations. Nevertheless, each President with his group of crisis managers showed considerable variation in the quality of decision making from one policy decision to another.

Table 2.1 also provides data pertinent to the main question investigated in the Herek, Janis, and Huth (1987) study: Are the symptoms of defective decision making (which reflect failures to carry out the essential steps of vigilant problem solving) predictive of unfavorable outcomes?

Ratings for the outcome of each crisis were obtained from two independent experts on international crises who held different political views about the Cold War. The experts were "blind" to the research hypotheses at the time they rated the effectiveness of crisis management by U.S. policy makers for each crisis. They provided two sets of ratings. First, they rated the effects on U.S. vital interests, specifically whether those interests were advanced, hindered, or unaffected during the days and weeks after the crises. Second, they rated the level of international conflict during the days and weeks after the ends of the crises, specifically whether there was an increase, decrease, or no change in tension, stability, hostility, or the likelihood of war between the United States and the Soviet Union or China. The two experts' ratings were combined to yield an outcome score that indicated a satisfactory degree of interanalyst reliability.

The results in Table 2.1 show a strong relationship between quality of decision making as manifested by number of symptoms of defective decision making (rated by a member of the research team who was kept "blind" to the research hypotheses at the time) and unfavorable outcomes (based on the average ratings of the two independent experts, who were also kept "blind"). Correlational analysis shows that higher symptom scores were significantly related to unfavorable outcomes for U.S. vital interests ($r = .64, p = .002$) and to unfavorable outcomes for international conflict ($r = .62, p = .002$). Thus the results indicate that the larger the number of symptoms of defective decision making, the less likely that the crisis outcome would be favorable. The findings are consistent with the hypothesis that when policy makers use vigilant problem-solving procedures they tend to make decisions that are likely to meet their goals. Contrary to the pessimistic views of Starbuck (1983, 1985) and other skeptics, who claim that the vigilant problem-solving approach is not effective for major policy decisions, the quality of the decision-making process is related to the policy decision's outcome.

While the correlations between process and outcome support the hypothesis that low-quality decision making leads to unfavorable outcomes, they do not prove a causal relationship. Significant correlations could result from the influence of a third (unobserved) variable. Very serious crises could be associated with grossly defective decision making and with less favorable outcomes because extremely serious crises are more stressful and are fraught with large, unavoidable traps. This alternative explanation seems improbable, however, on the basis of a stepwise regression analysis that took account of independent ratings of the seriousness of the crises and difficulty of the decision making (see Herek, Janis, & Huth, 1987, pp. 217–218).

In this study the two experts were also asked to rate the long-term outcomes of the crises, that is, the consequences in the months and years after the crisis ended. Although the experts showed fairly high agreement on their ratings of the short-term outcomes, they showed a considerable disagreement on the long-term outcomes. This is characteristic of the crisis management literature. For example, the immediate outcome of the Cuban Missile Crisis decisions, according to practically all analysts, was positive. But the analysts do not agree about the long-term outcome. Some say that Kennedy's decisions led to a lessening of the Cold War and other long-term positive effects; others say that the effects over the following years were extremely negative because Kennedy's decisions led Soviet leaders to increase their nuclear forces, which augmented the arms race.

Probably one reason why there is little agreement about long-term effects is that many additional factors come into play during the months and years after a crisis. Experts can only guess at which of the factors that come into play before and after the end of the crisis were the ones that ended up playing dominant causal roles. Observations of long-term changes after major crises therefore cannot be expected to provide dependable conclusions about the effects of the quality of crisis decision making. For major crises that pose the danger of outbreak of nuclear war, or any other immediate catastrophe, however, short-term effects are of crucial importance for vital interests, including national survival. Accordingly, evidence on short-term effects of major international crises is relevant for developing a basic theory of effective policy making and for drawing inferences about how crisis management might be improved.

There are, of course, certain types of policy decisions for which long-term effects are crucial. One such type consists of those policy decisions designed to reduce pollution and prevent ecocatastrophes. For these decisions, we expect a positive relationship between the decision-making process and the crucial long-term outcomes, but it is difficult for research investigators to collect and assess the cogent evidence. Perhaps dependable research data on the relationship could be obtained, however, from studies of other types of policy decisions, such as those made by large business corporations and public welfare organizations, with the goal of attaining their long-term objectives, including survival of the organization.

SUPPORT FROM OTHER SOCIAL SCIENTISTS

A few social scientists do not agree with our views about the effectiveness of vigilant problem solving (e.g., Lindblom, 1980; Starbuck, 1985), but our position is neither unique nor remarkable. A number of scholars who have conducted research on decision making in international crises agree with our views. For example, Stein and Tanter (1980) in their analysis of policy decisions made during international crises reach a conclusion similar to ours: "Other things being equal, 'good' procedures are more likely to produce 'good' outcomes" (p. 8).

Alexander George (1980) also shares our view from his extensive studies of presidential decision making in foreign and domestic policy issues. George concludes that a President's premature resort to or overreliance on simple decision rules, such as consensus (finding out what most people in the organization will accept), "can be dysfunctional insofar as it interferes with the search and analysis activities that should precede choice of policy" (p. 187).

Herbert Simon's (1976) account of how executives in business and government made "good" decisions is also compatible with our views. In practice, according to Simon, good policy makers who strive for high-quality decisions engage in analytic problem solving. Their procedures involve working to the best of their limited abilities within the confines of available organizational resources to exercise all the caution they can to avoid mistakes in the essential tasks of information search, deliberation, and planning.

Neustadt and May (1986), on the basis of their studies of decision making by corporate executives and government leaders, recommend the main steps of vigilant problem solving to improve outcomes. For example, they recommend that policy makers begin their deliberations by drawing up three separate lists of what is actually known, what remains unclear, and what is assumed. They suggest that policy makers test each assumption by explicitly asking: "What fresh facts . . . would cause us to change this presumption?" They also recommend that policy makers use a similar procedure when they reach the stage of examining the pros and cons of viable options. The case examples given by Neustadt and May indicate that such information search and appraisal can correct faulty assumptions and conceptual errors in working on policy decisions.

In sum, the postulate that vigilant problem solving increases the likelihood of desirable outcomes is consistent with the views of a number of social scientists, including George (1980), Lawrence (1985), Lebow (1981), Neustadt and May (1986), and Stein and Tanter (1980).

IMPORTANT FEATURES OF VIGILANT PROBLEM SOLVING

The assumptions we make about vigilant problem solving are not equivalent to those of "rational actor" models, although they have some components in common. The rational actor model espoused the notion that policy makers almost always deal with policy problems by trying to find the best possible alternative, the one that emerges from thorough information search and careful comparisons that take account of all the gains they want to maximize. Such a model has been subjected to continual criticism and cannot be sustained as a descriptive theory (cf. Kahneman & Tversky, 1979; Lebow, 1981; Slovic, Fischhoff, & Lichtenstein, 1977).

The discredited rational actor model has been replaced among some social scientists by a nonrational actor model that supposedly holds true for almost all policy decisions (see Lindblom, 1980). But the nonrational actor model appears to be as flawed as the rational actor model. Examples abound of chief executives who demonstrated clear, vigilant problem solving in dealing with some crises, but revealed fuzzy and even simple-minded thinking in dealing with others. Fred Greenstein's (1982) analysis of Dwight Eisenhower's presidential decision making in relation to the 1954 crisis of Quemoy and Matsu is a prime example of a leader who, despite his popular image as a pleasant but ineffectual policy maker, was capable of high-quality decision making.

Our assumption is that practically all policy makers show considerable variability in the way they arrive at policy decisions. Sometimes they rely on satisficing or other simple decision rules; sometimes they are swayed by self-serving and emotive biases; at other times they use a mixed approach with partial reliance on simple decision rules; and once in a while, under certain conditions, policy makers practice all the steps of vigilant problem solving. In short, we assume that the steps of vigilant problem solving are part of the repertoire of most policy makers. But we also assume that most of them seldom use full-blown vigilant problem solving (see Figure 2.2). It is reserved for challenges that they judge to be of major importance, ones they see as affecting the vital interests of the organization or nation. For decisions they judge to be of minor and even moderate importance, a simple or mixed strategy is used, which saves the time, cost, and effort involved in vigilant problem solving.

Figure 2.2 indicates that a major determinant of whether or not vigilant problem solving will be used is the perceived importance of the problem. When a problem is judged to be routine or relatively unimportant because no vital interests are at stake, policy makers use simple decision rules. But if they misjudge the importance of a highly consequential issue, their reliance on simple procedures makes for gross miscalculations, which increase the likelihood of a poor decision and an unfavorable outcome.

Another major determinant of whether or not vigilant problem solving will be used is the salience of powerful constraints that can obstruct vigilant problem solving even when the policy makers judge the issue to be of vital importance (cf. Janis, 1989). As shown in Figure 2.2, these include cognitive constraints (e.g., limited time and lack of expertise and resources for dealing with the issue), affiliative constraints (e.g., need for acceptability, consensus, and social support), and egocentric constraints (e.g., the leader's desire for prestige and need to maintain self-esteem to cope with stress and to satisfy other emotional needs). All of these factors influence the way policy decisions are made. The policy maker will trade off vigilant problem solving in favor, for example, of speed and the satisfaction of appearing decisive when deadlines are highly salient constraints.

Vigilant decision makers, rather than allowing any such constraints to dominate their thinking, treat them as additional requirements to be met, if possible. When confronted with time pressure they are likely to attempt to negotiate an extension of the deadline and use whatever limited time is available to collect and assess relevant information in their search for a sound solution. It has long been recognized, on the basis of a number of different types of research investigations, that a moderate degree of time pressure is one of the major situational determinants—along with moderate levels of threat and of information load—of a fairly complex information processing approach to decision making (cf. Janis & Mann, 1977; Tetlock, 1989).

When policy makers engage in vigilant problem solving they do not avoid using simple decision rules. Indeed, simple decision rules may be incorporated into vigilant policy making in many ways. First, they can serve as a source of preliminary ideas or first approximations to be examined further (e.g., "How would my opponent respond if I used a simple retaliation rule?"). Second, they can serve as a means for reconsidering coolly evaluated options that are not consistent with intuitions and gut reactions (e.g., "Instead of putting up a fight, should I get the hell out fast?"). Third, they can serve to reduce a large set of alternatives into a manageable number (e.g., "Should I start off discarding the unpromising alternatives that do not meet my minimal requirements, [which is part of the satisficing approach] before looking carefully into the pros and cons of the remaining alternatives?").

After most of the tasks required by vigilant problem solving have been completed and the choice has been narrowed down to a few viable alternatives, the policy makers might decide to adopt a simple affiliative rule, such as the groupthink rule (preserve group harmony), which can be beneficial because it makes for prompt and conscientious implementation of the group's decision by promoting high morale and loyalty among all the members.

In sum, simple decision rules can be used as helpful aids when policy makers are carrying out most or all of the steps of the vigilant problem-solving approach. The crucial requirement is that simple decision rules do not dominate the policy maker's thinking.

LIMITATIONS OF VIGILANT PROBLEM SOLVING

In some circumstances, as we have already indicated, a vigilant problem-solving approach is likely to be inefficient and even counterproductive. At least three shortcomings can be identified:

1. Vigilant decision makers tend to be information-hungry. Accordingly, vigilance can easily lead to information overload and the "dilution effect." Information overload distracts the policy maker from identifying the key issues. This occurs particularly when policy makers distrust their intelligence analysts and expose themselves to raw (unselected and unanalyzed) intelligence reports, as Henry Kissinger did in some of the crises during the Nixon administration. It also occurs when policy makers are inundated with huge amounts of undigested material gathered by the intelligence community and attempt to meet role expectations that they read and assimilate all of it. The dilution effect that we discussed earlier refers to the tendency for irrelevant information to influence the impact of useful information on decision makers (Nisbett, Zukier, & Lemley, 1981; Tetlock, 1989). Useless information is not disregarded, but tends to dilute the implications of relevant information. Decision makers exposed to a considerable amount of undifferentiated information may fail to grasp the full seriousness of a problem because it has been watered down by the addition of trivial and irrelevant facts.

2. Vigilant problem solving is inefficient when it is used to solve unimportant problems. Sometimes policy makers misjudge a problem to be very important when it is not, with no serious consequences for the individual or the organization. The application of vigilance to such problems is a waste of time, effort, and organizational resources. As there is little risk of serious loss from errors, a simple strategy would be more efficient (cost effective). For problems of moderate importance, quasi-vigilant and quasi-simplistic procedural strategies may be cost effective (Janis, 1989). These are mixed strategies that combine some of the essential tasks of vigilant problem solving with some reliance on simple decision rules. "Quasi" approaches are sometimes adopted when policy makers recognize their own cognitive limitations and the limited resources of their organization or when they make an initial "under-no-circumstances" declaration that certain options (e.g., surrendering to the enemy) are unthinkable. While "quasi" problem-solving approaches are unsuitable for major crises, they can be expected to produce fewer avoidable errors than the simplistic procedural strategy (cf. Herek, Janis, & Huth, 1987).

3. Vigilant problem solving cannot eliminate all human errors in policy making. Among the sources of error that persist are basic perceptual and judgmental processes that give rise to faulty inferences from intelligence reports, such as those bearing on risk and the probabilities of various outcomes. Kahneman and

ANTECEDENT CONDITIONS
(ILLUSTRATIVE TYPES OF
INFORMATIONAL INPUT)

MEDIATING PROCESSES

OBSERVABLE
CONSEQUENCES

START: PROBLEM POSED BY
CHALLENGING EVENT OR
COMMUNICATION (CONVEYING
THREAT OR OPPORTUNITY)

Experts' predictions elaborating on
expected losses from: (a) continuing
"business-as-usual" and/or (b)
making changes

Organizational reports about: (a)
inherent difficulties of solving the
problem and/or (b) lack of time or of
other resources for intelligence
gathering and analysis

Is the
problem a
routine or relatively
unimportant one that is
not worth the time and
other resources required
to search for a good
solution?

Are
there
overriding
constraints that
prevent searching for a
high-quality solution?
notably:

Any
cognitive
limitations
(such as inability
to comprehend complex
ramifications of the problem)
or any crucial lack of
organizational
resources that
makes the
search
futile?

Reliance on S.O.P.'s
or simple *cognitive*
decision rules (such as
"analogize" or
"satisfice")

YES

NO

YES

46

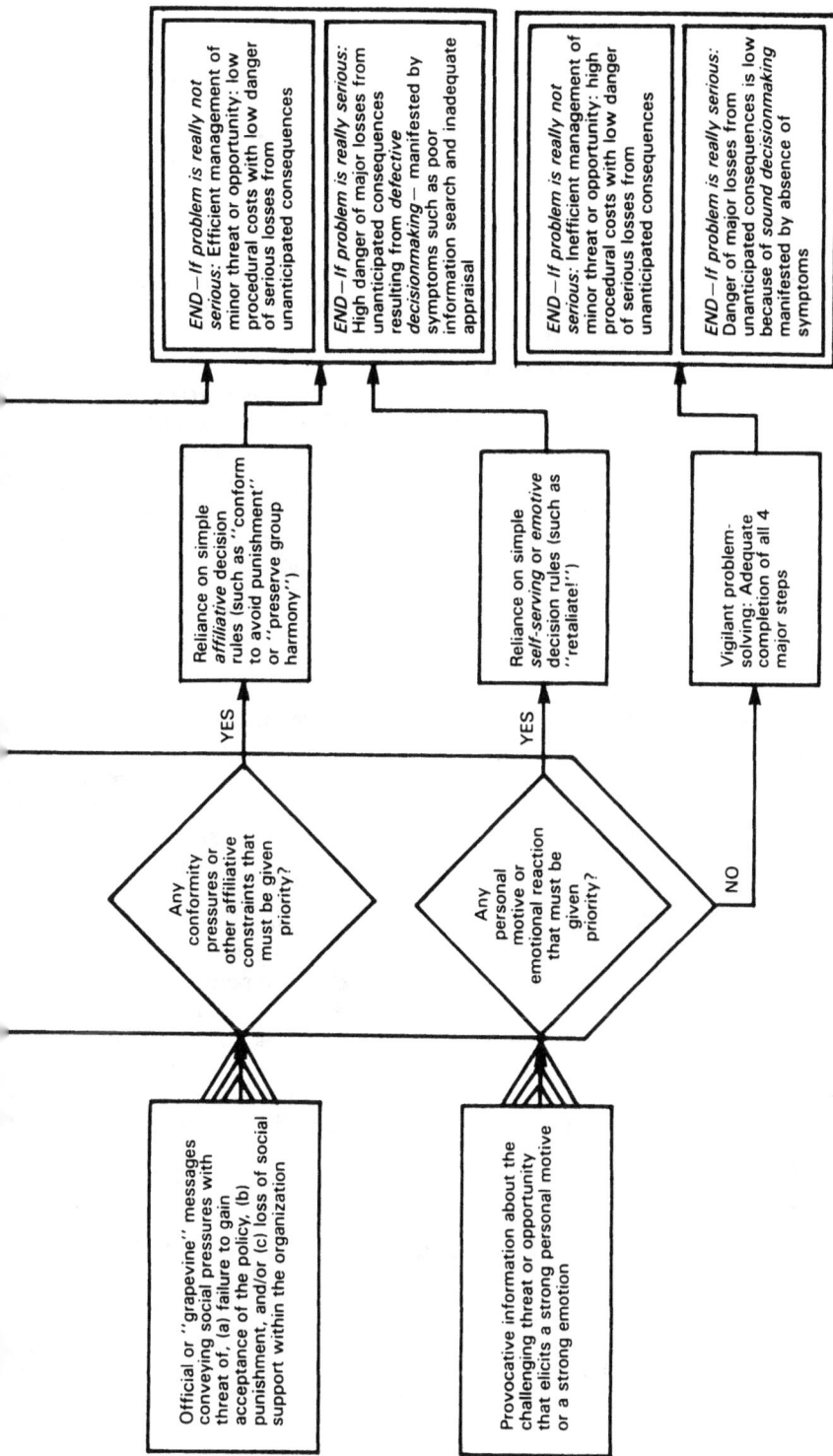

Figure 2.2 A descriptive model representing psychological effects of dominant constraints on policy making. (Reprinted from *Crucial decisions: Leadership in policy making and crisis management* by Irving L. Janis. Copyright © 1989 by The Free Press, a division of Macmillan, Inc.)

47

Tversky's (1979) prospect theory suggests that decision makers lack an understanding of extreme probabilities, such that large probabilities are underweighted. Thus, a probability of .80 may be treated psychologically as if it were a probability of .65 or .70. Small probabilities are either markedly overweighted or else ignored. Thus, a probability of .01 may be treated as if it were either a probability of .10 or 0. The overweighting of small probabilities may explain the attractiveness of long-shot odds to some military leaders.

Other conceptual errors highly resistant to vigilant problem-solving procedures include incomplete knowledge and faulty assumptions about an adversary's actions, which lead to misdiagnosis of the decision problem and misinterpretation of the available information. Information analysts and aides who edit and prepare material for reports may be another source of error, as they deliberately or inadvertently screen out discomforting and puzzling data from transmission to their leaders. The basic ideological beliefs and schemas policy makers hold about vital national interests are another source of error. They act as a "mind-set" filter for processing information and diagnosing problems. In sum, the vigilant problem-solving strategy cannot be expected to detect and rectify all sources of error. Yet it increases the likelihood that some of the worst distortions will be corrected before a final decision is made.

CONCLUSION

In sum, we maintain that it is more useful to examine the features of a moderately complex approach to decision making, known as vigilant problem solving, than to debate the strengths and weaknesses of simple decision rules (e.g., majority rule, satisficing, analogizing, or deciding on the basis of "consensus") versus highly complex decision strategies (e.g., mathematical decision analysis involving complicated and often unrealistic transformations of data). As we see it, an important task for social science research is to determine the conditions under which vigilant problem solving is effective and the conditions when it is not.

So far, two major determinants have been extracted from prior research: Perceived importance of the policy issue ("what is at stake?") and perceived manageability of constraints such as time pressures, conformity pressures, and the need to cope with psychological stress engendered by acute decisional conflict ("can we deal effectively with the constraints without giving any of them top priority?") A complementary set of problems for the research agenda is to determine when other types of procedural strategies, including relying on simple decision rules and applying highly complex mathematical procedures, would be more effective than vigilant problem solving.

REFERENCES

Abelson, R. P., & Levi, A. (1985). Decision-making and decision theory. In G. Lindzey & E. Aronson (Eds.), *Handbook of social psychology* (Vol. 1, pp. 231-310). New York: Random House.
George, A. (1974). Adaptation to stress in political decision making. In G. V. Coelho, D. A. Hamburg, & J. E. Adams (Eds.), *Coping and adaptation.* New York: Basic Books.
George, A. L. (1980). *Presidential decision making in foreign policy: The effective use of information and advice.* Boulder, CO: Westview.
Greenstein, F. I. (1982). *The hidden-hand presidency: Eisenhower as leader.* New York: Basic Books.

Herek, G., Janis, I. L., & Huth, P. (1987). Decision making during international crises: Is quality of process related to outcome? *Journal of Conflict Resolution, 31*, 203–226.

Hogarth, R. M. (1980). *Judgment and choice: The psychology of decision.* New York: Wiley.

Humphreys, P., & McFadden, W. (1980). Experiences with MAUD: Aiding decision structuring versus bootstrapping the decision maker. *Acta Psychologica, 45*, 51–69.

Janis, I. L. (1989). *Crucial decisions: Leadership in policymaking and crisis management.* New York: Free Press.

Janis, I. L., & Mann, L. (1977). *Decision making: A psychological analysis of conflict, choice, and commitment.* New York: Free Press.

Jervis, R. (1976). *Perception and misperception in international politics.* Princeton, NJ: Princeton University Press.

Kahneman, D., & Tverksy, A. (1979). Prospect theory: An analysis of decisions under risk. *Econometrica, 47*, 263–291.

Lawrence, P. R. (1985). In defense of planning as a rational approach to change. In J. M. Pennings (Ed.), *Organizational strategy and change* (pp. 373–382). San Francisco: Jossey-Bass.

Lebow, R. N. (1981). *Between peace and war: The nature of international crisis.* Baltimore: Johns Hopkins University Press.

Lindblom, C. E. (1980). *The policy-making process* (2nd ed.). Englewood Cliffs, NJ: Prentice-Hall.

May, E. R. (1973). *Lessons of the past.* New York: Oxford University Press.

Nisbett, R. E., Zukier, H., & Lemley, R. E. (1981). The dilution effect: Non-diagnostic information weakens the implications of diagnostic information. *Cognitive Psychology, 13*, 248–277.

Neustadt, R. E., & May, E. R. (1986). *Thinking in time: The uses of history for decision makers.* New York: Free Press.

Payne, J. W., Bettman, J. R., & Johnson, E. J. (1988). Adaptive strategy selection in decision making. *Journal of Experimental Psychology: Learning, Memory, and Cognition, 14*, 534–552.

Simon, H. A. (1976). *Administrative behavior: A study of decision-making processes in administrative organization* (3rd Ed.). New York: Free Press.

Slovic, P., Fischhoff, B., & Lichtenstein, S. (1977). Behavior decision theory. *Annual Review of Psychology, 28*, 1–39.

Starbuck, W. H. (1983). Organizations as action generators. *American Sociological Review, 48*, 91–102.

Starbuck, W. H. (1985). Acting first and thinking later: Theory versus reality in strategic change. In J. M. Pennings (Ed.), *Organizational strategy and change* (pp. 336–372). San Francisco: Jossey-Bass.

Stein, J. G., & Tanter, R. (1980). *Rational decision making: Israel's security choices.* Columbus, OH: Ohio State University Press.

Suedfeld, P. (1988). Authoritarian thinking, groupthink, and decision making under stress: Are simple decisions always worse? *Society, 25*(5), 25–27.

Tetlock, P. E. (1989). *Cognitive structure and political sophistication: Is it good or bad to be integratively complex?* Unpubl. manuscript, University of California, Berkeley.

Tetlock, P. E., & Boettger, R. (1989). Accountability: A social magnifier of the dilution effect. *Journal of Personality and Social Psychology, 57*, 388–398.

Ulvila, J. W., & Brown, R. V. (1982). Decision analysis comes of age. *Harvard Business Review, 60*(5), 130–141.

Van der Pligt, J. (1988). Applied decision research and environmental policy. *Acta Psychologica, 68*, 293–311.

Wisudha, A. D. (1985). Design of decision-aiding systems. In G. Wright (Ed.), *Behavioral decision making* (pp. 235–256). New York: Plenum.

Zeleny, M. (1981). Descriptive decision making and its applications. *Applications of Management Science, 1*, 327–388.

3

Psychological Advice about Political Decision Making: Heuristics, Biases, and Cognitive Defects

Peter Suedfeld and Philip E. Tetlock

Psychological studies of political leadership (not always conducted by professional psychologists) have a long history. Almost all biographers from Plutarch onward try to explain, not merely to describe, the behavior of their subjects, and these explanations usually invoke what we now classify as psychological variables.

In recent decades, the attempt has become more systematic, as the formal theories and research approaches of scientific psychology have been used in various political realms. The portion of this work with which we deal in this chapter is that which emphasizes the characteristics of cognitive processes—reasoning, thinking, memory, information search, and processing—in explaining how political leaders make important international policy decisions.

Although the concept of optimal decision-making performance has been summed up under several labels by different authors, its descriptions commonly include the range of features subsumed by cognitive, conceptual, or integrative complexity and vigilant decision making. It is free of preconceptions, rigidity, "symptoms of defective decision making," and preprogrammed tendencies that distort judgment. More positively, it is characterized by extensive information search, empathy for the positions of other participants, openness to disagreement, and the wish to find a mutually acceptable outcome. The good decision-maker can perceive many dimensions and legitimate points of view pertaining to any problem. He or she can combine these in a multifaceted and responsive solution, or, in the language of conceptual/integrative complexity theory, showing high levels of both differentiation and integration (Schroder, Driver, & Streufert, 1967; Suedfeld, Tetlock, & Streufert, in press; Tetlock, 1989).

How did this ideal person become the normative model of a decision maker? It was not always so. History abounds with admiration for the decisive "man of action," who stands the egg on its end by smashing it, solves the puzzle of the Gordian knot by slashing it, and deals with a hostile neighboring state by thrashing it. "It is better to do anything than nothing" is a precept held dear by many military training manuals; panache, élan, attack à l'outrance, "come back with your shield or on it," are all simple decision rules. If public opinion polls and election results are anything to go by, commonsense judges even today do not seem to admire the person with authority who delays and dithers in using it.

But psychologists and social scientists obviously are not commonsense judges.

Used to working meticulously and slowly, entertaining alternative hypotheses, collecting masses of data, considering all possibly relevant variables, and drawing only tentative conclusions, we have generalized these strategies as optimal for all problems, or at least all "complex" and important ones, and enshrined them as desiderata applicable to all problem solving. Not surprisingly, decision makers on the international and national level tend to fall short of these standards.

In this chapter, we will look at how psychologists, and particularly cognitively oriented psychologists, have analyzed high-level governmental decision making. We will also evaluate the adequacy of the data as a foundation for the recommendations purportedly extrapolated from them. It is important to remember that the purpose of this chapter is not to judge whether any particular kind of decision strategy is better than any other, but rather to judge whether currently available social science data justify making such a judgment.

The typical research project in this area has three major components, which appear in different order from one study to the next depending on the major interests of the author or authors. One step is the analysis of actual cognitive processes. This analysis may be anecdotal, biographical, or conjectural, but more frequently it follows the usual pattern of psychological research. Hypotheses about how people think are generated from observation or from a theoretical framework, empirical research is designed to test these hypotheses, data are collected and analyzed, and the results are interpreted in light of the original theories and predictions.

The relevant literature uses a wide range of methods. Some might be called microdecision studies: straight laboratory experiments on cognition, hypothetical case scenarios or vignettes, and simulations. The study of macrodecisions (i.e., important political events in the real world) may involve the interpretation of historical documents, either in the traditional case-study way; by more systematic content analytic methods; or through the use of complex statistical techniques, extensive and intensive interviews with important participants, and analog studies using actual decision makers in what the researcher considers to be comparable situations (e.g., corporate business decisions).

In another component, a person best described as a political psychologist (who may or may not be the original researcher) decides that these particular findings are relevant to political decision making. He or she describes an ideal cognitive process for arriving at decisions through an exhaustive information search, flexible and combinatorial consideration of that information, creative strategies based on the consideration, prophetic insight into how others will interpret each move, thorough monitoring of progress, and constant reconsideration and adaptation of the strategies to suit evolving circumstances. The political psychologist selects one or more episodes and/or leaders and, by analyzing the relevant decisions and their outcomes, demonstrates how the cognitive processes studied previously function in real life. Usually, they fall short of the prescribed ideal. With luck, one can show a range of such episodes, which demonstrate that actual decision-making strategies, unlike the ideal ones, lead to imperfect or even catastrophic outcomes.

The third component is speculation about why these people have not managed to do it right and explanations of their failures on the basis of psychological theory, whether based on unconscious death wishes, limited cognitive channel capacities, or innate laziness (for reviews, see Tetlock, Crosby, & Crosby, 1981; Tetlock & McGuire, 1986).

Last, suggestions are made as to how the calamitous effects of these characteristics can be avoided by new ways of selecting, training, or organizing decision makers.

As we indicated above, the order of these steps is variable. One scholar may begin with an interest in a particular cognitive style found in laboratory studies, test it in the political field, and show its (usually negative) effects. Another may start with a criticism of the current state of world or national affairs, speculate as to why leaders have gotten us into such a mess, and focus on the difference between perfect and actual decision making. A third may have a theory as to what optimal decision making is, find something different in actual research, and illustrate these differences with historical examples.

Below, we describe some of the cognitive and (more briefly) noncognitive tendencies that are thought to degrade the quality of decision making.

COGNITIVE RULES

The list of cognitive variables that have been alluded to in this context is long. Some of the more frequently cited ones are:

1. *Heuristics and biases* (e.g., Kahneman, Slovic, & Tversky, 1982). These include availability (the most easily remembered or imagined solutions are likely to be used, even though they may not be appropriate); representativeness (if an event seems similar to or representative of a class of events, we assume that it belongs to that class); anchoring (later decisions tend to be adjustments of earlier ones, whereas something completely different may be better); and framing (the way a question is posed influences the answer; for example, people will choose a sure small gain over a larger uncertain gain but will prefer to take a chance on a large loss rather than accept a certain smaller one; and so on). Subsequent workers have developed long lists of such cognitive shortcuts (e.g., a list of 29 in Hogarth, 1980). Heuristics and biases are considered to be universal and unthinking decision tendencies.

2. *Simple information processing* (e.g., Streufert & Swezey, 1986). Different authors may not use the same labels for these characteristics (see Stein, 1988), but there is agreement on a common core of components. These include the rigid following of internal rules (preconceptions, schemata, scripts, belief systems, or ideologies) or external ones (manuals, standard operating procedures, or precedents); intolerance of ambiguity and a need for rapid closure; inadequate information search; overgeneralized perceptions of the situation, such as ignoring unique aspects of different nations in one's own or the opposing bloc; resistance to tradeoffs; failure to empathize with other participants in the process; and an inability to integrate diverse components in either decision making or the actual decision.

3. *Symptoms of defective decision making* (Herek, Janis, & Huth, 1987; Janis, 1986). Although in a sense all of the cognitive characteristics described in this section can be considered to be this sort of symptom, the phrase specifically alludes to the work of Janis and his colleagues on international crisis decision making. There is overlap between Janis's list and those of others. The cognitive symptoms studied by Janis are: omissions in the survey of goals or values relevant to choice, omissions in the survey of alternatives, poor information search, bias in processing information at hand, failure to reconsider originally rejected alternatives, failure to examine the major costs and risks of the preferred choice, and

failure to work out detailed implementation, monitoring, and contingency plans (paraphrased from Janis, 1986, p. 205).

4. *Minimization of effort.* One way to summarize most, if not all, of the diagnoses noted above (as well as others of their ilk) is that they view the human information processor as a "cognitive miser" (Taylor, 1980). Such misers frequently pursue the first solution that appears to be reasonably close to satisfactory, rather than continuing to search for others that may be closer. This tendency, dubbed "satisficing" by Simon (1983), underlies many of the "rules of thumb," "making decisions by the seat of your pants," "cognitive shortcuts," etc., criticized by psychologists.

These descriptions are placed in opposition to the ideal of the rational actor, who acts in accordance with subjective expected utility theory: the decision maker who has a clear picture of how desirable various possible events or outcomes are, a thorough appreciation of the various alternative strategies and their probable consequences, and therefore a foundation for choosing optimal strategies to reach desired (and avoid undesired) results.

NONCOGNITIVE RULES

Some critics have taken decision studies to task for underemphasizing psychological factors other than those related to cognitive processing and have sometimes attempted to remedy this fault (e.g., Etzioni, 1988). It is clear that many strategies have both emotional and cognitive roots. Classifying decision rules under either category may be a matter of convenience or arbitrary choice (Tetlock & Levi, 1982). For example, how should one describe "motivated misperception of threat" (Stein, 1988)? The tendency to deny or underestimate danger is motivated by fear, which is certainly an emotion, but the resultant decision bias is cognitive. The same difficulty is posed by the ascription of cognitive biases to the workings of the unconscious as it continues to deal with psychosexual problems of early life, the theme of psychohistory (deMause, 1975; Lifton, 1974), or other intellectual tendencies derived from emotional experiences in childhood, youth, or early adulthood (Lasswell, 1930).

Bearing this caveat (as well as the cognitive focus of this chapter) in mind, we shall only briefly mention some of the better known taxonomies of motivated decision flaws.

1. *Emotive decision rules.* These degrade the quality of decisions, as emotions aroused by the situation guide the response. Among these are retaliation, the "can do" imperative (mobilizing all one's resources to overcome obstacles and risks), and the "Wow!" imperative (excessive enthusiasm for what appears to be a wonderful solution, to the point of not evaluating it carefully; Janis, 1986, pp. 212–216).

2. *Groupthink* (Janis, 1982; Janis & Mann, 1977). "Groupthink" is a clear and catchy label for what goes wrong in decision making as a consequence of small-group dynamics. In his later work, Janis refers to such processes as affiliative decision rules. They include the avoidance of recriminations by not making or not supporting any suggestion that may arouse the opposition of peers or superiors, setting aside one's own doubts about an emerging group consensus in order to

preserve harmony, and other rules that maintain the individual's "social support, power, compensation, or status within the organization" (Janis, 1986, p. 219).

3. *Mixed models.* Various scholars have combined items from several of these lists to describe the roots of poor judgment. Not all of the cognitive and other dangers to good decision making are extrapolated to the national/international scene by the original authors. Kahneman and Tversky, for example, have not specifically addressed themselves to how heuristic biases have affected high-level decision making. However, political psychologists have incorporated these and other cognitive shortcuts, originally studied in the laboratory, into their own generalizations. For example, Stein (1988) lists the availability and representativeness heuristics as factors that impair decision making. As illustrations of the first, Stein mentions the pre–World War II British overestimation of German air power and Israel's underestimation of the probability of an Egyptian attack in 1973. An illustration of the second is Anthony Eden's classification of Nasser as a threat similar to Hitler and Mussolini (as of 1991, Bush's similar categorization of Saddam Hussein may be added).

Stein goes on to cite the egocentric bias, overconfidence, proportionality bias, fundamental attribution error, and unrealistic attributions of coherence and centralization as other cognitive errors. In addition, motivated misperception of threat is discussed as an important emotional/motivational source of distortion.

Similarly, Frankenhaeuser (1988), Jervis (1976), Lebow (1981), and many others have taken observations from various psychological studies of cognition, perception, and motivation and transferred them to the international level in offering critiques of decision making. The tendency to error is emphasized by most authors in combining concepts from these various fields, and a lengthy list of cognitive and other factors that have been hypothesized to influence policy makers is given by Tetlock, McGuire, and Mitchell (1991). Tetlock et al. also point out examples of effective decision making under high stress and evaluate the usefulness of the literature as it specifically applies (or fails to apply) to deterrence as a strategy.

CRITICIZING THE CRITICISMS

Perhaps we should begin by explicitly stating our conclusions. In our judgment, the psychological literature (experimental and extrapolated) does not justify any serious belief that decision making is generally poor, nor that complex decisions (i.e., those not using shortcuts) are necessarily better than simple ones. This is true even for complicated situations and critical issues. We reject the view that human beings are cognitive misers, preferring to think of them (that is, us) as cognitive *managers* (see Suedfeld & Bluck, 1991). The distinction is crucial: whereas misers hoard their resources, failing to perceive where expenditures (which, in this context, means expenditures of time, energy, thought, and effort, rather than money) are worthwhile, managers react to specific challenges and opportunities.

We do not wish to imply that cognitive managers are perfect meta–decision makers who always invest exactly the right amount of effort and time in decision-making tasks. People obviously do make mistakes, just as even the best money managers err in their financial strategies. But we think that cognitive managers are correct more often than not and that being a prudent rather than a lavish manager is frequently the right strategy. Complexity has costs, which some theorists have downplayed or even ignored: costs in time, effort, opportunity to deal with other problems, confidence, momentum, etc., so that upward changes in complexity should be justified by appropriate cost/benefit ratios.

We do not argue that these decisions—actually, meta-decisions, as they are decisions about how to make decisions—are rationally or even consciously thought out in every instance. Decision making is affected by nonrational, endogenous factors and by many exogenous ones, as well as by multiple goals. Moreover, there is growing evidence that people do adjust the complexity of their information processing in response to variables such as the importance of the decision, the reversibility of the decision, the need to justify one's views to an audience or constituency, and the intensity of value conflict activated by the issue (Chaiken, 1980; Fiske & Neuberg, 1990; McAllister, Mitchell, & Beach, 1979; Petty & Cacioppo, 1986; Tetlock, 1983, 1986a, 1986b; Tetlock, Skitka, & Boettger, 1989).

In evaluating the descriptions of actual decision making and the prescriptions for improvement, we must first acknowledge that most decision scholars offer at least a token acknowledgment of the possible utility of shortcuts. For example, Harvey, Hunt, and Schroder (1961) cite a few situations where immediate simple decisions are better than extensive information search or the generation of alternatives. The examples tend to be along the lines of, "If you're a soldier on the battlefield, and someone yells, 'Hit the ground!,' the best response is to obey at once." The impression left with the reader is that, except for such highly limited and for most of us unusual circumstances, complexity is still the ideal.

Later generations of complexity researchers have been less devoted to one end of the continuum. In their treatment of managerial decisions, Streufert and Swezey argue that although cognitively complex executives may consider more alternatives in planning, it does not necessarily make them better executives. "Under some conditions, 'overplanning' can be just as detrimental as underplanning. In some cases, a simple, straightforward decision might be preferable to a well-considered strategic decision" (Streufert & Swezey, 1986, p. 71). Data from their simulation research support this point of view. Another researcher in this tradition has argued the case for an environmental interactionist approach to this issue, with the implication that many of even the most high-level and critical situations are more amenable to simple than to complex solutions (Suedfeld, 1988).

Tversky and Kahneman (1974) recognize that heuristics are generally useful and lead to efficiency, even though they also note the potential for systematic error. The actual research program, however, does tend to emphasize the errors: It is oriented toward identifying how heuristic rules diverge from statistical and logical ones and how they lead to inconsistencies based on logically irrelevant factors such as framing variables. Thus, it is difficult to escape the conclusion that in the view of these authors the drawbacks of relying on such rules are greater than the benefits.

Janis and his co-workers, in successive treatments of the issue, have at times acknowledged that simple rules have their advantages. In recent work, they have argued that moderately complex [or, in their terms, vigilant (Janis & Mann, 1977) or reflective (Herek et al., 1987)] decision making should be used in developing solutions to very important problems, although it may be unnecessary for routine or trivial issues. Herek et al. even admit that good decisions on important issues may exhibit some symptoms of defective decision making; the difference between good and bad decisions is that the latter are dominated by such symptoms. Once again, however, the concrete case studies and prescriptions emphasize the dangers of insufficient, never of excessive, complexity. Even at the abstract conceptual level, it is noteworthy that all of the seven symptoms are forms of simple, not complex, decision rules.

We think it is fair to conclude that some of the most prominent psychological scholars in this area give a *pro forma* acknowledgment that complex decision making is not always crucial, nor always superior. Their research, analysis, and historical interpretation, on the other hand, quite consistently depict complex information processing as normatively superior to simple modes of thought. Let us now see the counterarguments to the literature and to the inferences drawn from it.

Internal Validity

We will first look at the research from which the extrapolations are made. There are two major points to be considered: one is whether the data support the idea that human cognition is rife with systematic biases toward simplicity and the other is whether these biases systematically lead to erroneous outcomes.

Are Biases Universal?

The research focused on "heuristics" makes for good examples, partly because its procedures are clearly understandable and the bases of its predictions and conclusions are more objectively established than most. For example, subjects' responses can be compared with probabilistic calculations, so that, unlike in many simulations, right and wrong solutions can be identified. We will therefore use this approach to illustrate some of the problems alluded to above. The reader should remember that similar problems permeate the methodologies used in this field.

One example occurs in the use of scenarios to identify cognitive biases. Hypothetical situations are described and subjects are asked to judge issues such as probable outcomes and their own hypothetical reactions. This line of research has identified various commonly used cognitive decision rules or heuristics, shortcuts used automatically and perhaps without awareness. Most of these are conducive to logical, statistical, or other fallacies in decision making. Scenarios can be used to identify such shortcuts as well as their departures from strict logic or probability theory. However, the internal validity of this research has been subject to criticism.

To some extent, the findings may be specific to particular research procedures. A number of studies have addressed this issue, focusing on various cognitive biases. One of the fallacies reported to occur as a result of heuristic thinking is the conjunction fallacy, estimating as more probable the combined event A + B than the component event A. Thus, for example, subjects may rate the probability of a major war developing in the Middle East if Iraq attempts to invade Saudi Arabia as higher than that of a major war developing in the Middle East (without any specific antecedent condition named). Logically, the probability of the combined event can at most be equal to that of the less probable constituent event, yet 85–90% of subjects have been found to commit the conjunction fallacy. This occurs even among subjects who have had prior training in probability and statistics (Tversky & Kahneman, 1983).

Among criticisms of this research have been suggestions that subjects may not have understood the problem or may have understood it in unintended ways, for example, that they inferred the two probabilities to be judged were not "A + B" versus "A," but rather "A + B" versus "A but not B." In our example above, according to this explanation, subjects interpret the comparison to be between a case in which an Iraqi invasion occurs versus a case in which war breaks out in the absence of such an invasion. The error may be in how subjects understand the question, which is much less of a problem in the real world where decision makers communicate in normatively prescribed ways (Grice, 1975) and, when confused, can seek clarification.

The commonality of this cognitive error may also depend on the specific phrasing of the task. Fiedler (1988) reports that the conjunction fallacy is committed by considerably fewer subjects when the task is to judge the frequency of an occurrence (in a given number of cases) than when it is to judge the probability of the occurrence. In two experiments, the percentage of subjects committing the conjunction fallacy under the two conditions respectively were 28% versus 73% and 25% versus 70% (see Einhorn & Hogarth, 1981). Recent experiments have shown that other cognitive biases are similarly subject to wording and order effects in the particular experimental presentation (Krosnick, Li, & Lehman, 1990; Lehman, Krosnick, & West, 1990).

In a more general critique of this line of research, Cohen (1981) argued that failure to meet normative criteria cannot be used as conclusive evidence of human irrationality, because the criteria themselves cannot be established independently as "correct" in some absolute sense. A nonexistent fallacy may be perceived by the researchers because standards are applied inappropriately or the wrong standards are applied. In other cases, correct inferences may require special knowledge. Such studies may be investigating the subjects' education or intelligence rather than general human shortcomings. Recent research has shown that both brief focused training in the rules of logical inference and, more generally, university education produce large increments in people's ability to draw logically and probabilistically correct inferences (Lehman, Lempert, & Nisbett, 1988; Lehman & Nisbett, 1990; Nisbett, Fong, Lehman, & Cheng, 1987). Whether this necessarily leads to better decisions is arguable, but the results do cast doubt on the intractable universality of cognitive bias phenomena.

Are Biases Universally Undesirable?

Even at the research level, complex problem solving is not necessarily optimal. For example, Streufert and Swezey's simulation studies (1986) have not only shown the drawbacks of excessive planning, they also indicate the importance of adjusting one's level of complexity to the situation. In a developing emergency, rapid and clear-cut decisions are crucial. Porter (1987) has demonstrated that decisions made on the basis of implicit knowledge can be more accurate than those arrived at on the basis of explicit information processing. Tetlock and Boettger (1989) have reported that providing a great deal of irrelevant information will degrade judgment if decision makers, attempting to process all available information, allow irrelevancies not only to take up their time and capacity but also to distort conclusions that could be firmly based on relevant factors.

External Validity

One criticism of decision analysis is that the transfer of data from artificial and highly structured research situations to the world of international politics is a dubious enterprise. The usual warnings about psychology experiments and simulations apply here *a fortiori*. University student populations cannot be equated easily with international leaders. The stakes in any laboratory game are not comparable with those of keeping a national economy functioning or a world order at peace. The amount of information and resources available to policy makers cannot even remotely be approximated in the laboratory. Therefore, findings in laboratory situations—and even in the most convincing field experiments—can best be thought of as hypothesis generating, not hypothesis testing, in the study of high-level decision making. We may summarize the problems of moving from the database to policy advice under relatively few headings. Some of these, with tongue in cheek, we take from the literature that we are criticizing.

Defining Error

We have already looked at problems with the data derived from the research using vignettes to identify heuristics, which have been used to buttress arguments that political decisions influenced by heuristics are likely to be bad ones. When extrapolating these data to real problems, we face the possibility that what appear to be fallacies (and may be errors in the context of a specific vignette) may in fact be correct conclusions in a different context. Wolford, Taylor, and Beck (n.d.) argue that, in some instances, the issue is not the relative probability of the component and combined events, but the probability of each of these in a particular case relative to other events. Their example is a robbery occurring in a town small enough so that all suspects are known:

> The policeman "first learns that dynamite was used. . . . Person X is unlikely to use dynamite so the policeman doesn't place X very high on the suspect list. The policeman then discovers that the robber had bright red hair. Since X has bright red hair, he moves to a much higher spot on the suspect list. . . . The probability of the compound event that X has red hair and used dynamite is still less than or equal to the probability of the component event that X used dynamite, but the probability that X has red hair and used dynamite might well be greater than the probability of any other suspect having that joint event." (p. 9; emphasis in original).

In real life, solutions that are based on faulty logical or statistical reasoning are not necessarily wrong. One illustration of the representativeness heuristic is:

> Steve is very shy and withdrawn, invariably helpful, but with little interest in people, or in the world of reality. A meek and tidy soul, he has a need for order and structure, and a passion for detail.

In judging the probability that Steve is engaged in a particular one of a list of possible occupations, subjects overwhelmingly tend to pick one that seems compatible with Steve's personality (e.g., librarian), ignoring factors such as base rate frequencies (e.g., if one alternative is "farmer," the fact that there are many more farmers than librarians should enter into the calculation). However, it may still be the case that people with Steve's personality characteristics will seek out librarianship and avoid farming with sufficient consistency to make the popular guess the right one.

Even when we cannot clearly identify an alternative interpretation, we must face the challenge of how erroneous the supposed fallacies really are. In the real world of strategy, there are situations where base rate plays a very minor role compared to individual characteristics of the event, or makes no difference at all. There may be many more international threats that are not followed by military action than those that are. Nevertheless, there are two reasons why a prudent policy maker will not assign much weight to that general statistic when weighing the dangers of a particular threat. First, it is profoundly difficult to specify the "most relevant" base rate (Did the historical examples occur in a nuclear or pre-nuclear era? Were truly vital interests at stake? Had the threatening state previously carried through (or failed to carry through) other threats? . . .) Second, the policy maker must weigh the relative magnitude of making a Type I error (preparing for attack when the other side is not planning one) versus a Type II error (failing to prepare for an attack that is being planned). Given the ambiguity concerning the true probability of attack under these particular circumstances and the relative consequences of Type I and II errors, policy makers probably use base rates "to the extent that they [lead] to satisfactory solutions" (Ginossar & Trope, 1987).

In the same way, how inherently defective is the "Wow!" imperative, the enthusiastic adoption of what appears to be a simple and satisfying solution to an important problem (Janis, 1986)? Janis' primary example is the dropping of atomic bombs on Japan, which Truman and his advisors saw "as a master card, not only for the purpose of bringing a rapid end to the war in Japan, but also for demonstrating U.S. arms superiority in a way that would help contain the Soviet Union after the war" (Janis, 1986, p. 215). On this basis, where is the defect, and what is the rationale for classifying the "Wow!" imperative as fallacious? The nuclear attacks did in fact achieve all of the goals that Janis described and Truman presumably expected. Janis' criticism is both questionable (in that the readiness of Japan to surrender anyway is by no means historically established) and incomplete (in that it does not address the issue of impressing the U.S.S.R. with U.S. strength). The root of Janis' criticism, we suspect, is moral rather than cognitive. Is killing large numbers of enemy civilians with atomic weapons justified even if such an action, on balance, seems to save lives? An intriguing and important question, to be sure, but not the question that the critics claim to be addressing.

Defining Outcomes

One of the major problems in this entire literature is the evaluation of outcomes. How do we know which strategic decisions were successes and which failures, or to what extent such a simple dichotomy is even relevant (Suedfeld, 1988)?

Herek et al. (1987) judged the outcomes of their 19 crises by getting two experts to rate the impact of each crisis on the vital interests of the United States and on its effects on "tension, stability, hostility, or the likelihood of war between the United States and the Soviet Union or China" (p. 213). Although there was a correlation between these consequences and symptoms of defective decision making in the short term, the two experts were in so much disagreement on long-term outcomes (58% agreement on effects on U.S. interests, 26% agreement on effects on world tension!) that the authors did not bother to calculate correlations with cognitive symptoms. Given that national leaders are interested in long-term, not only immediate, results, we can understand the low impact of psychological research on decision makers (Blight, 1986).

We may also take another look at the Cuban Missile Crisis, the resolution of which was an example of nongroupthink processes (Janis, 1982) and showed only one symptom of defective decision making. Was its resolution in fact favorable to the United States? In the immediate short run, arguably so: The Soviet missiles were withdrawn without war. On the other hand, the United States in effect guaranteed the continuation of the Castro regime and agreed to withdraw its own missiles from Turkey, where they had been based for many years. It paid a price for the mere restoration of the status quo in regard to Soviet missiles in Cuba. These were the short- and medium-term outcomes.

In the long term, Castro remained as a source of trouble in the Caribbean and South America. The U.S.S.R. entered an intensive nuclear arms build-up to avoid any future loss of face. In the even longer term, this effort may have contributed to the Soviet Union's current disastrous economic and political condition. However we evaluate all of these consequences, a clear judgment of good or bad seems fantastic.

The Cuban Missile Crisis is probably the norm, not the exception, in this regard. Even when the immediate outcome seems obvious, secret agreements may be hidden traps for the evaluator. Long-term consequences are by definition unknown at the time, and in dispute even after the lapse of many years. If the criterion measure is thus unknowable, how then can we judge the goodness of the process that led to it? We should proceed, if at all, with extreme caution.

Side Effects

Decisions frequently have consequences other than their impact on the proximate problem. Such consequences may affect events, persons, and conditions that form a background to the focal issue; but not only are backgrounds often crucial, they may at some future time become focal themselves. If that happens, the side effects of the decision may turn out to be more important than its effects in the original situation.

At a national level, a mediocre foreign policy decision may have important beneficial effects for the domestic economy. In a more restricted vein, it may burnish the image of the ruler or his or her party; with a personal focus, it may strengthen his or her self-confidence. All of these outcomes may outweigh the fact that the decision might not have been the best way to deal with the particular problem. The positive side effects may in fact lead to better solutions to other problems than might have been found otherwise. Such consequences may also affect future events; this possibility is discussed later.

The use of standard operating procedures, or of historical precedents, can foster continuity, stability, and a feeling that one can predict and rely on certain contingent outcomes. *Stare decisis*, the judicial rule that precedents must be considered (although they may be violated if the situation warrants), is seen to reduce potential corruption and personal idiosyncracy and to increase fairness, predictability, and efficiency. As in law, so in government: ". . . we know that the last time thought and effort went into the problem, and it seems a good idea to have the benefit of that thought and effort now. The past banked its wisdom, and it is foolish not to draw on it" (Rembar, 1969, pp. 25–27).

It is worth remarking in this context that one's evaluation of a simple *stare decisis* or more complex decision rule hinges very much on both the historical context and one's moral and political values. In the 1950s and 1960s, many liberals applauded an activist U.S. Supreme Court that overturned a wide range of conservative precedents in a series of rather integratively complex opinions that simultaneously paid homage to the principle of precedent and created new branches of legal reasoning (Tetlock, Bernzweig, & Gallant, 1985). In the 1980s and 1990s, many conservatives look to the Supreme Court to undo the liberal precedents of earlier decades, an ideological assignment that requires complex exercises in legal reasoning from the conservative side of the bench. Cognitive psychology seems quite irrelevant to this normative debate.

The Unit of Analysis

All social scientists concerned with cognitive processes in high-level decision making proceed by analyzing a particular crisis, confrontation, or political problem, or a series of such events. However, national leaders deal with several such problems not only simultaneously, but continuously. The resolution of any one problem should be designed so as to avoid or reduce future problems related to the present one. Every choice of a strategy will affect not only the decision to which it is applied but also the decision environment in which future problems are faced. Thus, a solution that may be imperfect if judged in isolation may be seen as optimal if it is part of a series of decisions.

For example, Janis (1986) criticizes the retaliation imperative, which, under the label of aversive reinforcement, is known by psychologists to suppress undesired behavior in many instances. Retaliation may be a nonoptimal reaction to a particular provocation, but it may also establish an atmosphere where future aggression is deterred and a more cooperative relationship between the states involved is generated. How should such an outcome reflect back on the original correctness of the retaliatory response?

Inadequate Information Search

This label is actually somewhat unfair; we use it, nevertheless, to emphasize that it is no less unfairly applied to policy makers by social scientists. The unfairness is in the implication that it is the searcher who is inadequate, and that by dint of a little more effort or ingenuity the needed information could have been obtained. This is often not true either for the governmental leader or for the researcher.

By necessity, scholars base their analyses of the episodes with which they deal on the available information, which is frequently, if not always, incomplete. In fact, it could be argued that by its nature it can never be complete. More mundanely, much of the relevant material is classified and inaccessible to scholars for at least decades after the event; not all participants' perspectives and not all documents are preserved; and memoirs are affected by memory lapses, impression management goals, and ego defenses. Obviously, unavailable information cannot be used. The foundations of analysis are therefore shaky. Occasionally, embarrassment results when what appeared to be a firmly based conclusion is completely shattered by the publication of previously classified, lost, or untranslated documents. New light on aspects of the Cuban Missile Crisis, for example, is being shed by the recent publication of Robert F. Kennedy's and Nikita Khrushchev's memoirs. Some of this new light casts serious doubt on whether the cognitive strengths adduced by policy theorists such as Janis either existed or were in fact strengths (see Holsti, 1988).

A corollary problem is that of evaluating the information. Scholars, like decision makers, must winnow a mass of information, some of which may be misleading or inaccurate, and much of which may be contradictory. Decision makers, unlike scholars, have relatively little control over that information, know that some of it is deliberately intended to mislead them, and cannot put off decisions for very long.

The Availability Heuristic

We have already mentioned the availability heuristic, a tendency to "assess the frequency of a class or the probability of an event by the ease with which instances or occurrences can be brought to mind. For example, one may assess the risk of heart attack among middle-aged people by recalling such occurrences among one's acquaintances" (Tversky & Kahneman, 1974, p. 1125). The workings of the availability heuristic in the realm of strategic decision making have been cited in the use of inappropriate historical analogies and in failure to prepare for possible but not easily imaginable disasters (Janis, 1989, p. 174).

This cognitive rule of thumb is exemplified within the psychological analysis of decision making because decision analysts concentrate on a few highly salient decisions and events. As a rule, these are crises or other episodes with dramatic and at least potentially serious negative outcomes. Scholars tend to ignore the great number of daily if not hourly decisions whose favorable outcomes keep the national and international polities functioning.

Another aspect of the availability heuristic is the concentration of social scientists on the dimensions of behavior that we study most effectively in normal laboratory or field research. It is no wonder that we transfer to the analysis of decisions concepts such as logical or statistical validity, mainstays of cognitive psychology, or social conformity ("groupthink"), a major topic in social psychology. There are plenty of objections to the overemphasis on "cold" cognition as a normative ideal: "All that formal logic will tell you is whether a conclusion is valid; it won't tell you whether it's silly. So at the very least there must be something over and above logic to tell you what inferences to draw" (Johnson-Laird, 1988, p. 2).

We have been criticized for ignoring cultural and political forms and limitations, medical and physiological factors, and the influence of language as an independent (as opposed to a dependent) variable. Perhaps less excusably, we have ignored factors that are more purely psychological in nature but that have shown themselves recalcitrant to manipulation. Those factors are intuition, imagination, and implicit cognitive processes. These processes are powerful and surely shape many crucial decisions, yet no analyst of political strategy development has paid significant attention to them. A search through the indexes of books on political psychology is disappointingly fruitless. More broadly, the emphasis on cognition may have led to an undervaluing of other influences, theories, and research traditions in the study of decision making (see Jervis, 1989; Streufert, 1987).

Last, one may argue that the entire enterprise we have been addressing is but an interesting variant of this principle. Once a cognitive bias has been identified in the laboratory, it is tempting to look for it in governmental decisions. But finding it is no proof that the decision was significantly and negatively affected by the bias. If U.S. leaders developing policy toward Iraq in 1990 claim to see similarities between Saddam Hussein and Adolf Hitler, and therefore at least by implication between the invasion of Kuwait and that of Czechoslovakia, does that mean the availability heuristic is operating? Is the example of the Vietnam War less available to these policy makers than that of World War II? To ask the question is to answer it. The same kind of reasoning in psychohistory is trenchantly examined by Stannard (1980).

Selective Bias in Considering Information

This subtitle is taken from Herek et al. (1987); its more basic cognitive counterpart is the confirmation bias. Both phrases refer to the tendency to interpret events as being compatible with one's expectations and to ignore, reject, discount, explain away, or assimilate contradictory evidence. Beginning with the hypothesis that cognitive shortcuts are generally bad when used in important decisions, scholars tend to emphasize events and factors that support this analysis while ignoring (or reinterpreting) those that contradict it. We have previously discussed the work of Herek et al. (1987), who studied the quality of U.S. decision strategies in 19 post–World War II international crises. Scoring these strategies for the presence or absence of their seven symptoms of defective decision making and having the short- and long-term consequences of the decisions rated by two political scientists, the authors concluded that the presence of more symptoms (including heuristics and other characteristics of simple information processing) was associated with worse outcomes.

One of the outstanding examples of good decision making cited was the process that led up to the resolution of the Cuban Missile Crisis of 1962. It should be noted that this particular episode was also assessed favorably by other policy analysts and has been referred to as being relatively uncontaminated by groupthink (Janis, 1982). We have already considered whether the positive evaluation of the outcomes of the decision was justified; here, we shall look at another problem.

Herek et al. (1987) could find only one symptom of defective decision making in the process, the failure to reconsider originally rejected alternatives. But a more recent analyst (Welch, 1989) takes issue with this conclusion. In fact, Welch argues, five of the seven symptoms occurred in the decision process, but not the one Herek et al. said they found! According to Welch, the Executive Committee of the National Security Council, the policy-making body in this case, did commit gross omissions in surveying alternatives and objectives, failed to examine major costs and risks of the preferred choice, engaged in poor information search, and failed to work out detailed implementation, monitoring, and contingency plans. Welch thought that selective bias in processing the information at hand was not codable because of insufficient data, but that the Committee did reconsider previously rejected alternatives (the lack of which was the symptom Herek et al. reported).

Similar problems arise in other episodes of recent history. Lyndon B. Johnson's policy in Vietnam is widely considered to have been disastrous. Janis (1982) called it a fiasco, and three component crises included in Herek et al. (1987)—the 1964 decision to bomb North Vietnamese coastal areas, the air war against North Vietnam in 1964–1965, and the decision to commit U.S. ground forces to combat in 1965—were rated as displaying respectively, four, five, and four of the seven possible symptoms of defective decision making. It is difficult to believe that this is the same strategy characterized by another expert as "a moderately complex, balanced attempt to avoid the mistakes in Korea (namely, provoking massive Chinese entry into the conflict) and simultaneously contain Communist influence in Indochina. . . ." (Tetlock, 1991). In fact, repudiating the view that complex approaches to admittedly complex problems are necessarily better, Tetlock goes on to say that "one cannot help but wonder whether a simple dovish *or* hawkish policy would not have worked out better from an American standpoint. . . ." (emphasis in original). In a parallel case, the policies of the Eisenhower administration toward Middle East problems are characterized as "complex, innovative, well-organized, and profoundly unsuccessful" (Tetlock, 1991). In short, it is quite possible to be both simple and right or complex and wrong.

It should also be pointed out that relatively little attention has been paid to historical episodes that exemplify good outcomes of simple approaches. Suedfeld and Rank (1976) showed that successful revolutionary leaders displayed low levels of integrative complexity during their struggles, a phenomenon that makes considerable theoretical sense. Similarly, Chamberlain's level of integrative complexity during the 1938 negotiations leading to the Munich Agreements was considerably higher than Hitler's (2.2 versus 1.5; Suedfeld, unpublished data); nevertheless, the general consensus among historians is that Britain was the loser (e.g., Thorne, 1968).

Ignoring of Situational Factors

According to some critical social scientists (e.g., Stein, 1988), policy makers are likely to explain the hostile behavior of adversaries on the basis of inherent and stable characteristics, for example, "Capitalist countries are by nature imperialistic and exploitive," "China has always been and will remain authoritarian, because its culture fosters gerontocracy," or "Russian governments, Tsarist or Communist, are naturally expansionistic." These characteristics may be ascribed either to the country (economic system, political structure, or general culture) or to individual leaders. Explanations based on such assumptions ignore important situational patterns, both domestic and international, that may in fact be guiding the decision maker. On the other hand, one's own hostile behavior is usually ascribed to more specifiable causes, whether external ("Their mobilization forced us to follow suit") or internal ("We misunderstood what they were trying to tell us").

This tendency, which social psychologists call the *fundamental attribution error*, detracts from achieving a full awareness of crucial aspects of why the other side is acting as it is. In the foreign policy area, it is hypothesized to produce an overestimation of the threat posed by others, who are invested with a spurious intrinsic ill will toward oneself when they may actually be responding to a specific situation. This may make it difficult to understand that if the situation changes, their behavior may stop being hostile.

We will not debate the scientific status of the fundamental attribution error at this point. Its generality even in laboratory experiments is uncertain, and we understand too little about when and why people exhibit it and the extent to which it actually leads to erroneous conclusions. What we do consider relevant here is that too many of the policy criticisms we have been summarizing ignore situational influences and ascribe the errors perceived by the psychologist to inherent characteristics of the decision maker or decision-making group.

There is no point in presenting these in detail: most have already been mentioned. Poor decision making has been attributed to the authoritarian personality (Adorno, Frenkel-Brunswick, Levinson, & Sanford, 1950; Dixon, 1979) and other various neurotic or inadequate personality constellations (Barber, 1972; Lasswell, 1930; Ward, 1975); simple conceptual structure (Harvey et al., 1961); and Tversky and Kahneman's (1974) heuristics, among other constructs.

Even aside from voluminous analyses of the decision process from the point of view of political science and sociology, which do pay attention to situational factors, not all political psychologists studying leader behavior ignore environmental and other temporary influences on behavior (see Fiedler & Garcia, 1987; Hermann, 1977, 1979; Janis, 1982; Rejai, 1979; Simonton, 1984, 1987; Suedfeld, 1983; Suedfeld, Corteen, & McCormick, 1986; Suedfeld & Rank, 1976; Suedfeld & Tetlock, 1977; Tetlock, 1981; Walker, 1987; Walker & Watson, 1988; Wallace & Suedfeld, 1988). Nevertheless, many of the psychological recommendations on how to improve decision making either implicitly or explicitly discount contextual and other temporary dimensions and assume that information processing characteristics are internally determined and are general across time, across issues, and perhaps across individuals. This assumption may occasionally be warranted; we see mounting evidence, however, that it is often wrong. People frequently are able and motivated to adjust their styles of thinking to situational demands (Chaiken, 1980; Fiske & Neuberg, 1990; Kruglanski, 1989; McAllister et al., 1979; Payne, 1982; Petty & Cacioppo, 1986; Tetlock, 1986a, 1986b, 1989).

Post Hoc Ergo Propter Hoc

This logical fallacy, that a subsequent event is necessarily a consequence, has its psychological variant: the inference of causation from correlation. Errors of this type abound in the decision analysis literature. The entire edifice of psychohistory assumes that if we can find a particular type of early experience and what appears to be a theoretically compatible adult behavior pattern, the former caused the latter. The relationship between the number of symptoms of defective decision making and the judged favorableness of the decision (correlations in the low .60s; Herek et al., 1987) is interpreted in causal terms: ". . . when the high-quality procedures of reflective problem solving are used, . . . the likelihood of making *avoidable* errors is decreased, which in turn decreases the likelihood of obtaining an *unsatisfactory* outcome" (Janis, 1986, p. 210; emphases in original). There is, of course, no evidence that would lead us to eliminate other possibilities (e.g., that some third, unidentified factor within the situation or the decision makers was at the root of both high-quality procedures and good outcomes).

CONCLUSION

The literature examined in this chapter has posed some interesting questions about how important decisions are made and has provided some intriguing answers both directly and by analogy. It has expected leaders to follow scholarly modes of procedure that allow for considering one problem at a time, taking long periods to reach closure, maximizing rationality and minimizing emotional and personal considerations, controlling many environmental variables, searching for all available relevant information, and reaching only tentative conclusions. Psychological research has therefore set up a prescriptive model based not merely on an ideal, but on an ideal scientist. National decision makers do not live in a decision environment where these things are possible nor necessarily even desirable.

In fact, there is no overwhelming reason to think that complex decision strategies are generally preferable. "The simple-minded and determined pursuit of a single well-defined objective may sometimes yield better results than complex attempts to achieve many, poorly defined objectives" (Tetlock, 1991, p. 32). Even "in scientific research, neither the degree of one's intelligence nor the ability to carry out one's tasks with thoroughness and precision are factors essential to personal success and fulfillment. More important for the attaining of both ends are total dedication and a tendency to underestimate difficulties, which cause one to tackle problems that other, more critical and acute persons instead opt to avoid" (Levi-Montalcini, 1988).

In the actual world, values, alternatives, probabilities, and outcomes are not as clear as is required for ideal decision making. The need to make many choices in a short period of time, the complexity of the interactions that determine outcomes, and the uncertainty surrounding probabilities, all compel human beings to make their choices by bounded rationality: a simplified model of the decision environment. Simon's (1983) behavioral model of decision making is based on this concept, which emphasizes how people actually solve problems by focusing attention, generating solution alternatives, and collecting and interpreting information. The process is not based on ideal omniscience and is not governed by pure thought, but draws upon intuition and the emotional processes that direct attention.

We have already presented our own view, that human beings are cognitive managers. Managers are pragmatic and use means that are accessible and no more than appropriately demanding. These means may include limiting information search, learning routines, modeling one's behavior on that of a successful predecessor or counterpart, and repeating previously successful strategies. They also include using a convenient and satisfactory solution if searching for a somewhat better one costs more than the improvement is worth and utilizing intuition and imagination even in contradiction to formal rules of logic and probability.

How correct this view is is not the point of this chapter. The point, rather, is whether the body of scientific knowledge available at this time is sufficiently solid to warrant the recommendations that have been made as to the need for complexity in high-level decision making. The further implication is that decision makers should be selected or trained, or the decision process be organized, so as to maximize this characteristic. In our judgment, the verdict is "Not proved."

REFERENCES

Adorno, T. W., Frenkel-Brunswick, E., Levinson, D. J., & Sanford, R. N. (1950). *The authoritarian personality*. New York: Harper.

Barber, J. D. (1972). *The presidential character: Predicting performance in the White House*. Englewood Cliffs, NJ: Prentice-Hall.

Blight, J. G. (1986). How might psychology contribute to reducing the risk of nuclear war? *Political Psychology, 7*, 617–660.

Chaiken, S. (1980). Heuristic versus systematic information processing and the use of source versus message cues in persuasion. *Journal of Personality and Social Psychology, 39*, 752–766.

Cohen, J. L. (1981). Can human irrationality be experimentally demonstrated? *Behavioral and Brain Sciences, 4*, 317–370 (with commentary).

deMause, L. (Ed.). (1975). *The new psychohistory*. New York: Psychohistory Press.

Dixon, N. F. (1979). *On the psychology of military incompetence*. London: Futura.

Einhorn, H. J., & Hogarth, R. M. (1981). Behavioral decision theory: Processes of judgment and choice. *Annual Review of Psychology, 32*, 53–88.

Etzioni, A. (1988). *The moral dimension: Toward a new economics*. New York: Free Press.

Fiedler, K. (1988). The dependence of the conjunction fallacy on subtle linguistic factors. *Psychological Research, 50,* 123-129.

Fiedler, F., & Garcia, J. E. (1987). *New approaches to effective leadership: Cognitive resources and organizational performance.* New York: Wiley.

Fiske, S. T., & Neuberg, S. L. (1990). A continuum of impression formation from category-based to individuating processes: Influence of information and motivation on attention and interpretations. In M. P. Zanna (Ed.), *Advances in experimental social psychology* (Vol. 23, pp. 1-74). New York: Academic Press.

Frankenhaeuser, M. (1988). To err is human: Nuclear war by mistake? In A. Gromyko & M. Hellman (Eds.), *Breakthrough: Emerging new thinking* (pp. 53-60). New York: Walker.

Ginossar, Z., & Trope, Y. (1987). Problem solving in judgment under uncertainty. *Journal of Personality and Social Psychology, 52,* 464-474.

Grice, H. P. (1975). Logic and conversation. In P. Cole & J. L. Morgan (Eds.), *Syntax and semantics, 3: Speech acts* (pp. 41-58). New York: Academic Press.

Harvey, O. J., Hunt, D. E., & Schroder, H. M. (1961). *Conceptual systems and personality organization.* New York: Wiley.

Herek, G., Janis, I. L., & Huth, P. (1987). Decisionmaking during international crises: Is quality of process related to outcome? *Journal of Conflict Resolution, 31,* 203-226.

Hermann, M. G. (1979). Indicators of stress in policymakers during foreign policy crises. *Political Psychology, 1,* 27-46.

Hermann, M. G. (Ed., with T. W. Milburn). (1977). *A psychological examination of political leaders.* New York: Free Press.

Hogarth, R. M. (1980). *Judgment and choice: The psychology of decision.* New York: Wiley.

Holsti, O. R. (1988). *Crisis decision-making.* Report prepared for the National Research Council, Washington, DC.

Janis, I. L. (1982). *Groupthink: Psychological studies of policy decisions and fiascoes,* Rev. Ed. (original title, *Victims of groupthink*). Boston: Houghton Mifflin.

Janis, I. L. (1986). Problems of international crisis management in the nuclear age. *Journal of Social Issues, 42,* 201-220.

Janis, I. L. (1989). *Crucial decisions: Leadership in policymaking and crisis management.* New York: Free Press.

Janis, I. L., & Mann, L. (1977). *Decision making: A psychological analysis of conflict, choice and commitment.* New York: Free Press.

Jervis, R. (1976). *Perception and misperception in international relations.* Princeton, NJ: Princeton University Press.

Jervis, R. (1989). Political psychology—some challenges and opportunities. *Political Psychology, 10,* 481-493.

Johnson-Laird, P. N. (1988). *The computer and the mind.* Cambridge, MA: Harvard University Press.

Kahneman, D., Slovic, P., & Tversky, A. (Eds.). (1982). *Judgment under uncertainty: Heuristics and biases.* Cambridge, U.K.: Cambridge University Press.

Krosnick, J. A., Li, F., & Lehman, D. R. (1990). Conversational conventions, order of information acquisition, and the effect of base rates and individuating information on social judgments. *Journal of Personality and Social Psychology, 59,* 1140-1152.

Kruglanski, A. (1989). *Lay epistemics and human knowledge: Cognitive and motivational bases.* New York: Plenum Press.

Lasswell, H. D. (1930). *Psychopathology and politics.* Chicago: University of Chicago Press.

Lebow, R. N. (1981). *Between peace and war: The nature of international crisis.* Baltimore, MD: Johns Hopkins University Press.

Lehman, D. R., Krosnick, J. A., & West, R. L. (1990). *The focus on judgment effect: A question wording effect due to hypothesis confirmation bias.* Unpublished manuscript. University of British Columbia and Ohio State University.

Lehman, D. R., Lempert, R. O., & Nisbett, R. E. (1988). The effects of graduate training on reasoning: Formal discipline and thinking about everyday-life events. *American Psychologist, 43,* 431-442.

Lehman, D. R., & Nisbett, R. E. (1990). A longitudinal study of the effects of undergraduate training on reasoning. *Developmental Psychology, 26,* 952-960.

Levi-Montalcini, R. (1988). *In praise of imperfection: My life and work.* New York: Basic Books.

Lifton, R. J. (Ed.). (1974). *Explorations in psychohistory.* New York: Simon & Schuster.

McAllister, P. W., Mitchell, T. R., & Beach, L. R. (1979). The contingency model for the selection of decision strategies: An empirical test of the effects of significance, accountability, and reversibility. *Organizational Behavior and Human Performance, 24,* 228-244.

Nisbett, R. E., Fong, G. T., Lehman, D. R., & Cheng, P. W. (1987). Teaching reasoning. *Science, 238,* 625-631.

Payne, J. (1982). Contingent decision behavior. *Psychological Bulletin, 92,* 382-402.

Petty, R. E., & Cacioppo, J. T. (1986). The elaboration likelihood model of persuasion. In L. Berkowitz (Ed.), *Advances in experimental social psychology* (Vol. 19, pp. 124-206). New York: Academic Press.

Porter, D. B. (1987). *Classroom teaching, implicit learning, and the deleterious effects of inappropriate explication.* Paper presented at the meeting of the Human Factors Society.

Rejai, M. (with K. Phillips). (1979). *Leaders of revolution.* Beverly Hills: Sage.

Rembar, C. (1969). *The end of obscenity.* New York: Bantam.

Schroder, H., Driver, M., & Streufert, S. (1967). *Human information processing.* New York: Holt, Rinehart, & Winston.

Simon, H. A. (1983). *Reason in human affairs.* Stanford, CA: Stanford University Press.

Simonton, D. K. (1984). *Genius, creativity, and leadership.* Cambridge, MA: Harvard University Press.

Simonton, D. K. (1987). *Why presidents succeed: A political psychology of leadership.* New Haven, CT: Yale University Press.

Stannard, D. E. (1980). *Shrinking history: On Freud and the failure of psychohistory.* New York: Oxford University Press.

Stein, J. G. (1988). Building politics into psychology: The misperception of threat. *Political Psychology, 9,* 245-272.

Streufert, S. (1987). Decision making: Research and theory challenges for applied social psychology. *Journal of Applied Social Psychology, 17,* 609-621.

Streufert, S., & Swezey, R. W. (1986). *Complexity, managers, and organizations.* New York: Academic Press.

Suedfeld, P. (1983). Authoritarian leadership: A cognitive-interactionist view. In J. Held (Ed.), *The cult of power: Dictators in the twentieth century* (pp. 1-22). Boulder, CO: East European Monographs.

Suedfeld, P. (1988, July/August). Authoritarian thinking, groupthink, and decision-making under stress: Are simple decisions always worse? *Society, 25,* 25-27.

Suedfeld, P., & Bluck, S. (1991). *Value conflict as a factor in determining integrative complexity.* Unpubl. manuscript, University of British Columbia.

Suedfeld, P., Corteen, R. S., & McCormick, C. (1986). The role of integrative complexity in military leadership: Robert E. Lee and his opponents. In G. Y. Nogami (Ed.), Special Issue on Military Psychology, *Journal of Applied Social Psychology, 16,* 498-507.

Suedfeld, P., & Rank, A. D. (1976). Revolutionary leaders: Long-term success as a function of changes in conceptual complexity. *Journal of Personality and Social Psychology, 34,* 169-178.

Suedfeld, P., & Tetlock, P. E. (1977). Integrative complexity of communications in international crises. *Journal of Conflict Resolution, 21,* 169-184.

Suedfeld, P., Tetlock, P. E., & Streufert, S. (in press). Conceptual/integrative complexity. In C. P. Smith (Ed.), *Handbook of thematic analysis.* New York: Cambridge University Press.

Taylor, S. E. (1980). The interface of cognitive and social psychology. In J. H. Harvey (Ed.), *Cognition, social behavior, and the environment* (pp. 189-211). Hillsdale, NJ: Erlbaum.

Tetlock, P. E. (1981). Pre- to post-election shifts in presidential rhetoric: Impression management or cognitive adjustment? *Journal of Personality and Social Psychology, 41,* 207-212.

Tetlock, P. E. (1983). Accountability and complexity of thought. *Journal of Personality and Social Psychology, 45,* 74-83.

Tetlock, P. E. (1986a). Psychological advice on foreign policy: What do we have to contribute? *American Psychologist, 41,* 557-567.

Tetlock, P. E. (1986b). A value pluralism model of ideological reasoning. *Journal of Personality and Social Psychology, 50,* 819-827.

Tetlock, P. E. (1988). Monitoring the integrative complexity of American and Soviet policy statements: What can be learned? *Journal of Social Issues, 44,* 101-131.

Tetlock, P. E. (1989). Structure and function in political belief systems. In A. G. Greenwald & A. Pratkanis (Eds.), *Attitude structure and function* (pp. 129-151). Hillsdale, NJ: Erlbaum.

Tetlock, P. E. (1991). Learning in U.S. and Soviet foreign policy: In search of an elusive concept. In G. Breslauer & P. E. Tetlock (Eds.), *Learning in U.S. and Soviet foreign policy.* Boulder, CO: Westview.

Tetlock, P. E., Bernzweig, J., & Gallant, J. (1985). Supreme Court decision-making: Cognitive style as a predictor of ideological consistency of voting. *Journal of Personality and Social Psychology, 48*, 1227–1239.

Tetlock, P. E., & Boettger, R. (1989). Accountability: A social magnifier of the dilution effect. *Journal of Personality and Social Psychology, 57*, 388–398.

Tetlock, P. E., Crosby, F., & Crosby, T. (1981). Political psychobiography. *Micropolitics, 1*, 191–213.

Tetlock, P. E., & Levi, A. (1982). Attribution bias: On the inclusiveness of the cognitive-motivation debate. *Journal of Experimental Psychology, 18*, 68–88.

Tetlock, P. E., & McGuire, C. B. (1986). Cognitive perspectives on foreign policy. In S. Long (Ed.), *Political behavior annual* (Vol. 1, pp. 147–179). Boulder, CO: Westview Press.

Tetlock, P. E., McGuire, C. B., & Mitchell, G. (1991). Psychological perspectives on nuclear deterrence. *Annual Review of Psychology* (pp. 239–276). Palo Alto, CA: Annual Reviews, Inc.

Tetlock, P. E., Skitka, L., & Boettger, R. (1989). Social and cognitive strategies of coping with accountability: Conformity, complexity, and bolstering. *Journal of Personality and Social Psychology, 57*, 632–641.

Thorne, C. (1968). *The approach of war, 1938–1939*. New York: St. Martin's.

Tversky, A., & Kahneman, D. (1974). Judgment under uncertainty: Heuristics and biases. *Science, 185*, 1124–1131.

Tversky, A., & Kahneman, D. (1983). Extensional versus intuitive reasoning: The conjunction fallacy in probability judgment. *Psychology Review, 90*, 293–315.

Walker, S. G. (Ed.) (1987). *Role theory and foreign policy analysis*. Durham, NC: Duke University Press.

Walker, S. G., & Watson, G. (1988, March-April). *Groupthink and cognitive complexity in Britrish foreign policy decision making during the Munich and Polish crises*. Presented at the meeting of the International Studies Assoc., St. Louis, MO.

Wallace, M. D., & Suedfeld, P. (1988). Leadership performance in crisis: The longevity-complexity link. *International Studies Quarterly, 32*, 439–451.

Ward, D. (1975). Kissinger: A psychohistory. In L. deMause (Ed.), *The new psychohistory* (pp. 69–130). New York: Psychohistory Press.

Welch, D. A. (1989). Crisis decision making reconsidered. *Journal of Conflict Resolution, 33*, 430–445.

Wolford, G., Taylor, H. A., & Beck, J. R. (n.d.). *The conjunction fallacy?* Unpublished manuscript. Dartmouth College.

ADDITIONAL READING

Abelson, R. P., & Levi, A. (1985). Decision-making and decision theory. In E. Aronson & G. Lindzey (Eds.), *Handbook of social psychology* (3rd Ed., pp. 231–310). Reading, MA: Addison-Wesley.

Beach, L. R., & Mitchell, T. R. (1978). *The presidential character: Predicting performance in the White House*. Englewood Cliffs, NJ: Prentice-Hall.

Breslauer, G., & Tetlock, P. E. (Eds.). (1991). *Learning in U.S. and Soviet foreign policy.* Boulder, CO: Westview.

Peterson, S. A. (1985). Neuropsychology, cognition, and political thinking. *Political Psychology, 6*, 495–518.

Staw, B. M. (1980). Rationality and justification in organizational life. In B. M. Staw & L. Cummings (Eds.), *Research in organizational behavior* (Vol. 2, pp. 45–80). Greenwich, CT: JAI Press.

4

Nuclear Policies: Deterrence and Reassurance

Ralph K. White

ADVOCACY THROUGH WHAT CHANNELS?

In view of the overriding importance of the nuclear danger and the great relevance of psychology *at certain points* in any comprehensive discussion of how to cope with that danger, it seems to me that qualified psychologists—qualified by a basic knowledge of related disciplines—have both a right and an obligation to play an active part in that discussion, but not alone. Each of several other disciplines, political science, 20th century world history, Soviet studies, and the new discipline of "national security studies" (including nuclear hardware and strategy), has at least as much relation to such policy decisions as psychology. There are few, if any, nuclear policy decisions that follow directly from psychological considerations alone. The broad field of foreign and defense policy is like a great picture puzzle in which many psychologists hold one or more important pieces, but the pieces are meaningless until fitted in with others, and the others are much more numerous.

To give just one example: Jervis (1976) and Lebow (1981) have shown amply that armed deterrence sometimes works in preventing war and sometimes actually precipitates it. There is a very relevant psychological proposition: Explicit or implicit threats of force intended as deterrence may be perceived by the adversary as implying an imminent attack that calls for immediate countermeasures. Whether in a given situation this will be the adversary's reaction is a question that can be answered only by a rigorously analytical approach to historical examples, plus much knowledge of the adversary and of the immediate situation. Few psychologists, as psychologists, have much of that kind of knowledge.

Therefore, it seems to me inappropriate for the American Psychological Association or any other psychological organization to make nuclear policy statements on its own. In order to make wise recommendations, in order to express them and the reasons for them in ways the policy makers can understand, and in order to avoid being seen, correctly, as presumptuous, I think organized psychologists should make public statements in this area only in collaboration with representatives of other disciplines and after much interdisciplinary discussion. However, there are at least two important channels through which qualified psychologists can contribute. One is participation in the kind of interdisciplinary group thinking suggested above, and the other is writing and talking *as individuals*. This chapter deals with ways in which, through these channels, psychologists may be able to bring their special knowledge and insights to bear on nuclear and other aspects of national and international security.

THE RELEVANT KNOWLEDGE
OF PSYCHOLOGISTS

On a number of psychological subjects that are directly or indirectly related to war and peace, psychologists and psychiatrists have made substantial contributions. Some examples are:

• Negotiation and mediation (e.g., Pruitt, 1981; Pruitt & Kimmel, 1977; Pruitt & Rubin, 1986; Rubin, 1980)
• Attribution, which includes the formation of national self images and enemy images (e.g., Fiske & Taylor, 1984; Heider, 1958; Jones & Davis, 1965; Nisbett & Ross, 1980; Oskamp, 1965, 1971; Ross, 1977)
• Cognitive and integrative complexity (Suedfeld & Tetlock, 1977; Tetlock, 1988)
• Cognitive availability (Kahneman & Tversky, 1979; Tversky & Kahneman, 1973). The "lesson of Munich" is highly available, though it is less relevant to the present situation than several other historical events
• Goals and assumptions of the Soviet people (Bronfenbrenner, 1961)
• Goals and assumptions of the Soviet government (White, 1984, 1986)
• Goals and assumptions of the American people (Yankelovich & Doble, 1984)
• Psychological effects of the nuclear threat (Lifton & Falk, 1982; Mack & Snow, 1984)
• The roots of anger and hate (Ardrey, 1966; Bandura, 1973; Berkowitz, 1969; Lorenz, 1966)
• Collective pride and narcissism (Frank, 1967; Fromm, 1973; Kohut, 1977)
• Selective inattention (Sullivan, 1953)
• Projection and the enemy image (Keen, 1986; Silverstein & Holt, 1989; Volkan, 1985)
• Social-conflict experiments (Deutsch, 1983; Lindskold, Walters, & Koutsourais, 1983; Oskamp, 1965, 1971; Pruitt, 1981)
• Communication and persuasion (Hovland, Janis, & Kelley, 1953)
• Spiral processes (Deutsch, 1983; Osgood, 1962)
• Personality description at a distance (Hermann, 1980)
• Conflict-resolution workshops (Burton, 1972; Kelman, 1965, 1972)
• Group decision making in crises (Janis, 1973; Janis & Mann, 1977)

The list is decidedly incomplete, both as to the psychological topics it contains and as to the names mentioned under each topic. However, it may serve to suggest the range of puzzle pieces that psychologists and psychiatrists have produced and that a qualified psychologist might be able to fit into the larger picture of war causation and prevention in our nuclear age. It is a list of which to be proud. Those who sweepingly belittle even the indirect and potential contributions of psychology in this area (e.g., Blight, 1987) are very wide of the mark.

It is noteworthy, though, that the list does not contain either deterrence or reassurance. They are both essentially psychological topics; they represent two ways of influencing what goes on in the minds of adversaries. Very few psychologists have dealt with them directly. In fact, nearly all of the important work on them has been done by nonpsychologists: by nuclear strategists and "national security" specialists (Allison, 1971; Brodie, 1946, 1959; Cox, 1982; Ford, 1985; Freedman, 1981–1982; Kahn, 1961; Kaufmann, 1954; Kissinger, 1961; McNamara, 1983, 1986; Nitze, 1976–1977; Nye, 1987; Schelling, 1960, 1966; Snyder & Diesing, 1977; Steinbruner, 1981–1982; Wohlstetter, 1959); by historians and Sovietologists (Garthoff, 1985; Howard, 1981; Kennan, 1980, 1982; Newhouse, 1988; Talbott, 1984); by game theorists (Axelrod, 1984; Rapoport, 1960; Rapoport & Chammah, 1965); and especially by political scientists who have a strong interest in psychology (George, 1971; George & Smoke, 1974; Holsti, North, & Brody, 1968; Jervis, 1976; Jervis, Lebow, & Stein, 1985; Lebow, 1981, 1987; Lebow & Stein, 1987; Reichart & Sturm, 1982; Smoke, 1977, 1982; Stein, 1985a, 1985b).

The one psychologist who has made a major, empirically based contribution in this area, to my knowledge, is Stephen Kull, a clinical psychologist. His 84 interviews with nuclear policy makers, in some depth, and his psychological interpretations of those interviews, are outstanding (Kull, 1988). There is clearly a great gap between the potentially relevant subjects that psychologists have explored and the problems of deterrence and reassurance in our nuclear age. Psychologists need to learn more about how to bridge that gap.

BASIC CONCEPTS: DEFINITIONS
AND DISTINCTIONS

In accord with Lebow and Stein (1987), *deterrence* is defined here as an attempt to "prevent an undesired behavior by convincing the party who may be contemplating such an action that its cost will exceed any possible gain" (p. 6). In a word, it seeks to increase fear in an adversary. It includes *general* deterrence (arming, seeking allies, gaining buffer territory, etc.) and also *immediate* deterrence (explicit threats and acts such as mobilizing, alerting a strategic air command, or moving naval ships into an area, at a time when the adversary seems about to engage in undesired behavior). The purpose is always to show some kind of strength or resolve, or both. The distinction between general and immediate deterrence is basic. Most of the recent discussion casting doubt on the effectiveness of deterrence focuses on immediate deterrence. That is appropriate because both threats and actions such as mobilizations can easily be interpreted by the adversary as preparation for aggression and can precipitate rather than prevent war. The Russian mobilization in 1914 did just that. Nuclear threats during a crisis, intended as deterrence, might actually lead the other side to preempt, thereby precipitating nuclear war.

On the other hand, general deterrence, including adequate nuclear strength (which perhaps could be only a fraction of what each side in the East–West conflict now possesses), has much to be said for it. There is a strong case for the proposition that without such general deterrence the two superpowers might well have been at each others' throats at some time during the long period from 1945 to 1990. It is noteworthy that even Lebow and Stein, whose long article "Beyond deterrence" was published in the *Journal of Social Issues* in 1987, along with 13 commentaries, are more favorable to general than to immediate deterrence. In a follow-up article in the same issue, Lebow says that immediate deterrence has had "largely pernicious effects. General deterrence, by contrast, has had a moderating effect on superpower behavior. It rests on the realization in Moscow and Washington that there is nothing that can be done to protect either country from the near-certain annihilation that would result from a superpower nuclear war" (p. 184).

Reassurance has had nowhere near the amount of attention that deterrence has had in policy-making circles, but it deserves to be given at least equal emphasis. It can be defined as an attempt to reduce, in an adversary, the unhealthy, exaggerated, paranoid kind of fear that fuels arms races and often leads nations to engage in defensively motivated aggression. To sharpen the distinction between them we can also say that the right kind of deterrence means maintaining, in opponents' minds, a healthy fear of the consequences of attacking, while the right kind of reassurance means decreasing, in opponents' minds, exaggerated fears of being attacked. The two concepts are by no means opposites (although in some contexts they may be incompatible), and it is possible and urgently necessary to seek both at the same time.

It also seems plain that, in the post-1989 era, many forms of mutual reassurance that formerly seemed politically and psychologically impossible may have become possible and now deserve careful consideration. The emphasis should shift, perhaps dramatically, from emphasizing deterrence to emphasizing reassurance. That means that psychologists, like everyone else, should be weighing the pros and cons (the desirability and the feasibility) of a considerable number of concrete forms that reassurance might take. Some are negative and relatively easy: not pushing the arms race, not designing or building new first-strike weapons (those that can be devastatingly lethal to the other side's homeland and are also vulnerable), not striving for nuclear superiority under a pretense of seeking equality, not indulging in belligerent rhetoric, not intervening in Third World countries in ways that the chief opponent will be sure to perceive as aggression, and not violating the letter or spirit of agreements that have been made. Other items—the harder and more important ones, as a rule—are more active and positive. Some examples:

1. Reduction of each side's nuclear weapons, by fairly rapid stages, to a fraction of what they are now. McNamara (1986) suggests that the fraction might be one-twentieth. Nuclear weapons, far more than conventional ones, increase the unhealthy fear of being attacked. This means that in the current Strategic Arms Reduction Talks (START talks) the United States should have a great sense of urgency and willingness to compromise in order to achieve drastic reductions quickly.

2. Total elimination, by both sides, of first-strike nuclear weapons, such as MIRVd ICBMs, MXs in fixed silos, and antisatellite (ASAT) weapons. First-strike weapons, much more than other nuclear weapons, increase the unhealthy fear of being attacked, perhaps without warning. More than any other weapons they increase the other side's perceptions that one's own side could attack with total devastation and also that one's own side might be hostile enough to want to do so. And the typical vulnerability, far from deterring, tempts the other side to strike first (cf. Adelman, 1984–1985). This means that in the current START talks there should be a special sense of urgency about reducing first-strike weapons.

3. Rapid achievement of rough parity in conventional weapons. Because a chief rationale for having more than minimal nuclear weapons has been an assumed need to bolster the deterrent power of the West in defense of Western Europe, and because that need has been assumed on the basis of a perceived great superiority of the Soviet Union in conventional forces, achievement of parity in the current talks on conventional forces in Europe (CFE) should have a major reassuring effect in both Western Europe and the United States. Such reassurance, in turn, should help to make drastic nuclear cuts on the Western side psychologically possible.

4. Charles Osgood's GRIT—graduated and reciprocated initiatives in tension-reduction (1962), which is in effect an arms race in reverse.

5. Matching and exceeding such initiatives by the other side (e.g., Gorbachev's test moratoriums and his unilateral troop reductions).

6. A comprehensive test ban (CTB), covering underground tests as well as other tests.

7. In arms control negotiations, a general willingness to be more reasonable and forthcoming than the other side, for instance, not insisting, as the United States has insisted, that its own forward-based systems in Western Europe and the nuclear weapons of its West European allies should not be counted in judging the "strategic balance" (Newhouse, 1988, pp. 221–222). Also, persuading allies to accept such reasonable positions when necessary.

8. A joint no-first-use statement, backed up by elimination of first-strike weapons and tactical nuclear weapons. In order to make that change in policy psychologically and politically possible, publicizing the little-known fact that the United States does not now have a no-first-use policy (Yankelovich & Doble, 1984).

9. Favoring mobility, in whatever nuclear weapons still exist, as a way of reducing vulnerability (Newhouse, 1988, p. 406).

10. Opposing a launch-on-warning policy and the superfast, superaccurate weapons that might make launch-on-warning seem to be a rational damage-limiting measure in a crisis situation.

11. Following Gorbachev's lead in reducing especially the more offensive conventional arms, such as tanks, mobile heavy artillery, and river-crossing equipment—with adequate verification.

12. Several kinds of confidence-building measures (e.g., "hot line," exchanging military information).

13. Businesslike mutual-benefit economic relations (e.g., elimination of the Jackson–Vanik Amendment, which made free trade contingent on Jewish emigration from the U.S.S.R.).

14. Strenuous pursuit of nonproliferation agreements, by example (drastic reduction of nuclear arsenals by the superpowers) as well as by precept.

All of the items in this list have a common psychological characteristic: They all are intended to contribute to reassurance. They are designed to reduce exaggerated, unhealthy fears of being attacked by the other side. In doing so they should promote a reversal of the psychological vicious spiral (Deutsch, 1983, calls it the "malignant process" of hostile interaction) that, at least until recently, has characterized the East–West conflict. The items also have another common psychological characteristic: They are consistent with the most necessary forms of deterrence and are therefore not beyond the range of what might ultimately be acceptable to both sides. For instance, they do not preclude each side having an adequate second-strike capability (adequate considering that one nuclear-armed submarine could destroy all of the major cities on the other side), nor do they preclude equality of conventional strength, which should reassure West Europeans that they have not been left vulnerable to a Soviet conventional attack. In other words, combining sensible deterrence with sensible reassurance, defining both in these concrete ways, could be a win–win, mutual-benefit solution of the still-lingering problem of war between East and West.

Some Psychological Hypotheses Related to Nuclear Policy

In our bridge-building, between our own interests and those of the political scientists, we psychologists will be well-advised to pay close attention to certain bridging hypotheses that are derived mainly from the work of the psychologically oriented political scientists. Here are five of them:

When Deterrence Should Be Stressed

Deterrence should be stressed more when facing an empire builder like Hitler than when facing an adversary whose arming and aggressive actions, like those of the Germans in 1914, seem motivated mainly by fear. In other words, "the lesson of Munich" is valid in a situation like Munich, but not necessarily in many other situations. Jervis (1976) was perhaps the first to formulate this hypothesis clearly. In the chapter titled "Deterrence, the spiral model, and intentions of the adversary," in his classic *Perception and misperception in international politics*, he describes two models of international conflict behavior that he calls the deterrence model and the spiral model. The central argument of deterrence theory, he says, is that "great dangers arise if an aggressor believes that the status quo powers are weak in capability or resolve. . . . If the status quo powers retreat, they will not only lose the specific value at stake, but . . . will encourage the aggressor to press harder. To avoid this disastrous situation the state must display the ability and willingness to wage war" (p. 58).

The spiral model, on the other hand, takes as its central image an arms race in which each side is actually arming mainly in self-defense, because of fear, but each believes the other is arming because of an intention to attack. The actions on each side feed the other's image of an aggressive opponent, and the end is often a war unwanted by either. After giving several examples that fit each model, Jervis suggests that the spiral interpretation can be readily applied to the origins of World War I and that "deterrence theorists often hark back to, and derive much of their analysis from, the failure of appeasement in the 1930s" (p. 95).

Lebow, in his detailed analysis of 13 "brinkmanship crises" (1981) finds that the challenger of the status quo is actually more often driven by fear than by cold-blooded expansionist ambition. The fear, he finds, takes two main forms: policy makers' fears that they will lose politically if they do not take a firm, decisive stand in a crisis and fears that a national adversary will gain dangerously in relative power if a decisive stand is not taken (pp. 61–97). He too finds that German and Austrian aggression in World War I was motivated mainly by fear and adds that Russian mobilization, designed to deter, directly precipitated the German attack on France through Belgium.

Gorbachev Era

In the present "Gorbachev Era," the West's need for deterrence has become minimal, and the appropriateness of reassurance has become especially clear. At this writing (early 1990) the momentous events of 1989 have perhaps made that proposition self-evident. The present Soviet Union has neither the ability nor the desire to play an aggressive role in the rest of the world. Yet an important question remains: If Gorbachev were to die or be replaced, what would happen? Might the Soviet Union then return to the military strength and the aggressive ways of its past? And should the United States therefore remain heavily and expensively armed, in order to be realistically cautious, in spite of its own urgent unmet domestic needs? In the minds of a great many U.S. citizens, including President Bush, that question is probably the chief obstacle to a decisive turn from a policy of deterrence to a policy of reassurance.

An immediate political answer is that those who would take Gorbachev's place appear to be fairly similar to him in their renunciation of expansionist aims. It is a remarkable and little noticed fact that only a small part of the large amount of criticism of him inside the U.S.S.R. is directed at his conciliatory foreign policy and what there is comes mainly from the military. While the economic problems of the country under his leadership are objects of continual and very widespread attack, his arms-reduction policies and his willingness to see the empire in East Europe disappear are not.

A more fundamental psychological answer consists of the hypothesis that for many years, and until very recently, Western publics and elites have tended to exaggerate the inherent aggressiveness of the Soviet leaders. A strong case can be made that, partly because of the interest of the military-industrial complex in making and selling arms and partly because of spontaneous psychological tendencies in the general public, an unduly frightening image of the Soviet Union has been created. Or rather, the valid devil image that Stalin's behavior created, when he wielded despotic power, has been sustained and unconsciously clung to, partly because of a psychological need for an enemy.

Many psychologists and psychiatrists (e.g., Frank, 1967; Keen, 1986; Silverstein & Holt, 1989) have thought along that line and have suggested various psychological processes, especially projection, that could account for such a need. This is not the place to elaborate on their thinking; other psychologists are familiar with it. Something should be said, though, about how a fresh look at recent history may support their stress on the exaggerated "enemy image" and on projection as a factor in its formation. Surely in the Stalin period there was behind Soviet foreign policy not only a desire for buffer territory in order to be secure but also a desire for power for its own sake that bore some resemblance to Hitler's type of expansionism. Stalin was, like Hitler, a devil—or at least a dangerous paranoid—and deterring him was urgent. The period included the Finnish war, the takeover of most of Eastern Europe, the Berlin Blockade in 1948–1949, and the Korean War.

The case is different with regard to Soviet foreign policy in the post-Stalin period. Eastern Europe began to be held with a looser rein shortly after Khrushchev came to power. For 26 years (1953–1979) there were no takeovers comparable to those of the 1940s. There were confrontations on Berlin and Cuba, but in them the Soviet Union backed down. Actions in Hungary and Czechoslovakia were undoubtedly aggressive, but could be interpreted as holding buffer territory that the U.S.S.R. already possessed, in fear of a domino process in Eastern Europe, rather than as reaching out for more. The contrast in apparent motivation between those actions and Hitler's conquests is great, and there has been a real resemblance to some U.S. actions, such as those in North Korea, Iran, Guatemala, Cuba (the Bay of Pigs), Vietnam, and Nicaragua. Taken all together, there is much evidence that the degree of inherent aggressiveness usually attributed to the Soviet Union has been exaggerated.

Lebow's interpretation of the Cuban Missile Crisis (1981, pp. 64–66) and Garthoff's detailed, authoritative treatment of the motivation behind the Soviet invasion of Afghanistan (1985, pp. 887–965) as well as of the Angolan and Ethiopian events, are among the historical studies that lend support to this judgment. If such a revision of the typical U.S. interpretation of post-Stalin Soviet foreign policy is needed, then the typical expectation of what might happen when Gorbachev dies or is replaced also needs revision. In that case there could be a far larger diversion of U.S. resources from military to civilian needs.

A separate question is whether the deterrent policy of President Reagan, including his peace-through-strength arms buildup and his evil-empire theme, had good effects. In one way it probably had a very good effect. By forcing the U.S.S.R. to arm heavily if it wanted to maintain its status as a superpower, the President's policy intensified the economic predicament of the Soviet people, shocking them into a realization of how expensive (and futile) their arming was and how urgent it was to turn their attention inward to domestic reforms. His evil-empire theme also may have shocked them into somewhat more awareness of how evil their East European empire was and always had been.

A related question is: How can the reasonableness and conciliatory character of Gorbachev's foreign policy be accounted for, psychologically? He seems singularly free from a Stalin-like power drive (power as an end in itself) and also from the Khrushchev and Brezhnev type of occasional aggressiveness stemming, according to one interpretation, from insecurity (power in order to be safe). The chief motive, quite clearly, is economic necessity. But it also seems likely that Gorbachev's reasonableness and his unusual ability to empathize realistically with adversaries have enabled him to be unusually rational in his perception of ways to achieve economic well-being for his country. In brief, his thinking is characterized by a degree of integrative complexity that his predecessors lacked.

Exaggerated Strength

An adversary's strength, as well as its aggressiveness, is very often exaggerated, and this has occurred in Western thinking about the U.S.S.R. The exaggeration of an opponent's aggressiveness is part of the familiar, simplistic "good guys and bad buys" conception of a conflict and has been somewhat covered by the two hypotheses stated earlier. It is a major form of the unrealistic simplicity of thinking that Suedfeld and Tetlock (1977) have stressed. The tendency to exaggerate an opponent's power is not often recognized, and this is puzzling, since it seems to contradict the more familiar tendency to wishful thinking. Does a person want, even unconsciously, to have an opponent be more powerful than her- or himself?

There is much evidence of it, however: the "missile gap" that turned out to be the opposite of the truth (Cox, 1982, p. 95; Newhouse, 1988, pp. 121–124); the ignoring, mentioned earlier, of the fact that U.S. forward-based systems in Western Europe were not being counted in comparisons of strategic strength; and the similar ignoring of U.S. superiority in high technology, in long-range bombers, in quality of nuclear-armed submarines, in warheads, and in nuclear-armed allies. There have also been many exaggerated claims that Soviet conventional superiority is "overwhelming," ignoring especially the evidence that Soviet arms are often qualitatively inferior (Cox, 1982, pp. 104–126; Dean, 1987, pp. 27–28, 34–35; Newhouse, 1988, pp. 93, 119–124).

Two Ways of Thinking

Both national policy makers and the general public are in a state of inner conflict between two patterns of thinking: a traditional belief-system that does not fully recognize the implications of the existence of nuclear weapons and an up-to-date adaptive belief-system that does fully recognize them. For instance, one such implication is that, because of the enormous destructiveness of even one nuclear weapon, a relatively small number of them may be quite adequate for deterrent purposes, even if the adversary has a far larger number (assuming that the small number is relatively invulnerable to a first strike by the other side). In other words, parity in nuclear weapons, in contrast with parity in conventional forces, has become almost irrelevant.

This conflict between two belief-systems is the essence of what Kull discovered in his indepth interviews of 84 national policy makers (1988). It also applies to the general public, as is shown by the public opinion data on simultaneous public endorsement of two inconsistent propositions. On the one hand, 79% agree that "It doesn't matter if the United States or the Soviet Union is ahead in nuclear weapons because both sides have more than enough to destroy the other no matter who attacks first" (a *Washington Post*/ABC News poll, 1982, quoted by White, 1984, pp. 340–341). That judgment reflects the up-to-date, adaptive belief-system. On the other hand, many other polls show that the public insists "we must not lose the nuclear arms race" and must have a "strong defense" in nuclear as well as in conventional forces (Yankelovich & Doble, 1984). That view reflects the traditional belief-system, and in practice it means that the public is uncritically accepting the proposition, put forward as obvious by President Bush and Secretary Cheney, that until the Soviet Union agrees to make deep cuts in its nuclear weapons we cannot afford to do so unilaterally.

Fear of Preemption

A panicky fear of nuclear preemption by the other side, at a time of international crisis, could lead decision makers in any country to misinterpret ambiguous evidence and to preempt. It follows that a launch-on-warning policy, and the superfast, superaccurate first-strike weapons on both sides that might make launch on warning seem a rational damage-limiting policy, should be avoided like the plague. It follows also—and this is where psychology comes in—that a state of high international tension, with a high level of fear and suspicion on both sides, would predispose decision makers to misinterpret ambiguous evidence and to "press the button." Therefore this most plausible way for a nuclear war to start should be anticipated long before a crisis arrives, and the level of tension should be permanently kept as low as possible.

BIBLIOGRAPHY

In addition to serving the ordinary purposes of a reference list and bibliography, this one is an attempt to be useful to those psychologists who want to fit their kind of psychology appropriately into the great expanding picture puzzle of war and peace. They may want to focus quickly on the parts of the available literature that are most relevant to their individual purposes. Therefore the bibliography contains at least one illustrative example of the work of each of the psychologists and each of the nonpsychologists mentioned in the text.

Asterisks indicate that the author or chief author is a psychologist. The author(s)' name(s) in the most recommended sources (the chief basis being relevance to war and peace, not just nuclear war) are italicized.

Adelman, K. L. (Winter, 1984–1985). Arms control with and without agreement. *Foreign Affairs, 63,* 240–263.

Allison, G. T. (1971). *Essence of decision: Explaining the Cuban Missile Crisis.* Boston: Little, Brown.

Ardrey, R. (1966). *The territorial imperative.* New York: Dell.

Axelrod, R. (1984). *The evolution of cooperation.* New York: Basic Books.

*Bandura, A. (1973). *Aggression: A social learning analysis.* Englewood Cliffs, NJ: Prentice-Hall.

*Berkowitz, L. (Ed.). (1969). *Roots of aggression: A reexamination of the frustration-aggression hypothesis.* New York: Atherton Press.

*Blight, J. G. (1987). Toward a policy-relevant psychology of avoiding nuclear war. *American Psychologist, 42,* 11–29.

Brodie, B. (Ed.). (1946). *The absolute weapon.* New York: Harcourt Brace.

Brodie, B. (1959). *Strategy in the missile age.* Princeton, NJ: Princeton University Press.

*Bronfenbrenner, U. (1961). The mirror-image in Soviet-American relations. *Journal of Social Issues, 17,* 45–56.

Burton, J. (1972). Resolution of conflict. *International Studies Quarterly, 16*(1).

Cox, A. M. (1982). *Russian roulette: The superpower game.* New York: Times Books.

Dean, J. (1987). Military security in Europe. *Foreign Affairs, 66*(1), 22–40.

*Deutsch, M. (1983). The prevention of World War III: A psychological perspective. *Journal of Political Psychology, 4*(1).

*Fiske, S. T., & Taylor, S. E. (1984). *Social cognition.* Reading, MA: Addison-Wesley.

Ford, D. (1985). *The button: The Pentagon's strategic command and control system.* New York: Simon and Schuster.

*Frank, J. (1967). *Sanity and survival: Psychological aspects of war and peace.* New York: Vintage Books.

Freedman, L. (1981–1982, Winter). NATO myths. *Foreign Policy, 45,* 48–68.

*Fromm, E. (1973). *The anatomy of human destructiveness.* New York: Holt, Rinehart & Winston.

Garthoff, R. L. (1985). *Detente and confrontation: American-Soviet relations from Nixon to Reagan.* Washington, DC: The Brookings Institution.

George, A. L. (1971). *The limits of coercive diplomacy.* Boston: Little, Brown.

George, A. L., and Smoke, R. (1974). *Deterrence in American foreign policy: Theory and practice.* New York: Columbia University Press.

*Heider, F. (1958). *The psychology of interpersonal relations.* New York: Wiley.

*Hermann, M. G. (1980). Assessing the personalities of Soviet politburo members. *Personality and Social Psychology Bulletin, 6,* 332–352.

Holsti, O., North, R., & Brody, R. (1968). Perception and action in the 1914 crisis. In J. D. Singer (Ed.), *Quantitative international politics.* New York: The Free Press.

Hough, J. (1980, March 1). Why the Russians invaded. *The Nation,* pp. 225–232.

*Hovland, C., Janis, I., & Kelley, H. (1953). *Communication and persuasion.* New Haven, CT: Yale University Press.

Howard, M. (1981, November 3). The case for keeping a strong conventional arms capability. Letter to *The Times* (London). Quoted in Cox (1982), *Russian roulette,* pp. 147, 210.

*Janis, I. L. (1973). *Victims of groupthink.* Boston: Houghton Mifflin.

*Janis, I. L., & Mann, L. (1977). *Decisionmaking: A psychological analysis of conflict, choice, and commitment.* New York: The Free Press.

*Jervis, R. (1976). *Perception and misperception in international politics.* Princeton, NJ: Princeton University Press.

Jervis, R., Lebow, R. L., & Stein, J. G. (Eds.). (1985). *Psychology and deterrence.* Baltimore, MD: Johns Hopkins University Press. (Also contains articles by J. Snyder and P. Morgan.)

*Jones, E. E., & Davis, K. E. (1965). From acts to dispositions: The attribution process in person perception. In L. Berkowitz (Ed.), *Advances in experimental social psychology* (Vol. 2, pp. 219–266). New York: Academic Press.

Kahn, H. (1961). *On thermonuclear war.* Princeton, NJ: Princeton University Press.

*Kahneman, D., & Tversky, A. (1979). Prospect theory: An analysis of decision under risk. *Econometrica, 47,* 263–291.

Kaufmann, W. W. (1954). *The requirements of deterrence.* Princeton, NJ: Center of International Studies.

*Keen, S. (1986). *Faces of the enemy: Reflections of the hostile imagination.* San Francisco: Harper & Row.

*Kelley, H. H. (1971). *Attribution in social interaction.* Morristown, NJ: Silver Burdett.

*Kelman, H. C. (Ed.). (1965). *International behavior: A social-psychological analysis.* New York: Holt, Rinehart & Winston.

*Kelman, H. C. (1972). The problem-solving workshop in conflict resolution. In R. L. Merritt (Ed.), *Communication in international politics.* Urbana: University of Illinois Press.

Kennan, G. F. (1980, April). Imprudent response to the Afghanistan crisis? *Bulletin of the Atomic Scientists,* pp. 7–9. Reprinted from *New York Times Magazine,* February 1, 1980.

Kennan, G. F. (1982). *The nuclear delusion: Soviet-American relations in the nuclear age.* New York: Pantheon.

Kissinger, H. (1961). *The necessity for choice: Prospects for American foreign policy.* New York: Harper.

*Kohut, H. (1977). *The restoration of the self.* New York: International Universities Press.

*Kull, S. (1988). *Minds at war: Nuclear reality and the inner conflicts of defense policymakers.* New York: Basic Books.

*Lebow, R. N. (1981). *Between peace and war: The nature of international crisis.* Baltimore, MD: Johns Hopkins University Press.

Lebow, R. N. (1987). Conventional vs. nuclear deterrence: Are the lessons transferable? In G. Levinger (Issue Ed.), *Journal of Social Issues, 43,* 171–191.

Lebow, R. N., & Stein, J. G. (1987). Beyond deterrence. In G. Levinger (Issue Ed.), *Journal of Social Issues, 43,* 5–71.

*Lifton, R. J., & Falk, R. (Eds.). (1982). *Indefensible weapons: The political and psychological cases against nuclearism.* New York: Basic Books.

*Lindskold, S., Walters, P. S., & Koutsourais, H. (1983). Cooperators, competitors, and response to GRIT. *Journal of Conflict Resolution, 27,* 521–532.

*Lorenz, K. (1966). *On aggression.* New York: Harcourt Brace.

*Mack, J., & Snow, R. (1984). Psychological effects on children and adolescents. In R. K. White (Ed.), *Psychology and the prevention of nuclear war.* New York: New York University Press.

McNamara, R. S. (1983, Fall). The military role of nuclear weapons. *Foreign Affairs, 62,* 59–80.

McNamara, R. S. (1986). *Blundering into disaster: Surviving the first century of the nuclear age.* New York: Pantheon.

Newhouse, J. (1988). *War and peace in the nuclear age.* Companion book to the public television series. New York: Knopf.

*Nisbett, R. E., & Ross, L. (1980). *Human inference: Strategies and shortcomings of social judgment.* Englewood Cliffs, NJ: Prentice-Hall.

Nitze, P. (1976–1977, Winter). Deterring our deterrent. *Foreign Policy, 25,* 195–210.

Nye, J. S., Jr. (1987). Nuclear learning and U.S.–Soviet security regimes. *International Organization, 41,* 371–402.

*Osgood, C. E. (1962). *An alternative to war or surrender.* Urbana: University of Illinois Press.

*Oskamp, S. (1965). Attitudes toward U.S. and Russian actions: A double standard. *Psychological Reports, 16,* 43–46.

*Oskamp, S. (1971). Effects of programmed strategies on cooperation in the Prisoner's Dilemma and other mixed-motive games. *Journal of Conflict Resolution, 15,* 225–259.

*Pruitt, D. G. (1981). *Negotiating behavior.* New York: Academic Press.

*Pruitt, D. G., & Kimmel, M. J. (1977). Twenty years of experimental gaming. *Annual Review of Psychology, 28,* 363–392.

*Pruitt, D. G., & Rubin, J. Z. (1986). Social conflict: Escalation, stalemate, and settlement. New York: Random House.
Rapoport, A. (1960). Fights, games, and debates. Ann Arbor: University of Michigan Press.
Rapoport, A., & Chammah, A. M. (1965). Prisoner's dilemma. Ann Arbor: University of Michigan Press.
Reichart, J. F., & Sturm, S. R. (Eds.). (1982). American defense policy (5th Ed.). Baltimore, MD: Johns Hopkins University Press. (Articles on deterrence by Bull, Gray, Jervis, Lambeth, and G. Snyder.)
*Ross, L. (1977). The intuitive psychologist and his shortcomings: Distortions in the attribution process. In L. Berkowitz (Ed.). Advances in experimental social psychology (Vol. 10, pp. 174–241). New York: Academic Press.
*Rubin, J. Z. (1980). Dynamics of third party intervention: Interdisciplinary perspectives on international conflict. New York: Praeger.
Russett, B. (1967). Pearl Harbor: Deterrence theory and decision theory. Journal of Peace Research, 4, 89–105.
Schelling, T. (1960). The strategy of conflict. Cambridge, MA: Harvard University Press.
Schelling, T. (1966). Arms and influence. New Haven, CT: Yale University Press.
*Silverstein, B., & Holt, R. R. (1989). Research on enemy images: Present status and future prospects. In R. R. Holt & E. Silverstein (Issue Eds.), Journal of Social Issues, 45, 159–175.
Smoke, R. (1977). War: Controlling escalation. Cambridge, MA: Harvard University Press. Excerpts reprinted in R. K. White (Ed.), 1986, Psychology and the prevention of nuclear war. New York: New York University Press.
Smoke, R. (1982). The evolution of American defense policy. In F. I. Greenstein & N. Polsby (Eds.), Handbook of political science. Vol. 8: International politics. Reading, MA: Addison-Wesley. Reprinted with minor revisions in Reichart & Sturm, 1982.
Snyder, G., & Diesing, P. (1977). Conflict among nations. Princeton, NJ: Princeton University Press.
Stein, J. G. (1985a). Calculation, miscalculation, and conventional deterrence, I: The view from Cairo. In R. Jervis, R. N. Lebow, & J. G. Stein (Eds.), Psychology and deterrence (pp. 34–59). Baltimore, MD: Johns Hopkins University Press.
Stein, J. G. (1985b). Calculation, miscalculation, and conventional deterrence, II. The view from Jerusalem. In R. Jervis, R. N. Lebow, & J. G. Stein (Eds.), Psychology and deterrence (pp. 60–88). Baltimore, MD: Johns Hopkins University Press.
Steinbruner, J. (1981–1982, Winter). Nuclear decapitation. Foreign Policy, 45, 16–28.
*Suedfeld, P., & Tetlock, P. E. (1977). Integrative complexity of communication in international crises. Journal of Conflict Resolution, 28, 169–184.
*Sullivan, H. S. (1953). In H. S. Perry & M. L. Gawel (Eds.), The interpersonal theory of psychiatry. New York: Norton.
Talbott, S. (1984). Deadly gambits: The Reagan Administration and the stalemate in nuclear arms control. New York: Knopf.
*Tetlock, P. E. (1988). Monitoring the integrative complexity of American and Soviet policy rhetoric: What can be learned? Journal of Social Issues, 4, 101–131.
*Tetlock, P. E., Husbands, J. L., Jervis, J., Stern, P. C., & Tilly, C. (Eds.). (1989). Behavior, society, and nuclear war. New York: Oxford University Press.
*Tversky, A., & Kahneman, D. (1973). Availability: A heuristic for judging frequency and probability. Cognitive Psychology, 5,
Volkan. (1985). The need to have enemies and allies. Political Psychology, 6, 219–247.
*White, R. K. (1984). Fearful warriors: A psychological profile of U.S.-Soviet relations. New York: The Free Press.
*White, R. K. (Ed.). (1986). Psychology and the prevention of nuclear war. New York: New York University Press.
Wohlstetter, A. (1959). The delicate balance of terror. Foreign Affairs, 37, 211–234.
Yankelovich, D., & Doble, J. (1984, Fall). The public mood: Nuclear weapons and the U.S.S.R. Foreign Affairs, pp. 33–46.

5

Nuclear Crisis Psychologies: Still "Crazy" (and Still Irrelevant) after All These Years

James G. Blight

> *I would not be convicted by a jury of my peers—*
> *"still crazy, after all these years."*
>
> Paul Simon, 1974

Without a single nuclear weapon being fired in anger since World War II, and thus by means of thought experiments alone, the leaders and citizens of the nuclear superpowers have, in the presence of what has been called the "crystal ball effect," learned to abhor the prospect of any sort of nuclear war (Blight, 1990; Carnesale et al., 1983). But does abhorrence necessarily translate into avoidance? Few would argue that it does, although complacency in this regard seems to be on the rise in our glasnost-inspired age of East–West rapprochement (Fukuyama, 1989; Mueller, 1989). No serious student of nuclear risk, however, rates the probability of nuclear war at zero. For those who still, and correctly, worry about how to avoid a nuclear war we have already learned to abhor, the concern lies with two factors: first, a nonzero probability of an event with a potentially catastrophic outcome; and second, our belief that in certain situations—we usually call them *crises*—the probability of a nuclear war might rise alarmingly high. Such a paradoxically initiated nuclear war would occur by means of *inadvertence*: some not fully imagined, insidious concatenation of technology, psychology, and politics resulting in a situation that is so relentlessly perverse, so apparently devoid of satisfactory options, that nuclear war is actually initiated. When we speak, therefore, of the task of avoiding nuclear war nowadays, we generally mean avoiding *inadvertent* nuclear war (Blight, 1990, Ch. 7; McNamara, 1986, 1989).

The problem of framing our understanding of inadvertent nuclear war is bound up entirely with what we believe constitutes a nuclear crisis, and answers to both sets of questions, regarding inadvertence and regarding crises, will depend on our success in addressing what is fundamentally a psychological process. In the worst conceivable situation, often described as a crisis deeper than the Cuban Missile Crisis, leaders' basic beliefs will become inverted regarding the relative worth of initiating a nuclear war. It is an inadvertent process because in normal times, or even at the outset of such a crisis, leaders would not have imagined that they eventually would come to believe such a thing.

Adapted from Blight (1990), Chapter 4.

The difficulty encountered by anyone who tries to speak sensibly about inadvertent nuclear war arising out of a crisis can be illustrated in a set of propositions. The first four conditions are generally believed to apply uniformly in all noncrisis situations, and a fifth condition may, under the most desperate circumstances, apply in a nuclear crisis. The trick is to answer the question that follows the propositions (see below) in a way that has enough empirical content to be convincing.

Under Normal Conditions:

1. Nuclear deterrence, the mutual capacity for total annihilation, promotes caution and political stability.
2. No sane leader will want to start a nuclear war, under any circumstances.
3. Purely accidental nuclear war or nuclear war through a leader's insanity is practically inconceivable.
4. Nuclear deterrence is robust, stable, and very unlikely to fail.

Under Nuclear Crisis Conditions:

5. Numbers 1–4 stated above may be false.

Question: What will happen between statements 1–4 and statement 5? Or what is there about a nuclear crisis that makes "crazy" behavior seem required?

Somehow a nuclear crisis will work its black magic on leaders responsible for nuclear arsenals, and it will be psychological black magic. Minds will change; deeply held beliefs will be jettisoned. In this way, for reasons just barely imaginable, the most basic lesson of the nuclear age will somehow be forgotten or repudiated—that a nuclear war is the war that must never be fought. A psychological revolution will have occurred just before the world is blown up.

Thus a great strain is inevitably placed upon the imaginations of those studying paths to inadvertent nuclear war and upon the credibility of their enterprise. In certain respects, the task of avoiding nuclear war is somewhat akin to the tasks of avoiding earthquakes or falling meteorites. Everyone wants to avoid them, but no one really knows how. Schelling (1985–1986) has proposed an even more interesting metaphor that brings the discussion of avoiding nuclear disaster to some of the basic principles of deterrence. Our learning to abhor nuclear war and our need to avoid a nuclear war, according to Schelling, are very nearly functionally equivalent to one another. As Schelling argues:

> People regularly stand at the curb watching trucks, buses and cars hurtle past at speeds that guarantee injury and threaten death if they so much as attempt to cross against the traffic. They are absolutely deterred. But there is no fear. They just know better. (Schelling, 1985–1986, p. 233)

Because he believes we "know better" than to enter into a nuclear war, it is difficult for Schelling to imagine a situation in which this salient knowledge would be forgotten or superseded. Having once worked with film director Stanley Kubrick on the planning of the film *Dr. Strangelove*, Schelling believes the film turned out to be an absurdist comedy for precisely this reason: No one involved in conceiving it could imagine it as a believable tragedy (Schelling, 1983, p. 124). That is why the inadvertence in the character Dr. Strangelove became a function of certifiable craziness among all the major characters in the film. Thus, while one may find *Dr. Strangelove* entertaining, most of us do not believe that the highest levels of nuclear policy making are anything like analogous to the crazy goings-on in the movie. Thus we might conclude, as Schelling apparently has, that initiating a major nuclear war in a crisis is too crazy to worry about.

We should notice, however, the psychology that underlies Schelling's difficulty in imagining inadvertent nuclear war as a possibility. Traditionally, many of the most influential students of nuclear risk have had the same difficulty for the same reason. The psychology (the cluster of assumptions, concepts, and data used to interpret aspects of mental life deemed relevant to nuclear risk) is not derived from common sense psychology or from academic scientific or clinical psychology but rather from economics.

This made perfectly good sense in the late 1950s when Schelling (1960), Wohlstetter (1959), and a number of other nuclear strategists made their seminal contributions. The great fear in that dawn of the missile age was a nuclear surprise attack—a "bolt out of the blue." The task of Schelling and the others was to spell out the conditions under which rational individuals, continually calculating the ratio of costs and benefits to be derived from initiating a nuclear war, might actually arrive at a decision to do so. This was the imagined mental event of interest *par excellence,* and the contributions of Schelling and his colleagues may indeed have played a significant role in deterring nuclear war. This was done in part by revolutionizing what Schelling called in 1960 "the retarded science of international strategy" (Schelling, 1960, Ch. 1).

This psychology has proven to be very durable. It remains, in fact, the ostensible (though, as Schelling has recently pointed out, quite inconsistently applied) psychological basis for our arms control policies and for strategies for deterring nuclear war (Schelling, 1985-1986). The concrete result of applying this economics-derived rational actor psychology to nuclear strategy and arms control has been to render demonstrably irrational the initiation of a nuclear war by either superpower against the other. This is what we have learned (see Nye, 1987; Tetlock, 1991).

We believe in the salience, ubiquity, and power of human rationality. Inadvertent nuclear war to that extent may seem almost like a contradiction in terms and avoiding it as easy as not stepping in front of a speeding bus. In fact, continued deterrence of nuclear war is fully deducible from the rational actor psychology. That aspect, together with the presence of mutually redundant conditions, makes the initiation of a nuclear war very probably tantamount to committing irrational suicide. Everyone will just "know better." They're not crazy.

During his first term in office President Reagan, by his bellicose anti-Sovietism, inadvertently brought an end to the virtual hegemony of the rational actor psychology of avoiding nuclear war. Of course, there had been movement in this direction for years within the strategic and nuclear policy communities. Most notably, Allison (1971) and Steinbruner (1974) a decade or so earlier had begun to amend the rational actor "model" in important ways. They noted how rationality is constrained by the standard operating procedures of large bureaucracies. Steinbruner was especially concerned about inadvertent nuclear war deriving from a process analogous to that which he believed produced World War I: "An unintended and unexpected consequence of a limited strategic maneuver" (Steinbruner, 1976, p. 119).

But with the great nuclear fear that swept through the Western democracies in the early 1980s, this trickle of derationalization and attention to nuclear inadvertence became a flood. As professional psychologists and psychiatrists began to enter the nuclear debate in large numbers and as their views found their way into the arguments of nonpsychologists, the discussion became increasingly strident and radically divergent from the rational actor psychology and the policies for which it seemed to provide justification (Blight, 1987, 1988; Hoffmann, 1986).

Unlike students of nuclear policy who came to an interest in this subject from economics, game theory, or political science, the new psychological radicals tended greatly to minimize the role of rationality in planning, deployment, strategy, and, most of all, in crises. As a result, inadvertent nuclear war, which had previously been regarded by most as distinctly improbable, came increasingly to be regarded as almost a sure thing. As the hypothetical irrational actor came in some quarters to replace the hypothetical rational actor, inadvertent nuclear war suddenly seemed far from mysterious and improbable. The wonder, according to irrational actor psychologists, was that one had not already occurred.

This new psychology of avoiding nuclear war has focused almost exclusively on inadvertence, on some hypothesized process by which the mechanisms of deterrence become inverted, and thus deterrence becomes the cause of, rather than the antidote to, nuclear war. There are four paths along which nuclear war is imagined to occur. The first, and least plausible, is by a *conspiracy of circumstance* (Sayle, 1985). Roughly speaking, this is the argument that "Murphy's Law" is the guiding principle in international affairs, that accidents are bound to happen, and that any system as complex as that which buttresses mutual nuclear deterrence simply must fail (Perrow, 1984).

Advocates of this view often use as analogies the Soviet shoot down of Korean Air Lines 007 in September 1983 or, less plausibly, the nuclear accidents at Three Mile Island and Chernobyl. The argument is simple and, to some, compelling: Systems break down; nuclear deterrence is a system; deterrence will break down. Thus, this particular approach may be thought of almost as antirational antipsychology, in which the relative rationality of actors is not nearly as controlling as the law of large numbers. Sooner or later, if the wheel of fortune is spun often enough, it will come up with any number, including those as improbable as that representing a major nuclear war. When this occurs, it will simply have been mainly a case of fallible matter triumphing over unwitting, unintending minds.

A second path through the irrational actor psychology of causes of nuclear war may be called a *conspiracy of crazies or craziness*. A substantial number of antinuclear radicals apparently believe that the leaders of the superpowers are, in fact, crazy and desirous of provoking a nuclear war. Caldicott (1984) put forth an elaborate argument to demonstrate that former President Reagan and former Defense Secretary Caspar Weinberger were paranoid psychotics while both were in office. And Caldicott is far from alone in holding this view. It is quite popular among psychiatrists and clinical psychologists (Kovel, 1984). Thus, according to advocates of this perspective, the most likely sort of nuclear war will occur inadvertently in regard to the wishes of the vast majority of humanity, but hardly contrary to the wishes of certain sick leaders, many of whom are believed to crave the chance to fight a nuclear war. In this way, a Strangelovian scenario will actually unfold, as life imitates art in the most catastrophic fashion imaginable.

A more sophisticated version of this general approach holds that *systemic crazi-*

ness, not deranged leaders, will bring about an inadvertent nuclear war. Surprising as it may seem to many nonpsychologists, this view has become virtually paradigmatic in the U.S. psychological establishment. Deutsch (1983), a distinguished social psychologist, calls the process leading to nuclear war the "malignant superpower relationship." The central idea is this: The villain is the arms race that, because it requires one to "demonize" the enemy, leads to a phenomenon called by psychoanalyst Erikson (1984) "pseudo-speciation"—the belief that a national adversary is composed of subhuman devils. Erikson sees powerful parallels between the pseudo-speciation of the Jews in Nazi Germany and what he takes to be the advanced stages of the same process occurring at present between the United States and the Soviet Union (Erikson, 1986).

When this process runs its course, according to believers in malignant, systemic superpower craziness, it is easy to imagine war breaking out between the superpowers and ultimately leading to nuclear war and planetary catastrophe. The slightest spark could provide the impetus. Both sides would have become caught up in a crazy process of threat and counterthreat whose natural terminus is a war to eliminate an enemy who is by then regarded as both subhuman and very dangerous. In this kind of scenario, a nuclear war occurs in spite of the relevant leaders having full knowledge of its consequences, because of the irresistible evolution of enmity that derives from the crazy social process in which both sides are trapped.

None of these conspiratorial theories of nuclear inadvertence are given much credence by strategists or even by political scientists. Indeed, many of the best-known advocates of these views are almost unknown outside the subset of psychologists who concern themselves with nuclear matters. Yet there is a fourth conspiratorial view that is beginning to find a wide audience among the more traditional students of nuclear risk. Advocates of this view believe an inadvertent nuclear war is likely to begin because of what may be called a conspiracy of *circumstantial craziness.* The psychology informing this approach is focused on situation-specific lapses in the rationality of decision makers under the stress of trying to manage deep and dangerous crises. These scholars worry about decision-making pathologies such as defensive avoidance, "groupthink," cognitive closure, selective attention, and many other ways in which the quality of decision making in foreign policy can be degraded under the stress of crises (Janis, 1982, 1989; Lebow, 1981, 1987).

In an important book, Lebow has illustrated the ways in which crisis-induced stress may have been causally connected to radical lapses in the powers of perception and reason in the leaders of Great Britain and Argentina in the 1983 Falklands/Malvinas War (Lebow, 1985). In the same book, Stein has put forth an analogous argument in regard to the 1967 and 1973 wars in the Middle East (Stein, 1985). Moreover, the Harvard Project on Avoiding Nuclear War has identified crises and crisis-induced degradation of rationality as important but imperfectly understood factors that may contribute to raised risk of nuclear war. The Harvard group has begun to suggest measures for combatting what they call "Model II Factors." These are breakdowns of rationality in crises or of the *belief* in mutually ubiquitous rationality, which may lead to the initiation of a nuclear war. A war, at the outbreak of the crisis, was undesired by all parties to the conflict (Allison, Carnesale, & Nye, 1985, 1986).

For all these students of nuclear risk, crises are the enemy because under conditions of high risk, high stakes, and apparent shortage of time to decide, leaders may do (and have often done) what in retrospect look like very crazy things. They may even, as Betts (1985) has argued, conclude that nuclear war is inevitable, or that it has already begun. On this basis leaders may launch a nuclear attack that, under ordinary (noncrisis) conditions, would have been inconceivable to them (see Jervis, 1988, 1989).

Unfortunately, these new psychologies emphasizing crisis craziness may prove to be epiphenomenal to policy. Too much of the literature of these new psychologies is so logically flawed, empirically dubious, or esoterically psychological that it may, in some of its more extreme forms, be doomed to policy irrelevance. For example, arguments that rely on the putative craziness of leaders are unlikely to have much impact, particularly on leaders themselves. Moreover, arguments that rely, as do those of the pure circumstantialists, on analogies between international affairs and the spinning of roulette wheels or the flipping of coins are just plain false. These analogies fail to take into account the possibility of human learning. The risk of nuclear war might gradually be reduced because the superpowers have made conscious decisions that make war between them less likely (Nye, 1986). Furthermore, analogies between the clinical consulting room and international politics, which are extraordinarily popular among psychiatrists and psychologists, are also highly dubious. The quasi-anarchic world of sovereign states is nearly the inverse of the artificially supportive environment the psychological clinician tries to establish.

Finally, we must not fail to notice the significance of stress in crises. As many studies have shown, albeit indirectly, the psychological effects of stress in nuclear and in nonnuclear contexts may be quite different. Whereas the top level decision making in recent cases like the Falklands/Malvinas War and the 1967 and 1973 Middle East Wars seems to exhibit the full range of psychological devolution, rationality seems to have prevailed during the Cuban Missile Crisis (the classic case of nuclear danger; Blight & Welch, 1989; Welch & Blight, 1987–1988).

In the cases of conventional conflict, leaders' judgments seemed, as the crises wore on, to become ever more detached from the constraints of objective reality, and they increasingly were unable to distinguish between their fears and the adversarys' intentions. In the missile crisis, President Kennedy moved rapidly from relatively simplistic judgments about the Soviets to a very intense effort to discover Khrushchev's motivations and constraints.

It may well be that, psychologically speaking, nuclear danger really is unique in certain respects.[1] If it is, then we ought to be very skeptical about attempts to generalize the psychological analyses of nonnuclear crises to hypothetical nuclear cases (Blight, 1990, Ch. 9).

For various reasons, the new psychologies of avoiding nuclear war have so far shown themselves to be policy irrelevant. This has been admitted by several leading exponents of the conspiratorial approaches, especially Lebow (1985). In a

---

[1] I focus here only on U.S. and Soviet leaders in the missile crisis. Kennedy, Khrushchev, and their inner circles of advisers appear to have shared the experience of nuclear danger, the fear of inadvertent nuclear war, and the urgent need to resolve the crisis quickly and with compromise. This does not appear to have applied to Fidel Castro and the Cuban leadership, however (see Allyn, Blight, & Welch, 1989–1990). Lacking access to the nuclear weapons on their soil, and feeling a U.S. attack was imminent, the Cubans seem to have made few distinctions between nuclear and conventional weapons. The gross discrepancy between this Cuban view, and that shared by U.S. and Soviet leaders, is roughly the difference between experiencing a nonnuclear and a nuclear crisis. This would appear to have increased nuclear risks, especially at the climax of the crisis, October 26–28, 1962 (see Allyn, Blight, & Welch, 1989–1990).

passage remarkable for its courage and honesty, he has pointed out the source of the difficulty facing all those seeking to replace the rational actor psychology of avoiding nuclear war with a psychological perspective that permits a serious investigation of the risk of inadvertent nuclear war. His statement takes this possibility seriously as an event that, under certain (specifiable) conditions, is *very* likely to happen. According to Lebow:

> *Deterrence, which, relatively speaking, is easy to implement, may nevertheless not be a very effective strategy of conflict management, because it does not address the most important sources of aggression. On the other hand, efforts to alleviate the kinds of insecurities that actually encourage or even compel leaders to pursue aggressive foreign policies do not seem very likely to succeed. (Lebow, 1985, p. 192)*

This is Lebow's paradox: The rational actor psychology underlying classical deterrence theory is *psychologically* bankrupt. It has no place in its lexicon for the psychological implications of the fear engendered by attempts at deterrence. An irrational actor psychology focused on the degradation of rational decision making in crises is *pragmatically* bankrupt. Policy makers do not like its message, nor do they understand it, and hence they have no idea how to implement policies in accord with it. Lebow is quite direct about why the irrational actor psychologies, even those emphasizing stress and crises, are likely to remain pretty much academic exercises. Neither he nor anyone else so far has imagined a plausible means for intervening directly into the lives of leaders to reduce the intensity of the psychological needs that seem to motivate many failures of nonnuclear deterrence. These needs, by analogy, are believed to be primary psychological culprits in some hypothetical failure of nuclear deterrence. Leaders, even in crises, are unlikely to believe that they are becoming progressively less rational, let alone to believe that psychological counseling for *themselves* is the key to resolving crises successfully. Thus Lebow (1985) is correct, I believe, to ask: What is to be the practical point of the new irrational actor psychologies of avoiding nuclear war? How will the new understandings they generate eventually help to reduce the risk of inadvertent nuclear war?

Having briefly surveyed the rational/irrational actor psychologies of avoiding nuclear war, let us observe in conclusion why neither can provide any assistance to understanding how to prevent *inadvertent* nuclear war from arising out of a crisis. We have already seen that Schelling, the fountainhead of the rational actor psychology, believes that rational actors will survive through and beyond a nuclear crisis. He acknowledges the problems that might arise from "nervousness," but he finds the issue much less interesting than do the proponents of irrational actor psychology. This accounts for Schelling's interesting account of the Cuban Missile Crisis in *Arms and influence* (Schelling, 1966). Instead of trying to *describe* the sequence of psychological events possibly leading to a decision to launch, Schelling strategically explained why no such decision was ever reached (Schelling, 1966, p. 166). The reason he could not imagine it was that the observable data bearing most heavily on the outcome (the strategic nuclear balance), combined with the theory of rational actors, fully determined the (rational) decisions of leaders not to go to nuclear war. While we can dispute Schelling's interpretation, we must admit that it is consistent with the outcome of the Cuban Missile Crisis. Schelling's work shows that a "crisis" is only a linguistic convention with which he has reluctantly agreed to go along.

Certainly, people may become nervous during these particularly intense competitions in risk-taking, as Schelling first called them a generation ago and as they have generally been understood ever since. We never get the impression, however, that competitions of this sort are somehow or other qualitatively different sorts of enterprises. In fact, this was the point of Schelling & Halperin's collaborative book, *Strategy and arms control:* The same principles apply, whether in bargains in easy chairs in Geneva or deep in a so-called crisis (Schelling & Halperin, 1961).

The irrational actor psychologists say they reject all this. They believe that crises are special, qualitatively more dangerous episodes in the conduct of international relations. Why? Because risk of nuclear war will rise dramatically in a nuclear crisis. Yet, because they buy into a lot more of Schelling's assumptions than they know or admit, irrational actor psychologists are forced into an awkward situation that Schelling and other rational actor traditionalists have avoided. Schelling only had to observe the outcome of the Cuban Missile Crisis and conclude that people acted rationally. Khrushchev noted his own inferiority, backed down, and thus ended the crisis. However, the irrational actor psychologists must try to offer convincing *explanations*—general, vague, and usually drawn from data unrelated to the missile crisis—as to why in certain circumstances we might do what is inherently unimaginable. These psychologists must make do with vague truisms like "Murphy's Law" will prevail, or stress can often lead to clouded judgment, which, while perhaps true, tell us little about any particular crisis. Alternatively, they can imagine in great detail what might have happened, say, in the Cuban Missile Crisis that would have pushed the crisis into war (see Neustadt & Allison, 1971). It is impossible to attach meaningful probabilities to such possibilities, which leaves the arguments quite unconvincing.

Notice what happens as purveyors of the irrational actor psychology, deeply worried about the risk-inducing effects of nuclear crises, try unsuccessfully to fit this square irrational actor psychological peg into the round hole of a psychological approach that ubiquitously assumes rational action. The strategic balance of nuclear forces was *rationally* developed to deal with a totally different problem, that of a calculated surprise attack. For Schelling, the psychological variables remain constant and the actors remain rational (in theory); no craziness here. The central determining factors influencing a decision to launch a nuclear war, with or without a crisis, reside in the constituents of the strategic balance of nuclear forces. The values of these factors are empirically derivable within estimatable ranges of error.

For irrational actor psychologists worried about the decisive, catastrophic effects of a nuclear crisis, constants and variables are reversed. The strategic balance of forces will not change at all merely because of the onset of a crisis, so balance is taken as given and constant. If the risk of war is to rise dramatically, *psychological* variables must be altered: something must change fundamentally in the minds and hearts of leaders charged with nuclear responsibilities. The ultimate significant question is, of course, *what* changes? But the prior question, the one that presents a real problem, is: Where do we look for data, for evidence, concerning the nature of this supposed psychological revolution that is a logical prerequisite to a decision to launch a nuclear war? What is to be the analog to Schelling's empirically derivable description of *his* relevant variability, the state of the strategic balance? What is to be the psychological analog of the ground intelligence and satellite reconnaissance that would inform Schelling's rationally acting leaders, crisis or no?

The answer is that there is no such analog. Borrowing from every sort of psychological literature imaginable, arguments are put forward emphasizing the deleterious effects of stress, denial, and so forth. It might happen, you cannot say it cannot happen. This is the only conclusion one can justifiably be expected to draw from this literature. They are in fact hung up on the "$N = 0$" problem, the lack of an actual, two-sided nuclear crisis that exploded into war. The missile crisis, the closest call, only serves to reinforce Schelling's point that it would be very difficult, "crisis" or no, to have a nuclear war.

Those who emphasize the connection between crisis, fear, irrationality, and risk of nuclear war can say little more about the missile crisis other than that we were lucky. We may or may not have *been* lucky, but the irrational actor psychologists cannot provide the necessary proof to people who disbelieve them: an empirically rich description of the perverse psychological revolution required in a nuclear crisis to produce a nuclear war.[2]

Several things seem obvious. First, the rational actor psychology has done its job. Surprise attack, having been rendered totally irrational, is unlikely. Second, for those whose intuitions or experience tell them that nuclear risk rises in a crisis, the rational actor psychology has little or nothing to say. It is crisis irrelevant, in the sense that it has no place for a state called "crisis" that yields a qualitatively different and more dangerous psychological evolution. Third, the irrational actor psychology is crisis obsessed but is still crisis irrelevant. Its advocates would be right to conclude that something like a new discipline—an empirical psychology of nuclear crises—is now required to augment the venerable tradition of strategy and arms control (Blight, 1990, Ch. 5, 6).

The irrational actor psychologists have, for various reasons, chosen to emphasize imported theory over indigenous data. They have failed to appreciate that a crisis-relevant, and therefore potentially policy-relevant, psychology of avoiding nuclear war must begin with Schelling's question: Why have we *not* had a nuclear war explode from a crisis? Rather, they have, in effect, asked: How *would* we explain the nuclear war we have *not* yet had? In regard to the missile crisis, the irrational actor psychologists must ask: Why was the missile crisis resolved peacefully?

The Cuban Missile Crisis of 1962 indeed seems to have been fraught with nuclear danger. Leaders in the White House and the Kremlin felt it and remember it vividly. The state of mind experienced by leaders in October 1962 *was* different from any experienced by them before or since. Events seemed to be spinning out of control, as inadvertent nuclear war began to seem only days or hours away. It really could have "blown." That was the deeply disturbing revelation. But this drove the leaders to caution and to a heightened sense of responsibility, not to craziness. They found the way out. So must all who try to understand what happens to nuclear deterrence in crises. They must move beyond appeals to rationalist

[2]We can now be reasonably certain that, by the final weekend of the crisis, Kennedy was willing to pay a very high political price to avoid escalating the crisis any further (see Blight & Welch, 1989; Blight, 1990). He seems, for example, to have been willing to enter into a public trade of missiles—Soviet missiles in Cuba for North Atlantic Treaty Organization (NATO) missiles in Turkey—even though many of his advisers believed that such a move might lead to the destruction of NATO.

complacency and irrationalist, quite hypothetical, craziness. The outcome of the Cuban Missile Crisis, our closest call, had nothing to do with either complacency or craziness; neither should the psychology with which we try to understand it. If we believe the veterans of the missile crisis when they say that nuclear crises really are different, and dangerous, then we must turn our descriptive focus inward to the evolution of psychological life during that crisis. We must try to understand what it was like when, psychologically, the crystal ball seemed to be shattering, and how that is connected to the fact that the world did not (Blight, 1990).

REFERENCES

Allison, G. T. (1971). *Essence of decision: Explaining the Cuban Missile Crisis.* Boston: Little, Brown.

Allison, G. T., Carnesale, A., & Nye, J. S. (Eds.). (1985). *Hawks, doves, and owls: An agenda for avoiding nuclear war.* New York: Norton.

Allison, G. T., Carnesale, A., & Nye, J. S. (1986). The owl's agenda for avoiding nuclear war. *The Washington Quarterly, 9*(3), 45–58.

Allyn, B. J., Blight, J. G., & Welch, D. A. (1989–1990). Essence of revision: Moscow, Havana, and the Cuban Missile Crisis. *International Security, 14*(3), 136–172.

Betts, R. K. (1985). Surprise attack and preemption. In G. T. Allison, A. Carnesale, & J. S. Nye (Eds.), *Hawks, doves, and owls: An agenda for avoiding nuclear war* (pp. 54–79). New York: Norton.

Blight, J. G. (1987). Toward a policy-relevant psychology of avoiding nuclear war: Lessons for psychologists from the Cuban Missile Crisis. *American Psychologist, 42,* 12–29.

Blight, J. G. (1988). Can psychology help reduce the risk of nuclear war?: Reflections of a "little drummer boy" of nuclear psychology. *Journal of Humanistic Psychology, 28*(2), 7–58.

Blight, J. G. (1990). *The shattered crystal ball: Fear and learning in the Cuban Missile Crisis.* Savage, MD: Rowman & Littlefield.

Blight, J. G., & Welch, D. A. (1989). *On the brink: Americans and Soviets reexamine the Cuban Missile Crisis.* New York: Farrar, Straus & Giroux/Hill & Wang.

Caldicott, H. (1984). *Missile envy.* New York: Moscow.

Carnesale, A., Doty, P., Hoffmann, S., Huntington, S. P., Nye, J. S., & Sagan, S. D. (1983). *Living with nuclear weapons.* New York: Bantam.

Deutsch, M. (1983). The prevention of World War III: A psychological perspective. *Political Psychology, 4*(1), 3–31.

Erikson, E. H. (1984). Reflections on ethos and war. *Yale Review,* pp. 481–486.

Erikson, E. H. (1986, March). Remarks at a symposium on the psychology of U.S.-Soviet relations, Big Sur, CA.

Fukuyama, F. (1989). The end of history? *The National Interest, 16,* 3–18.

Hoffmann, S. (1986). On the political psychology of war and peace: A critique and an agenda. *Political Psychology, 7*(1), 1–22.

Janis, I. L. (1982). *Groupthink* (2nd ed.). Boston: Houghton-Mifflin.

Janis, I. L. (1989). *Crucial decisions: Leadership in policymaking and crisis management.* New York: Free Press.

Jervis, R. (1988). War and misperception. *Journal of Interdisciplinary History, 18,* 675–700.

Jervis, R. (1989). *The meaning of the nuclear revolution: Statecraft and the prospect of Armageddon.* Ithaca, NY: Cornell University Press.

Kovel, J. (1984). *Against the state of nuclear terror.* Boston: South End Press.

Lebow, R. N. (1981). *Between peace and war: The nature of international crisis.* Baltimore, MD: Johns Hopkins University Press.

Lebow, R. N. (1985). Conclusions. In R. Jervis, R. L. Lebow, & J. G. Stein (Eds.), *Psychology and deterrence* (pp. 203–232). Baltimore, MD: Johns Hopkins University Press.

Lebow, R. N. (1987). *Nuclear crisis management: A dangerous illusion.* Ithaca, NY: Cornell University Press.

McNamara, R. S. (1986). *Blundering into disaster: Surviving the first century of the nuclear age.* New York: Pantheon.

McNamara, R. S. (1989). *Out of the cold: New thinking for American foreign and defense policy in the 21st century.* New York: Simon & Schuster.

Mueller, J. (1989). *Retreat from doomsday: The obsolescence of major war.* New York: Basic Books.

Neustadt, R. E., & Allison, G. T. (1971). Afterword. In R. F. Kennedy, *Thirteen days: A memoir of the Cuban Missile Crisis* (pp. 109–150). New York: Norton.

Perrow, C. (1984). *Normal accidents.* New York: Basic Books.

Nye, J. S. (1986). *Nuclear ethics.* New York: Free Press.

Nye, J. S. (1987). Nuclear learning and U.S.-Soviet security regimes. *International Organization, 41,* 371–402.

Sayle, M. (1985). KE 007: A conspiracy of circumstance. *New York Review of Books, 32*(7), 44–54.

Schelling, T. C. (1960). *The strategy of conflict.* Cambridge, MA: Harvard University Press.

Schelling, T. C. (1966). *Arms and influence.* New Haven, CT: Yale University Press.

Schelling, T. C. (1983). Arrangements for reciprocal reassurance. In H. Roderick & U. Magnusson (Eds.), *Avoiding inadvertent nuclear war: Crisis management* (pp. 123–129). Austin, TX: LBJ School of Public Affairs.

Schelling, T. C. (1985–1986). What went wrong with arms control? *Foreign Affairs, 64,* 219–233.

Schelling, T. C., & Halperin, M. H. (1961). *Strategy and arms control.* New York: Twentieth Century Fund.

Stein, J. G. (1985). Calculation, miscalculation, and conventional deterrence, I: The view from Cairo; and II: The view from Jerusalem. In R. Jervis, R. L. Lebow, & J. G. Stein (Eds.), *Psychology and deterrence* (pp. 34–88). Baltimore, MD: Johns Hopkins University Press.

Steinbruner, J. D. (1974). *The cybernetic theory of decision.* Princeton, NJ: Princeton University Press.

Steinbruner, J. D. (1976). Beyond rational deterrence: The struggle for new conceptions. In K. Knorr (Ed.), *Power, strategy, and security* (pp. 103–125). Princeton, NJ: Princeton University Press.

Tetlock, P. E. (1991). Learning in U.S. and Soviet foreign policy: In search of an elusive concept. In G. Breslauer & P. E. Tetlock (Eds.), *Learning in U.S. and Soviet foreign policy.* Boulder, CO: Westview.

Welch, D. A., & Blight, J. G. (1987–1988). The eleventh hour of the Cuban Missile Crisis. *International Security, 12*(3), 5–29.

Wohlstetter, A. (1959). The delicate balance of terror. *Foreign Affairs, 37,* 211–234.

6

Fear of Nuclear War: "When I Grow Up, I Want To Be an Old Woman"

Lake McClenney

On mentioning the topic of this chapter to colleagues, I met with exclamations of surprise; after all, they intimated, now that detente with the Soviet Union is in the offing, who is afraid of nuclear war anymore? Many people feel reassured by recent developments in the Soviet Union and in Eastern Europe. Yet, quite apart from the possibility that current events in these countries could easily make for greater instability rather than less, there is the fact that no decrease in nuclear weaponry has actually taken place, nor has the likelihood diminished that other nations, or terrorist groups, could use nuclear weapons. In the long run, the fact that more than one billion people are starving in the world obviously will contribute to political instability. In addition, fear of nuclear war is highly correlated with fears of other technological hazards (Pilisuk & Acredolo, 1988), and these, unfortunately, seem as unlikely to disappear of their own accord as the radioactive waste products from nuclear weapons production (Boly, 1990).

For these reasons, despite the advice of my colleagues, I have reviewed recent psychological literature relevant to the topic "fear of nuclear war." In doing so, I have attempted to answer the following questions: Are people afraid of nuclear war? To what extent is this fear appropriate (that is, are defensive processes operating)? Is this fear, or the defense against it, harmful to mental health? I have divided the review into a consideration of research on attitudes of the general public, a section on attitudes of policy makers, and a summary section assessing the adequacy of the "psychotherapy" model of nuclear war prevention.

FEAR OF NUCLEAR WAR IN THE GENERAL PUBLIC

Overt Indices

Early studies using an interview format with children and adolescents (Escalona, 1965; Schwebel, 1965) suggested that fears of nuclear war were widespread. More recently, Goldenring and Doctor (1986) questioned more than 900 adolescents in suburban areas of California, using both an open-ended format ("list three things

Shocked, M. (1988). *When I Grow Up*. New York: Polygram Records, © 1988 by Michelle Shocked.

you worry most about") and Likert ratings of 20 possible worries, including nuclear war. Of the sample, 7% spontaneously listed nuclear war as a worry; however, when nuclear war was offered as a choice, nearly 32% rated themselves worried about nuclear war (compared to 53% for "parents dying" and 37% for "getting bad grades"). Younger children reported more worry than did older ones; there were no differences related to socioeconomic status or ethnicity. Interestingly, teenagers' worries about nuclear war covaried with concerns about the environment and getting cancer, rather than with fears about parents dying or personal injury or death. Similar studies in many other countries (Chivian et al., 1985; Holmborg & Bergstrom, 1985; Solanteus, Goldberg, Levinson, Ross, & LaCombe, 1985; Sommers, Goldberg, Levinson, Ross, & LaCombe, 1985) indicate somewhat greater worry about nuclear war, particularly in Sweden, Finland, and the Soviet Union. In the United States, fears about nuclear war also apparently increased rather dramatically between 1976 and 1982 and have since remained level—about 30% worry often about nuclear war (Diamond & Bachman, 1986). In general, these studies indicate that approximately one-third of children and adolescents do fear nuclear war when they think about it, that is, when it is brought to their attention in the form of a direct question. Fear may be greater in younger children (Chivian et al., 1985; Tizard, 1984), girls rather than boys (Goldenring & Doctor, 1986; Solanteus et al., 1985), and in northern Europe as compared to the United States (Chivian et al., 1985; Holmborg & Bergstrom, 1985; Solanteus et al., 1985).

Continuing the trend for age, adults appear less fearful about nuclear war than adolescents. Kramer, Kalick, and Milburn (1983) found that fear of nuclear war increased between 1945 and 1982, yet 71% of respondents said they never worried about the prospect. Despite Coles' (1984) claim that fear of nuclear war is a luxury of the elite, there is evidence to the contrary (Diamond & Bachman, 1986). Several researchers (Fiske, 1986; Newcomb, 1986) have found that women report more fear than men. In an elegant design using experimentation in national samples asking about "the most important problem facing the nation today," Schuman, Ludwig, and Krasnick (1986) concluded that an open versus closed format (low salience) of nuclear war explanation did not account for lack of concern about nuclear war in the general population. At least for adults, lack of fear is not merely due to the fact that nuclear war does not come to mind as an issue.

Cognitive Distortion and Defenses Against Fear

Lifton (1979) has suggested that the enormity of nuclear threat, like the actual nuclear catastrophe experienced by survivors of Hiroshima and Nagasaki, leads to "psychic numbing," an umbrella term that he uses to summarize various classical defense mechanisms, including "repression, suppression, isolation, denial, undoing, and reaction formation and projection"(p. 103). In a similar vein, Mack (1984) discusses resistances on both individual and collective levels to "knowing the truth about nuclear weapons and the arms race" (p. 2), citing evidence that the earth would be unlivable if nuclear war were to take place. Lifton and Mack each believe that lack of fear is pathological, both because it brings humans closer to nuclear annihilation as a species and because it has a direct negative effect on mental health. This explanation of lack of an appropriate level of fear is appealing to those who are frustrated in attempts to change nuclear policy, much as the concept of resistance is appealing to psychotherapists working with clients who frustrate their efforts to help. However, the constructs "psychic numbing" and "collective resistance," while perhaps suitable as ideological labels, are too poorly defined to serve as the basis for ongoing scientific dialog.

The notion of unconscious defenses has been a major source of confusion and controversy in psychology. For the purpose of this review, I adopt Bowers' (1984) eclectic definition: "Determinants of thought and action that are not noticed or appreciated as such constitute unconscious influences" (p. 22), which has the advantage of being consistent both with psychoanalytic concepts and with more contemporary notions (Nisbett & Ross, 1980).

Adopting this definition, the totality of evidence supports the operation of some unconscious defensive processes with respect to fear of nuclear war. Probably the best extant evidence is Schwebel's (1965) work showing that adolescents' fears of nuclear war actually decreased during the Cuban Missile Crisis when the danger of war was clearly very high. The increase in reported worry about nuclear war with lesser age, noted previously, also suggests that some sort of numbing may take place over time, or at least that people learn ways to avoid being afraid of nuclear war. The age data indicate that it is not lack of awareness of threat that minimizes adult fear (it is unlikely that children would have more information than adults), and there is also evidence that older children are better informed than younger children (Tizard, 1984). However, it is possible that adults, especially men, may not report fear from some sense that it is inappropriate to admit to such feelings (Fiske, 1986). Slemrod (1986) used a time series design to demonstrate a relationship between likelihood of nuclear war and decreases in private savings in the United States. This study implies the existence of unconscious threat that is kept out of awareness through hedonistic pursuits. Schuman et al. (1986) found that adults in national surveys had three explanations for not mentioning nuclear war as a problem: nuclear war is not an immediate problem, it is impossible, or there is nothing to be done about it. The first two explanations, the authors suggest, represent denial; that is, the majority of adults surveyed did not worry about nuclear war because they were engaged in unconscious defensive processes.

Factual misinformation regarding the Soviet Union abounds. For example, 28% of respondents in a *New York Times* survey believed that the Soviet Union fought against the United States in World War II (Silverstein, 1989), and 24% of a student sample thought that the Soviet Union had first invented the bomb (De Rivera, 1984). Although this level of ignorance does suggest that people organize information about nuclear policy schematically along simplistic lines such as "Four legs good, two legs bad" (Orwell, 1954), it does not necessarily imply the existence of defensive processes. However, other studies of enemy images (Silverstein, 1989) provide evidence that Americans process information about the Soviet Union in a biased manner. For example, several studies have demonstrated that U.S. students evaluate Soviet actions more negatively than they evaluate the same actions by the United States (Oskamp, 1965, 1968), and attributional biases regarding Soviet actions have been found repeatedly (Hirschberg, 1988; Sande, Goethals, Ferrari, & Worth, 1989). However, the motivational basis of these distortions has not been elucidated.

Evidence relating hostility toward the Soviet Union to fear about nuclear issues is contradictory. Feshbach and White (1986) found that nonsupporters of a nuclear moratorium showed more hostility toward the Soviet Union, more willingness to defer to experts, and more willingness to characterize freeze supporters as stupid and unpatriotic. In a thoughtful exploration of discrepancies in their longitudinal survey data from high school seniors, Diamond and Bachman (1986) differentiate *concern* about the risk of nuclear war and *despair* over its likelihood. Concern has increased steadily since 1975; despair has remained relatively stable. Bellicosity (e.g., beliefs about the United States' need for more military power relative to the Soviet Union) was not related to either construct.

A colleague and I (McClenney & Neiss, 1989) found that men were less likely to seek information about nuclear arms control after exposure to a fear-arousing communication than after an efficacy-enhancing or informational message, whereas women were more likely to seek information in response to fear arousal than in response to other types of communications. *Denial*, operationalized as lack of worry about nuclear war (thus, the opposite of Diamond & Bachman's *concern* construct) also predicted failure to engage in information-seeking about arms control. Neiss and I suggested the possibility that men engage in defensive "machismo" (Mosher & Sirkin, 1984) in response to a fear-arousing message. These results cannot be explained by a reporting bias because study participants were not required to report fear, nor is it likely that lack of awareness could account for differences. All participants were exposed to the same information regarding nuclear war. It is thus possible that bellicosity is related to fear of nuclear war in (some) men, but not in women.

Fear of Nuclear War and Mental Health

Is it pathological to respond to the threat of nuclear war with defensive processes? This is the most controversial question in the literature. The implications of using words such as "resistance" or "numbing" are that lack of worry about nuclear war should be associated with poor mental health. However, it is sometimes also asserted that worrying produces pathology. Members of the American Psychological Association Task Force on Nuclear Issues have argued that children's and adolescents' fears about nuclear war have a negative impact on their development (Escalona, 1982; Schwebel, 1982). I am not sure that we can have it both ways: For our mental health, should we worry or not?

Newcomb (1986) reported that the term *nuclear anxiety* is associated with "less purpose in life, less life satisfaction, more powerlessness, more depression, and more drug use" (p. 906). Similarly, Mayton (1985) found that students showing spontaneous concern about the probability of nuclear war scored lower on measures of self-esteem, sense of well-being, and perceived control. It should be noted that in neither study is there an indication that negative mental health effects are clinically significant. Also, general anxiety level was not used as a covariate; the evidence is mixed regarding the relationship between trait anxiety and anxiety about nuclear war (Goldenring & Doctor, 1986; Hamilton, Chavez, & Keilin, 1986). In a recent study, however, Dyal and Morris (1987) found a significant decrement in subjective well-being as a function of nuclear anxiety, beyond that contributed by trait anxiety and stressful life events.

The evidence is thus fairly consistent, if sparse, in demonstrating a connection between nuclear anxiety and general affective distress and dissatisfaction with life. Nevertheless, this may only indicate a general willingness to complain. Furthermore, "nuclear concern" and "fear of the future" were correlated in Newcomb's sample, whereas Diamond and Bachman (1986) found "nuclear concern" and "nuclear despair" to be orthogonal, and only "despair" was related to mental health problems such as low self-esteem, dissatisfaction with life, school absenteeism, lack of perceived control, and loneliness. Examination of items suggests that Diamond and Bachman's "despair" measure probably indicates extremely negative expectations about the future of the human race, whereas their "concern" item measures a behavior, frequency of worry. Newcomb's "nuclear anxiety" measure combines expectations (will survive a nuclear war), other beliefs (nuclear power and weapons linked), and emotions (depressed about nuclear war; 1986, p. 912). It will be important for purposes of validation to predict behavioral measures of adjustment from nuclear anxiety. For example, I assume Hamilton et al.'s (1986) "romanticists" and "disarmists" differ in level of nuclear anxiety; would romanticists also perform better in school, at work, and in interpersonal relationships? This seems unlikely. One of the possible effects of continual defense about fear of annihilation, which has not been investigated, is a loss of the ability to experience real joy. This may be worse than the anxiety engendered by awareness of threat.

Antinuclear activism itself may increase subjective well-being (Dyal & Morris, 1987; Mack, 1984). However, several studies (Hamilton et al., 1986; McGraw & Tyler, 1986; McKenzie & Dyal, 1985) report greater worry, fear, or anxiety among antinuclear activists. Thus, it is not clear that activism is a cure for anxiety, nor that anxiety necessarily motivates activism. Although many reviewers have asserted a role for perceived control or efficacy in generating activism (Gilbert, 1988), a sense of personal control is correlated with good mental health as well (Strickland, 1989). Watanabe and Milburn (1986) found that the best predictor of nuclear-relevant activism was previous political activity and that perceived efficacy was of minimal significance.

Similarly, Tyler and McGraw (1983) found that a sense of moral responsibility was a stronger predictor of antinuclear activism than personal control. McClenney and Neiss (1989) found that worry about nuclear war, a sense of control over political events, and a sense of responsibility for social changes were all mediated by intentions to act in their effects on activism. Gilbert (1988) suggested that certainty regarding the correctness as well as the impact of actions is required to justify activism. Activists may not have to believe that what they are doing will work; they may only have to believe that they are doing the right thing.

Reviewing this literature has led me to the following tentative conclusions: The general public could be characterized as only slightly afraid of nuclear war. Covert indices suggest that those who do not report fear may be using various cognitive distortions and defenses/coping strategies to avoid experiencing fear. Support is minimal for the contention that either the fear itself, or these forms of coping, are detrimental to mental health. This should come as no surprise; in other areas of psychology, defensiveness does not predict poor mental health (Bower, 1990), although it may be correlated with poor physical heath (Buck, 1984). Of course, so might it be in the case of nuclear policy, given the risk of nuclear annihilation as well as the long-term risks of exposure to radioactive waste. Poor physical health is also predicted, however, by depression and anxiety (Friedman & Booth-Kewley, 1987; Peterson, Seligman, & Vaillant, 1988).

Apart from being extremely difficult to support empirically, labeling those who are not antinuclear activists as pathologically unfeeling seems counterproductive if the goal is to change their behavior. A number of researchers have provided concrete suggestions about how that might be accomplished (Feshbach & White, 1986; Gilbert, 1988; McClenney & Neiss, 1989).

DECISION MAKERS

Lifton (1979), analyzing the statements of policy makers, has defined the condition "nuclearism: the passionate embrace of nuclear weapons as a solution to death anxiety and a way of restoring a lost sense of immortality" (p. 369). Mack (1981) has stated that the madness of nuclear proliferation is not merely an intrapsychic phenomenon, but a systemic problem. Similarly, Janis (1986) identified a pathological group process, "groupthink," in which members of a decision-making group support one another's cognitive defenses in the interests of maintaining shared illusions about reality. Frank (1987) hypothesizes that decision makers' drive for power is the major cause of the nuclear arms race.

Blight (1987) attacks these "depth psychologists" for explaining nuclear policy in terms of psychopathology, instead preferring to characterize international policy makers as a bunch of thugs, or (more hopefully) as two wrestling teams (p. 25); in both characterizations, participants are motivated by innate aggression. Certainly, the exchange between Blight and those whose naiveté he deplores, like international politics, contains elements of the games of boys, and perhaps the all-male character in both arenas has something to do with this. However, beneath the simplistic analogies, there are genuine differences between the two approaches to avoiding nuclear war, both of which must be honored.

Although Blight decries the "psychotherapy" model of avoiding nuclear war, he, in fact, proposes something very like therapy as an approach to changing policy: "In those situations leading potentially to, and through nuclear crises, we need to begin by getting as close as possible to the experiential facts regarding what is feared by decision makers in nuclear crises and what it is like to have such concerns in those situations" (1987, p. 27). Although psychologists do label their clients in terms of psychopathology, if they actually hope to establish a "context in which healing can occur" (Mack, as quoted by Blight, 1987, p. 24), they begin, regardless of therapeutic orientation, with the experience of the client. On the other hand, Blight himself might be accused of being naive by those who truly view international politics as similar to gang warfare. Neither empathy nor labeling appears to change the behavior of thugs; psychopathy seems remarkably resistant to treatment.

As in the case of theory and research on the responses of the general public to the threat of nuclear war, there seem to be two implicit, opposing perspectives in the literature on decision makers' responses to threat. One approach pathologizes this response, analyzes it in terms of unconscious defenses, and appears to believe in the power of interpretation as a therapeutic intervention. The other approach describes the response, analyzes it in social cognitive terms, and declines to treat the phenomenon.

ADEQUACY OF THE PSYCHOTHERAPY MODEL

If we are going to do therapy, let us do it well. Even if nuclear war is unique among social problems, preventing it may still have something in common with preventing AIDS, teenage pregnancy, or cardiovascular disease. Whether, in a particular case, the risk is minimal or the denial is pathological does not really matter. Behavior changes when the phenomenological world of the individual is understood, information relevant to this world is made salient, concrete alternatives to present behaviors are made available, and appropriate reinforcement, especially the support of significant others, is provided (Des Jarlais & Friedman, 1988). Whether we are trying to change the behavior of an apathetic public, decision makers, gang members, or two wrestling teams, these ingredients of successful prevention strategies should be well kept in mind.

Second, if the research on psychotherapy can teach us anything, it is that individual differences must be considered (American Psychiatric Association Commission on Psychotherapies, 1982). There is no reason to believe that changing behavior to prevent nuclear war is any different. No one treatment is appropriate for everyone. Some people are afraid, some are well-defended, some are pathologically anxious or defensive. In order to effect a change in nuclear policy, we will need all the techniques at our disposal.

In the case of decision makers, the psychotherapy model may break down, in that treating them could be viewed as somewhat akin to attempting psychotherapy with a gang of muggers. Although at times this degree of cynicism may seem justified, decision makers must also be viewed as a diverse group of human beings (Kull, 1988). Furthermore, even the behavior of muggers can be changed, if only, in the absence of more legitimate channels, by neighborhood vigilante committees.

Finally, I think it is important to acknowledge that in psychotherapy the client has decided to change and has sought help in doing so. This is not the case either for the general public or for decision makers in psychologists' attempts at change. Yet survey data consistently indicates that well over two-thirds of adults advocate a bilateral moratorium on nuclear testing (Gallup Poll, 1986; Kramer, Kalick, & Milburn, 1983). Although we cannot accurately assess the actual degree of threat of nuclear war, most reasonable people would agree that there is some threat and that a prevention model would apply. In the prevention of AIDS, the client is the general public or specific at-risk populations, who also do not give express permission for treatment; treatment is justified because of the potential danger and the cost to society of risk-denial and behaviors that increase risk. Perhaps a better model for promoting activism would be to focus on health enhancement rather than risk prevention. Like influencing people to get regular exercise, influencing them to flex their own political muscles on a regular basis requires that they learn to enjoy it for its own sake.

My father, whose work in nuclear chemistry helped make the first atomic bomb possible (Thompson, 1949; Thompson & Seaborg, 1956), believed deeply in the value of scientific truth. Although by writing this review I acknowledge its value as well, perhaps due to his example, I have less faith in the relationship between scientific evidence and truth. Whereas we know how to prevent AIDS, we have no certain knowledge about preventing nuclear war. Should this constrain action? Clinicians frequently make decisions about appropriate interventions on the basis of minimal evidence; good ones make ongoing evaluations of the effects of these interventions, changing ineffective ones rather than labeling the client as resistant. Psychologists doing psychotherapy, or promoting activism, are in a position similar to that of parents attempting to raise children to be happy adults in an uncertain future. We can only acknowledge the influence of our values on our decisions, recognizing as well that sitting on the fence also has consequences. There is no way to avoid a decision regarding our role in the prevention of nuclear war.

REFERENCES

American Psychiatric Association, Commission on Psychotherapies. (1982). *Psychotherapy research: Methodological and efficacy issues.* Washington, DC: Author.
Blight, J. G. (1987). Toward a policy-relevant psychology of avoiding nuclear war: Lessons for psychologists from the Cuban Missile Crisis. *American Psychologist, 42,* 12-29.
Boly, W. (1990). Downwind from the cold war. *In Health, 4*(4), 58-69.
Bower, B. (1990). Defensiveness reaps psychiatric benefits. *Science News, 137,* 309.
Bowers, K. S. (1984). On being unconsciously influenced and informed. In K. S. Bowers, & D. Meichenbaum (Eds.), *The unconscious reconsidered* (pp. 227-272). New York: Wiley.
Buck, R. (1984). *The communication of emotion.* New York: Guilford Press.
Chivian, E., Mack, J. E., Waletsky, J. P., Lazaroff, C., Doctor, R., & Goldenring, J. M. (1985). *American Journal of Orthopsychiatry, 55,* 484-512.
Coles, R. (1984, November 11). Freezniks are elitists. *Washington Post,* p. D4.
De Rivera, J. (1984). Facing nuclear weapons. *American Behavioral Scientist, 27,* 739-756.
Des Jarlais, D. C., & Friedman, H. S. (1988). The psychology of preventing AIDS among intravenous drug users: A social learning conceptualization. *American Psychologist, 43,* 865-870.
Diamond, G., & Bachman, J. (1986). High-school seniors and the nuclear threat, 1975-1984: Political and mental health implications of concern and despair. *International Journal of Mental Health, 15,* 210-235.
Dyal, J. A., & Morris, P. (1987, June). *Nuclear anxiety and issue-relevant behavior: Associations with mental health.* Paper presented at the Conference of the Canadian Peace Research and Education Association, Hamilton, Ontario.
Escalona, S. (1965). Children and the threat of nuclear war. In M. Schwebel (Ed.), *Behavioral science and human survival* (pp. 201-289). Palo Alto: Science and Behavioral Books.
Escalona, S. (1982). Growing up with the threat of nuclear war: Some indirect effects on personality development. *American Journal of Orthopsychiatry, 52,* 600-607.
Feshbach, S., & White, M. J. (1986). Individual differences in attitudes towards nuclear arms policies: Some psychological and social policy considerations. *Journal of Peace Research, 23,* 129-139.
Fiske, S. (1986). People's reactions to nuclear war: Implications for psychologists. *American Psychologist, 42,* 207-217.
Frank, J. D. (1987). The drive for power and the nuclear arms race. *American Psychologist, 42,* 337-344.
Friedman, H. S., & Booth-Kewley, S. (1987). The "disease-prone personality": A meta-analytic view of the construct. *American Psychologist, 42,* 539-555.
Gallup Report. (1986, May). *Greater war risk* (Report no. 24).
Gilbert, R. K. (1988). The dynamics of inaction: Psychological factors inhibiting arms control activism. *American Psychologist, 43,* 755-764.
Goldenring, J. M., & Doctor, R. (1986). Teenage worry about nuclear war: North American and European questionnaire studies. *International Journal of Mental Health, 15,* 72-92.
Hamilton, S. B., Chavez, E. C., & Keilin, W. G. (1986). Thoughts of Armageddon: The relationship between attitudes toward the nuclear threat and cognitive/emotional responses. *International Journal of Mental Health, 15,* 189-207.
Hirschberg, M. (1988, July). *Attributions for super power interventions: Were they forced to do it?* Paper presented at the meetings of the International Society for Political Psychology, Secaucus, NJ.
Holmborg, P. O., & Bergstrom, A. (1985). How Swedish teenagers think and feel concerning the nuclear threat. In T. Solanteus, E. Chivian, M. Vartanyan, & S. Chivian (Eds.), *Impact of the threat of nuclear war on children and adolescents. Proceedings of an international research symposium* (pp. 170-180). Boston: International Physicians for the Prevention of Nuclear War.
Janis, I. L. (1986). International crisis management in the nuclear age. In R. K. White (Ed.), *Psychology and the prevention of nuclear war* (pp. 381-396). New York: New York University Press.
Kramer, B. M., Kalick, S. M., & Milburn, M. A. (1983). Attitudes toward nuclear weapons and nuclear war: 1945-1982. *Journal of Social Issues, 39,* 7-24.
Kull, S. (1988). *How the policy makers think.* New York: Basic Books.
Lifton, P. J. (1979). *The broken connection: On death and the continuity of life.* New York: Touchstone Books.
Mack, J. E. (1981). Psycho-social effects of the nuclear arms race. *Bulletin of the Atomic Scientists, 37*(4), 18-23.
Mack, J. E. (1984). Resistances to knowing in the nuclear age. *Harvard Educational Review, 54*(3), 1-11.

Mayton, D. M., (1985, April). *Personality correlates of nuclear war threat perception.* Paper presented at meeting of Western Psychological Association, San Jose, CA.

McClenney, L., & Neiss, R. (1989). Psychological responses to the threat of nuclear war. *Journal of Applied Social Psychology, 19,* 1239-1267.

McGraw, K. M., & Tyler, T. R. (1986). The threat of nuclear war and psychological well-being. *International Journal of Mental Health, 15,* 172-188.

McKenzie, S., & Dyal, J. (1985, June). *Predicting who becomes involved in anti-nuclear activities: Implications for public education.* Paper presented at the Convention of the Canadian Psychological Association, Montreal, Canada.

Mosher, D. L., & Sirkin, M. (1984). Measuring a macho personality constellation. *Journal of Research in Personality, 18,* 150-163.

Newcomb, M. D. (1986). Nuclear attitudes and reactions: Associations with depression, drug use, and quality of life. *Journal of Personality and Social Psychology, 50,* 906-920.

Nisbett, R., & Ross, L. (1980). *Human inference: Strategies and shortcomings of social judgment.* Englewood Cliffs, NJ: Prentice-Hall.

Orwell, G. (1954). *Animal farm.* New York: Harcourt-Brace.

Oskamp, S. (1965). Attitudes toward U.S. and Russian actions—A double standard. *Psychological Reports, 16,* 43-46.

Oskamp, S. (1968). Relationship of self-concept to international attitudes. *Journal of Social Psychology, 76,* 31-36.

Peterson, C., Seligman, M. E., & Vaillant, G. E. (1988). Pessimistic explanatory style is a risk factor for physical illness: A thirty-five-year longitudinal study. *Journal of Personality and Social Psychology, 55,* 23-27.

Pilisuk, M., & Acredolo, C. (1988). Fear of technological hazards: One concern or many? *Social Behavior, 3,* 17-24.

Sande, G. N., Goethals, G. P., Ferrari, L., & Worth, L. (1989). Value-guided attributions: Maintaining the moral self-image and the diabolical enemy-image. *Journal of Social Issues, 45,* 91-118.

Schuman, H., Ludwig, J., & Krasnick, J. A. (1986). The perceived threat of nuclear war: Salience, and open questions. *Public Opinion Quarterly, 50,* 519-536.

Schwebel, M. (1965). Nuclear cold war: Student opinion and professional responsibility. In M. Schwebel (Ed.), *Behavioral science and human survival* (pp. 20-23). Palo Alto, CA: Science and Behavioral Books.

Schwebel, M. (1982). Effects of the nuclear war threat on children and teenagers: Implications for professionals. *American Journal of Orthopsychiatry, 52,* 608-618.

Silverstein, B. (1989). Enemy images: The psychology of U.S. attitudes and cognitions regarding the Soviet Union. *American Psychologist, 44,* 903-913.

Slemrod, J. (1986). Saving and the fear of nuclear war. *Journal of Conflict Resolution, 30,* 403-419.

Solanteus, T., Goldberg, S., Levinson, D., Ross, C., & LaCombe, S. (1985). Young people and the threat of war: Overview of a national survey in Finland. In T. Solanteus, E. Chivian, M. Vartanyan, & S. Chivian (Eds.), *Impact of the threat of nuclear war on children and adolescents* (pp. 94-103). Boston: International Physicians for the Prevention of Nuclear War.

Sommers, F. G., Goldberg, S., Levinson, D., Ross, C., & LaCombe, S. (1985). Children's mental health and the threat of nuclear war: A Canadian pilot study. In T. Solanteus, E. Chivian, M. Vartanyan, & S. Chivian (Eds.), *Impact of the threat of nuclear war on children and adolescents* (pp. 61-93). Boston: International Physicians for the Prevention of Nuclear War.

Strickland, B. R. (1989). Internal-external control expectancies: From contingency to creativity. *American Psychologist, 44,* 1-12.

Thompson, S. G. (1949). Relation between half life and disintegration energy in orbital electron capture by heavy nuclei. *Physics Review, 76,* 319.

Thompson, S. G., & Seaborg, G. T. (1956). Progress in nuclear energy, Series III. In *Process Chemistry* (Vol. 1). London: Pergamon Press.

Tizard, B. (1984). Problematic aspects of nuclear education. *Harvard Educational Review, 54,* 271-282.

Tyler, T. R., & McGraw, K. M. (1983). The threat of nuclear war: Risk interpretation and behavioral response. *Journal of Social Issues, 39,* 25-40.

Watanabe, P. Y., & Milburn, M. A. (1986). Activism against Armageddon: Determinants of nuclear-related political behavior. *Political Psychology, 7,* 661-674.

7

The Great Nuclear Terror Bubble: A Memoir

Joseph B. Adelson

In June 1989 the press carried accounts of a project that had encouraged adolescents to write to the U.S. Congress about the issues of most concern to them. More than 5,000 seventh and eighth graders had written. The top seven issues mentioned were substance abuse (25%), sexual issues (17%), the environment (10%), crime (7%), education (5%), child abuse (5%), and suicide (5%). Other issues adduced ranged from health care to helmet and skateboard laws.

There was, however, an extraordinary omission—there was no mention of nuclear warfare and how to avoid it. How could that be? It had been drummed into us that the fear of a nuclear Armageddon haunts the adolescent imagination. Less than a year before we had learned from the *New England Journal of Medicine* that "Nuclear war is one of the greatest concerns of American children and adolescents" (Chivian, Robinson, Tudge, Popov, & Andreyenkov, 1988). The implications were said to be profound. In an accompanying guest editorial, a well-known professor of psychiatry at the Harvard Medical School said that these apprehensions might well affect "impulse control and capacity to delay gratification, the formation of long-term ideals, the ability and willingness to form relationships, views of death, the capacity for intergenerational trust, the development of social responsibility, and interest in planning for the future" (Mack, 1988). In short, just about everything.

Consider that, in 1988, nuclear anxiety was said to be nearly ubiquitous in its reach and utterly malignant in its effects. Less than a year later it had seemingly vanished, leaving few traces save some stray citations in *Psychological Abstracts* and *Excerpta Medica*. How can we account for it? One might say that the discrepancy is more apparent than real, that those 5,000 letters do not confute the questionnaire data, that the nuclear terror has not diminished, and that the worries reported are more real than the issues addressed in the letters. Clearly that theory will not wash. Why should we impute more "reality" to check marks on a questionnaire than to the energy required to write a hortatory letter? Or we might say that the changes are genuine enough since nuclear anxiety has been brought to an end by the easing of the cold war. It may well be so, but that leads us to question whether nuclear terror was so deeply rooted in the first place. After all, the burden of the argument was that these fears had come close to destabilizing the adolescent mind.

There is a third possibility, which underlies the argument of this paper: There

Preparation of this article was made possible by a grant from the Lynde and Harry Bradley Foundation.

was no psychological crisis, it was invented as a vast exercise in self-deception, and it tells us a great many sorrowful things about our discipline.

NUCLEAR ANXIETY

My interest in nuclear anxiety came about unexpectedly, when I was telephoned by a Minority (Republican) aide to the House Select Committee on Children, Youth, and their Families. The Committee, she told me, had been established to study problems such as divorce, illegitimacy, domestic violence, child abuse, and other misfortunes besetting U.S. families. That was more than enough to take up completely the Committee's time and energy. Yet the chair of the committee had insisted on pushing through a special hearing whose essential purpose, she thought, was to support the nuclear disarmament proposals coming before Congress. It was to be argued that nuclear terror among the young was so severe as to constitute a national crisis in mental health. Not only were our children terrified by fears of a nuclear catastrophe, but these fears were also a major cause of other afflictions, including the rising rates of suicide, drug abuse, and school failure. Some of the Minority members were upset, largely because the real work of the Committee was to be delayed in order to put on a television event. Children were to testify along with some celebrity psychiatrists. The television networks had been invited in and it might well turn into a media circus.

She was calling to see whether I agreed that the nation's young were in crisis. She herself thought the idea farfetched. She had seen nothing untoward in her own children, nor among their friends, but then again she was not a psychologist, so perhaps was missing something. What did I think? What I thought, without telling her so, was that she had misunderstood or exaggerated the claims being made. I thought it unlikely that I would fail to see signs of nuclear anxiety in my clinical cases, or those of my students, colleagues, and friends, were anxieties present in such severe intensity. Still, it was possible, and so I told my caller I would look into it and get back to her.

Looking into the literature I discovered that she had in no way overstated the case. It was in fact being claimed that the American young were in the grip of despair, induced by their fear of an inescapable nuclear calamity. Yet this conclusion had been reached almost gratuitously, and it was based on an array of more-or-less inadequate studies. These studies varied; some entirely anecdotal, some amateurish, a few no more than passable technically, and as a group they showed few signs of inferential prudence. In some studies the samples had been chosen nearly willynilly (e.g., youngsters had been recommended by acquaintances of the interviewer, themselves passionate advocates of antinuclear politics; Escalona, 1982; Mack, 1988). In much of the work, the youngsters studied were of the "new class," upper-middle-class and suburban, from the seedbed of the peace movement. Nor were investigator effects taken into account, most of the early studies having been carried out by persons deeply devoted to the peace movement.

These were the more obvious errors, most clearly visible in the clinical research. The other common genre was the opinion survey, wherein youngsters were asked to write in, check off, or rate their concerns, worries, or fears. That would seem to be a straightforward approach, yet it is not, and when used without sufficient care can provide extremely misleading data. These studies, then and later, showed little awareness of how tricky it can be to measure complex or fugitive states of mind. Being worried is not the same as being concerned or fearful. Furthermore, being worried may mean entirely different things to different children. This is not a trivial problem. One of the leading studies in the antinuclear literature found that the fear of getting poor grades is greater than the fear of nuclear warfare. This is a fairly clear sign of how much variation there can be in how such questions are understood (Goldenring & Doctor, 1984). Nor is merely saying you are worried quite the same as the depth of "worry" that might reveal itself on a projective test. There was not much recognition of context effects, either. Many children, surveyed at school, will tend to view the experience as a current-events quiz, hence accounting for the surprisingly high frequency of worries about matters such as pollution, overpopulation, and world starvation.

Still, the clinical studies were the most troublesome, given their casual and at moments reckless habits of inference. Clinical theory had taken a hard look at those habits in recent years and had developed some doctrines of self-consciousness and caution. Yet none of that delicacy of touch could be seen in the antinuclear literature. If the person (interviewee, patient) was openly fearful, that made the case; if he or she feared something else, that was a derivative, and also made the case; if there were no signs of fear, that pointed to "psychic numbing," a concept that acted as a universal solvent to wash away all contradiction.

Its implausibility could be forgiven if the reader could feel that somehow the work was onto something, that it had captured, however imperfectly, an important and neglected truth. If it had been argued that there was an increasing apprehensiveness among the young and that it bore watching, then one would not be so concerned. Yet much more was being claimed. One writer, in an approving summary of the literature, saw the nuclear bomb as

> A major force behind increased apathy, conformity, hedonism and lack of faith; the source of powerlessness, nervousness, sensationalism, alienation and dehumanization; the creator of a weakness in the distinction between reality and unreality, information overload, psychic numbing, expectation of holocaust, rejection of materialism, rejection of technology and the religion of nuclearism. (Carey, 1982)

Such assertions raised the question of why a terror so devastating had gone unnoticed by others. Yet I could find no references to nuclear panic outside the work of those engaged in the antinuclear movement. I found a fairly recent book reporting studies on childrens' ideas of death as depicted in their drawings (Lonetto, 1980). These pictures showed no sign of nuclear disaster at all (despite the available, vivid icon of the mushroom cloud), and in fact there was scarcely any mention of death in war—fewer than 2% among those 9 to 12 years of age. Surveying a dozen texts in child and adolescent psychology and psychiatry I found that the topic simply did not appear. Even the fear of war was rare. Among children of latency age it was found only in 8% of the girls and was scarcely mentioned by boys (Lonetto, 1980).

One can easily imagine an advocate's rejoinder to these findings: They were out of date, and they did not penetrate deeply enough into the subterranean torments the newer clinical research had uncovered. The most compelling evidence against accepting the nuclear-terror claims was precisely that, its absence in *current* clinical observations. I saw no sign of it in my own cases, those of my graduate interns, or those of the young psychologists I supervised, nor in presentations at case conferences. My colleagues did not report it when I questioned them and neither did the child and adolescent therapists I spoke to. I went so far as to examine all of the process notes from the therapy supervisions I had done during the past year (about 1,000 hours) and found only one reference to nuclear matters, and that to a patient talking about someone else. I gave special attention to fantasies and dreams, to see whether I could discern even faint derivatives of nuclear anxiety. It was not there.

Most of the patients were young adults. They lived in Ann Arbor, Michigan, a major college town, at a time in its history where one could not stroll down its main campus street without being asked to sign a petition to make the city a nuclear-free zone. Even so there were no nuclear perturbations to be felt in psychotherapy. By way of contrast, it was at that very moment, 1983, that AIDS was just beginning to seep into public awareness, though as yet it was no more than a distant cloud on the horizon. The perturbations of AIDS were almost immediately evident in psychotherapy, and not among homosexuals alone.

When we next talked, I offered the Minority (Republican) aide my opinion that nuclear fears did not pose a threat to the mental health of the young and that the data supporting that notion were flawed or nonexistent. I agreed to prepare a report to become part of the record of the court hearings (Adelson, 1984). After the hearings were over, she called to say that they had gone surprisingly well. The media coup she feared did not happen. The child witnesses, though winsome and articulate, were clearly atypical, clearly fledgling members of the antinuclear culture. They were not taken seriously as representative of children in general. The Majority's (Democratic) mental health experts were effectively countered by the Minority's; there was a stand-off. The next day there was a little news coverage on the hearings.

At the time, I could not see how nuclear anxiety could sustain itself, without a serious conflict between the superpowers—something like the Cuban Missile Crisis—and there seemed no sign of that. Political disputes, national and international, about nuclear strategy would keep those issues prominent and concern high, but there was no reason to feel that nuclear anxiety would induce terror, as peace doctrine held it had. When that became evident, the anxiety about nuclear anxiety would diminish and the topic would fade from view.

NUCLEAR TERROR

So much for prescience. The doctrine I thought would soon be moribund was alive and vigorous, and indeed it was at the beginning of a growth spurt that was to produce an explosion of psychological writing. It was not to be an explosion of new thinking, however, only much more of the same. Nevertheless, the rapid growth in quantity provided the illusion of quality, as the topic acquired committed authors and audiences.

Some months after the Committee hearings, the transcript was published (Select Committee on Children, Youth, and Their Families, 1984). I found it discouraging and at moments appalling, for several reasons. I felt the child witnesses were being exploited, being displayed, for effect alone, to illustrate the motif of the suffering child that played so large a role in the imagery of the movement. The children were willing to tell us that they were suffering and that they were haunted by the prospect of their imminent annihilation. Yet we saw few signs of that. We had, for example, a forceful 12-year-old boy who lectured the assembly before him on

Democritus, Newton, and Einstein; on how one constructs a nuclear weapon; and on why nuclear energy cannot be used safely. What comes to mind is an image not of a terrified child but of a child evangelist preaching the gospel of hellfire and salvation.

Even more troubling was the nature of the psychiatric testimony. I had imagined that the *gravitas* of a Congressional hearing would induce rhetorical restraint. There were the usual polite murmurs about preliminary findings and more research needed, but these served merely to launch even more astonishing assertions. For example, the recent interest in video games was a displacement from nuclear fears, or an interest in working hard academically was "the only alternative to despair" about the world's blowing up. We were also offered the familiar mind-boggling clinical anecdotes, that is, of children aged 5 and 6 expressing fears of nuclear destruction and of an 11-year-old girl asking her parents if she would have time to commit suicide upon hearing that nuclear bombs were on their way.

The most troubling element of the transcript was that it clearly revealed the root intention of the hearing, which was not merely to support the nuclear freeze resolution but also to pave the way for a national program of political education. That was the constant refrain, that the U.S. young are thwarted by a conspiracy of silence that keeps them from learning the truth about our common nuclear peril. All discussion of the topic is taboo and the effects are poisonous. There is a building-up of doubt, desperation, hopelessness, and helplessness because of a fierce suppression of honest discussion. Parents would not talk about it to the kids. The schools would not talk about it to the kids. The kids were now demanding that the curtain be lifted and the truth be told.

It will not strain the reader's credulity to learn that programs of pedagogy were in place and ready to go. Curricular units on nuclear education had been developed by powerful groups such as the National Education Association (NEA) and were soon to be employed in thousands of schools. Shortly thereafter the leading journals of education devoted entire issues to the need for such education. At about the same time, several of the larger foundations announced that they would sponsor munificent programs on peace research and education.

This is not the place for a full discussion of the nuclear curricula. A bibliography compiled by the California Department of Education lists 64 published by the year 1986. The unit *Choices* (National Education Association Professional Library, 1983), apparently the most widely used, offers a heavy dose of shock treatment. Since nuclear psychiatry holds that children live in a state of denial, the syllabus depicts as gruesomely as possible the terrible damage occasioned by nuclear war. Children are invited to imagine, even forced to gaze upon, horrific pictures of devastation and to read the most lurid tales of human suffering. Though we must assume its good intentions, it is finally an exercise in sadism.

The other stated purpose for the curricula is pedagogic, to meet the yearning of youngsters for more information on the nuclear impasse. There is an irony here—the very establishment that presided over the collapse of U.S. education is nevertheless prepared to teach the Byzantine complexities of arms control. Remember that most of our high school seniors cannot, on a four-part multiple-choice test, choose the five-year period during which D-Day occurred or when the United Nations was founded and that only a bare majority know the quarter-century of the Eisenhower or Roosevelt presidencies or can identify Stalin as the Soviet ruler during World War II (Ravitch & Finn, 1987). How then are they to be instructed on world history and geopolitics? Assuming against all likelihood that it can be done, how can it be done in an even-handed manner? Would the views of both Richard Perle, former National Security advisor, and Richard Barnet, peace activist, be treated, as well as those of both Paul Nitze and Paul Warnke?

Even a cursory scan of the major curricula makes it plain that they are disingenuous exercises in indoctrination. The students are told that there are two competing nuclear powers, with one rather more to blame than the other, that one being the United States. It will not recognize how much the Russians have suffered, how beleaguered they feel, and how strong their interest in peace really is. Soviet efforts at conciliation are rebuffed, leaving them little option but to continue an arms race they have no interest in. All this, remember, took place during the time the Afghanistan brutalities were being carried out. In some cases the nuclear curricula also traffic in what can only be called weird ideas, for example, the notion that "the West" is disposed to violence because of its bloodthirsty religious tradition (Judeo-Christian), while the religions of the East conduce to tranquility. That the religions of the East conduce to tranquility is an incredible observation, given that the bloodiest massacres and genocides in the post–World War II period took place in the East—in Korea, Indochina, China, and Cambodia, millions upon millions were slaughtered wantonly. How does it happen that people so ignorant of recent world history are deputed to write educational programs on history? Why were there no second thoughts among school boards and superintendents, why was there no close examination of these materials in mainstream periodicals?

Antinuclear belief was then in such favor in the establishment culture that second thoughts were heretical. Even disconfirming events had little effect. Consider *The day after* episode. That television play, dramatizing the effects of a nuclear exchange on a small U.S. city, received enormous preshowing publicity. Many in the antinuclear movement believed the program would trigger mass hysteria, given the reservoir of hidden panic said to be present among so many of our citizens. The belief was strong enough that a national hotline was established, to offer reassurance and advice to the many psychiatric casualties expected. As we know, *The day after* was shown, and everyone watching it was able to go to bed and wake the next morning with no sign of disrepair—no outpouring of calls to the hotline, no increased activity at the emergency rooms, and no rise in suicides. Despite such spectacular disconfirmation, there was no sign that peace movement psychiatry had learned any lessons from its failure of prophecy.

NUCLEAR PSYCHOLOGY

It was during this period that the nuclear issue became attractive to a great many psychologists and psychiatrists. A bibliography published in 1985 (Kramer, 1985) reported about 750 items, and there would soon be many more in print. Nuclear psychology became a standard topic at the national conventions of the mental health associations. However, the papers did not contribute much beyond a sense of outrage, usually by generalizing exotic events such as an 8-year-old who threatened suicide to avoid nuclear death. (That child, or some equivalent, was becoming a stock figure of the movement, a kind of poor little match girl.)

The more restrained voices rarely offered anything new. A famous psychologist proposed a long, banal list of suggestions, including talk to one's students, create discussion groups, speak and write about the arms race for the general public, and "encourage others to follow our example" (Klineberg, 1984). Another paper advised stepping outside one's professional assumptions, though it was not at all clear what would or should follow thereafter (Morawski & Goldstein, 1985). Still another explained that an all-out nuclear exchange would be a most unsettling event psychologically (Allen, 1985). It is hard not to sympathize with the motive that drove the writing of these articles—the urge to contribute something from our discipline to this momentous problem. Yet it is not at all clear how much psychologists were able to contribute beyond moral earnestness and good intentions. One sometimes senses that the authors themselves vaguely sense that to be so, to judge by the frequency with which "further research" is called for and the infrequency with which useful research suggestions are made.

There was heightened activity but little genuine progress in dealing with the issue of nuclear anxiety among the young. The public opinion surveys became more sophisticated in method, but the limitations persisted. They tended to provide different findings depending on minor variations in phrasing. As an example, at a peak period of antinuclear publicity, one survey of 8,000 students (fifth and ninth grades) found "nuclear destruction" well down the list of worries, in fact 12th behind the front-runners (school performance, one's looks, being liked, parental death, and how one was treated by friends).

But even if nuclear fear were to be Number One, we would still be unclear about its depth psychology. Any number of catastrophes—local and planetary—can overtake us. If you live in earthquake country or on the edge of a volcano, that should affect your sense of the future, although unless there has been actual trauma, it does not seem to. Why then should nuclear fears be any different? Peace psychiatry insisted it was different, not only in degree but in essence. Nuclear anxiety had generated unique psychological effects, about all nihilism and a sense of futurelessness so severe as to unhinge the average child. Was that true? The evidence was entirely anecdotal. Could one devise a more exacting test? It did not have to be the perfect test. All one needed was a modest study providing some elementary controls. Such efforts were simply not to be found.

A good example is the much-praised book by Greenwald and Zeitlin, *No reason to talk about it: Families confront the nuclear taboo* (1987). It could not have better credentials. Under the imprint of a most distinguished publishing house, its dust jacket carries ecstatic commendations by household names such as Karl Menninger. Yet the research turns out to be the usual assemblage of anecdotes, though pretending otherwise; in fact, it is almost a textbook case of how not to do a serious study. The writers, both specialists in family therapy, interviewed 25 families, discussing with them their reactions to a nuclear threat. There are the superficial trappings of systematic research: the interviews were videotaped and later transcribed. Yet it manages to repeat every error made in the early and presumably exploratory stages of work in the area. The investigators are dedicated members of the peace movement. The families studied were in no way chosen randomly, but were found by word of mouth, or "networking." A clear majority of them were political activists, many in the peace movement. An even larger majority (80%) were middle- to upper-middle-class in social status—a psychoanalyst, a physician, a lawyer, a college dean, an investment counselor, and several engineers, technicians, and businessmen. There seems to have been no systematic interview format and apparently no intention of making systematic comparisons. The analysis of the data is summed up in a single sentence: The analysis reported in this book is the result of repeatedly viewing tapes and reading transcripts. As the authors insist on telling us, they are doing *clinical* but not *pure* research (another way of saying that they were not doing research at all).

So we have one more caricature of disinterested inquiry. The work begins not from hypothesis, not even from expectation, but from a fixed belief that, as one of the blurbs on the book jacket puts it, "The American family is haunted by the nuclear spectre." That being so, there seems no need to discover whether it is in fact so, or for whom it is so, or when, or how that spectre relates to the many other spectres of contemporary life. The task is to confirm and illustrate what is already known. The inferential pattern discussed earlier obtains here as well. If the person is haunted by the spectre, that makes the case; if he or she does not seem to be, denial and numbing are at work; if he or she follows the adage of Sir Sydney Smith, to trust in God and take short views, a childlike passivity may be inferred. If there has not been much talk about the spectre at the dinner table, it means the children have not been given permission by the parents and that has interfered with "the struggle for mastery" and with "identity formation." On the parental side, the spectre has destroyed their ability to guide the next generation, which amounts to "an assault on generativity." And so it goes, every developmental crisis imagined by Erik Erikson being brought into play. How do we know any of this is so? We are told it is so. It is research by asseveration, by the accumulation of selected interview excerpts—sound bites.

It is clear enough that given the same assumptions, methods, and modes of inference, an equivalent case can be made for a great many other spectres. Imagine a pair of scholars from the "Meryl Streep Institute," eager to show us that the U.S. family is haunted by unavowed fears of carcinogens. They gather a group of largely upscale families, someone to run the camcorder, and set about finding out how much is known about the substances that befoul the air, the water, the food, and the earth itself—the pesticides, the toxic wastes, the acid rain. Some children will tell them that they know something about it but not that much. They have heard that there are so many substances around that they cannot be avoided and they expect to die of cancer, since that's what everybody gets, though in the meantime they expect to go to the state university and study marketing. Others will say that they do not know what carcinogens are, since they haven't come to it in their civics class. Some parents will confess that they are worried but have not yet discussed it with the kids since they don't really understand it. Other parents will say that they don't worry about it because the government would not let it get out of hand. All the categories we need are already in place: futurelessness, denial, psychic numbing, the childlike belief in government, parental powerlessness, and the assault on generativity.

NUCLEAR AND ABORTION SPECTRES

To accept the idea of a nuclear spectre, one must first accept that there is enough likelihood of a nuclear war that most people must come to terms with the prospect. Now imagine someone who considers the prospect remote and the idea itself an illusion. I introduce you to an acquaintance of mine, an academic with an academic's sensibility and sophistication, yet with a moral and political outlook radically different from my own.

He is a zealous foe of abortion, which he views as the quintessential moral problem of our time, in every way as horrible as the Holocaust and all the other genocides of the century, indeed the culmination of those genocides. Abortion is murder. At any point in the unborn's life, it is a murder carried out with utter insouciance and accompanied by a propaganda campaign justifying and at times celebrating the act. This man is contemptuous of the antinuclear movement, which he considers hysterical. Why carry on about entirely hypothetical deaths when we cast so cold an eye on well over a million homicides each year in this country alone?

However, he believes the movement is right in one matter—their ideas on psychic numbing, futurelessness, and the death culture. Antinuclear supporters grasp what is going on, but are blind to its origins. What they are numb to, he thinks, is the domestic death machine, grinding out millions of tiny corpses, with more lives lost in a decade than at the death camps and killing fields taken together.

Why can't they grasp that these killings have horrendous psychological effects upon us collectively, he wonders. Much of the popular culture is given over to displacements and reworkings of the abortion terror. Look at that staple of adolescent entertainment, the horror movies that depict a young girl endangered by an evil older man preparing to stab her. The man pushes us to think about that remarkable space-horror movie *Alien,* which begins and ends with its figures comfortably asleep in womblike beds, their space idyll destroyed by a malevolent snakelike creature that invades first the safely enclosed ship and later the bodies of the crew members. Its most memorable scenes depict the savage, bloody rendering of their innards. The man says that if you dare to look at that, you will see enacted a parable about abortion, about the invasion and destruction of a secure inner space. Is it an accident that the movie is made shortly after the beginning of mass abortions in this country?

He continues somewhat like this:

Those family studies you tell me about, and the supposed nuclear taboo. Let me tell you that the real taboo will be found in the secular family's refusal to confront its complicity in this murderous industry, its pretense that there is nothing amiss. Probe carefully and you will discover hidden wellsprings of shame, guilt, and remorse. If there is such inner turmoil about an imaginary event, how much will you find about the quotidian, relentless shedding of innocent blood? If you tell me that most people view the unborn as unliving, as worthless lumps of protoplasm, then I tell you that they are shielding themselves from what they know to be true, and if serious psychological consequences follow from nuclear denial, far more serious ones will emerge from our willed incapacity to confront the abortion horror.

In any case, there are tens of millions of Americans who do deem abortion to be murder and who are tormented by it. Why are their concerns ignored? Why no special hearings by a House Select Committee? Let me tell you, we can produce thousands of troubled children, and their parents, and obstetricians, and pediatricians, and clergy—all ready and able to testify on the psychological ravages of abortion. Why are there no curricular units on abortion? We can produce some splendid ones, complete with intrauterine photography of the executions, and films of the body bags at Planned Parenthood. You tell me there is little enough research on abortion and almost none reflecting our view of it. Why not? You know as well as I do. It is not a chic topic at this fashionable university of ours. Your colleagues think of people like myself as ludicrous—an intellectual underclass.

NUCLEAR PERSPECTIVE

We have just had an exercise in what literary critic Kenneth Burke calls "perspective by incongruity," where we juxtapose apparent opposites to uncover what is otherwise concealed in both objects of study. The preceding section is a summary and paraphrase of several conversations. The interlocutor is in the humanities, conversant in a general way with psychoanalytic ideas, though unaware before our conversations of the uses made of those ideas by the antinuclear movement. Yet he catches on quickly to its rhetorical strategy, so much so that he turns it on its head and expropriates it for his own ends. In some respects he is more compelling than the antinuclearists, particularly in his comments on the cultural resonances of abortion. (There has in fact been a striking increase, in horror films, of the theme of the endangered fetus.) Yet whether we are persuaded by him is another matter entirely, which will depend less on the merits of the case and more on one's political beliefs. Those feeling allied to the liberal political culture will find his antiabortionism alien if not indeed offensive. Nuclear activists will dismiss his claims for the pathogenic effects of abortion as scornfully as he dismisses what he calls their hysterical fears of nuclear catastrophe.

Putting that aside, who will doubt his tacit claim that he can demonstrate, on abortion, the same deep anxiety that the nuclear-terror canon claims exists among the young and their families? It is done easily, and in fact I have done it myself, quite recently, in the course of trying out interview items for a study on adolescent reasoning. The fairly simple question "what do you think about abortion?" elicits vivid responses from many youngsters, particularly those from religious or politically conservative families. A devoutly religious 16-year-old girl says she prays for the souls of the murdered children. A conservative 14-year-old boy says abortion is morally wrong, and when asked whether he worries about it, replies sarcastically that if he worried about all the things liberals favor, he would commit suicide. A 12-year-old gives a more characteristic response, saying that he doesn't like it because it is "like killing," but as long as it is legal, "people have a right to do it if they want to—it is freedom of choice." If these are the answers we provoke by superficial questions, imagine what we could obtain with deeper probing. Does anyone doubt that a compelling case could be made for abortion anxiety, or abortion guilt, given children preprogrammed by their families or an investigator eager to make the case?

How would we go about demonstrating the pandemic malevolence of abortion guilt? By committing the elementary error of taking correlation to imply causation, assuming a connection between two events coincident in time. It is that rather simple mistake we find throughout the nuclear-spectre studies. Carried to its extreme it produces some startling examples, for example, a researcher in organizational psychology asserts that the reason athletes have become so exhibitionistic (high fives, dancing in the end zone) is that they feel helpless because of the possibility of nuclear war and because of other overwhelming problems (Greenberg, 1989). The nuclear possibility is the *primum mobile* of all noteworthy or deplorable psychological events. In a further extention of this idea, all events are conditioned by their being part of the Nuclear Age. I recently discovered an essay discussing Anna O., the first psychoanalysis patient. In speculating on what she might be like if she were a patient today, the authors twice speak about "Anna O. in the Nuclear Age" (Rosenbaum & Muroff, 1984). The allusion makes no sense.

What does the Nuclear Age have to do with Anna O.? Why not the Biogenetic Age, the Computer Age, the Age of Space Travel, the Audiovisual Age, or for that matter the Anorexic Age, or the Psychobabble Age, or, come to think of it, the Age of Abortion?

To return to our *gedenk* (thought) research. Suppose I were to gather a group of interviews, choose vivid and touching excerpts, and write up the findings. I would characterize them as preliminary or clinical, but of such ominous import as to warrant the attention of the discipline. Suppose I were to send the paper to a journal. What would the editorial response be? That the study is impressionistic, weak methodologically, needing a control group or some double-blind procedure, a modicum of statistical treatment, etc. Or suppose I were to ask the American Orthopsychiatric Association if they would schedule a special session on the mental health effects of the Abortion Holocaust, along the lines of their many previous special sessions on the Nuclear Holocaust? To ask the question is to answer it.

NUCLEAR POLITICS

Is there a more politicized topic in psychology? It is hard to think of one. In other cases politics biases the work, tilts it, by various not-quite-conscious devices—through the samples chosen, the questions asked, the methods used, the inferences made. Here we feel the topic itself was created to serve political aims. It is politics masquerading as psychology.

How did that happen? The impulse is to look to prominent figures, to represent them as Pied Pipers leading the innocent astray. In fact, nuclear psychology is a collective construction, reflecting the monotonic politics of the academy and of the softer social sciences. On all nuclear matters, whether it be the presumed enervation of the young by apocalyptic fear or the larger questions of strategy and policy, there is near unanimity of openly expressed opinion among psychologists and psychiatrists. As always, those with intense beliefs set the agenda and the terms of disclosure. They are cheered on by many fervent supporters. A great many more sympathize less vocally. They are for peace, so they do not look too closely at the evidence. What counts is the goodness of the cause itself.

There are some skeptics and some critics, but their voices are rarely evident, for one reason or another. Hence there is almost no dissent, and what little there is is not often heard. The most bemusing experience I have had during this adventure was to learn that an *eminence grise* of nuclear psychology had refused to participate in a proposed symposium at a psychiatric convention if I were to be on the panel. That should tell us a great deal. Those are not the manners or the mores of science and scholarship, even among devout enemies. They are far closer to one-party politics.

The absence of dissent may lift the spirits momentarily but will sooner or later deaden thought. Without an adversary to keep in mind, the argument loses its force and sharpness. Inanition sets in. We repeat ourselves. Professional gatherings preach to the converted and become rallies, revival meetings, prayer services.

To the self-indulgence produced by the absence of opposition, we add the self-indulgence permitted by clinical modes of inquiry. The free and easy means of discovery and proof we find throughout this body of work provides—to the life-long clinician—a truly depressing confirmation of the harsh critiques advanced by Grünbaum (1984), Crews (1986), and so many others. Discovery: seek and ye shall find; proof: right you are if you think you are. The solipsistic temptations of the clinical method are too easily realized. That disinterest hard enough to attain under ordinary conditions of clinical work can disappear completely given sufficient zeal.

Episodes such as these take their toll. We squander our credibility. Among our sophisticated audiences, among journalists, legislators, jurists, and natural scientists, we can discern a growth of skepticism about our work, not merely about our opinions or about specific findings, but about the entire enterprise of psychological research. To some degree that reflects the recognition that our reach exceeds our grasp, that we do not have the means to answer really difficult or complex questions. Yet the more important reason is the suspicion that were we able to answer those questions, we would not do so in good faith. We would load the dice. Bias in, bias out. There are too many cases where findings dovetail much too neatly with ideological interests. We have had unpleasant findings evaded or denied. We have had scholars penalized for making those findings. And so we find that the more cynical observers of our discipline have come to view us as they do lawyers—as advocates, as hired guns, though procurable not by money but by the love of a cause.

REFERENCES

Adelson, J. (1984). Prepared statement to U.S. House of Representatives, Select Committee on Children, Youth, and their Families. In *Children's fears of war* (pp. 108–120). Washington, DC: U.S. Government Printing Office.

Allen, B. P. (1985). After missiles: Sociopsychological effects of nuclear war. *American Psychologist, 40,* 927–937.

Carey, M. (1982, January). Psychological fallout: Growing up nuclear. *Bulletin of the Atomic Scientists,* pp. 20–24.

Chivian, E., Robinson, J., Tudge, J., Popov, N., & Andreyenkov, V. (1988). American and Soviet teenagers' concerns about nuclear war and the future. *The New England Journal of Medicine, 319,* 407–413.

Crews, F. (1986). *Skeptical engagements.* New York: Oxford University Press.

Escalona, S. (1982). Children and the threat of nuclear war. In M. Schwebel (Ed.), *Behavioral science and human survival* (pp. 201–209). Palo Alto, CA: Behavioral Science Press.

Goldenring, J., & Doctor, R. (1984). Statement to House Select Committee on Children, Youth, and their Families. In *Children's fears of war* (pp. 55–65). Washington, DC: U.S. Government Printing Office.

Greenwald, D. S., & Zeitlin, S. J. (1987). *No reason to talk about it: Families confront the nuclear taboo.* New York: Norton.

Grünbaum, A. (1984). *The foundations of psychoanalysis: A philosophical critique.* Berkeley: University of California Press.

Klineberg, O. (1984). Public opinion and nuclear war. *American Psychologist, 39,* 1245–1253.

Kramer, B. (1985). *Nuclear psychology: A preliminary bibliography.* Unpubl. manuscript, University of Massachusetts, Dorchester.

Lonetto, R. (1980). *Children's conceptions of death.* New York: Springer.

Mack, J. (1988). American and Soviet teenagers and nuclear war. *New England Journal of Medicine, 319,* 437–438.

Morawski, J., & Goldstein, S. (1985). Psychology and nuclear war: A chapter in our legacy of social responsibility. *American Psychologist, 40,* 276–284.

National Education Association Professional Library. (1983). *Choices: A unit on conflict and war* (144 pp.). West Haven, CT: Massachusetts Teachers Association and National Education Association.

Ravitch, D., & Finn, C. (1987). *What do our seventeen-year-olds know?* New York: Harper & Row.

Rosenbaum, M., & Muroff, M. (1984). Anna O. (Bertha Pappenheim): Her history. In M. Rosenbaum & M. Muroff (Eds.), *Anna O.: Fourteen contemporary reinterpretations.* New York: Free Press.

Select Committee on Children, Youth, and Their Families. U.S. House of Representatives, Ninety-Eighth Congress. (1984). *Children's fears of war.* Washington, DC: U.S. Government Printing Office.

II

DOMESTIC POLICY

AFFIRMATIVE ACTION
Overcoming Resistance to Affirmative Action in Industry: A Social
  Psychological Perspective

Affirmative Action: Social Policy as Shibboleth

PORNOGRAPHY IN THE MASS MEDIA
Civil Liberties and Research on the Effects of Pornography

Pornography Research, Social Advocacy, and Public Policy

DEPICTION OF VIOLENCE ON TELEVISION
Television Violence and Aggression: What Psychologists Should Tell
  the Public

The Effects of Television Violence on Aggression: A Reply to a
  Skeptic

GUN CONTROL
The Weapons Effect Revisited: The Effects of Firearms on Aggressive
  Behavior

Research and Policy: The Case of Gun Control

II

DOMESTIC POLICY

8

Overcoming Resistance to Affirmative Action in Industry: A Social Psychological Perspective

Hugh Jordan Harrington and Norman Miller

Affirmative action has remained an important and controversial social issue in the United States for 25 years. We, the authors, wish to establish a continuing case for affirmative action and describe how social psychological theory and research can contribute to strategies for its success in industry. The values on which we premise our support of affirmative action are redressing past injustices, protecting against contemporary prejudice, and enlightening self-interest for the long-term peace and prosperity of society.

EQUAL OPPORTUNITY—AND AFFIRMATIVE ACTION TO ACHIEVE IT

A Rationale for Equal Opportunity

Equal job opportunity is the core of one's ability to enjoy the benefits of society. Title VII of the Civil Rights Act of 1964 establishes the Equal Employment Opportunity (EEO) Commission and bans discrimination based on race, religion, color, sex, or national origin. In addition to the concern for equal treatment at the individual level, some framers of this legislation recognized considerable gaps between Blacks and Whites at the national level on important measures of equality—economic status, unemployment rates, and occupational distributions. Some legislators also acknowledged that this systematic pattern of unequal participation in employment was the result of 250 years of legalized slavery followed by 100 years of institutionalized segregation. "Systematic exclusion became embedded in the attitudes, values, and behavior of virtually all institutions of American life" (Hawkins, 1987). If compensatory justice to people of color is to occur, these gaps must be reduced. Companies can either contribute to this national problem or to its resolution.

Affirmative Action to Achieve EEO

It was also evident that equal opportunity for the individual would not reduce these economic gaps in a timely manner nor could a policy eradicate the effects of prejudice. Executive Order 11246 (1965) requires a proactive effort from companies that want federal contracts to ensure that discrimination does not occur, irrespective of whether they exhibited past evidence of discrimination. Companies who bid on federal contracts must submit affirmative action plans and document relevant action. Competitive contractors need clear contract standards for these plans, and therefore, in 1969, numerical goals and specific regulations such as timetables were introduced as criteria. These are company-established goals, whereas in cases where judicial intervention becomes necessary, plans are court-ordered.

Goals versus Quotas

Goals for specific job categories are to be established on the basis of discrepancies between current levels of utilization and the availability of candidates for those positions in a protected class—that is, goals address specific areas of underutilization. Considerable debate has questioned whether goals are really quotas in disguise. Goals are established by comparing existing utilization of protected class members with their availability, and are then targeted to reduce any levels of underutilization. Without some way to measure goals, however, they can be meaningless. The maximum federal requirement is good faith effort by contractors to achieve their affirmative action goals as they would any company goal. Good faith effort is a process, not a result (Jones, 1987). Failure to meet affirmative action goals does not constitute a violation, but it may call for an investigation into the efforts taken to achieve them. On the other hand, meeting affirmative action goals satisfies a contractor's formal obligation. The law does not establish quotas nor has any legal opinion ever required an employer to hire or promote unqualified people or to discriminate against nonminorities. Furthermore, the use of timetables is based on the assumption that progress takes time. Timetables imply that correction of the historical problem will be temporally limited. Historical inequities will take longer to redress, however, than some companies have estimated (Feinberg, 1984).

Reverse Discrimination

A related issue is the claim that affirmative action constitutes reverse discrimination (Glazer, 1975). It is true that the probability of employment and promotion decreases for White men as more minorities and women enter the labor pool. However, their previous advantaged opportunity rested on the exclusion of minorities and women. It is also true that actions taken to reduce disparity will involve some form of preference to qualified candidates from groups that have been traditionally excluded, much as preference to veterans is given, although with much less controversy (Glasser, 1988). Some who believe the eventual goal of color-blindness in employment decision making to be appropriate question whether color-conscious affirmative action is an appropriate means for reaching it (Glazer, 1988). The U.S. Supreme Court, nevertheless, has stated (*Fullilove v. Klutznick*, 1980) that it is not unconstitutional to use race as a basis for decision making in situations where affirmative action plans are appropriately designed. Merit and seniority remain part of the decision-making process, and as long as no one is excluded from consideration, then the rights of majority members will not be violated.

Two Forms of Discrimination

There are two legal uses of the term *discrimination*—disparate treatment at the individual level (the traditional notion), and disparate impact at the group level. Any company practice involving employment decisions (i.e., hiring, terminations, layoffs, transfers, rates of pay, promotions, training, performance appraisals) can be examined for promoting disparity between majority and protected class groups. This latter concept takes discrimination out of the quagmire produced by a focus on intentions with respect to individual decisions into the more objective dimension of equality.

The Dilemma of Equality

How would one know (measure) whether equal opportunity exists? Simply posting an EEO policy or developing an affirmative action plan will not create it. A measure based on the number of EEO complaints filed by employees is misleading because evidence of few complaints might simply reflect a climate of fear of retribution rather than an absence of discrimination. Yet if one examines results and finds inequality, then how does one know if it is because of discrimination or instead, if there are actual group-level differences in ability, motivation, education, interest, etc.? We suggest that many, if not all, existing differences are due to the legacy of systematic exclusion. Alternatively, we ask what conditions would constitute equality and what company actions would produce these conditions. First, assuming that job requirements and employment practices are valid, absence of discrimination at the individual level and equal qualifications at the group level would provide equal opportunity. Existing disparities, however, would persist. If there are existing disparities in particular job categories, then companies can give limited preference to protected class members over equally qualified White men to ensure increased minority and women's inclusion in those targeted areas. This shift from equal opportunity at the individual level to an additional consideration for protected class status is designed to promote equality at the group level.

Second, group level differences in expectations, preparation, or qualifications can be addressed by compensatory efforts such as training, job assignments, mentoring, and educational support, to help a larger percentage of potential candidates in the protected class meet job qualifications and performance levels. Finally, we can ask at what point is affirmative action no longer necessary and reply "when there is no longer evidence of underutilization of the available pool of previously excluded applicants." We believe that the government has a moral obligation to eliminate disparities of opportunities and that affirmative action is an effective mechanism for targeting underutilization. Although many extraneous factors can contribute to inequality, results will test whether a good-faith effort was made to promote equality of opportunity. It should be evident that affirmative action in industry, in itself, cannot (nor was it designed to) eliminate all the inequities produced by institutionalized racism.

Objective Data on Progress

There has been some progress in inclusion of minorities and women in employment shares, income level, and occupational distribution (Smith & Welch, 1984). The gaps that remain in these areas, however, are greater than the gains. There has been no such improvement in unemployment levels—Blacks comprise 10% of the employed but 22% of the unemployed. Black incomes have risen from about 60% to 75% of White incomes. There has been no relative change for White women, and Black women are now at parity with White women—both earn about 60% of White male earnings. The most serious evidence of exclusion is in the executive ranks. Only one Black leads a Fortune 500 or Service 500 company and less than 1% of corporate vice presidents are minorities (Farnham, 1989).

A series of econometric studies by Leonard show that Black male, Black female, and White female employment shares increased significantly faster in federal contractor than noncontractor companies, those required to have an affirmative action plan versus those not required to (Leonard, 1984a). Thus, affirmative action plans can make a difference in progress. Compliance reviews of affirmative action plans are formal investigation processes and a frequent form of sanction by the Office of Federal Contract Compliance Programs. Positive impact on Black male employment was greater in reviewed than nonreviewed contractors, and the effect of being reviewed was twice as great as the effect of affirmative action plan requirements (Leonard, 1985a). Title VII litigation (discrimination cases) also plays a significant role in increasing Black employment, particularly in professional and management positions (Leonard, 1984b). Thus, direct pressure makes an even greater impact on progress. Companies promise more in their goals than they deliver in their results (Leonard, 1985b). Nevertheless, those who promise more also achieve more. Indeed, a company's affirmative action goal is the single best predictor of subsequent employment demographics, far better than its own past history. Company commitment, then, is a critical component of affirmative action success. Opponents of affirmative action may claim that employers discriminate on the basis of merit rather than race. If this were true, then one would expect lower levels of productivity associated with higher levels of minority inclusion. Leonard (1984b) found no evidence to support this and no other research has been done to investigate this basis of opposition.[1]

In conclusion, an assessment of current status is that the progress toward eradicating gaps on economic indicators has been smaller than the gaps that remain. Beyond gradual progress, requirements for affirmative action plans significantly increase progress, but federal pressure has an even larger effect. Affirmative action goals do not equate in principle or in practice to quotas; however, more ambitious company-set goals produce more substantial results. Sustained progress can be ensured by both corporate commitment and federal agency surveillance.

ATTITUDES TOWARD EQUAL OPPORTUNITY AND AFFIRMATIVE ACTION

Neither law nor company policy can prescribe or prohibit privately held attitudes. If regarded as dispositions to act, then prejudiced attitudes can be conceived as dispositions to discriminate. Thus, they can serve to guide legally prohibited actions in the workplace. In addition, the implementation and success of affirma-

---

[1]The editors have raised an interesting pair of questions: a) would liberals still support affirmative action if it did have significant productivity costs? and b) would conservatives still oppose it (on procedural grounds) if it actually stimulated productivity? Until such data are collected, these questions remain rhetorical.

tive action depends on the cooperation and commitment of employees in general and management in particular.

Conventional racial prejudice, the denial of legal and social rights to equality, has greatly declined and there is now near unanimous belief that Blacks should have equal opportunity (Burnstein, 1979). Despite the increased acceptance of the principle of equality for Blacks, there has been little change in attitudes toward affirmative action. Based on economic indicators of equality, three-fourths of White Americans hold unrealistic beliefs about the progress that has been made and the degree to which equality of opportunity currently exists for Black Americans. It follows that most Whites believe: "if there isn't a problem, you don't need a solution" (Kluegel, 1985). Three of four Whites believe that there are no longer unfair employment conditions and that Blacks are now favored. One of two believes that reverse discrimination exists (Kluegel & Smith, 1982). Finally, in 1978, only 11% of Whites favored preferential treatment to make up for past discrimination (Lipset & Schneider, 1978). Essentially confirming the persistence of this opposition, more recently (Kantrowitz & Springer, 1988), only 14% of Whites support preferential treatment of Blacks over equally qualified Whites because of past discrimination.

Racial Similarities and Differences of Opinion

In order to understand more clearly attitudes of Whites toward affirmative action, it is useful to consider attitudes of Blacks as well. Racial/ethnic groups differ in their attitudes toward the amount of progress, its rate, and support for implementation. As Whites increasingly see more progress toward equality, Blacks increasingly see less (Schuman, Steeh, & Bobo, 1985). Consistent with this, increasingly more Whites believe that change is "moving at the right pace," whereas increasingly more Blacks believe it is "moving too slowly." Black support of implementation is generally much higher than that by Whites. Nevertheless, the gap between principle and implementation, although only half as great as for Whites, is also present for Blacks. Although 40% of Blacks support preferential treatment to redress inequality (Kantrowitz & Springer, 1988)—a larger percentage than that of Whites—nevertheless, the majority of both groups share the same opinion. Reasons given by Blacks for opposition to busing (half oppose it) are the same as those given by White opponents (Schuman et al., 1985). Finally, many of the temporal trends in White attitudes are paralleled by the trends in Black attitudes (Schuman et al., 1985). These similar opinions between racial groups suggest that not all opposition to affirmative action can be attributed to racism. Other factors need to be considered.

Sociodemographic Variation

Significant age differences are found on conventional racial prejudice, with younger cohorts being less prejudiced (Davis, 1980). There are similar age differences in support of principles of equality (Schuman et al., 1985) as well as in perceived causes of Black–White socioeconomic disparity (Kluegel & Smith, 1982). Thus, successive cohorts appear to be less prejudiced toward Blacks, although recent survey data suggest an increase in prejudice among younger cohorts.[2] In contrast, however, there is no evidence of age differences in perceived limits to Black opportunities at the social or structural level (Kluegel, 1985) and no differences in support of affirmative action (Schuman et al., 1985). Jackman (1978) noted that education correlates with support of general principles but not with applied policies. Kluegel (1985), however, found that realistic beliefs (e.g., that Blacks have less than average opportunity and this has not improved a great deal) are related to more education, as well as living outside the South, and, to a lesser degree, to age, income, and occupational status. Again, the different patterns of opinion toward principle and practice suggest a more complex picture.

WHY DO PEOPLE OPPOSE AFFIRMATIVE ACTION?

Opposition to affirmative action can rest on any of several independent reasons: racism, economic threat, conservative values, opposition to government intervention in general, justification of the in-group's relatively superior position, personal self-interest, or meritocracy (to each according to one's accomplishments). Since many minorities do not support it either, one must ask if some similar reasons might not apply. Sociopsychological research on racism, values, stereotyping, attributions, perceived threat, divergent perceptions, social projection, in-group favoritism, and stigmatization, however, can provide a framework for understanding opposition and a basis for devising strategies of intervention.

Racism, Old-Fashioned and Modern

The classical definition of prejudice is negative affect (toward Blacks) coupled with belief systems that are stereotype-driven. Racism, then, results in discrepancies in level and type of participation in the institutions of society. In a review of experimental studies (Crosby, Bromley, & Saxe, 1980), consistent evidence shows that many Whites, when given the opportunity to discriminate against Blacks, will do so in unobtrusive conditions, particularly when face-to-face interaction is not involved. Several recent studies (Dovidio, Mann, & Gaertner, 1989) show a consistent pattern of White subjects evaluating both Black and White targets similarly on negative dimensions. In contrast, on positive dimensions White targets are evaluated more favorably—"Blacks are not worse, but Whites are better." Reviews of studies in which both Black and White behavior is assessed, however, find that same-race preference is equally displayed (Crosby et al., 1980; Krager & Ford, 1985).

Symbolic Racism

Kinder and Sears (1981) propose that old-fashioned racism has been replaced by "symbolic racism," a new and different form that fuses negative sentiment and stereotypes with traditional American values. It is pernicious precisely because it can masquerade (to self and to others) as a legitimate and socially acceptable expression of values without any appearance of racial sentiment. Symbolic racism theorists argue that apparent progress in attitudes toward equality for Blacks from

[2]The editors have informed us that John Robinson has collected recent data that indicates the relationship between age and conservativeness takes an inverted U form.

survey data merely reflects a social desirability response bias and that "true" beliefs find their expression in such things as opposition to busing and affirmative action. The construct of symbolic racism is criticized on several grounds by Sniderman and Tetlock (1986a, 1986b), particularly for the confounding of independent and dependent variables. Defining opposition to affirmative action as racism precludes establishing any relationship between the two and automatically negates the question of whether there are reasons for opposition to affirmative action that are nonracist.

Stereotypes and Attributions

Stereotypic beliefs about the characteristics associated with certain groups contribute to the formation and maintenance of prejudice. In a 1978 survey, half of Whites believe Blacks are less ambitious than Whites and one-fourth of Whites believe Blacks are less intelligent (cited in Sniderman & Tetlock, 1986b). Additionally, one-third of Whites see Blacks as breeding crime, living off the handout, and being more violent. Only one in eight Whites does not agree with any racial stereotype and 80% of men, compared to 18% of women, do not agree with any gender stereotype (Fernandez, 1988). V. E. Schein (1973, 1975) found that both female and male managers share a stereotype of the successful manager—one that is decidedly masculine. It is difficult to imagine that Blacks and women have as equal an opportunity as White men when they must compete against stereotypes not only about their group but about ideal candidates as well, neither of which may be valid or appropriate.

Kluegel and Smith (1982) examined Whites' explanations of poverty and found that four internal reasons (e.g., lack of effort) were endorsed more often than four external reasons (e.g., not enough jobs). Similar patterns occurred with respect to reasons for wealth. Thus, the ideology of economics displays the fundamental attribution error (Ross, 1977), that is, the tendency for internal causes to be more salient than external causes. Consequently, people hold individuals responsible rather than social, historical, and structural conditions. This is consistent with the belief in a just world—people receive what they deserve, and so most people blame the victim (Ryan, 1971). Two-thirds of Whites believe that Blacks have worse jobs, income, and housing because of lack of motivation; one-fourth attribute these conditions to innate abilities. Whites are seen as relatively more successful because they work harder, whereas laziness accounts for the Blacks' plight (Kluegel & Smith, 1982). Disparity in attribution occurs in the face of identical behavior by Black and White actors (Duncan, 1976). The "ultimate attribution error" is the reinforcement of group differences with selective explanations that justify the ingroup's advantaged position (Pettigrew, 1977).

Threat and Conflict of Interest

Threat increases intragroup cohesiveness (Campbell, 1958) and thereby increases intergroup category distinctiveness. The stronger the feeling of relative deprivation among Whites, the greater are the denial of past discrimination against minorities and the belief in reverse discrimination (Kluegel & Smith, 1982). Conflict of interest, such as that produced by layoffs, generates aggressive intent

(Struch & Schwartz, 1989) and creates additional challenge to affirmative action by making it a target for displaced hostility. When attitudes toward affirmative action in industry were assessed (Kluegel & Smith, 1983), self-interest (the perceived risk of being laid off) significantly affected attitudes of young employees toward affirmative action, specifically those with less seniority and at greater risk. Layoffs are a difficult issue. Seniority, which is unrelated to merit, can have a major impact on layoff decisions, thereby threatening to undermine the ground slowly gained under affirmative action plans. Minorities and women may be hurt less by layoffs, however, when companies are under affirmative action requirements (Leonard, 1987).

Different Perspectives and Social Projection

The process of social projection operates to support beliefs. In the absence of knowledge about what similar others believe, one assumes that they share similar beliefs. On the issue of segregation, however, although only one in seven Whites supports it, half believe the majority supports it (O'Gorman, 1979). This is because segregationists overestimate how many agree with them, whereas opponents of segregation underestimate how many Whites also oppose it. Attitudes can be reinforced when they are perceived to be normative. Although some researchers have been quick to dismiss increased favorability toward Blacks in surveys as a social desirability response bias, this in itself suggests the potential of perceived norms to shape behavior.

Attitudes can also be shaped by knowledge, empathy, or personal experience. There is little evidence on how these sources influence attitudes toward affirmative action, but, in general, direct experience with an attitude object leads to more positive attitude change (Fazio & Zanna, 1981). There seems to be an absence of both public and personal sources of objective information about national conditions of disparity, for example. It is not known if employees even understand what affirmative action legislation requires or know the actual hiring and promotion disparities within their own company. It is known, for example, that many men do not have a practical knowledge of sexual harassment laws, and men's perceptions of what behaviors constitute harassment differ markedly from women's (Konrad & Gutek, 1986). Only three in five men think that "touching meant to be sexual" or "sexual looks or gestures meant to be insulting" constitute harassment, compared to five in six women. Harassment is legally defined as conduct that unreasonably interferes with an individual's work performance or creates an intimidating, hostile, or offensive working environment (Simmons, 1985).

Category Distinctiveness and the Stigma of Affirmative Action

Literature on intergroup relations shows the preference given to members of one's own group, independent of any past history between the groups or personal gain. Social identity theory (Tajfel & Turner, 1985) posits that individuals need to feel good about themselves, about their personal and social identity. In situations where group membership is salient, people identify with and favor their in-group members at the cost of devaluing out-group members (Brewer, 1979). This is evidenced even when an otherwise homogeneous group is divided on some trivial basis into an in- and an out-group. There are processes more basic than those covered earlier that can account for this bias—specifically categorization and competitive social comparison. Thus, there is evidence that prejudice is not target specific, but rather is a generalized hostility toward out-groups (Weigel & Howes, 1985). A dilemma, then, is that affirmative action makes group boundaries salient; it polarizes the workforce into social in- and out-groups. Factors that increase the salience and distinctiveness of social categories will augment prejudice and bias. To defuse the situation, Brewer and Miller (1984) recommend strategies for reducing category salience and promoting personalization of individuals. The implementations of these strategies are considered in the following section.

One of the objections to affirmative action is that it stigmatizes minorities and women with its emphasis on category-based rather than merit-based treatment. It conveys the impression that minorities receive help because they need it. Therefore, it implies they are less qualified, thus reinforcing existing stereotypes (Heilman & Herlihy, 1984). Evidence of the negative impact of this stigma has been obtained (Chacko, 1982; Kanter, 1977). Opposition to affirmative action among minorities may be based on this additional burden. Not only are they often in a "solo" position, they are also accorded "token" status, both of which can debilitate performance and limit opportunities (Crocker & McGraw, 1984; Pettigrew & Martin, 1987).

POLICY IMPLICATIONS

Affirmative action is an appropriate response for redressing historical inequalities. Company-set goals and timetables in affirmative action plans help this progress, and federal pressure in terms of compliance reviews and sanctions further facilitates it. White Americans, however, express considerable opposition to affirmative action, only part of which can be attributed to racism. We do not propose that racism can be eradicated. Other basic sociopsychological processes, however, act to buttress opposition to affirmative action, and these can be addressed. Companies need a strategy to produce positive attitude change, reduce threat, minimize stereotypes, alter norms, foster accurate perceptions and attributions, reduce ingroup favoritism, develop intergroup cooperation, and avoid stigmatization. The challenge is complex.

In a survey of Fortune 500 CEOs, two-thirds saw the effect of affirmative action in U.S. business as good, very good, or outstanding, and only 8% expect to extend more effort to promote affirmative action (Farnham, 1989). Only 2% and 1% of human resource executives consider EEO and sexual harassment, respectively, to be one of the three major human resources management issues (L. Schein, 1986). Why should companies invest more in this effort? First, legislative, executive, and judicial attention is an important incentive. Second, dramatic changes in new entrants to the labor pool indicate that only one in three will be a native-born White man ("A second look at America's workers," 1990). Companies must come to grips with the changing nature of the available labor pool. Third, disruptions to productivity and innovation can occur as a result of intergroup conflict (Cohen, Arechavala-Vargas, Nobel, & Shenhav, 1985). Lowered morale among all groups could result from perceptions of a company's affirmative action plan. One in eight of the CEOs mentioned above say their affirmative action plan has produced contention and controversy. Fourth, failure to utilize the talents of female and minority employees must be costly. Fifth, when one focuses on numbers and not on persons, the "revolving-door syndrome" can occur— dissatisfied women and minorities leave only to be replaced by others without company concern about the conditions fostering dissatisfaction. Half of those same CEOs said the "pirating away of their minority managers has thwarted their affirmative action efforts." This was the most frequent description of the programs, but mobility is a facet of middle management that is equally present among White managers. Finally, opponents can undermine the company as well as the affirmative action efforts, for example, by promoting those who are unprepared or unsupported or by using the "grapevine" to distort company policy or actions.

Although the issues are complex and we do not have the solution, we do offer some recommendations for a corporate strategy. We consider four groups: executives, supervisors and managers, employees in general, and protected class members in particular. We recognize the problems at different employment stages and organizational levels, particularly top management positions. We focus on the policies, plans, practices, structures, and systems that can support successful affirmative action efforts. Conditions that have ameliorative effects on intergroup relations are used as organizing principles (Allport, 1954; Cook, 1978; Miller & Brewer, 1984). These are:

1. Normative support from authorities and leaders who affirm egalitarian principles and personally endorse these other activities,
2. Cooperative interaction and participation in group decision making,
3. Shared goals that require interdependent interaction,
4. Identification with a superordinate group that encompasses those who would otherwise remain in-group or out-group members,
5. Equal status contact or equal opportunity to contribute,
6. Personal contact that promotes individualizing interaction,
7. Information that helps to disconfirm stereotypes,
8. Successful outcomes, and
9. Interdependent rewards that allow all participants to share in the team success.

Our recommendations are in eight areas. Each is designed to promote one or more of the conditions above. We do not propose that any one, by itself, will produce positive results, or that enough is known about any one to avoid problems and failures, but rather, that collectively they represent a useful concerted effort. We start with the assumption that a company-specific plan is based on objective data within the company on distributions and levels of jobs, responsibilities, pay, performance appraisals, and promotion histories, and on information about availabilities within the workforce and the community.

Executive Commitment

Companies need to state clearly why they have an EEO policy and an affirmative action plan. That includes the philosophies, objectives, methods of implementation, interrelationships, and the evidence and values upon which they are based. Executives play a central role in establishing egalitarian norms and the priority of affirmative action goals. Perceived commitment to affirmative action by top management is a key factor for its successful implementation (Hitt & Keats, 1984;

Marino, 1980). While maintaining visible normative support for affirmative action, we disagree with Dovidio et al. (1989) that companies should label resistance to affirmative action as racist. We have attempted to demonstrate that this may not always be accurate. Such incendiary comments are likely to fuel the fire and increase perceived threat.

Employee Awareness

An employee awareness program can articulate the company's policy and plan. If all groups of employees have the opportunity for participation in the development of a company strategy, a company can overcome resistance to change and promote greater acceptance (Coch & French, 1948; Weigel & Cook, 1975). In addition, awareness sessions can sensitize employees to the ubiquitous and insidious natures of stereotypes, harassment, discrimination, and stigmatization, as well as to explain what is expected of all employees and what will not be tolerated.

Valid Practices

Companies can help by demythologizing career development. It is often as much a result of social networks (the good old boy club), favoritism, selective sharing of informal rules, and serendipity as it is a product of qualifications. Legislative and judicial actions have forced companies to improve understanding of what qualifications are validly required for a position, to develop better methods for measuring them, and to devise practices for applying them fairly. Organizational psychologists have contributed much to these areas (Arvey, 1979; Cascio & Bernardin, 1981; Thompson & Thompson, 1982). Companies need to articulate their affirmative action position and practices clearly so all employees know that minorities and women who are hired or promoted have met the qualifications for the position and that standards have not and need not be lowered to promote equality in those areas where it has been found lacking.

Supervisory Training

Supervisors and managers need training in dealing with subordinates on harassment issues, in understanding their own role in implementing EEO/affirmative action policy and in human relations, as well as their personal accountability. Human relations training can be an effective tool (Burke & Day, 1986). Supervisors and managers need to know that they are accountable at all levels.

Recruitment and Orientation

Recruitment of minorities and women will require greater cooperation with the community and support of education to increase qualified candidates within the labor pool. Employment interviews promote the personalization of minority and female applicants (Dovidio et al., 1989). In practice, however, such inquiries could be taken as attempts to identify protected-class information, making them indefensible as job-relevant, and therefore, proscribed by law. Recruiters, personnel, and line managers who conduct interviews, therefore, need to be trained in fair and appropriate methods designed to reduce potential bias. New members of the work group should be personalized in their introductions, and their personal sense of self should be presented as well as their qualifications, experience, or education (Pettigrew & Martin, 1987).

Training and Career Development

A method should be developed to identify high-potential minority and female candidates and programs should be designed to facilitate their development by training them in precisely those skills most valued by the company. Minority and female professionals and managers, in particular, will need greater support of their development to remain and to advance. Mentoring of minority new hires can be an effective method of orientation and development (Ford, 1988).

Incentives and Sanctions

Incentive programs should support company goals in activities such as recruitment, training, mentoring, and promotion of minorities and women in order to communicate their importance. Likewise, appropriate sanctions need to be applied uniformly and visibly in cases of harassment and discrimination. Policy needs to be reinforced by appropriate systems. Procedures whereby complaints can be presented without fear of retribution and receive fair and timely resolution need to be in place and perceived as credible.

Cooperative Workgroups

Planned workgroup interventions that focus on teamwork within ethnicly diverse groups can be developed to promote mutual respect. Conditions and activities that decrease the salience and relevance of one's social category membership and that promote the personalization of individuals will promote the positive acceptance of out-group members (Brewer & Miller, 1984). When appropriate to the task and given adequate support, cooperative heterogeneous teams can be effectively utilized to facilitate positive intergroup relations (cf. Miller & Harrington, 1989, for implementation issues and strategies). Diversity of talents, viewpoints, and backgrounds bring innovation to the team. Team projects are also an appropriate place to develop the leadership skills of minorities and women. Given the resources for success, shared goals can solidify a diverse group. Individual contributions can be recognized and team efforts can be rewarded.

Companies face a difficult challenge. The tendency to underestimate the seriousness of the issue, however, can diminish corporate responsibility to society. Furthermore, policy makers need a greater understanding of the extent and complexity of resistance to affirmative action in particular and to change in general. Armed with greater awareness, companies will need to raise the priority of affirmative action goals to increase progress. They will need strategic plans that are, on the one hand, sufficiently tailored, and on the other hand, extensive enough to provide the conditions that promote both positive results and intergroup acceptance. Given the success of corporate America's ingenuity, resourcefulness, and persistence, it would appear that greater willingness is the critical factor.

REFERENCES

Allport, G. W. (1954). *The nature of prejudice.* Reading, MA: Addison-Wesley.
Arvey, R. D. (1979). Unfair discrimination in the employment interview: Legal and psychological aspects. *Psychological Bulletin, 86,* 736–765.
Brewer, M. B. (1979). In-group bias in the minimal intergroup situation: A cognitive–motivational analysis. *Psychological Bulletin, 86,* 307–324.
Brewer, M. B., & Miller, N. (1984). Beyond the contact hypothesis: Theoretical perspectives on

desegregation. In N. Miller & M. B. Brewer (Eds.), *The psychology of desegregation* (pp. 281–302). New York: Academic Press.

Burke, M. J., & Day, R. D. (1986). A cumulative study of the effectiveness of managerial training. *Journal of Applied Psychology, 71*, 232–245.

Burnstein, P. (1979). Public opinion, demonstrations, and the passage of antidiscrimination legislation. *Public Opinion Quarterly, 79*, 152–172.

Campbell, D. T. (1958). Common fate, similarity, and other indices of stress of aggregates of persons as social entities. *Behavioral Science, 3*, 14–25.

Cascio, W. F., & Bernardin, H. J. (1981). Implications of performance appraisal litigation for personnel decisions. *Personnel Psychology, 34*, 211–226.

Chacko, T. T. (1982). Women and equal employment opportunity: Some unintended effects. *Journal of Applied Psychology, 67*, 119–123.

Civil Rights Act of 1964 (Title VII). 78 Stat.

Coch, L., & French, J. R. F. (1948). Overcoming resistance to change. *Human Relations, 1*, 512–532.

Cohen, B. P., Arechavala-Vargas, R., Nobel, D. R., & Shenhav, Y. A. (1985). *Organization and productivity in R & D teams: A report of research findings.* Unpublished report, Stanford University, Stanford, CA.

Cook, S. W. (1978). Interpersonal and attitudinal outcomes in cooperating interracial groups. *Journal of Research and Development in Education, 12*, 97–113.

Crocker, J., & McGraw, K. M. (1984). What's good for the goose is not good for the gander: Solo status as an obstacle to occupational achievement for males and females. *American Behavioral Scientist, 27*, 357–369.

Crosby, F., Bromley, S., & Saxe, L. (1980). Recent unobtrusive studies of Black and White discrimination and prejudice: A literature review. *Psychological Bulletin, 87*, 546–563.

Davis, J. A. (1980). *General social surveys, 1972–1980: Cumulative data.* New Haven, CT: Roper Public Opinion Research Center.

Dovidio, J. F., Mann, J., & Gaertner, S. L. (1989). Resistance to affirmative action: The implications of aversive racism. In F. A. Blanchard & F. J. Crosby (Eds.), *Affirmative action in perspective* (pp. 83–103). New York: Springer-Verlag.

Duncan, B. L. (1976). Differential social perception and attribution of intergroup violence: Testing the lower limit of stereotyping of Blacks. *Journal of Personality and Social Psychology, 34*, 590–598.

Executive Order No. 11246. (1965). 3 C.F.R. 339.

Farnham, A. (1989, March 13). Holding firm on affirmative action. *Fortune, 119*, 87–88.

Fazio, R. H., & Zanna, M. P. (1981). Direct experience and attitude-behavior consistency. In L. Berkowitz (Ed.), *Advances in experimental social psychology* (Vol. 14, pp. 161–202). New York: Academic Press.

Feinberg, W. E. (1984). At a snail's pace: Time to equality in simple models of affirmative action programs. *American Journal of Sociology, 90*, 168–181.

Fernandez, J. P. (1988). Racism and sexism in corporate America: Still not color- or gender-blind in the 1980s. In D. Thompson & N. DiTomaso (Eds.), *Ensuring minority success in corporate management* (pp. 71–99). New York: Plenum Press.

Ford, D. L. (1988). Minority and nonminority MBA progress in business. In D. E. Thompson & N. DiTomaso (Eds.), *Ensuring minority success in corporate management* (pp. 57–69). New York: Plenum Press.

Fullilove v. Klutznick. (1980). 448 U.S. 448.

Glasser, I. (1988). Affirmative action and the legacy of racial injustice. In P. A Katz & D. A. Taylor (Eds.), *Eliminating racism: Profiles in controversy* (pp. 341–357). New York: Plenum Press.

Glazer, N. (1975). *Affirmative discrimination.* Cambridge, MA: Harvard University Press.

Glazer, N. (1988). The future of preferential affirmative action. In P. A Katz & D. A. Taylor (Eds.), *Eliminating racism: Profiles in controversy* (pp. 329–339). New York: Plenum Press.

Hawkins, A. F. (Chair). (1987). *A report of the study on affirmative action to the Committee on Education and Labor.* Washington, DC: U.S. Government Printing Office.

Heilman, M. E., & Herlihy, J. M. (1984). Affirmative action, negative reaction? Some moderating conditions. *Organizational Behavior and Human Performance, 33*, 204–213.

Hitt, M. A., & Keats, B. W. (1984). Empirical identification of the criteria for effective affirmative action programs. *Journal of Applied Behavioral Science, 20*, 203–222.

Jackman, M. R. (1978). General and applied tolerance: Does education increase commitment to racial integration? *American Journal of Political Science, 22*, 302–324.

Jones, J. E. (1987). The origins of affirmative action. In A. F. Hawkins (Chair), *A report of the study* group on *affirmative action to the Committee on Education and Labor* (pp. 160–211). Washington, DC: U.S. Government Printing Office.

Kanter, R. M. (1977). Some effects of proportions on group life: Skewed sex ratios and responses to token women. *American Journal of Sociology, 82,* 965–991.

Kantrowitz, B., & Springer, K. (1988, March 7). A tenuous bond from 9 to 5. *Newsweek, 111,* 24–25.

Kinder, D. R., & Sears, D. O. (1981). Prejudice and politics: Symbolic racism versus racial threats to the good life. *Journal of Personality and Social Psychology, 40,* 414–431.

Kluegel, J. R. (1985). If there isn't a problem, you don't need a solution. *American Behavioral Scientist, 28,* 761–784.

Kluegel, J. R., & Smith, E. R. (1982). Whites' beliefs about Blacks' opportunity. *American Sociological Review, 47,* 518–532.

Kluegel, J. R., & Smith, E. R. (1983). Affirmative action attitudes: Effects of self interest, racial affect, and stratification beliefs on Whites' views. *Social Forces, 61,* 797–824.

Konrad, A. M., & Gutek, B. A. (1986). Impact of work experiences on attitudes toward sexual harassment. *American Sociological Quarterly, 31,* 422–438.

Krager, K., & Ford, J. K. (1985). A meta-analysis of ratee effects in performance ratings. *Journal of Applied Psychology, 70,* 56–65.

Leonard, J. S. (1984a). The impact of affirmative action on employment. *Journal of Labor Economics, 2,* 439–463.

Leonard, J. S. (1984b). Anti-discrimination or reverse discrimination: The impact of changing demographics, Title VII, and affirmative action on productivity. *Journal of Human Resources, 19,* 145–174.

Leonard, J. S. (1985a). Affirmative action as earnings distribution: The targeting of compliance reviews. *Journal of Labor Economics, 3,* 363–384.

Leonard, J. S. (1985b). What promises are worth: The impact of affirmative action goals. *Journal of Human Resources, 19,* 145–174.

Leonard, J. S. (1987). The impact of affirmative action regulations and equal opportunity law. In A. Hawkins (Chair), *A report of the study group on affirmative action.* Washington, DC: U.S. Government Printing Office.

Lipset, S. M., & Schneider, W. (1978). The Bakke case: How would it be decided at the bar of public opinion? *Public Opinion, 1,* 38–44.

Marino, K. E. (1980). A preliminary investigation into behavioral dimensions of affirmative action compliance. *Journal of Applied Psychology, 65,* 346–350.

Miller, N., & Brewer, M. B. (1984). The social psychology of desegregation: An introduction. In N. Miller & M. B. Brewer (Eds.), *The psychology of desegregation* (pp. 1–8). New York: Academic Press.

Miller, N., & Harrington, H. J. (1989). *Diversity and teamwork in industry: Recommendations from a social-psychological framework.* Unpublished manuscript, University of Southern California.

O'Gorman, H. O. (1979). White and Black perceptions of racial values. *Public Opinion Quarterly, 43,* 48–59.

Pettigrew, T. F. (1977). The ultimate attribution error: Extending Allport's cognitive analysis of prejudice. *Personality and Social Psychology Bulletin, 5,* 461–476.

Pettigrew, T. F., & Martin, J. (1987). Shaping the organizational context for Black American inclusion. *Journal of Social Issues, 43,* 41–78.

Ross, L. (1977). The intuitive psychologist and his shortcomings: Distortions in the attribution process. In L. Berkowitz (Ed.), *Advances in experimental social psychology* (Vol. 10, pp. 174–220). New York: Academic Press.

Ryan, W. (1971). *Blaming the victim.* New York: Pantheon.

Schein, L. (1986). Current issues in human resource management. *The Conference Board Research Bulletin, 190,* 1–14.

Schein, V. E. (1973). The relationship between sex role stereotypes and requisite management characteristics. *Journal of Applied Psychology, 57,* 95–100.

Schein, V. E. (1975). The relationship between sex role stereotypes and requisite management characteristics among women. *Journal of Applied Psychology, 60,* 340–344.

Schuman, H., Steeh, C., & Bobo, L. (1985). *Racial attitudes in America.* Cambridge, MA: Harvard University Press.

A second look at America's workers. (1990, November 19). *U.S. News and World Report.*

Simmons, R. J. (1985). *Employment discrimination and EEO practice manual.* Van Nuys, CA: Castle Publications.

Smith, J. P., & Welch, F. (1984). Affirmative action and labor markets. *Journal of Labor Economics, 2*, 269–301.

Sniderman, P. M., & Tetlock, P. E. (1986a). Symbolic racism: Problems of motive attribution in political analysis. *Journal of Social Issues, 42*, 129–150.

Sniderman, P. M., & Tetlock, P. E. (1986b). Reflections on American racism. *Journal of Social Issues, 42*, 173–187.

Struch, N., & Schwartz, S. H. (1989). Intergroup aggression: Its predictors and distinctions from in-group bias. *Journal of Personality and Social Psychology, 56*, 364–373.

Tajfel, H., & Turner, J. C. (1985). The social identity theory of intergroup behavior. In S. Worchel & W. Austin (Eds.), *Psychology of intergroup relations* (pp. 7–24). Chicago: Nelson-Hall.

Thompson, D. E., & Thompson, T. A. (1982). Court standards for job analysis in test validation. *Personnel Psychology, 35*, 865–874.

Weigel, R. H., & Cook, S. W. (1975). Participation in decision making: A determinant of interpersonal attraction in cooperating interracial groups. *International Journal of Group Tensions, 5*, 179–195.

Weigel, R. H., & Howes, P. W. (1985). Conceptions of racial prejudice: Symbolic racism reconsidered. *Journal of Social Issues, 41*, 117–138.

9

Affirmative Action: Social Policy as Shibboleth

William R. Beer

Social scientists have generally refused to study the effects of affirmative action in the United States. Although certainly it is one of the most controversial policies ever implemented, and abundant raw data on the subject are available, most researchers have been reluctant to study its consequences. This lack is particularly grievous because affirmative action's justifications rest on misconceptions that could be corrected by scrupulous scholars. One explanation for our ignorance is that affirmative action was never seriously intended to serve as a policy to ameliorate the condition of Black Americans. It is primarily a gesture of expiation made by White liberals to assuage their guilt over past wrong suffered by Blacks and a form of emotional extortion employed by some Black leaders to advance their own agendas. As other minority groups have climbed onto the affirmative action bandwagon, their dynamic has been the same.

I begin with an illustration of the virtual neglect of the subject by social scientists. This stands in sharp contrast to the many surveys showing public hostility about affirmative action, described second. The need for scientific comment is particularly acute because the public debate, as I show in the third part of the chapter, is full of confusions our science can and must clarify.

First, a clarification of the term *affirmative action* is in order. Title VII of the Civil Rights Act of 1964 authorized courts to identify and remedy proved instances of discrimination and take "such affirmative action as may be appropriate." It specifically denied that preferential treatment was authorized [Section 703(j)]. Furthermore, the legislation denied that any kind of racial balance was thereby to be achieved.

Nevertheless, the antipreferential treatment provisions of the act have been systematically ignored. Almost immediately, Executive Order 11246 required businesses contracting with the U.S. government to keep records of the race and sex (the latter after a 1967 amendment) of their employees for the purposes of assessing whether nondiscrimination had been achieved. The Office of Federal Contract Compliance (which was established under the Department of Labor by Executive Order 11246) specified in 1968 that employers must have a plan, including "goals and timetables," for correcting statistical disparities between percentages of protected groups among their employees and a desirable proportion based on a theoretically available labor pool.

Judicial decisions about the constitutionality of these legislative and executive measures have followed a meandering course. In general, until 1989 the U.S. Supreme Court endorsed the preferential treatment aspects of affirmative action, notably in two 1986 decisions that, respectively, permitted Blacks to be hired over more qualified Whites and women to be hired over more qualified men for the specific purpose of achieving statistical balance in a workplace. In 1989, the Court handed down a series of decisions that undermined, but by no means eliminated, the legal basis for racial preference.

An authoritative estimate is that half of all workers in the United States are now subject to these regulations (Smith & Welch, 1986, p. 87). The groups deemed deserving of preferential treatment now include Blacks, women, Hispanics, Asians, Pacific Islanders, Aleuts, Eskimos, and other Native Americans.

In short, affirmative action was originally conceived as a measure aimed at helping Black Americans overcome the effects of past discrimination. It has been transformed into a racially and sexually based hiring system of preferential treatment that aims for comparable statistical representation of all protected groups at all levels of U.S. society.

One of the most surprising aspects of this political and institutional mutation is that its consequences have been left virtually unexamined by social scientists. This is not to say that there is any lack of desire to talk about the subject. In a literature review, Beer (1987a) found that there are roughly four rubrics under which commentary on affirmative action can be classified: polemics, legal analyses, organizational studies, and true empirical studies of affirmative action's societal effects. For brevity, I will give a few examples of the sociological comments that have been made. I will concentrate primarily on affirmative action for Blacks. For a fuller commentary, see also Beer (1987b, 1988).

POLEMICS

Almost by definition, argumentative pieces are of little use in empirical research, because such authors usually tailor facts and logic to fit their arguments. Some claim scholarly status, and three of these will be cited.

Exum (1983) asserts that there are not enough qualified Blacks to fill racial hiring quotas on university faculties, because universities have "standards not easily surmounted by historically disadvantaged minorities" (Exum, 1983, p. 393). In addition to his confusion between the terms *Black* and *minority,* Exum's argument cannot be sustained in the face of the impressive success of Asians in American universities, particularly because for many of them English is not their native language. His inference that the problem lies not in poor educational achievement by minorities but in unreasonably high standards would make it impossible to reconcile affirmative action and academic excellence.

Lincoln (1980, p. 374) says that "affirmative action is an instrument of justice," a compensation by "White America" for past discrimination against Blacks. For him, all of White America is privileged and must atone for the past, a view that is sociologically incorrect if only because there are roughly twice as many poor Whites as poor Blacks. He also ignores the remarkable success of Black West Indians, who are also eligible for preferential treatment according to his argument.

One last citation should suffice for the flavor of scholarly polemics. Sexton (1979, p. 323) claimed, "Affirmative action in an admissions program does not mean that unqualified minority students will gain admission to professional schools." It is hard to see how Sexton could have known this, because at the time there had been no empirical research on the subject. Since then, a study for the Rand Corporation (Keith, Bell, & Williams, 1987) found that, in fact, affirmative action students in medical schools had demonstrably inferior records, both as students and as doctors.

In sum, writers who give opinions under the guise of scholarship do scant service to scholarship and provide little guidance in evaluating the effects of affirmative action.

LEGAL ANALYSES

One of the most prevalent types of commentary on affirmative action has been legal, most of it sociologically questionable.

For example, one of the most articulate juridical defenses of affirmative action was presented by Fullinwider. He offers what he calls "a theory of affirmative action which is nondiscriminatory" (Fullinwider, 1980, p. 170). To justify setting goals for minority hiring by employers, Fullinwider attributes present inequality to past discrimination and asks us to imagine what the selection profile of an employer would look like if there were no discrimination. "The employer should set his goals at that figure one would expect to be realized under nondiscrimination" (Fullinwider, 1980, p. 173).

Affirmative action is necessary because simply not discriminating would keep minorities in the historically subordinate position where they find themselves. Fullinwider argues that employers have a bad habit of discriminating, like a baseball pitcher has a bad habit with pitches. The task of government-imposed affirmative action plans is like that of a coach who has to break a player's bad pitching habit. Without these goals, discrimination will continue.

Fullinwider's mistake is to attribute all racial inequality to discrimination, whereas myriad other factors produce unequal outcomes between different social groups. He also neglects to distinguish between past and present discrimination. Removal of negative barriers does not guarantee that a group will remain in a subordinate position unless it gets special help from the government. The enormous success of Jews in the United States should be enough to give the lie to that notion. Once freed from Tsarist or Arab or communist fetters they have flourished, without a shred of affirmative action.

MANPOWER STUDIES

Numerous studies assess the extent to which statistical disparities between groups have been erased in single organizations as results of programs imposed by outside authorities. These are of little use in assessing the society-wide impact of affirmative action. For example, Owen (1985) carried out open-ended interviews with 1,190 people in San Quentin Prison to find out the effects of affirmative action on prison workers. She found that the policy tended to aggravate tensions in the potentially explosive world of the penitentiary. Milward and Swanson (1979) look at affirmative action in a single urban county in Kansas. Lansky (1978) studied a program that existed for one year in Cincinnati. Booth (1978) studied

2,000 people in the U.S. Navy. Such studies do little besides illustrate some effects of affirmative action in individual polities or organizations.

EMPIRICAL STUDIES

Affirmative action is often mentioned speculatively by sociologists with regard to its overall societal effects. One of the first iconoclasts was Glazer (1976, 1979), who questioned the possible effects of the policy. Similarly, Sowell (1981) and Wilson (1978, 1987) question whether affirmative action will help any but up-wardly mobile college-educated younger Blacks, who may not need preferential treatment. Such questions are well taken, but they merely beg the question of why more research has not been done. Part of the answer is provided by Lynch, who has documented (Lynch, 1984) the extraordinary reluctance of journal editors to deal with the subject.

Two nonsociological findings, by Johnson and by Smith and Welch, underscore sociology's silence. In a psychological report, Johnson (1980a) described how he tested 62 White male subjects in an experimental situation of reverse discrimina-tion. He found that "reverse discrimination is indeed seen as unjust" and that for these young men, at least, "a major reaction to reverse discrimination is the notion that one's actions have less to do with one's successes or failures than one once thought."

In a second report, he concluded that the experiment produced considerably greater amounts of racial animosity toward Blacks who won a competition through preferential treatment rather than through ability (Johnson, 1980b). If these results are reproduced on a societal scale, affirmative action is likely to produce exactly the opposite effect (greater White hostility against Blacks) to that it was intended to produce.

Likewise, an economic study underscores the need for a sociological counter-part. Smith and Welch (1986) document that affirmative action has caused enor-mous increases in Black employment in firms covered by the guidelines and a sharp drop in noncovered firms. This does not mean that affirmative action has increased opportunities for Blacks, it simply means that Blacks go where the pref-erential hiring policies are imposed. It also does not demonstrate that Black oppor-tunities would not have expanded without affirmative action. Finally, Smith and Welch sound an ominous note of reverse discrimination when they say that "Blacks are more likely than White men to work at these [covered] firms" (Smith & Welch, 1986, p. 90). A similar pattern was reported by Leonard (1984a, 1984b).

One of the only truly empirical studies of the effects of affirmative action on American society is a special issue of the *American Behavioral Scientist* edited by Lynch and devoted to assessing the effects of affirmative action (Lynch, 1985). Among others, it includes articles by Jencks and Kluegel that talk about the pol-icy's impact on society.

Jencks reports that the economic effects of affirmative action for Blacks are mixed. While there is evidence that it may have improved the salaries of highly educated Blacks, it did not benefit Black male high school graduates at all. Pres-sure from the government led to intense competition to hire the best-educated Blacks, but since Blacks have much higher school dropout rates this obviously did not benefit Blacks overall. During the period of active affirmative action enforcement, the unemployment rate among young Black men grew sharply, while that for young White men did not. At the same time, there were serious drawbacks. "Affirmative action programs have often led to discrimination against Whites. . . . In some cases a double standard in hiring leads to clear differences in performance between Blacks and Whites doing the same sort of work. . . . The same thing happens in elite private colleges that admit marginal Black students. The presence of such students convinces many students and faculty that Blacks just are not very bright" (Jencks, 1985, p. 753).

Kluegel reviews some survey data on Whites' attitudes about affirmative action, but the material is out of date in comparison to the survey data listed below. Curiously absent is consideration of Blacks' attitudes about preferential treatment. He concludes that Whites' beliefs are based on a "dominant ideology" that prizes individual ambition and that Whites are naively misinformed about the universality with which Blacks suffer from discrimination. Since he favors preferential treatment for Blacks, Kluegel calls for better public relations: "White support is likely to continue to have only the degree of passion that can be generated to make up for a past injustice that is seen as fading in its current impact" (Kluegel, 1985, p. 780).

The special issue also contains legal commentary by Rossum and an essay on the prospect for nondiscriminatory affirmative action by Glazer. Lynch concludes, "The contributors to this volume all seem to share the view that affirmative action must change if it is to survive at all" (Lynch, 1985, p. 841).

SURVEY DATA

There are abundant survey data on the topic, should any social scientist choose to study them. Opinion polls usually ask one of four types of question about this issue:

1. General questions about affirmative action: These usually get endorsements from majorities of Blacks and Whites. In 1977, for example, a CBS/*New York Times* poll found that 68% of Whites and 85% of Blacks agree that "the government should see to it that people who have been discriminated against in the past get a better break in the future." Likewise, in 1984, a Louis Harris poll that found 67% of likely voters favor "affirmative action programs for women and minorities, provided there are no rigid quotas."

2. Questions that explicitly contrast ability with preferential treatment or lowered standards in hiring and school admissions: These usually show strong opposition to preferential treatment among Whites, and weak majorities or minorities among Blacks. In 1986, a Gallup poll asked respondents about their opinions on the Supreme Court decisions of that year permitting hiring and promotion of women and minorities over more qualified White men. Overall, 25% of Whites approved and 69% disapproved. Women were overwhelmingly opposed (67% against); Blacks were more favorable, with 45% in favor. A 1988 Gallup poll asked if Blacks should receive "preference over equally qualified Whites in matters such as getting into college and getting jobs." Only 14% of Whites were in

142   DOMESTIC POLICY

favor and 80% opposed; among Blacks, 40% favored preferential treatment and 50% opposed it.

3. Questions asking whether preferential treatment is called for in specific instances where there has been discrimination in the past: Here one finds the greatest degree of Black support for anti-White discrimination, though a positive answer to this question is not necessarily an endorsement of preferential treatment of Blacks across the board. In a 1988 survey, CBS/*New York Times* found 37% of Whites approved preference for Blacks in these circumstances, compared to 75% of Blacks.

4. Questions asking about the experience or likelihood of anti-White discrimination as a result of preferential affirmative action: Large minorities of Whites believe that such anti-White bias is very likely, and smaller minorities of Whites assert that they personally have been victimized. In a 1984 Gordon Black Associates survey of White registered voters, 1 out of 10 said they had lost a job opportunity or an educational opportunity as a result of affirmative action. In the 1986 National Election Study of the Institute for Social Research, respondents were asked about the chances that a White person does not get admitted to a school while an equally or less qualified Black person gets admitted instead. Those saying anti-White discrimination was very likely account for 27.6% of White respondents, and those saying somewhat likely, for 41.4%. When the same question was asked about a job or promotion, the proportions were nearly identical. When Whites were asked what they thought of the likelihood that they or someone in their families would not get a job or a promotion while an equally or less qualified Black gets one instead, 12.4% of Whites thought it very likely and 28.7% thought it somewhat likely. Again, the responses were nearly identical when the question referred to school admissions.

One other type of survey subject needs to be mentioned—the possible stigma attached to affirmative action as a result of doubts about the qualifications of its beneficiaries. In 1976 a Louis Harris poll asked whether medical schools should lower their standards to increase the proportion of Black doctors. "Should lower standards" was accepted by 10% of Whites and 37% of Blacks, but 86% of Whites and 40% of Blacks said "should not." More recently, a 1988 Gallup poll said that some Blacks benefit from preferential treatment over equally qualified Whites, but that some people feel their achievements are not fully earned. "How big a problem do you think this is for Blacks?" Fully 38% of Blacks thought this was a very serious problem, 53% thought it was somewhat serious, and only 14% thought it was not serious at all.

In short, the survey data show that U.S. citizens endorse affirmative action only when it does not require preferential treatment. When it requires anti-White discrimination, Whites are strongly opposed and Blacks split but tend to be opposed. There is strong Black support for anti-White discrimination only in specific cases where past discrimination has been identified. There is a strong current of belief among Whites that they suffer as a result of affirmative action policies, and there is deep doubt among Blacks about the stigma that affirmative action attaches to them. In light of these figures, the routine practice of racially based recruitment and promotion policies by U.S. municipalities, universities, and corporations does not bode well for future racial harmony.

SOCIOLOGICAL MISCONCEPTIONS

Public debate, both lay and scientific, about affirmative action is clouded by imprecision and confusion. There is great conceptual ambiguity about who the alleged beneficiaries are supposed to be. This is owing largely to the fact that past discrimination, one of the problems the policy is supposed to alleviate, is usually inferred and not objectively measured. And the evidence shows that there is much doubt that present discrimination is a significant problem for Blacks. In fact, affirmative action cannot even be sustained on logical grounds.

Conceptual Ambiguity

Since 1972, the beneficiaries of affirmative action include *minorities*, a term that is seldom defined. In Equal Employment Opportunity Commission policy, for instance, minorities include Black Americans, Hispanics, Aleuts, Asians, and Pacific Islanders, but not Jews, Greek-Americans, or Polish-Americans. A newly arrived immigrant of South American origin is eligible for preferential hiring and school admissions over any young, White, non-Hispanic American whose forebears may have been citizens for generations. Simply being Hispanic bestows oppressed status in the United States, a practice that greatly amuses wealthy Cuban-Americans. There is no sociologically valid explanation for it.

The criterion used for establishing which groups are minorities is often simply a question of political pressure. At the City University of New York, Italian-Americans recently were designated a minority for affirmative action purposes for the first time. In some midwestern cities, Appalachians, that is, Whites whose forebears are from the poverty-stricken Appalachian Mountain areas, have been called a minority for affirmative action (Lansky, 1978).

Much of this ambiguity can be blamed on social scientists who use the term *minority* in an attempt to lump into a homogeneous class all those who are allegedly oppressed in the United States:

> A minority group *is a subordinate group whose members have significantly less control or power over their own lives than the members of a dominant or majority group. . . . A minority group does not share in proportion to its numbers in what a given society, such as the United States, defines as valuable. (Schaefer, 1988, p. 5)*

The weakness of such definitions consists in the assumption that there is a single majority group in the United States. Moreover, the only measure of subordination Schaefer proposes is that of statistical disparity, which in no way can be considered proof of subordination. If statistical disparity were proof of subordination, men should be considered a minority because almost all prison inmates are male. One doubts if Schaefer would accept this use of his definition.

Methodological Crudity

One ostensible purpose of affirmative action is to alleviate the effects of past discrimination, yet no adequate measure of past discrimination has ever been devised. Most analyses and polemics rely on what can be called *the fallacy of inferred past discrimination,* whereby present unemployment or poor educational achievement is allegedly the result of past hardship. Although the connection between past discrimination and present deprivation has a certain intuitive appeal, it cannot be substantiated scientifically.

Sowell has pointed out the mistake of imputing a relation between past discrimination and present prosperity or lack thereof. In his words, "The *moral* offensiveness of discrimination has attracted much attention, but whether its *cause-and-effect* role is equally important is another question" (Sowell, 1981, p. 6). He presents a table, reproduced here, that lists ethnic groups according to where their family incomes lie in relation to the U.S. national average (see Table 9.1).

Three of the four most prosperous groups in Table 9.1 (Jewish Americans, Chinese-Americans, and Japanese-Americans) suffered from systematic discrimination in the past, and two of those three are nonwhite. Black Americans, conversely, have low family incomes, but West Indians, who are also Black, have incomes close to the national average. The historical record shows that slavery was much harsher in the West Indies than in the southern United States. Where is the connection between race, past discrimination, and poverty in this table?

Jencks provided a narrower test of the hypothesis connecting past discrimination and present relative poverty by comparing immigrant groups of European origin. Family incomes of groups are presented by national origin in Table 9.2.

If we used Table 9.2 to infer past discrimination on the basis of present statistical disparities, we would have to conclude that Americans of British origin suffered from far more past discrimination than Jews, that Italian immigrants suffered from practically no discrimination, that Scandinavian-Americans remain an oppressed minority, and that Irish Protestants suffered from far more discrimination than Irish Catholics. All such inferences would be gross falsifications of history. Jencks concludes, "Far from suggesting that discrimination kept its European victims impoverished, [the table] suggests that it spurred them on to greater success" (1985, p. 743). Sowell suggests the same pattern pertains to some non-European immigrants.

Table 9.1   Incomes of ethnic groups in relation to U.S. national average

Group	Family income index (U.S. Average = 100)
Jewish	172
Japanese	132
Polish	115
Chinese	112
Italian	112
German	107
Anglo-Saxon	107
Irish	103
Total U.S.	100
Filipino	99
West Indian	94
Mexican	76
Puerto Rican	63
Black	62
Indian	60

Source: U.S. Census and National Jewish Population Survey, quoted from Sowell, 1980, p. 5.

Table 9.2   Incomes of European ethnic groups in the United States,
            1972–1980

Ethnic group	Income as percentage of European average
Jews	138
Irish Catholics	114
French	104
Italians	102
Czechs	101
British (including Scottish)	101
Germans	96
Poles	95
Irish Protestants	91
Dutch	88
Scandinavians	88

Source: GSS, adapted from Jencks, 1984, p. 742.

Historically, some groups such as Black Americans suffered from discrimination in the past and have not shown upward mobility, and some, such as British- and German-Americans, who were relatively free from discrimination are about average. Yet many groups that suffered from discrimination in the past, such as Chinese, Japanese, Irish Catholics, and Jews, are doing very well today, and many groups relatively free from past discrimination, such as the Scotch-Irish and the Dutch, have today only modest achievements.

The simple fact is that there is no connection between present success or failure and past oppression. There is no proof of the causal importance of the principal problem affirmative action is supposed to combat.

Empirical Weaknesses

Another ostensible purpose of affirmative action is to combat present discrimination. Yet there is scant evidence of the decisive importance of contemporary discrimination. Of course, there are individual cases of anti-Black discrimination, just as there are cases of anti-White discrimination by affirmative action quotas. It is highly questionable if present discrimination accounts significantly for group statistical disparities.

If we look at opinion polls, a majority of Black Americans consistently say they have never suffered from racial discrimination. For example, in a January 1986 ABC News/Washington Post poll, 75% of Blacks said they had never suffered educational discrimination, 73% said they had never suffered housing-related discrimination, and 57% said they have never suffered from wage discrimination.

Objective measures, too, show that there are only slight differences in achievement between comparable Blacks and Whites. For example, most differences in income between the two are due to extraneous variables that must be controlled in order to assess the impact of discrimination: age, marital status, family composition, education, and region. In fact, there is little difference between the incomes of comparably educated young, Black married couples and White married couples living outside the South. This has been true for more than 10 years.

Logical Contradictions

Finally, affirmative action cannot stand up to logical scrutiny. In imposing preferences for Blacks and women over Whites and men, it contradicts itself in four ways. It punishes young White men who have never discriminated against anybody. It does not punish those older Whites and men who may have practiced discrimination, since it applies largely to school admissions, initial hiring, and promotion. It benefits young women and Blacks, who because of their age obviously did not suffer from past discrimination. And it does not benefit older women and Blacks who did suffer from discrimination in the past; for most of them, it is too late. In sum, affirmative action punishes the innocent, spares the guilty, benefits those who were not victims, and does not benefit those who were victims.

CONCLUSION

There is little empirical research on which the effects of affirmative action can be evaluated. There is no adequate measure of the alleged impact of the past discrimination for which affirmative action is supposed to atone. Public opinion is clearly hostile to affirmative action in the established form of preferential treatment. Measures of discrimination show its effects to be extremely modest. None of the underlying concepts used to justify and elaborate the policy is publicly and rationally articulated. In sum, affirmative action is a social policy without a scientific base.

Social scientists have refused to look at its effects for two sets of reasons. First, there is self-interest. Most academic social scientists, being older and tenured, are not affected by affirmative action and are therefore not interested in damages it may inflict. Indeed, they can and often do make exhortations about its moral rightness without suffering its consequences. At the same time, younger and untenured academic social scientists are likely to be female and Black beneficiaries of a policy they are not inclined to examine critically. The few White untenured men are in a precarious enough position to want to avoid taking the contentious stand of questioning the biases of mainstream academia, since their careers are at stake.

Second, biased toward the liberal/left wing of the political spectrum as they are, most social scientists do not choose to examine the effects of one of the most cherished policies of liberalism's "Great Society" for fear of what they might find. Accordingly, affirmative action has become a shibboleth, and opponents of it can be, by definition, identified as racists (Sniderman & Tetlock, 1986, pp. 145–147). Since affirmative action is primarily a way of expiating Whites' guilt about Black suffering, a guilt artfully stimulated by shrewd Black politicians, it is evidently a policy aimed at White atonement, rather than at real Black achievement. The effects of affirmative action therefore are irrelevant—its existence is its own justification. The constant call for more minority hiring and college admissions is an incantation, not a rationally examined policy.

REFERENCES

Beer, W. R. (1987a, May). *Sociology and affirmative action: A case of resolute ignorance.* Paper presented at meeting of the Eastern Sociological Society, Boston, MA.
Beer, W. R. (1987b, May/June). Resolute ignorance: Social science and affirmative action. *Society,* pp. 63–69.

Beer, W. R. (1988). Sociology and the effects of affirmative action: A case of neglect. *The American Sociologist, 19,* 218–231.

Booth, R. (1977). Social status and minority recruitment performance in the Navy. *Sociological Quarterly, 18,* 567–573.

Civil Rights Act of 1964 (Title VII). 78 Stat.

Executive Order No. 11246. (1965). 3 C.F.R. 339.

Exum, W. (1983). Climbing the crystal stair: Values, affirmative action and minority faculty. *Social Problems, 30,* 383–399.

Fullinwider, R. (1980). *The reverse discrimination controversy: A moral and legal analysis.* Totowa, NY: Rowman and Littlefield.

Glazer, N. (1976). *Affirmative discrimination.* New York: Basic Books.

Glazer, N. (1979). Affirmative discrimination: Where is it going? *International Journal of Comparative Sociology, 20,* 13–14.

Jencks, C. (1985). Affirmative action for Blacks. *American Behavioral Scientist, 28,* 731–760.

Johnson, S. (1980a). Consequences of reverse discrimination. *Psychological Reports, 47,* 1035–1038.

Johnson, S. (1980b). Reverse discrimination and aggressive behavior. *Journal of Psychology, 104,* 11–19.

Keith, S., Bell, R., & Williams, A. (1987). *Assessing the outcome of affirmative action in medical schools.* Santa Monica, CA: Rand.

Kluegel, J. (1985). If there isn't a problem, you don't need a solution: The bases of contemporary affirmative action attitudes. *American Behavioral Scientist, 28,* 761–784.

Lansky, D. (1978). External (legal) coercion and internal commitment: A case study of an affirmative action training program in municipal government. *Journal of Applied Behavioral Science, 14,* 27–41.

Leonard, J. (1984a). *The impact of affirmative action on employment* (Working paper 1310). Cambridge, MA: National Bureau of Economic Research.

Leonard, J. (1984b). *Splitting Blacks? Affirmative action and earnings inequality within and across races* (Working paper 1327). Cambridge, MA: National Bureau of Economic Research.

Lincoln, C. (1980). Beyond Bakke, Weber, and Fullilove: Peace from our sins. *Soundings, 63,* 361–380.

Lynch, F. (1984). Totem and taboo in sociology: The politics of affirmative action research. *Sociological Inquiry, 54,* 124–141.

Lynch, F. (1985). Affirmative action: Past, present, and future [special issue]. *American Behavioral Scientist, 28*(6), 731–841.

Milward, H., & Swanson, C. (1978). The impact of affirmative action on organizational behavior. *The Policy Studies Journal, 7,* 208–213.

Owen, B. (1985). Race and gender relations among prison workers. *Crime and Delinquency, 31,* 147–159.

Schaefer, R. (1988). *Racial and ethnic groups.* Boston, MA: Scott, Foresman.

Sexton, J. (1979). Minority admissions programs after Bakke. *Harvard Educational Review, 49,* 313–339.

Smith, J. P., & Welch, F. (1986). *Closing the gap: Forty years of economic progress for Blacks.* Santa Monica, CA: Rand.

Sniderman, P., & Tetlock, P. (1986). Symbolic racism: Problems of motive attribution in political analysis. *Journal of Social Issues, 42,* 129–150.

Sowell, T. (1981). *Ethnic America.* New York: Basic Books.

Wilson, W. J. (1978). *The declining significance of race.* Chicago: University of Chicago Press.

Wilson, W. J. (1987). *The truly disadvantaged.* Chicago: University of Chicago Press.

10

Civil Liberties and Research on the Effects of Pornography

Daniel Linz, Neil M. Malamuth, and Katherine Beckett

INTRODUCTION

Americans are concerned about the problem of pornography,[1] particularly *violent* pornography. A total of 73% of Americans say they would ban magazines that show sexual violence, 68% would bar theaters from showing movies that depict sexual violence, and 63% would bar the sale or rental of video cassettes that feature sexual violence (Burton, 1989). For the last seven years, policy advocates from the conservative right and the traditional left and many feminists have engaged in a fierce debate about the appropriate legal solution to the problem of pornography, in both violent and nonviolent forms. Research and expert testimony from social psychologists in one form or another has been used by virtually all parties involved in the debate.

In this chapter we assess what we feel psychologists can legitimately contribute to this dispute by focusing their research on media effects. We have an obligation to share our findings but also, concomitantly, to vigorously assert our opinions about the inconsistencies in the results and the methodological shortcomings of the relevant studies. This obligation may become more or less pressing, depending on our perception of the policy goals of a particular group.

On the surface, the debate about the relevance of social science data for policy decision making in this area seems to be between two relatively distinct positions: Do we speak out despite the problems with the database we have? Or, do we refrain from speaking out until the database is sufficient? But these positions have one assumption in common, that policy making proceeds in a deductive way. Evidence accumulates and then, faced with overwhelming proof for a given effect, we (society) make a decision to take action that is congruent with the data.

To frame the debate in these ideal terms ignores some facts about policy decisions in the area of pornography (and perhaps in any domain where social science research is applied to social policy). Legal judgments and policy decisions concerning pornography are philosophical, moral, or political in nature. They often

[1]The term *pornography* is used herein to refer to sexually explicit media without any pejorative meaning necessarily intended. Terms such as *violent pornography* and *sexually violent media* are used to refer to media that combine sexual and violent content. We also sometimes use the term *sexually violent media* to refer to materials that fuse sex and violence but do not necessarily have a high degree of sexual explicitness.

reflect the power and values of one group versus another in our society (i.e., the rights of women who might be harmed because of certain forms of pornography versus the costs incurred by society as a whole when certain forms of speech are banned), or they are moral principles, about what is right or wrong behavior, advanced by one group or another.

In this chapter, we discuss the development of social policies about pornography in the United States and the interface of these policies with social science research. We argue that fundamentally the decisions in this area have been moral/political ones, augmented by social science evidence only when it suited the policy makers. We note that in some situations social science evidence on the effects of pornography has been ignored altogether, explicitly labeled irrelevant, or used selectively to confirm certain moral/political beliefs.

This puts us, as potential policy advisers, in a curious position. Given the fact that, for political or moral reasons, a given policy alternative will be pressed regardless of our input, we have no choice but to contribute what we know in the hopes of steering the debate toward the consideration of carefully collected scientific evidence. But, because the research has such a high potential for misuse, we must do so in a cautious way, pointing out whenever possible the methodological shortcomings of the research we cite.

In order to come to a conclusion about when and to whom social science data should be disseminated, we consider two guiding ethics. These principles have helped us frame our decisions about when it is necessary to emphasize the shortcomings and inconsistencies of the research rather than the consistencies among the findings. They involve searching for alternatives to censorship and being cautious whenever the policy making body is predisposed toward the deprivation of traditional First Amendment rights. We suggest a rank ordering of situations, from least to most "safe," for researchers to provide expert advice in light of these principles.

Finally, we suggest some broad guidelines for future research in this area. Our suggestions are intended for social scientists who wish to devise research projects that are both theoretically relevant and policy oriented.

RESEARCH ON SEX AND VIOLENCE IN THE MASS MEDIA AND PUBLIC POLICY

In recent years there have been several domains where social policy and social science evidence on the effects of pornography and sexual violence in the media have converged. We will consider three of these: the 1970 Pornography Commission, the 1984 Minneapolis/Indianapolis antipornography civil rights ordinance, and the 1986 Attorney General's Commission on Pornography. Although the laws and recommendations that have emerged from each of these domains appear to have been sometimes informed and guided by psychological research, they have at least as often proceeded in a given direction despite the research evidence.

1970 Pornography Commission

In 1970 the Presidential Commission on Pornography and Obscenity sponsored many basic science empirical studies on the effects of exposure to sexually explicit materials. In fact, as others have noted (Einsiedel, 1989), one of the primary contributions of the commission was that it put human sexual behavior on the agenda for continuing scientific inquiry. The studies undertaken by the commission suggested few antisocial effects from exposure to sexually explicit material (see Howard, Reifler, & Liptzin, 1971). They concluded that persons exposed to most forms of the pornography widely available then did not show significant changes in their attitudes toward women and showed no increases in tendencies toward sexual violence. These scientific findings could have been used reasonably to substantiate a policy of no legal intervention.

Instead, obscenity law flourished. By 1973, the United States Supreme Court, under the leadership of Chief Justice Warren Burger, had fashioned a more restrictive obscenity standard than any that existed in the 1960s. In a landmark case, *Miller v. California* (1973), Chief Justice Burger argued that each community had the right to establish its own obscenity standard. According to many legal theorists, this case made obscenity law stricter because it permitted local courts to find persons guilty for distributing materials that could not plausibly be found obscene in other, more sophisticated, jurisdictions (Feinberg, 1979).

Obscenity law may have flourished despite the commission's null findings in part because the premise of obscenity law was not actually challenged by the research findings. The law assumes that the danger from exposure to certain materials lies in the sexual explicitness and appeal to prurient interest of the material itself. Obscenity law rests on the idea that the harm caused by exposure to obscene materials is done to the viewer, rather than to any other party who might be injured because of the viewer's more calloused attitudes or predisposition to antisocial behavior. Obscene materials offend community standards of decency and therefore fall outside the range of speech protected by the First Amendment. This premise is not challenged by the 1970 commission's finding that exposure to pornography has no effect on antisocial attitudes and behavior toward women (Howard et al., 1971).

It is interesting to note that there is some indication that the court wished to have it both ways, that is, to justify obscenity standards both in terms of the harm done to the viewer and harm done to other parties. Chief Justice Burger bolstered the *Miller* decision by citing the Minority Report of the 1970 commission. This report argued that there was evidence of at least an arguable correlation between the consumption of pornography and antisocial behavior toward women.

1984 Minneapolis/Indianapolis Civil Rights Ordinance

The attempt by some feminists to fashion a civil law to regulate pornography was a direct response to the ineffectiveness of obscenity law in the 1980s. The amount of pornography in American society in the decade after the 1970 commission had mushroomed. Feminist theorists Catherine MacKinnon (1985) and Andrea Dworkin shifted the debate from the idea of harm done to the viewer of pornography to the idea of harm accruing to women by the existence of pornography in our society. Scientific studies (for reviews, see Donnerstein, Linz, & Penrod, 1987; Malamuth & Donnerstein, 1984) on the effects of exposure to sexually violent media were cited by these theoreticians to support their claims in cases such as *American Booksellers Association v. Hudnut* (1984, 1985).

These studies indicated that, in the laboratory, exposure to certain forms of violent pornography resulted in changed perceptions of rape, attitudes, and aggression against women. In the typical study focusing on short-term or relatively immediate effects on aggressive behavior, male subjects were first exposed to depictions showing the female victim enjoying or reacting in a positive fashion to sexual aggression or similar mistreatment. Then subjects were given the opportunity to administer electric shocks or other forms of punishment to a female victim. The results of these studies have generally indicated that in comparison with control subjects, male subjects exposed to sexual violence of this sort showed increases in aggression. However, the only study of this type that examined more long-term effects of such exposure (by having repeated exposure to sexually violent materials and measuring aggression a considerable time after the exposure phase had been completed) did not find increased aggression (Malamuth & Ceniti, 1986).

Other research focusing on perceptions and attitudes shows (a) changes in the perception of the rape victim (e.g., seeing her as less injured and more responsible for her assault); (b) effects on perceptions of a rapist as less responsible for his actions and as deserving less punishment; and (c) greater acceptance of violence against women and of certain rape myths (see Donnerstein et al., 1987; Malamuth, 1984, 1989). Research on exposure to sexually explicit materials that were not overtly violent but were arguably degrading to women yielded less consistent effects (Linz, 1989), but some data suggested that long-term exposure to these materials might also result in more lenient attitudes toward rapists (Zillmann, 1986).

Dworkin and MacKinnon persuaded the Minneapolis City Council to adopt a civil rights ordinance permitting women to recover damages from the alleged harms resulting from pornography, which was defined as the sexually explicit subordination of women through pictures or words that also presents women as dehumanized sexual objects who enjoy pain, humiliation, or rape (MacKinnon, 1985). Accordingly, pornography was seen as constituting a violation of women's civil rights. Under certain circumstances, women were permitted to sue the producers of such material for damages. Such an ordinance was ultimately passed in Indianapolis with the help of political conservatives. The ordinance was successfully challenged by the American Booksellers Association and the American Civil Liberties Union (*American Booksellers v. Hudnut*, 1984).

Although the feminist argument about harm appears to dovetail nicely with some of the scientific findings regarding sexually violent media, nearly all observers of the events in Indianapolis agree that there was little evidence that conservative supporters of the ordinance had abandoned assumptions upon which traditional obscenity law rests in favor of a harm-to-women approach. In other words, the danger of pornographic materials lay in their sexual explicitness, appeal to prurient interests, and tendency to morally corrupt consumers. Conservatives were convinced that the proliferation of pornographic materials was proof that existing obscenity law was an ineffective means of restricting access to pornographic materials and saw this new approach as potentially viable. For many of the ordinance's supporters, the results of scientific experiments were essentially irrelevant to their support for the legislation. They endorsed the legislation primarily because it promised a practical solution to what they considered an old problem.

1986 Attorney General's Commission on Pornography

Rather than adopt the feminist legal approach, political conservatives (who appeared to form the majority of the 1986 Attorney General's Commission on Pornography), in keeping with their social philosophies, recommended more vigorous enforcement of traditional obscenity law. To its credit, the 1986 commission maintained that the most harmful material was that which was sexually *violent*. They concluded that there was a causal relationship between exposure to sexually violent pornography and negative changes in certain attitudes, perceptions, and aggression toward women. With respect to aggressive behavior, this is an accurate statement as long as we are referring to results of laboratory studies examining the short-term effects of sexually violent images (also see Linz, Donnerstein, & Penrod, 1987).

As we noted earlier, there is currently no research to show long-term effects on aggressive behavior (Malamuth & Ceniti, 1986). The main body of the 1986 commission's report (Attorney General's Commission on Pornography, 1986) did not include any reference to or discussion of this study, although it is cited in a different section of the report, the "Social and behavior science research analysis" section (p. 985), prepared separately by a social scientist.

The commission's conclusions regarding the effects of violent sexual media on attitudes are more consistent with our own literature reviews (e.g., Malamuth, 1989) than with their generalizations regarding violent behavior. As noted below, there are aspects of their generalizations about attitudes that we feel may be premature.

There are at least two important considerations that the commission did not emphasize sufficiently in its application of social science research to their conclusions about pornography and aggression against women. First, the question is whether the changes in attitudes and behavior after exposure to sexually violent material are a function of both the violence in the depiction and the pornographic nature of the material per se (i.e., the fact that the material contains sexually explicit images) or are due primarily to messages about the violence against women regardless of sexual explicitness. Second, a methodological qualification (not discussed here) involves the familiar critiques of laboratory investigations of aggressive behavior (see Fredrich-Cofer & Huston, 1986; Freedman, 1984, 1986).

Many of the scientific studies cited by the commission as evidence for the effects of pornography strongly suggest that in order to find harmful effects, sexual explicitness need not attain a level anything like that which would be judged obscene or pornographic by virtually any standard (e.g., Malamuth & Check, 1981). Studies in which subjects have been exposed to materials that are sexually explicit and violent toward women, sexually explicit but purged of violence, and violent but not sexually explicit have indicated that materials with a message of violence against women presented in sexually nonexplicit contexts are capable of producing some of the same antisocial effects as violent pornography (e.g., Donnerstein, Linz, & Penrod, 1987). We are not denying that the combination of sex and violence may have some unique and troublesome effects, but this issue needs to be more systematically investigated prior to any conclusive generalizations. As well, research on the effects of "slasher" films that portray extreme forms of violence against women in mildly erotic contexts has also revealed antisocial effects (Linz, Donnerstein, & Penrod, 1984, 1988).

In fact, the commission itself noted that the preponderance of the evidence suggests that the effects of violent pornography "do not vary with the extent of sexual explicitness so long as the violence is presented in an undeniably sexual context" (Attorney General's Commission on Pornography, 1986, p. 328). According to the commission, "the so-called slasher films, which depict a great deal of violence connected with an undeniably sexual theme but less sexual explicitness than pornographic materials, are likely to produce the consequences discussed here to a greater extent than most materials available in 'adults only' pornographic outlets" (p. 329). The most reasonable conclusion that one can reach from the commission's own statements is that depictions of violence against women, whether in a sexually explicit context or not, should be the primary focus of concern.

In addition to violent pornography, the commission issued statements regarding what it termed nonviolent but degrading pornography, nonviolent and nondegrading pornography, and nudity. The commission stated that substantial exposure to degrading pornography will (a) lead individuals to view rape as less serious, (b) encourage individuals to view rape victims as more responsible for their own plight, and (c) increase the likelihood that men will say that they would "force" women into sexual practices. The social science research conducted to date is not, by any means, conclusive on the effects of exposure to materials that are nonviolent but may be degrading to women. Although some research has found that exposure to this type of material changes an individual's perceptions of rape (e.g., Zillmann & Bryant, 1982), other studies, with both male and female viewers (e.g., Intons-Peterson, Roskos-Ewoldsen, Thomas, Shirley, & Blut, 1989; Krafka, 1985; Linz, Donnerstein, & Penrod, 1988; Padgett, Brislin-Slutz, & Neal, 1989), have not shown such effects. The commission selectively attended to the results of research that obtained effects while largely disregarding those studies producing null effects.

Lacking solid scientific proof, the commission argued, on the basis of their "own insights and experience with these types of pornography," that substantial exposure to materials of this type "bears some causal relationship to the level of sexual violence, sexual coercion, or unwanted sexual aggression in the population so exposed" (Attorney General's Commission on Pornography, 1986, pp. 333–334). Ironically, the commission noted that, as with the sexually violent materials, these effects may not be dependent on any sexual explicitness contained in the depictions. Despite the conclusion that the harm associated with pornography had little to do with sexual explicitness, the commission's legal recommendations were primarily directed at strengthening existing obscenity law, the focus of which is explicit sexuality, appeal to prurient interest, and the moral corruption of the individual viewer. Obscenity law does not specifically address the harm accruing to women as a result of others viewing sexually violent media, which is the primary focus of the scientific research. The primary legal recommendations made by the commission for strengthening traditional obscenity laws belied its own assertions about what the data revealed. The research shows and the commission's own opinion is that the sexual explicitness of the portrayal is of only secondary concern. Obscenity laws are traditionally directed to the prosecution of purveyors of sexually explicit materials. To strengthen these laws makes little sense in light of the data.

In summary, there have been some occasions where policy and psychological research appear to have meshed in a logical way. The Minneapolis antipornography ordinance developed by feminists Andrea Dworkin and Catherine MacKinnon was consistent to some degree with the social scientific evidence. In other words, the fusion of sexually explicit material and violence, rather than being objectionable because it was offensive or tended to corrupt the morals of those who viewed it, might produce its greatest harm to third parties, namely women. However, the ordinance encompassed a range of materials (i.e., degrading pornography in general rather than sexually violent media) that was not specifically tied to the type most clearly implicated by the research as having potential negative effects. Furthermore, the ordinance eventually passed by the Indianapolis City/County Council was passed through the sponsorship and endorsement of politically conservative council members whose primary interest was in controlling the spread of objectionable sexually explicit material.

Other legal policies appear to have been formulated and implemented regardless of what social science research demonstrated. The most significant obscenity decision, *Miller v. California* (1973), was largely in conflict with the findings of the 1970 Presidential Commission on Pornography and Obscenity, whose studies suggested that exposure to sexually explicit materials available at the time did not produce antisocial effects (see Howard et al., 1971). The recommendations of the 1986 Attorney General's Commission on Pornography to strengthen traditional obscenity law 16 years later flies in the face of its admission that it is the message of violence against women, regardless of sexual explicitness, that is at issue.

DISTINGUISHING BETWEEN
A POLITICAL/MORAL QUESTION
AND AN EMPIRICALLY ANSWERABLE QUESTION

Why has social science evidence been applied to policy decision making in such a seemingly haphazard way? We submit that it is because policy makers have sought first to advance a political or moral position and then have tried to support these positions with the necessary scientific evidence. When the evidence has been consistent they have emphasized it; when it has proven contrary to their case they have usually chosen to ignore it or to denigrate its value.

Quite often research has been ignored altogether. This has been especially true for the U.S. courts. What the social scientist contemplating the value of research on the effects of pornography must bear in mind is that no matter how compelling or inconclusive the data might be, the courts view the issue as a legal and moral one and only tangentially as an empirical one.

The Southern District Court made this point quite clearly when it considered the legality of the Indianapolis antipornography ordinance once the measure was passed by the city council and challenged by the American Booksellers Association and the American Civil Liberties Union. In its discussion of the social psychological findings entered as evidence in the Indianapolis hearings, the court asserted:

> *[The] defendants argue that there is more than enough "empirical" evidence in the case at bar to support the City-County Council's conclusion that "pornography" harms women . . . it is not the Court's function to question the City-County Council's legislative finding. The Court's solitary duty is to ensure that the ordinance accomplishes its purpose without violating constitu-*

tional standards or impinging upon constitutionally protected rights. (American Booksellers Association v. Hudnut, *1984, p. 46)*

The same distinction was made in the decision regarding the constitutionality of the antipornography ordinance by the Seventh Circuit Court of Appeals. In this decision, the court did not challenge the premise of the legislation (based in part on the results of social psychological experiments), that pornographic depictions of violence toward and subordination of women tend to perpetuate such subordination. In fact, the Seventh Circuit Court noted, "this subordination [may in turn lead] to lower pay at work, insult and injury at home or even battery and rape on the streets" (*American Booksellers Association v. Hudnut,* 1985, p. 9). In this regard the court compared pornography to other forms of speech that promote hatred and bigotry, such as manifestos by the Ku Klux Klan or even violent TV programs.

The court maintained that even though harmful effects are likely to arise from materials like these, they are nonetheless protected by the First Amendment. According to the Seventh Circuit Court:

Racial bigotry, anti-Semitism, violence on television, reporters' biases—these and many more influence the culture and shape our socialization. None is directly answerable by more speech, unless that speech too finds its place in the popular culture. Yet all is protected speech, however insidious. Any other answer leaves the government in control of all of the institutions of culture, the great censor and director of which thoughts are good for us. (American Booksellers Association v. Hudnut, *1985, p. 9)*

What such courts have made clear is that they believe the harms resulting from pornography and/or sexual violence, even when empirically demonstrated, are not as devastating to society as harms that might be incurred if the government were to regulate such material in any manner other than through existing obscenity laws. According to the courts, the danger of accepting sex discrimination as a more compelling state interest than First Amendment protections is that it may open the door for any legislative body to regulate speech concerning nearly any group. Even if scientific research produced empirical evidence that unequivocally demonstrated that exposure to particular forms of pornography resulted in a recognizable harm and assessed the degree of harm resulting from restrictions to free speech, the U.S. courts may still decide that additional regulation beyond the traditional restraints contained in the criminal obscenity statutes are not desirable or permissible. The empirical evidence, while useful for clarifying the issue, cannot resolve the essential moral and political questions involved in balancing which harms are less acceptable.

This distinction between the empirical and the political is not unique to social science research and public policy. Biological scientists involved in inquiries into topics about which there is considerable philosophical debate have often found themselves in similar situations, despite the greater certainty usually accorded the findings of workers in these disciplines. For example, in recent history attempts have been made to transform the question of the propriety of abortion from a moral question into an empirical one. Nineteenth century physicians claimed that new scientific evidence demonstrated that the fetus was the moral equivalent of a child; in reality, the scientific facts themselves did not and could not demonstrate that such a claim was true. Rather, the truth of this claim depended on the subjective definition of terms such as *moral equivalence, life,* and *human.* While the new evidence did indicate that pregnancy was a continuous process and therefore dispelled the notion that a 40- or 80-day-old fetus could be considered unformed, this new knowledge did not help resolve the moral question of how the rights of the fetus were to be compared with the rights of the mother.

The abortion debate was not, and still is not, about the scientific facts, but rather about how to interpret, weigh, and assess them (Luker, 1985). For example, the dispute about whether the zygote constitutes a human being depends on one's conception of what it means to *be* a human being, of the proper role of women in society, and whether adherence to a moral rule about the political rights of the unborn is valued more highly than the political right of individual choice. While medical science can clarify the issue and define the parameters of the debate, the scientific facts themselves cannot demonstrate the "rightness" of either the prolife or the prochoice position.

What constitutes harm to a particular society, and how the legal system redresses this harm, is always debatable. In the United States, the courts have traditionally demanded that media depictions of violence be shown to cause tangible and immediate harm to a specific individual rather than to a class of individuals. The U.S. courts have upheld a narrow definition of harm as well as the position that criminal law should limit itself to the proscription of certain types of behavior that impinge on the rights of others. An alternative approach, advocated by certain policy makers in Canada, allows that criminal law should be a reflection of a society's broader values.

Rather than limiting itself to the protection of what are termed First Amendment freedoms in the United States, such as freedom of speech, thought, religion, and expression, Canada's Fraser Commission, a policy advisory group given the mandate to explore how existing obscenity and prostitution laws fit into Canada's newly acquired constitution, suggested a different approach (*Pornography and Prostitution in Canada,* 1985). They suggested that rights to freedom of speech and expression can be protected only insofar as they do not conflict with other rights such as equal protection under the law and equal benefit of the law.

By this way of thinking, feminists' attempts to frame the issue of harm emerging from pornography as a question of civil liberties, and their assertion that women suffer discrimination as a result of men viewing pornography, would have at least equal standing with the rights of freedom of speech and press. It is ironic, but consistent with our previous assertion that policy decision making is largely independent of social scientific findings, that the Fraser Commission came to accept much of the feminist position regarding the effects of pornography and the function of the law while disavowing the validity of the social science evidence on this subject. See McKay & Dolff (1984).

The idea that certain forms of speech actually undermine others' rights to equality has not been addressed by the U.S. courts. Thus far, the U.S. courts have supported the right to formal equality for women, but have not recognized, at least in the context of the pornography debate, the substantive inequality that exists between men and women in society. The validity of one group's harm relative to another may be aided by social science research—we can try to evaluate whether the harms exist—but, as we have noted, we cannot empirically demonstrate which group's harm should be heeded, and at what expense to another group's rights. Deciding how to apply the law to address these harms once they are demonstrated cannot be aided by scientific studies. The role of the social scientist is to assess and comment on whether evidence is consistent with assertions of harms and their magnitudes.

POLICY INTERVENTIONS
AND THE PSYCHOLOGIST'S RESPONSIBILITY

As psychologists who study the effects of pornography, we are in a position to provide information to policy makers at many levels. This might include dissemination of information to: (a) other social scientists, (b) trained clinicians, (c) educators for sex education programs, (d) the mass media, (e) attorneys for use in individual legal cases, (f) governmental commissions and legislative bodies, and (g) political or religious groups. We feel that information dissemination to each of these types of groups implies a unique set of responsibilities. In particular, it is important to discuss the limitations of the research with those groups involved in policy making, especially those using the law. We have, therefore, deliberately listed the groups in the above order, roughly corresponding to a rank ordering in terms of policy-making orientation. Two guiding principles can be articulated as the foundation for this rank ordering: First, a search for alternatives to censorship; and second, a consideration of the fact that when we attempt to predict certain types of low-base-rate behaviors, such as violent behavior, we encounter methodological problems that could lead to restricting the rights of many while accurately identifying only a few persons who may be incited to violence.

Alternatives to Censorship

Although we must always be wary of problems of distortion and sensationalizing of the research, the safest targets for the dissemination of social scientific research findings may be other scientists, since they have been trained to evaluate research of this type. The next level might include clinicians, educators, the media, and attorneys, as these groups are least likely to be in a position to attempt to limit access of individuals to certain forms of speech. Information disseminated to governmental commissions, legislative bodies, and political or religious groups, in contrast, may be particularly likely to be used to support legislation aimed at increased regulation. Thus, we should be particularly vigilant to note potential flaws, inconsistencies, and limits to generalizability. It may be particularly challenging to accomplish this, since these groups may be seeking expert advice that would simplify the information. They may, therefore, directly or subtly pressure scientists to provide bottom line statements to justify particular policy options.

We have an obligation to explore alternatives to restricting the flow of information for two reasons. First, it is congruent with the tenets of academia. In our positions as scientists, we should be looking for ways to inform and encourage more communication, rather than discouraging it. Science is premised on the belief that the free exchange of ideas is the basis of truth and progress. Second, predicting who could be adversely affected by media exposure in a manner that might justify legal restrictions raises problems.

Deprivation of Civil Liberties and Scientific Prediction

Policies advocating restrictions in media content may be based on rationales other than direct incitement effects on violent behavior, although this may be the most likely basis for justifying such restrictions. Even social scientists who argue that exposure to some types of pornography directly causes aggression (e.g., Russell, 1988) will probably acknowledge that only a small percentage of the population is likely to be directly incited to violence in the "clear and present danger" sense (*Schenck v. United States,* 1919). If this type of effect were the basis for restricting media, the problem of restricting the First Amendment rights of a large number of media consumers because of the potential effects on only a small proportion arises. Conceivably, we could try to identify those individuals most "at risk" to incitement and apply a particular social policy only to them. Setting aside for the moment obvious and legitimate concerns of the "1984 Orwellian" nature of such an approach, from a scientific perspective this raises the familiar low-base-rate problem (Meehl & Rosen, 1955), which occurs in trying to predict a behavior that occurs infrequently. Even if our predictions were highly accurate, we would always have a substantial number of false positives where we restrict the rights of a large number of individuals who would not actually have been incited to violence.

GUIDELINES FOR FUTURE POLICY-RELEVANT RESEARCH

We have suggested that, as social scientists, our legitimate role in the pornography and sexual violence debate may be to provide policy makers with information about the findings of research pertaining to the questions of harms and their magnitudes. Once this empirical question has been addressed, it is left to policy makers to decide the moral question, whose harms count most. Despite the fact that our role is somewhat circumscribed, it is nonetheless critical. The central question now becomes: How do we produce research that we find theoretically meaningful and academically interesting, but that policy makers find useful? We suggest several ways in which researchers can triangulate methods, theory, and practical questions in such a way as to allow us to explore theoretically relevant questions while providing information useful in helping to resolve policy dilemmas.

Identify Critical Policy Assumptions

Critical policy assumptions often hinge on testable assumptions about human nature. The primary assumption of obscenity law is that lewdness in sexual explicitness is harmful. The assumption of feminists advocating civil ordinances is that sexual explicitness is not critical, but that the portrayal of women as the objects of violence, humiliation, and degradation produces harm. It has been possible to design research pertaining to these assumptions by investigating the effects of exposing subjects to materials that were sexually explicit and violent toward women, sexually explicit but purged of violence, and violent but not sexually explicit (Donnerstein et al., 1987). Of course, we recognize that the manner by which harm was defined and measured in this research focused on a particular type of potential harm, aggressive behavior. It did not specifically examine other harms that might be argued by proponents of obscenity laws, such as greater acceptance of lewd behavior. We believe, however, that it is feasible to devise experiments to test critical assumptions underlying legal policies. Most pressing at this point would be further tests of the assumptions made by policy makers regarding the harms of degrading materials that are not overtly violent.

Understanding Theoretical Mechanisms

Experiments designed to test basic psychological processes, far from being irrelevant to policy, often suggest directions for policy interventions. For example, we have found that repeated exposure to slasher films results in a tendency for viewers to exhibit less sensitivity to female victims of violence in other contexts. We have hypothesized that this effect is due to subjects involuntarily becoming emotionally and physiologically desensitized to violence against women from watching the films and that this desensitization then carries over to other situations (Linz, Donnerstein, & Adams, 1989; Linz, Donnerstein, & Penrod, 1988). But our data are not entirely consistent with this explanation. A better explanation may involve the notion of a cognitive priming effect whereby certain ideas about the appropriateness of aggression against women are *temporarily* activated, and these ideas are carried over to other situations. Another explanation might hold that the viewer undergoes more enduring belief and attitude changes, rather than the temporary activation of certain thoughts.

Each of these basic psychological processes suggests a different type of social intervention. If repeated exposure to slasher films results in physiological desensitization that viewers then use as a guide for their attitudes toward women in the films as well as in other contexts, one policy implication that follows is that viewers should be informed of the desensitization process, which may be inevitable given repeated exposure and may not be noticeable to the viewer. Once informed that they can become desensitized, viewers may choose not to expose themselves to this type of film. If exposure to sexually violent films results in enduring attitude change, then the appropriate policy response might be the provision of countermessages designed to change the beliefs about women engendered by the films. If effects are only temporary and do not have cumulative long-term impact, no intervention may be needed.

Maximize External Validity

The point may be rather obvious, but it is worthwhile to stress that our research ideally should generalize across settings, persons, and times to be useful to policy makers. It is our obligation to point out when the data are not generalizable in any one of these domains. The less obvious point is that by taking external validity concerns seriously we are often led in interesting directions. Generalizing across people, for example, might mean that we need to examine the impact of exposure with persons of both sexes and of varying ages and backgrounds. We know little about women's reactions and little about adults other than college students. We also know little about the effects of sexually violent material on adolescents, a group that may be especially vulnerable to mass media effects.

Theoretical mechanisms are needed to account for the different effects of exposure to violence in each of these groups. Wilson and Cantor (1987), for example, suggest that desensitization to fearful stimuli may occur rapidly when older children are asked to imagine detailed, changing scenes involving a fear object. Younger children, on the other hand, appear to experience no desensitization when asked to imagine a fear object, but do experience desensitization when actually in the presence of the object. Wilson (1990) has proposed an information processing perspective that provides a unified approach to desensitization that can account for the findings regarding children of both age groups. By expanding our research objectives in order to demonstrate that our effects are robust across age groups, times, or places, we may discover anomalies, or indeed consistencies, that compel us to develop and test new theories.

Multiplicity of Causation and Methods

Most dependent variables of interest to policy makers in the area of pornography and sexual violence are multiply determined. As current research illustrates (see Huesmann & Malamuth, 1986), it is becoming increasingly apparent that exposure to violent mass media may increase the probability of aggressive behavior. However, aggressive behavior after a violent media depiction will most often be mediated and moderated (Baron & Kenny, 1986) by several intervening variables. These might include a prior history of personal aggressiveness, approval or disapproval of media violence by fellow observers, availability of a victim after seeing violence, and similarity between available targets and victims portrayed in the media event. Also included are subject anger at the time of the exposure to media violence, the degree to which the viewer believes the media depictions to be realistic, and demographic characteristics such as age and sex. Each of these variables plays a role in whether actual violence will ensue after exposure to media violence and is important for determining which types of individuals are most susceptible to media effects. Similar factors are likely to affect the impact of sexually violent media and of various types of pornography. If we accept that exposure to sexually violent media can significantly affect some men's attitudes (e.g., Malamuth & Check, 1981) and that such attitudes may in turn affect aggressive behavior (Malamuth, 1989), it is important to note that the effects of such attitudes are likely to be substantially moderated by other factors (e.g., Malamuth, 1986, 1989).

Our studies are also strengthened by a multitude of methodological approaches. To the extent that we see a consistent pattern of results across varied methods, we as scientists are convinced of the robustness of our findings. In our opinion, five types of information must coalesce before social scientists studying the effects of pornography and sexually violent media can be truly confident that there are socially harmful effects on aggressive behavior. These are:

1. Laboratory studies indicating that such exposure "could" be a significant cause of aggression (Berkowitz & Donnerstein, 1982).
2. "Causal" modeling studies that examine the role of such media in the context of other factors (Malamuth, Sokoloskie, & Koss, 1991).
3. Longitudinal studies that are more suited for identifying cause and effect relationships than cross-sectional designs (Mulvey & Haugaard, 1986).

4. Field studies that incorporate content analyses of the media with assessment of naturally occurring behaviors (e.g., Iyengar & Kinder, 1987).

5. Intervention studies that verify the theoretical mechanisms proposed by producing prosocial changes (e.g., Huesmann, Eron, Klein, Brice, & Fischer, 1983).

This may sound like an unrealistic prospect, but it might be argued that such convergence of findings across methods already exists in the area of children and televised (nonsexual) violence (Huesmann & Eron, 1986), although there continues to be disagreement regarding critical aspects of those data (e.g., Freedman, 1984, 1986).

CONCLUSIONS

As researchers we should not endorse a particular legal policy position pertaining to the control of pornography. If pressed to take a position we should admit that the data in this area do not, at this time, justify taking a particular policy position, unless it involves an educational type of intervention that would more adequately inform consumers about the findings of research and the potential of negative effects of certain materials. This is not to imply, however, that our influence on policy decision making in this area would be likely to change substantially once the data are improved further. Even if the data were highly consistent there are certain extra-scientific factors in the debate about the effects of pornography that make it unlikely that the policy decision will be calibrated with great precision to the data we collect. The best we can hope for, at least in this policy domain, is that by designing methodologically sound studies that examine the potential harms produced by exposure to certain forms of mass media, we provide data relevant to the assumptions and claims of those advocating various policies.

REFERENCES

American Booksellers Association v. Hudnut, 598 F. Supp. 1316 (S.D. Ind. 1984).

American Booksellers Association v. Hudnut, 771 F.2d 323 (7th Cir. 1985).

Attorney General's Commission on Pornography. (1986). *Final Report*, Department of Justice. Washington, DC: U.S. Government Printing Office.

Baron, R., & Kenny, D. A. (1986). The moderator–mediator variable distinction in social psychological research: Conceptual, strategic, and statistical considerations. *Journal of Personality and Social Psychology, 51*, 1173–1182.

Berkowitz, L., & Donnerstein, E. (1982). External validity is more than skin deep. *American Psychologist, 37*, 245–257.

Burton, D. (1989). Public opinion and pornography policy. In S. Gubar & J. Hoff-Wilson (Eds.), *For adult users only: The dilemma of violent pornography* (pp. 133–146). Bloomington: Indiana University Press.

Donnerstein, E., Linz, D., & Penrod, S. (1987). *The question of pornography: Research findings and policy implications.* New York: Free Press.

Einsiedel, E. F. (1989). Social science and public policy: Looking at the 1986 Commission on Pornography. In S. Gubar & J. Hoff-Wilson (Eds.), *For adult users only: The dilemma of violent pornography* (pp. 87–107). Bloomington: Indiana University Press.

Feinberg, J. (1979). Pornography and criminal law. In D. Copp & S. Wendell (Eds.), *Pornography and censorship* (pp. 105–137). New York: Prometheus.

Fredrich-Cofer, L., & Huston, A. C. (1986). Television violence and aggression: The debate continues. *Psychological Bulletin, 100*, 364–371.

Freedman, J. L. (1984). Effect of television violence on aggressiveness. *Psychological Bulletin, 96*, 227–246.

Freedman, J. L. (1986). Television violence and aggression: A rejoinder. *Psychological Bulletin, 100,* 372–378.

Howard, J. L., Reifler, C. B., & Liptzin, M. B. (1971). Effects of exposure to pornography. In *Technical report of the Commission on Obscenity and Pornography* (Volume 8, pp. 97–132). Washington, DC: U.S. Government Printing Office.

Huesmann, L. R., Eron, L. D., Klein, R., Brice, P., & Fischer, P. (1983). Mitigating the imitation of aggressive behaviors by changing children's attitudes about media violence. *Journal of Personality and Social Psychology, 44,* 899–910.

Huesmann, L. R., & Eron, L. D. (Eds.). (1986). *Television and the aggressive child: A cross-national comparison.* Hillsdale, NJ: Erlbaum.

Huesmann, L. R., and Malamuth, N. M. (1986). Media violence and antisocial behavior: An overview. *Journal of Social Issues, 42*(3), 1–6.

Intons-Peterson, M. J., Roskos-Ewoldsen, B., Thomas, L., Shirley, M., & Blut, D. (1989). Will educational materials reduce negative effects of exposure to sexual violence? *Journal of Social and Clinical Psychology, 8,* 256–275.

Iyengar, S., & Kinder, D. R. (1987). *News that matters: Agenda setting and priming in a television age.* Chicago: University of Chicago Press.

Krafka, C. L. (1985). *Sexually explicit, sexually violent, and violent media: Effects of multiple naturalistic exposures and debriefing on female viewers.* Unpublished doctoral dissertation, University of Wisconsin-Madison.

Linz, D. (1989). Exposure to sexually explicit materials and attitudes towards rape: A comparison of study results. *The Journal of Sex Research, 26,* 50–84.

Linz, D., Donnerstein, E., & Adams, S. (1989). Physiological desensitization and judgments about female victims of violence. *Human Communication Research, 15,* 509–522.

Linz, D., Donnerstein, E., & Penrod, S. (1984). The effects of long-term exposure to filmed violence against women. *Journal of Communication, 34,* 130–147.

Linz, D., Donnerstein, E., & Penrod, S. (1987). The findings and recommendations of the Attorney General's Commission on Pornography: Do the psychological facts fit the political fury? *American Psychologist, 42,* 946–953.

Linz, D., Donnerstein, E., & Penrod, S. (1988). Long-term exposure to violent and sexually degrading depictions of women. *Journal of Personality and Social Psychology, 55,* 758–768.

Luker, K. (1985). *Abortion and the politics of motherhood.* Berkeley: University of California Press.

MacKinnon, C. (1985). Pornography, civil rights, and speech: Commentary. *Harvard Civil Rights–Civil Liberties Law Review, 20,* 1–70.

Malamuth, N. M. (1984). Aggression against women: Cultural and individual causes. In N. Malamuth and E. Donnerstein (Eds.), *Pornography and sexual aggression* (pp. 19–52). Orlando, FL: Academic Press.

Malamuth, N. M. (1986). Predictors of naturalistic sexual aggression. *Journal of Personality and Social Psychology, 50,* 953–962.

Malamuth, N. M. (1989). Sexually violent media, thought patterns and antisocial behavior. In G. Comstock (Ed.), *Public communication and behavior* (Vol. 2). Orlando, FL: Academic Press.

Malamuth, N. M., & Ceniti, J. (1986). Repeated exposure to violent and nonviolent pornography: Likelihood of raping ratings and laboratory aggression against women. *Aggressive Behavior, 12,* 129–137.

Malamuth, N. M., & Check, J. (1981). The effects of mass media exposure on acceptance of violence against women: A field experiment. *Journal of Research in Personality, 15,* 436–446.

Malamuth, N. M., & Donnerstein, E. (Eds.). (1984). *Pornography and sexual aggression.* Orlando, FL: Academic Press.

Malamuth, N. M., Sokoloskie, R., & Koss, M. (1991). *Assessing the role of pornography using structural equations modeling.* Manuscript in preparation.

McKay, H. B., & Dolff, D. J. (1984). The impact of pornography: An analysis of research and summary of findings. In *Working papers on pornography and prostitution: Report 13.* Canada: Department of Justice.

Meehl, P., & Rosen, A. (1955). Antecedent probability and the efficacy of psychometric sign, patterns, or cutting scores. *Psychological Bulletin, 52,* 194–216.

Miller v. California, 413 U.S. 15 (1973).

Mulvey, E. P., & Haugaard, J. L. (Eds.). (1986, August 4). *Report of the Surgeon General's Workshop on Pornography and Public Health* (U.S. Department of Health and Human Services, Office of the Surgeon General). Washington, DC: U.S. Government Printing Office.

Padgett, V. R., Brislin-Slutz, J. A., & Neal, J. A. (1989). Pornography, erotica, and negative attitudes towards women: The effects of repeated exposure. *Journal of Sex Research, 26,* 479–491.
Pornography and Prostitution in Canada. (1985). *Report of the special committee on pornography and prostitution (Vol. 1).* Ottawa, Canada: Canadian Government Publishing Centre.
Russell, D. E. H. (1988). Pornography and rape: A causal model. *Political Psychology, 9,* 41–73.
Schenck v. United States, 249 U.S. 47 (1919).
Wilson, B. J. (1987). Reducing children's emotional reactions to mass media through rehearsed explanation and exposure to a replica of a fear object. *Human Communication Research, 14,* 3–26.
Wilson, B. J. (1990). *Desensitization techniques for treating children's fears: A developmental review.* Unpublished manuscript, University of California, Santa Barbara.
Wilson, B. J., & Cantor, J. (1987). Reducing fear reactions to mass media: Effects of visual exposure and verbal explanation. In M. McLaughlin (Ed.), *Communication yearbook 10* (pp. 553–573). Newbury Park, CA: Sage.
Zillmann, D. (1986, June). *Effects of prolonged consumption of pornography.* In E. P. Mulvey & J. L. Haugaard (Eds.), *Report of the Surgeon General's Workshop on Pornography and Public Health* (U.S. Department of Health and Human Services, Office of the Surgeon General). Washington, DC: U.S. Government Printing Office.
Zillmann, D., & Bryant, J. (1982). Pornography, sexual callousness, and the trivialization of rape. *Journal of Communication, 32,* 10–21.

11

Pornography Research, Social Advocacy, and Public Policy

Dolf Zillmann

In this chapter, we shall briefly examine how, in recent years, psychological research has been used to derive guidelines for public policy concerning pornography and to what extent the research may have influenced adopted policies and legislation. We shall concentrate on procedures that were used to integrate and summarize available research findings for those recommending and/or deciding on policy, as well as on these agents' apparent partialities in extracting information in the necessary process of data reduction. Finally, we shall present alternative, potentially superior procedures and discuss their advantages.

POLICY FORMATION IN PRACTICE

A policy issue is created by citizens who deem particular happenings undesirable for society and who seek their curtailment or elimination. The pornography issue is no exception. Many citizens took offense at what readily available pornography presents and were concerned about the effects on sexual behavior, especially on violent sexual behavior, that might result from exposure. Influential people brought their concerns to the attention of policy and law makers who, in this case, decided to consider the merits of the pleas. In accord with common practice, committees were formed to ascertain the facts and, under the assumption that the facts bear out the citizens' concerns, to recommend remedial actions for consideration by law makers. This involves inspection of the scientific evidence—in this instance, inspection of the sociological and psychological research findings concerning the uses and effects of pornography.

The first Commission on Obscenity and Pornography was formed in 1970. It was composed of 18 commissioners, and it was supported by 22 staff members and a budget of $2 million. In addition to conducting hearings, this commission supported original empirical research as well as reviews of the pertinent literature by social scientists and legal scholars. The committee was given 2 years to produce recommendations. At the end of this period it concluded that there was insufficient evidence to consider pornography implicated in the causation of antisocial effects and refrained from recommending more stringent regulation of pornography (*Report of the Commission on Obscenity and Pornography*, 1970).

The issue did not go away, however. Pressures to regulate pornography continued, and deficiencies in the 1970 report became apparent. In particular, it became clear that the commission had based its verdict of "no ill effects" on few and tentative findings, many of which had been generated in haste for the commission. There also were the usual charges of partiality in composing the commission, culminating in allegations that "potentially difficult" leading scholars had been ostracized (Cline, 1974). However, in all probability it was the availability of new research findings that gave impetus to the formation of a new commission with the mandate to reexamine the scientific evidence and to recommend regulatory policy. Psychological investigations figured prominently among the new evidence (e.g., Donnerstein, 1980, 1983; Malamuth, 1981, 1984; Zillmann & Bryant, 1982) because their findings seemed to challenge the assessment of the 1970 commission and to warrant different recommendations.

The new commission, the Attorney General's Commission on Pornography, was formed in 1985. Eleven commissioners were appointed. They were supported by a budget of $400,000, assisted by a staff of 9, and given 1 year to complete their mandate. Because of budget and time limitations, empirical research could not be commissioned, nor could extensive reviews of the literature. The 1986 commission was thus restricted to conducting hearings. One of the hearings primarily presented and discussed social science research on the effects of pornography. This hearing was held on 11 September 1985 in Houston, Texas. Numerous psychologists were invited to testify. Many of those who had conducted empirical research on the uses or effects of pornography presented summaries of their findings, and many of those with relevant clinical experience reported their observations. In addition, "pornography addicts" testified, and victims of pornography-related sexual abuse described their agony, torment, anguish, and grief.

The Attorney General's Commission on Pornography was to be assisted by a committee of the U.S. Surgeon General. This committee was to ascertain the state of the art in pornography research and report to the Commission on Pornography. Mainly because of complications in the budget appropriation, the Surgeon General's committee was not formed in time. Eventually it came into being on a budget that barely covered the commission of five reviews of the pertinent research literature and the travel of about 15 invited participants. The committee was referred to as the Surgeon General's Workshop on Pornography and Public Health. It met for just three days, on 22–24 June 1986 in Arlington, Virginia.

The Surgeon General's workshop was not attended by members of the Attorney General's Commission. However, the chairman of the Attorney General's Commission took part in the proceedings by informing the workshop participants of happenings in the Attorney General's Commission. The release of final reports is of interest because it shows that, counter to intentions, the efforts of the Surgeon General's workshop were without consequence for the conclusions and recommendations of the Attorney General's Commission on Pornography. Release of the final report of the commission (Attorney General's Commission on Pornography, 1986) predated that of the workshop's report (Mulvey & Haugaard, 1986) by about one month.

PREDICTABLE CRITICISM

From its inception, the 1986 commission was under attack. Those representing the pornography industry considered the very formation of a commission an indictment of pornography (Nobile & Nadler, 1986). Those aligned with the American Civil Liberties Union took a similar stand (Hertzberg, 1986; Linsley, 1989). Most of the immediate criticism concerned the composition of the commission, however. It was deemed intolerable that six commissioners had made public statements to the effect that some restrictions of pornography might be desirable; the commission's chair was considered unacceptable because he had been a successful prosecutor in a campaign against pornography in theaters and bookstores (Hertzberg, 1986; Paletz, 1988). Others found it objectionable that only three commissioners— a psychologist, a psychiatrist, and a legal scholar—could document professional expertise with pornography (Wilcox, 1987). Yet others saw problems in the way in which the commission conducted its deliberations (Gouran, 1988; Paletz, 1988).

Politically speaking, most of the immediate criticism came from liberal quarters. The conservative side was surprisingly uninquisitive and quiet about the committee, its composition, and its deliberations. It went unnoticed, for example, that one of the expert commission members cosponsored the proposal that for some sex offenders exposure to pornography would "transiently decrease the likelihood to commit sex crimes" (Abel, Becker, & Mittelman, 1985). Nonetheless, considerable discontent with the commission and the proceedings has been expressed as well (Scott, 1985).

Perhaps somewhat less predictable was the instant criticism of the commission's conclusions and recommendations on the part of psychologists. Minority reports and critical appraisals had been published before—in connection with the 1970 commission (Cline, 1970, 1974). The new report, however, prompted accusations of misrepresentation of critical findings. In particular, investigators whose own findings and views on policy differed from the 1986 commission's conclusions and recommendations published detailed accounts of how, in their view, the data at hand should have been interpreted and what policy should have been recommended. Linz, Donnerstein, and Penrod (1987), for example, took issue with the commission's report: "the authors find several of the commission's findings and recommendations incongruent with available research data" (p. 946).

A case in point is the commission's expressed conviction that the evidence concerning antisocial effects of violent pornography is particularly strong and that "societal consensus (concerning these effects) is greatest" (Attorney General's Commission on Pornography, 1986, p. 376). Such data interpretation led the committee to "urge that the prosecution of legally obscene material that contains violence be placed at the top of both state and federal priorities in enforcing the obscenity laws" (p. 377). Linz et al. (1987) objected to this advocacy of "stricter legal controls" and favor a "call for educational programs to mitigate *the effects of sexual violence in the media*" (p. 946, emphasis added).

Although these investigators seem to acknowledge undesirable effects of exposure to sexual violence in their plea for education, they question the 1986 commission's assessment of the available evidence (see also Donnerstein & Linz, 1986; Donnerstein, Linz, & Penrod, 1987). Specifically, they challenge the attribution of particular effects, such as an increased likelihood of aggression against women, to the sexuality portrayed in violent pornography. They suggest that these effects are created, instead, by the portrayal of violence, irrespective of sexual content and context. Their suggestion derives from the findings of two unpublished studies (Donnerstein, Berkowitz, & Linz, 1986; cited in Linz, Donnerstein, & Penrod,

1987). In these studies it has been observed that men tend to express more retaliatory aggression against women after exposure to either sexually violent or purely violent films than after exposure to innocuous control films.

In contrast, exposure to films showing nonviolent sexual activities was not found to facilitate retaliatory aggression. Other experiments have produced quite different outcomes (cf. Zillmann & Bryant, 1988a). But these investigations were declared inconclusive and dismissed. For example, Check's (1985) demonstration of increments in reported rape proclivity after repeated exposure to either violent or nonviolent pornography, compared with no such exposure, was said to involve "several methodological procedures that prevent us from placing as much confidence in the outcome of the experiment as we would like" (Check, 1985, p. 951). The procedures are not appreciably different, however, from those used in studies that enjoy broad acceptance (e.g., Malamuth & Ceniti, 1986). Such partiality in the interpretation and acceptance of pertinent findings has prompted the accusation that those who have alleged others' misrepresentations are themselves guilty of misrepresentation (Page, 1989).

Moreover, from within the social sciences came assaults on investigations that had generated findings that some apparently viewed as supportive of policies deemed unacceptable, if not abhorrent (Brannigan & Goldenberg, 1987). Christensen (1986), for instance, condemned demonstrations of antisocial effects of pornography—on intuitive grounds—as "flatly false" and "socially irresponsible" (p. 182). He cited historical examples, "such as the antimasturbation hysteria of earlier years, to show what harm this culture's traditional sexual fears can do" (p. 183). Investigators who obtained and reported evidence of antisocial effects of pornography were accused of antiquated, repressive sexual morality. Christensen's contempt for research demonstrations of pornography effects inspired a call for more restrictive criteria for the publication of such demonstrations and for informational protection of the public. Research in this realm, he suggested, "should be subjected to especially careful scrutiny before being promulgated to the general public" (p. 183).

The criticism of the effects demonstrated produced several published colloquia that are laden with false accusations and marked by a degree of hostility rarely found in the social science literature (Brannigan, 1987; Christensen, 1987; Linz & Donnerstein, 1988). For example, Christensen (1987) accused Zillmann and Bryant (1982) of deliberate deception in citing nonexistent data. The data in question had been presented at a conference (Donnerstein, 1984) but were later deemed unimportant, and they vanished (Linz, 1985). After numerous highly charged exchanges between the disputing parties, the data's existence was acknowledged (Linz & Donnerstein, 1988). Efforts at discounting apparently undesirable research demonstrations have led to similarly rash, unwarranted allegations. Brannigan (1987), for instance, advanced elaborate alternative explanations for such demonstrations on presumptions about selective subject attrition in experimental groups. It turned out that there had been no attrition at all. In related allegations, Donnerstein, Linz, and Penrod (1987) insinuated that findings different from their own must have been artificially created by exposure to strings of snippets showing "sexually explicit images with no context" (p. 79). But typical, intact pornographic films had been used, and the research report said so.

Most of the criticism focused on procedural details, and especially on details that could support charges of experimental artificiality and lack of generalizability. Criticism often transcended methodological considerations, however, and became innuendo of the investigators' political motives, if not their religious beliefs. Christensen (1987), for example, seemed apprehensive about "fundamentalist conspiracies" when investigators met with former Surgeon General Koop, a born-again Christian, to discuss their findings.

Some rather unexpected criticism of pornography research, finally, came in the form of a general analysis of methodology. Byrne and Kelley (1986) examined all facets of research procedures that had been employed, and they concluded that all findings on the effects of pornography are exceedingly tentative and unacceptable as a basis for policy recommendations. The fact is that the criteria applied in this analysis are so stringent that, if used to judge psychological research at large, they would reduce psychology from a science to an art form. Such humbling self-criticism reveals a decided unwillingness to influence regulatory policy for pornography, an unwillingness that seems to be prevalent among psychologists with a research interest in sexual behaviors.

Reluctance to influence policy is also evident in the evaluation of the work of the Surgeon General's Workshop on Pornography and Public Health. The Surgeon General's committee refrained from making policy recommendations and qualified its conclusions about effects so far as to make them meaningless. For instance, violent pornography was said to affect *laboratory* aggression. Statements about effects outside the laboratory were conspicuously absent (Linz & Donnerstein, 1988). Additionally, the report (Mulvey & Haugaard, 1986) cautioned that pornography would constitute only one of numerous potential influences on behavior, and it suggested that conceivable interactions among the potential influences would have to be investigated before general statements about the behavioral effects of pornography would be warranted. Presumably because of such caution, the committee's work has been hailed as excellent (Wilcox, 1987), and essentially because psychologists declared their work inconclusive and inconsequential for policies concerning pornography, psychology was thought to have "acquitted itself well" (Wilcox, 1987, p. 943).

The selective self-curtailment of psychology's potential influence on policy has not gone entirely unnoticed. Page (1989) noted the apparent "cop-out" and took issue with it. He suggested, in direct opposition to the frequent claims of research limitations and calls for more and better data, that the definitive research in this area "has in fact been conducted ad nauseum" (p. 580), and he explained the cop-out in political terms. For the research on pornography effects, "the most serious drawback of the cumulative evidence is that it could be taken as support for perspectives and positions advocated by unpopular political groups within the social science and academic communities" (p. 580).

All this is not intended to deny the usefulness of more and superior research data. Nor is it to call the merits of caution into question or to promote unwarranted bold action. The objective, instead, is to point out that caution is not without political implications. Caution, especially in extreme forms, is not by necessity prudent procedure. One should be cognizant of the fact that it can be a strategy favoring the status quo. In short, the call for more inclusive, more decisive, and absolutely definitive research may be an effective strategy in support of a policy of inaction.

PRINCIPAL DIFFICULTIES

If nothing else, the debate over pornography research and the possible regulation of pornographic material has made it clear that most of those who gather policy-relevant information, especially psychologists who seek to delineate the causal conditions of behavioral consequences of exposure, find it difficult, if not impossible, to separate presumed facts about effects from personal views on desirable social policy concerning these effects. The problem is a fundamental one for the social sciences that serve the welfare of citizens. There is, after all, no legitimacy in deriving social precepts from so-called facts about the real world. Imperatives do not follow from declaratives. And what ought to be done about particular circumstances cannot be inferred from knowledge about them, irrespective of how penetrating and veridical that knowledge might be. The endorsement of a precept or the acceptance of a policy, then, simply does not follow from social science data, no matter how obvious the connection might seem to some. If, for instance, it were established that drunk driving kills or maims one-tenth of the population, it would not follow that efforts should be made to change the situation. Or if it were established that fictional violence on U.S. television inspires acts of brutality on an average per year in only seven youngsters, it would not follow that nothing should be done about it. More to the point, if it were compellingly and irrefutably established that pornography promotes rape, that in the United States it leads to the traumatization of 80,000 women each year, it would not follow that we ought to curtail its distribution. In terms of science, the connection between knowledge of causal circumstances and policy is a *strictly arbitrary* one. The justification of social policy is necessarily outside science proper. It is moral at the individual level and political at the societal level.

It appears that, in dealing with the pornography issue, policy makers and social scientists, as well as their critics from various camps, have been rather confused about the relationship between facts and policy. Had they not been, the results of the proceedings and the criticism thereof should have been different.

Commission Composition and Policy

If it is recognized that the mandate of the Attorney General's 1986 commission was to recommend policy partly in light of social science information, any citizen capable of comprehending the pertinent information should qualify for membership. Expertise in the area of pornography is of no consequence for the value-based endorsement of policy. Hence, it should have been treated as immaterial.

Concerns about policy-related convictions of individual commission members, and about the distribution of these convictions in the commission, are probably well founded. If committees are dominated by persons already committed to particular policies, impartial deliberation of policy options is unlikely and policy recommendations may be foregone conclusions.

In principle, the fair-trial paradigm of criminal justice cannot be applied to policy deliberations, and no one should pretend that it does. The informational conditions are strikingly different. Jurors may be kept uninformed, prior to court proceedings, about the specifics of cases. They thus may enter these proceedings without having prejudged innocence or guilt of defendants. In contrast, public policy issues are public issues by definition. The circumstances creating these issues are common knowledge, and potential members of policy committees cannot be kept in the dark about them.

It must be assumed that, as a rule, such committee members are cognizant of the circumstances in question; furthermore, that members have contemplated and judged the societal desirability or undesirability of these circumstances. Citizens who can be recruited for policy committees are therefore neither ignorant of the issue nor unlikely to have appraised it and adopted a stand that amounts to a willingness to support some policies more than others.

This precondition creates considerable problems. Because a committee composed of truly impartial members cannot be constituted, and because any member imbalance that might favor particular policies has been deemed intolerable by many critics, a balanced committee is implicitly suggested as a solution. But is it a solution? Quite obviously, if a committee were composed such that half its members favor a particular policy and the other half oppose it, the committee is bound to be deadlocked. This likely result of balancing is by no means a neutral outcome, however. It should be recognized that any stalemate in policy-recommending committees favors the status quo. It favors a policy of inaction. The insistence on balanced committees can thus be construed as a strategy for inaction.

All this is not to say that imbalance in policy committees is desirable. The argument is that the insistence on balance is not, as often implied, a clarion call for fairness and neutrality; it can be, and often is, a policy strategy.

As there is no apparent solution concerning the composition of policy committees, the best that can be hoped for is that the members of committees are open to pertinent information and do adjust their policy-relevant convictions in accord with that information, and not just occasionally, but regularly.

Expert Testimony and Policy

The composition of expert groups for so-called testimony before policy committees is not without problems either. It is often inconceivable to invite all who might qualify. The necessary exclusion of some then opens the doors for criticism. The Attorney General's 1986 commission was promptly criticized for limiting expert testimony (Wilcox, 1987).

The opposite stand seems more meaningful. The commission may have been exposed to far too much social science testimony—in too short a period of time, anyway. At the Houston hearings, almost all psychologists who had done empirical work on pornography uses and effects, along with a large number of clinicians with experience in these matters, had their say. In a string of academic presentations, interrupted only by the occasional testimony of victims of sexual abuse seemingly related to pornography, they compressed their knowledge into brief summaries of their research or experience.

The commission must have been overwhelmed. Absorption of all the evidence presented, and the thorough critical appraisal of this evidence, would seem to exceed human capabilities. Moreover, only a small minority of commissioners, at best, had the training to judge the merits of research findings. The result of such conditions (that is, of conditions of information overload and inability to separate compelling research findings from dubious ones and expert opinion) was that overall impressions were formed on the basis of obtrusive assertions and vivid displays.

Media coverage of the hearings is telling in this regard. It focused on victim testimony (e.g., the TV cameras were rolling when victims, anonymous behind screens, revealed their fascinating ordeals and were not when academicians presented research). The commissioners similarly may have focused their attention on images and highly dramatic, yet probably nonrepresentative, clinical cases, rather than on the comparatively abstract, general information. This, at least, is what one would expect on the basis of the heuristic principles and shortcuts in information processing that have been explored in cognitive psychology (Fiske & Taylor, 1984; Zanna, Olson, & Herman, 1987).

The relative neglect of particular research findings in proceedings of this kind is unavoidable. This circumstance gives almost all testifying investigators cause for complaints. It explains the frequent allegations of under- or misrepresentation of their stands (Donnerstein, Linz, & Penrod, 1987). However, considering the policy process at large, such grievances are quite unimportant. The significant and principal dilemma in the relationship between research evidence and public policy is the enormous loss of social science information in hearings of policy committees that do not give sufficient time for the evaluation of findings and are composed of members with little qualification to evaluate the findings presented.

It should be mentioned in this connection that in the Surgeon General's Committee a panel of experts was given three hours to generate recommendations and reach consensus on the recommendations. The panel decided to refrain from making policy recommendations and sought to reach agreement on statements summarizing the pertinent research evidence. The stipulation that consensus be reached gave every member veto power and resulted in the panel's failure to agree on any generalization of relevance.

The panel's decision to refrain from making policy recommendations, in opposition to its mandate, contrasts sharply with the behavior of the social scientists who testified before the Attorney General's Commission. Most were eager to urge particular policies. Few were deliberate in avoiding policy statements and adhered to their mandate of presenting whatever findings they had aggregated. The behavior of most, then, shows that social scientists are often confused about the conceptual boundaries between science and public policy. They have few reservations about combining the two and, given a chance to testify, want to speak as both scientists and citizens.

Effects of Presumptions about Policy

The fact that at the Houston hearings so many social scientists felt compelled to urge the commission to adopt or reject certain policies concerned with the availability of pornography in society would seem to indicate how strongly they felt personally about the issue. In violation of their limited assignment, to enlighten the commission about uses and effects of pornography as known from research or clinical experience, they expressed their views on what ought to be done. In so doing, they essentially voted their own erotic preferences. Whatever evidence of uses and effects they may have presented, it cannot have justified recommendations concerning the regulation or deregulation of pornography.

Most of those social scientists who pleaded for particular policies behaved as if the Attorney General's Commission was set up to determine whether or not the research evidence warrants a total ban on pornography of any kind. Under this presumption, some urged that something finally be done about pornography and others pleaded for leaving things alone. Such apparent eagerness to influence policy proved highly divisive. It produced factions of censorship supporters, censorship opponents, and censorship-indifferent investigators. Additionally, the latter group was suspected of favoring censorship if their findings showed consequences deemed undesirable, and of opposing it if their findings showed consequences that could not be deemed undesirable or if they failed to show relevant consequences altogether. Such unfortunate dominance, of political conviction over scientific judgment, would be less likely if social scientists realized that expert testimony before policy-recommending committees does not call for their citizen views on desirable policy, if only because they so obviously do not represent the population at large.

Research Limitations and Policy

As indicated earlier, research on the consequences of exposure to pornography has been subjected to extreme scrutiny and criticism (Brannigan & Goldenberg, 1987; Byrne & Kelley, 1986). Quite obviously, descriptive research may help define the societal phenomenon of pornography usage, but it is uninformative as far as behavioral effects are concerned. Case studies may be illustrative, but their incidental and arbitrary aggregation does not allow the generalization of findings, including accounts of stimulus-response connections, to populations of interest.

Surveys of opinions and beliefs about effects of pornography exposure can inform us about distributions of opinions and beliefs, but not about the etiology of behavioral contingencies. Actually, they do not reliably inform us about opinion distributions either, nor about the distribution of pornography-related habits (e.g., frequency, circumstances, and purpose of usage). Surveys of erotic and sexual preferences are patently unreliable (Eysenck, 1976), mostly because a good portion of the surveyed population is unwilling to reveal its inclinations and habits in the sexual realm. The exploration of natural (i.e., uninfluenced, unmanipulated) relationships between pornography consumption and possible behavioral consequences, whether by way of naturalistic inquiry or in quantitative terms, again cannot prove anything definitively about the causation of behavior. It is suggestive at best. The devastating remark that it is "only correlational" is liberally applied to regression studies that seek to determine which aspects of pornography exposure might influence particular behaviors.

Similar studies on other, less controversial policy issues are often treated with considerable compassion. The statistical relationship between drunk driving and car accidents is a case in point. It does not provide causal proof. But nobody seems to want to argue that drivers who drink are reckless people, and that reckless people cause accidents whether or not they are intoxicated. In contrast, the fact that rapists tend to be heavy consumers of pornography and often use it as a turn-on prior to committing rape (Marshall, 1989) is deemed immaterial because it can be argued that exposure to pornography is incidental and rapists, being reckless people, would commit rape independent of exposure.

The burden of proof of behavioral consequences of pornography exposure is thus squarely placed on experimental methodology. Causal relationships are accepted only if exposure to pornography is followed by particular policy-relevant behavior, and no exposure to pornography is not, or is to a different degree.

The usefulness of this paradigm for the determination of the behavioral consequences of exposure to pornography is severely limited. Ethical considerations simply rule out the experiments that could provide definitive proof and resolve the issue. Most obvious is that sexual violence cannot be used as a dependent variable. For instance, men cannot be placed at risk of developing sexually violent inclinations by extensive exposure to violent or nonviolent pornography, and women cannot be placed at risk of becoming victims of such inclinations. As anything short of demonstrating behavioral changes in these terms has been found wanting (Byrne & Kelley, 1986), we have to accept that compelling proof of a causal connection between the consumption of different types of pornography and sexually violent behaviors, should such a connection exist, is not forthcoming.

Ethical considerations not only prevent experimentation on sexually violent behavior, but also apply to the study of sexual callousness manifest in social dispositions or attitudes. Early studies have shown, for instance, that repeated exposure to pornography trivializes rape as a criminal offense (Zillmann & Bryant, 1982) or relaxes inhibitions in the contemplation of coercive acts in the pursuit of sexual access (Check, 1985). Experimental subjects thus had been placed at risk; and now that such consequences are known, it would be irresponsible to conduct similar investigations to further our understanding of the dynamics of the observed dispositional changes.

Furthermore, ethical considerations prevent any experimental work with children and precollege adolescents. This may seem unimportant, but actually it has significant implications. It turns out that most men, prior to entering college (or prior to reaching college age), already had substantial exposure to various forms of pornography (Bryant & Brown, 1989). If such exposure influences sexual callousness or particular erotic orientations, these influences may have taken hold before these men could become experimental subjects. The result is that experimental manipulations of exposure are ineffective. Conditions of no exposure cannot be created, and no exposure versus exposure manipulations in experiments would result in comparisons between similarly heavily exposed groups. These conditions are bound to produce null findings in future research, null findings that are likely to be used as evidence for no effects (Linz & Donnerstein, 1988).

Experimentation on pornography effects faces numerous other difficulties. Most notably, the apparent temporal separation between cause and effect creates problems (i.e., exposure may have a delayed impact, and numerous exposures may be required to bring it about), and the relationship between measures that can be used and what they are to measure (i.e., measurement validity) tends to be poor.

The bottom line is that research on many potentially significant aspects of the influence of pornography on beliefs, attitudes, and behaviors cannot be definitive. It cannot satisfy the demands for rigor and compellingness that have been placed on it. Not now, and in a free society, not ever. The research leaves us with considerable uncertainty about exposure consequences at the societal level.

On the other hand, it provides us with a good deal of understanding of *some* of the issues involved. Numerous effects demonstrations do meet the demands for reliability, validity, and generalizability that the social science community places on research in other domains of human endeavor. Fragmented and limited in scope as these demonstrations may be, they constitute and convey integratable and accumulating information about facets of the etiology of erotic orientations and their behavioral consequences that is superior to hearsay, guessing, and unchecked common sense. In these terms, research findings that derive from empirical investigations that use the best available methodology may be considered the best available basis for the contemplation and construction of public policy.

Research Eclecticism and Policy

If left to its own devices, social science research is likely to produce highly eclectic evidence for policy considerations. Investigators select and address research issues for varied, rather personal reasons. They may, for instance, pick something that intrigues them, impresses their peers, promises an easy publication, brings fame, or relates to a deeply felt concern of theirs. Whatever the particular criteria for their choices, the resulting body of knowledge does not necessarily serve the public interest and cannot possibly be considered an optimal basis for policy decisions.

Regarding pornography uses and effects, the available research has failed to address many issues of potential significance for public policy. Issues likely to incite intense controversy have not been touched, and topics deemed safe in these terms have attracted a disproportionate amount of attention. For instance, social scientists elected to ignore possible effects of pornography on the formation of erotic orientation and sexual preference in adolescents. Likely effects on the development and modification of erotic orientation and preference in women has received no attention at all. The possible creation of unrealistic, unfulfillable sexual expectations and temptations, along with their implications for coping, has been neglected. Only one published study deals with matters such as sexual satisfaction or dissatisfaction resulting from prolonged pornography consumption (Zillmann & Bryant, 1988b). Effects of early exposure (i.e., during childhood) remain largely unknown. The involvement of pornography in sexual child abuse has been ascertained in descriptive terms only (Lanning & Burgess, 1989). Effects of pornography consumption on values concerning family and marriage, as well as on the desire for progeny, also have received little attention (Zillmann & Bryant, 1988a). In contrast, the least objectionable research item, the effect of the worst kind of pornography (i.e., sexually violent material) on the worst kind of sexual behavior (i.e., rape), has been explored in numerous studies (Check, 1985; Donnerstein, 1980; Malamuth, 1986).

Oddly enough, this obtrusive eclecticism in the research on pornography uses and effects has been overlooked in the otherwise thorough and seemingly exhaustive aforementioned academic self-criticism. Setting one's own research agenda is apparently considered an essential part of academic freedom that is not to be questioned. From a policy perspective, however, the yield of sporadic research without a defined agenda is of limited value.

Committees that pondered the pornography issue, with a mandate to recommend regulatory policy, were thus confronted with eclectic evidence whose validity has been severely questioned by those who generated this evidence. Given such a dilemma, how can anybody be surprised that committees in the United States, in Canada, and in Britain decided to give little credence to the so-called expert testimony by social scientists and, instead, based their decisions on alternative sources of information (Einsiedel, 1988)?

A RESEARCH POLICY FOR POLICY RESEARCH

As indicated earlier, recent efforts toward the formation of policy regulating or deregulating pornography have gone wrong on many counts. One of them is social science input, which simply proved inconsequential for policy recommendations and, hence, legislation. The Attorney General's commission was ill-equipped to review social science evidence, and the Surgeon General's committee, composed of social scientists potentially able to assist in a meaningful way, reported only after the Attorney General's commission had made its recommendations.

The process could have been more productive if the Surgeon General's committee had summarized the state of the art of research on the uses and effects of pornography more exhaustively and without pressures toward consensus (also without engaging in self-destructive methodological criticism that was apparently motivated by fears of regulatory consequences), and if the Attorney General's commission had worked from this summary rather than from assorted testimony by experts and victims and from their own personal views on regulatory policy.

Such a procedure would still have been far from satisfactory, however, mainly because policy objectives would have remained unclear, and the research evidence would have remained eclectic. To remedy this situation, it would seem to be necessary to proceed in three stages:

1. A policy-exploring committee should be formed and charged with (a) the assessment of citizens' grievances pertaining to the issue under consideration, (b) the specification of perceived problems in all their manifestations, and (c) the projection of possible regulatory policy. From a social science perspective, the second part of this charge is crucial. The assignment calls for an exhaustive listing of presumed effects. Research could obviously assist the search for presumed consequences of pornography consumption (surveys of beliefs and reviews of the available research literature). But most important, the listing would serve as a research agenda. As this agenda would be comprehensive and exhaustive, as well as focused, the problem of eclectic and unfocused research could be overcome. However, it can be overcome only if funds are provided to conduct the necessary investigations.

It should be noted that such an agenda in no way limits the freedom of investigators to conduct whatever studies they deem important, even studies that are extraneous to the agenda. Research extraneous to the agenda would, in fact, complement agenda research in a most positive fashion, potentially serving as a corrective for incomplete agendas.

2. After a period of time allowing for the execution of needed investigations, a social science committee should be constituted. Its mandate should be to assess all pertinent research findings, irrespective of what policy implications they might have. This committee should be composed of social scientists capable of judging the technical merits of the available research. The committee's principal task would be to critically evaluate and integrate all pertinent research findings and to present a summary of findings in terms intelligible to lay persons.

3. A policy-recommending committee then should be formed and given the mandate to propose policies that, in full view of the research evidence at hand, would best serve the public at large. The formulation of such policies necessarily

entails value judgments and thus is best left to those experienced in anticipating reactions of constituencies and in caring for the welfare of these constituencies.

Surely, the evidence at hand will not be definitive in the sense that none of its aspects could be questioned by someone. And just as surely, no set of recommended policies can satisfy all the people, when the issue is as charged and controversial as pornography. Some will feel that their erotic birthright is threatened (Money, 1985) and others will fear the decay of morality and the decline of culture (Scott, 1985). Uncertainty will remain, and controversy is ensured. The outlined procedure would generate results, however, that should be superior to public policy recommended on the basis of fickle public opinion or the views of a handful of politicians and lawyers.

REFERENCES

Abel, G. G., Becker, J. V., & Mittelman, M. S. (1985, September 18). *Use of pornography and erotica by sex offenders*. Paper presented at the eleventh annual meeting of The International Academy of Sex Research, Seattle, WA.

Attorney General's Commission on Pornography. (1986, July). *Final Report* (Department of Justice). Washington, DC: U.S. Government Printing Office.

Brannigan, A. (1987). Pornography and behavior: Alternative explanations. *Journal of Communication, 37*(3), 185–192.

Brannigan, A., & Goldenberg, S. (1987). The study of aggressive pornography: The vicissitudes of relevance. *Critical Studies in Mass Communication, 4*, 262–283.

Bryant, J., & Brown, D. (1989). Uses of pornography. In D. Zillmann & J. Bryant (Eds.), *Pornography: Research advances and policy considerations* (pp. 25–55). Hillsdale, NJ: Erlbaum.

Byrne, D., & Kelley, K. (1986). Psychological research and public policy: Taking a long, hard look before we leap. In E. P. Mulvey & J. L. Haugaard (Eds.), *Report of the Surgeon General's Workshop on Pornography and Public Health* (U.S. Department of Health and Human Services, Office of the Surgeon General). Washington, DC: U.S. Government Printing Office.

Check, J. V. P. (1985). *The effects of violent and nonviolent pornography*. Ottawa: Department of Justice for Canada.

Christensen, F. (1986). Sexual callousness re-examined. *Journal of Communication, 36*(1), 174–188.

Christensen, F. (1987). Effects of pornography: The debate continues. *Journal of Communication, 37*, 186–188.

Cline, V. B. (1970). *Minority report of the U.S. Commission on Obscenity and Pornography*. New York: Bantam.

Cline, V. B. (Ed.). (1974). *Where do you draw the line?* Salt Lake City, UT: Brigham Young University Press.

Donnerstein, E. (1980). Pornography and violence against women: Experimental studies. *Annals of the New York Academy of Sciences, 347*, 277–288.

Donnerstein, E. (1983). Erotica and human aggression. In R. G. Geen & E. I. Donnerstein (Eds.), *Aggression: Theoretical and empirical reviews. Vol. 2. Issues in research* (pp. 127–154). New York: Academic Press.

Donnerstein, E. (1984). Effects of pornography. In D. Scott (Ed.), *Symposium on media violence and pornography: Proceedings and resource book* (pp. 78–94). Toronto: Media Action Group.

Donnerstein, E., Berkowitz, L., & Linz, D. (1986). *Role of aggressive and sexual images in violent pornography*. Unpublished manuscript, University of Wisconsin-Madison.

Donnerstein, E., & Linz, D. (1986, December). The question of pornography. *Psychology Today*, pp. 56–59.

Donnerstein, E., Linz, D., & Penrod, S. (1987). *The question of pornography: Research findings and policy implications*. New York: Free Press.

Einsiedel, E. F. (1988). The British, Canadian, and U.S. pornography commissions and their use of social science research. *Journal of Communication, 38*(2), 108–121.

Eysenck, H. J. (1976). *Sex and personality*. Austin: University of Texas Press.

Fiske, S. T., & Taylor, S. E. (1984). *Social cognition*. New York: Random House.

178   DOMESTIC POLICY

Gouran, D. S. (1988). *Questionable inferences in the Attorney General's Commission on Pornography: A case study of unwarranted collective judgment and faulty group decision making.* Unpublished manuscript, Penn State University, University Park, PA.

Hertzberg, H. (1986, July 14). Big boobs: Ed Meese and his pornography commission. *The New Republic,* pp. 21-24.

Lanning, K. V., & Burgess, A. W. (1989). Child pornography and sex rings. In D. Zillmann & J. Bryant (Eds.), *Pornography: Research advances and policy considerations* (pp. 235-255). Hillsdale, NJ: Erlbaum.

Linsley, W. A. (1989). The case against censorship of pornography. In D. Zillmann & J. Bryant (Eds.), *Pornography: Research advances and policy considerations* (pp. 343-359). Hillsdale, NJ: Erlbaum.

Linz, D. (1985). *Sexual violence in the media: Effects on male views and implications for society.* Unpublished doctoral dissertation, University of Wisconsin, Madison.

Linz, D., & Donnerstein, E. (1988). The methods and merits of pornography research. *Journal of Communication, 38*(2), 180-192.

Linz, D., Donnerstein, E., & Penrod, S. (1987). The findings and recommendations of the Attorney General's Commission on Pornography: Do the psychological "facts" fit the political fury? *American Psychologist, 42,* 946-953.

Malamuth, N. M. (1981). Rape proclivity among males. *Journal of Social Issues, 37*(4), 138-157.

Malamuth, N. M. (1984). Aggression against women: Cultural and individual causes. In N. M. Malamuth & E. Donnerstein (Eds.), *Pornography and sexual aggression* (pp. 19-52). Orlando, FL: Academic Press.

Malamuth, N. M. (1986). Do sexually violent media indirectly contribute to antisocial behavior? In E. P. Mulvey & J. L. Haugaard (Eds.), *Report of the Surgeon General's Workshop on Pornography and Public Health* (U.S. Department of Health and Human Services, Office of the Surgeon General). Washington, DC: U.S. Government Printing Office.

Malamuth, N. M., & Ceniti, J. (1986). Repeated exposure to violent and nonviolent pornography: Likelihood of raping ratings and laboratory aggression against women. *Aggressive Behavior, 12,* 129-137.

Marshall, W. L. (1989). Pornography and sex offenders. In D. Zillmann & J. Bryant (Eds.), *Pornography: Research advances and policy considerations* (pp. 185-214). Hillsdale, NJ: Erlbaum.

Money, J. (1985, December 30). *Statement on pornography.* Unpublished manuscript, Johns Hopkins University, Baltimore, MD.

Mulvey, E. P., & Haugaard, J. L. (1986, August 4). *Report of the Surgeon General's Workshop on Pornography and Public Health* (U.S. Department of Health and Human Services, Office of the Surgeon General). Washington, DC: U.S. Government Printing Office.

Nobile, P., & Nadler, E. (1986). *United States of America vs. Sex.* New York: Minotaur Press.

Page, S. (1989, March). Misrepresentation of pornography research: Psychology's role. *American Psychologist,* pp. 578-580.

Paletz, D. L. (1988). Pornography, politics, and the press: The U.S. Attorney General's Commission on Pornography. *Journal of Communication, 38*(2), 122-137.

Report of the Commission on Obscenity and Pornography. (1970). Washington, DC: U.S. Government Printing Office.

Scott, D. (1985, March). *Family policy and insights, Vol. 4: Pornography and its effects on family, community, and culture.* Washington, DC: Free Congress Foundation.

Wilcox, B. L. (1987). Pornography, social science, and politics: When research and ideology collide. *American Psychologist, 42,* 941-943.

Zanna, M. P., Olson, J. M., & Herman, C. P. (Eds.). (1987). *Social influence: The Ontario Symposium* (Vol. 5). Hillsdale, NJ: Erlbaum.

Zillmann, D., & Bryant, J. (1982). Pornography, sexual callousness, and the trivialization of rape. *Journal of Communication, 32*(4), 10-21.

Zillmann, D., & Bryant, J. (1988a). Effects of prolonged consumption of pornography on family values. *Journal of Family Issues, 9,* 518-544.

Zillmann, D., & Bryant, J. (1988b). Pornography's impact on sexual satisfaction. *Journal of Applied Social Psychology, 18,* 438-453.

12

Television Violence and Aggression: What Psychologists Should Tell the Public

Jonathan L. Freedman

In 1985 the American Psychological Association (APA) issued a press release entitled "Psychologists warn of potential dangers of TV violence" (APA, 1985). The release stated that ". . . the conclusions drawn on the basis of 25 years of research and a sizable number of experimental and field investigations is that viewing televised violence may lead to increases in aggressive attitudes, values, and behavior, particularly in children." In their submissions to the National Institute of Mental Health (NIMH; 1982) report on television, all of the psychologists (with the exception of a group employed by NBC) stated that television violence causes an increase in aggressiveness. The Ontario Psychological Association (1976) told the Canadian Royal Commission on Violence in the Communications Industry that "It has been clearly demonstrated that violence presented in the media increases aggressive, and probably later violent behaviour of consumers" (p. 145). According to these official statements, the negative effect of watching television violence thus is not a matter of opinion, not a careful weighing of conflicting information, not a best guess based on limited research, but a clear and definite scientific fact.

If this were true, it would surely be our responsibility as psychologists to inform the public about it. Although psychologists rarely discover effects that are as immutable and certain as those found by physicists, many of our findings are highly reliable. When we have information of this kind, I think we should have full confidence in ourselves as scientists and should be willing, even anxious to share what we know with anyone who might be able to use it. However, I believe that before taking a public stand as scientists, we should require that the findings be highly consistent and reliable. We should not expect absolutely definitive evidence from research on such a complex issue as the effect of television violence, but we should have as our criterion the requirement that the evidence be such that any reasonable scientist would be convinced by it. If it is, we should tell the world; if it is not, we should keep quiet or qualify our public statements accordingly.

As I have argued at some length (Freedman, 1984, 1986), the evidence for the causal effect of TV violence on aggression does not meet this criterion. Some of those who read the available research carefully may conclude that the effect probably exists, others will find that they are unable to make a reasonable guess, and still others will be led to think that watching TV violence probably does not affect aggression. But the research has not produced the kind of strong, reliable, consistent results that we usually require to accept an effect as proved. It may be that watching violent programs causes increased aggressiveness, but from a scientific point of view, this has not been demonstrated. Our public statements should reflect this.

REVIEW OF THE FINDINGS

Laboratory Experiments

By far the largest group of studies are laboratory experiments in which subjects are exposed to violent films or video tapes and are given the opportunity to express aggression. Most of these experiments have found more aggression after viewing violent material than after viewing neutral material. The results are not entirely consistent. Some of the published studies have failed to find significant effects in all or some conditions (e.g., Collins, 1973; Hapkiewicz & Roden, 1971; Lovaas, 1961). Moreover, sometimes viewing violence increased aggressiveness only when subjects were first frustrated or made angry (Berkowitz & Geen, 1966; Berkowitz & Rawlings, 1963; Geen and O'Neal, 1969), but other very similar experiments found the effect without either frustration or anger (Hapkiewicz & Stone, 1974; Kniveton, 1973; Liebert & Baron, 1972). Nevertheless, there is little doubt that it is possible in the laboratory to increase subjects' scores on various measures of aggressiveness by first showing them violent films (see Andison, 1977, for a review).

There is, however, some question whether it is the violence in the films that causes the increased aggression. Zillmann (1971) has provided evidence that the effect may be due to the fact that violent films are generally more exciting and arousing than the neutral films to which they have been compared. If true, this suggests first that the effects would be very short-lived because arousal would decrease rapidly, second that the effects are not specific to aggression but would hold for any response, and third that the problem (if there is one) is not with violent material on television but with any kind of exciting or arousing program.

Despite this alternative explanation, let us accept that the laboratory studies do indicate that one can increase scores on various measures of aggression by exposing subjects to violent material. Unfortunately, laboratory experiments have only limited relevance to our basic question, which is whether watching the programs that actually appear on television (or in the movies) causes children or adults to become more aggressive. That researchers can produce this effect in the laboratory suggests that it might also occur in the uncontrolled environment of the home, but it does not prove it.

The first difficulty with generalizing from the laboratory studies is that they rarely measure actual aggression. Hitting a "Bobo doll" or pressing a "shock" button in a laboratory study does not involve actual physical aggression toward another person. In addition, this aggression is allowed and even encouraged in the laboratory, whereas it tends to be discouraged outside.

Second, there is inevitably a serious problem with experimenter influence in the laboratory. The subject is shown a film selected by the experimenter. Presumably the subject can conclude that the experimenter approves of this film and may even conclude that he or she is asking or encouraging the subject to behave in the manner it portrays. In contrast, children who watch television in their homes tend to select the programs themselves, and no one there is suggesting that they should behave in the way the people do in the film.

The most profound difficulties stem from the fact that the subjects are shown only one or at most a few short bits of material selected by the experimenter to be violent or nonviolent. There is a big difference between a 10-minute exposure to a violent video tape and a regular diet of television that includes all sorts of material—violent, nonviolent, cartoons, news, and so on. Eating only broccoli would probably make you sick, but this does not mean that it would be harmful to add broccoli to your regular diet. The same might be said for viewing violence on TV.

In addition, the content of the particular violent program must be taken into account. Social learning theory might suggest that children would learn to be aggressive by watching violent films because they see violence rewarded. But in many programs the violent people are punished, not rewarded. Few programs portray indiscriminate aggression. Instead, they show the "bad guys" being aggressive and getting punished, while the "good guys" who are aggressive are usually policemen, detectives, or others who have a legal right to use force. Rather than learning to be aggressive, children may learn to discriminate between legitimate and nonlegitimate use of force. Their own tendency to be aggressive might not be affected or might even be reduced. The point is that without knowing the actual content of the programs children watch and the mix of these programs, it is impossible to make any logical prediction about how they might be affected.

Thus, this laboratory research merely raises the possibility that watching violence on television may cause subjects to be more aggressive. The scientific case for the harmful effects of television violence must rest primarily on research done in natural settings. Although some researchers would disagree with this, giving the laboratory research more weight than I do, the fact remains that most of the active scientists in this area have chosen to do field research. In any case, if the field studies do not replicate the results of the laboratory experiments, it would seem to indicate that the effect does not generalize beyond the laboratory.

Correlational Studies

The second source of evidence is a group of correlational studies that obtained measures of how aggressive children are and how much television violence they watch (Eron, Huesmann, Lefkowitz, & Walder, 1972; Hartnagel, Teevan, & McIntyre, 1975; Huesmann & Eron, 1986; McIntyre & Teevan, 1972; McLeod, Atkin, & Chaffee, 1972; Milavsky, Stipp, Kessler, & Rubens, 1982). Despite considerable variability in the size of the effect, virtually all of the studies have found that children who watch more violent programs on television tend to be more aggressive. This finding is extremely important, because it raises the possibility that watching violence on television *causes* people to be more aggressive. Demonstrating causality has not been so successful.

Search for Causation

The most promising piece of evidence in favor of a causal effect of violent TV comes from a longitudinal study (Eron et al., 1972) that followed children from third grade to college level. The key finding was a correlation between watching TV violence at grade 3 and aggressiveness at grade 13 that was actually greater than that between TV violence and aggressiveness at grade 3 and a reverse relation between later TV violence viewing and early aggression. This pattern is consistent with and tends to support the idea that the effect on aggression of watching violent television is cumulative. That would explain why early TV viewing was more strongly related to later aggression than to early aggression. Although other inter-pretations of this result are possible, this is certainly the most plausible one.

However, this set of correlations did not replicate within the Eron study and has never been replicated by anyone else. In the original study, this pattern was found for only one of three measures of aggression and only for boys, not girls. Similar research has not produced an equivalent pattern (e.g., Huesmann, 1982), and these researchers have abandoned this particular kind of analysis in favor of others (e.g., Huesmann & Eron, 1986; Huesmann, Lagerspetz, & Eron, 1984). Whatever the reason for the failures, this pattern of relations stands alone and therefore cannot carry much weight.

The more typical method of trying to demonstrate causality is to assess the relation between early viewing of violent TV and later aggression over and above the effect due to the stability of aggression. An impressive cross-national study was conducted in the United States, Finland, Poland, Australia, Israel (Huesmann & Eron, 1986), and The Netherlands (Wiegman, Kuttschreuter, & Baarda, 1986). The most relevant analyses are multiple regressions in which early aggression is held constant and the effect of early viewing of violence on later aggression is assessed. Of 14 analyses of this sort (for boys and girls in each country, including two different samples in Israel), only three were significant. Huesmann and Eron take some comfort from the fact that the relations were all positive, but surely this is not an encouraging set of data for the notion that watching TV violence causes aggression. In fact, the researchers from Australia and The Netherlands conclude that there is no evidence for a causal relation.

Milavsky et al. (1982) conducted a massive study of the same kind in the United States. Four different measures of aggression were used, and complete analyses were done on the data. Although as usual aggressiveness was related to preference for violent television, early TV viewing contributed little or nothing to later ag-gressiveness.

Several other studies are sometimes cited as evidence for a causal link between viewing violence on TV and aggression. The first (Belson, 1978) found a relation between TV violence and only one of four measures of aggressiveness. Even this result was greatly weakened because the relation between viewing nonviolent TV and this measure of aggression was just as great as with viewing violent TV.

Two small-sample studies (Singer & Singer, 1980, 1986) also looked at the relation between viewing and aggression but found no consistent pattern indicating that early viewing affected later aggression. The authors did report that later ag-gression was predicted (though not necessarily caused) by earlier heavy viewing of a combination of violent cartoons such as *Superheroes* and *Woody Woodpecker* and what they characterize as the "fast-paced" *Sesame Street*. That almost everyone's favorite educational program, *Sesame Street*, supposedly affects aggression might make one wonder about the process by which watching television is supposed to make children aggressive. Indeed, it might suggest that if there is an effect, it is due to arousal (as discussed earlier) rather than to the violent content.

In summary, these correlational studies demonstrate that a preference for violent television is related to a tendency to be aggressive. In contrast, they do not support the idea that one causes the other. There is perhaps one strong positive result (the pattern of cross-lagged correlations in Eron et al., 1972), but this does not replicate even in that study and is never found again. Other attempts have produced contradictory results. Thus, this approach to the problem, employing very large numbers of subjects and highly sophisticated statistical techniques, has failed to provide consistent evidence that watching television affects subsequent aggression.

Field Experiments

The first field experiment was the most ambitious. Feshbach and Singer (1971) assigned boys in seven residential schools to a diet of either violent or nonviolent television for 6 weeks. The results were that boys who watched violent programs were generally *less* aggressive than those who watched nonviolent television. This study has been harshly criticized on several counts, and it was certainly not perfect. However, it was as good as or better than most of the work in this field.

Leyens, Parke, Camino, and Berkowitz (1975) and Parke, Berkowitz, Leyens, West, and Sebastian (1977) reported three studies done by this group, one in Belgium and two in the United States. In all three, boys in residential schools were shown either violent or nonviolent films and their aggressiveness was observed. There are quite a few problems with the analyses of the data so that it is more than usually difficult to know just what was found. It seems fair to say that the Belgian study found an effect mainly for initially aggressive boys; the first U.S. study found an effect mainly for low aggressive boys; and the second U.S. study found no overall effect, but perhaps a small increase after the violent films for boys who were initially low in aggressiveness.

Friedrich and Stein (1973) did a similar study in a nursery school. There were no effects of type of film on any of five measures of aggression. On one measure there was a barely significant interaction showing that the initially highly aggressive subjects who saw violent films *decreased* in aggressiveness less than those who saw neutral films, while low-aggressive subjects who saw the violent films increased *less* than those who saw the neutral films.

Finally, a study by Loye, Gorney, and Steele (1977) found some very weak evidence in favor of the causal effect, while a series of studies by Milgram and Shotland (1973) found no such evidence.

In addition to these field experiments, there are two quasi-experiments that should be mentioned. Hennigan et al. (1982) compared crime rates in U.S. cities that had television with those that did not during the period 1949 to 1952, when there was a freeze on new channels. The study found no effect of television on homicide, aggravated assault, burglary, or auto theft but some indication of an increase in minor theft, which the authors attributed to envy caused by poorer viewers who observed the relatively affluent people pictured on television. Whatever the correct explanation of this effect, the study produced no evidence of an effect of television on aggression.

The other study (Phillips, 1983) looked at the number of murders that occurred following world championship heavyweight prize fights between 1973 and 1978. The author reported that the number of homicides increased on day 3 following a fight, and to a lesser extent on days 4, 6, and 9, but not on any other day. The complex statistical procedures in this study have been criticized (Baron & Reiss, 1985). Moreover, it is difficult to imagine why there should be an increase on days 3 and 9 but not on days 2 and 8, or why the effect should occur only if the fights took place outside the United States. In short, while this is an interesting approach to the problem, the results are difficult to interpret.

Summary

This set of field experiments produced a few findings that were consistent with the causal effect of viewing TV violence on aggression, but also several that showed no such effect or even, in one case, a reverse effect. Considering all of the research, there is some evidence of a causal effect from the laboratory studies, very little from the correlational studies, and mixed results from the field experiments. Taken together, these data do not provide the kind of consistent findings that would ordinarily be required to give us confidence in an effect.

PUBLIC STATEMENTS VERSUS THE EVIDENCE

Other researchers may disagree with my descriptions of some of the studies and the weight I give to each. Nevertheless, I think it should be clear to any objective reader of the research that there is a considerable amount of inconsistency in the findings. Indeed, in a careful review of the evidence, Cook, Kendzierski, and Thomas state, "Our analysis of the past evidence for a causal link between television violence and aggression suggests that there is less consistency in the results than claimed. . . ." (1983, p. 191).

Assuming for the moment that I am not suppressing a whole body of supportive evidence or totally misrepresenting the research I did review, how can we explain APA's and others' categorical acceptance of the view that watching TV violence causes aggression? One possibility might be that I am requiring perhaps more perfect results than is reasonable. But it seems to me that the findings are far more inconsistent than one would need to consider an effect established. Remember that the cross-national study, conducted and written by psychologists who are strong believers in the harmful effect of viewing television violence (Huesmann & Eron, 1986) found a significant effect in only 3 of 14 possible analyses and that many of the field experiments found no effect. Thus, it is not a matter of simply wanting stronger evidence in favor, but also a matter of accounting for all of the failures to demonstrate an effect. It seems that if the effect were there, it would not be so difficult to find it. People may read the evidence carefully and still decide that, on balance, they believe that viewing violence causes an increase in aggressiveness. In fact, that is what Cook et al. (1983) decided. It is difficult for me to believe, however, that anyone can conclude that there is overwhelming or even strong, solid support for that effect, yet that is what APA stated.

Another explanation is that others place much more weight on the laboratory studies. For me they indicate only the possibility that the laboratory findings showing increased aggression after exposure to violent material effects generalize; for other researchers, laboratory studies seem to indicate that the effects almost surely generalize, and it is only a matter of showing that they do. Nevertheless, I would have thought that such other researchers would be discouraged by the results of the field studies. If there had never been any field studies, I could understand researchers being reasonably confident of the causal effect; but once the field studies had failed to confirm the effect, it would seem that they should inevitably become less confident.

Why are researchers so sure? I would suggest that part of the explanation is that many, perhaps most, psychologists came to this issue with strong personal dislike of TV violence and a belief that it is harmful. Starting with that, they read some of the early experimental work that was consistent with their feelings. When the contradictory evidence began to appear, psychologists were predisposed to reject it. They sharply criticized the Feshbach and Singer (1971) study and were thus able to ignore it, but they did not criticize the studies that got the effect, and were therefore impressed by them. Psychologists were delighted by the finding by Eron et al. (1972) and did not notice or were unconcerned that the effect was found in only one of six analyses. Researchers then criticized the study by Milavsky et al. (1982) and were ready to reject it anyway because it was supported by National Broadcast Corporation (NBC). And they were reassured by the cross-national study even though the crucial effect was significant in only a few of the many analyses. By giving great weight to the positive results and discounting the negative results, they remained convinced that the evidence strongly supported their position. Otherwise how can one explain that in 1986 a distinguished psychologist can still write "Anyone who looks at the accumulated research into the consequences of observed violence must be impressed by the consistency of the findings" (Berkowitz, 1986, p. 93)?

Moreover, it seems likely that the field as a whole tended to be more accepting of research showing the harmful effect of TV violence than research that did not show it. Feshbach (1988) relates reviewing an article for a journal and recommending it be published. It was a field study that found no effect or a positive effect of viewing TV violence. The editor rejected it, saying "This study presents one more field experiment that contradicts laboratory findings—it adds to the debate, but does not resolve it." I have had several similar experiences. Of course, these negative results do not resolve the debate. But keeping them out of the journals may give undue weight to the positive findings.

Individuals and the field as a whole have been predisposed to believe in the effect. I certainly am not suggesting any conspiracy or collusion or deliberate bias. But it is entirely natural to be more open to evidence that supports one's beliefs than to evidence that contradicts them. Thus, by some reading selective both in terms of what was read and how it was read, people managed to strengthen their beliefs in the harmful effect of TV violence despite the increasing number of nonsupportive results.

This is a difficult and complex literature. Few people who are not intimately involved in the work have the time and energy to read it all carefully. Thus, almost everyone relies on the experts in the field. When the experts said that the results were consistent, the nonexperts were happy to accept it. And the experts were so involved themselves, with their scientific careers and belief systems committed to the effect, that they too were relatively uncritical except of negative findings.

This interpretation is supported to some extent by public statements. Having said that the effects were clear, the spokesperson sometimes offered testimony that was simply inaccurate. For example, APA testimony to the United States Senate

(APA, 1984) stated that Friedrich and Stein found that the youngsters who watched the *Batman* and *Superman* cartoons were more likely to hit their playmates, whereas in fact there was no overall effect of type of program on physical aggression. Similarly, in its submission to the Royal Commission, the Ontario Psychological Association (1976) cites Lovaas (1961) as one study that found a negative effect of violent material, whereas in three separate experiments this study showed no significant effects. It cites another study as showing that after an aggressive film subjects delivered more shocks, but actually in that study there was no overall effect of type of film.

I mention these errors not because they are crucial to the argument. Only a full review of the literature can reveal what the evidence has found. As shown earlier, this kind of review indicates that the research has not produced consistent support for the causal effect of viewing violent television on aggression. However, I think that these errors suggest that the public statements on this issue have been less careful than they ought to have been. I believe this shows a tendency to accept the negative effect of TV violence and not to worry too much about the details of the evidence. This pattern makes sense only if those making the statements are certain that the effect exists even before they read the evidence. This is not the way we should use scientific inquiry, and I think it has done a disservice to the public and to our field.

WHAT SHOULD WE SAY?

How should psychologists deal with the results of research in talking to the public or to government agencies? The most important principle to keep in mind is that when we psychologists make public statements as experts, we should not advocate a position but present fully the scientific facts. Giving an impartial, accurate statement means discussing all of the results, not just those that support one position, and describing all of the weaknesses and inconsistencies. If the evidence is strong enough, there will be few qualifiers necessary; if there are many qualifiers required, the evidence is probably weak.

I should add that to some extent psychologists should take into account the responsibility of protecting or at least warning potential victims. If there is evidence that people are at risk, researchers should try to assess the seriousness of that risk as well as the strength of the evidence. The more serious the risk, the greater the need to inform the public.

Even with the possibility of very grave risk, psychologists should still follow the basic principle of telling the public everything. Thus, psychologists might say that they have some evidence that suggests a very serious threat, but then say that the evidence is still quite weak and inconsistent. They might go further and warn against taking action on the basis of such weak evidence, but add that it was important to communicate even weak evidence because of the severity of the risk. If this were done carefully and responsibly (not announced in a press release or a popular magazine), it would then be the job of government and others to decide whether to take action.

With regard to television violence, we can say with full confidence that children who watch more violent television also tend to be more aggressive. The evidence for this is almost perfectly consistent and I think we would be justified in saying this relation is proved beyond a reasonable doubt, with no qualifiers. We can also say that in the laboratory it appears that watching violent television increases aggressiveness, but the effect is not entirely consistent and we do not know why it occurs in some experiments and not in others. Moreover, we as psychologists should further qualify our position by telling the public that we are not certain whether anger is necessary for the effect or whether the effect is due to the violence or to the arousal. Despite these qualifications, we are confident that researchers can produce this effect in the laboratory.

There is little to say about the causal effect on aggression of viewing television violence except that it has not been demonstrated. Since there is no convincing evidence of an effect on actual crime, the possible risks are probably minimal, and we should require substantial evidence of a causal effect. If there were substantial evidence of an effect on crime, we would be willing to inform the public about it. In any case, because there is some risk (perhaps considerable if even a few people commit a violent act because of television violence), it seems perfectly reasonable for those psychologists who believe in the effect to inform the public. However, when those psychologists express opinions about the dangers of viewing television violence, they should make it clear that, while their opinions are based on their reading of the research, the evidence does not allow them to make definitive statements. This can probably be accomplished best by pointing out the various inconsistencies in the data and then adding that although they may be quite confident of the effect as persons, as scientists they are not. Of course, this kind of testimony will probably not have much weight with government or in court, but given the evidence, that is the way it should be.

In general, I believe that the more cautious and objective we are in presenting our research to the public, the more impact we will have when we have something to say. Going beyond the data or advocating a position that is not fully supported, like crying "wolf," will only discredit psychology as a scientific field and eventually will weaken whatever impact we might have.

REFERENCES

American Psychological Association. (1984, October 25). Testimony before the United States Senate Subcommittee on Juvenile Justice.

American Psychological Association. (1985, February 22). *Psychologists warn of potential dangers of TV violence* (Press release).

Andison, F. S. (1977). TV violence and viewer aggression: A cumulation of study results, 1956–1976. *Public Opinion Quarterly, 41*, 314–331.

Baron, J. N., & Reiss, P. C. (1985). Same time, next year: Aggregate analyses of the mass media on violent behavior. *American Sociological Review, 50*, 347–363.

Belson, W. (1978). *Television violence and the adolescent boy.* Hampshire, England: Saxon House.

Berkowitz, L. (1986). Situational influences on reactions to observed violence. *Journal of Social Issues, 42*, 93–106.

Berkowitz, L., & Geen, R. G. (1966). Film violence and the cue properties of available targets. *Journal of Personality and Social Psychology, 3*, 525–530.

Berkowitz, L., & Rawlings, E. (1963). Effects of film violence on inhibitions against subsequent aggression. *Journal of Abnormal and Social Psychology, 66*, 405–412.

Collins, W. A. (1973). Effect of temporal separation between motivation, aggression, and consequences: A developmental study. *Developmental Psychology, 8*, 215–221.

Cook, T. D., Kendzierski, D. A., & Thomas, S. V. (1983). The implicit assumptions of television research: An analysis of the 1982 NIMH report on television and behavior. *Public Opinion Quarterly, 47*, 161–201.

Eron, L. D., Huesmann, L. R., Lefkowitz, M. M., & Walder, L. O. (1972). Does television violence cause aggression? *American Psychologist, 27*, 253–263.

Feshbach, S. (1988). Television research and social policy. In S. Oskamp (Ed.), *Applied social psychology annual 8* (pp. 198-213). Newbury Park, CA: Sage.

Feshbach, S., & Singer, R. D. (1971). *Television and aggression: An experimental field study.* San Francisco: Jossey-Bass.

Freedman, J. L. (1984). Effect of television violence on aggressiveness. *Psychological Bulletin, 2,* 227-246.

Freedman, J. L. (1986). Television violence and aggression: A rejoinder. *Psychological Bulletin, 3,* 372-378.

Friedrich, L. K., & Stein, A. H. (1973). Aggressive and prosocial television programs and the natural behavior of preschool children. *Child Development Monograph, 38* (No. 4).

Geen, R. G., & O'Neal, E. C. (1969). Activation of cue-elicited aggression by general arousal. *Journal of Personality and Social Psychology, 11,* 289-292.

Hapkiewicz, W. G., & Roden, A. H. (1971). The effect of aggressive cartoons on children's interpersonal play. *Child Development, 42,* 1583-1585.

Hapkiewicz, W. G., & Stone, R. D. (1974). The effect of realistic versus imaginary aggressive models on children's interpersonal play. *Child Study Journal, 4,* 47-58.

Hartnagel, T. F., Teevan, J. J., Jr., & McIntyre, J. J. (1975). Television violence and violent behavior. *Social Forces, 54,* 341-351.

Hennigan, K. M., Del Rosario, M. L., Heath, L., Cook, T. D., Wharton, J. D., & Calder, B. J. (1982). Impact of the introduction of television on crime in the United States: Empirical findings and theoretical implication. *Journal of Personality and Social Psychology, 42,* 461-477.

Huesmann, L. R. (1982). Television violence and aggression behavior. In D. Pearl, L. Bouthilet, & J. Lazar (Eds.), *Television and behavior: Ten years of scientific progress and implications for the eighties. Vol. 2. Technical reviews* (pp. 126-137). Washington, DC: U.S. Government Printing Office.

Huesmann, L. R., & Eron, L. D. (1986). *Television and the aggressive child: A cross-national comparison.* Hillsdale, NJ: Erlbaum.

Huesmann, L. R., Lagerspetz, K., & Eron, L. D. (1984). Intervening variables in the TV violence-aggression relation: Evidence from two countries. *Developmental Psychology, 20,* 746-775.

Kniveton, B. H. (1973). The effect of rehearsal delay on long-term imitation of filmed aggression. *British Journal of Psychology, 64,* 259-265.

Leyens, J. P., Parke, R. D., Camino, L., & Berkowitz, L. (1975). Effects of movie violence on aggression in a field setting as a function of group dominance and cohesion. *Journal of Personality and Social Psychology, 32,* 346-360.

Liebert, R. M., & Baron, R. A. (1972). Some immediate effects of televised violence on children's behavior. *Developmental Psychology, 6,* 469-475.

Lovaas, O. I. (1961). Effect of exposure to symbolic aggression on aggressive behavior. *Child Development, 32,* 37-44.

Loye, D., Gorney, R., & Steele, G. (1977). An experimental field study. *Journal of Communication, 27,* 206-216.

McIntyre, J. J., & Teevan, J. J., Jr. (1972). Television violence and deviant behavior. In G. A. Comstock & E. A. Rubinstein (Eds.), *Television and social behavior: Vol. 3. Television and adolescent aggressiveness* (pp. 383-435). Washington, DC: U.S. Government Printing Office.

McLeod, J. M., Atkin, C. K., & Chaffee, S. H. (1972). Adolescents, parents, and television use: Self-report and other measures from the Wisconsin sample. In G. A. Comstock & E. A. Rubinstein (Eds.), *Television and social behavior: Vol. 3. Television and adolescent aggressiveness* (pp. 239-313). Washington, DC: U.S. Government Printing Office.

Milavsky, J. R., Stipp, H. H., Kessler, R. C., & Rubens, W. S. (1982). *Television and aggression: A panel study.* New York: Academic Press.

Milgram, S., & Shotland, R. L. (1973). *Television and antisocial behavior: Field experiments.* New York: Academic Press.

National Institute of Mental Health. (1982). *Television and behavior: Ten years of scientific progress and implications for the eighties. Vol. I. Summary report.* Washington, DC: U.S. Government Printing Office.

Ontario Psychological Association. (1976). *Report of the Royal Commission on Violence in the Communications Industry: Vol. I. Approaches, conclusions, and recommendations.* Toronto, Ontario: Ministry of Government Services.

Parke, R. D., Berkowitz, L., Leyens, J. P., West, S., & Sebastian, R. J. (1977). Some effects of violent and nonviolent movies on the behavior of juvenile delinquents. In L. Berkowitz (Ed.), *Advances in experimental social psychology* (Vol. 10, pp. 135-172). New York: Academic Press.

Phillips, D. P. (1983). The impact of mass media violence on U.S. homicides. *American Sociological Review, 48,* 560–568.

Singer, J. L., & Singer, D. G. (1980). *Television, imagination, and aggression: A study of preschoolers' play.* Hillsdale, NJ: Erlbaum.

Singer, J. L., & Singer, D. G. (1986). Family experiences and television viewing as predictors of children's imagination, restlessness, and aggression. *Journal of Social Issues, 42,* 107–124.

Wiegman, O., Kuttschreuter, M., & Baarda, B. (1986). *Television viewing related to aggressive and prosocial behaviour.* The Hague: SVO.

Zillmann, D. (1971). Excitation transfer in communication-mediated aggressive behavior. *Journal of Experimental Social Psychology, 7,* 419–434.

13

The Effects of Television Violence
on Aggression: A Reply to a Skeptic

**L. Rowell Huesmann, Leonard D. Eron, Leonard Berkowitz,
and Steven Chaffee**

In his 1984 *Psychological Bulletin* article, "Effect of television violence on aggressiveness," Freedman reached several specific conclusions:

> *It seems clear that . . . viewing violent material on television or film in the laboratory can increase aggressive responses in the laboratory.* (p. 228)

He concluded:

> *Exposure to and preference for violent programming on television is correlated with aggressive behavior.* (p. 243)

However, he also concluded:

> *There is little convincing evidence that viewing violence on television in natural settings causes an increase in subsequent aggressiveness.* (p. 243)

Finally, he qualified his conclusion by writing:

> *My conclusion does not mean or imply that the causal hypothesis is incorrect.* (p. 244)

While these specific conclusions may seem judicious when examined in isolation, Freedman presented them in an overall context that was clearly intended to reject the causal hypothesis. Unfortunately, many who have read the article in the past six years missed the subtleties of the specific conclusions and retained only this general negative theme. The article has been cited frequently ( ) as showing that media violence does not stimulate aggressive behavior. Such a conclusion was not justified by the existing research at the time and is not justified now. In fact, it is at odds with the opinions of most developmental and social psychologists working in the field, who have come to believe that media violence increases the chance that individuals in the audience, adults as well as children, will subsequently behave aggressively themselves.

Contrary to Freedman's assertion on page 228, his article is not (and was not at the time) the only comprehensive review available. A number of equally thorough reviews of the literature had been published in the immediately preceding years (Chaffee, 1972; Comstock, 1980; Hearold, 1979; Huesmann, 1982; Lefkowitz &

Huesmann, 1980). Since the publication of Freedman's article several other excellent reviews have been produced. The most recent are two meta-analyses, one by Comstock and Paik (in press) and one by Wood, Wong, and Chacheri (in press). Freedman's article is distinguished only by the fact that its conclusions were different from the others. Unfortunately, because of this characteristic it attracted sufficient attention that even six years later, a chapter such as the current one is necessary to set the record straight.

NEGLECT OF LABORATORY RESEARCH

In his article Freedman agrees with most researchers that it has been proven beyond reasonable doubt that exposing children to media violence causes an increase in their aggressive behavior under the controlled laboratory conditions in which causation can be tested most convincingly. Freedman also agrees that in the real world, children who watch more violence on TV generally behave more aggressively. However, Freedman does not agree with most researchers on the implications to be drawn from longitudinal field studies. Unfortunately he then bases his general conclusions almost entirely on interpretations of this one subset of research. He simply disregards laboratory experiments, mentioning them only briefly. Such selective attention reveals a misplaced confidence in field studies, and although field studies may have greater external validity than laboratory studies and in some cases allow greater generalization of results, this is not always the case (Berkowitz & Donnerstein, 1982). Further, those who believe that a causal theory can be proved or disproved solely by field studies are bound to be disappointed. Yet this is just what Freedman has attempted to do by ignoring laboratory studies. A field study may suggest that one causal theory is more plausible than another, but it cannot prove a theory true or false. What is most impressive about the media violence research is the way in which the laboratory experiments, correlational single-wave field studies, and longitudinal developmental studies all complement each other in linking exposure to media violence with subsequent aggression. Freedman misses this convergence of evidence from different sources entirely by concentrating solely on field studies.

Freedman's reasons for rejecting laboratory evidence include the presumed artificiality of the laboratory experiments. First, noting that the aggression measures used in these studies are "only analogues of naturalistic aggression," he questions whether the findings obtained with these measures can be generalized to real-world aggression. However, Berkowitz and Donnerstein (1982) have surveyed the research bearing on just this matter and have shown that there is indeed an empirical basis for generalizing such laboratory results to the real world.

Freedman also asserts that the "laboratory work suffers from strong experimenter demands." That is, the subjects, on seeing the aggressive nature of the film shown to them, behave aggressively "because in a sense they have been told to or perhaps given permission by the experimenter." This criticism, however, runs counter to the empirical evidence. Turner and Simons (1974) have shown that participants in aggression experiments are much more likely to be affected by evaluation apprehension than by supposed demand characteristics. The "permission giving" posited by Freedman has never been demonstrated in aggression experiments. As a matter of fact, Turner and Simons (1974) note that if subjects suspect that the experimenter is interested in their aggressive reactions, they are apt to suppress these responses. Apparently they believe they can make a better impression on the experimenter by acting cool, calm, and collected than they can by displaying open aggression. There is no evidence that subjects behave as if they believe the experimenter's interest in their aggression gives them permission to act aggressively. Still, experimenters in this field have always been aware of the possibility of demand effects, so from the earliest experiments on film violence they have taken great care to avoid obtrusive measurement (e.g., Bandura, Ross, & Ross, 1963).

SELECTIVE REPORTING AND CHANGING CRITERIA

Freedman justified his exclusion of laboratory experiments by saying that he wanted to examine only the research conducted in natural settings. It is often claimed that investigations carried out in natural settings have an inherent advantage over laboratory experiments because their conditions are presumably more representative of the real world, and thus their findings supposedly can be better generalized to other natural situations. However, the degree of generalization depends more on similarity of meaning across different situations than on appearance. The situations established in laboratory studies can have much the same meaning as situations existing in many natural settings (Berkowitz & Donnerstein, 1982). Furthermore, even though in principle Freedman wrote that he favored highly representative research, he actually included some studies in his sample that were conducted in quite unusual situations. Examples include the experiments reported by Feshbach and Singer (1971); Parke, Berkowitz, Leyens, West, and Sebastian (1977); and Leyens, Parke, Camino, and Berkowitz (1975). Each of these studies involved boys incarcerated in special institutions for adolescents who have violated the law—subjects and settings that are far from representative of what most TV and movie viewers encounter in their homes and in theaters. The authorities in these reform institutions typically frown on any aggressive displays. Not only were the teenagers unlikely to think that movies shown to them gave them permission to assault each other, they were also apt to believe that they could be disciplined as troublemakers if they pushed, shoved, or fought with others around them. All this suggests that the aggressive actions recorded by the observers in the Parke and Leyens experiments occurred in spite of the restraining influences in the situation—certainly not because of any supposed "permission giving."

Freedman also disregarded at least one experiment that meets his major objections, a report of an experiment by Parke et al. on the second phase of their American research (1977). In this study, those who had been exposed to violent movies were verbally more aggressive to their partners than were the boys in the neutral movies conditions (regardless of whether they had been harassed). The chief difference between this study and others had to do with the relatively controlled nature of the interaction with the partner, a control that heightens the study's internal validity. In excluding the effects of past history (the other boy was a stranger) and by making sure that the boys' actions were not affected by other youngsters around them, the researchers could be more certain that the verbal aggression displayed by the subjects resulted from the movie treatment alone. This field experiment with positive results was ignored by Freedman, while he included less well controlled field experiments that produced null or reverse results (e.g., Feshbach & Singer, 1971; Milgram & Shotland, 1973).

It is unwarranted to assume that every naturalistic study is more representative than any laboratory study. For example, Freedman refers to the experiment by Friedrich and Stein (1973) that deals with children in an unusual summer nursery school. Was this naturalistic enough that the findings from this investigation would be more generalizable to other populations and settings than, say, results from experiments conducted in university laboratories?

Bias in Selective Reporting

Any survey of research must exclude some findings and focus on others. However, Freedman's review seems unduly slanted, often suggesting that positive results were more inconsistent than they were and negative results more clearcut. As one example, consider Freedman's comments about an investigation by Parke et al. (1977). Although the published article indicated a main effect for type of movie on the general aggression index, Freedman insisted there was no such effect (1984, p. 231). He correctly noted that the boys initially low in aggressiveness seemed to be somewhat more affected by the violent films than were those initially high in aggressiveness, but overlooked the finding (shown in Fig. 4 of Parke et al., 1977, p. 151) that both the highly aggressive and the less aggressive youngsters displayed more general aggression after the violent movies than after the neutral films.

There also seems to be bias in the way Freedman summarized the findings in Leyens et al.'s (1975) replication of the Parke et al. (1977) research. In reporting the adolescents' behavior during the evening (the time they saw the movies), Leyens and his colleagues noted that the residents of the two cottages shown the violent movies exhibited a significant increase in physical aggression from the baseline period to the week of movie viewing; the residents of the two cottages in the neutral film condition displayed virtually no physical aggression. Further, the posttests demonstrated that the boys in both aggressive movie cottages were physically more aggressive than their neutral movie counterparts during the movie week. Freedman, to the contrary, emphasizing what he said were differences between the cottages within a film category concluded, "One of the violent-film cottages showed a general increase in aggressiveness; the other violent-film cottage showed an increase only in physical aggression" (p. 230), implying some inconsistency. In other words, while most of the results of these experiments point in the same direction (with relatively minor variations), Freedman de-emphasized the converging findings, in part by failing to report some of the results, and instead emphasized the variations.

While some might regard Freedman's summary as showing that he is a hard-headed "naysayer," it is clear that Freedman was selective in his skepticism. He was rigorous in evaluating investigations reporting a connection between media violence and aggressive behavior, but remarkably gentle toward the few published studies that conclude there is no such influence. This is apparent in the way the anomalous field experiment by Feshbach and Singer is discussed (Freedman, 1984, pp. 229–230).

Critics of the Feshbach and Singer (1971) study have noted, among other things, that the nonviolent TV programs were significantly less enjoyable to the viewers than were the aggressive programs. The youngsters in the former condition clearly resented not being able to see their favorite programs. In fact, in several schools the boys in the nonviolent programs condition complained so much about not being able to watch their favorite shows that the researchers relented and allowed them to see one popular violent program, *Batman*. Freedman acknowledged this as a reasonable criticism but thereafter ignored it entirely. What is important, he said, was that the boys who were limited to viewing the nonviolent programs were subsequently more aggressive than boys who were allowed to watch the violent programs in six of the seven replications involved in the study. However, the reasonable criticism cannot be ignored and does explain the aberrant results of this study parsimoniously as frustration effect: the youths in the nonaggressive TV diet condition were relatively frustrated in these replications, and predictably acted out as a result.

Because of this substantial threat to the internal validity of the Feshbach/Singer experiment, one really cannot draw any conclusions from the reported results. One should not even say, as Freedman did, that at least the difference between the violent and nonviolent TV diet conditions was in the wrong direction. The aggression scores may have been in the wrong direction because in this study the frustration-induced instigation to aggression was stronger than the aggression-enhancing effects of the violent programs.

It is also worth noting how Freedman treated essentially the same problem in his discussion of the Parke et al. (1977) experiments. In the first phase of their research, Parke and his associates found that the nonviolent movies were regarded as less interesting and less enjoyable than the violent films, and therefore they selected more interesting neutral movies for their second investigation. Freedman considered this a potentially serious problem. If this difference in the movies' interest value was a serious source of uncertainty in the Parke research, it must have been at least as serious a problem in the Feshbach/Singer experiment. But Freedman concluded instead that it was generous to say the Leyens et al. (1975) and Parke et al. (1977) studies had obtained some evidence for the notion that observed aggression could induce aggression. At the same time Freedman claimed that the highly aggressive boys in the Feshbach/Singer experiment had shown "a major decrease in aggression after viewing violent television." In fact, the boys in question were a control group whose viewing habits were left undisturbed by the investigators, and there is no before–after evidence of any decrease in their aggressive behavior.

Unfortunately, this is not the only case where Freedman's summary misrepresents the actual results obtained by investigators reporting a linkage between media depictions of violence and subsequent aggression. There are several important errors in his review of Phillips' (1983) study indicating that widely publicized prize fights tend to be followed by a rise in homicides under certain conditions. (See Phillips, 1985, for a further discussion of Freedman's errors in this regard.)

Another instance of Freedman's selectivity bias in favor of negative results is his inclusion of the Milgram and Shotland (1973) experiment testing the notion that the portrayal of stealing on TV would induce stealing in natural situations. This particular investigation has a number of serious methodological problems that were ignored by Freedman (see Liebert, Sprafkin, & Davidson, 1982, p. 115). For one thing, this experiment did not deal with aggression. Did Freedman bring in this study because he wanted to say there was no evidence that TV programs could induce any kind of illegal behavior? If so, he should have mentioned Phillips' studies of the contagion of mass media suicides as well as homicides (Phillips, 1974, 1979, 1982). These studies may also have flaws (Kessler & Stipp, 1984), but that does not distinguish them from many of the studies Freedman reviewed. Only the direction of the results distinguishes them. The paper by Berkowitz and Macaulay (1971) reporting a mass media–induced contagion of criminal violence is also relevant but was ignored by Freedman.

Freedman also neglects the available data on real-world intervention studies that have attempted to reduce the effect of TV violence on aggressive behavior. Such planned interventions not only have social value if successful, but also serve as experiments to confirm or falsify the causal relation between TV violence and aggression. One such study was that by Huesmann, Eron, Klein, Brice and Fischer (1983). Using an attitude change procedure in a field experiment, they reduced both the aggressiveness of high violence viewers and the correlation between their violence viewing and their aggression. In a comparable control group the relation of violence viewing to aggression did not change, nor was the level of aggressive behavior diminished. The success of this intervention adds to the validity of the thesis that viewing violence stimulates aggression, yet Freedman did not mention the study.

Two other important articles published almost simultaneously with Freedman's were missed. Huesmann, Lagerspetz, and Eron (1984) presented cross-national data from Finland and the United States implicating media violence in the development of aggression. Freedman was aware of the study, as his comments on early partial reports reveal, but he never requested the complete report. Similarly, Freedman included a superficial, partial report of the Singer and Singer research but did not cite their readily available published complete results (Singer & Singer, 1980; Singer, Singer, & Rapaczynski, 1984). These papers contain several critical analyses that implicate TV violence as an instigator of aggression even when early aggressiveness is partialed out. Perhaps unaware of these results, Freedman concluded the opposite about the Singers' research.

LACK OF DEVELOPMENTAL THEORY

Another major error Freedman makes is to ignore developmental theory. Freedman treats every study, whether its subjects were toddlers, children, teenagers, or adults, as equally important for examining the relation between media violence and aggression. Indeed, he seldom mentions the ages of subjects or survey respondents. But, within most models for the development of aggression, one would expect quite different effects at different ages. Freedman does recognize that a cumulative developmental process might be a plausible theory (even though he incorrectly asserts that no one has made this argument before), but he draws the wrong conclusions from such a theory. For example, he asserts that under a cumulative theory synchronous correlations between violence viewing and aggression must increase with age. This might happen, but it is not a necessary implication. As children mature, their viewing patterns change substantially; time spent with TV generally increases throughout childhood, then decreases through adolescence (Comstock et al., 1978). Viewing patterns are not very stable over time and their variability may change (Huesmann & Eron, 1986). It is perfectly plausible for heavy early violence viewing to have a cumulative effect in promoting later aggression, while the later aggression may not always correlate highly with the later violence viewing (Lefkowitz et al., 1977). However, adults are also vulnerable to the effects of violent displays on television. Transient effects of considerable magnitude have been demonstrated with adult subjects. Although long-term learning may not be implicated in these studies with adults, other processes do contribute, for example, priming, response elaboration, and disinhibition (Berkowitz, 1984).

The development theory that Huesmann and Eron (Eron, 1982; Huesmann, 1982, 1986, 1988; Huesmann & Eron, 1984, 1986; Huesmann et al., 1983; Huesmann, Eron, Lefkowitz, & Walder, 1984) have hypothesized suggests that aggression, as a characteristic way of solving social problems, is learned at a young age and becomes more and more impervious to change as the child grows older. A substantial body of data support this view (e.g., Olweus, 1979; Huesmann, Eron, Lefkowitz, & Walder, 1984). Under this developmental model, one would expect exposure to media violence at a young age to be correlated with concurrent and later aggression; whether media violence viewing and aggression were correlated among older teenagers or adults would be irrelevant. Media violence affects aggression in adulthood by teaching young children lasting aggressive habits, not by changing adults' habits. Freedman has not approached the problem from a developmental perspective, and, therefore, he misses a number of such critical points. We note that even in Milavsky, Kessler, Stipp, and Ruben's (1982b) supposedly null data, the strength of the longitudinal effects from early violence viewing to later aggression is greatest for the longest lags.

STATISTICAL MISEMPHASES

Freedman does not seem to appreciate recent advances in techniques for the analysis of longitudinal data. He emphasizes the results of cross-lagged correlational analyses, for example, while most researchers have agreed with Rogosa (1980) that this technique is suspect. Huesmann, Lagerspetz, and Eron (1984); Milavsky, Kessler, Stipp, and Rubens (1982a); and Singer, Singer, and Rapaczynski (1984) have turned to using a form of regression or path analysis in their recent research. One predicts as much of later aggression as possible from early aggression and then examines whether TV violence viewing adds significantly to the prediction. This is a very conservative approach, especially when dealing with a relatively stable characteristic such as aggression. Almost all the path coefficients obtained in this manner from early violence viewing to later aggression are positive in the recent Huesmann, Lagerspetz, and Eron (1984), Singer and Singer (1990), and Milavsky et al. (1982a, 1982b) studies. Most of Huesmann et al.'s and Singer and Singer's path coefficients are statistically significant. Still, Freedman treats these as weak results because the coefficients are not large relative to the coefficient for early aggression on later aggression. His mistake is to view the stability of aggression over time as a competing theory rather than as a contextual fact of human development and behavior. In terms of developmental theory, the results would be highly suspect if the coefficient from early viewing of TV violence to later aggression were higher than that from early aggression itself to later aggression.

Freedman, like many other skeptics, also falls into the trap of discounting correlations that seem small in absolute value, no matter how significant they are. Abelson (1985) and Rosenthal (1986) have both argued against this discounting especially when it comes to socially significant phenomena. Correlations that seem to explain relatively little variance may in fact indicate very socially significant effects.

PREFERENCE FOR WEAK THEORIES

In his article Freedman reveals a limited conception of the potential universe of theories for explaining the relation between television violence viewing and aggression. His theories do not describe psychological processes but simply relations among variables. This neglect of process theory becomes a serious deficit when it leads to attempts to explain what must be a psychological phenomenon without any concern for psychological processes.

Freedman also finds imprecise, nonspecific theories plausible even if they are not falsifiable. For example, one reason why Freedman calls the evidence for TV violence causing aggression weak is the following conjecture:

> There is little difficulty in providing an alternative explanation of the relation between viewing television violence and aggressiveness: Those individuals who prefer violent television programs also tend to be aggressive. More simply, something in their personalities or behavior patterns, some predisposition, trait, combination of environmental pressures, learning history, or whatever, causes people to like aggressive programming and also to be aggressive. (Freedman, 1984)

But this is not an explanation at all. What "something"? Many somethings have been tested empirically but have failed to explain the effect. What Freedman is really saying is, as long as one is not required to be precise, it is easy to speculate that there are alternative reasons for the correlation between TV violence and aggression.

Freedman sets an impossible criterion for studies he wants to reject, viz. that they "demonstrate a causal effect" (p. 228) or "definitive proof" (p. 242). This is a logically unreachable conclusion, according to Popper's (1959) falsificationist analysis. At the same time, Freedman sets no standards of evidence at all for his preferred hypothetical explanations, such as "something in their personalities or behavior patterns," which he concludes "receives especially strong support" (sic) because one study shows little time-lagged effect in a bivariate analysis. In short, results that are consistent with the effects hypothesis are never to be accepted as supportive because they are not conclusive in a positivist sense, while null findings are taken as strong evidence in favor of practically any other explanation one might invoke. His standard of evidence seems to be that of a criminal trial, with TV violence on trial; better let its crime go unpunished than to castigate it for a crime it might not have committed. This is a strange way to handle a review of a scientific literature.

There are at least two other errors in Freedman's article that, while not of critical importance, add to the generally negative tone. On page 236, Freedman includes a paragraph explaining the methodological danger of combining genders in correlating aggression with violence viewing. His implicit suggestion is that many important results are artifacts of such a procedure. Not only is this untrue, but this issue has in fact been addressed previously by the very researchers Freedman criticizes (Huesmann, Lagerspetz, & Eron, 1984). And Chaffee (1972), for example, found positive correlations in six of seven samples of boys and in five of six samples of girls. In the discussion of cross-lagged correlations in the Eron, Huesmann, Lefkowitz, and Walder (1972) 10-year study, Freedman is critical because of the cross-lagged pattern for TV violence viewing with self-reported measures of aggression (MMPI-F49 and Physical Aggression) were not presented while the lagged correlations with peer-nominated aggression were (Freedman, 1984, p. 241). He failed to note that self-report measures were not given to the children at age 8. Thus no cross-lags could possibly have been computed.

SUMMARY

In his widely cited 1984 review article, Freedman concluded that while viewing of media violence was correlated with aggressive behavior, there was no compelling evidence that it stimulated aggressive behavior. In this chapter we have argued that Freedman's conclusion of no causal effect was not justified at that time and is not justified now. It was a result of his misunderstanding of some data, his dismissal of laboratory experiments as irrelevant, his selective disregard of data contrary to his view, his overreliance on atypical field experimental data, his fluctuating criteria for evaluating positive and negative evidence, and his failure to approach the problem from an adequate theoretical perspective.

REFERENCES

Abelson, R. P. (1985). A variance explanation paradox: When a little is a lot. *Psychological Bulletin, 97,* 129–133.

Bandura, A., Ross, D., & Ross, S. (1963). Imitation of film-mediated aggressive models. *Journal of Abnormal and Social Psychology, 66,* 3–11.

Berkowitz, L. (1984). Some effects of thoughts and anti- and prosocial influences of media events: A cognitive-neoassociation analysis. *Psychological Bulletin, 95,* 410–427.

Berkowitz, L., & Donnerstein, E. (1982). External validity is more than skin deep: Some answers to criticisms of laboratory experiments. *American Psychologist, 37,* 245–257.

Berkowitz, L., & Macaulay, J. (1971). The contagion of criminal violence. *Sociometry, 34,* 238–260.

Chaffee, S. H. (1972). Television and adolescent aggressiveness (overview). In G. A. Comstock & E. A. Rubinstein (Eds.), *Television and adolescent aggressiveness.* Washington, DC: U.S. Government Printing Office.

Comstock, G. A., et al. (1978).

Comstock, G. A. (1980). New emphases in research on the effects of television and film violence. In E. L. Palmer & A. Dorr (Eds.), *Children and the faces of television: Teaching, violence, selling.* New York: Academic Press.

Comstock, G., & Paik, H. (in press). The effects of television violence on aggressive behavior: A meta-analysis. In J. A. Roth (Ed.), *A preliminary report to NRC Panel on the understanding and control of violent behavior.* Washington, DC: National Research Council.

Eron, L. D. (1982). Parent–child interaction, television violence, and aggression of children. *American Psychologist, 37,* 197–211.

Eron, L. D., Huesmann, L. R., Lefkowitz, M. M., & Walder, L. O. (1972). Does television violence cause aggression? *American Psychologist, 27,* 253–263.

Feshbach, S., & Singer, R. D. (1971). *Television and aggression.* San Francisco: Jossey-Bass.

Freedman, J. (1984). Effect of television violence on aggressiveness. *Psychological Bulletin, 96,* 227–246.

Friedrich, L. K., & Stein, A. H. (1973). Aggressive and prosocial television programs and the natural behavior of preschool children. *Child Development Monograph, 38*(4).

Hearold, S. L. (1979). *Meta-analysis of the effect of television on social behavior.* Unpublished doctoral dissertation, University of Colorado.

Huesmann, L. R. (1982). Television violence and aggression behavior. In D. Pearl, L. Bouthilet, & J. Lazar (Eds.), *Television and behavior: Ten years of scientific progress and implications for the eighties.* (pp. 126–137). Washington, DC: U.S. Government Printing Office.

Huesmann, L. R. (1986). Psychological processes promoting the relation between exposure to media violence and aggressive behavior by the viewer. *Journal of Social Issues, 42,* 125–140.

Huesmann, L. R. (1988). An information processing model for the development of aggression. *Aggressive Behavior, 14,* 13–24.

Huesmann, L. R., & Eron, L. D. (1984). Cognitive processes and the persistence of aggressive behavior. *Aggressive Behavior, 10,* 243–251.

Huesmann, L. R., & Eron, L. D. (Eds.). (1986). *Television and the aggressive child: A cross-national comparison.* Hillsdale, NJ: Erlbaum.

Huesmann, L. R., Eron, L. D., Klein, R., Brice, P., & Fischer, P. (1983). Mitigating the imitation of aggressive behaviors by children's attitudes about media violence. *Journal of Personality and Social Psychology, 44,* 899–910.

Huesmann, L. R., Eron, L. D., Lefkowitz, M. M., & Walder, L. O. (1984). The stability of aggression over time and generations. *Developmental Psychology, 20,* 1120–1134.

Huesmann, L. R., Lagerspetz, K., Eron, L. D. (1984). Intervening variables in the TV violence-aggression relation: Evidence from the two countries. *Developmental Psychology, 20,* 746–755.

Kessler, R. C., & Stipp, H. (1984). The impact of fictional television suicide stories on U.S. fatalities: A replication. *American Journal of Sociology, 90,* 151–166.

Lefkowitz et al. (1977).

Lefkowitz, M. M., & Huesmann, L. R. (1980). Concomitants of television violence viewing in children. In E. L. Palmer & A. Dorr (Eds.), *Children and the faces of television: Teaching, violence, selling.* New York: Academic Press.

Leyens, J. P., Parke, R. D., Camino, L., & Berkowitz, L. (1975). Effects of movie violence on aggression in a field setting as a function of group dominance and cohesion. *Journal of Personality and Social Psychology, 32,* 346–360.

Liebert, R., Sprafkin, J., & Davidson, E. S. (1982). *The early window: Effects of television on children and youth* (2nd Ed.). New York: Pergamon.

Milavsky, J., Kessler, R., Stipp, H., & Rubens, W. (1982a). *Television and aggression: The results of a panel study.* New York: Academic Press.

Milavsky, J. R., Kessler, R., Stipp, H., & Rubens, W. (1982b). Television and aggression: Results of a panel study. In D. Pearl, L. Bouthilet, & J. Lazar (Eds.), *Television and behavior: Ten years of scientific progress and implications for the eighties. Volume 2. Technical review.* Washington, DC: U.S. Government Printing Office.

Milgram, S., & Shotland, R. L. (1973). *Television and antisocial behavior.* New York: Academic Press.

Olweus, D. (1979). The stability of aggression reaction patterns in human males: A review. *Psychological Bulletin, 85,* 852–875.

Parke, R. D., Berkowitz, L., Leyens, J. P., West, S., & Sebastian, R. S. (1977). Some effects of violent and nonviolent movies on the behavior of juvenile delinquents. In L. Berkowitz (Ed.), *Advances in experimental social psychology* (Vol. 10, pp. 135–172). New York: Academic Press.

Phillips, D. (1974). The influence of suggestion on suicide: Substantive and theoretical implications of the Werther effect. *American Sociological Review, 39,* 340–354.

Phillips, D. (1979). Suicide, motor vehicle fatalities, and the mass media: Evidence toward a theory of suggestion. *American Journal of Sociology, 84,* 1150–1174.

Phillips, D. (1982). The impact of fictional television stories on U.S. adult fatalities: New evidence on the effect of mass media on violence. *American Journal of Sociology, 87,* 1340–1359.

Phillips, D. P. (1983). The impact of mass media violence on U.S. homicides. *American Sociological Review, 48,* 560–568.

Phillips, D. (1985). Natural experiments on the effects of mass media violence on fatal aggression: Strengths and weaknesses of a new approach. In L. Berkowitz (Ed.), *Advances in experimental social psychology* (Vol. 19). Orlando, FL: Academic Press.

Popper. (1959).

Rogosa. (1980).

Rosenthal, R. (1986). Media violence, antisocial behavior, and the social consequences of small effects. *Journal of Social Issues, 42,* 141–154.

Singer, J. L., & Singer, D. G. (1980). Television viewing and aggressive behavior in preschool children: A field study. *Annals of the New York Academy of Sciences, 347,* 289–303.

Singer, J. L., Singer, D. G., & Rapaczynski, W. S. (1984). Family problems and television viewing as predictors of children's beliefs and aggression. *Journal of Communication, 34,* 73–89.

Turner, C. W., & Simons, L. S. (1974). Effects of subject sophistication and evaluation apprehension on aggressive responses to weapons. *Journal of Personality and Social Psychology, 30,* 341–348.

Wood, W., Wong, F. Y., & Chacheri, J. G. (in press). Effects of media violence on viewers' aggression in unconstrained social interaction. *Psychological Bulletin.*

14

The Weapons Effect Revisited: The Effects of Firearms on Aggressive Behavior

Charles W. Turner and Jacques-Philippe Leyens

INTRODUCTION

Many popular accounts have suggested that the ready availability of firearms is a major factor contributing to criminal violence. This supposed effect has led some individuals to claim that sharp restrictions in gun ownership could reduce the availability of weapons for crime. Others have proposed that ownership of firearms is the result rather than the cause of violence. Still other accounts have argued that no direct relationship exists between ownership of firearms and violence. According to these latter two perspectives, efforts to restrict the availabilities of guns are not likely to reduce and might even increase the rates of criminal violence. The present chapter reviews scientific research that relates firearms availability to impulsive, aggressive behavior. We propose that the aggressive meanings attached to firearms are a major determinant of a weapon's influence on impulsive, aggressive responses. Policy recommendations to reduce criminal violence need to consider the aggressive meaning as well as the availability of firearms.

FIREARMS AVAILABILITY AND CRIMINAL VIOLENCE

Compared to other modern industrialized countries, the United States has a high rate of private firearms ownership as well as firearms-related deaths. The total number of firearms deaths in the United States approached 30,000 in 1986. This number includes homicides (43%) and suicides (55%) as well as accidents (2%). In 1986, 7.5 out of 100,000 Americans killed themselves by firearms; this rate is the highest ratio in the world. There are approximately 400 deaths (Treanor & Bijlefeld, 1989) and more than 2,500 injuries each year to children who are under the age of 14 (Baker, O'Neill, & Karpf, 1984). Turner, Simons, Berkowitz, and Frodi (1977) estimated that 90% of all firearms deaths resulted from a gun that belonged to the victim's immediate social circle. This circle included the victim, a family member, a friend, or an acquaintance. We will focus on the high rates of ownership and death associated with firearms in the United States.

The authors are indebted to Leonard Berkowitz and Judith W. Turner for the comments that they made on an earlier draft of the manuscript.

As compared to other countries, the United States has one of the highest rates of firearms present in private homes. In responses given to several national surveys, 50% of the people reported that they owned at least one firearm; nearly 30% said that they had a handgun in the home. These survey responses suggest that there were approximately 120 million privately owned firearms in the United States in 1978 (Wright, Rossi, & Daly, 1983, p. 9). The number of firearms in private homes has continued to increase since 1978 (Shields, 1981). Other societies have comparable rates of firearms present in the homes (e.g., Israel, Norway, and Switzerland). However, citizens in these countries possess weapons as part of the national military service rather than for private use.

Handguns are more likely than other firearms to be involved in homicides (Newton & Zimring, 1969). Handgun ownership is infrequent in homes outside the United States, even in other formerly "frontier" societies such as Canada and Australia. For example, researchers compared the firearms homicide rates of Seattle, Washington, and Vancouver, British Columbia (Sloan et al., 1988). These two cities appear to be quite similar on most demographic indices. Yet the citizens of Seattle were much more likely than the citizens of Vancouver to own firearms and to commit homicides.

One publication has estimated that guns kill more people per year in the United States than in the rest of the world combined, especially if the estimates include only nonwartime deaths (Massachusetts Council on Crime and Correction, 1974). The co-occurrence of high rates of firearms possession and violent deaths in the United States has led many writers to argue that widespread availability is directly responsible for the firearms deaths ("Seven deadly days," 1989).

Some researchers have provided an alternative perspective. They offer scientific evidence that the availability of firearms is not a simple, causal factor in these firearms deaths (Wright et al., 1983). According to their reasoning, the vast majority of gun owners do not use their weapons for violent acts toward themselves or other persons. These authors propose that the widespread availability of arms may be a consequence rather than a cause of violence. They also suggest that some third factor such as the social or economic situation may be responsible both for violence and gun ownership. Wright et al. (1983) reject the idea that social policy directed toward reduction in firearms availability is either necessary or possible in order to decrease violence.

IS FIREARMS AVAILABILITY RESPONSIBLE FOR CRIMINAL VIOLENCE?

The Firearms Availability Premise

As we indicated in the introduction, the United States has a very high number of firearms owners as well as a high rate of criminal violence. Investigators have proposed that the widespread availability of firearms may be one major cause of criminal violence (Newton & Zimring, 1969; Turner, Simons, et al., 1977). Two other findings support this premise. First, the annual frequency of criminal violence in the United States increased at least tenfold from 1960 to 1975 (Turner, Cole, & Cerro, 1984; Turner, Fenn, & Cole, 1981). Firearms ownership also increased during this period. For example, the United States domestically manufactured or imported 65 million new firearms between 1969 and 1978 (Wright et al., 1983). Writers sometimes cite this dramatic increase in weapons availability as evidence that the United States is becoming an armed camp. Presumably, the greater availability of firearms in this armed camp is partly responsible for the increasing rate of criminal violence.

Figure 14.1 portrays the annual frequency of homicides in the United States for the years 1950–1989 and the number of new handguns for the years 1958–1982. Figure 14.2 portrays the homicide rate per 100,000 population for the years 1955–1989. We obtained these data from the annual *Uniform Crime Reports* (1955–1989). Figure 14.2 also portrays the annual percentage of homicides from 1960–1989 that involved firearms (as reported in FBI statistics in the *Uniform Crime Reports*, 1955–1989). As the figure indicates, the period from 1960–1975 involved a dramatic increase in the annual rate of firearms-related homicides.

We attempted to determine whether an association exists between new handgun ownership and firearms-related homicides. We estimated the annual number of new handguns introduced into the United States for the years 1959–1982 (Bureau

Frequency of Handguns and Homicide

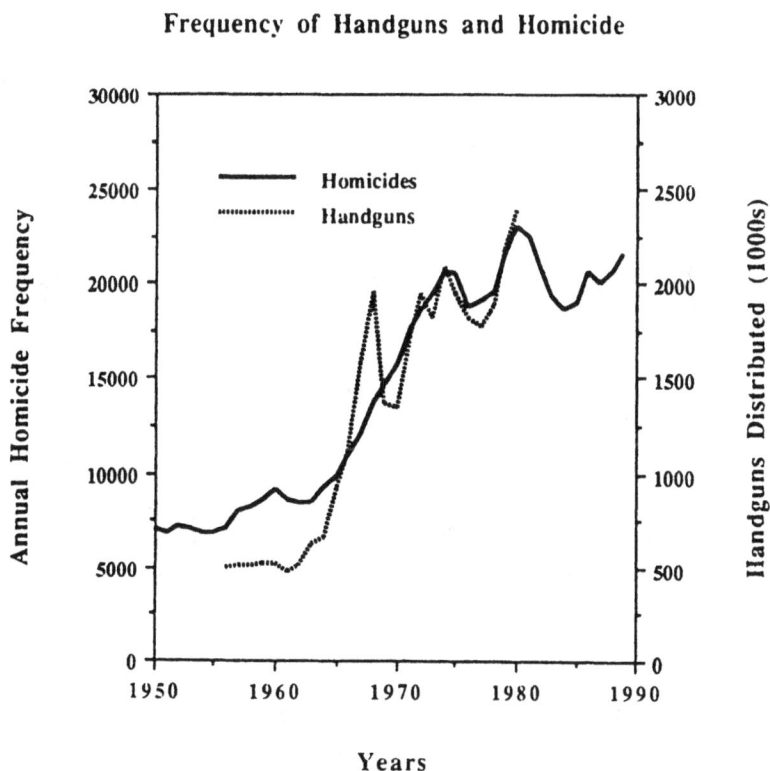

Figure 14.1 The annual frequency of homicide within the United States for the years 1955–1989 (*Uniform Crime Reports*) and the annual frequency of new handguns distributed in the United States from 1959 to 1982 (Bureau of Alcohol, Tobacco, and Firearms, 1959–1982; Newton & Zimring, 1969; Shields, 1981).

Homicide Rates and Firearms Percents

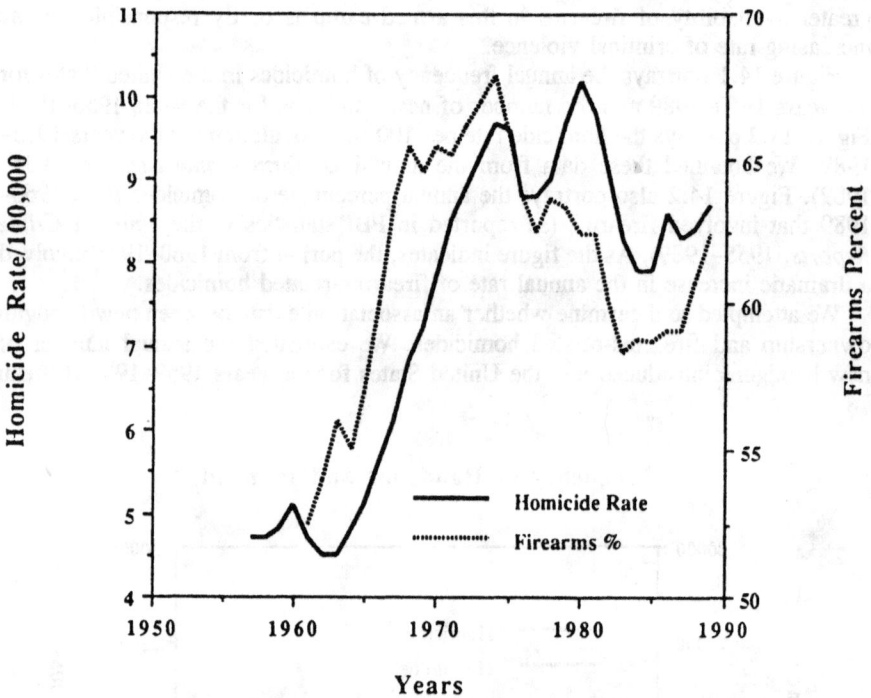

Figure 14.2   The annual homicide rate per 100,000 from 1955 to 1989 and the percentage of homicides within the United States that are firearms related from 1960 to 1989 (*Uniform
Crime Reports*, 1955–1989).

of Alcohol, Tobacco, and Firearms, 1959–1982; Newton & Zimring, 1969;
Shields, 1981). We were unable to obtain consistent estimates for the years prior to
1959 or after 1982. Next, we formed a 3-year moving average based on the sum of
the new handguns introduced in the prior 3 years (producing scores for the years
1961–1982). We divided this 3-year moving average score by the estimated United
States population for that year (derived from the *Uniform Crime Reports*, 1955–
1989). We also determined the percentage of homicides in which a murderer used
a firearm for each of these years. These estimates appear in the statistics reported
in the *Uniform Crime Reports* (1960–1983). These data provided estimates of the
annual frequency of homicide, of the annual homicide rate per 100,000 population, and of the annual percentage of firearms-related homicides.

Using these estimates for the 1961–1982 period, we computed a linear correlation coefficient between the index of "new" handguns and the percentage of homicides committed with firearms. The results indicated that a significant correlation
existed between the 3-year handgun index and the firearms-related homicide percentages [$r = .93$; $F(1, 20) = 136.25$, $p < .001$]. These findings are consistent
with the argument that a greater availability of firearms creates a greater likelihood
that firearms are used to commit murders.

A second source of data provides support for the firearms availability hypothesis. Analyses of geographical differences within the United States indicated that regions with higher rates of firearms availability also have higher levels of criminal violence. A state-by-state comparison reveals that southern states have higher rates of firearms ownership and of criminal violence than other states (Newton & Zimring, 1969).

An Alternative Perspective

Wright et al. (1983) argued that the supposed association of firearms availability and criminal violence is spurious. For example, these researchers note that the sharp increase in criminal violence from 1969 to 1978 cannot be explained simply by the 65 million new firearms that had become available in the United States. Three independent factors contributed to the new purchases. First, Americans purchased approximately 25 million new firearms to replace those that had become defective or that the police had confiscated.

A second factor accounted for another 20 million of the 65 million increase. The total number of households in the United States increased by 25% during the 1968–1978 period. These new residents purchased 25 million firearms for their own homes. However, the actual percentage of homes with firearms changed very little from 1968 to 1989 (Wright et al., 1983). The sudden increase in households occurred because the postwar baby-boom generation had matured enough to establish independent housing. These individuals were likely to purchase a firearm for their home if their parents had also owned one (Wright et al., 1983).

This second factor of household increase for the 1969–1978 period accounted for 20 million of the new firearms. Of the remaining 20 million increase in new weapons, approximately half were rifles and shotguns. These shoulder weapons are infrequently used in criminal violence.

A third factor may account for much of the remaining increase in new handgun ownership. This factor includes increased sports and recreational use of handguns as well as the augmentation of the police force. When all of these factors are included, all but 5 million of the 65 million new gun purchases can be explained without supporting the assumption that the new firearms have turned the United States into an armed camp (Wright et al., 1983).

Increased Firearms Ownership and Violent Crime

As the baby-boom generation matured through various age-specific stages of development, they flooded each of those specific age groups. Any behavior that characterized a specific age group abruptly increased as the baby-boom generation reached that age group. Violent crime is a behavior that occurs in a fairly narrow age range of 15–30 years (Turner & Dodd, 1979; Turner et al., 1981, 1984). When the baby-boom birth cohorts reached ages 15–30, the age range of violent crime, in the years 1960 to 1975, the rate of violent crime surged in the United States. After the baby-boom generation matured beyond the age of 30, the rate of violent crime actually decreased, in the years 1980 through 1986. The homicide rate has been increasing since 1986 (*Uniform Crime Reports,* 1986–1989).

The baby-boom generation established independent households during the period 1960–1975. As we just noted, the apparent correlation between the increased numbers of firearms purchased and numbers of crimes committed may be a spurious association. That is, each increase might have occurred because the number of young adults suddenly increased and they became available to commit crime and to purchase firearms.

Wright et al. (1983) also questioned regional statistics that supposedly show an association between firearms availability and criminal violence. Although a higher proportion of people in southern states than in all other states own firearms and a higher proportion commit criminal violence, the two events may not be causally related to each other. The high rate of firearms ownership in the South primarily involves shoulder weapons, although handgun ownership is also more frequent. People in rural communities own these shoulder weapons primarily for sports and recreational purposes. However, the high rates of violent crimes in the South are committed with handguns and occur in urban rather than rural areas. According to Wright et al. (1983), the high rate of firearms availability in the southern states does not appear to be responsible for the high rates of criminal violence.

Wright et al. (1983) conclude that the presence of firearms in private homes is not a sufficient explanation for the high levels of criminal violence in the United States. These authors also reason that efforts to reduce the availability of firearms will not decrease the rates of criminal violence. Wright and his colleagues have made some important contributions to the debate about firearms effects and aggressive behavior. They have provided evidence that the relationship between these variables is certainly not one of a simple and direct causal association.

Even if firearms availability does not provide a sufficient explanation for criminal violence, other variables may influence the relationship to availability. These variables are the lethality, the impulsivity, and the violent meaning of firearms. We examine these variables in the subsequent sections of this chapter.

LETHALITY OF FIREARMS ASSAULTS

One possible reason that firearms contribute to so many homicides is that these weapons produce more destructive injuries to victims than occurs with other weapons. If an assaulter uses a firearm instead of a knife as a weapon, the resulting injuries are five times as likely to be lethal for the victim. Knives are more plentiful than firearms; virtually every home in the United States has at least one sharp knife while only 50% of the homes have firearms. Assaults with knives also are at least twice as frequent as assaults with firearms. However, Newton and Zimring (1969) noted that twice as many people died each year from gunshot wounds as from knife wounds; this ratio of gun-to-knife homicides continues today (*Uniform Crime Reports,* 1970–1989).

Newton and Zimring (1969) proposed that reductions in the number of lethal weapons might lower the homicide rates. Indeed, while the chances of a successful suicide are 5% overall, the chances are 92% when a gun is used. If fewer firearms were readily available, presumably fewer people would select them as weapons, and consequently, fewer victims would die.

However, a potential problem exists for Newton and Zimring's (1969) argument. Suppose that murderers select firearms rather than knives because they intend for their victims to die rather than simply suffer injuries (Wright et al., 1983). Killers may select the most lethal weapons that they can find in order to try to kill someone. Even if firearms were not readily available, these individuals might find some other effective method for killing their victims. In short, murderers may select firearms as weapons because of their lethality rather than because they happened to be readily available (Wright et al., 1983).

Newton and Zimring (1969, pp. 43–44) provided evidence designed to refute the premise that killers seek the most lethal weapon possible. They analyzed police reports about the apparent motives and circumstances surrounding 152 knife assaults and 265 firearms assaults in Chicago. Their findings suggest that knife and firearms assaults do not differ in terms of the assaulters' intentions to kill their victims. In fact, a higher portion of knife than gun attacks occurred to vital areas of the body (e.g., neck, head, or chest). Knife attacks involved more injuries but fewer fatalities to the victim than gun attacks. If Newton and Zimring's (1969) reasoning is correct, reductions in firearms availability would reduce homicides. Assaulters would have less lethal weapons to use when they attack their victims. As a consequence, more of the victims would survive assaults.

Toch (1969) has presented evidence consistent with the claims of Newton and Zimring (1969). After interviewing numerous killers, Toch concluded that most killers meant to hurt but did not mean to kill their victims. The killers reported that they had hurt their victims much more than they intended. People committed most murders during escalating altercations, and these attacks appeared to be impulsive acts of violence. If attackers had used a weapon less lethal than a firearm, presumably many of their victims would have survived these impulsive attacks.

Berkowitz (1974) has also proposed that many acts of violence reflect impulsive rather than intentional acts. The situational cues may have instigated more intense acts of violence than intended by the killers. One of these situational cues is a weapon. That is, it is not simply the killer who pulls the trigger; rather, in a sense, the "trigger pulls the finger rather than the finger pulling the trigger" (Berkowitz, 1968).

IMPULSIVITY OF FIREARMS ASSAULTS

Extensive experimental research has examined the effects of weapons on aggressive behavior. The research was conducted in laboratory and field settings across a number of countries; the subjects have included young children, adolescents, and adults. As with other research on aggression, researchers used men as subjects in nearly all of the research. Because of this limitation in the sampling, the results summarized in the present chapter may not generalize to women. Collectively, the aggression research provides evidence that the mere presence of firearms can induce aggressive responses in individuals. The stimulating effects of weapons on aggression occurred even when the subjects did not use the weapons to express their aggressive responses. Berkowitz called this phenomenon the "weapons effect" (Berkowitz & LePage, 1967).

The experimental research suggests that guns not only increase the chances of doing serious injury but also heighten some people's incitation to aggression. Berkowitz (1968) speculated that the effects of firearms in aggressive acts could result because firearms stimulate impulsive aggression-facilitating reactions. The research has also demonstrated a complex association between firearms and aggression. Although firearms can create reactions including anger and aggression, they can cause other reactions such as fear and intimidation or even provoke a response of cooperation. The effects of firearms depend upon the meanings that individuals have learned to attach to these objects.

RESEARCH ON THE WEAPONS EFFECT

Numerous experiments have investigated the effects of weapons on aggressive behavior. This research has focused upon possible stimulating effects of weapons on impulsive aggressive behavior. Researchers have completed studies in at least nine countries. Several experiments were conducted in field settings to minimize the potential contributions of experimental demand effects. These effects can occur when subjects know they are being studied (as in the laboratory settings). Collectively, the findings of the experimental research suggest that guns heighten some people's instigation to aggression.

The Original Weapons Effect Experiment

Berkowitz and LePage (1967) conducted the original study that produced findings called the "weapons effect." First, an experimental accomplice, who was acting as a fellow subject, provoked half of the subjects by giving them a harsh evaluation using electric shock; the remaining subjects received a favorable evaluation. Next, the experimenters varied the presence of weapons by exposing some subjects to a .38 caliber pistol and a 12-gauge shotgun. Subjects seeing the weapons learned either that the weapons belonged to (associated weapons group) or did not belong to (unassociated weapons group) their supposed fellow subject. In two other conditions, subjects saw either a neutral object (badminton racquet) or no objects at all. Subjects learned that someone had mistakenly left the weapons or racquets in the experimental room. The weapons appeared in a conspicuous place near the apparatus that the subject used for administering shocks to the partner.

The researchers found that provoked subjects responded more aggressively when the subjects saw weapons rather than nonaggressive objects. Subjects gave the most shocks to their partners when the weapons ostensibly belonged to the partners. Moreover, the angry men in both weapons conditions displayed significantly more punishment to the confederate than their provoked counterparts displayed in the neutral-object group.

Theoretical Explanations of the Weapons Effect

Berkowitz (1974, 1984) explained the weapons effect findings in terms of an associative learning model. He reasoned that weapons may become associated with aggressive stimuli through their frequent pairing with aggressive acts in real life and in books, newspapers, movies, and television. When an aroused and uninhibited person subsequently sees a weapon, he or she is likely to react with a response that they have associated with guns, that is, with aggressive behavior.

Learned associations occur early in a child's life and persist for many years. Indeed, young children with strong aggressive habits are likely to grow up to be aggressive adults (Dodge, 1980; Huesmann, 1988). Children's learning of aggressive behavior patterns can occur either through their personal actions (enactive learning) or through observational learning (Huesmann, 1988).

Enactive learning can occur when a child discovers that aggressive behavior can be an effective strategy in achieving desired goals or avoiding punishing situations (Patterson, 1982). This enactive learning frequently occurs in the context of painful experiences. Research with a wide variety of animals shows that painful and aversive experiences can lead to two different types of reactions that appear as fight or flight (Azrin, Hutchinson, & Hake, 1967; Cannon, 1929). Aversive experiences may cause the individual to be afraid and to attempt to flee from the painful experience. When flight is not possible, the individual may turn and attack whatever appears to be the source of the pain. Similar processes occur in humans. A child frequently reacts to painful experiences with crying and fearful reactions. Many young children also learn that aggressive or coercive actions are effective in terminating painful or aversive experiences (Patterson, 1982).

The child may also learn to use aggressive behavior by watching others who are successful in using these behaviors (Bandura, 1986; Huesmann, 1988; Turner, Hesse, & Peterson-Lewis, 1986). A typical child in a modern industrialized country is likely to observe thousands of assaults and homicides using firearms in the mass media. Heroic figures commit many acts of homicide, and they receive praise and respect for their actions. Other heroic figures portray the use of weapons as the only solution possible to escape from their desperate situations. After witnessing thousands of these episodes, some children may come to believe that firearms can provide an effective solution to their problems.

A large marketing effort encourages children to purchase replicas of the cartoon characters, their clothes, and their weapons. For example, the three major U.S. networks aired more than 175 toy commercials on a single Saturday morning a few weeks before Christmas in 1969 (Liebert, Neale, & Davidson, 1973, p. 124). Some of these toys are replicas of the aggressive characters in the Saturday morning cartoons. The replicas may increase the likelihood that the child will imitate and rehearse the cartoon aggressive behavior in their own play behavior. Furthermore, as the children carry the toys away from the television set, they may be more likely to generalize the learned behavior to novel settings (away from the television set).

Aggressive Scripts and Schemata

Huesmann (1988) proposed that these enactive or observational learning experiences become encoded in memory as scripts and schemata. A script is a type of behavior program similar to a computer program. This program guides the sequence of actions that are to take place in a particular setting, much as a script for a play guides the sequence of actions on the stage. A child may rehearse a script overtly in actual behavior or covertly in fantasized behavior. Children's aggressive play may be another method by which they rehearse a script. Children's play behavior involved many different types of aggressive games (e.g., Cowboys and Indians). Children frequently use various props or costumes while playing these games. These items include guns, cowboy hats, feathered bonnets, or bows and arrows.

Initial rehearsal of a script may require conscious effort with undivided attention (also called controlled processing). As the child continues to rehearse the script, it becomes easier to recall. With sufficient rehearsal, the script becomes "automated" so that the child requires little conscious effort or attention for enactment of the script. When activated, these automated scripts may create behavior that appears to be impulsive aggressive responses (Berkowitz, 1984). The script may become integrated with other scripts to form complex schemata for dealing with aversive situations.

Since many scripts eventually become encoded in memory, not all of them can influence behavior at the same time. Environmental cues are one important determinant of whether a child recalls a particular script from memory. The most recently recalled scripts are likely to influence overt behavior. Furthermore, any cues associated with the initial encoding and rehearsal of the script may stimulate recall and lead to its enactment (Turner & Layton, 1976).

Weapons can serve as one cue to prompt the retrieval of well-rehearsed scripts. Media portrayals of violent episodes can create learned associations between aggressive acts and films. For example, children's cartoons contain many instances of gun play. Cartoon characters usually are able to intimidate others by brandishing weapons. However, when these characters are shot, none of them are ever permanently injured.

Aggressive scripts portray both successful aggressors and unsuccessful victims. When children rehearse aggressive scripts, they may identify with either one of these roles. Thus, some children may react with aggression while others react with fear to the same aggressive script. In adult cowboy movies or television programs, a drawn pistol or rifle signals that a fist fight, swearing, knifing, or shooting will follow shortly afterwards. Objects such as hats, spurs, or western clothes are also associated with violent scenes, but these objects are also connected with many nonaggressive behaviors. Hence, these objects may elicit many diverse, possibly incompatible, reactions so that no single script or reaction is sufficiently dominant to influence overt behavior.

For some individuals, nearly all exposure to firearms may occur when they see media portrayals of aggressive episodes. For example, people whose exposure to firearms occurs only by television are likely to have this experience. These weapons may acquire aggressive meanings (or associations) that could stimulate recall of the aggressive scripts individuals have learned.

Some individuals may see firearms primarily in nonaggressive contexts. For example, they may spend many hours practicing target shooting. These target shooters may not associate firearms with aggressive episodes on television or other media presentations. Hence, they would be unlikely to recall aggressive scripts or to act aggressively when they see firearms. Viewers, on the other hand, may recall the aggressive scripts even when they have not recently viewed a violent film or TV series. Anticipation of the program may be a sufficient condition.

In a study conducted by Leyens and Dunand (1990), undergraduate students expected to watch either a very violent or very romantic film. However, the students learned that the equipment broke and the experimenter needed to repair the equipment. As an alternative activity, the students could participate in a psychological experiment that involved competition between two subjects on a manual ability task. To impair the opponents' performances, the subjects could send electric shocks of varying intensities to them. The subjects who originally anticipated seeing the violent film selected higher intensities than those who had expected to watch a romantic movie. In other words, thinking about the violent movie appeared to be sufficient to activate the aggressive script.

OTHER STUDIES OF THE WEAPONS EFFECT

Numerous studies have replicated the Berkowitz and LePage (1967) findings (see Carlson, Marcus-Newhall, & Miller, 1990; Turner, Simons, et al., 1977). Although diverse subject groups participated in these studies (young children, high school students, military recruits, automobile drivers, and college students), most of the subjects have been men. Researchers have used different types of aggressive cues (e.g., guns, knives, a blackjack, and pictorial depictions of guns). The weapons effect also occurred in cultural settings, other than the United States (e.g., Belgium, Canada, France, Italy, Lebanon, Sweden, Syria, and Yugoslavia). The present review is an attempt to categorize the relevant studies and to discuss the conditions under which the weapons effect may occur or be inhibited.

A Cross-Cultural Replication in Sweden

Frodi (1973) partially replicated Berkowitz and LePage's (1967) procedure using Swedish high school students. An experimental accomplice either angered or did not anger the subjects. Next, the subjects received one of three treatments: (a) exposure to a pistol and rifle, (b) exposure to "aggression-inhibiting" stimuli (e.g., a baby bottle and a teething ring), or (c) no exposure to these objects. Both the angered and nonangered subjects gave more shocks to their partners when weapons were present on the table rather than no objects or the baby items. These findings differed from Berkowitz and LePage (1967) in that weapons stimulated aggression in the nonangered subjects as well as in the angered subjects. Heightened aggressiveness occurred in the presence of weapons even when an accomplice had not provoked the subjects (Caprara, Renzi, Amolini, D'Imperio, & Travaglia, 1984; Page & O'Neal, 1977; Simons et al., 1976; Turner & Goldsmith, 1976).

Replication of the Weapons Effect in Field Settings

Other support for the weapons effect has come from field research. Turner, Layton, and Simons (1975) examined the effects of weapons on the horn honking of Utah drivers who were blocked by an apparently stalled vehicle at a traffic light. In this experiment, an accomplice drove an old pickup truck displaying one of three levels of aggressive stimulation: (a) the truck had nothing on it (no aggressive stimulation), (b) the truck had a rifle in a gun rack and a bumper sticker with the message "Friend" attached to the tailgate (moderate stimulation), or (c) the truck had a rifle with the message "Vengeance" attached to the tailgate (high aggressive stimulation). The bumper stickers manipulated the rifle's aggressive meaning; the weapon was expected to elicit more aggressive ideas when it was coupled with the "Vengeance" than the "Friend" bumper sticker.

The driver of the truck could be hidden from the subject by a curtain across the rear window. This procedure was introduced to lower subjects' inhibitions. When the confederate was not visible (curtain closed), the weapon together with the "Vengeance" bumper sticker led to significantly more honking than the average of the other two levels of aggressive stimulation.

In a second study, an observer recorded the subject's sex and the age of the subject's car. In this investigation, new-car drivers in the rifle/vengeance condition honked at their frustrater significantly more often than did the subjects who were exposed either to the rifle or vengeance bumper sticker alone. Since the rifle only increased honking in the context of an aggressively phrased bumper sticker, Turner, Layton, and Simons (1975) speculated that rifles did not have a sufficiently salient aggressive meaning to some people unless the guns occurred in an aggressive context.

For old-car drivers, the rifle/vengeance sticker condition produced significantly lower rates of honking than did the other manipulations. This particular finding may have been due to the perceived higher status of the target relative to the potential aggressor. The old-car drivers apparently restrained their honking at someone driving a truck newer than their own cars. In addition, women were found not to respond differentially to the manipulation, possibly because they inhibited aggressive reactions in the presence of firearms. All in all, the results suggest that the aggression-enhancing effects of the mere presence of weapons frequently may be masked in some people by situationally evoked inhibition.

Boyanowski and Griffiths (1982) also conducted a field experiment on the effects of weapons. These researchers arranged for Canadian police either to wear or not to wear a holstered pistol as part of their normal patrol activities (wearing a weapon is optional for these officers). Drivers were stopped either for routine information checks (a neutral condition) or for a traffic violation (a negative condition). An observer rated the subjects' facial expression of emotion and then had subjects complete a Mood Adjective Check List. The facial expressions and self reports of traffic violators revealed greater aggressiveness when the police officer carried a pistol than when he or she did not carry one.

Simons, Fenn, Layton, and Turner (1976) investigated the aggressive behavior of young adult males at two college spring carnivals. These men did not know that they were participating in an experiment. The men were insulted or not insulted by a target person as they took part in a carnival game in which they were to throw wet sponges at the insulter. Supposedly as a prop for the carnival scene, a rifle was placed near the target person, who was dressed as a cowboy. The presence of the weapon increased the number of times that the men threw the wet sponges at the target in both investigations. However, the relatively weak insult manipulation had no effect, and the weapon effect arose in both the noninsulted and insulted groups.

The results from four field studies suggest that the mere presence of guns can increase the aggression displayed by people who do not know they are being studied.

The Stimulating Effects of Toy Weapons in Children

Several studies employing children of different ages have also shown that aggressive play with toy weapons can promote aggressive behavior. For these children, moreover, anger arousal does not seem to be a necessary condition to produce these heightened aggressive reactions.

Feshbach (1956) had children listen to stories with either an aggressive theme or a neutral theme and then permitted them to play with aggressive or neutral toys consistent with the earlier story. Children who had heard the aggressive theme and played with aggressive toys displayed more inappropriate or antisocial, aggressive behavior than those who had heard the neutral story. Adding support to this finding, Mendoza (1972) demonstrated that children playing with aggressive toys such as guns, tanks, and soldiers engaged in significantly more aggressive play behavior than children playing with neutral toys.

Turner and Goldsmith (1976) extended these findings by exposing young children to toy guns as part of their free play session in kindergarten. These researchers found that the toy guns were more likely than toy airplanes or neutral toys to stimulate antisocial free play behavior. Conventional thematic play (e.g., saying "Bang, bang, you're dead") was not counted as antisocial play behavior. These authors proposed that toy or real weapons may function much like retrieval cues, reminding children of their previous contact with the toys. These exposures might have come from television, adult movies, children's cartoons, books, or other free play sessions.

Mahjoub, Leyens, and Yzerbyt (1989) recently conducted experiments with groups of Palestinian children in Syria and Lebanon. While a toy weapon was present among nonaggressive toys for some groups, no weapon or a flute was present for the other groups. In both studies, the presence of the toy weapon increased the rate of *thematic* aggressive play but did not increase *nonthematic* aggression. In fact, in one study, the weapon decreased the rate of aggression in the groups; in the other, it increased the amount of cooperation. Further comments will be provided about these experiments in a later section.

Pictorial Depictions of Weapons

Leyens and Parke (1974) reasoned that pictures of weapons in gun advertisements and various other visual displays may well serve as aggression-eliciting cues. These cues also may create less anxiety and inhibitions than actual weapons. Leyens and Parke (1974) hypothesized that aggressive behavior increases proportionately to the increasing aggressive meaning of the display. Thus, they varied this dimension of meaning by using slides that had been prerated as low (e.g., a box of milk), medium (e.g., a whistle), or high (e.g., a revolver) in aggressive meaning.

The experiment was conducted in Belgium. Subjects first saw one of the sets of slides, and then they were either insulted or not insulted. Finally, they were asked to choose the intensity of electric shock that they wanted to deliver to their partners as punishment for errors in a supposed learning task. Although the slide's aggressive meaning had no effect on the noninsulted subjects, a weapons effect occurred for the insulted subjects. These provoked subjects selected a significantly higher shock level for their frustrater if they had viewed the gun slides rather than the less aggressive slides. Apparently, the sight of the weapons had heightened the punishment that they wanted to administer to their tormentor. Leyens and Parke's (1974) procedure was replicated in Italy (Caprara et al., 1984), the United States (Page & O'Neal, 1977), and France (DaGloria, personal communication, 1989).

Tannenbaum (1972) incorporated pictures of weapons as aggressive cues into one of four movie versions with erotic content. All subjects were angered by an experimental accomplice and then viewed one of the four films. These films varied in content in the following way: (a) aggressive commentary and portrayal of weapons in a film, (b) aggressive commentary only, (c) erotic commentary only, (d) no aggressive commentary or weapons portrayal. The movie with the aggressive comments and the visual inserts of weapons led to higher shock intensity delivered by subjects to their partners than the other three films. Tannenbaum reasoned that the erotic cues induced arousal that interacted with the additional aggressive cues to facilitate aggressive behavior.

Individual Differences Related to the Weapons Effect

Not all individuals are likely to react to weapons with increased aggressive behavior. For example, some individuals may experience anxiety or fear rather than instigation to aggression in the presence of weapons. These people are likely to inhibit rather than express aggressive responses in the presence of weapons.

Fraczek and Macauley (1971) provided evidence to support this line of reasoning. They stated that highly emotional individuals would be likely to inhibit aggressive reactions to weapons. First, they measured emotionality in male subjects using a word association test; a subject's responses in the test were rated for the level of his emotionality. Based on these ratings, the experimenters then classified subjects as either high or low in emotionality. Next, the men received part of the "weapons effect" procedure. All subjects were angered and half were exposed to weapons. The weapons effect occurred only in subjects who had low emotionality responses to aggressive words in the word association test. The researchers reasoned that the highly emotional subjects might have experienced aggression-related anxiety in the experiment. When these individuals were provoked, they were likely to inhibit any aggressive impulses resulting from the weapons.

A Replication Attempt Employing Knives as Aggressive Cues

Fischer, Kelm, and Rose (1969) attempted a replication of the weapons effect using knives rather than firearms. First, half of the subjects were provoked by an experimental accomplice serving as the subject's peer. Next, subjects were exposed to one of four conditions: a switchblade, a carving knife, a table knife, or no knife at all. Finally, subjects completed a paper-and-pencil self-report measure and an evaluation of the confederate. The switchblade led to higher hostility, depression, and anxiety ratings but to less negative evaluations of the innocent peer. Perhaps the highly aggressive cues elicited anxiety so that the subjects restrained their harmful behavior (Berkowitz, 1976).

UNSUCCESSFUL REPLICATIONS OF THE WEAPONS EFFECT

Several researchers have failed to reproduce the weapons effect (Buss, Booker, & Buss, 1972; Cahoon & Edmonds, 1985; Ellis, Weinir, & Miller, 1971; Page & Scheidt, 1971). These findings are of some importance because they draw our attention to potential limitations of the weapons effect. Turner, Simons, et al. (1977) proposed that the subjects in some of these experiments might have been anxious or apprehensive; this anxiety might have reduced their aggressive response in the presence of weapons.

After trying to replicate the weapons effect, Page and Scheidt (1971) reasoned that the original weapons effect might have been an experimental artifact. They reached this conclusion because a weapons effect occurred only in nonapprehensive, sophisticated subjects. These subjects previously had participated in an unrelated deception experiment. The researchers reasoned that their subjects had simply responded to implicit experimental demands to administer electric shock in the presence of weapons. They further speculated that Berkowitz and LePage (1967) also might have used nonapprehensive, sophisticated subjects in obtaining a weapons effect. If their speculation was correct, then perhaps the original finding was not due to the stimulating effects of weapons. Rather, the weapons effect finding might have been a result of experimental demand effects.

Alternative research findings suggest that Page and Scheidt were correct in reasoning that apprehensive subjects in a laboratory setting would not display the weapons effect. However, their proposal that the findings were artifacts is not consistent with most of the available research. First, two experiments directly varied the subject's evaluation apprehension (Simons & Turner, 1976; Turner & Simons, 1974). Subject sophistication was varied in one study and assessed in the other experiment. The results of these studies indicated that the weapons effect was unlikely to occur either in apprehensive or in sophisticated subjects. The weapons effect was actually obtained for the nonapprehensive, unsophisticated subjects. Second, and as we have seen, several field studies examined adults who were unaware of their participation in a psychological experiment. These studies have also found the weapons effect (Boyanowski & Griffiths, 1982; Simons et al., 1976; Turner, Layton, & Simons, 1975). Third, the same is true for young children who are unlikely to be sophisticated subjects (Mahjoub et al., 1989; Turner & Goldsmith, 1976).

THE MEANING OF THE WEAPONS

Actually, a close examination of the *unsuccessful* replications for the weapons effect shows that there was usually a decrease, significant or not, of aggression. This pattern of findings led Leyens and Parke (1975) to think that the weapons in those studies stimulated an anxiety meaning rather than an aggression meaning. To avoid this anxiety problem, Leyens and Parke (1975) used slides of weapons rather than the weapons themselves. The researchers found that the weapons slides stimulated more aggression. The researchers noted that the procedure is similar to the method used in desensitization procedures with anxiety-provoking cues. Other experiments have since shown that the mere presence of weapons does not necessarily induce an instigation toward aggression, possibly because of anxiety-induced reactions. Some studies have shown that weapons can sometimes stimulate prosocial reactions.

The Weapons Effect Among Palestinian Children

Often, the media portray children living in war environments as enjoying war games. The implicit message is that they have learned to behave aggressively and that they are, in fact, especially aggressive. Mahjoub et al. (1989) conducted two studies to determine whether young Palestinian children living in refugee camps (varying in insecurity) would be especially reactive to the presence of a toy weapon. The first study involved children from two kindergartens in Yarmouk camp (Damascus); the second study comprised kindergarten children from Yarmouk (Damascus), Chatila (Beirut), and Ain El Heloue (near the Israeli border). Children participated in groups of six. Some of the groups received six or nine toys for their play period and the other groups received only three toys. This manipulation was introduced to vary the level of frustration that would be experienced by the availability of toys.

In the first study, a toy rifle was included among the otherwise nonaggressive toys for one-half of the groups. In the second study, a revolver was included for one-third of the groups and a flute with the same shape as the revolver was included for another one-third of the groups. All of the other children received small cars as toys for play. The children's play sessions were videotaped. Subsequently, observers in Belgium reviewed these tapes and classified the children's behavior as being either aggressive or cooperative. While the number of toys did not have any reliable effect, the presence of the weapon significantly decreased aggression in the first study and significantly increased the cooperative behaviors in the second study. In both cases, an association was obtained between the presence of toy weapons and imitation of military acts, that is, playful (thematic) aggression.

The authors explained their results by examining the meaning that weapons have for these groups of Palestinian children. These children are rarely exposed to the same types of films as children in other cultures where weapons are associated with acts of violence by one person toward another. Rather, the Palestinian children may have a very different type of association with firearms. Weapons have become a symbol of freedom for Palestinians. Quite often, these children see or participate in national dances where a machine gun is passed on from older dancers to younger ones. In these homogeneous groups of young Palestinians, the weapon may serve as a symbol of cohesion rather than competition. In this context, a weapon may lead to less aggressive acts toward each other and to more prosocial acts for members of their social group. Of course, increased cohesion within a group may lead to greater conflict with people outside the group.

A Replication in Yugoslavia

In Yugoslavia, Zuzul (unpublished data) also showed that children tested in groups were sensitive to the meaning of weapons that they had seen before their playtime. More aggression occurred when the weapons were presented without comment or as very good and useful than if they were presented as dangerous and associated with bad persons. These findings for Palestinian and Yugoslav children suggest that weapons may have very different effects depending on the meaning that the weapon has for the individual.

MITIGATING THE WEAPONS EFFECT

Firearms are a major cause of death and injury in the United States and kill approximately 30,000 people per year. Most (90%) of the firearms causing these deaths belong to the victim or family (Turner, Simons, et al., 1977). These findings suggest that people have more to fear from the firearms in their immediate social circle than from firearms in the hands of strangers. As we indicated earlier, one possible method for reducing firearms-related aggressive behavior would be to reduce the exposure of the public to firearms. However, one of the major problems in mitigating the effects of weapons on aggressive behavior is predicting who will be stimulated to violence. Although millions of people own firearms, only a very small proportion will ever use these weapons in an aggressive manner (Wright et al., 1983). Thus, efforts to restrict firearms ownership may primarily affect individuals who would use firearms in a safe and reasonable manner.

Another method is to change the meanings associated with firearms. As long as weapons are associated with sports and hunting, they are not likely to cause many injuries or deaths. Instead firearms are much more likely to be associated with injury when they are purchased for so-called "self-defense." The actual cases of successful self-defense involving a firearm are not frequent. In a study of 464 gun-related deaths in one week in the United States, *Time* magazine ("Seven deadly days," 1989) counted only 14 cases in which the death occurred as a result of self-defense. The message implied by these findings is that gun ownership is more likely to increase danger than to increase safety.

Because firearms are often lethal and instigate impulsive, aggressive reactions, laws might be passed to reduce these impulsive acts. These laws might make it impossible to buy weapons much as we buy an alcoholic drink; that is, we would not be able to buy one on the spot simply because we want one. By creating rules and laws that delay purchase of a firearm, the procedures would give time for the aggressive script to be deactivated before the weapon can be obtained. These laws would not impede those who are "professional" or safe users of firearms. Of course, these legal requirements also would not deter a firearm owner from having an aggressive script activated after the firearm is purchased. Still, the laws may prevent some unfortunate accidents.

Any effort to reduce firearms availability is likely to meet with very stiff opposition from public interest groups. We need not be discouraged by the relative difficulty of changing firearms availability for the society at large. Consider the fact that the most dangerous firearms to an individual are those in the immediate social environment. We might be able to affect the use of the firearms in our social environment even if we can not affect society at large. The following sections describe some methods of mitigating the effects of firearms on behavior.

Decentration

Leyens, Cisneros, and Hossay (1976) proposed a procedure to mitigate the effects of weapons on aggressive behavior. They reasoned that the effect of a stimulus depends on the way an individual attends to the cue at any point in time. A change in the focus can modify someone's response even when he or she is exposed to cues that are normally associated with aggression. Leyens et al. (1976) applied these principles to the weapons effects for Belgian military recruits. When recruits were trained to attend primarily to the aesthetic qualities of aggressive slides, they rated the slides as better, less violent, less aggressive, and less wicked than subjects not so trained. Decentration might change either the meaning assigned to the cues leading to a decrease in arousal or to an accentuation of the fictitious dimension of the cues.

Leyens et al. (1976) then demonstrated that decentration can lessen the weapons effect. Subjects first saw either aggressive or neutral slides, then were insulted by an experimental accomplice, and finally were permitted to deliver shocks to their partners. In addition to this variation, some of the men were asked to evaluate the aesthetic qualities of the slides (the decentration manipulation). The results indicated that subjects not directed to attend to the aesthetic features gave a significantly higher intensity of shock when exposed to aggressive rather than to neutral slides. On the other hand, subjects asked to focus on the aesthetic qualities of the slides showed no more aggressiveness in response to the aggressive slides than to the neutral slides.

Child Training

Describing a procedure similar to decentration, Huesmann, Eron, Klein, Brice, and Fischer (1983) developed an intervention that was effective in mitigating the effects of television on children's aggressive behavior. This procedure was designed to change children's attitudes about television violence. Since so many of the lessons learned about firearms occur on television, the same methods might be applied to the effects of firearms.

First, the researchers identified a potential violence-prone group of children who experienced a heavy diet of television violence. Half of these children received the mitigating treatment. This intervention taught the children about the fictional nature of television, the inappropriateness of the solutions used in television programs, and the undesirability of acting in a manner similar to the televised characters. Huesmann et al. (1983) found that the treated group received significantly lower peer-rated aggression scores than the untreated group. Here again, the experimenters somewhat changed the aggressive meaning of the programs shown on TV. These mitigation procedures might be extended to the firearms portrayals on television. That is, further efforts could be made to demonstrate the dangers of owning firearms. These messages might emphasize that firearms ownership increases one's danger rather than increasing one's safety.

Civil Liability of Manufacturers

Civil litigation (rather than criminal laws) may be used to reduce the likelihood of firearm-related injuries. A recent civil-liability litigation effort has been made to shift the responsibility for injuries from firearms to the manufacturer (Turley, 1983). Social science data can be useful in establishing the basis for the suit (Linz, Turner, Hesse, & Penrod, 1984). Using the legal principle of strict product liability in torts, attorneys have alleged that firearms manufacturers should be held accountable for avoidable injuries caused by their products (Turley, 1983). Essentially, the product liability principle states that manufacturers have a duty to minimize any dangers associated with their products. These legal challenges rely on social science research to demonstrate the potential dangers of firearms.

The first legal requirement is that a manufacturer must foresee that the product is dangerous in its reasonable use (Turley, 1983). High death and injury rates associated with firearms clearly demonstrate that the product meets this first legal standard. Second, the manufacturer must be able to manufacture the product so that it is less dangerous (Turley, 1983). Numerous design improvements have been proposed that could minimize firearms injuries. The most obvious safety measure is to make firearms more difficult to discharge by children (under the age of 14). Currently, the "western" revolver has no effective safety mechanism to prevent children from discharging it. A number of effective safety mechanisms have been invented and could be installed on revolvers. However, manufacturers have failed to make these improvements (Turley, 1983).

Third, to be liable for the injuries, the manufacturer must continue producing the dangerous product even though he or she knows how to improve the product (Turley, 1983). The person who sells the weapon also may be liable for any injuries resulting from the dangerous product. Numerous suits have been filed in United States courts against firearms manufacturers. These lawsuits are likely to substantially change the way firearms are manufactured, sold, and stored in private homes. As a consequence, these lawsuits may discourage the private ownership of firearms and, subsequently, also decrease the likelihood of criminal violence.

CONCLUSION

Although popular accounts have suggested that the ready availability of firearms is a major factor contributing to criminal violence, empirical evidence does not directly support the premise. If availability explained criminal violence, then the reduction in firearms availability might reduce violence. In the absence of more clearcut evidence, we have no basis for recommending efforts to restrict the availability of guns as a means to reduce the rates of criminal violence. This chapter does provide evidence of an alternative approach to the association of firearms and violence. We propose that the aggressive meaning attached to firearms is one of the major determinants of a weapon's influence on impulsive, aggressive responses. We propose that policies to reduce criminal violence need to consider the aggressive meaning as well as the availability of firearms.

REFERENCES

Azrin, N. H., Hutchinson, R. R., & Hake, D. F. (1967). Attack, avoidance, and escape reactions to aversive shock. *Journal of the Experimental Analysis of Behavior, 10*, 131–148.

Baker, S. P., O'Neill, X., & Karpf, R. S. (1984). *The injury fact book.* Lexington, MA: D. C. Heath & Co.

Bandura, A. (1986). *Social foundations of thought and action: A social cognitive theory.* Englewood Cliffs, NJ: Prentice-Hall.

Berkowitz, L. (1968). Impulse, aggression, and the gun. *Psychology Today, 2*, 19–22.

Berkowitz, L. (1974). Some determinants of impulsive aggression: Role of mediated associations with reinforcements for aggression. *Psychological Review, 81*, 165–176.

Berkowitz, L. (1976). The "weapons effect," demand characteristics, and the myth of the compliant subject. *Journal of Personality and Social Psychology, 20*, 332–338.

Berkowitz, L. (1984) Some effects of thoughts on anti- and prosocial influences of media events: A cognitive-neoassociational analysis. *Psychology Bulletin, 95*, 410–427.

Berkowitz, L. (1988). Frustrations, appraisals, and aversively stimulated aggression. *Aggressive Behavior, 14*, 3–11.

Berkowitz, L. & LePage, A. (1967). Weapons as aggression-eliciting stimuli. *Journal of Personality and Social Psychology, 7*, 202–227.

Boyanowski, E. O., & Griffiths, C. T. (1982). Weapons and eye contact as instigators or inhibitors of aggressive arousal in police–citizen interaction. *Journal of Applied Social Psychology, 12*, 398–407.

Bureau of Alcohol, Tobacco, and Firearms. (1959–1982). *Alcohol, tobacco, and firearms summary statistics* (Department of the Treasury). Washington, DC: U.S. Government Printing Office.

Buss, A. H., Booker, A., & Buss, E. (1972). Firing a weapon and aggression. *Journal of Personality and Social Psychology, 22*, 296–302.

220   DOMESTIC POLICY

Cahoon, D. D., & Edwards, E. M. (1985). The weapons effect: Fact or artifact? *Psychonomic Society, 23,* 57–60.
Cannon, W. B. (1929). *Bodily changes in pain, hunger, fear and rage: An account of researches into the function of emotional excitement* (2nd ed.). New York: Appleton-Century-Crofts.
Caprara, G. V., Renzi, P., Amolini, P., D'Imperio, G., & Travaglia, G. (1984). The eliciting cue value of aggressive slides reconsidered in a personological perspective: The weapons effect and irritability. *European Journal of Social Psychology, 14,* 313–322.
Carlson, M., Marcus-Newhall, A., & Miller, N. (1990). Effects of situational aggression cues. *Journal of Personality and Social Psychology, 58,* 622–633.
Dodge, K. (1980). Social cognition and children's aggressive behavior. *Child Development, 53,* 620–635.
Ellis, D. P., Weinir, P., & Miller, III, L. (1971). Does the trigger pull the finger? An experimental test of weapons as aggression eliciting stimuli. *Sociometry, 34,* 453–465.
Feshbach, S. (1956). The catharsis hypothesis and some consequences of interaction with aggressive and neutral play objects. *Journal of Personality, 24,* 449–462.
Fischer, D., Kelm, J., & Rose, A. (1969). Knives as aggression-eliciting stimuli. *Psychological Reports, 24,* 775–760.
Fraczek, A., & Macauley, J. R. (1971). Some personality factors in reaction to aggressive stimuli. *Journal of Personality, 39,* 163–177.
Frodi, A. (1973). The effects of exposure to aggression-eliciting and aggression-inhibiting stimuli on subsequent aggression. *Goteburg Psychological Reports, 3,* No. 8.
Huesmann, L. R. (1988). An information processing model for the development of aggression. *Aggressive Behavior, 14,* 13–24.
Huesmann, L. R., Eron, L. D., Klein, R., Brice, P., & Fischer, P. (1983). Mitigating the imitation of aggressive behavior by children's attitudes about media violence. *Journal of Personality and Social Psychology, 44,* 899–910.
Leyens, J. Ph., Cisneros, T., & Hossay, J. F. (1976). Decentration as a means for reducing aggression after exposure to violent stimuli. *European Journal of Social Psychology, 6,* 459–473.
Leyens, J. Ph., & Dunand, M. (1990). *Cognitive anticipation of viewing an aggressive movie: The instigation effect is already there.* Submitted for publication.
Leyens, J. Ph., & Parke, R. D. (1974). Aggressive slides can induce a weapons effect. *European Journal of Social Psychology, 5,* 229–236.
Liebert, R. M., Neale, J. M., & Davidson, E. S. (1973). *The early window: Effects of television on children and youth.* New York: Pergamon Press.
Linz, D., Turner, C. W., Hesse, B. W., & Penrod, S. D. (1984). Bases of liability for injuries by media portrayals of violent pornography. In N. M. Malamuth & E. Donnerstein (Eds.), *Pornography and sexual aggression* (pp. 277–305). New York: Academic Press.
Mahjoub, A., Leyens, J. Ph., & Yzerbyt, V. (1989). *The weapons effect among children living in an armed-conflict environment.* Submitted for publication.
Massachusetts Council on Crime and Correction. (1974). *Firearms and violence in American society.* Boston, MA: Author.
Mendoza, A. (1972). *The effects of exposure to toys conducive to violence.* Unpublished doctoral dissertation, University of Miami.
Newton, G. G., & Zimring, F. E., (1969). *Firearms and violence in American life.* Washington, DC: U.S. Government Printing Office.
Page, D., & O'Neal, E. C. (1977). "Weapons effect" without demand characteristics. *Psychological Reports, 41,* 29–30.
Page, M. M., & Scheidt, R. J. (1971). The elusive weapons effect: Demand awareness, evaluation apprehension, and slightly sophisticated subjects. *Journal of Personality and Social Psychology, 20,* 591–596.
Patterson, G. R. (1982). *Coercive family process.* Eugene, OR: Castalia Publishing.
"Seven deadly days." (1989, July 17). *Time,* pp. 30–60.
Shields, P. (1981). *Guns don't die—people do: The pros, the cons, the facts.* New York: Arbor House.
Simons, L. S., & Turner, C. W. (1976). Evaluation apprehension, hypothesis awareness, and the weapons effect. *Aggressive Behavior, 2,* 77–87.
Simons, L. S., Fenn, M. R., Layton, J. F., & Turner, C. W. (1976). Verhalten in eninem aggressions—Spiel auf dem vergnugunsplatz. In J. J. Koch (Ed.), *Altruismus und aggression: Der feld experiment in der sozial psychologie* (vol. 1), Weinheim und Basel: Beltz Verlag.
Sloan, J. H., Kellerman, A. L., Reay, D. T., Ferris, J. A., Koepsell, T., Rivara, F. P., Rice, C., Gray, L., & LoGefro, J. (1988, November 10). Handgun regulations, crime, assaults, and homicide: A tale of two cities. *The New England Journal of Medicine.*

Tannenbaum, P. H. (1972). Studies in film- and television-mediated arousal and aggression: A progress report. In G. A. Comstock, E. A. Rubinstein, & J. P. Murray (Eds.), *Television and social behavior. Vol. 5. Television effects: Further explorations* (pp. 309–350). Washington, DC: U.S. Government Printing Office.

Toch, H. H. (1969). *Violent men: An enquiry into the psychology of violence.* Chicago: Aldine Publishing Co.

Treanor, W. W., & Bijlefeld, M. (1989). *Kids and guns: A child safety scandal.* Washington, DC: American Youth Work Center.

Turley, W. (1982). Manufacturers' and suppliers' liability to handgun victims. *Northern Kentucky Law Review, 10,* 41–62.

Turner, C. W., Cole, A. M., & Cerro, D. S. (1984). Contributions of aversive experiences to robbery and homicide: A demographic analysis. In R. M. Kaplan, V. J. Konecni, & R. W. Novaco (Eds.), *Aggression in children and youth* (pp. 296–341). The Hague: Martinus Nijhoff Publishers.

Turner, C. W., & Dodd, D. K. (1979). The development of anti-social behavior. In R. L. Ault (Ed.), *Selected readings in child development.* Santa Monica, CA: Goodyear.

Turner, C. W., Fenn, M. R., & Cole, A. M. (1981). A social psychological analysis of violent behavior. In R. B. Stuart (Ed.), *Violent behavior: Social learning approaches to prediction, management, and treatment* (pp. 31–67). New York: Brunner/Mazel.

Turner, C. W., & Goldsmith, D. (1976). Effects of toy guns and airplanes on children's antisocial free play behavior. *Journal of Experimental Child Psychology, 21,* 303–315.

Turner, C. W., Hesse, B. W., & Peterson-Lewis, S. (1986). Naturalistic studies of the long-term effects of television violence. *Journal of Social Issues, 42,* 51–74.

Turner, C. W., & Layton, J. F. (1976). Verbal imagery and connotation as memory induced mediators of aggressive behavior. *Journal of Personality and Social Psychology, 33,* 755–763.

Turner, C. W., Layton, J. F., & Simons, L. S. (1975). Naturalistic studies of aggressive behavior: Aggressive stimuli, victim visibility, and horn honking. *Journal of Personality and Social Psychology, 31,* 1098–1107.

Turner, C. W., & Simons, L. S. (1974). Effects of subject sophistication and evaluation apprehension on aggressive responses to weapons. *Journal of Personality and Social Psychology, 30,* 341–348.

Turner, C. W., Simons, L. S., Berkowitz, L., & Frodi, A. (1977). The stimulating and inhibiting effect of weapons on aggressive behavior. *Aggressive Behavior, 3,* 355–378.

Uniform Crime Reports. (1955–1989). Washington, DC: U.S. Government Printing Office.

Wright, J. D., Rossi, P. H. & Daly, K. (1983). *Under the gun: Weapons, crime and violence in America.* New York: Aldine.

15

Research and Policy: The Case of Gun Control

Hans Toch and Alan J. Lizotte

ADVOCATING GUN CONTROL

In 1971 one of the authors of this chapter served as consultant to the National Commission on the Causes and Prevention of Violence. In this capacity, he participated in a study group whose views were transmitted to the commission. The commission in turn reported to the President that "after extensive study we find that the availability of guns contributes substantially to violence in American society." The commission also noted, "our studies have convinced us that the heart of any effective national firearms policy for the United States must be to reduce the availability of the firearm that contributes the most to violence. *This means restrictive licensing of the handgun* . . . reducing the availability of the handgun *will* reduce firearms violence*" (National Commission on the Causes and Prevention of Violence, 1964, pp. 169–188; emphasis in the original).

This commission proposed (Recommendation #52) that federal legislation be enacted to "encourage the establishment of state licensing systems for handguns" and to impose federal standards in states that failed to respond. The commission also suggested (Recommendation #56) that a ban be enacted against the importation, production, and sale of "junk guns." As buttressing, the commission mandated (Recommendation #50) that "further research be undertaken on the relationship between firearms and violence and on the measures that can reduce firearms sales" (National Commission on the Causes and Prevention of Violence, 1984 pp. 278–279).

Recommendations #52 and #56 still await implementation, but Recommendation #50 has come home to roost, in that the further research that has been done has weakened the certitude of any inferences we can draw from data. This is so because the facts that seemed simple in 1969 have acquired complexity by now and yield imperfectly to simplistic conclusions.

The authors of a recent review of the empirical literature (Wright, Rossi, & Daly, 1983) emerge from their exploration with the conclusion:

> . . . *that the probable benefits of stricter gun controls (itself a nebulous concept) in terms of crime reduction are at best uncertain, and at worst close to nil, and that most such measures would pose rather high social costs.*
>
> *For these and other reasons . . . our view is that the prospects for ameliorating the problem of criminal violence through stricter controls over the civilian ownership, purchase, or use of firearms are dim. (p. 22)*

Among the other reasons referred to are concerns that have little to do with guns, crime, or violence, but instead have to do with social control. There are perhaps 20,000 gun laws now in effect in this country. That these laws have had limited or no effect on the rate of violent crime is apparent. Wright et al. (1983) conclude that stricter laws are likely to foster widespread evasions and noncompliance by citizens, by the police, and by other criminal justice agencies. As with Prohibition, "laws that cannot be enforced, that violate what citizens perceive to be their rights, or that invite widespread noncompliance cannot help but undermine the foundations of a society attempting, sometimes fitfully, to exist under the rule of law" (Wright et al., 1983, p. 323).

NATURE OF THE PROBLEM

Part of the difficulty lies in the nature of the problem. At least half of U.S. households own one or more firearms. Most of this burgeoning arsenal is used for leisure pursuits, but a sizable fraction (25% of all guns, and 40% to 50% of handguns) are regarded by the owners as means of self-protection. The assumption is probably fallacious, but the security it offers nevertheless can be real.

Of the commission's arguments for gun control, the hardest to demolish is that the many lethal crimes of passion (chiefly intrafamily and other nonstranger violence) could be lessened by reduced availability of handguns. The argument is undergirded by two sets of facts: There is similarity in the patterning of assault and homicide incidents, which suggests that the weapon that is deployed rather than the type of person who uses it presages the lethal aspect of serious incidents; and minor altercations tend to spark intrafamily homicide, which suggests that motives for murder escalate in the encounter, rather than entering it in full-blown form. These facts matter because the scenarios they describe imply a spur-of-the-moment recourse to whatever weapon is available.

THE "WEAPONS EFFECT"

Psychology's special claim to being able to document a gun control stand rests on experimental studies of angry or retaliatory aggression. In most of these studies the subjects—typically college students—are verbally degraded, or subjected to mild electric shocks. They are then given the opportunity to be aggressive or hostile, should they feel (understandably) so inclined. Additional stimuli can be introduced, but care must be taken to disguise the connection between such stimuli and the experiment. A cover story is also needed to prevent subjects from guessing that aggression is the subject of the study.

The most publicized of these experiments was conducted by a team headed by Leonard Berkowitz, a behavioral social psychologist. Berkowitz hypothesized that an angry person would be more likely to express aggression in the presence of stimuli that in the past had been associated with aggression. The most interesting aspect, given our concerns, was the assumption that weapons would figure prominently among stimuli that should carry violent connotations.

The advertised source of injury to subjects in the experiment (Berkowitz & LePage, 1967) was an experimental accomplice, who rated advertising slogans drafted by the subject. The injury he inflicted consisted of up to seven shocks (the maximum allowable number) reflecting an unfavorable assessment of the subject's work. The subject in turn "shocked" the accomplice, though no electric shocks were actually delivered. In the weapons condition, a shotgun and a large revolver were highly visible, lying on a table.

As in other studies of this kind, subjects who were gratuitously injured (with seven shocks) behaved more aggressively than those who had been more reasonably treated. The frustrated subjects who displayed what has become known as the "weapons effect" administered significantly more shocks than other frustrated subjects to the accomplice who had been identified as the owner of guns.

In a number of publications, Berkowitz has fleshed out what he regards as policy inferences he can draw from this research. He has written that:

> A society that wants fewer violent outbursts should reduce frustration, leave inhibitions intact and remove immediate cues that can set off aggressive acts. . . . The third possibility, reducing the number of aggressive stimuli people encounter from day to day, is probably the easiest one to effect, and the fastest. . . . The task seems more manageable when one realizes that most aggressive stimuli fall into only a few large categories, one of the largest of which bears the label "guns." Guns not only permit violence, they can stimulate it as well. The finger pulls the trigger, but the trigger may also be pulling the finger. (Berkowitz, 1968, p. 22)

More recently, Berkowitz has written:

> I contended, and still contend, that we sometimes react mindlessly and impulsively to the presence of guns. Since that is so, the more control the law exercises over the availability of guns, the better. . . .
> In all, the import of the weapons-effect studies remains. Guns carry with them meanings that increase aggression: They create aggression that in the absence of guns would not exist. It is in this sense that the trigger can pull the finger. One important way to diminish such tragic occurrences is through stricter gun controls limiting the availability of guns. (Berkowitz, 1981, p. 12)

One fact that has made these policy inferences less than compelling is that many studies have failed to replicate the Berkowitz and LePage (1967) findings, and some have even reported opposite findings. The second of these two contingencies had been anticipated by Berkowitz and LePage (1967), who noted that their hypothesis would be confirmed only "assuming that the weapons do not produce inhibitions that are stronger than the evoked aggressive reactions (as would be the case, e.g., if the weapons were labeled as morally 'bad')" (Berkowitz & LePage, 1967, p. 203).

One of the clearest disconfirmations of the weapons effect was that of Ellis, Weiner, and Miller (1971). In this study, the accomplice was costumed as a policeman. Ellis, Weiner, and Miller (1971) report that:

> We tried various ways of convincing the subject that the weapons he saw belonged to his student-partner—he was going hunting after the experiment, he was from ROTC, and so on. None of these worked. On more than one occasion subjects actually burst out laughing at our efforts. The reaction seemed to us to be perfectly justified. It was only because of our failure here that we decided to use a policeman for the weapons-associated condition. In all but two cases the manipulation was completely successful. The two exceptions were students who recognized our confederate, and almost fell over backwards because they believed he really was a policeman and had been working undercover in their dorm. (p. 454)

The study confirmed that injury was correlated with angry retaliation, but found that weapons inhibited aggression where anger-levels were low. The experimenters (Ellis et al., 1971) concluded, tongue-in-cheek, that their research should not be read "as providing support for *increasing* the sale of weapons and thereby producing a generalized inhibition of violent behavior" (pp. 464–465, emphasis added).

Another devastating disconfirmation of the weapons effect was reported by Buss, Booker, and Buss (1972), who had set out to explore the effects of firing a weapon on subsequent aggression, in experienced and nonexperienced gun users. A lack of clear findings in the weapons-firing conditions led the experimenters to replicate the Berkowitz and LePage (1967) study. The conditions they used were identical to the original, though they changed the cover story about the confederate's use of weapons, since "this instruction resulted in a large proportion of subjects being eliminated from the experiment as being too suspicious" (Buss et al., 1972, p. 300). Despite care taken in replicating the original study, the weapons effect was not obtained or a significant opposite finding was registered.

Buss et al. (1972) dismissed the weapons effect as a statistical artifact. They concluded that "it is well known that samples drawn from a college population do tend to vary" and that "given the usual variations in sampling, it is not surprising that statistically significant findings fail to replicate." They also pointed out that successive experiments "yielded just the kind of data found in statistics texts to illustrate a population mean of zero: weapons increase aggression, no weapons increase aggression, and no difference between weapons and no weapons" (p. 301).

Subsequent experiments have yielded a somewhat different picture. What the sum of these experiments suggest is that a weapons effect is obtained with some subjects under some circumstances, but that other subjects and other circumstances can produce no effect or an opposite effect. Berkowitz and his colleagues have commented on these findings, and concluded that

> . . . *weapons do not always stimulate aggression. In fact, many individuals frequently seem to "bend over backward" to avoid aggressive reactions in the presence of weapons. These individuals may experience aggression-related anxiety in the presence of firearms due to fears of retaliation from their victim or because they think aggressive responses might portray an unfavorable impression to those around them. Based on people's previous experience with firearms, they may have very different associations to firearms which may determine whether inhibitory reactions or stimulating effects will predominate. Further research is required to better understand individual differences in people's reactions to firearms. (Turner, Simons, Berkowitz, & Frodi, 1977, pp. 375–376)*

What this summary implies is that the weapons effect is a weak effect that may be produced only under sharply delimited conditions. More confusingly, weapons under some conditions reliably inhibit aggression and under other conditions reliably disinhibit aggression, which does not invite unambiguous policy-related inferences. In the words of Cahoon and Edmonds (1984)

> *In view of the conflictual, if not contradictory, results in this important area, it seems prudent for psychologists to avoid further public policy recommendations based upon an apparently elusive variable. To do otherwise may serve to weaken the credibility of psychology as a data resource with respect to social issues. (p. 307)*

The focus of literature has most recently shifted to a discussion of the conditions that promote the weapons effect or, rather, that promote one of two weapons effects. Much of this focus is not relevant to policy inferences about gun control, in that it deals with artificial experimental conditions that have no counterpart in violent incidents.

It has become obvious, to take an example, that aggression in the laboratory can be affected if subjects infer that experimenters have a weapons-related hypothesis. Such suspicion can produce either uncongenial or congenial responses. One set of experimenters (the weapons effect critics) seem to emphasize the tendency of subjects to comply (Page & Scheidt, 1971) while other experimenters (the Wisconsin group and its allies, such as Turner & Simons, 1974; Berkowitz, 1971) highlight subject resistance. This difference in emphasis is not accidental, in that inhibition of the weapons effect through contrariness presupposes that there is something (the original effect) to be inhibited, whereas compliance with demand can explain the effect as an artifact. Either process also relates to the subject's self-esteem. This is so because subjects may comply with the hypothesis to gain acceptance or prove themselves as "junior scientists." They may also resist compliance to demonstrate their autonomy or to protest the experimenter's encroachment.

There is another self-esteem–related variable that has policy relevance, but not in the gun control direction. This variable has to do with a replicated observation to the effect that subjects equate respectability with restraint, and bend over backward to avoid appearing bloodthirsty. The inference is that lack of inhibition is unfashionable, and that it is resisted in the presence of stimuli that are designed to promote it.

Experiments have suggested that aggression invites anxiety, and that this anxiety extends to guns used as stimuli. One set of studies, mostly done in Europe, shows that slides featuring aggression-related stimuli are seemingly more potent in the laboratory than the objects themselves. Pictures of guns produce a "depicted gun effect" (although that is not what it is called), and do so reliably. The authors of one study (Leyens & Parke, 1975) note that:

> One reason for the success of the pictorial paradigm may be due to the lowering of anxiety produced through this procedure. As previous research on desensitization has indicated, slides of anxiety-producing objects will arouse less anxiety than the objects themselves. (p. 234)

The inference—at least for persons who are not desensitized gun aficionados— is that the built-in lethality of weapons in real life can have a sobering effect, whereas pictures (or even toy guns used in child studies) permit displays of carefree rambunctiousness. Leyens and Parke (1975) draw a dubious policy inference from this fact, which is that "serious consideration should be given to the regulation of [weapons] advertising. Secondly, the impact of books which contain pictures of guns which are generally considered harmless, and often appropriate, for children need to be carefully evaluated" (p. 235).

An unrelated but overlapping point has to do with personality differences in susceptibility to the weapons effect. Several studies suggest that subjects who are habitually irritable tend to respond to aggression-enhancing stimuli (Caprara, Renzi, Amolini, D'Imperio, & Travaglia, 1984) while high-anxiety (highly emotional) subjects inhibit aggression in the presence of guns (Fraczek & Macaulay,

1971). These studies point away from the original effect and suggest that it is only a select group of persons, such as aggression-prone men (never women), who experience the effect. Other persons either tend not to experience the effect or manifest its opposite.

There are further differences that relate to stimulus conditions. The original weapons effect was an "associated-weapons effect," meaning that significant differences linked the weapon with the confederate who was the object of retaliation in this study. The instructions for this condition are summarized as follows: "The experimenter said that the weapons were being used in some way by this person [the confederate] in his research . . . the guns were to be disregarded" (Berkowitz & LePage, 1967, p. 204).

It follows that the meaning assigned to the guns was that they belonged to a person who not only delighted in frustrating subjects (instant experiment) but who ran other experiments in which he showed a propensity for violence or sadism. This configuration is not highlighted by Berkowitz and his associates, which is particularly troublesome given that Berkowitz has correctly noted that experiments lend themselves to surfacing assigned meanings by experimental subjects. In a seminal article about experimentation, Berkowitz and Donnerstein (1982) point out that "the most influential analyses of human behavior in experimental social psychology today emphasize the role of the individual's thought processes and assume that he or she is an active seeker after meaning and often tries to control what is happening" (p. 247).

Such emphasis invites attention to how subjects perceive guns when they react to them and how subjects perceive guns when they do not react to them, such as when the original (Berkowitz and LePage) instructions are changed. There are some research studies that are rich in information about these assigned meanings. One study that explores such meanings, including the meaning of the impotent "pure" (nonassociated) weapons connotations, is a field experiment (Turner, Layton, & Simons, 1975) that has been acknowledged by Berkowitz (1981) to be an exploration of the weapons-effect in real life.

The Turner, Layton, and Simons (1975) experiment centered on a busy intersection during nonrush-hour traffic. The confederate (experimenter) in the study appeared in a truck, timing his arrival to coincide with a red light. When a suitable subject-motorist arrived before the light turned, the confederate stepped on his brakes and remained standing for 12 seconds.

If the subject in this study honked at the confederate, he was deemed to have expressed aggression. Differences were anticipated in response to a rifle in the truck's window, reinforced by a bumper sticker that read "Vengeance." In a second condition the rifle was paired with a nonaggressive bumper sticker ("Friend") in the same location.

In one set of experiments, the truck was an old one, and the subjects selected were male drivers of new cars. The confederate was sometimes hidden from view by a closed curtain; in another condition, the confederate was visible. Increases in honking were found where the gun was paired with the aggressive sticker and the confederate's curtain was drawn. With regard to the curtain, Turner, Layton, and Simons (1975) point out that other researchers in aggression experiments "typically isolate the subject in order to lower inhibitions about giving shocks" (p.

1102). Berkowitz (1974), however, argues that information about target pain (assuming the pain is not excessive) can be reinforcing.[1]

Turner, Layton, and Simons (1975) ran a second set of experiments using a later model truck and imposing "no restrictions . . . on the age of drivers' vehicles or sex of subjects" (p. 1103). They obtained the highest honking rate (80%) for female drivers in the control condition, which featured neither bumper sticker nor gun.[2] The most dramatic difference appeared for male drivers of old vehicles, who virtually never honked when they encountered the "Vengeance" sticker and rifle. The experimenters point out that "the present findings tentatively suggest that the presence of a rifle in an aggressive context (like the bumper sticker) for some male subjects may produce inhibitions rather than stimulate more aggression" (Turner, Layton, and Simons, 1975, p. 1105). This means that policy inferences are discouraged, though Berkowitz (1981) cites the honking study to support gun control recommendations.

If Turner, Layton, and Simons' (1975) findings prove reasonably replicable (they have not survived replication in a small town), they mean at best that a gun associated with a frustrating agent who is also a certified aggressor (as defined by a bumper sticker) can enhance the annoyance of some frustrated persons and intimidates others who fear retaliation from a self-advertising bully. Guns sported by frustrating nonaggressors produce no impact, and some subject attributes (such as status and gender) are correlated with inhibition or disinhibition. Nothing in any of the field experiments in which guns were used suggests that the *mere presence of a weapon* has an impact, as the phrase *weapons effect* implies. There is also no justification for assuming that guns in the hands of subjects (a condition that has not been deployed in the experiments, except unsuccessfully by Buss et al., 1972) exercise an effect in experiments. This fact matters because there is no gun control argument that contends that guns are dangerous because persons who wield them (confederates associated with guns) subject themselves to aggression from persons they have antagonized.

EXTERNAL VALIDITY

A more general issue (broached by Berkowitz & Donnerstein, 1982) is whether laboratory studies of aggression have external validity. The answer to this question depends on what *external validity* means. It is clear that psychological processes can be isolated in the laboratory where conditions can be controlled. The problem is that conditions may be *too* controlled for processes to be relevant in life. Berkowitz and Donnerstein (1982) admit, for example, that

---

[1] A more likely explanation for the difference between the curtained and noncurtained conditions is a principle enunciated by the syndicated news columnist Mike Royko, who advised (in a column dated November 15, 1988), "never give the finger to someone with a tattoo on his arm who is driving a clunker which looks uninsurable."

[2] The high honking rate among women obscures the standard interpretation of what honking means. Turner, Layton, and Simons (1975) themselves note that "anecdotal evidence suggests that drivers often honk at others to attract their attention or to warn them about some danger." (p. 1106). This means that some honking may be friendly whereas other honking is distinctly unfriendly.

Experiments in the area of aggression usually attempt to minimize the subjects' inhibitions against aggression, whereas these restraints are often quite strong in natural social settings. Because of the lessened inhibitions in the former cases, it may actually be somewhat easier to see the weapons effect in the laboratory than in most social situations. . . . As a consequence, we cannot use our laboratory findings to estimate the likelihood that a certain class of responses will occur in naturalistic situations. . . . Experiments are not conducted to yield such an estimate. (p. 255)

The problem of prevalence of a process is not important where the process studied is so powerful that we can depend on its survival in complicated real life situations. But we cannot depend on the survival of very weak effects, which are easily overwhelmed when the parameters we have deleted in the sandbox are reinstated in the battlefield. Violence in the laboratory can have little consequence since it does not maim, kill, mobilize counteraggression, or send subjects to prison. Hence, why not lessen inhibitions that exist elsewhere?

A second issue has to do with the transferability of connotations that attach to the subjects' behavior in the laboratory. Berkowitz and Donnerstein (1982) contend that

Although the responses they make in the experiment certainly do not physically resemble the attacks they display in their daily lives, all of these actions appear to have much the same meaning to the participants; they know they are intentionally hurting someone else. This common meaning relates the laboratory behavior to the conduct shown in more naturalistic settings. (p. 254)

But how common is common? Is pressing a shock button with abandon an experience that is suffused with consequential rage? And what about the weapons? Is any variable that matters to the experimenter a factor in the subject's decision? Does the trigger push the finger on the shock button or give it a nudge? Do guns hasten, or enhance, the frustrated subject's retaliatory resolve? What is more likely is that guns redefine the confederate to whom they are attributed, making him somewhat less worthy of gentlemanly consideration accorded to fellow-subjects in experiments. If this is so, what sort of external validity does this have, particularly in life, where rage is real?

PATTERNS OF GUN OWNERSHIP

Guns play a role through their fateful availability for use where their bearers' or owners' destructive urges or resolves culminate. This sad fact is indisputable, and psychology is not needed to highlight it. But psychology may be obscuring this effect by simplifying it in the laboratory. In contrast with the laboratory paradigm, the role of guns in violent incidents is not serendipitous (as are guns lying next to the shock button), nor cross sectional, nor short term, nor discrete.[3] Guns do not *happen* to be present where they are used and they are not disembodied stimuli that contribute to the aggressor's mood. Guns are lethal instruments wittingly carried

[3]Should weapons effects in nonlaboratory situations exist, they are unlikely to last over time. As with the titillating impact of pornography (which is closely analogous to the postulated weapons effect), satiation can be expected with prolonged exposure.

into situations that can explode. They are owned and retained and kept available with expectations of violence. Whatever effect guns have spans time and has to do with motives and expectations relating to gun acquisition, ownership, and deployment. The kinds of questions to ask about this effect are different from questions that can be posed in the laboratory, because they must be addressed to gun bearers and gun owners and not to indentured students.

There is an enormous literature on patterns of firearms ownership and use that can shed more light on the importance of the weapons effect in real life relative to other concerns. A weapons effect implies that subjects in a laboratory give meanings to firearms that translate into aggressive behavior. Sociologists have been interested in the meanings that are attached to firearms in aggregate populations. More often they reflect on the causes of the attachment of specific meanings in the society at large (Tonso, 1982), in the culture, or in some subculture (Bordua & Lizotte, 1979; Gastil, 1971; Hackney, 1969; Lizotte & Bordua, 1980; Reed, 1972). The assumption is that firearms take on differing meanings depending on one's demographic, structural, and, in the end, cultural placement in the social order. It is assumed that a clearer understanding of the causes of these various meanings comes from a fuller knowledge of patterns of firearms ownership and use.

We have noted that slightly more than half of the households in the United States have at least one firearm, with most of those having more than one. This means that there are somewhere between 100 million and 250 million firearms in the country. No one really knows exactly how many there are, but the ballpark is very large indeed.

It is also known that patterns of ownership vary enormously depending on demographic, structural, and cultural characteristics of people and places. Southerners own more guns (60% of households) than northerners, while those in the Northeast are least likely to own firearms: In that part of the country gun ownership is confined to one-third of households (Newton & Zimring, 1968; Wright et al., 1983). There is good historical reason for such discrepancies. In general, the earlier a frontier region was settled, the higher the likelihood that ancestors of the settlers have owned guns and their progeny will still own them today. As with other cultural artifacts, there is substantial cultural momentum to firearms ownership.

In the early days of our history, guns were acquired in response to direct need associated with a specific place. As a result, the types of guns owned are specific to each region of the country. Southerners are most likely to own shotguns, while those in the West are more likely to own rifles. One assumes that shotguns made good sense in the Old South since they were most effective in hunting the small game indigenous to that region. Pioneers in the West, on the other hand, required rifles that could bring down big game such as buffalo, grizzly bear, and mountain lion at long range.

After artifacts or firearms become cemented into the culture, the original need can wither, with the culture itself becoming the reason for ownership. Even though the original reason for owning an implement may have passed, the meaning that members of the culture place on the artifact would remain substantially the same (Tonso, 1982). Cultures can be quite resilient and do not change overnight. Since the meanings and possession of firearms are a part of the culture, giving up guns is not easy; the gun and its meaning have become part of one's heritage. The Second

Amendment to the Constitution is a good example of this cultural momentum.[4] No doubt the founders intended to guarantee the defense of the country through a citizens' militia, this having been an effective tool in the Revolution. Gun enthusiasts do not count themselves among those who would reject the need for the Second Amendment in contemporary society, but this does not mean that they envisage the need for a militia today.[5]

Historically, shotguns and rifles have been preferred by rural people, while city dwellers prefer handguns. Again, this reflects the connotations of firearms as tools both in the past and in contemporary society. In addition to the long-run cultural meanings that are attached to firearms, there are also short-run meanings that are current and situationally located. For a farmer, a shotgun is a farm tool to use to deal with wild dogs or rats. Handguns take on different meanings for the urbanite troubled by "dogs" and "rats" of another variety. Even in the latter example, however, the meaning is determined by a person's position regarding the business end of the handgun.

Very similar firearms can take on dramatically different meanings depending on the cultural, situational, and demographic profile of the individual. The trigger might pull the finger to the button in the laboratory. But for the collector of rare and expensive hand-crafted firearms, one bullet discharged can destroy the value of a prized possession in much the same way that opening a rare bottle of wine destroys its value for the wine collector. No collector's finger would pull a time-honored trigger, yet a criminal might not hesitate to fire the same gun in a crime. Certainly the meanings associated with the firearm for the student, collector, or criminal differ.

Of course, demographic variables are also strongly related with patterns of firearms ownership. Wealthy people are more likely to own guns than poor people. Firearms are expensive and the wealthy find them more affordable. Protestants are more likely to own guns than members of other religions. This is not just because Protestants tend to live in more rural places than others, but also because such persons settled the continent earlier and therefore have a richer cultural history of firearms ownership that sustains motives underlying current ownership. Men are much more likely to own guns then women, but rates of male firearms ownership tend to be inversely correlated with violent crime rates, a curious fact if firearms stimulate aggression (Bordua & Lizotte, 1979). It is hard to explain that where firearms are most dense violent crime rates are lowest, and where guns are least dense violent crime rates are highest.

Women who own guns are another matter. When violent crime rates are below average, women's gun ownership looks like men's—low crime is associated with high rates of female ownership. When violent crime rates are above average,

---

[4]The Second Amendment reads: "A well regulated Militia, being necessary to the security of a free State, the right of the people to keep and bear Arms, shall not be infringed." In no way do we mean to slight a "strict construction" interpretation of the Second Amendment. See Bately (1986), Halbrook (1986), Kates (1986), and Shalhope (1986) for interesting legal and historical discussions of the Second Amendment.
[5]For example, in the now familiar "I'm the NRA" advertisements by that organization, the actor states: "Why am I comfortable as a member of the NRA? Because I'm comfortable with the Bill of Rights. It says the right of the people to keep and bear arms shall not be infringed. . . . I support the freedoms the Constitution guarantees. But democracy is fragile. It's threatened all the time from many quarters. Eternal vigilance is the price of liberty."

however, quite the opposite is true, and rates of female firearms ownership come to be positively associated with violent crime rates. This does not imply that urban women are responsible for the urban crime problem; it demonstrates that when violent crime rates are high, women arm themselves for protection.

There is some reason to believe that young, Black, urban women who live in high crime areas are the most likely to own firearms for protection (Bordua & Lizotte, 1979), and this is, of course, a group at high risk for victimization. In addition to the efficacy of keeping a gun for protection,[6] we have mentioned that gun owners presumably enjoy some psychological benefit as well. This is so because those who keep guns for protection are less fearful of crime than those who do not (Lizotte & Bordua, 1980; Lizotte, Bordua, & White, 1981). The Beatles may have recognized this psychological benefit when they sang "Happiness is a warm gun," unless they intended this dictum tongue in cheek.

GUN SUBCULTURES

There is some speculation that subcultures exist that center on violent behavior and firearms ownership. In addition to violent behavior and gun ownership, members of such a subculture should have violent attitudes, and the theory states that these violent attitudes would be prized themes of the subculture. In other words, attitudes are not a result of the gun ownership, which is itself just another aspect of the subculture. However, it would do no harm to subcultural theory to assume that the violent attitudes were a result of firearms ownership, itself an aspect of the subculture. Then the violent attitudes manifested by members of the subculture could be interpreted as a weapons effect.

Research on the southern subculture of violence makes assumptions in this vein. Gastil (1971), Hackney (1969), and Reed (1972) all attribute high rates of gun ownership and violent crime in the South to a southern subculture of violence. Analyses by Gastil and Hackney show higher rates of homicide in the South, and Reed finds significant regional differences in firearms ownership. This research has lent some plausibility to the assumption that guns and violent attitudes coalesce in a violent subculture to produce violent behavior. However, Loftin and Hill (1974) reanalyzed the Gastil and Hackney data, finding that the higher homicide rates in the South could be attributed totally to higher rates of structural poverty in that region. Other economic factors being equal, the South's homicide rate turns out to be no higher than the North's.

Similarly, using national survey data, O'Connor and Lizotte (1978) and Dixon and Lizotte (1987) show that the higher probability of firearms ownership in the South is a result of its more rural nature. Again, other things being equal, Southerners are no more likely to own guns than Northerners. Using scales measuring violent and protective attitudes, Dixon and Lizotte have also found that Southerners are no more or less violence-minded than Northerners. More important, violent attitudes appear to be unrelated to firearms ownership for either Northerners or Southerners.[7]

---

[6]Women who are confronted with a sexual assault are significantly less likely to experience a completed rape if they resist with a weapon (Lizotte, 1986). See also Kleck (1988) on the protective efficacy of firearms.

[7]In other studies, Lizotte and Bordua (1980) and Lizotte et al. (1981) find that for a random sample of individuals in Illinois, violent attitudes are unrelated to firearms ownership.

Protective attitudes or chivalry are related to southern firearms ownership. Southerners who own guns are more willing than others to allow a person to defend women, children, and property from unwarranted aggression by striking the attacker. It is worth noting that the vast majority of all respondents in surveys (more than 90%), whether gun owners or not, southern or not, favor defending women, children, and property with force. Southerners are just a little more strident than respondents in other regions.

This is not to say that subcultures of firearms ownership do not exist. Dixon and Lizotte (1987) found some evidence of a southern subculture that centered on protection and firearms ownership. Similarly, Lizotte and Bordua (1980) and Lizotte et al. (1981) have pinpointed subcultures of sporting and protective gun use. These subcultures are characterized by four necessary conditions. First, individuals in the subculture must possess behaviors, attitudes, and norms that are different than those of the larger culture. For instance, they may own guns for sport and protection.[8] Second, these persons must have contact with other members of the culture. A group of people must interact to constitute a culture. Next, there must be an intergenerational transmission of the behavior, attitude, or norm. In other words, there must be cultural momentum, and gun ownership must be handed down from parent to child. Finally, all three of these conditions must exist independent of conditions that operate in the short run. This is just another way of saying that the first three conditions must be met, *ceterus paribus*. Cultures and subcultures are tenacious, and they do not dissipate easily or quickly.

These subcultures of firearms ownership do not possess the violent attitudes indicative of violent gun cultures such as gun-toting gangs. Rather, there is a happy-go-lucky subculture of sport and a not so happy, but certainly less fearful, subculture of protective ownership. People in the sporting culture of firearms ownership have usually acquired their first guns at early ages. They hunt together and read the same hunting magazines. Their friends own guns for sport, as do their parents and their children. They do these things independent of other demographic and situational variables. Similarly, members of the protective gun culture own guns because they are concerned about crime. They have friends who own guns for protection, their parents have owned guns, and so do their children. Again, this pattern of ownership is quite independent of other concerns.

Another point to consider is that, when used for protection, firearms can seriously inhibit aggression and can provide a psychological buffer against the fear of crime.[9] Furthermore, the fact that national patterns show little violent crime where guns are most dense implies that guns do not elicit aggression in any meaningful way.[10] This is not to say that guns are not used in crime, but that these guns may have a dramatically different meaning in the culture. Finally, there is no evidence that members of subcultures of firearms ownership, whether those of sport or protection, possess the violent attitudes indicative of a subculture of violence.

[8]It is something of a misnomer to call these groups of gun owners subcultures since more than half of the families in the United States own at least one gun. It would be more proper to call those who do not own guns the subculture and those who do the main culture. Hofstadter (1970) noted this in his work, "America as a gun culture."

[9]Moreover, criminals frequently use firearms in crime in order to discourage resistance on the part of the victim.

[10]Quite the contrary, these findings suggest that high saturations of guns in places, or something correlated with that condition, inhibit illegal aggression.

One reason why the issue of subcultures is so important is that if gun cultures do exist, it should be especially difficult to convince their members to give up their guns. Subcultures are by definition tenacious, intergenerational, and insensitive to short-run concerns. Convincing culturally motived gun owners to give up guns would be as difficult as convincing individuals to change religions. In fact, about 75% of gun owners say that they would not turn in their guns in the event of a gun ban (Bordua, Lizotte, Kleck, & Cagle, 1979). Many gun owners volunteer that they might turn in one or two guns, since they are known to own firearms, but would keep as many as they could. This order of magnitude of resistance to control is consistent with a subculture of firearms ownership.

To reinforce the point one need only consider the membership of the National Rifle Association (NRA). The NRA has 2 3/4 million members, each of whom pays $20 per year in dues. Political and lobbying money is donated totally. The subculture of firearms ownership and the grassroots support that it provides makes the NRA powerful, a fact that is rarely understood by its detractors. By contrast, the opposition, 200,000 members of Handgun Control Incorporated, pay $15 every 2 years, and it has no subculture from which to draw membership. Faced with the threat of extinction, members of the subculture of firearms ownership can successfully flex their political muscle, making gun control very difficult to enact.

GUN POLICY COSTS AND BENEFITS

Any social policy has its associated costs and benefits, and in the policy realm there is no quick fix. Policy initiatives take time, have costs, and frequently fail. Because of this, the costs and benefits of policies must be evaluated. Only then can it be determined if the policy is worth the consequences or if the cost is too high. Sometimes a policy may be abandoned or modified because the costs and possible outcomes, which were initially hidden, are discovered to be unacceptable.[11]

Mandatory prison sentences for those who commit crimes with firearms are one good example of a policy initiative that has failed. These laws are relatively simple. They provide that people who commit gun crimes are to be sentenced to prison. No exceptions are allowed.

These laws have several crime-reducing aspects. The society could benefit from special and general deterrence as well as from the incapacitative effects of the policy. Lives could also be saved, since fewer gun crimes would translate into fewer homicides. One would therefore think that this policy could be instituted relatively easily. With the exception of gun criminals, there seems to be no opposition.

Exhaustive research, however, shows that these laws have not worked, and that once passed they are not implemented. For example, in Massachusetts, Carlson (1982) reports that after passage of a mandatory sentence law the police "were now more selective about who to frisk because they did not want to risk involving 'otherwise innocent' persons" (p. 6). In addition, "in some instances an even greater degree of power was granted to arresting officers, who could decide when to look for a gun, and if they found one, whether to report" (p. 3). Moreover, some sentencing discretion "was transferred to the district attorneys since the charge at conviction now determined the length of the prison sentence if there was

---

[11]See Lizotte (1986) for a more detailed discussion of possible costs associated with gun control.

one" (p. 3). In other words, to circumvent the law the district attorney could ignore the gun charge.

Even though judges in Massachusetts had no sentencing discretion in gun crimes, they bypassed the law by increasing the number of not guilty verdicts in bench trials. Lizotte and Zatz (1986) report that "in Massachusetts it seems that limiting discretion at one point in the system (sentencing and parole) merely shifted discretion to other points (arrest, charge, guilt/innocence)" (p. 202). It appears that, in essence, the criminal justice system maintains a state of homeostasis in sentencing. The system compensates for change, maintaining a constant level and type of output. Massachusetts is not alone in this respect: Similar displacements of sentencing discretion on gun charges have been found in Detroit (Loftin, Heumann, & McDowall, 1983) and in California (Lizotte & Zatz, 1986).

Both pro- and anti-gun-control forces agree that mandatory sentencing for gun criminals is a good thing, but actors in the criminal justice system do not like losing their discretion. As a result, they find it easy to sabotage noncontroversial policy initiatives. It is infinitely more difficult to initiate a policy where 75% of those to be regulated say they will not comply, as is the case with gun bans.

Very often individuals or institutions call for gun control without specifying precisely what form the control would take. This tactic is tempting because it allows one to highlight benefits while ignoring the specifics of the policy and hiding the attendant costs.

There are at least five types of costs that can accrue to gun control policies. They include human lives and suffering, monetary costs, civil liberties costs, crime control costs, and emotional costs. These costs may or may not accrue to any particular policy initiative, but they should at least be considered.

We have already discussed one psychological cost of handgun control. Those who own guns for protection enjoy reduced levels of fear of crime. The gun gives a feeling of psychological well-being, and if it were removed the feeling would be reduced.

Monetary costs could also be considerable, depending upon the exact nature of the policy of interest. Only 4–5% noncompliance in a ban would result in 5–10 million illegal guns, requiring millions of household searches, trials, prison sentences, and the like. If guns were turned in there would need to be compensation at fair market value (200 billion × $300 = $60 trillion). If the guns turned in were not compensated, the compliance rate would probably be lower, requiring more expenditures at the law enforcement end.

Any gun control policy would require sufficient enforcement to deter noncompliance. There are obvious monetary costs associated with these levels of enforcement. There are also civil liberties costs, especially if large numbers of individuals do not comply. The Fourth Amendment of the Constitution protects against illegal search and seizure.[12] Some argue that these protections would bar any de facto control of existing guns. There are at present so many firearms that the number of searches necessary to police even a low level of noncompliance might be constitutionally unacceptable.

[12]The Fourth Amendment reads: "The right of the people to be secure in their persons, houses, papers and effects, against unreasonable searches and seizures, shall not be violated, and no Warrants shall issue, but upon probably cause, supported by Oath or affirmation, and particularly describing the place to be searched, and the persons or things to be seized.

There may also be crime control costs to banning firearms. Kleck (1988) argues that armed citizens are actually more likely than the police to deter crimes, catch criminals, and interrupt victimizations, and Wright and Rossi (1986) report that felons are more concerned about armed citizens than they are about the police. Elsewhere, Kleck (1985) points out other tantalizing crime control costs of gun control. He notes that armed criminals have the luxury to victimize hardened targets where the payoff is larger. Without the gun, however, they might be forced to prey on weaker targets where the payoff is smaller. This might result in an increase in the crime rate, because more offenses would be necessary to generate the same amount of money. In addition, weaker targets are those who can least afford victimization, such as the poor and aged.

Cook (1980) finds that injury rates are higher in knife attacks than in gun attacks, even though attacks with guns are more likely to result in death.[13] If handgun confiscation were somehow implemented, some criminals might substitute knives and other less efficient weapons, increasing injury rates. On the other hand, surveys of gun felons (Wright & Rossi, 1986) indicate that a substantial number of criminals state that they would substitute sawed-off rifles and shotguns if they could not obtain handguns.[14] If these self-characterizations are accurate, the increased deadliness of sawed-off rifles and shotguns would result in an increase in the death rate in crime. A possible paradoxical result of just handgun control might thus be increases in the injury rate and in the death rate, along with increases in crime rates. The exact amount of the increases in death or injury, if any, would depend upon the precise amount of substitution of sawed-off long guns or of knives.[15] If Kleck (1985, 1988) and Wright and Rossi (1986) are correct, it implies that handgun-only bans may not be the most desirable solution to the problem, and more sweeping measures involving all guns, or smaller more focused initiatives, such as banning military hardware, may be in order.

We conclude that social policies should be guided by historical, political, psychological, cultural, and sociological parameters of the phenomenon to be regulated, as well as the costs and benefits. The monetary, civil liberty, and other costs must be balanced against related benefits before accepting or rejecting a policy initiative.

PSYCHOLOGY, GUNS, AND VIOLENCE

Psychology has much to contribute to illuminating the links between guns and violence, provided we respect the complexity of the problem. There is much to be gained for us if we seek to learn from this area, which is different from applying ready-made principles (processes we have studied elsewhere) that fit uneasily when transplanted.

---

[13]Firearms allow criminals to practice their trade at a distance, giving them a degree of security and comfort. Of course, once fired the gun produced a serious result. Other weapons require more proximate contact to the victim, and therefore, a faster reaction time, less comfort, and more threat to the assailant. This results in more injury, but other weapons are less deadly than guns.

[14]It should be kept in mind that the individuals surveyed are not known for their honesty. They are certainly dishonest and probably liars and braggarts.

[15]This scenario depends on a number of assumptions about the psychological motivations of criminals. For example, only the most serious gun criminal would possess the sustained motivation to saw off a long gun.

We have to start by admitting that the policy implications we are likely to derive from research will be negligible, because policy deals with what ought to be while data tell us what actually is. Policy also must be couched in clearcut terms, while data are often confusing or ambiguous.

Some examples of research questions may provide the flavor of what is possible, assuming that we are interested in understanding the gun–violence problem, without resolving the question of gun control.

Disaggregating Gun Ownership

Given the wide prevalence of gun ownership in the United States, psychological characterizations of "the gun owner" do not make sense, although they have been attempted (Diener & Kerber, unpublished). (Gun owners may not be representative of the U.S. population, but such lack of representativeness is at best demographic, with heterogeneous subpopulations very slightly overrepresented among owners of weapons (Diener & Kerber, unpublished). But even though studies of gun owners in general would be useless, scrutiny of subsets of gun owners might yield inferences and insights. One subset of interest, for example, is the gun-using violent offender, whose attitudes have been explored in prison surveys (Wright & Rossi, 1986).

A second interesting subset is the owner of military hardware such as semiautomatic assault weapons, who (notwithstanding the claims of the NRA) is unlikely to be a typical sportsman or conservationist. Other, more psychological disaggregation could consider parameters such as (a) the salience assigned to guns, including time and attention invested in them; (b) motives for core membership in gun-related movements such as the NRA; (c) perceptions of danger to which self-arming responds; (d) connotations assigned to killing in recreational gun use; (e) self-esteem connotations that derive from gun ownership; and (f) involvement patterns in gun-related socialization.

Describing Violent Incidents in which Guns Are Used

The literature contains untested assumptions about the way guns are deployed in violent incidents. Speculation about choice of substitute weapons, for example, presupposes that violence can be calculated and instrumental, meaning that weapons are prioritized tools. The experiments on the weapons effect focus on affront-induced angry impulsivity, which suggests blind recourse to whatever weapon is available. Given categories of incidents, such as domestic conflicts in which guns are used, one could ascertain which model is applicable to the majority of incidents.

Psychological experiments could help to determine the sequence of events in domestic disturbances that escalate over a series of incidents to lead to weapons use. Other questions are: How do guns enter violence scenarios? At what juncture are they invoked? What frame of mind governs their invocation? How do expectations or anticipations of gun use translate into gun deployment? How do motivations for gun ownership relate to gun use?

Exploring Reactions to Interventions

There are researchable questions that impinge on policy, although not on the issue of which policy to pursue. These explore the psychological context in which reforms take place, or the driving and resisting forces that face the change agent (Lewin, 1947) irrespective of preferences and persuasion. Does the public favor gun control? Polls suggest that a majority of Americans favor some sort of action but oppose stringent measures. More to the point, any gun control that a segment of the public favors impinges invariably on others (Wright et al., 1983).

Equally tantalizing, but less easy to research are these questions: How strongly would *which* segment of the public feel about *which* aspect of hypothetical interventions? How would such attitudes translate into certain types of behavior? Which reactions would be short term and evanescent and which long term and continuing? What behavior would survive our efforts to control it, given available disincentives? Answers to such questions would tell policy makers what tradeoffs they must make, if they become convinced that serious violence levels could be reduced by curtailing gun ownership. It may well be that policy makers faced with data could decide to modify their proposals or not to intervene, because the resistance they anticipate might be considered too high a price for otherwise worthy achievements.

REFERENCES

Bately, R. (1986). Strict construction of firearms offenses: The Supreme Court and the Gun Control Act of 1968. *Law and Contemporary Problems, 49,* 163–198.

Berkowitz, L. (1968). Impulse, aggression, and the gun. *Psychology Today, 2,* 19–22.

Berkowitz, L. (1971). The 'weapons effect,' demand characteristics, and the myth of the compliant subject. *Journal of Personality and Social Psychology, 20,* 332–338.

Berkowitz, L. (1974). Some determinants of impulsive aggression: Role of mediated associations with reinforcements for aggression. *Psychological Review, 81,* 165–176.

Berkowitz, L. (1981). How guns control us. *Psychology Today, 15,* 11–12.

Berkowitz, L., & Donnerstein, E. (1982). External validity is more than skin deep. *American Psychologist, 38,* 245–257.

Berkowitz, L., & LePage, A. (1967). Weapons as aggression-eliciting stimuli. *Journal of Personality and Social Psychology, 7,* 202–207.

Bordua, D. J., & Lizotte, A. J. (1979). A subcultural model of legal firearms ownership in Illinois. *Law and Policy Quarterly, 2,* 147–175.

Bordua, D. J., Lizotte, A. J., Kleck, G., & Cagle, V. (1979). *Patterns of firearms ownership, use and regulation in Illinois.* Report to the Illinois Law Enforcement Commission, Springfield, IL.

Buss, A. H., Booker, A., & Buss, E. (1972). Firing a weapon and aggression. *Journal of Personality and Social Psychology, 22,* 296–302.

Cahoon, D. D., & Edmonds, E. M. (1984). Guns/no guns and the expression of hostility. *Bulletin of the Psychonomic Society, 22,* 305–308.

Carlson, P. (1982). *Mandatory sentencing: The experience of two states.* Washington, DC: National Institute of Justice.

Caprara, G. V., Renzi, P., Amolini, P., D'Imperio, G., & Travaglia, G. (1984). The eliciting cue value of aggressive slides reconsidered in a personological perspective: The weapons effect and irritability. *European Journal of Social Psychology, 14,* 313–322.

Cook, P. (1980). Reducing injury and death rates in robbery. *Policy Analysis, 6,* 21–45.

Diener, E., & Kerber, K. W. (year). *Personality characteristics of gun owners.* Unpublished manuscript, University of Illinois, Champaign.

Dixon, J., & Lizotte, A. J. (1987). Gun ownership and the southern subculture of violence. *American Journal of Sociology, 93,* 383–405.

Ellis, D. P., Weiner, P., & Miller, L. (1971). Does the trigger pull the finger? An experimental test of weapons as aggression-eliciting stimuli. *Sociometry, 34,* 453–465.

Fraczek, A., & Macauley, J. R. (1971). Some personality factors in reaction to aggressive stimuli. *Journal of Personality, 39,* 163–177.

Gastil, R. (1971). Homicide and a regional culture of violence. *American Sociological Review, 36,* 412–427.

Hackney, S. (1969). Southern violence. In H. D. Graham & T. Gurr (Eds.), *The history of violence in America* (pp. 505–527). New York: Praeger.

Halbrook, S. (1986). What the framers intended: A linguistic analysis of the right to 'bear arms.' *Law and Contemporary Problems, 49,* 151–162.

Hofstadter, R. (1970). America as a gun culture. *American Heritage,* October, pp. 4–11.

Kates, D. B. (1986). The Second Amendment: A dialogue. *Law and Contemporary Problems, 49,* 143–150.

Kleck, G. (1985). Policy lessons from recent gun control research. Meeting of the American Society of Criminology, San Diego.

Kleck, G. (1988). Crime control through private use of armed force. *Social Problems, 35,* 1–21.

Lewin, K. (1947). Group decision and social change. In T. M. Newcomb, and E. L. Hartley (Eds.), *Readings in social psychology,* New York: Holt and Company.

Leyens, J. P., & Parke, R. D. (1975). Aggressive slides can induce a weapons effect. *European Journal of Social Psychology, 5,* 220–236.

Lizotte, A. J. (1986). Determinants of completing rape and assault. *Journal of Quantitative Criminology, 2,* 203–218.

Lizotte, A. J., & Bordua, D. J. (1980). Firearms ownership for sport and protection: Two divergent models. *American Sociological Review, 45,* 229–244.

Lizotte, A. J., Bordua, D. J., & White, C. S. (1981). Firearms ownership for sport and protection: Two not so divergent models. *American Sociological Review, 46,* 497–503.

Lizotte, A., & Zatz, M. (1986). The use and abuse of sentence enhancement for firearms offenses in California. *Law and Contemporary Problems, 49,* 199–221.

Loftin, C., & Hill, R. H. (1974). Regional subculture and homicide: An examination of the Gastil–Hackney thesis. *American Sociological Review, 39,* 714–724.

Loftin, C., Heumann, M., & McDowall, D. (1983). Mandatory sentencing and firearms violence: Evaluating an alternative to gun control. *Law and Society Review, 17,* 287–318.

Loftin, C., & McDowall, D. (1981). "One with a gun gets you two": Mandatory sentencing and firearms violence in Detroit. *Annals of the American Academy of Political and Social Science, 455,* 150–167.

National Commission on the Causes and Prevention of Violence. (1964). *To establish justice, to insure domestic tranquility: Final report.* Washington, DC: U.S. Government Printing Office.

Newton, G. D., & Zimring, F. E., (1968). *Firearms and violence in American life.* Washington, DC: U.S. Government Printing Office.

O'Connor, J. F., & Lizotte, A. J. (1978). The 'southern subculture of violence' thesis and patterns of gun ownership. *Social Problems, 25,* 420–429.

Page, M. M., & Scheidt, R. J. (1971). The elusive weapons effect: Demand awareness, evaluation apprehension, and slightly sophisticated subjects. *Journal of Personality and Social Psychology, 20,* 304–318.

Reed, J. S. (1972). *The enduring South.* Lexington, Mass: D. C. Heath.

Shalhope, R. E. (1986). The armed citizen in the early republic. *Law and Contemporary Problems, 49,* 125–141.

Tonso, W. R. (1982). *Gun and society.* Washington, DC: University Press of America.

Turner, C. W., Layton, J. F., & Simons, L. S. (1975). Naturalistic studies of aggressive behavior: Aggressive stimuli, victim visibility, and horn honking. *Journal of Personality and Social Psychology, 31,* 1098–1107.

Turner, C. W., & Simons, L. S. (1974). Effects of subject sophistication and evaluation apprehension on aggressive responses to weapons. *Journal of Personality and Social Psychology, 30,* 341–348.

Turner, C. W., Simons, L. S., Berkowitz, L., & Frodi, A. (1977). The stimulating and inhibiting effect of weapons on aggressive behavior. *Aggressive Behavior, 3,* 355–378.

Wright, J. D., & Rossi, P. (1986). *Armed and considered dangerous: A survey of felons and their firearms.* Hawthorne, NY: Aldine de Gruyter.

Wright, J. D., Rossi, P. H., & Daly, K. (1983). *Under the gun: Weapons, crime, and violence in America.* New York: Aldine.

III

THE CRIMINAL
JUSTICE SYSTEM

16

Tipping the Scales Toward Death: The Biasing Effects of Death Qualification

Robert Mauro

Capital punishment is popular. It is so popular that many legislatures and courts have been willing to ignore and distort facts, contort logic, and abandon basic principles of justice to protect it. Even the United States Supreme Court is not immune. It has ruled that the death penalty is constitutional even it if is applied in a discriminatory fashion (*McCleskey v. Kemp*, 1987) by juries that are biased toward conviction (*Lockhart v. McCree*, 1986).

In any trial, potential jurors who cannot be fair and impartial in deciding the guilt or innocence of the defendant are excluded.[1] In capital cases, citizens who are opposed to the death penalty are also excluded, even if they would be fair and impartial in deciding the guilt or innocence of the defendant. All jurors who remain would consider sentencing the defendant to death. There is considerable evidence that these jurors are prone to convict.

Trial lawyers have long assumed that juries composed entirely of these death-qualified jurors are biased. According to the lore of the courtroom, jurors who support capital punishment favor the prosecution while those who oppose capital punishment favor the defense. Prosecutors have even admitted to charging capital murder (in addition to first degree murder) to have the benefit of a death-qualified jury. Nevertheless, the courts have been reluctant to admit that death-qualified juries are biased.

In the first major case that dealt with death qualification, *Witherspoon v. Illinois* (1968), the Supreme Court ruled that the evidence of bias was too tentative and fragmentary to prove that death-qualified juries were conviction prone. At the time, the Court had before it preliminary reports of three studies (Goldberg, 1970; Wilson, 1964; Zeisel, 1968), and this conclusion was probably justified. By the time the issue returned before the Court in 1986, 15 studies, including simulations, surveys, and analyses of the decisions of actual jurors, supported the hypothesis that death-qualified juries are biased (American Psychological Association, 1987; Bersoff, 1987).

I thank Jennifer Alansky Mauro for her help in the preparation of this chapter.

[1]The jury selection process in the United States can be quite complex, frequently taking days to complete. In Britain, little or no questioning is involved. Jurors are usually drawn almost indiscriminately from those summoned for jury duty.

WHO IS EXCLUDED?

The criteria used to determine who is excluded from capital juries have changed considerably. Prior to *Witherspoon*, potential jurors could be barred from serving on capital juries if they had conscientious scruples against the death penalty. The Court in *Witherspoon* decided that this standard was too broad and ruled that the state may exclude potential jurors for this cause only if they made it unmistakably clear that:

> 1. *they would* automatically *vote against the imposition of capital punishment without regard to any evidence that might be developed at the trial of the case before them, or*
> 2. *that their attitudes toward the death penalty would prevent them from making impartial decisions as to the defendant's guilt.* (Witherspoon, *1968, p. 522*)

In *Wainwright v. Witt* (1985), these exclusion criteria were relaxed, thus preventing more citizens from serving on juries in capital cases. The *Witherspoon* standard allowed the exclusion of those whose attitude would "prevent" them from being impartial or those who would "automatically" vote against the death penalty. The *Witt* standard allows for the exclusion of anyone whose attitude toward the death penalty would "prevent or substantially impair the performance of his duty as a juror in accordance with his instructions and oath" (*Wainwright v. Witt*, 1985, p. 850).

The answer to the question "Who is excluded?" has changed over time. Most inmates sentenced for capital crimes between 1968 and 1985 were tried before juries death-qualified under the *Witherspoon* standard. Under *Witherspoon*, potential jurors can be divided into four groups:

1. *Nullifiers.* These individuals would refuse to vote for guilt if there was a chance that the defendant would be sentenced to death. Almost no one argues that these individuals should be included in capital juries.[2]
2. *Guilt-phase includables.* These individuals would be fair and impartial in deciding on guilt or innocence but would never vote for the death penalty.
3. *Death-qualified jurors.* These individuals would be fair and impartial in deciding on guilt or innocence and would vote for the death penalty in some cases.
4. *Automatic death penalty jurors.* These individuals would always vote for the death penalty for capital crimes, without regard for any mitigating evidence.

Nullifiers and guilt-phase includables are occasionally grouped together as *Witherspoon* excludables. Some states use a standard that excludes automatic death penalty jurors (e.g., California; see *Hovey v. Superior Court*, 1980), and other states do not.

Several surveys have been conducted to determine the demographic and psy-

---

[2]In his dissent from *Witherspoon v. Illinois* (1968), Justice Douglas argued that a jury could not be truly representative of the community unless all members of the community had a chance to serve on the jury during the penalty trial.

chological characteristics of those who are excluded under the *Witherspoon* standard (Bronson, 1970, 1980; Harris & Associates, 1971). Fitzgerald and Ellsworth (1984) conducted the most rigorous of these studies. In their study, a sample of 811 jury-eligible men and women in Alameda County, California, were randomly selected and interviewed by an independent survey research firm. Over one-quarter (26.6%) of the sample would have been barred from serving on a jury in a capital case. Of these, 43.5% were nullifiers.

Once the nullifers are removed from the sample (because they would be excluded under any standard), 717 respondents remain. Of these, 17% were guilt-phase includables. This number included 21% of the women and 26% of the Blacks. Other surveys (Harris & Associates, 1971; Precision Research, 1981, cited in American Psychological Association, 1987) have produced similar results.[3] Thus, not only does death qualification prevent a substantial portion of the jury-eligible population from serving on juries in capital cases, but it disproportionately excludes Blacks and women.

Furthermore, death-qualified respondents differed from guilt-phase includables on a number of attitudes that are directly linked to the duties of a juror (see Table 16.1). For example, death-qualified participants were most likely to believe that if a defendant fails to take the stand, he or she is probably guilty; that illegally obtained evidence should not be excluded from a trial; and that the insanity defense is a loophole (compare also Ellsworth, Bukaty, Cowan, & Thompson, 1984). Death-qualified participants were also more likely to state that they would consider a confession they heard in the news media but not in court even though the judge instructed them to base their decisions only on what they heard during the trial.

WHAT IS THE EFFECT?

These attitudinal differences translate into actions. Several studies have examined whether death-qualified jurors are more prone to convict than those who are excluded (e.g., Cowan, Thompson, & Ellsworth, 1984; Jurow, 1971). In the best of these studies (Cowan et al., 1984), 288 adults eligible for jury service viewed a 2.5 hour videotape of a simulated homicide trial. These jurors then gave an initial verdict, deliberated for one hour in 12-person juries that were either death-qualified or that contained 2 or 4 guilt-phase includables, and then gave a final verdict. Death-qualified jurors were significantly more likely to vote guilty both before and after deliberating (see Table 16.2).

The differences between death-qualified and excludable jurors affect the decisions of juries as well as jurors. In one study (Horowitz & Seguin, 1986), 528 jury-eligible adults in 44 juries listened to an audiotaped robbery–homicide trial and then rendered a verdict. Seventeen of these juries were death-qualified prior to hearing the trial; the remainder were not. Some of the death-qualified and non-death-qualified juries were told that they would decide only guilt or innocence. Others were told that if they found the defendant guilty, they would be asked to

---

[3]Percentage of *Witherspoon* excludables reported by Harris (1971): 46% of Blacks, 29% of Whites, 37% of women, 24% of men. Percentages of guilt-phase includables reported by Precision Research (1981; cited in American Psychological Association, 1987): 11% of the population, 29% of Blacks, 9% of Whites, 13% of women, 8% of men.

Table 16.1 Attitudinal Differences Between Death-Qualified and Excludable Respondents in Fitzgerald and Ellsworth (1984)

Item	Respondents who agreed		
	Excludables (%)	Death-qualified (%)	*p*
Better to let guilty go free than to convict innocents	62.5	44.0	< .001
Defendent who doesn't testify is probably guilty	23.5	32.3	< .006
Even worst criminal should be considered for mercy	77.8	44.0	< .001
District attorneys need to be watched, because they will do anything to convict	53.1	48.9	< .05
All laws should be strictly enforced, no matter what the results	46.3	57.1	< .003
People on trial are probably guilty	26.5	32.3	—
Illegally obtained evidence should be kept out of court	63.9	56.5	< .09
Insanity plea is a loophole	59.2	78.0	< .001
Harsher treatment of criminals is not the solution to crime	80.0	59.0	< .001
Defense attorneys need to be watched, because they will do anything to get their clients off	64.7	73.5	< .003
If you were a juror, would you consider a confession reported by the news media but not in court against the judge's instructions?	39.8	50.9	< .04
Should you infer guilt from the defendant's silence?	14.0	24.0	< .02

Note. Both the questions and the results reported in this table have been abbreviated. The proportion agreeing for the first 10 items is a combination of the "agree strongly" and "agree somewhat" categories used in the survey. The probability values reflect the values of chi-square obtained from analyses of the original data, not the collapsed categories reported here.

Table 16.2 Death-Qualified and Guilt-Phase Includable Jurors in Cowan et al. (1984) Voting for Guilt

	Jurors voting for guilt	
	Death-qualified	Guilt-phase includables
Before deliberating[a]	77.9% (258)	53.3% (30)
After deliberating[b]	86.3% (197)	65.5% (29)

Note. Values in parentheses are total numbers of subjects in cells.
[a]Chi-square = 7.46, $p < .01$.
[b]Chi-square = 7.79, $p < .01$.

Table 16.3 Juries in Horowitz and Seguin (1986) Voting for Guilt by Type of Procedure

	Type of jury	
Procedure	Death-qualified	Non–death-qualified
Trial & penalty phase	88.9% (9)	73.7% (19)
Trial only	75.0% (8)	37.5% (8)

Note. Values in parentheses are total numbers of subjects in cells. The differences between these groups can be tested by constructing the ratio of the arcsine transforms of the proportions to their standard errors and comparing this to the standard normal distribution (Winer, 1971; Langer & Abelson, 1972). This yields a $z = 1.824$. Because the appropriate test is one-tailed (i.e., the hypothesis is that the proportion of death-qualified juries voting to convict is *greater* than the proportion of non-death-qualified juries voting to convict), the associated *p*-value is .034.

decide on the penalty as well.[4] Death-qualified juries were significantly more likely to convict the defendant (see Table 16.3).

Of course, demonstrating that death-qualified juries are more likely to convict than mixed juries is not equivalent to demonstrating that death-qualified juries are less accurate than mixed juries. One could argue that it is the mixed juries that are biased toward acquittal. However, analyses of responses on a postdeliberation questionnaire from the Cowan et al. (1984) study, controlling for initial death penalty attitudes, revealed that individuals who had served on the mixed juries were generally more critical of the witnesses and better able to remember the evidence. This suggests that the mixed juries were more thorough in their consideration of the case. It is hard to conceive how being more sensitive to the evidence could lead to less accurate decisions.

The evidence of the biasing effect of death qualification is not limited to surveys and laboratory simulations. Death-qualified jurors in actual cases demonstrate a proconviction bias. Of course, the decisions of death-qualified jurors in actual capital murder cases cannot be compared to the decisions of excludable jurors in these cases because by law excludable jurors are excluded. However, the decisions made by death-qualified jurors serving on noncapital juries can be compared to the decisions of the other jurors hearing these cases.

Zeisel (1968) interviewed jurors in Chicago and New York who had served on felony juries. These jurors were asked to report the number of first ballot votes for and against conviction, their vote on the first ballot, and whether they had conscientious scruples against the death penalty (Zeisel conducted this study before the *Witherspoon* decision and used the criterion appropriate at that time). Because the jurors had heard many different cases, Zeisel classified the 464 votes reported by his sample into 11 groups depending on the number of votes for conviction. This provides a rough control for the strength of the case against the defendant. In 9 of the 11 groups, the proportion of death-qualified jurors voting for conviction exceeded the proportion of jurors with scruples against the death penalty who voted for conviction (binomial $p = .03$; see Table 16.4).

More recently, Luginbuhl, Kadane, and Powers (1990) examined the decisions

---

[4]These are only some of the results of this study. It was actually much more complex. The authors examined the effect of various forms of bifurcation on both conviction rate and penalty using various measures. All of the jurors were asked about their ability to be impartial. There was a specific question designed to detect nullifiers (Horowitz, personal communication, June 1990).

Table 16.4 Proportion of Jurors Voting for Guilt in Zeisel (1968) by Total Number of Jurors Voting for Guilt and Attitudes Toward the Death Penalty

	Jurors voting for guilt on the first ballot (%)	
Jurors voting for guilt (*n*)	Jurors without scruples against the death penalty	Jurors with scruples against the death penalty
1	33.3	28.6
2	3.7	27.8
3	28.6	12.5
4	46.2	33.3
5	75.0	20.0
6	37.0	38.5
7	57.9	37.5
8	74.3	69.2
9	85.7	73.3
10	87.8	85.3
11	100.0	87.9

Note. The differences between these groups can be tested by constructing the ratio of the arcsine transforms of the proportions to their standard errors and comparing this to the standard normal distribution (Winer, 1962; Langer & Abelson, 1972). This yields a $z = 2.10$. Because the appropriate test is one-tailed (i.e., the hypothesis is that the proportion of jurors without scruples voting for guilt is greater than the proportion of jurors with scruples voting for guilt), the associated *p*-value is .018.

of 478 jurors in 57 criminal trials. These trials included cases of noncapital murder, assault with a deadly weapon, sexual assault, drug trafficking, robbery, fraud, forgery, and driving under the influence of an intoxicant. The jurors completed a questionnaire that (among other items) asked for information on the first ballot vote. Later, they were interviewed by telephone. On the basis of their responses to a structured interview protocol, the jurors were classified according to the *Witherspoon* criteria. Using a complex statistical analysis designed to account for missing data, Luginbuhl et al. (1990) determined that while death-qualified jurors were generally more likely to convict than guilt-phase includables, the reverse was true when the charge was driving under the influence of an intoxicant.[5] This suggests that excludable jurors are not simply anticonviction and prodefense.

It is impossible to determine from these data why excludable jurors in drunk-driving cases are more likely to convict than death-qualified jurors. However, one intriguing possibility is that excludable jurors may be more sensitive to the strength of the evidence than death-qualified jurors. In cases in which the evidence is strong (such as breathalyzer results in drunk-driving cases), jurors who are particularly sensitive to the strength of the evidence would be expected to be more likely to convict. In cases in which the evidence is weaker, the opposite is true: Jurors who are particularly sensitive to the strength of the evidence would be less likely to convict. This is precisely what excludable jurors appear to do.

[5]Luginbuhl et al. (1990) report that in driving under the influence cases, 75% of the death-qualified jurors voted for guilt on the first ballot compared to 100% of the guilt-phase includable jurors. On other types of cases, 64.1% of the death-qualified jurors voted for guilt compared to 42.1% of the guilt-phase includables. They report that the differences in the raw proportions between groups are significant, but that given the large amount of missing data, the more complex analysis is preferable.

There have been four studies that have failed to demonstrate the conviction-prone bias of death-qualified jurors. Osser and Bernstein (1968) compared the conviction rate of juries that decided robbery and burglary cases to the conviction rate of juries that decided first-degree murder cases in Los Angeles during a six-month period. They found that these rates did not differ and concluded that death-qualified juries are not biased. This conclusion depends on several assumptions that are almost certainly false. First, it assumes that all of the juries in the murder cases were death-qualified and that all of the other juries included some excludables. However, only capital-murder juries are death-qualified by law; it is unlikely that all of the juries in all of the murder trials were death-qualified. Furthermore, the proportion of excludables in the population is not large enough to guarantee the inclusion by chance of an excludable on all of the robbery and burglary juries. Second, the conclusion assumes that robbery, burglary, and murder cases are identical in every meaningful way except in the composition of the juries. This is absurd. Even if the authors' first assumption were correct, all that could be concluded from this study is that the biasing effect of death qualification is not large enough to completely overcome all of the other differences among types of felony cases.

The other three studies that fail to find an effect of death qualification are unpublished. They were conducted by Elliot (reported in a footnote in Elliot, 1991) and his colleagues in an attempt to replicate Cowan et al.'s (1984) simulation study. In one study (Elliot, 1991), undergraduate students in a psychology and law class viewed the videotaped homicide trial used by Cowan et al. (1984). A few hours or days later they rendered a verdict, then deliberated in groups of varying sizes, and gave a second verdict. In the other studies (Hirsch, 1985; Reid, 1987; cited in Elliot, 1991), undergraduate honors students showed a 1-hour videotape of a homicide trial to undergraduates enrolled in an introductory psychology class, who then rendered their verdicts.

There are serious flaws in these studies. Most important, none of these studies has sufficient statistical power to demonstrate an effect of the size found by Cowan et al. (1984). In each case, the investigator failed to use sufficient numbers of subjects.[6] In addition, Elliot, Hirsch, and Reid each altered a number of the important elements used in Cowan et al.'s (1984) design. For example, the subjects in the Cowan et al. (1984) study were jury-eligible adults who were paid to participate; Elliot (1991), Hirsch (1985), and Reid (1987) relied on undergraduate psychology students.

Cowan et al. (1984) carefully controlled all aspects of their simulation including the length of time devoted to each phase of the experiment and the number of subjects in each jury. Elliot (1991) allowed the length of time between the trial and the first verdict to vary from hours to days and allowed the subjects to discuss the case in groups of varying sizes. The noise introduced into the simulations by any

---

[6]To observe a difference in conviction rates between death-qualified and guilt-phase includable jurors of the size reported by Cowan et al. (1984), one would need approximately 200 subjects (α = .05, $1 - \beta$ = .80). There were 107 individuals who participated in Elliot's (in press) study; 110 subjects participated in Hirsch's (1985) study; and 56 participated in Reid's (1987) study. The probability of observing an effect the size of that reported by Cowan et al. (1984) in Elliot's (in press), and Hirsch's (1985) studies is approximately 59% (α = .05, $1 - \beta$ = .80). The probability of observing an effect of this size in Reid's (1987) study is approximately 32% (α = .05, $1 - \beta$ = .80).

or all of these factors may have obscured any differences that were present between the death-qualified and excludable jurors.

In sum, the results of 17 studies conducted over 26 years using various methodologies converge on one inescapable conclusion: In most cases death-qualified jurors are biased toward conviction.[7] Only one published study (Osser & Bernstein, 1968) failed to demonstrate this effect and it has been widely discredited (e.g., Cowan et al., 1984; Moran & Comfort, 1986).

THE COURTS' RESPONSE

The majority of this evidence was presented in an evidentiary hearing before the U.S. District Court for the Eastern District of Arkansas. The court evaluated the research and concluded that the practice of death qualification created juries that were unconstitutionally biased against the defendant (*Grigsby v. Marbry*, 1983). The state (Arkansas) appealed, but the Eighth Circuit Court affirmed the lower court's decision (*Grigsby v. Marbry*, 1985).

The Supreme Court ruled on the issue in *Lockhart v. McCree* (1986). McCree's attorneys argued that death qualification violated McCree's right to a fair and impartial jury guaranteed to him by the Sixth Amendment as applied to the states by incorporation through the Fourteenth Amendment. In previous cases (e.g., *Duncan v. Louisiana*, 1968), the Supreme Court had ruled that the Sixth and Fourteenth Amendments also conferred upon a defendant the right to a jury selected from a representative cross-section of the community. McCree's attorneys argued that a death-qualified jury was not composed of a representative cross-section of the community. However, a 6–3 majority of the Supreme Court disagreed. The lower courts were overruled and the constitutionality of death qualification was upheld. Writing for the majority, Chief Justice Rehnquist argued, in essence, that the data were inadequate and that even if they were not, death qualification would still be constitutional.

The arguments used by the Supreme Court are instructive.

Serious Flaws in the Evidence

The Chief Justice began his argument by considering the social science evidence. He found a flaw in every study except one and concluded that one study provides an insufficient base upon which to decide a constitutional issue. According to the Supreme Court, eight of the studies dealt ". . . solely with generalized attitudes and beliefs about the death penalty and other aspects of the criminal justice system . . ." (*Lockhart*, 1986, p. 1762).

Next, the Court dismissed a study (Haney, 1984) that demonstrated that the questioning process involved in death qualification itself tends to bias jurors because "standing alone" it would not "give rise to a constitutional violation"

---

[7]Although mixed juries are less likely to convict than death-qualified juries, they are not necessarily more likely to acquit than convict. For example, Cowan et al. (1984) found that more death-qualified jurors and guilt-phase includables voted for guilt than for innocence (cf. Table 16.2) but that the percentage of death-qualified jurors favoring guilt was larger than the percentage of guilt-phase includables voting for guilt. The overall probability of conviction will depend on the characteristics of each case. Given a particular case, death-qualified jurors are generally more likely to convict than are guilt-phase includables.

(*Lockhart*, 1986, p. 1763). Three of the remaining studies had been before the Court in *Witherspoon*. At that time the Court found the evidence too tentative and fragmentary to substantiate a claim of constitutional error. Therefore ". . . the same studies, unchanged but for having aged some 18 years, are still insufficient to make out such a claim in this case" (*Lockhart*, 1986, p. 1763). The remaining three studies were found to be unfit because they did not use ". . . actual jurors sworn under oath to apply the law to the facts of an actual case involving the fate of an actual capital defendant" (*Lockhart*, 1986, p. 1763). In addition, two of these studies did not ". . . even attempt to simulate the process of jury deliberation . . ." (*Lockhart*, 1986, p. 1764). Finally, only one of the final three studies (Cowan et al., 1984) had accounted for the presence of nullifiers.

There are several inaccuracies in the Court analysis. For example, one of the studies dealing with generalized attitudes was the Fitzgerald and Ellsworth (1984) study. Some of the questions asked in this study dealt directly with the juror's role in a capital trial. For example, the respondents were asked whether failing to take the stand in one's own defense is an indication of guilt, whether the insanity defense is a loophole, and whether they would ignore a judge's instructions and consider a confession reported in the media but not in court. The three studies presented to the Court in *Witherspoon* had in fact, changed. Preliminary drafts had been replaced by complete reports. The decisions of death-qualified jurors cannot be compared to the decisions of excludable jurors in an actual case involving the fate of an actual capital defendant because excludable jurors are prevented from serving on juries in these cases.

These studies do have flaws, although not fatal ones. It is rare for one study in any discipline to provide a complete explanation; rather, each study contributes a piece of the puzzle. The gaps in the puzzle left by one study are filled by another. Apparently, the majority of the Justices believed that unless a study is flawless, nothing can be learned from it. This demonstrates complete ignorance of the concept of convergent validity. By the Chief Justice's logic, a person could never complete a journey of a thousand miles because it cannot be made in one step.

Having disposed of the social science evidence, the Chief Justice attempted to find a logical basis for the majority's decision in constitutional law. The arguments that he made are remarkable.

No Bias Exists Because No Juror Is Biased

According to the Court, if each juror says that he or she could be impartial, then the jury must be impartial. Thus, even if the evidence showed that over many juries a distinctive pattern of bias existed, it would not matter.

Representation Can Be Instantaneous

Lawyers for McCree argued that the pool of potential jurors for capital cases was not representative of the community because guilt-phase includables had been systematically excluded. The Court disagreed, stating that the pool need only include a fair cross-section of the community at the time that ". . . the names are put in the box from which the panels are drawn" (*Lockhart*, 1986, p. 1765, citing *Pope v. United States*, 1967, p. 725). That excludable jurors are always prevented

from serving on capital juries is immaterial. Because their names had once been in
the box, the pool is representative of the community. This implies that a completely White or male jury pool could be declared to be representative of the
community. All that is required is that the names of women and minority group
members be placed in the box before they are immediately removed.

Excludables Are Not a Distinction Group

A fair cross-section of the community in a jury pool is obtained when all
distinctive groups are adequately represented in the pool. Excludable jurors are
clearly distinguishable on the basis of their attitudes, but the Court argued that
groups defined solely on the basis of shared attitudes are not distinctive groups and
therefore need not be represented in jury pools. According to the Court, the difference between distinctive groups and excludables is that "Unlike other groups such
as Blacks, women, and Mexican-Americans, *Witherspoon*-excludables are singled
out for exclusion in capital cases on the basis of an attribute that is within the
individual's control" (*Lockhart*, 1986, p. 1766). By this standard, it would be
permissible to exclude all Catholics or Jews or members of any other group that is
defined by an attribute that is within the individual's control.

The Luck of the Draw

The majority found "It . . . hard . . . to understand the logic of the argument
that a given jury is unconstitutionally partial when it results from a State-ordained
process, yet impartial when exactly the same jury results from mere chance"
(*Lockhart*, 1986, pp. 1767). In this argument, the Chief Justice confused the fairness of a process with the appearance of the outcome. By this standard, the state
could exclude Blacks and women from serving on juries because it is possible that
by chance a jury could be comprised entirely of White men.

The State Has a Legitimate Interest in Using One Jury

This argument is straightforward. A bifurcated system in which capital defendants are tried before one jury and (if found guilty) sentenced by another might
prove troublesome to administer. However, a bifurcated jury system does not require two entirely separate juries. A single group of jurors can be used if during
the jury selection process enough alternates are chosen so that if the defendant is
found guilty, there are enough death-qualified jurors to decide on the sentence. In
any case, the additional costs incurred would seem to be a small price to pay for an
impartial jury.

CONCLUSION

The Supreme Court clearly did not appreciate the social scientific evidence of
the biasing effects of death qualification. The Court has frequently expressed a
distrust of social scientific evidence (cf. Ellsworth, 1988); the *Lockhart* decision
may simply be another result of this hostility. Many of the justices do not understand the basic principles of social science. They are unable to evaluate the evi-

dence presented to them and they avoid it whenever possible. When social scientific evidence is considered, it is (in the words of Andrew Lang) frequently used "as a drunken man uses lampposts, for support rather than for illumination." This distrust of social science is not limited to the Supreme Court, but it does not afflict all jurists. The federal district and circuit courts that reviewed the evidence in *Lockhart* made very careful evaluations of the data. Justice Marshall clearly recognized the importance of convergent validity in concluding that:

> *The chief strength of the respondent's evidence lies in the essential unanimity of the results obtained by researchers using diverse subjects and varied methodologies. Even the Court's haphazard jibes cannot obscure the power of this array.* (Lockhart, 1986, Marshall, J. dissenting, p. 1773)

However, the Court did not rule on the basis of the social science evidence. Instead, the Court argued that even if there were sufficient evidence that death-qualified juries were biased, they would not be unconstitutional:

> *. . . we will assume for purposes of this opinion that the studies are both methodologically valid and adequate to establish that "death-qualification" in fact produces juries somewhat more "conviction-prone" than "non-death-qualified" juries. We hold, nonetheless, that the Constitution does not prohibit states from "death-qualifying" juries in capital cases.* (Lockhart, 1986, p. 1764)

Yet the legal arguments, like the attacks on the social scientific evidence that preceded them, are unconvincing. One can only conclude that the Court's ruling is based not on logic, but on expedience.

If the Court had found that death-qualified juries were not impartial, the convictions of thousands of defendants tried before death-qualified juries might have been reversed. If the Court had tried to limit its ruling to future cases, it would have been confronted with the specter of men and women being executed subsequent to trials by a jury system that the Court had acknowledged was unfair. If the Court had simply denied the adequacy of the data, more studies would have been conducted and another challenge mounted. The only way to make the issue go away and stay away while leaving the death penalty intact was for the Court to rule that even if death-qualified juries were biased, it did not matter. The majority distorted facts, perverted logic, and finally sacrificed the principle of jury neutrality rather than rule against the death penalty. Perhaps the *New York Times* said it best:

> *What more could be said against the death penalty than the Supreme Court has just said in upholding it? According to a 6–3 majority, it is perfectly constitutional in capital cases to decide guilt or innocence with juries that are more likely to convict than acquit. The Court once demanded special safeguards for the accused in cases involving capital punishment. Now it rigs matters against them. A system that must rely on biased juries hardly needs opponents to condemn it. . . . The silver lining is that decisions like this are illogical on their face. If the only way capital punishment can be administered is by rigged juries, sooner or later a more patient Court will have to undo both.* ("Loading the argument for death," 1986, p. A30)

REFERENCES

American Psychological Association. (1987). In the Supreme Court of the United States: *Lockhart v. McCree. American Psychologist, 42,* 59–68.

Bersoff, D. (1987). Social science data and the Supreme Court: Lockhart as a case in point. *American Psychologist, 42*, 52–58.

Bronson, E. (1970). On the conviction proneness and representativeness of the death-qualified jury: An empirical study of Colorado veniremen. *University of Colorado Law Review, 42*, 1–32.

Bronson, E. (1980). Does the exclusion of scrupled jurors in capital cases make the jury more likely to convict? Some evidence from California. *Woodrow Wilson Law Journal, 3*, 11–34.

Cowan, C., Thompson, W., & Ellsworth, P. (1984). The effects of death qualification on jurors' predisposition to convict and on the quality of deliberation. *Law and Human Behavior, 8*, 53–79.

Duncan v. Louisiana, 391 U.S. 145 (1968).

Elliot, R. (1991). Social science data and the APA: The Lockhart brief as a case in point. *Law and Human Behavior, 15*, 59–76.

Ellsworth, P. (1988). Unpleasant facts: The Supreme Court's response to empirical research on capital punishment. In K. Haas & J. Inciardi (Eds.), *Challenging capital punishment: Legal and social science approaches*. Beverly Hills, CA: Sage.

Ellsworth, P., Bukaty, R., Cowan, C., & Thompson, W. (1984). The death-qualified jury and the defense of insanity. *Law and Human Behavior, 8*, 81–93.

Fitzgerald, R., & Ellsworth, P. (1984). Due process vs. crime control: Death qualification and jury attitudes. *Law and Human Behavior, 8*, 31–51.

Grigsby v. Marbry, 569 F. Supp. 1273 (E.D. Ark. 1983).

Grigsby v. Marbry, 758 F.2d 226 (8th Cir. 1985).

Goldberg, F. (1970). Toward expansion of *Witherspoon*: Capital scruples, jury bias, and the use of psychological data to raise presumptions in the law. *Harvard Civil Rights–Civil Liberties Law Review, 5*, 53–69.

Haney, C. (1984). On the selection of capital juries: The biasing effects of the process effect. *Law and Human Behavior, 8*, 121–132.

Harris & Associates, Inc. (1971). Study No. 2016. Reported in White, W. (1973). "The constitutional invalidity of convictions imposed by death-qualified juries." *Cornell Law Review, 58*, 1176–1220.

Hirsch, G. (1985). *Eyewitness identification and jury decision-making: A reevaluation of the psychologist's impact in the courtroom*. Unpublished honors thesis reported in Elliot (1991).

Horowitz, I., & Seguin, D. (1986). The effects of bifurcation and death qualification on assignment of penalty in capital crimes. *Journal of Applied Social Psychology, 16*, 165–185.

Hovey v. Superior Court, 28 Cal. 3d 1 (1980).

Jurow, G. (1971). New data on the effect of a death-qualified jury on the guilt determination process. *Harvard Law Review, 84*, 567–611.

Langer, E., & Abelson, R. (1972). The semantics of asking a favor: How to succeed in getting help without really dying. *Journal of Personality and Social Psychology, 24*, 26–32.

Loading the argument for death. (1986, May 7). *New York Times*, p. A30 (editorial). Copyright © 1986 by The New York Times Company. Reprinted by permission.

Lockhart v. McCree, 106 S. Ct. 1758 (1986).

Luginbuhl, J., Kadane, J., & Powers, T. (1990). *Death scrupled jurors: They are not always more lenient*. Technical Report, Dept. of Statistics, Carnegie-Mellon University, Pittsburgh, PA.

McCleskey v. Kemp, 107 S. Ct. 1756 (1987).

Moran, G., & Comfort, J. (1986). Neither "tentative" nor "fragmentary": Verdict preference of impaneled felony jurors as a function of attitude toward capital punishment. *Journal of Applied Psychology, 71*, 146–155.

Osser, A., & Bernstein, B. (1968). The death-oriented jury shall live. *University of San Fernando Valley Law Review, 1*, 253–358.

Pope v. United States, 372 F.2d 710 (1967).

Reid, C. (1987). *Situational construal and social judgment: A case study*. Unpublished honors thesis reported in Elliot (1991).

Wainwright v. Witt, 105 S. Ct. 844 (1985).

Wilson, W. (1964). *Belief in capital punishment and jury performance*. Unpublished manuscript.

Winer, B. (1971). *Statistical principles in experimental design*. San Francisco: McGraw-Hill.

Witherspoon v. Illinois, 391 U.S. 510 (1968).

Witt (see *Wainwright v. Witt*).

Zeisel, H. (1968). *Some data on juror attitudes towards capital punishment*. Chicago, IL: University of Chicago.

17

On the Alleged Prosecution-Proneness of Death Qualified Jurors and Juries

Rogers Elliott

INTRODUCTION

In 1960 William Witherspoon was found guilty of capital murder and condemned to death by a jury from which all venirepeople who had expressed opposition to the death penalty had been excluded. In *Witherspoon v. Illinois* (1968) the United States Supreme Court did not accept Witherspoon's claim that the jury that found him guilty, because it had been thus "death qualified," therefore also had been unfairly disposed to ignore the presumption of innocence, to accept the prosecution's version of the facts, and to return a verdict of guilt. Only three studies of the issue (Goldberg, 1970; Wilson, 1964; Zeisel, 1968) had been introduced in an earlier stage of litigation, and they were considered too tentative and fragmentary to sustain the argument. The Court did, however, footnote (*Witherspoon v. Illinois*, 1968, 391 U.S. 520) an invitation to social scientists to pursue the matter: "A defendant convicted by such a jury in some future case might still attempt to establish that the jury was less than neutral with respect to guilt" (p. 520).

Thus a public policy issue touched profound moral sentiments with a psychological question—the relation between attitudes and behavior—that had long been a central focus of theory and data in social psychology. Data addressed specifically to the issue posed by the Court were not long in coming, and a decade after *Witherspoon* there were three more quite substantial studies (Harris, 1971; Jurow, 1971; and what would be published as Cowan, Thompson, & Ellsworth, 1984). All of these studies found that mock jurors who opposed the death penalty were less likely to judge a defendant guilty than those who did not. Testimony on these studies formed the basis of an appeal to the California Supreme Court, which in *Hovey v. Superior Court* (1980) reviewed them in detail and with approval. The court's quotation of Zeisel's testimony reflects its own opinion of the data: "And since all of the studies show the same result, no matter with whom, no matter what the stimulus, no matter with what closeness of simulation, there is really only one conclusion that we can come to. The relationship is so robust . . . that no matter how strongly or how weakly you try to discover it in terms of your experimental design, it will come through" (*Hovey v. Superior Court*, 1980, p. 40).

The same testimony was presented in the federal system in *Grigsby v. Mabry* (1983), and it persuaded the district court to hold that the exclusion of jurors (termed *Witherspoon* excludables, or WEs) who say that they would hear the evidence fairly and impartially, even though they would never vote for death in the sentencing phase of a capital case, was an unconstitutional denial of an impartial jury. The holding was upheld by the Eighth Circuit (*Grigsby v. Mabry*, 1985), and it was appealed to the U.S. Supreme Court in *Lockhart v. McCree* (1986).

When the Supreme Court accepted the case for review, the American Psychological Association (APA) decided to file an amicus brief (Bersoff & Ogden, 1987; hereafter, Brief) on the side of the defendant, McCree. The chief psychological contention of the Brief (p. 60) was that "the data show that death-qualified juries [i.e., those from which WEs have been excluded] are conviction prone." Its argument echoed the statement by Zeisel quoted previously, and it included the very recent study by Moran and Comfort (1986), also interpreted as supportive of the other six studies.

The conclusions of the lower courts and the Brief were also finding their way into psychology texts. Thus, from Kassin and Wrightsman (1988, p. 39): "Turning to the relationship between death penalty attitudes and verdicts, the findings without exception converge on the same simple conclusion: Death-qualified juries are more likely to convict than normally selected juries. Over the years this result has surfaced across a wide variety of subject populations, methods, and trials." And from Hans and Vidmar (1986, pp. 233–234): "The accumulated evidence, then, suggests that from the outset capital murder juries . . . are likely to be predisposed toward conviction."

In the end the lower courts were reversed, and the studies that had been carrying everything before them left Chief Justice Rehnquist, the author of the *Lockhart* opinion, thoroughly unpersuaded. He did not feel that mock-juror studies had sufficient verisimilitude to be the basis for generalization, and he criticized both the dearth of studies involving jurors deliberating together and the absence of any information on jury outcome as a function of jury composition. Was he correct? One way to evaluate the Brief, a method approved by its author Bersoff (1986), is to judge it as science, that is, review it as an ordinary manuscript making a particular claim about an attitude–behavior relation.

ARE DEATH QUALIFIED JURIES CONVICTION PRONE?

The Brief, as noted, adduces seven studies on this question, none of which, strictly speaking, compares the verdicts of death-qualified (DQ) and non-DQ *juries* and only one of which includes the final, or legal, verdict as a variable. The general research strategy has been to correlate either death penalty attitudes (typically measured on a four- or five-point Likert scale from strong approval to strong disapproval) or WE or DQ status (unwillingness or willingness ever to impose the death penalty) with individual disposition to vote for guilt or acquittal. Subjects have responded to cases varying in verisimilitude from short written scenarios (three studies) through audio- and videotapes (two studies) to real service on felony juries (two studies). All but one study suffer from the fact that there are unknown numbers of nullifiers (persons so affected by the possibility of a death sentence that they would not be impartial in the determination of guilt or innocence) among groups opposed to the death penalty. Too much can be made of that objection, because most of the cases being judged do not even raise the specter of the death penalty, at least not in any direct or vivid way, and it is that specter that creates nullifiers. Only three of the studies can be said to have asked questions that define WE status rather than simply death penalty attitudes, although with *Wainwright v. Witt* (1985) this distinction may have lost some of its importance (in *Wainwright* the test is whether opposition to the death penalty might substantially impair one's performance as a juror).

Studies Using Brief Written Cases

Wilson (1964) and Goldberg (1970) used several written cases and showed differences, in the number of defendants convicted, between subjects (students) who said they did or did not have conscientious scruples against the death penalty. Scrupled students rendered fewer guilty verdicts to a significant degree in the first study and to a marginally significant one in the second. (The scrupled versus nonscrupled dimension has to be classified as a death penalty attitude rather than a WE status variable, because it is neither precise nor limiting enough to define the latter class.) Casting the variance accounted for by the mean differences into correlational terms gives correlations of the order of .15 between death penalty attitude and individual tendency to convict. In neither of these studies, nor in the next, was there any group deliberation.

Harris and Associates (1971) used a question that approximated a WE status question, and his sample was unusually large ($N = 2,068$). On average, in four written cases, 56% of his WE respondents convicted; 63% of his DQ respondents did. The difference is clearly significant with so large a number, but the associated phi correlation is only about .07.

Studies Based on the Recall of Real Jurors

Zeisel's (1968) study had carried great weight with the California Supreme Court and the lower federal courts because it was the only one introduced into evidence that used real jurors who had voted in real cases. He interviewed several hundred jurors, after their completion of jury service, as to whether they were scrupled against the death penalty (this, again, is a death penalty attitude question) and whether they had voted to convict or acquit or had been undecided on the first ballot of the jury they served on. He reported data only from juries that were not unanimous on their first ballot and broke the sample up into 11 groups on the basis of the reported number of votes for conviction on the first ballot taken. This was done to control to some extent the possibly confounding effect of strength of evidence for or against conviction.

In 9 of the 11 groups, greater proportions of nonscrupled than of scrupled jurors voted to convict. The result obscures the fact that 2 of the 9 groups had numbers of 10 or fewer, while the 2 groups in which nonscrupled jurors had been less likely to vote to convict (including the group having the initial voting pattern of six votes for guilt) had numbers of 40 or more. One might provide a more stable test of the death penalty attitude–conviction relation by recombining the 11 "strength of evidence" groups into 3 larger, coherent, and theoretically interesting categories: *Strong for acquittal* (1 to 4 initial votes for guilt); *strong for conviction* (8 to 11 initial votes for guilt); and *uncertain* (5, 6, or 7 initial votes for guilt).

Table 17.1 shows the data and the accompanying chi-square values. With pre-

Table 17.1 Recategorization of Zeisel's Data into Three Categories of Strength of Initial Vote for Conviction

Strength of initial vote	Attitude toward death penalty and individual decisions as to guilt						
	Not opposed			Opposed			
	G	%G	NG/U	G	%G	NG/U	χ^2
Strong to acquit: (1G–4G)	14	22%	50	18	26%	50	.37
Uncertain: (5G, 6G, 7G)	24	48%	26	9	35%	17	1.24
Strong to convict: (8G–11G)	116	87%	17	99	80%	24	2.15

Note. G stands for guilty, NG for not guilty, and U for undecided.

sumptively weak evidence for conviction (*strong for acquittal*), the scrupled jurors were actually slightly more given to conviction, and with strong evidence, slightly less. In the *uncertain* cases, which presumably give the greatest scope for the play of attitude, they were also less given to conviction, but in no comparison is the difference close to being significant. Phi values range from $-.06$ to $.13$ in the comparisons tabulated. It is difficult to find much support for the Brief's assertion in this study; and, of course, it cannot tell us anything about the differences between DQ and mixed (WEs included) juries.

Moran and Comfort (1986) are cited by the Brief as supporting Zeisel's (1968) results. They mailed questionnaires to two samples of felony jurors in Miami, Florida, with returns of 23% and 40%, $N = 319$ and $N = 346$. Variables included a four-point death penalty attitude scale, first verdict preference, and final jury verdict. In each sample the correlation between death penalty attitude and initial verdict preference was .11, marginally significant in the first case and significant ($p < .05$) in the second. This is the only study reporting correlations of death penalty attitude with final legal verdicts. They were, of necessity when the criterion is a unanimous vote, small: .00 and $-.04$.

Moran and Comfort (1986) performed an analysis of a subgroup of 44 jurors in the second sample who had sat on capital homicide juries and found among them a correlation of .51 ($p < .001$) between death penalty attitude and predeliberation verdict. This is a highly relevant and intriguing result, and it needs replication. For example, the authors also had found a sex difference in the correlation between death penalty attitude and predeliberation verdict in their first sample, but it did not reappear in their second one. Moreover, it is not clear whether the term *capital homicide* refers to a category of crime in which the death penalty could be sought, or to cases in which the prosecution actually asked for the death penalty, with attendant death qualifying voir dire (the preexamination of a possible juror) and the exclusion of WEs. Nor is it known how many, if any, of the 44 jurors sat on the same cases. It is an unusual feature of the literature reviewed in the Brief that it rarely measures death penalty attitude–behavior relations in a context in which the prospect of death is salient. If the Moran and Comfort finding is an indication of what the relation might look like, those interested in the issue ought to be designing appropriate studies.

But as matters stand, the studies by Zeisel (1968) and by Moran and Comfort (1986), taken as a whole, imply that death penalty attitude accounts for a little more than 1% of the variance in predeliberational verdicts, with a positive relation in 4 of 5 samples if the recategorization of the Zeisel data is accepted, or 11 or 13 if it is not.

Studies Using Audiotaped or Videotaped Trial Presentation

Two studies utilized presentations similar to what an actual juror might encounter, specifically dramatized versions complete with opening and closing arguments, direct and cross-examined testimony, and judicial instructions to the juror.

The first study was by Jurow (1971), who sampled 211 Sperry Rand (Long Island) employees, playing them audiotaped enactments of two cases (33 minutes for the robbery–murder of Case 1 and 1 hour for the rape–murder of Case 2). Jurow asked an appropriate WE-status question, and 10% (21) of his subjects were in fact WEs. The five categories of attitudes toward imposing the death penalty included the WEs; the mildly reluctant but occasionally willing; those open to consideration in all cases; those usually disposed to impose; and those who would automatically impose whenever possible. The Brief notes that when the WEs were compared with all others they were less likely to vote for guilt. The Brief fails to note, however, that such differences were not significant, being associated with chi-square values of 1.03 and 2.29 ($df = 1$ in each case) for the two cases, respectively, and associated phi correlations of .07 and .10. Nor, of course, were the results independent. As to death penalty attitude, I have calculated the point-biserial correlations between it and verdict, and they are .19 for Case 1 ($p < .01$) and .11 for Case 2 (not significant).

The most complete and important test of the hypothesis, and the centerpiece of the Brief, is the study by Cowan, Thompson, and Ellsworth (1984). They employed the dramatization based upon a real homicide case produced by Hastie, Penrod, and Pennington (1983). The 2.5-hour videotape consisted originally of a complete trial concerning a fatal stabbing that occurred during a fight. Cowan et al. edited out one witness and replaced the Massachusetts instructions with California instructions.

The tape was shown to a set of 288 subjects from which nullifiers had been screened out. Most were nonstudent volunteers from Stanford, California, and the communities around it, and 30 were WEs. Nearly two-thirds were women, and the educational and socioeconomic status levels were unusually high. After the viewing, subjects filled out attitude scales and gave predeliberation verdict preferences. They were then formed into two kinds of juries for deliberation for an hour—either completely DQ or mixed and having two to four WEs. No jury arrived at a unanimous verdict, but all subjects gave a postdeliberation verdict preference.

It was clear that the WEs were more willing to acquit than the DQs, both before and after deliberation. Nearly 47% of the WEs, compared with 22% of the DQs, voted for acquittal just after seeing the trial; the corresponding figures were about 35% and 14% on the postdeliberational ballot. The chi-square values were above 7 in each case ($df = 1$, $p < .01$), with associated phi correlations of .16 and .19, respectively. Cowan et al. (1984) also reported a correlation of .19 between death penalty attitude and first verdict severity.

DISCUSSION

There are two sets of relations reported in the Brief. One concerns death penalty attitude and juror predeliberational verdict, and the other WE status and juror predeliberational verdict. In the first set are 9 entries: Wilson (1964); Goldberg (1970); Zeisel (1968; 3 studies if the present category scheme is accepted); Moran and Comfort (1986; 2 studies); Jurow (1971; average of 2 studies); and Cowan et al. (1984). Eight of the 9 are positive ($p < .05$, two-tailed), with a median value of .13. On the basis of the literature reviewed in the Brief it can be said with confidence that the relation, though small, is reliable (and if the Zeisel cases are counted as 11 rather than 3 it is even more reliable).

For WE status there are only three independent and relevant findings. They are Harris (1971), Jurow (1971), and Cowan et al. (1984). All are positive, and the average size of the relation can be represented as a median correlation (averaging Jurow's cases) of about .09. Three cases, however, are not enough to support any conclusion other than "not proved."

The practice of using jurors instead of juries as the unit of analysis results from considerations of practicality in obtaining and running subjects. Its validity depends on an argument made in the Brief: to wit, "that jurors' initial vote preference predicts the jury's ultimate decision to a highly significant extent" (Bersoff & Ogden, 1987, p. 63, citing Kalven & Zeisel, 1966). That slightly misstates the finding, which is that a *jury's* initial *majority* vote predicts its final unanimous one.

The difference may be larger than it seems. Juries come to initial votes in various ways, the most common being a "go-around" or straw poll where everyone in turn expresses some opinion as to guilt. Many such initial votes will have occurred after some amount of discussion, and all will be taken in the context of deliberation, no matter how much of it may actually have taken place. That means that the first expressed verdict of many real jurors may have been affected by actual or impending consideration of the evidence in the case, with correspondingly less scope for the influence of general attitude. Several views of the evidence and the credibility of witnesses will be expressed that, along with pressures of consensus, will have substantial effects on individual votes. The connections between initial individual verdict preference, early stated opinions in a jury, first openly stated vote, and final jury vote are almost certainly much looser than the argument appears to credit. Of the studies reviewed, only three involved deliberation, and in Cowan et al. (1984), predeliberation verdicts were offered before the juries were formed. Only in Zeisel (1968) and in Moran and Comfort (1986) were initial verdicts given in the deliberative context of real juries.

Let us summarize the data conservatively. Seven studies have found a reliable relationship, accounting for perhaps as much as 2% of the variance between death penalty attitude and initial attitude toward guilt among individuals who have been given written or taped evidence from trials in which the death penalty was not an issue. Only two studies have assessed the relation between death penalty attitude and final verdict (finding literally none), and none has cleanly tried to do the same with WE status and final verdict. Finally, nothing in the attitude–behavior literature would suggest that the relations between death penalty attitude or WE status and voting would not become progressively smaller throughout the course of events from expression of initial attitude about guilt to final vote.

Even in the absence of clear rules for generalizing from laboratory to policy setting, one is entitled to be skeptical of the degree to which such a showing supports the Brief's assertions. Chief Justice Rehnquist said, "We have serious doubts about the value of these studies in predicting the behavior of actual jurors," (*Lockhart v. McCree*, 1986, p. 1761), and it is difficult not to share his doubts. If this collection of studies had been submitted to a reputable journal, it seems doubtful that they would have passed review as supporting what they claimed. Most literature reviews of a hypothesis offer analyses of dozens of relevant studies. A sample as small as the one reviewed would have required vastly more strength to sustain its large claim.

MORE RECENT RESULTS

Robust findings ought to portend repeatable results, but the data that have accumulated since the Brief was filed serve only to provide grounds for deepened skepticism about its main assertion. There have been several failures to replicate even the weak relations that existed between death penalty attitude or WE status and verdict choice. In my own laboratory five studies (three samples of undergraduates, two samples of older alumni, responding in three cases to the Cowan et al., 1984, videotaped trial) have failed to support such relations. The correlations between death penalty attitude and verdict choice were .17, $-.02$, $-.26$; .00, and .09, the weighted average being .06, or a bit lower than the .13 calculated for the studies cited in the Brief. In four of these studies chi-square could be computed to assess the relation between WE status and verdict: The values were .12, .14, .57, and .28, none coming remotely close to significance, and with the direction of difference in three of them opposed to the hypothesis (these are reported in Elliott, Robinson, Hirsch, & Reid, 1990). Similarly, Robinson (reported in Elliott et al., 1990) found no difference ($\chi^2 = 0$) between the verdict preferences of WE and DQ Stanford undergraduates who responded to a slide–tape version of the Cowan et al. (1984) trial.

As Chief Justice Rehnquist pointed out, none of the studies reviewed in the Brief concerned the outcomes of real juries hearing the same case, some made up entirely of DQ jurors and others including one or more WEs. The Brief (p. 66, footnote 32) suggested the possibility of such a study, but opined that it would be only marginally useful given the consistency of the other findings. Two other studies have been reported recently in which subjects have been formed into deliberative juries that either came to verdicts or hung within some defined time. The first was by Bernard and Dwyer (1984), who chose three kinds of undergraduates as mock jurors: Type A (DQs); Type B (DQs opposed to the death penalty but willing to consider it); and Type C (WEs, possibly including some nullifiers). They were to respond before deliberation to the issue of guilt/innocence from a written scenario of a murder trial. They were then to deliberate to unanimity, if possible, in juries composed to include either 0, 3, or 6 Type C jurors, the rest being As and Bs in a one-to-two ratio. All but 1 of the 15 juries (5 of each type) found the defendant guilty (the exception, which hung, had no WEs on it), so the case did not really permit sufficient variance to test the hypothesis. There was no difference among types of jurors in predeliberation opinions as to guilt, although with the evidence as strong for guilt as it was, there was little scope for such a difference to appear. The authors' conclusion (Bernard & Dwyer, 1984, p. 114) is this: ". . . pre-existing attitudes toward capital punishment do not affect judgments regarding guilt or innocence in a mock capital trial."

Horowitz and Seguin (1986) carried out an extensive study of the issue. Mock jurors first heard a voir dire, convened as juries, heard an audiotaped trial, and finally deliberated to a verdict. For some juries there were death qualifying questions in the voir dire, with exclusion of WEs, nullifiers, and those who would automatically impose the death penalty if given the opportunity to do so. For other juries, there was no death qualifying voir dire, hence no exclusion of any who might have been adamantly opposed to the death penalty.

Fourteen of 17 DQ juries found for guilt, as did 17 of 27 non-DQ juries. This difference in rate of conviction is not significant (i.e., $\chi^2 = 1.88$, not significant), although the outcome is in the hypothesized direction with an associated phi value of about .20. The main design problem is that we do not know how many, if any, WEs or nullifiers may have been on the non-DQ juries. The study remains the most sensitive and ecologically valid test so far of the main hypothesis that a DQ jury will convict more often than a mixed jury.

Here, then, are seven more studies, carried out in the 1980s, the significance of which is almost entirely negative with respect to the central assertion of the Brief. As stipulated by the Brief (Bersoff & Ogden, 1987) for its studies, these studies also measure behavior, not just attitude; they use diverse subjects, stimulus materials, and methods; the results are reliable and stable over the period; and it is implausible that they result from researcher bias. Nor do they fail entirely to replicate earlier studies. In the five studies that measured such correlations, there were moderate to strong correlations among attitudes toward the death penalty and sociolegal attitudes, precisely of the sort reported by several others (see Fitzgerald & Ellsworth, 1984). None of the recent studies questioned real jurors, as Zeisel (1968) had done. On the other hand, unlike those in the Brief, two of them made it clear that death might follow a finding of guilt.

How might we account for the difference between the two sets of studies? First, it is possible that prior to *Hovey* and the litigation that followed it, negative results on the issue, being perhaps both less exciting and less publishable than positive ones, never got farther than the file drawer. Second, because the positive results were dramatized by the highly visible policy uses to which they were applied, they stimulated attempts to replicate and extend them and created a context in which negative results would take on enhanced significance.

THE FAIRNESS ISSUE

One may wonder, if there is little or no relation between death penalty attitude and initial or final verdict, why it is necessary to exclude WEs. The short answer is that WEs say they would never impose death in the penalty phase of a two-part trial in which the defendant has been found guilty, and various studies (Bernard & Dwyer, 1984; Elliott et al., 1990; Horowitz & Seguin, 1986; Jurow, 1971) make it clear that they mean what they say—death penalty attitudes do predict decisions about imposing the death penalty, even if they don't predict verdicts. Thus WEs cannot carry out their duties as jurors when the same jury sits in both parts of a capital case.

Another reason, more pertinent to the concerns of this argument, is that the attitude–behavior relation claimed by the Brief might yet be shown to exist in appropriate studies. Suppose a series of studies of jury (not juror) decisions in capital cases like that done by Horowitz and Seguin (1986) was carried out, with the average and significant result that 80% of DQ juries convicted, but only 60% of mixed (i.e., WEs included) juries did so. Which kind of jury is to be considered to be closer to the truth? In other words, is one conviction prone, or is the other acquittal prone?

A fairly direct test might be to use trials where, because of the confession of the defendant or some other person afterward, the truth came to be known after the trial verdict, and see which kind of jury comes closer to that truth. Failing that, no one knows which would be the more valid jury, but it is the suspicion of several courts (e.g., *Spinkellink v. Wainwright*, 1978) that the WEs are more likely to be acquittal prone than the DQs are to be conviction prone. There is evidence that WEs say they would raise the thresholds for finding guilt (by making it harder to get past reasonable doubt, or by demanding more evidence) significantly more than DQ jurors say they would raise them, if death rather than life imprisonment without parole is the sentence being sought (Elliott et al., 1990). Since an impartial determination of guilt based on the law and the evidence ought not to vary with the possible sentence that might be imposed, the WEs are here admitting (or affirming) a marked degree of what looks like acquittal proneness.

Finally, with respect to the fairness issue, the Brief suggested, on the basis of the Cowan et al. (1984) study, that DQ juries do not function as well as mixed juries in recollection of facts and the skepticism toward witnesses. The main problem with the Cowan et al. analysis is that the responses of different jurors cannot be considered independent (i.e., the statistical tests ought to have been on the data of juries, with 17 degrees of freedom, rather than on the data of jurors, with 224, but they are not). If one juror recalls a piece of evidence, all jurors then will know it, but the recall of each cannot be considered independent of the recall of the others. What we need to know are the mean average responses of each kind of jury with respect to memory for evidence, belief in witnesses, and the other dependent variables reported. This includes mean average verdict, or, even better, the final verdict, which the juries in the study did not get to give.

CONCLUSIONS

The major assertion of the Brief (i.e., that the data show DQ juries to be conviction prone) cannot be said to be supported. Even the milder assertion that the data suggest, that DQ juries are relatively ineffective, is too strong. There is support for the proposition that a weak relationship exists between death penalty attitude and predeliberation verdict preferences. It is probably true that death qualification reduces the strength and presence not only of views opposing the death penalty (of course), but also of related sociolegal views. It is anybody's guess right now how much effect such contraction might have on deliberation and outcome. There is, finally, some possibility that including WEs at the guilt/innocence phase of a death penalty case might create as much unfairness as it would cure, if by fairness is meant relative lack of effect of the prospect of death on the weighing of evidence.

It is difficult to see how the APA could have argued that the "stability and convergence of the findings over three decades lend impressive support to their validity" (Bersoff & Ogden, 1987, p. 68), but I assume that the zeal to have an effect on policy must have played a role both in the decision to submit the Brief and in that view of the data. The showing in the Brief, in what is said to rate as one of the stronger areas of policy-relevant research, is really a set of hypotheses in the guise of proved assertions that would, I believe, be judged inadequately demonstrated by the standards of most scientists in the APA. The claim made here is not that scientific organizations should not take moral positions. Rather, it is that if they do so, they should not pretend to base them on scientific foundations when such foundations are insufficient to bear the argument.

Is it appropriate to apply the usual standards of peer evaluation to these briefs? Should there perhaps be a different standard when going public? Monahan and Walker (1988) suggest that the authority of social science derives from the single standard of its adequacy as assessed in the conventional ways of the science, in terms of reliability, internal validity, external validity, and so on. That is, a double standard ought not apply. Gardner, Scherer, and Tester (1989), in a critical analysis of the APA's abortion briefs (which seem similarly to have generalized far beyond what the empirical foundation could support), concur (p. 899): "When we claim to speak with scientific authority, it is implicit that our discourse is motivated by the epistemic values of science, rather than by extrascientific values." That is the view of this argument, but there needs to be an additional rule to resist the distorting effects of the adversary system, namely, that the scientific case should be essentially invariant regardless of the side or court presenting or receiving it.

Bersoff (1986) called attention to those sections of the *Ethical principles of psychologists* (APA, 1981) that require psychologists reporting their results in public forums to provide a thorough discussion of the limitations of their data and full recognition of the limits and uncertainties of their evidence. He went on to offer what seems unexceptionably good advice (1986, pp. 162–163): ". . . belief in the rightness of a particular cause does not justify abandonment of evenhandedness, dispassion, and neutrality. . . . [I]f experimental psychologists are to be respected by the courts and treated as more than mere numerologists attempting to convince the judiciary of doctrinaire positions, they must offer more situation-specific, ecologically valid, objective data that serve science, not a particular adversary." That the Brief of which he was coauthor fell as short as it did of meeting these standards is a telling commentary on the hazards that attend taking science into policy settings inhospitable to its values.

REFERENCES

American Psychological Association. (1981). *Ethical principles of psychologists*. Washington, DC: Author.

Bernard, J. L., & Dwyer, W. O. (1984). *Witherspoon v. Illinois*: The Court was right. *Law and Psychology Review, 8,* 105–114.

Bersoff, D. N. (1986). Psychologists and the judicial system: A broader perspective. *Law and Human Behavior, 10,* 151–165.

Bersoff, D. N., & Ogden, D. W. (1987). In the Supreme Court of the United States: *Lockhart v. McCree. American Psychologist, 42,* 59–68.

Brief (see Bersoff & Ogden, 1987).

Cowan, C. L., Thompson, W. C., & Ellsworth, P. C. (1984). The effects of death qualification on jurors' predisposition to convict and on the quality of deliberation. *Law and Human Behavior, 8,* 53–79.

Elliott, R., Robinson, R. J., Hirsch, G., & Reid, C. (1990). *Death penalty attitudes and the tendency to convict or acquit: Some data.* Unpublished manuscript, Dartmouth College, Hanover, NH..

Fitzgerald, R., & Ellsworth, P. C. (1984). Due process vs. crime control. *Law and Human Behavior, 8,* 31–51.

Gardner, W., Scherer, D., & Tester, M. (1989). Asserting scientific authority: Cognitive development and adolescent legal rights. *American Psychologist, 44,* 895–902.

Goldberg, F. (1970). Toward expansion of *Witherspoon*: Capital scruples, jury bias, and the use of psychological presumptions in the law. *Harvard Civil Rights Law Journal, 5,* 53.

Grigsby v. Mabry. (1983). 569 F. Supp. 1273.

Grigsby v. Mabry. (1985). 758 F.2d 226.

Hans, V., & Vidmar, N. (1986). *Judging the jury.* New York: Plenum

Harris, Louis & Associates, Inc. (1971). Study No. 2016 (unpublished).

Hastie, R., Penrod, S. D., & Pennington, N. (1983). *Inside the jury.* Cambridge, MA: Harvard University Press.

Hovey v. Superior Court. (1980). 28 Cal 3d 1.

Horowitz, I. A., & Seguin, D. G. (1986). The effects of bifurcation and death qualification on assignment of penalty in capital crimes. *Journal of Applied Social Psychology, 16,* 165–185.

Jurow, G. (1971). New data on the effect of a death-qualified jury on the guilt determination process. *Harvard Law Review, 84,* 567–611.

Kalven, H., & Zeisel, H. (1966). *The American jury.* Chicago, IL: University of Chicago Press.

Kassin, S. M., & Wrightsman, L. S. (1988). *The American jury on trial: Psychological perspectives.* Washington, DC: Hemisphere.

Lockhart v. McCree. (1986). 106 S. Ct. 1758.

Monahan, J., & Walker, L. (1988). Social science research in law: A new paradigm. *American Psychologist, 43,* 465–472.

Moran, G., & Comfort, J. C. (1986). Neither "tentative" nor "fragmentary": Verdict preference of impaneled felony jurors as a function of attitude toward capital punishment. *Journal of Applied Psychology, 71,* 146–155.

Spinkellink v. Wainwright. (1978). 578 F.2d 582.

Wainwright v. Witt. (1985). 105 S. Ct. 844.

Wilson, W. C. (1964). *Belief in capital punishment and jury performance.* Unpublished manuscript, University of Texas.

Witherspoon v. Illinois. (1968). 391 U.S. 510.

Zeisel, H. (1968). *Some data on juror attitudes toward capital punishment.* Monograph, Center for Studies in Criminal Justice, University of Chicago Law School.

18

Judgment and Memory: The Role of Expert Psychological Testimony on Eyewitness Accuracy

Jane Goodman and Elizabeth F. Loftus

INTRODUCTION

Wrongful criminal identifications persist (Gorman, 1987) despite improvements in police procedures and legally imposed safeguards to minimize the likelihood of misidentification (*Gilbert v. California*, 1967; *Manson v. Braithwaite*, 1977; *Neil v. Biggers*, 1972; *Stovall v. Denno*, 1967; *United States v. Wade*, 1967). Although precise estimates of the proportion of misidentifications in criminal cases cannot readily be made, some alarming examples have been documented (Loftus, 1984; Wall, 1965). Consider the case of Steve Titus. The day after a 17-year-old female hitchhiker was raped south of the Seattle airport by a bearded male, the victim studied a six-person photo montage for several minutes before pointing to the shots of Steve Titus and saying "This one is the closest one. It has to be this one" (Henderson, 1981a). A second victim raped 6 days earlier in the same locale failed to identify Titus from the photo montage. Nonetheless, Titus was arrested and charged with raping the 17-year-old. Some months later, at his trial, the victim was shown the photo montage again and asked whether she recognized the pictures. She replied that she did. Then, the prosecutor asked whether she recognized the person who had raped her and she pointed to Steve Titus in the courtroom (Henderson, 1981a). Based on this identification, Titus was convicted.

In the ensuing months, two more rapes were committed in the same district. One of the victims identified "Danny Stone" (Loftus & Ketcham, 1991), who also wore a beard, as the rapist. When Stone's photograph was shown to the 17-year-old woman who had testified that Titus raped her, she began to cry and exclaimed, "My God, what have I done to Mr. Titus?" (Henderson, 1981b). However, she failed to identify Stone as her attacker after viewing him in person in a lineup. Ultimately, Stone confessed to several rapes committed in the same area, qualifying him for a suspended sentence conditioned upon completion of a sexual psychopath treatment program. In the meantime, at the age of 35, Steve Titus died of a heart attack. Particularly perplexing from a psychological point of view is the conduct of the 17-year-old victim at a subsequent civil deposition in the wrongful death suit by Titus' estate. Under oath, she persisted in her conviction that Steve Titus was the man who had raped her, even though Titus was legally exonerated in 1981.

Similar persisting commitment to documented faulty recollection was noted in a field study in which actual eyewitnesses to a downtown shooting incident in a Canadian shopping mall were interviewed. One eyewitness who was driving by in her car at the time of the shooting erroneously insisted that the perpetrator of the robbery was the victim, even though statements by more than 20 other eyewitnesses and various newspaper accounts contradicted her version of the events (Yuille & Cutshall, 1986).

Real-world examples of mistaken memory such as these are important not only because they provide proof corroborative of the fact that eyewitness errors occur outside of psychological laboratories, but because they reveal the commitment and attachment of eyewitnesses to faulty memories even when faced with clear, incontrovertible evidence of their mistaken judgment.

Few legal safeguards exist to prevent convictions based on confident adherence to faulty accounts. Psychologists have made considerable progress in three distinct areas of empirical work about eyewitness identifications (Sanders, 1986). First, researchers have produced a body of information concerning the processes and factors that influence the ability of a witness to identify a suspect correctly or that may lead to misidentifications (Cutler, Penrod, & Martens, 1987; Shapiro & Penrod, 1986). Second, the ability of witnesses to judge the accuracy of their own identifications has been studied, including research that accounts for the unswerving confidence witnesses may hold in their mistaken perceptions (Fox & Walters, 1986; Lieppe, 1980; Wells & Lindsay, 1983; Wells & Murray, 1984). Third, psychologists have examined the ability of law enforcement officers or others to influence the accuracy of identification testimony (Lindsay & Wells, 1980; Malpass & Devine, 1981, 1983). Precisely how the legal system should best take into account a body of psychological research that addresses empirical questions arising in the course of litigation, such as questions concerning eyewitness fallibility and eyewitness confidence, has spawned considerable discussion among both legal scholars and social scientists.

THE CONTRIBUTION OF A RESEARCH PSYCHOLOGIST IN AN EYEWITNESS CASE

A number of commentors have questioned what a psychologist may contribute in a case in which eyewitness testimony is the major evidence identifying the defendant as the perpetrator of the crime charged. Basically, the expert's role is to become acquainted with the facts of the case pertaining to identification, to review available scientific research literature to select those issues that pertain to identification in the case, and to emphasize the elements that are known to be counterintuitive or contrary to many laypersons' beliefs about memory. Three broad areas of scientific inquiry are pertinent: (a) research on estimator variables, internal or external factors shown to influence the accuracy of eyewitness perception and recall; (b) research on system variables, such as lineup procedures or interviewing procedures shown to influence the accuracy of identification and recall; and (c) research on common misconceptions of laypersons concerning the accuracy of eyewitness testimony.

A psychologist may assist lawyers or the court in several ways, and the contribution will vary according to the capacity in which the expert help is sought. For example, a psychologist may serve as a consultant. He or she will offer advice on types of questions to ask of witnesses, types of interviewing or questioning techniques that will prove most fruitful, and probe areas in which memory accuracy has been shown to be most reliable or most vulnerable. The psychologist may also provide information about common misconceptions about memory for use in voir dire or provide material for lawyers to incorporate in opening statements, witness examinations, closing arguments, and proposed jury instructions. The first step is often to prepare a written or oral offer of proof establishing the presence in the case at hand of variables that researchers have found to impair the accuracy of eyewitness identification.[1] Based on a review of the pertinent scientific literature, the expert witness can: (a) summarize the literature; (b) critique the literature; and (c) make data generalizations from the literature (Gorman, 1987).

The admissibility of expert testimony in court is governed by the "helpfulness" standard set forth in Federal Rule of Evidence 702:

> If scientific, technical or other specialized knowledge will assist the trier of fact to understand the evidence or to determine a fact in issue, a witness qualified as an expert by knowledge, skill, experience, training, or education, may testify thereto in the form of an opinion or otherwise.

In considering the admissibility of testimony by an eyewitness expert, the Ninth Circuit Court of Appeals (*United States v. Amaral*, 1973) established a four-prong test that explicitly incorporates both Federal Rule of Evidence 702 and the *Frye v. United States* (1923) standards: (a) the expert must be qualified, having attained knowledge beyond that of the average layperson; (b) the testimony must address a proper subject; (c) the testimony must conform to a generally accepted explanatory theory;[2] and (d) the probative value of the evidence must outweigh its prejudicial effect.

THE USE OF SOCIAL SCIENCE IN THE COURTROOM

The particular way in which a court may use social science findings varies, although oral testimony in court by an expert witness based on his or her professional opinion is most typical, whether in a bench or jury trial (Colquitt, 1988). One source of tension in applying social science findings in the law derives from the different goals of the two disciplines. Science strives to be neutral, objective, and truth seeking; the legal advocacy system, based on partisan representation, is designed to bring about just (fair and legal) resolution to a particular dispute (Loftus, 1986). Many social scientists, familiar with the rigors of the former discipline, have expressed discomfort with the exactitude of the latter. Some social scientists have argued that a trial simply is not a suitable forum for the presentation

---

[1]For a more extensive substantive review of psychological research that has a bearing on eyewitness memory, see Laughery and Wogalter (1989) and Loftus and Doyle (1987). Some areas of specialization include developmental memory and applications in child sex abuse cases (Ceci, Toglia, & Ross, 1987).

[2]The fact that not all psychologists may hold the same opinion regarding the relevant scientific knowledge does not render the testimony inadmissible. The California Supreme Court held that a trial judge erred in excluding expert testimony on psychological factors that affect the accuracy of eyewitness observations (*People v. McDonald*, 1984), notwithstanding a minority view within the psychological community that insufficient research has been conducted to permit the conclusion that expert psychological testimony may improve jurors' abilities to evaluate eyewitness testimony.

and interpretation of scholarly research, thus prompting a closer examination of the uses of social science in law.

Three uses of social science in law were distinguished by Monahan and Walker (1988). First, social science may inform the court about social or adjudicative facts involving the parties in a case. For example, in a trademark infringement suit, an expert may present results of a scientific survey to assess whether the trademark of one product is readily confused by consumers with the trademark of another product. Case-specific research that addresses factual issues before the court is rarely opposed because its relevance is undisputed. Included in this category of social science is the testimony of clinical psychiatrists or psychologists regarding determinations of the mental state of individuals involved in a criminal or civil case, pertinent, for instance, to an insanity defense or a competency determination.

Second, a court may use social science findings as a source of authority, as occurred in *Brown v. Board of Education* (1954) when the Supreme Court in a unanimous opinion relied on seven social science references in support of its finding that segregation in public schools deprived minorities of equal educational opportunities. Here, the research cited did not directly involve the parties to the lawsuit. Social science findings in this category may be presented to the court by means of expert testimony or in the form of a written Brandeis Brief (Driessen, 1983).

The third use of social science findings distinguished by Monahan and Walker (1988) occurs when social science provides a context or frame of reference for particular facts in a case, but the relevant research was not conducted specifically for the parties in litigation. Rather, it provides a context or frame of reference in light of which legal and factual issues in the current case can be assessed. For instance, a psychologist familiar with experimental literature on perception and memory may testify about general factors affecting most eyewitnesses, or a psychologist familiar with literature on battered women may testify about general characteristics affecting most battered women. Monahan and Walker (1985) refer to this as "social framework" testimony.

This third area or category of social science in law is the most contentious, in particular in cases in which an expert witness is called to testify before a jury concerning factors that influence the accuracy of eyewitness memory (*Law and Human Behavior*, 1986). This chapter focuses on issues central to that controversy, although these comments clearly apply to other forms of "social framework" testimony, such as evidence concerning the battered wife syndrome, rape trauma syndrome, or personnel decisions tainted by sex stereotyped perceptions (Goodman & Croyle, 1989).

OPPOSITION TO SOCIAL FRAMEWORK TESTIMONY

In some instances social framework testimony is opposed because of confusion between the nature of expert testimony regarding adjudicative facts and that concerning social framework testimony. One clear example is confusion over differences in the role of a clinical psychologist or psychiatrist who offers an expert opinion on the mental competence of a party to a lawsuit and the role of an experimental psychologist who offers an expert opinion on general factors known to influence the accuracy of human perception and memory (Goodman & Loftus, 1988).

Opposition to social framework testimony may also be based on perceived interference by psychologists with the legal system. In cases in which expert testimony on eyewitness memory is proffered, one source of such opposition has been concern over whether the expert testimony addresses the *competency* of the eyewitness, traditionally a matter for the trial judge to decide, or the *credibility* of the eyewitness, traditionally a matter for the jury to decide (Colquitt, 1988). A class of common objections, often presented as a legal basis to exclude expert testimony, is that the court should not permit "academia to usurp the fact-finding function of the jury" (Loftus & Schneider, 1987). From a practical standpoint, in cases in which an expert on eyewitness memory is permitted to testify, it is the exception and not the general rule for the expert to offer an opinion on the accuracy of the identification testimony in the case at hand (Goodman & Loftus, 1988).

Since Federal Rule of Evidence 704 abolished the "ultimate issue rule" barring an expert from expressing an opinion on the ultimate issue in a case, numerous courts have ruled that expert testimony cannot be deemed inadmissible on the ground that credibility of the witness is an ultimate issue (*United States v. Downing*, 1985). In any event, jurors remain free to reject the expert testimony (Goodman & Loftus, 1988). Thus, the legal viability of this objection is questionable.

Another class of objections focuses on the possible outcome or impact of the expert testimony, rather than the content of the testimony. In the case of expert testimony that highlights the fallibility of eyewitness memory, to the extent that fact finders are more persuaded by the expert and less persuaded by the eyewitness, they may have increasing doubt about the guilt of the defendant, resulting in fewer criminal convictions if they convict only when persuaded "beyond a reasonable doubt" (Loh, 1984). An entirely different objection has to do with the values of the particular expert who is consulted. Opposition of this sort is most apparent in cases of alleged child sex abuse (Ceci, Toglia, & Ross, 1987) and in cases in which expert testimony concerning the battered wife syndrome is introduced.

HOW CAN A PSYCHOLOGIST ASSIST JURORS IN EVALUATING EYEWITNESS TESTIMONY?

To illustrate the controversy that may ensue when one party to a lawsuit wishes to call a psychologist to testify about factors that influence the memory of eyewitnesses, consider a recent slander suit filed by a 1988 presidential candidate, teleevangelist Pat Robertson. Robertson alleged that slanderous, disparaging remarks were made by Paul McCloskey, a former fellow serviceman, regarding conversations and events that took place approximately 38 years ago during the Korean War (*Robertson v. McCloskey*, 1988). In his defense, McCloskey planned to call four corroborating witnesses to testify that they heard statements by Robertson to the effect that he was going to seek the assistance of his father, a United States Senator, to avoid combat duty. Among these witnesses were some individuals who worked closely with Robertson, such as his Commanding Officer during a 2-week period aboard the *U.S.S. Breckinridge*, and one of Robertson's bunkmates.

After deposing McCloskey and other defense witnesses and to discredit the testimony of the alleged slanderers, Robertson contacted Dr. Matthew Erdelyi, "an expert on psychodynamics of memory and perception, to provide an overview statement on the factors that bear on the reliability of recollections proffered by Messrs. Gearheart, Rogers, Steinmeyer, McCaffrey and Marache concerning events associated with the Korean War in the period 1950–1951." Expert testimony in the *Robertson* case might have cautioned jurors that uncorroborated recollections of complex events long ago may be unreliable, based on general research findings that people tend to reconstruct or even fabricate events that occurred in the distant past, that memory diminishes over time, and that memory for stressful events is less reliable than memory for nonstressful events.

McCloskey's counsel opposed the expert testimony, arguing that (a) it would not assist the jury and would usurp the jury's role; (b) it was irrelevant because it was not based on an individualized examination of each witness; (c) it was prejudicial because it would tend to mislead or confuse the jury; (d) it was not based on a scientifically reliable body of knowledge. In addition, the defense argued that the evidence was novel and untested, and thus failed to meet the *Frye* standard of general acceptance. The District Court of Columbia reviewed the available case law, concluded there was no magic formula for determining admissibility, and held that the determination had to be made on a case-by-case basis by assessing whether the testimony would be helpful to the jury. The court distinguished as factually inapposite the legal authorities relied upon by both the plaintiff and the defendant, on grounds that those cases involved criminal eyewitness identifications as opposed to memories and perceptions of participants in complex events and conversations at issue in the *Robertson* case. The court pointed out that the testimony at issue in this case concerned memories of events 37 years ago and involving an individual who had a special relationship with the witnesses, for McCloskey and his associates were not strangers to Robertson, as is typical in most eyewitness identification cases.

In sum, Dr. Erdelyi's testimony was excluded because the court concluded it would not be helpful to the jury on three grounds: (a) the testimony was squarely within the common sense of the average juror, that is, everyone knows that memory deteriorates over time; (b) the generality of the testimony would not assist the jury, and thus the testimony would be irrelevant; and (c) a battle of the experts would probably ensue, which was likely to confuse the jury.

A second and separate basis for excluding the expert testimony was that the plaintiff failed to demonstrate the general acceptance of the scientific evidence (*Frye* test) since the prior cases cited in which expert testimony had been admitted dealt with research findings on eyewitness identification in criminal cases, not the psychodynamics of memory and perception. Each rationale of the court will be discussed in turn.

The Common Knowledge of the Jury

How accurate judges may be in assessing what is or is not within the common knowledge of jurors is not without question. Judges who are not well acquainted with the psychological research findings may hold beliefs that run counter to the data. For instance, both *Neil v. Biggers* (1972) and *Manson v. Braithwaite* (1977), which contain leading United States Supreme Court opinions listing factors to consider in determining whether to exclude identification testimony on grounds that it is unreliable, also contain erroneous assumptions about psychological factors. In *Neil v. Biggers*, the Court stressed that the reliability of the eyewitness identification could be assessed by examining the accuracy of the witness's prior description of the suspect and the confidence of the witness in his or her identification testimony. In *Manson*, the majority outlined a "totality of circumstances test" enumerating five factors to assess the reliability of the identification testimony: (a) opportunity to view the criminal at the time of the crime; (b) the witness's degree of attention; (c) the accuracy of the description given before the suggestive pretrial identification procedure; (d) the level of certainty demonstrated in identifying the suspect; and (e) the time between the crime and the identification confrontation.

Analysis of research regarding the impact on recall accuracy of several of the *Neil* and *Manson* factors reveals that justices, too, may be susceptible to common misconceptions about the psychology of misidentification. For example, reliance on the witness's own testimony about the length of time they viewed the criminal at the scene of the crime is unsound, since research has revealed that witnesses consistently overestimate the duration of brief periods of time, and that the overestimations are more extreme when the violence of the events in issue increases (Loftus, Schooler, Boone, & Kline, 1987). Witnesses frequently claim they had several minutes to observe the suspect when, in fact, only a few seconds elapsed. Second, underlying the notion that the attention paid by the witness to the crucial events predicts identification accuracy are two misconceptions about memory performance. Many people believe that witnesses who have special training to be observant, such as police officers, will demonstrate more accurate recall. Experimental research has not supported the notion that police training improves eyewitness ability. However, the common misconception that police are superior in identification ability persists (Loftus, 1984). In cases in which the witnesses have no special training, many people believe that a witness who can accurately recall details peripheral to the crucial events will prove to be a more reliable identification witness. Research on the correlation between memory for peripheral details and identification accuracy has not supported this hypothesis (Lieppe, 1980; Wells & Lieppe, 1981). Cutler, Penrod, and Martens (1987) reported that recall of details of a facial description was weakly correlated with recognition performance, but accuracy of the witness's prior description was not correlated with correct identification of a target. Memory for peripheral detail was positively correlated with choosing one of the faces in the lineup as the suspect but negatively correlated with identification accuracy.

Possibly the most serious judicial misconception is the assumption, in both *Neil* and *Manson*, of a strong positive correlation between confidence and accuracy of the eyewitness, although this factor was questioned by some of the dissenting justices in *Manson*: "the witness' degree of certainty in making the identification . . . is worthless as an indicator that he is correct" (Marshall, J., and Brennan, J., dissenting). Their view is supported by research that has revealed that confidence does not vary in response to the presence or absence of the perpetrator in an identification test, but appears to be a variable manipulated by the difficulty of the task (similarity to other faces in the lineup, Fox & Walters, 1986; Wells, 1978) or the amount of briefing, rehearsal, and witness preparation for cross-examination (Wells, 1984). To date, considerable investigation of this relationship revealed, at most, a weak correlation of witness confidence and witness accuracy (Shapiro & Penrod, 1986). A witness may be accurate and tentative, inaccurate and confident.

A sizeable body of empirical survey research has confirmed the prevalence of numerous commonly held misconceptions about memory performance. While this avenue of research has tended to focus on beliefs about eyewitness memory pertinent to criminal cases, several of the findings apply equally to civil cases and have a more direct bearing on the facts presented in the *Robertson* case. For instance, jurors tend to believe that postevent information enhances the accuracy of recall, while research shows that postevent contamination of memory is common, whether the information is visually or verbally presented (Belli, 1989). A second popular misconception about memory, pertinent to any civil or criminal case, is the belief that an eyewitness who relates what he or she perceived with great confidence is more likely to be accurate than a witness who relates the same content, but whose demeanor is hesitant or less confident. Another issue of fact in the *Robertson* case was the influence of stress and the level of stress experienced by Robertson and the trial witnesses during the Korean War. Studies have shown that people tend to believe memory performance is enhanced in situations of stress or violence, or that a violent event will be more accurately recalled than a nonviolent event, whereas research has established that stress can impair memory performance (Wells, 1984).

Many people believe they are sufficiently well acquainted with the fragility and foibles of memory through their personal experience, and thus general psychological research findings can add little to what they and presumably most jurors already know. However, Sanders (1986) pointed out that few of us have had the opportunity to assess our memory performance in situations of extreme stress or a life-threatening crime, and thus we lack direct experience that might specifically provide insight into the memory processes of witnesses in most criminal cases. Similarly, few of us have had the opportunity to assess our memory performance in situations parallel to those at issue in evaluating the memory of the key witnesses in the *Robertson* case, that is, conversations that took place approximately 37 years ago and having little autobiographical salience for the witnesses. Knowledge about the possible effects of postevent information on the accuracy of memory is not intuitive. For instance, testimony of the defense witnesses in this case may have been shaped or biased by conversations the witnesses had with one another, or with their attorneys in preparing for depositions and the trial. Accordingly, limitations exist concerning the extent to which common knowledge or experience will assist jurors in assessing the reliability of an eyewitness account crucial to a case presented in court.

For instance, since research has shown that people tend to overestimate the accuracy of their own autobiographical memories, it is safe to predict that jurors may generalize from their own experience. The accuracy of recall for events without personal autobiographic significance will be comparable to the perceived accuracy for events with personal autobiographic significance. A considerable number of psychological studies on nonstatistical heuristics, such as the base rate fallacy, predict the susceptibility of laypersons to make such biased generalizations and judgments concerning memory performance.

Many years ago, the French maximist, La Rochefoucauld, noted that everyone complains about his or her memory but that few of complain about his or her judgment. Psychological research has established that unconscious judgmental biases are as prevalent as poor memory (Loftus & Beach, 1982). Judgmental biases about memory performance are common. Nonetheless, some psychologists believe that what a psychologist can offer at trial will invade the province of the jury and that the prejudicial effects of the testimony will outweigh any probative value (Pachella, 1988). Pachella's view that the testimony will invade the province of the jury is based on his opinion that most educated people have taken introductory psychology courses, which permits them to induce what any expert might say as a matter of common sense.

Of course, not all juries are filled with college-educated citizens, and among those who are college educated, there is no guarantee that all will have completed comparable introductory psychology courses. Moreover, available research indicates that many people selected to serve as jurors hold a number of misconceptions about memory performance. Thus, while we agree that much of what a psychologist might say sounds like common sense, Pachella's assumptions about jurors' inferences remain unsupported.

The Relevance of the Expert Testimony to Specific Eyewitnesses

The argument by the *Robertson* court concerning relevancy problems of testimony by an expert on memory performance has been raised previously by psychologists McCloskey and Egeth (1983). This argument, we believe, is often premised on the failure to recognize the distinction between expert testimony specific to the parties and expert social framework testimony. Typically, the objection is stated as a variant on the theme that the proffered social science research can offer nothing of value in one particular case because the expert cannot tell whether a particular witness is or is not accurate, which is the very issue before the finder of fact (Goodman & Loftus, 1988).

Given the convention established by testifying medical doctors or psychiatrists as to whether a particular set of symptoms is present in a patient with whose case they are personally familiar, some courts and lawyers erroneously expect the cognitive or social psychologist offering social framework testimony to make the same genre of statements or opinions that is permissible by a clinical psychologist who has made a competency determination based on evaluative tests of a particular individual. In other words, they expect clinical testimony such as "I have interviewed the witness, and in my professional opinion, he is incapable of distinguishing right from wrong" to analogize directly into "I have interviewed this eyewitness, and in my professional opinion, his memory is unreliable."

Of course, research findings on the parameters of memory performance in general cannot predict the performance of a single eyewitness any more than general insurance findings that 16-year-old drivers pose the highest accident risk can be used to predict the accident-prone driving of any one 16-year-old driver. When it is made evident that the social framework expert has not interviewed or evaluated the memory performance of the eyewitness and will make no statement regarding the reliability of the particular witness' memory, some courts exclude all testimony concerning social science research. If the testimony is admitted, cross-examination is often focused on the fact that the expert cannot comment on the accuracy of any particular witness's performance.

A variation of the relevance objection is the argument that laboratory studies conducted by experimental psychologists have no external validity (Konecni & Ebbesen, 1986). In other words, testimony is opposed on grounds that the research findings do not generalize to events and circumstances outside of the laboratory, let alone to the specific individuals whose memories are at issue in the trial at hand. A

number of field studies and experiments designed specifically to address concerns
about the generalizability of the relevant data have led researchers to conclude that
this issue is less of a problem than some contend (Cutler, Penrod, O'Rourke, &
Stuve, 1988).

Pachella (1988) argues that even if an expert is permitted to testify and explains
phenomena that he believes are available to jurors through their common experience, this explanation cannot assist jurors "in arriving at the truth." Ergo, the
expert invades the province of the jurors. We believe that the role of the expert
witness is not to determine the truth in a case but to offer information that provides
a plausible explanation for the events perceived by the eyewitness. The task of fact
finding and the final determination of the ultimate issue in a case remain with the
jury. Moreover, few courts consider truth-determination within their province or
that of jurors. Rather, jurors engage in probabilistic decision making concerning
past events (Mogill, 1987).

We believe there is room for a contrary viewpoint concerning the relevance of
research findings despite the fact that prior studies will not be dispositive of the
issue of memory accuracy in any particular case. If the research assists the fact
finder in assigning more or less weight to eyewitness testimony, we believe it is
relevant. So long as the expert does not state that a particular witness is or is not
accurate, but merely informs the jury of certain factors that may affect the accuracy of an identification, the expert does not invade the province of the jury
(*People v. McDonald*, 1984). Federal Rule of Evidence 704 does not permit a
court to exclude expert testimony on the grounds that it usurps the province of the
jury, that is, the "ultimate issue" objection.

A Battle of the Experts Confuses the Jurors

The third reason the *Robertson* court excluded the expert testimony was to
avoid a battle of the experts over matters within every juror's grasp, which the
judge believed would serve only to delay the trial unnecessarily and to confuse the
jurors. Conversely, other justices have held the view that it is precisely the opportunity to cross-examine an expert or to present opposing testimony that facilitates
the most efficient discovery of the relevance and weight of the research (Colquitt,
1988; *People v. Wright*, 1988), and therefore expert testimony is the best way for
evidence on the frailty of memory to enter trial. Thus, a battle of the experts is not
to be seen as a negative, but as a strength of the advocacy system of justice. We
know of no reason why expert testimony on memory processes should have any
greater potential for jury confusion than testimony by other experts.

The General Acceptance of the Scientific Evidence

As the *Robertson* case made patently clear, applying Federal Rule of Evidence
702 to assess the admissibility of expert testimony in a civil case means rigorous
standards, just as in a criminal case. In practice, to assess whether a research
finding has been generally accepted, the testifying expert will often be asked
whether a finding has been established to a reasonable degree of scientific certainty, although it is not required that the expert use this phrase explicitly (*Sentilles
v. Inter-Caribbean Corp.*, 1959). The phrase, properly understood, means

whether the expert, in deriving his or her opinion, relied on an explanatory theory that experts in the discipline substantially accept (*Boose v. Digate*, 1969). This consensus requirement reflects values underlying the *Frye* test of general acceptance (Kassin, Ellsworth, & Smith, 1989). In construing this requirement, courts have held that there is room for differing minority opinions among qualified experts.

This standard can be applied in the *Robertson* case. Despite the court's ruling that the proposed testimony was novel because prior testimony concerned eyewitness identification in criminal cases, most psychologists would not dispute that the research on memory and perception, on which the *Robertson* expert would have relied, entails substantially the same explanatory theory and basic research as that underlying expert testimony on eyewitness memory admitted in criminal trials. Unfortunately, neither the trial briefs of the plaintiff nor of the defendants successfully brought to the attention of the court the vast number of studies on autobiographical memory (Rubin, 1986) and the impact of postevent information on long-term memories. Thus the court based its ruling on limited data.

The *Robertson* situation must be distinguished from cases in which an expert testifies to an opinion contrary to those of other experts in the field, or in which the expert is unaware whether other experts share this opinion. In these instances, admissibility is a separate issue. In our opinion, the *Robertson* case did not come within either of these categories. However, because no trial took place, and the expert testimony would have been excluded had the case come to trial, the precise nature of the pertinent expert testimony remains somewhat hypothetical.

In excluding the expert testimony, the *Robertson* court took pains to distinguish criminal cases in which similar expert testimony had been admitted, on grounds that the factual circumstances in criminal cases are different, and the philosophical underpinnings in criminal cases are so fundamentally different from those in civil cases that the same admissibility standards do not obtain. The factual circumstances in criminal cases differ from the facts of the *Robertson* case in length of time that has elapsed since the crucial events at issue. Unquestionably, there are more available research data on memory for recent events than for events long since passed. However, it is conceivable that a criminal case may involve witness recall for events in the distant past, such as the 1987 trial of John Demjanjuk, thought to be Ivan the Terrible, for Nazi war crimes committed more than 40 years ago (Loftus, 1987). It is probable that events crucial in a civil trial may involve witness recall for events in the more recent past than those at issue in the *Robertson* case. Accordingly, we see no reason why social framework research on percipient witness memory should not apply to testimony in a civil controversy.

The court's second point, that the philosophical underpinnings of civil versus criminal trials differ, argues for more lenient standards of admissibility of social framework testimony in criminal cases in which identification of the perpetrator must be proved beyond a reasonable doubt. The expert testimony tends to cast doubt on the accuracy of the eyewitness identification. Thus the *Robertson* court's view that important Constitutional rights are at stake in criminal cases leads the court to endorse a standard by means of which expert testimony on eyewitness accuracy is more likely to be admitted in criminal than in civil trials. Curiously, some psychologists have argued that social framework testimony on eyewitness memory should be excluded *only* in criminal cases, because of the more stringent criminal burden of proof and the fact that more important rights are at stake in criminal cases (Pachella, 1988). This viewpoint is apparently premised on the mistaken notion that in criminal cases, expert testimony must be based on reasonable scientific certainty, whereas in civil cases no such rigor applies and experts may testify based merely on their subjective professional opinion.

In fact, the legal standard regarding the reliability of expert testimony is identical in criminal and civil cases, as borne out by the *Robertson* court, for the same rules of evidence apply to civil and criminal cases. In other words, the requirement that scientific or medical opinions must be based on a reasonable degree of scientific certainty applies both to civil and to criminal cases. In many civil trials in which social science evidence is routinely admitted, extremely rigorous standards of reliability pertain. For instance, in employment discrimination litigation, when statistical evidence is admitted, courts commonly require three standard deviations or statistically significant findings based at a minimum on probability levels of $< .01$ or $< .001$ before an inference of probative discriminatory conduct may be drawn. This stringent requirement that the evidence be reliable is quite distinct from the court's application of the civil preponderance of the evidence standard to the testimony presented by both parties.

ALTERNATIVES TO EXPERT TESTIMONY ON EYEWITNESS MEMORY

Monahan and Walker (1988) propose that expert testimony that presents social framework evidence should be abandoned. In its place, they favor the use of written briefs to make the relevant empirical work available. They argue that research data should be treated like legal precedent and not like other testimonial evidence. While this method has not yet been tested, some commentators oppose it because this would eliminate the opportunity to cross-examine the experts. Cross-examination of witnesses is of fundamental importance in the advocacy system of justice (Colquitt, 1988).

Alternatively, Monahan and Walker (1988) advocate that psychological experts should participate in drafting jury instructions that take into account the relevant empirical findings. In 1972, a jury instruction listing factors that influence the accuracy of eyewitness memory was first adopted (*Telfaire v. United States*, 1972), and most federal circuit courts follow this approach (Loftus & Doyle, 1987). However, one problem with such instructions is that no information is provided regarding the way in which certain factors influence the accuracy of eyewitness memory (Greene, 1988). Without such clarification, some jurors will draw the wrong inferences. In some cases, the instruction itself provides the wrong inference. Thus, some courts have attempted to draft cautionary instructions that make the impact of the factors explicit.

The issue of inexplicit instructions was addressed in 1987 by the California Supreme Court, which held (6 to 1) that rejection by the trial court of an eyewitness "factors" instruction on the accuracy of eyewitness identification constituted reversible error in an armed robbery case. A group of men armed with handguns and wearing stocking masks burst into a company's warehouse, forced the employees to lie on the floor, and demanded their money and jewelry. One employee was forced to open the company safe so the robbers could remove money from it. The robbery lasted 20 minutes. Eight victims were unable to identify the defendant as one of the masked robbers. Three victims identified the defendant as one of the robbers. One witness identified the defendant's photo on the day of the robbery and at a lineup a week later, but did not sign her lineup card because she was only 75% certain the defendant was the robber. At trial, she was 100% certain.

The instruction proposed by the defendant listed three factors supported by the evidence in the case, relevant to the jury's evaluation of the eyewitness testimony:

1. the witness's ability to observe the person being identified at the time of the crime;
2. the reliability of the witness's subsequent identification of the defendant; and
3. inconsistent or erroneous identifications the witness may have made before trial.

The six justices revised the proposed model jury instruction specifying the direction or impact of certain eyewitness identification factors upon recall accuracy. For instance, the proposed model instruction stated that cross-racial identifications tend to be less reliable than same-race identifications, that memories tend to fade over time, that identifications based on a lineup parade are more reliable than identifications based on a single photograph or showup, and that witnesses may subconsciously incorporate into their memory information from sources other than the events they witnessed (e.g., information from descriptions given by other witnesses).

In a vigorous dissent, Justice Lucas disapproved the proposed model instruction as highly inappropriate, because "it not only invades the domain of the expert witnesses and the jury, but it also comes perilously close to prohibited judicial comment on the evidence" (*People v. Wright*, 1987, p. 297). The dissent argued that instructions of this nature eliminated the need for expert testimony, thereby generating jury confusion because only partial information was provided. Without expert testimony, jurors would not hear a wide range of questions on direct and cross-examination that would assist them in judging the credibility and qualifications of each expert and eyewitness. The opportunity to call an opposing expert was also eliminated. Instructions of this nature invaded the domain of the expert witness because they adopted expert opinion as incontrovertible fact without requiring testimony from any expert. The domain of the jury was invaded because information presented as a charge from the judge compelled jurors to accept that view unconditionally, depriving the jury of independence to consider and weigh the expert evidence. This interfered with the jury's exclusive function as the arbiter of questions of fact and the credibility of witnesses. (Similar objections to instructions that attempt to substitute for expert testimony were noted in *United States v. Amaral*, 1973).

After the composition of the California Supreme Court changed (resignation of Chief Justice Rose Bird), the prior majority opinion was withdrawn and a new opinion in the case was issued, adopting much of Justice Lucas' dissent. In the new *People v. Wright* (1988), the California Supreme Court retained the holding that it was error to reject the proposed factors instruction but added that the jury instruction should not take a position as to the impact of the each of the psychological factors listed and instead should list them in a neutral and nonargumentative way. The rationale for this reconsideration and subsequent limitation on the content of the instruction was the court's reluctance to incorporate the results of certain studies while discounting the results of others. The court was also reluctant to require the judge to endorse, and the jury to follow, a particular psychological theory relating to the reliability of eyewitness identifications. The court concluded that this would improperly invade the province of the jury and would confuse the roles of expert witnesses and judge. Instead, the court proposed that this type of neutral instruction should accompany expert testimony, and that cross-examination and argument of counsel should explain the effects of those factors to the jury.

A dissenting opinion by Judge Mosk, author of the original opinion containing the proposed directional instruction, argued that there was scientific consensus about the effects of some of these factors enumerated in the new instruction, and that if jurors were left to determine the effects of the factors based on their intuitions, they might reach conclusions contrary to the research findings. Specifically, Judge Mosk noted that the new factors instruction failed to mention: (a) that cross-racial identification is less reliable than same-race identification; (b) that an identification of someone familiar to the witness is more reliable than identification of a stranger; (c) that postevent information acquired from other sources may be incorporated into memory; or (d) that accuracy of recall may be adversely affected by unconscious biases in identification procedures.

In the new *People v. Wright* (1988) the court also upheld the trial court's rejection of a proposed instruction to the effect that eyewitness testimony "may be mistaken and should be received with caution."[3] The major rationale for this determination was that expert testimony is the appropriate and preferred manner to present information to the jury on the unreliability of eyewitness identifications under a certain set of circumstances. The court explained that it is not an appropriate function of a jury instruction to present such issues because jurors are bound to follow the court's instructions, whereas they are not bound to follow the testimony of trial witnesses. Thus, an instruction may properly alert jurors to factors that may affect eyewitness identifications, while expert testimony may be used to further elucidate the effects of the factors listed. A jury instruction that incorporates an expert's views would improperly bind the jury to that expert's views. The court added that the use of expert testimony over jury instructions has a number of advantages over jury instructions. For instance, because the expert is subject to cross-examination and rebuttal, the jury has the opportunity to determine the weight to give to the expert testimony.

CONCLUSION

A review of case law reveals that admissibility of expert testimony on eyewitness identification, like that of other social framework testimony, has been fraught with legal confusion, while reports of disagreement among research scientists have been exaggerated. The debate over appropriate standards for admission under the Federal Rules of Evidence and the *Frye* test continues. However, the issues surrounding the acceptance of this testimony have been clarified by an increase in the types of social framework testimony proffered as evidence. Alternatives to expert testimony that have been proposed (written briefs to the court or jury instructions

---

[3]The requested instruction reads: "Where the prosecution has offered identification testimony, that is, the testimony of an eyewitness that he saw the defendant commit the act charged, such testimony should be received with caution. An identification by a stranger is not as trustworthy as an identification by an acquaintance. Mistaken identification is not uncommon, and careful scrutiny of such testimony is especially important."

from the court) all have been criticized for eliminating the opportunity to cross-examine the expert. Although initially courts focused on the use of jury instructions as a less costly alternative to expert testimony, courts appear to have come full circle. The current trend is to admit expert testimony because the approved instructions are uninformative about the influence of specific factors on eyewitness performance. For the time being, there is a role for research psychologists in the courtroom when eyewitness testimony is at issue.

REFERENCES

Belli, R. F. (1989). Influence of misleading postevent information: Misinformation interference and acceptance. *Journal of Experimental Psychology: General, 118,* 72–85.
Boose v. Digate. (1969). 107 Ill. App. 2d 418, 423, 246 N.E. 2d 50, 53 (3d Dist.).
Brown v. Board of Education. (1954). 347 U.S. 483.
Ceci, S. J., Toglia, M., & Ross, D. (1987). *Children's eyewitness testimony.* New York: Springer.
Colquitt, J. A. (1988). Judicial use of social science evidence at trial. *Arizona Law Review, 30,* 51–84.
Cutler, B. L., Penrod, S. D., & Martens, T. K. (1987). The reliability of eyewitness identifications: The role of system and estimator variables. *Law and Human Behavior, 11,* 233–258.
Cutler, B., Penrod, S. D., O'Rourke, T. E., & Stuve, T. E. (1988, August). *The external validity of eyewitness identification research.* Paper presented at the Annual Meeting of the American Psychological Association, Atlanta, Georgia.
Driessen, P. A. (1983). The wedding of social science and the courts: Is the marriage working? *Social Science Quarterly, 64,* 476–493.
Fox, S. G., & Walters, H. A. (1986). The impact of general versus specific expert testimony and eyewitness confidence upon mock juror judgment. *Law and Human Behavior, 10,* 215–228.
Frye v. United States. (1923). 293 F. 1013 (D.C. Cir.).
Gilbert v. California. (1967). 388 U.S. 263.
Goodman, J., & Croyle, R. T. (1989). Social framework testimony in employment discrimination cases. *Behavioral Sciences & the Law, 7*(2), 227–241.
Goodman, J., & Loftus, E. F. (1988). Commentary: The relevance of expert evidence on eyewitness testimony. *Journal of Interpersonal Violence, 3,* 115–121.
Gorman, M. A. (1987). Evaluating eyewitness testimony in criminal trials: Can jurors use help from experts? *Chicago Kent Law Review, 63,* 137–158.
Greene, E. (1988). Judge's instruction on eyewitness testimony: Evaluation and revision. *Journal of Applied Social Psychology, 18,* 252–278.
Henderson, P. (1981a, May 15). One man's battle to clear his name. *The Seattle Times,* pp. D1, D2.
Henderson, P. (1981b, Oct. 23). The Titus case comes full circle. *The Seattle Times,* p. C1.
Kassin, S. M., Ellsworth, P. C., & Smith, V. L. (1989). The "general acceptance" of psychological research on eyewitness memory: A survey of the experts. *American Psychologist, 46,* 1089–1098.
Konecni, V. J., & Ebbesen, E. B. (1986). Courtroom testimony by psychologists on eyewitness identification issues: Critical notes and reflections. *Law and Human Behavior, 10,* 117–126.
Laughery, K. R., & Wogalter, M. S. (1989). Forensic applications of facial memory research. In A. W. Young & H. E. Ellis (Eds.), *Handbook of research on face processing.* Amsterdam: North Holland Publishing Co.
Law and Human Behavior. (1986). *10*(1–2).
Lieppe, M. R. (1980). Effects of integrative memorial and cognitive processes on the correspondence of eyewitness accuracy and confidence. *Law and Human Behavior, 4,* 261–274.
Lindsay, R. C. L., & Wells, G. L. (1980). What price justice? Exploring the relationship of lineup fairness to identification accuracy. *Law and Human Behavior, 4,* 303–314.
Loftus, E. F. (1984). Eyewitnesses: Essential but unreliable. *Psychology Today, 18,* 22–26.
Loftus, E. F. (1986). Ten years in the life of an expert witness. *Law and Human Behavior, 10,* 241–263.
Loftus, E. F. (1987, June 29). My turn: Trials of an expert witness. *Newsweek,* pp. 10–11.
Loftus, E. F., & Beach, L. R. (1982). Human inference and judgment: Is the glass half empty or half full? *Stanford Law Review, 34,* 901–918.
Loftus, E. F., & Doyle, J. M. (1987). *Eyewitness testimony: Civil and criminal.* New York: Kluwer.

Loftus, E. F., & Ketcham, K. (1991). *Witness for the defense: The accused, the eyewitness, and the expert who puts memory on trial* (pp. 33–60). New York: St. Martins Press.

Loftus, E. F., & Monahan, J. (1980). Trial by data: Psychological research as legal evidence. *American Psychologist, 35,* 270–283.

Loftus, E. F., & Schneider, N. G. (1987). "Behold with strange surprise": Judicial reactions to expert testimony concerning eyewitness testimony. *University of Missouri–Kansas City Law Review, 56,* 1–45.

Loftus, E. F., Schooler, J. W., Boone, S. M., & Kline, D. (1987). Time went by so slowly: Overestimation of event duration by males and females. *Applied Cognitive Psychology, 1,* 3–13.

Loh, W. D. (1984). *Social research in the judicial process: Cases, readings, and text.* New York: Russell Sage Foundation.

Malpass, R. S., & Devine, P. (1981). Eyewitness identification: Lineup instruction and the absence of the offender. *Journal of Applied Psychology, 66,* 482–489.

Malpass, R. S., & Devine, P. (1983). Measuring the fairness of eyewitness identification lineups. In S. Lloyd-Bostock & B. R. Clifford (Eds.), *Evaluating witness evidence* (pp. 81–102). Chichester: Wiley.

Manson v. Braithwaite. (1977). 432 U.S. 98.

McCloskey, M., & Egeth, H. E. (1983). Eyewitness identification: What can a psychologist tell a jury? *American Psychologist, 38,* 550–563.

Mogill, K. M. (1987). Some reflections on the relationship between the jury system, truth, and Charles Ives. *Cooley Law Review, 4,* 610–616.

Monahan, J., & Walker, L. (1988). Social science research in law. *American Psychologist, 43,* 465–472.

Monahan, J., & Walker, L. (1985). *Social science in law: Cases and materials.* New York: Foundation Press.

Neil v. Biggers. (1972). 409 U.S. 188.

Pachella, R. G. (1988). On the admissibility of psychological testimony in criminal justice proceedings. *Journal of Interpersonal Violence, 3,* 111–114.

People v. McDonald. (1984). 690 P.2d 709, 37 Cal. 3d 351.

People v. Wright. (1987). 729 P.2d 280 (Cal.).

People v. Wright. (1988). 88 Daily Journal D. A. R. 8764.

Robertson v. McCloskey. (1988). 676 F. Supp. 351 (D.D.C.).

Rubin, D. C. (1986). *Autobiographical memory.* Cambridge, UK: Cambridge University Press.

Sanders, J. (1986). Expert witnesses in eyewitness facial identification cases. *Texas Tech. Law Review, 17,* 1409–1471.

Sentilles v. Inter-Caribbean Corp. (1959). 361 U.S. 107, 109.

Shapiro, P. N., & Penrod, S. (1986). Meta-analysis of facial identification studies. *Psychological Bulletin, 100,* 139–156.

Stovall v. Denno. (1967). 388 U.S. 293.

Telfaire v. United States. (1972). 469 F.2d 552 (D.C. Cir.).

United States v. Amaral. (1973). 488 F.2d 1148 (9th Cir.).

United States v. Downing. (1985). 753 F.2d 1224 (3d Cir.).

United States v. Wade. (1967). 388 U.S. 218.

Wall, P. (1965). *Eyewitness identification in criminal cases.* Springfield, IL: Charles C Thomas.

Wells, G. L. (1978). Applied eyewitness testimony research: System variables and estimator variables. *Journal of Personality and Social Psychology, 36,* 1546–1557.

Wells, G. L. (1984). How adequate is human intuition for judging eyewitness testimony? In G. L. Wells & E. F. Loftus (Eds.), *Eyewitness testimony: Psychological perspectives* (pp. 256–272). Cambridge, UK: Cambridge University Press.

Wells, G. L., & Lieppe, M. R. (1981). How do triers of fact infer the accuracy of eyewitness identifications? Using memory for peripheral details can be misleading. *Journal of Applied Psychology, 66,* 682–687.

Wells, G. L., & Lindsay, R. C. L. (1983). How do people judge the accuracy of eyewitness identifications? Studies of performance and a metamemory analysis. In S. Lloyd-Bostock & B. R. Clifford (Eds.), *Evaluating witness evidence* (pp. 41–55). Chichester: Wiley.

Wells, G. L., & Murray, D. M. (1984). What can psychology say about the *Neil v. Biggers* criteria for judging eyewitness accuracy? *Journal of Applied Psychology, 68,* 347–362.

Yuille, J. C., & Cutshall, J. L. (1986). A case study of eyewitness memory of a crime. *Journal of Applied Psychology, 71,* 291–301.

19

Expert Psychological Testimony on Eyewitness Reliability: Selling Psychology Before Its Time

Judith McKenna, Molly Treadway, and Michael E. McCloskey

Since at least the time of Munsterberg (1908), experimental psychologists have endeavored to point out the implications of their science for the law. Eyewitness identification in particular has been held up as an example of the applicability of psychological research to real-world problems. Recent years have seen a virtual explosion of research bearing on issues of eyewitness identification and juror evaluation of eyewitness testimony. The results of this research are being brought into the courtroom with increasing frequency, in the form of expert psychological testimony. Most commonly, the expert testimony is introduced by the defense in criminal cases involving eyewitness identifications of a defendant by one or more prosecution witnesses. In such cases the expert typically testifies about the general unreliability of human perception and memory and also points to specific factors present in the case (e.g., stress, cross-racial identification) that, at least according to the expert, may contribute to inaccurate eyewitness identifications.[1]

Expert psychological testimony on eyewitness performance has generated substantial controversy among psychologists (e.g., Loftus, 1983a, 1983b, 1986; McCloskey & Egeth, 1983a, 1983b; McCloskey, Egeth, & McKenna, 1986). The issues in the debate are manifold and complex, and we will not attempt in this chapter to provide an exhaustive survey. Rather, we will focus on one of the central points of contention: the adequacy of the scientific foundation for the expert testimony. We begin by reviewing briefly the response of the judicial system to expert testimony on eyewitness performance, noting that the fundamental question with respect to admission of expert testimony is whether the testimony will be helpful to the jury. We then examine expert testimony on eyewitness performance in light of this question, suggesting that scientific knowledge about eyewitness perception and memory has not advanced to the point where psychologists can offer useful advice to jurors.

[1]Many of the factors discussed by experts (e.g., stress, delay) could conceivably contribute not only to identification errors in which witnesses mistakenly identify innocent suspects, but also to errors in which witnesses fail to identify guilty suspects. In practice, however, expert testimony has been applied only to situations that may potentially involve the former type of error. That is, expert psychological testimony concerning identification of criminal suspects has been limited to situations in which the defense alleges that a misidentification has occurred.

JUDICIAL RESPONSE TO EXPERT TESTIMONY
ON EYEWITNESS RELIABILITY

The U.S. judicial system has not always been eager to receive expert psychological testimony on eyewitness performance. Correctly perceiving the expert's role to be that of attacking the credibility of eyewitnesses, judges frequently rebuffed the efforts of defense attorneys to introduce eyewitness experts. Decisions about the admissibility of expert testimony are largely within the discretion of the trial judge, and therefore, appeals based on the exclusion of the eyewitness expert were (and in most jurisdictions remain) largely unavailing.

In *United States v. Amaral* (1973), the Ninth Circuit Court of Appeals stated a test for admission of expert psychological testimony on eyewitness performance:

1. the witness must be a qualified expert;
2. the matter must be a proper subject for expert testimony;
3. the testimony must be in accordance with a generally accepted explanatory theory;
4. the probative value of the testimony must not be outweighed by its prejudicial effects.

Referring to the *Amaral* criteria or other similar formulations, appellate courts for many years uniformly upheld trial court exclusions of eyewitness experts, typically on grounds that eyewitness reliability was not a proper subject for expert testimony. In particular, the courts were receptive to arguments to the effect that everyone knows that eyewitnesses can be mistaken. Many courts also agreed that the expert's testimony would invade the province of the jury and would constitute an impermissible attack on the credibility of eyewitnesses. Few courts directly addressed the scientific basis for the testimony, but in jurisdictions adhering to the test of *Frye v. United States* (1923), it was frequently found that there had been no showing of general acceptance of the proffered testimony by the relevant scientific community.

In the early 1980s, however, routine affirmation of trial court decisions to exclude expert testimony on eyewitness identification came to an end. The highest courts of Arizona and California ruled that, at least under the circumstances before them, the trial court's exclusion of an eyewitness expert was an abuse of discretion (*People v. McDonald*, 1984; *State v. Chapple*, 1983). In each case the court concluded that the expert witness would have provided scientifically well-founded testimony that would have assisted the jurors in evaluating the eyewitness testimony in the case. Despite indications, particularly by the Arizona Supreme Court, that the admission of such testimony was required only in exceptional circumstances, these decisions have led to a dramatic increase in expert testimony on eyewitness reliability in Arizona and California and have influenced courts in other jurisdictions as well.

In *United States v. Downing* (1985), the Third Circuit Court of Appeals vacated the conviction of John Downing, who was identified by 12 eyewitnesses as the perpetrator of a fraud. Concluding that the trial court's grounds for excluding a proffered eyewitness expert were insufficient, the appeals court remanded the case to the lower court for a hearing on the admissibility of the expert testimony.[2]

In discussing the admissibility of expert testimony on eyewitness identification, the appeals court in *Downing* focused on the "helpfulness" criterion codified in Rule 702 of the Federal Rules of Evidence:

> *If scientific, technical, or other specialized knowledge will assist the trier of fact to understand the evidence or to determine a fact in issue, a witness qualified as an expert by knowledge, skill, experience, training, or education, may testify thereto in the form of an opinion or otherwise.*

THE ARGUMENT FOR EXPERT TESTIMONY

Advocates of expert testimony on eyewitness performance argue that the testimony does in fact assist the jury (e.g., Ellison & Buckhout, 1981; Loftus, 1979, 1983a, 1983b; Wells, 1984; Woocher, 1977). Pointing to more than 100 years of scientific research on human perception and memory, they argue that this research has revealed many important factors that may influence the reliability of eyewitness testimony. However, the argument continues, laypersons are unaware of, or have misconceptions about, these factors. Hence, it is concluded, expert psychological testimony that informs jurors about the effects of the factors will improve their ability to assess the credibility of eyewitnesses.

Unfortunately, this argument does not withstand scrutiny. For a jury to gain appreciable help from the testimony of an expert, the testimony must provide information that has an adequate scientific foundation, goes beyond the knowledge of the average juror, and is usable by jurors in evaluating the credibility of eyewitnesses. However, examination of the various statements typically made in expert testimony on eyewitness performance suggests that these statements fall short on one or more of the above criteria. In the following section we illustrate this point by considering a few examples of the factors discussed by eyewitness experts.

FACTORS DISCUSSED IN EXPERT TESTIMONY

Stress

A common claim of experts testifying about eyewitness behavior is that the stress experienced by a witness to a crime impairs the ability of the witness to encode and later remember information about the crime and the perpetrator. However, the available data do not suggest the existence of such a simple relationship between stress and performance.

Most researchers agree that the effects of stress on performance conform to the Yerkes-Dodson Law, which holds that the function relating stress and performance is an inverted U (e.g., Deffenbacher, 1983; Ellison & Buckhout, 1981; Loftus, 1979). In particular, the Yerkes-Dodson Law states that as arousal or stress increases from very low to very high levels, performance at first improves but then, as stress increases beyond some optimal level, declines. The problem in applying

---

[2]After holding the hearing, the trial judge again ruled the defense expert's testimony inadmissible and reinstated Downing's conviction. This decision was upheld on appeal.

this law to actual eyewitnesses is that the optimal level of stress varies across situations (and probably also across individuals). That is, a level of stress that is optimal in one particular set of circumstances may be above or below the optimal level in different circumstances. Thus, even if it were possible to ascertain the level of stress experienced by a witness in a particular situation, the Yerkes-Dodson Law alone could not tell us whether that level of stress would tend to impair, improve, or have no effect on performance.

Nor does research concerned specifically with the relationship between stress and eyewitness performance permit more definitive conclusions. An obvious difficulty in this research is that ethical considerations preclude studies in which people are subjected to levels of stress comparable to those experienced by witnesses to violent crimes. Thus, laboratory studies typically involve relatively low levels of stress induced by means such as the presentation of an "upsetting" videotape or series of slides. These contrived situations are necessarily quite different from a situation in which someone actually witnesses a crime.

Of course, if stress-induced impairments were consistently observed even at the low stress levels in the laboratory studies, it might be reasonable to conclude that actual witnesses to violent crimes, because they were subjected to much higher levels of stress, would also show impairment. However, the laboratory studies by no means paint such a simple picture. Although some studies have found poorer performance for stressed than for nonstressed subjects (e.g., Brigham, Maass, Martinez, & Whittenberger, 1983; Clifford & Hollin, 1981; Clifford & Scott, 1978), other studies have found no effect, or even a facilitatory effect, of stress (e.g., Heuer & Riesberg, 1988; Leippe, Wells, & Ostrom, 1978; Tooley, Brigham, Maass, & Bothwell, 1987).

Furthermore, in a study involving eyewitnesses to an actual violent crime (i.e., a shooting incident in which one person was killed and a second seriously wounded), Yuille and Cutshall (1986) found that witnesses who reported having experienced high levels of stress in observing the crime were significantly *more* accurate in police interviews than witnesses reporting lower levels of stress. Although this result is confounded by the fact that the witnesses reporting higher levels of stress were also more centrally involved in the incident, the finding nevertheless suggests that even at the levels of stress experienced by witnesses to violent crimes, the relationship between stress and performance may not be a simple one, and that eyewitnesses who have experienced significant stress will not necessarily demonstrate inferior memory performance as a consequence.

It is plausible that terrified witnesses may be impaired in their ability to perceive and remember a crime and its perpetrator. However, it must be recognized that this is an intuition and not a conclusion that follows from the available scientific research. In fact, the Yuille and Cutshall (1986) results raise questions about the validity of the intuition. In any event, intuition is certainly not an adequate basis for expert testimony; there is no reason to give more credence to the intuitions of a psychologist than to those of jurors.

At present, the strongest conclusion warranted by the available research is the following:

> *Stress probably affects eyewitness performance, but there is no scientific basis for judgments about whether the level of stress experienced by a particular witness would improve performance, have no effect, or impair performance.*

Retrograde Amnesia

Claims made in expert testimony about the detrimental effects of stress on eyewitness memory have been extended to address memory for events preceding the critical stressful event. That is, expert testimony has been offered to the effect that a severe psychological stress or shock can impair a witness's ability to remember events that occurred prior to the stressful event. For example, this testimony has been used to suggest that even though a witness viewed the perpetrator of a crime for some time before the crime took place, his or her memory of that person may have been impaired by the subsequent stress. This purported memory impairment for events preceding a shock has been referred to as *retrograde amnesia*.

The psychological literature pertaining to stress-induced retrograde amnesia comprises only a handful of studies. The term retrograde amnesia was first used in the context of psychological stress in a study by Loftus and Burns (1982). College students watched a 2-minute film that ended with either a violent or nonviolent episode, and were then tested on their memory for details from the film. Questions were asked about details that occurred throughout the film prior to the violent or nonviolent ending. In reporting their results, Loftus and Burns concentrate on one peripheral detail, the number on a boy's football jersey, which was shown for two seconds just prior to the violent or nonviolent ending. For this detail subjects who viewed the violent ending showed poorer memory (4.3% correct) than subjects who viewed the nonviolent ending (27.9% correct). However, on tests of memory for other details viewed prior to the film's ending, only a trivial effect was found: Subjects who viewed the violent ending were 80% correct, whereas those who viewed the nonviolent ending were 84% correct. Clearly, this study does not provide an adequate foundation for expert testimony to the effect that stress impairs the ability of eyewitnesses to remember people or events encountered prior to the stressful experience.

The lack of an adequate scientific basis for expert psychological testimony on stress-induced amnesia becomes even more evident considering the other relevant studies. In a study by Christianson and Nilsson (1984), students viewed a series of slides of faces. Each face was accompanied by four descriptive words: the person's name, occupation, a hobby, and a personality trait. For the control subjects all faces were neutral, whereas for experimental subjects the faces in the middle of the series were horribly disfigured. These slides were intended to produce stress in subjects, and physiological measurements suggest that they did. The relevant question was whether this stress would impair memory for words associated with the earlier faces. In four experiments with this procedure, none showed a retrograde amnesia effect.

A study by Christianson (1984) also failed to provide clear evidence of stress-induced retrograde amnesia. Subjects viewed a slide sequence depicting an event that began with a mother and her son walking through a town. The slides in the middle of the sequence were either neutral or stress-inducing (i.e., a series of explicit photographs showing the son seriously injured after being hit by a car). Memory for material presented prior to the stressful or neutral slides was tested in four different ways. Across the four tests all possible patterns of results were obtained. In two tests there was no difference in performance between stressed and nonstressed subjects, in one test the stressed subjects performed more poorly than the nonstressed subjects, and in one test the stressed subjects did better than the nonstressed subjects.

It is apparent that the effects of stress on an eyewitness's memory for prior events are currently not well understood. The available studies not only involved circumstances quite different from those experienced by witnesses to violent crimes, but also produced inconsistent results. In our view, the available evidence leads to the following conclusion:

> *There is currently no scientific basis for claims about when, how, or even whether stress impairs memory for events preceding the stress.*

Confidence and Accuracy

Another staple of expert testimony on eyewitness performance is the contention that the confidence expressed by a witness is unrelated to the accuracy of the witness's testimony. A witness who is very confident is no more likely to be correct than a witness who expresses uncertainty. This sweeping claim is clearly not justified by the available psychological research. The available data are mixed. Some studies show a clear confidence/accuracy relationship, and other studies do not. For example, Deffenbacher (1980) reviewed 25 studies that collectively involved 43 assessments of confidence/accuracy relationships. In 22 of the assessments a positive correlation between confidence and accuracy was found, whereas in the remaining 21 assessments either no correlation or a slight negative correlation was obtained. Although several attempts have been made to account for the disparate results (e.g., Deffenbacher, 1980; Leippe, 1980; Wells & Murray, 1984), none has proven notably successful.

At present, the strongest conclusion justified by the available research is the following:

> *Witness confidence may be positively correlated with accuracy under some conditions but not under others. However, the conditions under which confidence does and does not predict accuracy are poorly understood.*

It does not seem that this conclusion would be of much help to jurors weighing the testimony of eyewitnesses.

It might be argued that regardless of the precise nature of the confidence/accuracy relationship, confidence is a weak and unreliable predictor of accuracy, and therefore should be ignored by jurors assessing the credibility of an eyewitness. On this argument, expert testimony that instructed jurors to ignore witness confidence would be valuable even in the absence of a clear understanding of the confidence/accuracy relationship. However, the conclusion that jurors should ignore confidence does not follow from the premise that confidence is only weakly related to accuracy. The relationship between accuracy and confidence may be no weaker than the relationship between accuracy and most other factors available for jurors to consider. In the absence of factors strongly related to accuracy, it is not inappropriate for jurors to take into account admittedly imperfect predictors such as witness confidence.

An expert witness might caution jurors that confidence is not necessarily indicative of accuracy. However, there is no basis for assuming that jurors are unaware of this point. Furthermore, given that weak predictors of accuracy should not necessarily be ignored, it is unclear how jurors profitably could make use of advice that states in essence that the confidence of a witness may or may not be related to the witness's accuracy.

Delay

Finally, consider briefly the effects of delay on the accuracy of eyewitness testimony. Eyewitness experts often testify that memory fades over time and hence that identifications made after significant delays are less reliable than identifications made very shortly after a crime. This testimony would appear to be adequately grounded in psychological research. A large body of data shows with reasonable consistency that memory performance decreases as the retention interval increases. However, it is clearly a matter of common sense that memory fades with the passage of time. Hence, it seems unlikely that expert testimony is needed to inform jurors of this point.

Expert testimony on effects of delay might be warranted if the expert could go beyond common sense, providing more specific information about how much of an effect a particular delay would be expected to have on the memory of a witness who observed a crime under a particular set of circumstances. However, the available data provide no basis for this sort of specific testimony. The strongest conclusion warranted by the available research is that memory for a face or event declines over time.

RISKS OF INADEQUATELY GROUNDED EXPERT ADVICE

The examples we have discussed illustrate a general point. Specifically, if we survey the conclusions typically drawn by psychologists in expert testimony on eyewitness performance, we find that virtually all of these conclusions fall into one of two categories. In the first category are conclusions that, although scientifically well-established, are common sense: Memory fades over time. In the second category are conclusions that, although not common sense, lack an adequate scientific foundation and sometimes even do violence to the available research: Confidence and accuracy are unrelated.

The statements in the second category are especially troubling. When experts present as scientific facts conclusions that are not warranted by the available research, their testimony carries substantial risk of confusing and misleading those it is supposed to assist. This concern is underscored by the *State v. Chapple* (1983) and *People v. McDonald* (1984) cases mentioned earlier, in which state supreme courts reversed murder convictions on grounds that the trial court's exclusion of a defense eyewitness expert was an abuse of discretion. In each case the appellate court was led to accept unsupported assertions as scientific fact.

In *State v. Chapple*, the Arizona Supreme Court considered the defense proffer of the expert testimony of Elizabeth Loftus and concluded:

> *Dr. Loftus' testimony would have informed the jury that there are many variables which affect the accuracy of identification and which apply to the facts of this case. . . . We cannot assume that the average juror would be aware of the variables concerning identification and*

memory about which Dr. Loftus was qualified to testify. (State v. Chapple, *1983, pp. 1220–1221*)

The court then went on to examine the specific factors Loftus would have discussed in her testimony. On the relationship between confidence and accuracy, the court noted that

> *Dr. Loftus' testimony and some experimental data indicate that there is no relationship between the confidence which a witness has in his or her identification and the accuracy of that identification. Again, this factor was specifically tied to the facts in the case before us since both Scott and Buck [i.e., the eyewitnesses in the case] indicated in their testimony that they were absolutely sure of their identification.* (State v. Chapple, *1983, p. 1221*)

As discussed above, however, the available research does not warrant the conclusion that confidence is unrelated to accuracy.

The court also mentioned that Loftus would have testified that stress impairs the ability of a witness to perceive and remember events. This testimony, the court concluded, would have been helpful to the jury. As we have seen, however, the claim that stress impairs witness performance lacks an adequate scientific foundation.

The *State v. Chapple* court's discussion of the "forgetting curve" provides an especially interesting example of judicial confusion in the face of expert testimony on eyewitness performance. The court summarized the proffered testimony as follows:

> *Dr. Loftus presented data from experiments which showed that the "forgetting curve" is not uniform. Forgetting occurs very rapidly and then tends to level out; immediate identification is much more trustworthy than long-delayed identification.* (State v. Chapple, *1983, p. 1220*)

From this information about the form of the forgetting curve the court drew conclusions about memory at particular intervals after the crime in the case:

> *Scott's failure to identify Chapple's photograph when it was first shown to him on March 26, 1978 (four months after the crime) and when Scott's ability to identify would have been far greater [than when he did identify Chapple thirteen months after the crime], is of key importance.* (State v. Chapple, *1983, p. 1220–1221*)

The assumption the court made is that after a delay of 4 months, a witness is still on the part of the forgetting curve where forgetting occurs rapidly, so that a great deal of forgetting would occur between 4 and 13 months. This conclusion is, of course, completely unjustified. The time span over which memory performance declines rapidly before leveling off is not constant over situations but varies as a function of factors such as the circumstances of initial exposure, the type of material being remembered, and the type of memory test. The available psychological research does not tell us anything about how to weigh the witness's performance at 4 months as opposed to 13 months. It may be, as the court concluded, that the witness remembered much more after 4 than after 13 months. On the other hand, the forgetting curve may have flattened out well before 4 months, so that his memory was nearly as good after 13 months as after 4 months. Thus, the *State v. Chapple* court drew unwarranted conclusions from the information it was provided about the forgetting curve.

In *People v. McDonald* the California Supreme Court overturned a murder conviction because the defendant had not been permitted to introduce expert psychological testimony on eyewitness reliability. The court offered a highly positive assessment of the proffered expert testimony, noting with approval not only the expert's contentions about several of the factors we have discussed but also claims about the difficulty of cross-sex and cross-age identification, claims for which there is utterly no scientific foundation. The court even went so far as to refer to the impressive consistency of the research on the various factors (*People v. McDonald*, 1984, p. 718). As we have seen, there is no such consistency.

If sophisticated judges are confused and misled by statements of the sorts offered in expert psychological testimony on eyewitness performance, it seems likely that jurors would be confused and misled, too.

CONCLUSION

Disagreements between proponents and opponents of expert psychological testimony on eyewitness reliability primarily may reflect differences in political or professional philosophy. Perhaps, for example, proponents place more weight than opponents on the importance of avoiding wrongful convictions; or perhaps proponents feel more strongly than opponents the professional responsibility to apply their expertise to real-world problems. In our view, however, the fundamental disagreements concern the strength of the available scientific evidence and the sorts of conclusions that can properly be drawn from this evidence. Bermant (1986, p. 98) expresses a similar view: "The opponents of expert testimony by experimental psychologists do not differ from the proponents in their senses of citizenship or professional responsibility. But they have considerably less confidence than the proponents do in the accuracy and generality of the psychological information that the proponents present in court."

Proponents of expert testimony implicitly assume that the world is a simple place, a place where questions such as, "How does stress affect eyewitness performance?" and "How are confidence and accuracy related?" have simple answers that hold true across all circumstances. If the world were that simple, then a single well-done experiment on each factor would provide a sufficient basis for expert testimony. If stress were found to impair performance in one set of circumstances, we could be sure that stress would also impair performance in any other set of circumstances. If confidence and accuracy were found to be unrelated in one situation, we could be sure that they would be unrelated in all other situations.

Unfortunately, the world is not that simple. The accumulating body of research, as well as common sense, tells us that the answers to questions about stress, confidence, and so forth, are not straightforward. The effects of factors vary across situations, in ways we do not understand yet. This unfortunate fact will not go away, no matter how much we may wish that it would.

It might be objected that our negative evaluation of expert testimony on eyewitness reliability has its origin in the unreasonable premise that expert testimony is appropriate only if scientific understanding of eyewitness performance is absolutely complete. In fact, however, we are not suggesting that all the i's must be dotted and all the t's must be crossed before psychologists should agree to testify as experts. Rather, our contention is that the field of eyewitness psychology is nowhere near the point of needing only to dot the i's and cross the t's. Psychologists interested in eyewitness perception and memory are only beginning to explore a set of complex and difficult questions that will not be resolved by a few simple experiments. Before we can claim to have even a preliminary understanding of factors affecting witness accuracy, we will have to study the factors under varied circumstances. More important, we will have to develop theories that provide a basis for predicting what effects a factor will have in any particular set of circumstances. Until we have progressed considerably further in both data collection and theory development we will not be in a position to offer useful advice to jurors.

REFERENCES

Bermant, G. (1986). Two conjectures about the issue of expert testimony. *Law and Human Behavior, 10,* 97–100.

Brigham, J. C., Maass, A., Martinez, D., & Whittenberger, G. (1983). The effect of arousal on facial recognition. *Basic and Applied Social Psychology, 4,* 279–293.

Christianson, S.-A. (1984). The relationship between induced emotional arousal and amnesia. *Scandinavian Journal of Psychology, 25,* 147–160.

Christianson, S.-A., & Nilsson, L.-G. (1984). Functional amnesia as induced by a psychological trauma. *Memory and Cognition, 12,* 142–155.

Clifford, B. R., & Hollin, C. R. (1981). Effects of the type of incident and number of perpetrators on eyewitness memory. *Journal of Applied Psychology, 66,* 364–370.

Clifford, B. R., & Scott, J. (1978). Individual and situational factors in eyewitness testimony. *Journal of Applied Psychology, 63,* 352–359.

Deffenbacher, K. A. (1980). Eyewitness accuracy and confidence: Can we infer anything about their relationship? *Law and Human Behavior, 4,* 243–260.

Deffenbacher, K. A. (1983). The influence of arousal on reliability of testimony. In S. Lloyd-Bostock & B. R. Clifford (Eds.), *Evaluating witness evidence: Recent psychological research and new perspectives* (pp. 235–251). New York: Wiley.

Ellison, K. W., & Buckhout, R. (1981). *Psychology and criminal justice.* New York: Harper & Row.

Federal rules of evidence for United States courts and magistrates. (1975). St. Paul, MN: West Publishing Co.

Frye v. United States. (1923). 293 F. 1013 (D.C. Cir.).

Heuer, L., & Riesberg, D. (1988). *Vivid memories of emotional events: The accuracy of remembered minutiae.* Unpublished manuscript.

Leippe, M. R. (1980). Effects of integrative memorial and cognitive processes on the correspondence of eyewitness accuracy and confidence. *Law and Human Behavior, 4,* 261–274.

Leippe, M. R., Wells, G. L., & Ostrom, T. M. (1978). Crime seriousness as a determinant of accuracy in eyewitness identification. *Journal of Applied Psychology, 63,* 345–351.

Loftus, E. F. (1979). *Eyewitness testimony.* Cambridge, MA: Harvard University Press.

Loftus, E. F. (1983a). Silence is not golden. *American Psychologist, 38,* 564–572.

Loftus, E. F. (1983b). Whose shadow is crooked? *American Psychologist, 38,* 576–577.

Loftus, E. F. (1986). Ten years in the life of an expert witness. *Law and Human Behavior, 10,* 241–263.

Loftus, E. F., & Burns, T. E. (1982). Mental shock can produce retrograde amnesia. *Memory and Cognition, 10,* 318–323.

McCloskey, M., & Egeth, H. (1983a). Eyewitness identification: What can a psychologist tell a jury? *American Psychologist, 38,* 550–563.

McCloskey, M., & Egeth, H. (1983b). A time to speak or a time to keep silence? *American Psychologist, 38,* 573–575.

McCloskey, M., Egeth, H., & McKenna, J. (Eds.). (1986). The ethics of expert testimony [Special issue]. *Law and Human Behavior, 10*(1/2).

Munsterberg, H. (1908). *On the witness stand.* New York: McClure.

People v. McDonald. (1984). 208 Cal. Rptr. 236, 690 P.2d 709.

State v. Chapple. (1983). 135 Ariz. 281, 660 P.2d 1208.

Tooley, V., Brigham, J. C., Maass, A., & Bothwell, R. K. (1987). Facial recognition: Weapon effect and attentional focus. *Journal of Applied Social Psychology, 17,* 845–859.

United States v. Amaral. (1973). 488 F.2d 1148 (9th Cir.).

United States v. Downing. (1985). 753 F.2d 1224 (3rd Cir.), on remand, 609 F. Supp. 784, aff'd, 780 F.2d 1017.

Wells, G. (1984). A reanalysis of the expert testimony issue. In G. Wells & E. F. Loftus (Eds)., *Eyewitness testimony: Psychological perspectives* (pp. 304–314). Cambridge, UK: Cambridge University Press.

Wells, G., & Murray, D. M. (1984). Eyewitness confidence. In G. Wells & E. F. Loftus (Eds.), *Eyewitness testimony: Psychological perspectives* (pp. 155–170). Cambridge, UK: Cambridge University Press.

Woocher, F. D. (1977). Did your eyes deceive you? Expert psychological testimony on the unreliability of eyewitness identification. *Stanford Law Review, 29,* 960–1030.

Yuille, J. C., & Cutshall, J. L. (1986). A case study of eyewitness memory of a crime. *Journal of Applied Psychology, 71,* 291–301.

20

Polygraph Techniques: History, Controversies, and Prospects

John C. Kircher and David C. Raskin

Polygraph techniques for the detection of deception and verification of truthfulness have a long history of use and abuse within the public and private sectors. Polygraph testing has become the source and focus of much debate within the political, legal, and scientific communities. Supporters and critics of polygraph techniques have pointed out many limitations and misapplications of polygraph techniques (e.g., Iacono & Patrick, 1988; Raskin, 1986a, 1988). However, we believe that many of the most vocal critics (e.g., Furedy & Heslegrave, in press; Lykken, 1981, 1988; Saxe, 1987) have overstated the case against the polygraph, in part because of their lack of direct experience with the techniques and their applications (Raskin & Kircher, 1988).

From a scientific and social responsibility perspective, it makes little sense to remain fixated on past problems. It is neither useful nor responsible to simply engage in diatribes against a technique that has a long history of scientific research and extensive recent development and improvements that have proven it to be a valuable tool with positive impacts on law enforcement and the administration of justice (Raskin, 1986a, 1989). Recent research has clearly demonstrated that properly conducted polygraph tests have sufficient reliability and validity to be of considerable value to individuals, the criminal justice process, and society.

In this chapter, we briefly review the historical development of polygraphy and current scientific knowledge concerning the reliability and validity of various polygraph techniques. We discuss the strengths and weaknesses of various approaches and techniques and when their application may or may not be justified on the basis of scientific research. In so doing, we comment on various problems that arise in the field, we describe what has been accomplished toward correcting the problems that have plagued attempts to use psychophysiological methods to assess credibility, and we suggest ways to improve their accuracy and applications.

Polygraphy is one of the oldest areas of research in applied psychology, and its history is distinguished by the stature of those who have worked in the area (e.g., Davis, 1961; Lindsley, 1955; Luria, 1932; see Trovillo, 1939, for a detailed review of the early history). Modern physiological methods for assessing truth and deception began in Italy near the end of the 19th century (Lombroso, 1895), and in the United States, polygraph techniques were developed for use as an investigative tool by the law enforcement community. Early work by Marston (1917) and subsequent improvements by Larson (1932) and Keeler (1933) resulted in a portable

295

polygraph instrument and a general method known as the relevant–irrelevant technique.

RELEVANT–IRRELEVANT TESTS

In the relevant–irrelevant test, two types of questions are presented to the subject. Relevant questions directly address the matter under investigation (e.g., "Did you take that $10,000 from the safe?"), whereas irrelevant questions concern neutral topics, such as the subject's name, place of birth or residence, or simple statements of fact (e.g., "Are you sitting down?"). As in all polygraph deception tests, questions must be answered "Yes" or "No." Respiration, electrodermal, and blood pressure responses to the relevant questions are compared to those produced by the irrelevant questions. If the reactions to the relevant questions are generally stronger, the subject is judged to be deceptive to the relevant questions. On the other hand, if the reactions to the relevant and irrelevant questions are similar in magnitude, the subject is considered truthful to the relevant questions.

The relevant–irrelevant test was originally developed as an aid to law enforcement agencies and the courts. However, from the 1950s until recently, it gained greatest acceptance and application in the commercial sector. By 1986, it was estimated that approximately 2 million U.S. citizens were tested annually as a condition of employment (Raskin, 1986b). Tests that focused on the job applicant's past behaviors, lifestyle, and employment history were used by employers to attempt to minimize the risk of hiring persons who might steal or engage in other behaviors deemed undesirable by the employer. The relevant–irrelevant technique was also used to test employees periodically in order to keep them honest and to reduce the risk of employee theft.

The relevant–irrelevant test gained widespread use in the commercial sector as a preemployment screening device despite the lack of credible evidence that it can distinguish between truthful and deceptive answers with a reasonable degree of accuracy, and there is recent evidence that it does not (Raskin, Kircher, Horowitz, & Honts, 1989). Moreover, the results of such tests are typically used to *predict* employee theft or security risks, which is a much more difficult problem than assessing the veracity of statements made about specific past events (Raskin, 1986b). These problems are compounded by the failure of the technique to include adequate safeguards against errors of concluding that truthful subjects were deceptive on the test (false positive errors); the general lack of training, skill, and competence of the polygraph examiners who conduct the tests; the lack of concern about the welfare and rights of the job applicant; and the coercive nature of the test (Raskin, 1978). Because of these problems, we provided substantial assistance to the U.S. Congress in the drafting and passage of the Polygraph Protection Act of 1988, which essentially banned the use of polygraph techniques for preemployment screening and periodic testing within the commercial sector (Raskin, 1986b).

Several flaws in the relevant–irrelevant technique also argue strongly against its use in criminal investigations (Raskin, 1986a, 1989). Most serious is the naive and transparent rationale underlying the relevant–irrelevant test. Although deceptive individuals are likely to produce relatively strong physiological reactions to the relevant questions and be diagnosed as deceptive, many truthful individuals perceive the relevant questions as more threatening, causing them to react more strongly to them. As a result, the relevant–irrelevant test can be expected to produce highly accurate decisions on deceptive subjects (true positives) and a large percentage of incorrect decisions on truthful subjects (false positives).

A recent laboratory experiment (Raskin, Kircher, Horowitz, & Honts, 1989) confirmed those predictions concerning the relevant–irrelevant test. In this study, some subjects committed a realistic mock theft and others were innocent of the theft. The relevant–irrelevant technique yielded 100% correct decisions on the guilty subjects but only 22% correct decisions on the innocent subjects. In the field, the false positive rate may be even higher since relevant questions have greater significance for innocent suspects of real crimes than for innocent subjects tested about a mock crime.

The use of the relevant–irrelevant technique has declined substantially in recent years, and in most jurisdictions it has fallen into disuse (Office of Technology Assessment [OTA], 1983). The Polygraph Protection Act of 1988 essentially eliminated its widespread use by commercial polygraph examiners. Although it offers little protection against false positive errors and the available scientific research argues against its use, the relevant–irrelevant technique is still occasionally employed by polygraph examiners in some federal programs (e.g., the Federal Bureau of Investigation and the National Security Agency). However, some jurisdictions have recognized the limitations of the relevant–irrelevant technique and have either prohibited its use as evidence (New Mexico Rule of Evidence 707) or its use for any purpose (Utah licensing regulations).

CONTROL QUESTION TESTS

To overcome the weaknesses of the relevant–irrelevant technique, Reid (1947) devised the control question test. The control question test differs from the relevant–irrelevant test in that physiological reactions to relevant questions are compared to those produced by control questions. Control questions are designed to arouse the concern of innocent subjects, and it is expected that they will react more strongly to them than to the relevant questions. For example, if the subject were suspected of a theft, a control question might be, "During the first 22 years of your life, did you ever take something that did not belong to you?" Control questions are intentionally vague, cover a long period of the subject's life, and include acts that most individuals have committed but are too embarrassed or afraid to admit during a properly conducted polygraph examination. During the pretest review of all questions to be asked on the test, control questions are introduced by the polygraph examiner in such a way that the subject will initially or eventually answer "No" to each of them.

Innocent subjects answer the relevant questions truthfully but are likely to be deceptive or uncertain about their truthfulness when answering the control questions. Therefore, innocent subjects are expected to react more strongly to the control questions than to the relevant questions. In contrast, guilty subjects are expected to be concerned about failing the test because their answers to the relevant questions are deceptive, and they are likely to show stronger reactions to the relevant questions. For a more detailed description of the control question test, see Raskin (1989).

Recently, the term *control question* has been the subject of controversy and confusion in the scientific literature (Furedy & Heslegrave, in press; Lykken, 1979; Raskin & Kircher, in press; Raskin & Podlesny, 1979). Control questions are misnamed because they do not function as controls in the strict scientific sense of the term, that is, they do not elicit reactions that indicate how subjects would react if their answers to the relevant questions were truthful. Rather, they may provide an estimate of how innocent subjects would react if their answers to relevant questions were actually deceptive. The fundamental issue is not whether control questions function as controls in the usual scientific sense, but if they elicit larger reactions from innocent subjects than relevant questions and thereby reduce the risk of false positive errors.

Accuracy of the Control Question Test

Prior to 1970, there had been virtually no scientific research on the reliability and validity of the control question technique for criminal investigation. The first study was conducted in our laboratory at the University of Utah (Barland & Raskin, 1975). By 1983, the Office of Technology Assessment (1983) had identified 14 analog studies and 10 field studies of the control question technique, some of which can reasonably be used to make inferences about the accuracy of control question tests in the field.

The accuracy of diagnoses made by polygraph examiners in actual criminal cases must be evaluated against an independent criterion of truth or deception. Two types of criteria have been used in field research on polygraph validity: judgments of guilt and innocence made by a panel of experts who reviewed all of the available evidence without the results of the polygraph tests, or confessions that inculpated or exculpated the examinee (Raskin, 1987).

The major problem with most field studies is the difficulty of establishing whether the subject was actually truthful or deceptive on the test. Disagreement between the polygraph outcome and the criterion could indicate that the polygraph test was incorrect or that the criterion was incorrect. Even when there is agreement between the decision by the polygraph examiner and the criterion, it is possible that both the test outcome and the criterion were incorrect. To remedy this problem, one recent field study required that the confessions be independently substantiated by compelling physical evidence (Raskin, Kircher, Honts, & Horowitz, 1988).

As is common in all fields of natural science, psychologists have often used laboratory simulations to assess the accuracy of polygraph tests. In the typical laboratory analog study, subjects are randomly assigned to guilty and innocent treatment groups. Guilty subjects commit a mock crime, such as a theft, and innocent subjects are given a general description of the crime but do not enact it. Subjects in both conditions are instructed to deny having committed the crime and are motivated to appear truthful on the polygraph test, usually by the offer of a cash reward for achieving a truthful result (Kircher, Horowitz, & Raskin, 1988; Raskin, 1989).

The major advantage of laboratory paradigms is that the actual truthful or deceptive status of subjects (ground truth) is known. Under these circumstances, it is possible to determine the accuracy of decisions made by the original examiners and by blind evaluators of the polygraph charts. The major problem with analog studies is that the motivational structure of the typical field polygraph examination is difficult to simulate in the laboratory (Podlesny & Raskin, 1977). An individual suspected of having committed a real crime is likely to be more concerned about the outcome of the test and the consequences of failing the test than a person who participated in a mock crime. Recent research that compared data obtained from laboratory and field situations suggests that patterns of physiological responses are qualitatively very similar in the two contexts. However, in field settings, truthful as well as deceptive subjects seem to show heightened reactions to relevant questions (Raskin, Kircher, Honts, & Horowitz, 1988).

Field studies and laboratory simulations have limitations, and neither type of study by itself can answer all of the questions about polygraph test validity. However, to the extent that both types of research yield results that converge on similar detection rates, we can be confident in our estimates of test accuracy. Despite the specific problems and limitations of existing field studies and the heated debates about their scientific merits (e.g., Lykken, 1979, 1988; Raskin & Kircher, 1988; Raskin & Podlesny, 1979), a reasonable approximation can be obtained by combining results from field studies that shared the objective of assessing polygraph test accuracy (OTA, 1983). Table 20-1 presents combined results of the 10 field studies that the OTA report considered to have some degree of scientific merit. Since these results were obtained by examiners whose competence ranged widely, they probably underestimate the accuracy of polygraph examinations conducted by well-trained examiners in criminal investigation.

Table 20.1 also presents results obtained in laboratory simulations. Because laboratory experiments are often designed to investigate various theoretical and applied issues, their methods may not be representative of standard field conditions, and it probably is not justified to aggregate detection rates across all experimental conditions (Kircher, Horowitz, & Raskin, 1988). Therefore, Table 20.1 presents the mean detection rates obtained only from standard guilty and innocent treatment conditions in six analog studies, five of which met our criteria for having established reasonable facsimiles of real crimes and having used standard field techniques (Kircher, Horowitz, & Raskin, 1988). We also included the results of a recent study by Patrick and Iacono (1989) that may have met those criteria but was published subsequent to our meta-analysis. Their study was included even though

Table 20.1 Mean Percentage Correct Decisions in Field and Laboratory Studies of the Control Question Technique

	Guilty	Innocent
Field studies (OTA, 1983)[a]	90	80
Laboratory studies[b]	93	87
Field study (Raskin, Kircher, Honts, & Horowitz, 1988)	95	96

Note. Percentage correct decisions was obtained by excluding inconclusive outcomes and calculating percent correct using only definite decisions, Correct/(Correct + Wrong).

[a]The field studies are Barland & Raskin (1976), Bersh (1969), Davidson (1979), Horvath (1977), Horvath & Reid (1971), Hunter & Ash (1973), Kleinmuntz & Szucko (1984), Raskin (1976), Slowik & Buckley (1975), and Wicklander & Hunter (1975).

[b]The laboratory studies are Ginton, Netzer, Elaad, & Ben-Shakhar (1982), Kircher & Raskin (1988), Patrick & Iacono (1989), Podlesny & Raskin (1978), Raskin & Hare (1978), and Rovner, Raskin, & Kircher (1979).

inadequate techniques may have been used by the two commercial polygraph examiners whom they hired to conduct the polygraph examinations.

The results of the laboratory and field studies presented in Table 20.1 converge on similar accuracy rates for guilty and innocent subjects, and they suggest that the accuracy of the control question technique is approximately 90% on guilty subjects and 85% on innocent subjects. Although these figures indicate that the control question technique has sufficient validity to justify its use in forensic settings, accuracy on innocent subjects is somewhat lower than on guilty subjects. Since it is less likely for a guilty subject to beat the test than it is for an innocent subject to fail the test, confidence in truthful polygraph outcomes is greater and more weight should be given to truthful as compared to deceptive test results on criminal suspects (Raskin, 1986a).

The polygraph examiners in the 10 field studies had a broad range of experience and expertise and their techniques also varied substantially. Better-trained and highly experienced field polygraph examiners and scientists probably achieve higher accuracies than those reported by OTA, whereas poorly trained and inexperienced examiners probably achieve lower overall accuracy than indicated in the OTA study. However, the field situation is improving. Legislation recently enacted by the U.S. Congress dramatically restricted the use of polygraph techniques by private corporations and has substantially reduced the number of poorly trained and incompetent field polygraph examiners. The majority of remaining polygraph examiners are employed by federal, state, and local law enforcement and investigative agencies. In general, they are better educated and trained than those whose primary source of income had been derived from preemployment and periodic tests of employees in the private sector.

Recent Congressional and administrative reviews of the use of polygraph techniques by the federal government have resulted in the establishment of research programs and training centers that are administered by psychophysiologists with appropriate academic credentials and practical experience. This should help to ensure that their research is well-designed and meaningful and that graduates of their training programs will be more sophisticated in the administration of polygraph tests and better qualified to interpret the physiological recordings. Some federal and state agencies have also begun to use computers to quantify physiological responses to test questions and to render objective, quantified diagnoses of truth and deception. The implementation of computer techniques promotes standardization of testing procedures and interpretations and provides more powerful and objective analyses of the physiological data (Kircher & Raskin, 1988; Raskin, Horowitz, & Kircher, 1989).

The detection rates reported by OTA were obtained from tests conducted by field polygraph examiners and laboratory researchers whose training, competence, and experience in administering the tests and interpreting the polygraph recordings varied greatly. Our recent field study with the U.S. Secret Service on the accuracy of control question tests (Raskin, Kircher, Honts, & Horowitz, 1988) suggests that the data reported in Table 20.1 provide conservative estimates of the detection rates that may be achieved when the tests are performed by well-trained examiners. This study sampled cases that included polygraph examinations in criminal investigations conducted during a 3-year period beginning in 1983. Polygraph examinations were selected if they met two criteria. The first criterion was a confession that inculpated or exculpated one or more suspects who had been given a polygraph test. The second criterion required corroboration of the confession by physical evidence, such as seizure of counterfeit money described in the confession or a fingerprint of the suspect on a forged check. Using these criteria, subjects were classified as confirmed truthful or deceptive on one or more of the relevant questions on the test.

The polygraph test outcomes were classified on the basis of the interpretations by the original examiners and also by blind evaluations performed by other Secret Service examiners. Accuracy of the test outcomes was evaluated at the level of individual questions, and the results are presented in Tables 20.1 and 20.2. The original examiners were highly accurate on confirmed truthful and deceptive responses to individual relevant questions. Their false negative rate was 5%, and their false positive rate was only 4%. Accuracy of decisions by blind interpreters on confirmed deceptive subjects was similar to that achieved by the original examiners, but blind evaluations were somewhat less accurate on confirmed truthful subjects.

It is possible that the original examiners outperformed the blind interpreters because they may have used information in addition to the physiological recordings, such as the case facts and the subject's verbal and nonverbal behavior. However, the results of our recent follow-up study (Raskin, Horowitz, & Kircher, 1989) showed that diagnoses derived from computer analyses of the physiological recordings were more accurate than diagnoses made by the original Secret Service examiners, suggesting that the results of the 1988 study were based solely on the physiological recordings. The results of both of these studies also indicate that the original examiners, the blind interpreters, and the computer methods had greatest difficulty in classifying responses from subjects who were confirmed as deceptive to one or more relevant questions and were also confirmed as truthful to other relevant questions on the same test.

In general, our field data demonstrate that well-trained and competent polygraph examiners are capable of producing very high levels of accuracy. The data also suggest that it is more difficult to distinguish between truth and deception when the suspect is deceptive to only some of the relevant questions. Laboratory studies by Podlesny and McGehee (1987) and Barland, Honts, and Barger (1989) produced similar results when different issues or roles were tested simultaneously. Consequently, mixed issue tests should be avoided, when possible.

Applications of Control Question Tests

The control question test is currently the most widely used technique in criminal investigations and judicial proceedings (Raskin, 1986a). Almost every major federal, state, and local law enforcement agency employs the control question technique to reduce the number of suspects so that limited resources can be focused on likely suspects, that is, those who have failed polygraph examinations. Control question tests are also used to examine prime suspects and people formally charged with criminal acts.

In many jurisdictions, prosecutors and defense attorneys make informal agreements that if the suspect or defendant passes a polygraph examination from a competent and well-qualified examiner, the prosecutor will seriously consider dismissing the charges. Alternatively, prior to the conduct of a polygraph examination, prosecutors and defense attorneys in most jurisdictions may enter into formal

Table 20.2 Percentage Outcomes on Individual Relevant Questions for Original Examiners and
Blind Interpreters

	n	Correct	Incorrect	Inconclusive	Correct decisions
Confirmed deceptive					
Original examiners	76	79	4	17	95
Blind interpreters	83	65	4	31	94
Confirmed truthful					
Original examiners	62	76	3	21	96
Blind interpreters	68	52	9	39	85

stipulations that the results will be admissible as evidence at trial. Under these arrangements, costly trials are often avoided by guilty pleas or dismissals based in part on the results of polygraph tests. Polygraph tests are sometimes used by prosecutors to assess the veracity of individuals involved in the crime who may testify for the prosecution in exchange for immunity or reduced charges if they demonstrate their truthfulness on the polygraph test. Also, some courts use polygraph evidence in postconviction proceedings, such as sentencing, and when considering motions for new trials. A comprehensive compilation and discussion of the federal and state case law and legislation concerning the admissibility of polygraph evidence and the polygraph examiner licensing regulations in the United States has recently been provided by Morris (1989).

NATIONAL SECURITY AND THE POLYGRAPH

National security programs use polygraph tests primarily to screen applicants for access to classified information and to assist in identifying individuals who have made unauthorized disclosures of sensitive information. Some of the arguments against the use of polygraphs in commercial preemployment contexts also apply to national security programs that use them to assess general lifestyle and suitability for employment. Although government polygraph examiners are generally well-trained and usually exercise reasonable standards of care in the administration of their tests, there is insufficient research on the reliability, validity, and utility of polygraph examinations for national security screening. Furthermore, the accuracy of such tests is likely to be low when the issues are vague, and it may be difficult to formulate adequate control questions for sophisticated subjects who have been tested many times.

Tests conducted during investigations of espionage and specific unauthorized disclosures are generally similar in purpose, structure, and probable accuracy to tests conducted in investigative and forensic settings. The relevant questions address specific, well-defined activities and events, and the test protocols and procedures developed for criminal investigations are readily applied to that situation. Therefore, such national security tests do not suffer from the same limitations inherent in screening tests.

CONCEALED KNOWLEDGE TESTS

The concealed knowledge or guilty knowledge test is another method for detecting deception (Lykken, 1959; Raskin, 1989). In contrast to the relevant–irrelevant and control question tests, the concealed knowledge test does not attempt to directly assess the veracity of a person's statements concerning knowledge of or involvement in a crime. Instead, this technique is used to determine if the subject is concealing knowledge of details of the crime that would be known only to a guilty person.

The test for concealed knowledge consists of a series of multiple-choice questions, each of which addresses a different aspect of the crime. For example, if the subject is suspected of stealing a ring, a question on the test might be, "Regarding the type of ring that was stolen, do you know if it was: (a) a ruby ring, (b) a gold wedding ring, (c) a pearl ring, (d) a diamond ring, (e) a sapphire ring, or (f) a silver and turquoise ring?" (Podlesny & Raskin, 1978). A guilty subject who knows the correct alternative is expected to show a relatively strong physiological reaction to that item. However, an innocent subject who has no specific knowledge is not expected to respond differentially to correct and incorrect alternatives.

Typically, only electrodermal responses to the questions are scored. Reactions to the first alternatives are not evaluated because the first item in a series typically produces a large orienting reaction that is independent of any specific knowledge that may be possessed by the subject. Thus, for one multiple-choice question, the probability that the subject's strongest electrodermal response will occur by chance to the correct alternative is 1 in 5, or 20%. With several multiple-choice questions, the chance probability that a subject who has no concealed knowledge will consistently react most strongly to the correct alternatives is vanishingly small (for a detailed description of the concealed knowledge test, see Raskin, 1989).

Accuracy of the Concealed Knowledge Test

The major strength of the concealed knowledge test is the protection it provides against false positive outcomes. Using conventional scoring rules (Lykken, 1959), the theoretical probability of a false positive is between 8% and 10%, depending on whether five or six questions are presented. However, empirical investigations of the concealed knowledge technique have generally produced false positive rates on the order of only 1%, which is puzzling. Thus, laboratory research has shown the concealed knowledge test to be more accurate on innocent subjects than theory predicts.

As with any type of decision problem, attempts to reduce the risk of one type of error usually increase the risk of another type of error. Reducing false positive errors by increasing test length or raising the cutoff score for a decision necessarily increases the probability that a guilty person will defeat the test (false negative error). Laboratory studies that used conventional scoring and decision cutoffs with the concealed knowledge technique indicate that the false negative rate is approximately 16%, and there are no data from field studies to estimate the validity of the technique in actual criminal investigations (Raskin, 1989).

Application of the Concealed Knowledge Test

There are several practical problems that prevent widespread use of the concealed knowledge test, some of which concern the circumstances surrounding many crimes. Details of a crime that may seem quite distinctive and memorable to an investigator or polygraph examiner may have gone unnoticed or been forgotten by the perpetrator because of emotional stress, confusion, inattention, or intoxication during the crime. It is often a difficult task for an investigator or polygraph examiner to identify details of a crime that are likely to be recognized by the guilty suspect during the test. Thus, the false negative rate of concealed knowledge tests in criminal investigation is likely to be higher than the 16% estimated from laboratory analog studies.

The utility of the concealed knowledge test is also limited because innocent subjects frequently are informed about the details of the crime prior to taking a polygraph test. It is common practice for police investigators to disclose details of crimes to suspects in the process of interrogation, news media publicize the details of many crimes, and defense attorneys usually discuss the details of police reports and allegations with their clients. Thus, the majority of criminal suspects have knowledge of the critical crime information and are not suitable subjects for concealed knowledge tests.

Many criminal investigations do not lend themselves to concealed knowledge tests because there is no special information that is unknown to potential polygraph subjects. Such situations include allegations of forcible sexual assault when the accused claims that the sexual acts were consensual, claims of self-defense in physical assault and homicide cases, and crimes in which the suspect admits having been present at the scene but denies any criminal participation. Because of its high rates of false negative errors and inapplicability in most investigative situations, the concealed knowledge test is not likely to become a viable substitute for control question tests.

RECENT DEVELOPMENTS
AND FUTURE PROSPECTS

As a result of efforts by scientists and policy makers, many of the inappropriate and most objectionable applications of polygraph tests have been eliminated or severely curtailed by recent legislation and administrative decisions. Along with the reduction in undesirable applications, a large proportion of the least competent polygraph practitioners have been forced to leave the field. This has had a salutary effect on the level of competence and practice in the field, and it has also fostered an increase in research funds and growth of research programs in universities and government agencies. These programs have also served to improve the training and competence of government and law enforcement polygraph examiners.

A second set of beneficial effects has been the development and implementation of computer techniques and improvements in physiological measures and examination procedures. These improved methods not only have enhanced the reliability and accuracy of polygraph tests, but they have raised the quality of training and practice, especially in agencies such as the Secret Service, the U.S. Department of Defense, the Royal Canadian Mounted Police, and state, provincial, and local law enforcement in the United States and Canada.

New question structures and examination procedures are being developed to overcome some of the problems that have plagued traditional control question techniques. The most promising of these is the directed lie test that has been developed at the University of Utah (Honts & Raskin, 1988; Raskin, 1989; Raskin, Kircher, Horowitz, & Honts, 1989). Instead of relying on the effectiveness of traditional control questions that require special skills on the part of the polygraph examiner and may be somewhat intrusive and ineffective with some subjects, the directed lie test employs a more straightforward approach that has clear face validity and is easier to standardize.

The directed lie test includes questions to which the subject is instructed to lie. These directed lie questions are introduced after the administration of a number test in which the subject had chosen a number and was then instructed to lie about the number that was chosen. The subject had been told that the number test enables the examiner to determine the subject's characteristic response patterns when lying and when answering truthfully. The examiner then explains that the directed lie questions will ensure that the subject will be correctly classified as truthful or deceptive on the subsequent polygraph test. These procedures reduce the number of false positive errors (Honts & Raskin, 1988), and they also increase standardization and ease of administration of polygraph examinations (Raskin, 1989).

SUMMARY

The various applications of polygraph techniques have engendered substantial debate and disagreement among scientists, practitioners, legal commentators, and politicians. Some of these problems are rooted in premature and naive conceptualizations of the psychophysiological bases of the tests and their interpretation. The acceptance of polygraph techniques has also been hindered by a historical lack of adequate training and competence among polygraph practitioners. Other issues seem to have grown out of differing opinions about the social desirability and public acceptance of using polygraphs in criminal investigations, and, more significantly, the widespread uses of polygraph techniques for selection and retention of employees, which rapidly increased between 1970 and 1985.

A scientific poll of the U.S. public conducted by the Associated Press ("Most Americans," 1986) indicated general acceptance of polygraph testing in criminal investigations and national security programs accompanied by strong negative attitudes toward their use by private employers for employee selection and retention. The latter applications were severely criticized at hearings on the Polygraph Protection Act of 1988 (Raskin, 1986b), the passage of which has greatly reduced the extent of polygraph abuses and the number of poorly trained and incompetent polygraph practitioners. Hopefully, the focus of the debate about polygraphs can now shift to the scientific and practical issues surrounding their applications in criminal investigations and national security programs.

Progressive polygraph training programs present current scientific knowledge and have generally upgraded their training, but many polygraph schools and their graduates continue to rely on outmoded approaches and misunderstandings of the psychological processes and physiological mechanisms (see Raskin, 1986a). Unfortunately, polygraph myths are continually reinforced by inaccurate descriptions of current techniques promulgated by members of the scientific community, who frequently rely on such misdescriptions when attacking current applications of the polygraph (see Furedy & Heslegrave, in press; Raskin & Kircher, in press).

Other aspects of the polygraph debate center on differing interpretations of the adequacy of the methods and the results obtained in research on the accuracy of polygraph examinations (e.g., Iacono & Patrick, 1988; Kircher, Horowitz, & Raskin, 1988; Lykken, 1988; Raskin, 1987, 1988; Raskin & Kircher, 1988). Historically, polygraph research has lagged behind applications of the techniques (Barland & Raskin, 1973). The first scientific study of the control question test was conducted at the University of Utah 25 years after Reid introduced it to the polygraph field (Barland & Raskin, 1975; Reid, 1947).

Until recently, most polygraph research had been conducted in a laboratory context, and the quality and amount of field research was minimal and was based on questionable methods and procedures (OTA, 1983; Raskin, 1987). However, recent field research seems to indicate that control question tests can be quite accurate when performed and interpreted by skilled examiners (Raskin, Kircher, Horowitz, & Honts, 1989). As more high-quality field research becomes available, we hope that the debate about test accuracy will become less acrimonious and more productive.

We expect that further refinements in the construction and administration of polygraph examinations coupled with advances in physiological recording techniques and computer technology will contribute to increases in accuracy and greater acceptance and applications of polygraph techniques in law enforcement, judicial proceedings, and government programs. We have little doubt that carefully structured and thoughtful polygraph programs will provide greater benefits to society in the years to come.

REFERENCES

Barland, G. H., Honts, C. R., & Barger, S. D. (1989). *Studies of the accuracy of security screening polygraph examinations.* Anniston, AL: Department of Defense Polygraph Institute.

Barland, G. H., & Raskin, D. C. (1973). Detection of deception. In W. F. Prokasy & D. C. Raskin (Eds.), *Electrodermal activity in psychological research* (pp. 417–477). New York: Academic Press.

Barland, G. H., & Raskin, D. C. (1975). An evaluation of field techniques in detection of deception. *Psychophysiology, 12,* 321–330.

Barland, G. H., & Raskin, D. C. (1976). *Validity and reliability of polygraph examinations of criminal suspects* (Report to the National Institute of Law Enforcement and Criminal Justice, Contract 75-NI-99-001). Salt Lake City: University of Utah, Department of Psychology.

Bersh, P. J. (1969). A validation study of polygraph examiner judgments. *Journal of Applied Psychology, 53,* 399–403.

Davidson, W. A. (1979). Validity and reliability of the cardio activity monitor. *Polygraph, 8,* 104–111.

Davis, R. C. (1961). Physiological responses as a means of evaluating information. In A. D. Biderman & H. Zimmer (Eds.), *The manipulation of human behavior* (pp. 142–168). New York: Wiley.

Furedy, J. J., & Heslegrave, R. J. (in press). The forensic use of the polygraph: A psychophysiological analysis of current trends and future prospects. In P. K. Ackles, J. R. Jennings, & M. G. H. Coles (Eds.), *Advances in psychophysiology* (Vol. 4). London: Jessica Kingsley.

Ginton, A., Netzer, D., Elaad, E., & Ben-Shakhar, G. (1982). A method for evaluating the use of the polygraph in a real-life situation. *Journal of Applied Psychology, 67,* 131–137.

Honts, C. R., & Raskin, D. C. (1988). A field study of the validity of the directed lie control question. *Journal of Police Science and Administration, 16,* 56–61.

Horvath, F. S. (1977). The effect of selected variables on interpretation of polygraph records. *Journal of Applied Psychology, 62,* 127–136.

Horvath, F. S., & Reid, J. E. (1971). The reliability of polygraph examiner diagnosis of truth and deception. *Journal of Criminal Law, Criminology, and Police Science, 62,* 276–281.

Hunter, F. L., & Ash, P. (1973). The accuracy and consistency of polygraph examiners' diagnoses. *Journal of Police Science and Administration, 1,* 370–375.

Iacono, W. G., & Patrick, C. J. (1988). Assessing deception: Polygraph techniques. In R. Rogers (Ed.), *Clinical assessment of malingering and deception* (pp. 205–233). New York: Guilford.

Keeler, L. (1933). Scientific methods of criminal detection with the polygraph. *Kansas Bar Association, 2,* 22–31.

Kircher, J. C., Horowitz, S. W., & Raskin, D. C. (1988). Meta-analysis of mock crime studies of the control question polygraph technique. *Law and Human Behavior, 12,* 79–90.

Kircher, J. C., & Raskin, D. C. (1988). Human versus computerized evaluations of polygraph data in a laboratory setting. *Journal of Applied Psychology, 73,* 291–302.

Kleinmuntz, B., & Szucko, J. (1984). A field study of the fallibility of polygraphic lie detection. *Nature, 308,* 449–450.

Larson, J. A. (1932). *Lying and its detection.* Chicago, IL: University of Chicago Press.

Lindsley, D. B. (1955). The psychology of lie detection. In G. J. Dudycha (Ed.), *Psychology for law enforcement officers* (pp. 89–125). Springfield, IL: Charles C Thomas.

Lombroso, C. (1895). *L'homme criminel* (2nd Ed.). Paris: Felix Alcan.

Luria, A. R. (1932). *The nature of human conflicts.* New York: Liverwright.

Lykken, D. T. (1959). The GSR in the detection of guilt. *Journal of Applied Psychology, 43,* 385–388.

Lykken, D. T. (1979). The detection of deception. *Psychological Bulletin, 86,* 47–53.

Lykken, D. T. (1981). *A tremor in the blood.* New York: McGraw-Hill.

Lykken, D. T. (1988). The case against polygraph testing. In A. Gale (Ed.), *The polygraph test: Lies, truth, and science* (pp. 111–125). London: Sage.

Marston, W. M. (1917). Systolic blood pressure symptoms of deception. *Journal of Experimental Psychology, 2,* 117–163.

Morris, R. A. (1989). The admissibility of evidence derived from hypnosis and polygraphy. In D. C. Raskin (Ed.), *Psychological methods in criminal investigation and evidence* (pp. 333–376). New York: Springer.

"Most Americans wouldn't object to taking lie detector tests." (1986, March 4). *Deseret News* (Salt Lake City, UT), p. A-6.

Office of Technology Assessment [OTA]. (1983). *Scientific validity of polygraph testing: A research review and evaluation.* Washington, DC: U.S. Government Printing Office.

Patrick, C. J., & Iacono, W. G. (1989). Psychopathy, threat, and polygraph test accuracy. *Journal of Applied Psychology, 74,* 347–355.

Podlesny, J. A., & McGehee, C. M. (1987). Investigative detection of deception: Role discrimination with a general question technique. *Psychophysiology, 24,* 605–606 (abstract).

Podlesny, J. A., & Raskin, D. C. (1977). Physiological measures and the detection of deception. *Psychological Bulletin, 84,* 782–799.

Podlesny, J. A., & Raskin, D. C. (1978). Effectiveness of techniques and physiological measures in the detection of deception. *Psychophysiology, 15,* 344–358.

Raskin, D. C. (1976). *Reliability of chart interpretation and sources of errors in polygraph examinations* (Report to the National Institute of Law Enforcement and Criminal Justice, Contract 75-NI-99-001). Salt Lake City: University of Utah, Department of Psychology.

Raskin, D. C. (1978, September 19). Statement presented at hearings on S. 1845, *Polygraph Control and Civil Liberties Protection Act,* Committee on the Judiciary, United States Senate.

Raskin, D. C. (1986a). The polygraph in 1986: Scientific, professional, and legal issues surrounding applications and acceptance of polygraph evidence. *Utah Law Review, 1986,* 29–74.

Raskin, D. C. (1986b, April 23). Statement presented at hearings on S. 1815, *Polygraph Protection Act of 1985,* Committee on Labor and Human Resources, United States Senate.

Raskin, D. C. (1987). Methodological issues in estimating polygraph accuracy in field applications. *Canadian Journal of Behavioural Science, 19,* 389–404.

Raskin, D. C. (1988). Does science support polygraph testing? In A. Gale (Ed.), *The polygraph test: Lies, truth, and science* (pp. 96–110). London: Sage.

Raskin, D. C. (1989). Polygraph techniques for the detection of deception. In D. C. Raskin (Ed.), *Psychological methods in criminal investigation and evidence* (pp. 247–296). New York: Springer.

Raskin, D. C., & Hare, R. D. (1978). Psychopathy and detection of deception in a prison population. *Psychophysiology, 15,* 126–136.

Raskin, D. C., Horowitz, S. W., & Kircher, J. C. (1989). *Computerized analysis of polygraph out-*

comes in criminal investigation. (Contract TSS 86-18, U.S. Secret Service). Salt Lake City: University of Utah, Department of Psychology.

Raskin, D. C., & Kircher, J. C. (1988). The validity of Lykken's criticisms: Fact or fancy? *Jurimetrics, 27,* 271–277.

Raskin, D. C., & Kircher, J. C. (in press). Comments on Furedy and Heslegrave: Misconceptions, misdescriptions, and misdirections. In P. K. Ackles, J. R. Jennings, & M. G. H. Coles (Eds.), *Advances in psychophysiology* (Vol. 4). London: Jessica Kingsley.

Raskin, D. C., Kircher, J. C., Honts, C. R., & Horowitz, S. W. (1988). *A study of the validity of polygraph examinations in criminal investigation.* (Grant No. 85-IJ-CX-0040, National Institute of Justice). Salt Lake City: University of Utah, Department of Psychology.

Raskin, D. C., Kircher, J. C., Horowitz, S. W., & Honts, C. R. (1989). Recent laboratory and field research on polygraph techniques. In J. C. Yuille (Ed.), *Credibility assessment* (pp. 1–24). Dordrecht, The Netherlands: Kluwer.

Raskin, D. C., & Podlesny, J. A. (1979). Truth and deception: A reply to Lykken. *Psychological Bulletin, 86,* 54–59.

Reid, J. E. (1947). A revised questioning technique in lie detection tests. *Journal of Criminal Law, Criminology, and Police Science, 37,* 542–547.

Rovner, L. I., Raskin, D. C., & Kircher, J. C. (1979). Effects of information and practice on detection of deception. *Psychophysiology, 16,* 197–198 (abstract).

Saxe, L. (1987). Transcript of testimony in *Commonwealth of Massachusetts v. Rosenberg, Otero, and Mendes.* Criminal Nos. 86-4257, 86-4201, 85-2858, Superior Court, Cambridge, MA.

Slowik, S. M., & Buckley, J. P. (1975). Relative accuracy of polygraph examiner diagnosis of respiration, blood pressure, and GSR recordings. *Journal of Police Science and Administration, 3,* 305–309.

Trovillo, P. V. (1939). A history of lie detection. *Journal of Criminal Law, Criminology, and Police Science, 29,* 848–881; *30,* 104–119.

Wicklander, D. E., & Hunter, F. L. (1975). The influence of auxiliary sources of information in polygraph diagnoses. *Journal of Police Science and Administration, 3,* 405–409.

21

Controversy: The Fight-or-Flight Response *in* Homo scientificus

David T. Lykken

I became interested in polygraphy in the 1950s through an association with my university's campus police chief, "Chick" Hanscomb, one of the Old Guard of polygraphers trained by the great polygrapher Leonarde Keeler himself. I am a psychophysiologist, and polygraphic interrogation is an example of applied (misapplied) psychophysiology. Hanscomb believed that, through recordings of peripheral physiological responses, it was possible to detect lying with high accuracy: "Most of the boys talk about 99 + % accuracy, Dave, but I try to be more conservative. I know *my* conclusions are right at least 95% of the time."

I thought then, as I do now, that these claims were psychologically implausible. We cannot distinguish even such radically different emotions as fear and anger with much better than chance accuracy from autonomic measurements alone. Given the wide individual differences in emotional reactivity, and the equally wide variation in peripheral accompaniments of emotion, it seemed to me futile to hope to distinguish the guilty fear of detection shown by a liar from the fear reaction that an innocent and truthful person might show in response to an accusatory question. As most of us know from personal experience, truthfully denying a false accusation can be accompanied by a kind of self-conscious guilty feeling. The idea that real guilt and neurotic guilt will produce reliably different polygraphic signatures—different patterns of changes in blood pressure or respiration or palmar skin resistance—seemed ludicrous to me.

Those early users of polygraphy were police investigators whose main interest was in obtaining a confession. Polygraphers succeed in obtaining confessions from a significant proportion of guilty suspects and, unfortunately, from a few innocent suspects as well, persons who feel all hope is gone once the lie detector has denounced them. In a landmark study of Royal Canadian Mounted Police polygraphers in Vancouver, Iacono and Patrick (1988) have clarified how it is that experienced polygraph examiners, some of whom have given thousands of these deeply flawed tests over the years, can honestly believe that their methods are as accurate as fingerprints in separating the guilty from the innocent. Iacono and Patrick found that virtually the only way in which polygraphers get definite feedback about the validity of a test is through these occasional confessions. But confessions result from interrogations administered when a test has been scored as "deception indicated." Therefore, the test just given will necessarily be verified as correct whenever there is a confession.

Sometimes a prior test is simultaneously verified by the confession, a test given to another suspect in the same crime. But these prior tests will have been scored as truthful because, if they were not, the suspects who confessed would not have been tested. Therefore, the only tests verified as truthful will be ones the examiner had previously scored correctly. Since criterion data are rarely available for tests that are in error, this occasional feedback that an examiner receives seems to indicate almost perfect validity for his methods. It would do so even if he were actually performing at a chance level of accuracy and were wrong about half of the time!

It has long been known that human judges overestimate their own accuracy, fail to seek or notice negative evidence, and code and retain feedback data as frequency rather than as probability of confirmation. Einhorn and Hogarth (1978) show how this "illusion of validity" is commonly learned and maintained in real world decision making. Their analysis indicates that experienced polygraphers would probably be grossly overconfident even if their accuracy feedback were random and unselective. Provided as they are instead with sanitized feedback from which all the bad news has been systematically excluded, polygraph examiners should not be derided for their delusions of infallibility. They, too, are victims of their delusive trade.

Yet, in 1960, I felt that, if the "20th century witchcraft" of polygraphy (former Senator Sam Ervin's phrase) succeeds in leading guilty suspects to confess, the self-delusion of the small fraternity of police polygraphers was relatively harmless. By the 1970s, however, polygraphy had changed from a forensic backwater into an industry of alarming proportions. Polygraphers in private practice were doing pre-employment screening of applicants for jobs in retail, banking, trucking, and other industries and, most pernicious, "solving" for employers cases of specific thefts or other employee misconduct. In these trials-by-polygraph, conducted without consideration of due process, the polygrapher served as prosecutor, judge, and jury. The hapless employee who made the polygraph's pens dance most vigorously was often punished more severely than the usual first-offender found guilty by a court of law: He or she lost his or her job, character, and perhaps all hope of further employment in a chosen profession.

By 1975 the lie detector had been a part of American mythology for more than 50 years, and polygraphy had become a big business, outpacing in dollar volume most other categories of applied psychology. All of the federal security agencies relied heavily on polygraphy for screening personnel. In many states it was difficult to get an entry-level job without first passing a polygraph test. Although polygraph evidence was not generally admissible in U.S. courts, a large loophole existed in many jurisdictions—a loophole through which criminal defendants were being sent to prison every year. In cases where prosecutors had a suspect but were unable to assemble enough admissible evidence to justify going to trial, they were offering deals: "If you pass a polygraph test, we'll drop the charges. But you must agree in advance that we can use the evidence against you if you fail the test." Courts understandably are inclined to admit any evidence stipulated to by both parties. My first experience as an expert witness involved just such a case.

THE CASE OF THE SELF-INVALIDATING LIE TEST

The defendant, Sam, had met the plaintiff, Mary, in the bar of a Phoenix motel where both were staying on business. According to Sam, they stayed until the bar closed. They then went to Mary's room where they had sexual intercourse. Sam returned to his own room about 4 a.m. carrying with him, in Mary's handwriting, her home phone number in anticipation of a future meeting. About 6 a.m., Mary called first the local newspaper, then the Phoenix police, saying she had been raped. Her story was that she had left the bar with Sam, who walked her to her room. She had invited him in because he needed to use the toilet; once inside he had threatened to choke her and, by this threat, had his way with her. Mary's story and her other behavior led the prosecutor to doubt that he could convict Sam on her testimony so he offered the lie detector deal. Defense counsel was convinced his client was innocent but took the precaution of having Sam tested privately, a test that Sam easily passed. Therefore, the stipulation was agreed to, Sam was examined by the police polygrapher—and he failed.

Asked by defense counsel to help in this case, I was dismayed to discover that not a single scientifically credible study of polygraph validity had appeared in the literature (it was then 1974). The nearest approximation, a study of U.S. Army polygraphers by Bersh (1969), was hopelessly ambiguous. Bersh himself acknowledged that it was impossible to determine from his findings what role, if any, the polygraph charts played in helping his examiners to achieve above-chance success.

Luckily for Sam, the police polygrapher had misunderstood the details of the criminal charges. The three relevant questions he designed referred to Sam's forcing his way into Mary's room, threatening to choke her, and raping her. Sam undeniably responded to each of these questions, showing far more disturbance than he showed to any of the control questions, such as "Have you ever committed an unusual sex act?" (Control questions vaguely refer to possible misdeeds that few people can altogether truthfully deny; polygraphers assume that persons who can answer the relevant questions truthfully will be relatively more disturbed by the control questions.) But we knew from the alleged victim herself that Sam didn't force his way into her room; she invited him in. The jury found it reasonable to conclude that Sam's reactions to the questions about rape and threats, like his reaction to the forced-entry question, were due to his natural alarm at being accused of a serious crime rather than to his actually having committed that crime. Sam was found to be not guilty.

LYING ABOUT LIE DETECTION

One neglected defect of the polygraph test is that any validity it has depends on the examiner's ability to deceive his subject in certain crucial ways. First, the examinee must be persuaded that the technique is highly accurate, thus augmenting fear of detection in the guilty suspect or increasing the confidence of an innocent person that he or she will be exonerated. Here is how one of the leading polygraph theorists explains it:

> *[The subject is] assured that if he knows in his own mind that he is being truthful, then there will not be any substantial reaction to [the relevant] questions on the polygraph instrument. [This explanation] is further reinforced by presenting a number test in which the subject is instructed to lie about the number that he has chosen and recordings are made on the polygraph instrument while he denies having chosen that number. He is then told that the charts show what his pattern of reaction looks like when he is telling the truth and when he is lying and there should be no problem on the actual test if he is truthful to all of the questions. (Raskin, 1982, pp. 319–371)*

As I have pointed out in another article (Lykken, 1988b), there are two deceptions here. The first is the assurance that a truthful answer will not be accompanied
by "any substantial reaction." *Most* innocent people respond emotionally to the
allegations contained in the relevant questions, and every examiner knows this.
Second, the charts obtained during the number or pick-a-card test do *not* show the
subject's "pattern of reaction" when he is lying or telling the truth. Every competent polygrapher knows that people do not have distinctive patterns of reaction for
lying or being honest. In fact, in the usual card test, where the polygrapher pre-
tends to discover the chosen card from an examination of the polygraph record, it
is necessary to cheat by employing a marked deck or some similar ruse, since the
"lie" about the chosen card cannot be reliably determined from the charts (Reid &
Inbau, 1977, p. 193).

A fundamental deception involved in the control question lie test is the following:

> The control questions are presented to the subject in a manner designed to lead him to believe
> that admissions would negatively influence the examiner's opinion and that strong reactions to
> those questions during the test would produce a deceptive result. (Raskin, 1986)

The truth is just the opposite of this. Only by giving strong reactions to the
control questions can the subject hope to pass the test. For this reason, no sensible
polygraph examiner would agree to submit to a lie detector test himself in any
consequential matter because he knows that he could not be deceived in these
essential ways. I have a letter in my files from an experienced police examiner in
Alabama who was accused of a felony and asked to submit to a lie test. Finding
himself really under the gun for the first time, it had dawned on him that his
examiner could not prepare him (i.e., deceive him) in the necessary way, and he
was writing to ask my advice. He elected to stay in jail for a number of weeks,
until the case had been solved, rather than risk taking a lie test.

Apart from any ethical qualms we might have about these necessary deceptions,
a test whose validity depends upon the successful deception of each subject is
vulnerable, not only to the likelihood that not every examiner is going to be able to
successfully hoodwink every subject, but also to the probability that the truth about
the test will become widely known. There are now dozens of books and articles in
print that contain this information. After reading this chapter, if at some future
time you are unjustly accused of a crime and asked to prove your innocence on the
polygraph, the examiner will not be able to mislead you as he or she must if he or
she hopes to get a valid result.

You won't be reassured when the examiner successfully guesses which card you
chose because you now know that the trick is a fake, and you will wonder why he
or she has to cheat if the polygraph can do what he or she claims. When the
examiner tells you that you won't respond to questions answered truthfully, you
will recognize his or her assurance to be fraudulent. In any serious matter, most
innocent people find those accusatory relevant questions to be very disturbing
indeed and the effect is magnified when one is sitting with all those attachments to
the body, hearing the polygraph pens dancing along, revealing involuntary but
perfectly innocent and natural internal disquiet.

Most important of all, now you no longer can be deceived into thinking that
your only threat has to do with those control questions. They pertain to alleged

misdeeds in your past life and are deliberately vague and general so that most people cannot answer "No" with total certainty. However, you know now that what the examiner is doing is comparing your cardiac and electrodermal and respiratory responses to the relevant questions with those to the control questions. The examiner will call you deceptive (and therefore guilty) if he or she decides that the relevant questions disturbed you more. You are innocent—you did not steal the money, give the secrets to the KGB, sexually abuse the child—but you know that if these questions make your heart pound or your hands sweat then you are likely to fail the polygraph and be prosecuted as a thief, a traitor, or a criminal pedophile. In light of all this, are you willing to entrust your fate to a trial by polygraph?

CONFESSIONS OF A SOCIAL ADVOCATE

Since that 1974 rape trial, I have testified as an expert on the polygraph in at least 50 civil and criminal trials and courts martial and have assisted counsel in perhaps 200 additional cases. I have published 12 articles on polygraphy in refereed scientific journals (Lykken, 1959, 1960, 1974, 1978a, 1979a, 1984b, 1984c, 1984d, 1985f, 1987a, 1987b, 1988c), chapters on polygraphy in 5 edited volumes (Lykken, 1978c, 1983b, 1985a, 1988b, 1990), plus a book of my own (Lykken, 1981a) that is still the only scientific monograph on this topic. I have written 10 articles on invitation for various journals (Lykken, 1975a, 1975b, 1976, 1981b, 1981c, 1981d, 1981f, 1982a, 1984e, 1985b) plus 5 invited editorials for national newspapers (Lykken, 1977a, 1983a, 1985e, 1985g, 1987c). I was asked to write the "Lie detector" entry for 2 scientific encyclopedias (Lykken, 1980, 1984a) and to review 3 books by professional polygraphers (Lykken, 1978b, 1981e, 1985d). I have lectured on the polygraph before various audiences, including members of the British Parliament in London (Lykken, 1982c), a convention of the American Association for the Advancement of Science in New York (Lykken, 1985b), the Bar Association of Puerto Rico in San Juan (Lykken, 1986), the 38th International Course in Criminology in Montreal (Lykken, 1988a), and the Interservice Military Judges Seminar in Montgomery, Alabama (Lykken, 1988d),

I have been asked to testify on the scientific status of the polygraph by legislative committees of three states, a Canadian Royal Commission (Lykken, 1975c), three committees or subcommittees of the U.S. House and Senate (Lykken, 1977b, 1979b, 1985c), and the President's Foreign Intelligence Advisory Board (Lykken, 1982b). I estimate that I have spent one-fourth to one-third of my professional time in social advocacy on this issue, attempting to educate the public, lawyers, journalists, and other psychologists; assisting victims of the polygraph; and advocating restrictive legislation.

The Mandate for Social Advocacy

When I first became involved in this issue, there was almost no useful literature, credible validity data, or empirical basis for asserting that the polygraph lie test was far too invalid to serve as a basis for important social or individual decisions. Most scientific critics of the Strategic Defense Initiative (SDI or Star Wars) do not have access to the classified findings of Pentagon researchers; should they therefore hold their peace even though convinced on logical and theoretical grounds that SDI is a trillion-dollar boondoggle that cannot work?

Of the thousands of polygraphers now practicing in North America, most are ex-police or security people and only a dozen or so have any significant training in psychology or related areas. All of the methods now in use for lie detection were invented, not by psychologists or other scientists, but by policemen or lawyers. I knew that their claim to have an accurate test for detecting lying was implausible. No other psychological test ever devised has accuracy approaching that claimed for the polygraph, and there was not a shred of credible evidence to support these claims. Yet, because of scientific apathy and the journalistic appeal of "lie detectors," every time a notable criminal defendant or politician passes or fails, takes or refuses to take, a polygraph test there is a guaranteed news story and each such story reinforces the myth. The polygraphers managed to shift the burden of proof from their own shoulders to those of a potential critic.

Innocent people were being hurt by polygraphy, losing their livelihoods and their reputations and suffering serious emotional distress. People were being prosecuted and even convicted of crimes they did not commit. In some of the cases in which I have been personally involved it was possible to prove that the lie test was in error.

For example, one elderly man accused of repeated sexual abuse of a 14-year-old girl was able to produce medical evidence that cancer surgery 10 years earlier had rendered him incapable of the sexual feats described by his accuser. Such dispositive evidence is not always available, and I have a drawer full of letters from other victims. Although no good validity research was yet available, I knew that the public was being deceived and that the polygraphers' claims could not be substantiated. I became involved in the effort to debunk the lie detector.

I have been personally associated with three different cases where men were convicted of first-degree murder by juries who had been allowed to hear a polygrapher testify: "I have given thousands of polygraph tests and, in my expert opinion, this defendant lied when he denied being the killer." In each of these three cases, the defendant was sentenced to life imprisonment but subsequently exonerated.

In one other murder case I became involved in time to testify for the defense (*New Mexico v. James Archer,* 1983). The jury had already heard the prosecution's expert, a professor of psychology and a well-known polygrapher, who testified that the young airman had assuredly lied in denying that he had stabbed his girlfriend. I explained how the polygraph is supposed to work and the assumptions on which it is based, and by this time there were also a few validity studies that I could discuss (see Lykken, 1987a, for a recent review of the evidence). My testimony balanced that of the prosecution's expert. The jury decided the case on its merits and within 2 hours found the defendant not guilty.

Was he innocent? Perhaps I helped a murderer go free. I do not know for certain the truth of this case. I do know that the decedent had an acquaintance who had been previously convicted of assault by stabbing, and that an old car similar to this acquaintance's vehicle had been seen driving off at high speed from the scene of the crime. The defense's investigators had established these facts, neglected by the prosecution, which relied on the polygraph results. It was not my job to tell the jury that this man was innocent. Rather, I testified that the polygraph findings had negligible probative value. I gave the jury information necessary to form their own opinions, and this implied that they should ignore that portion of the evidence. I cannot believe that any serious, disinterested observer would question either the ethics or the logic of my stand.

Asking for Trouble

Social advocacy implies the existence of an opposition and, the more persuasive the advocacy, the more likely is it that opponents will fight back with unexpected and unpleasant tactics. Academics are taught to eschew the *ad hominem* arguments that are commonplace outside the universities. In the law courts, "impeaching the witness" is a standard practice and both opposing counsel and opposing witnesses, while testifying under oath, can offer the most scandalous charges without fear of being sued for slander. One particularly feisty opponent, from the safety of the witness box, has accused me of being unprofessional, unethical, and even mentally unbalanced! (These personal attacks, incidentally, are bad tactics. I am convinced that jurors find them offensive.)

I believe that most professional examiners are decent and honorable people who, because they are protected from discovering most of their mistakes, honestly believe that they make very few mistakes.

One recurring and unavoidable irritant, however, is the allegation that a person who is not a licensed polygrapher, trained at an accredited polygraph school, is not competent to criticize the technique. There are dozens of polygraph schools in the United States, 30 of which are accredited by the American Polygraph Association. Most of these schools offer courses of instruction that last 6–8 weeks. (The Reid school in Chicago requires 25 weeks of training, and the U.S. Army school at Fort McClellan, Alabama, requires 14 weeks.)

These courses cover the operation of the polygraph instrument, some elementary psychophysiology and psychopathology, plus instruction in the various testing techniques favored by the polygraphers who serve as faculty. As a psychophysiologist I have worked with polygraphs for 30 years. It would be a grotesque waste of my time to spend 8 weeks attending such a school since I have no desire to become a licensed examiner or to augment my income giving tests that I consider to be invalid. I have no doubt, however, that I shall encounter this objection in courtrooms yet unvisited. It is a Catch-22 provision: You cannot be a critic unless you are a member of the guild, and members of the guild are unlikely to be critics.

Advocacy, Pro and Con

If the lie detector had not been heard of before the 1970s and was being newly promulgated as a high-tech solution to the problems of society, my colleagues would have been less likely to question my activism because almost any psychologist would find such claims incredible. Most Americans have grown up with the myth of the lie detector. Its roots are deeply intermingled with those of respected social institutions, including the police, the courts, the press, the FBI, the security agencies, and 20% of the Fortune 500 corporations (Belt & Holden, 1978). At least a few card-carrying psychologists, in the polygraph business themselves, are also believers. Credible supporting evidence is still absent, but it is dangerous to oppose anything with such momentum. It would lead to controversy, probably even to intramural controversy, one psychologist against another. It is my experience that most scientists abhor controversy and are suspicious of those who become involved in it. They apparently believe that controversy is not the way of science, that it is in the nature of science that differences of opinion are readily resolved by gentlemanly discussion and appeals to logic and evidence.

In the mid-1970s, before this controversy waxed hot, the Society for Psychophysiological Research appointed an ad hoc committee to investigate polygraphic interrogation and offer a position paper to better inform the public. This committee was chaired by a respected and truly impartial scientist and included two polygraphers and two critics. The result was predictable. Instead of accepting separate majority and minority reports that the membership could evaluate for themselves, the society disbanded the committee and turned its face away from this unexpectedly nasty problem that, being controversial, as they now realized, could not be scientific. Later, when as president of the society I proposed that the board should appoint a new committee consisting entirely of respected scientists who had not yet taken a position on the controversy, who would use polygraphers and critics only as witnesses, the board recoiled at once into its collective carapace: once burned, twice shy.

No one with even a rudimentary knowledge of the history of science believes that this history has been free of controversy, often bitter and protracted and involving some of the most eminent of scientists and the most fundamental of scientific questions. I incline to the view that those who are too shy of controversy may be ill equipped for making genuine scientific contributions themselves. To be creative involves an inevitable arrogance, an ineluctable obligation to be able to assert: "I am right and the rest of you are wrong, or at least stumped." This arrogance, this willingness to stand against received opinion, permits scientists to entertain heretical ideas in the first instance, to send them out into the world if they seem valuable, and to defend them against doubters and opponents. Those who believe that science deals in truths and facts that are noncontroversial are philosophically naive. Research yields not facts but empirical generalizations whose scope is never entirely definite and whose likelihood is never perfect. Theories are always false, differing only in verisimilitude or in their interim usefulness. Science, like other human affairs, is a matter of opinions, of judgment, and of controversy.

THE SCIENTIST-ADVOCATE AS TEACHER VERSUS AUTHORITY FIGURE

A familiar scenario is the courtroom drama in which two psychiatrists or two psychologists appear on opposite sides and reach opposite conclusions. This kind of controversy is distressing and embarrassing, but can it be avoided? Probably not, in my opinion, but the embarrassment can be mitigated. If I believe, based on adequate assessment, that the plaintiff suffered a genuine post-traumatic stress reaction caused by a polygraph test that he or she failed and that cost him or her a job, should I refuse to testify on the plaintiff's behalf merely because the defense plans to offer an expert who disagrees with my diagnosis? I doubt that it would be useful for the two experts to caucus privately in hopes of reaching a consensus. Scientists, like other people, find it difficult to give up fixed positions and they readily become polarized in the arena of the courtroom. An ideal solution, but a prohibitively costly one, would be to interpose a jury of experts to evaluate the testimony of the expert witnesses and pass on their consensus to the regular jury. The best feasible approach is for the expert to explain or teach rather than merely to opine. Any sensible juror can understand the assumptions on which the so-called control-question test (CQT, the mostly widely used polygraphic lie test format) is based, if the procedure is clearly explained, and can then make an independent judgment of the plausibility of these assumptions. The criteria for a credible experimental test of CQT accuracy are not hard to understand and teaching them would permit the jurors to evaluate the available studies for themselves.

A number of published studies (Horvath & Reid, 1971; Hunter & Ash, 1973; Slowik & Buckley, 1975; Wicklander & Hunter, 1975) that seem to indicate quite high validity share a defect that is not immediately obvious, even to many psychologists (but see Brett, Phillips, & Beary, 1986). In all of these studies, polygraph charts that had been verified by confessions were blindly rescored by one or more polygraphers. The criterion confessions were obtained either from the person tested, verifying that chart as deceptive, or from another suspect, verifying the given chart as truthful. In each of these studies, the original examiners had scored the charts correctly, indicating that, at least for these selected charts, the tracings conformed to polygraph theory. Therefore, when additional examiners rescored the same charts according to the same theory, they tended to score them correctly.

However, such studies merely assess interscorer agreement or reliability rather than polygraph accuracy. To assess accuracy, one must begin with a set of charts that are representative of polygraph tests generally. Jurors can understand this point. I find it helps to use astrology as a parallel. Some horoscope-based predictions will be correct just by chance. If we select a group of horoscopes that led to such correct predictions and ask other astrologers to evaluate them, by following the standard astrological rules the other astrologers will tend to make the same predictions, thus falsely verifying astrology as a valid method of reading the future.

Polygraphers on the witness stand do not tend to explain things but, instead, appeal to their own long experience and expert opinions. When polygraph charts are displayed for the jurors to wonder at, the polygrapher-expert will point to the activity following the relevant or "Did you do it?" question and assert that: "Here we see a typical deceptive response." What the jury needs to know is that there is no such thing as a"typical deceptive response," no Pinocchio-reaction that people show when and only when they are lying. All the chart shows is that the defendant was disturbed by that relevant question. It is anyone's guess why he was disturbed.

I once testified for the defense in a case in which a woman (divorced and a mother of a 5-year-old boy) had been accused by the new wife of her ex-husband of sexually abusing her own son. There was no actual evidence of sexual abuse and the prosecution was based almost entirely on the results of a stipulated polygraph test, which of course the defendant had failed. The judge ruled that by the woman's stipulation she had waived the right to question the accuracy of polygraph tests generally, and my testimony must be limited to the accuracy of her own test in particular.

Displaying the charts to the jury, we pointed out where her heart rate and blood pressure had increased when she was asked: "During the visit of May 15th, did you take Johnny's penis in your mouth?" This question had been preceded by the question: "Have you ever lied to someone in authority in order to get out of trouble?" We showed the jury that her response to this control question involved less disturbance than she showed when asked about taking Johnny's penis in her mouth. We explained that the polygrapher had diagnosed her as deceptive for this reason alone; he would have called her truthful only if her reaction to the control question had been stronger than the one to the relevant question. Jurors are not foolish; these jurors found this woman not guilty of the charges.

THE FUTURE OF POLYGRAPHY

It seems most unlikely that our species has evolved a Pinocchio reflex. No specific lie response has yet been discovered nor is likely to be even in the high-tech future. If all we can measure is the relative disturbances produced by different questions, as seems to be the case, then it is likely that a highly valid lie test may be impossible in principle. And a test on which such important social consequences ride *must* be highly valid or it should not be employed at all. Consider urine testing for illicit drug use by airline pilots: If one can show sensitivity and specificity of 99%, then most passengers and pilots would consider testing to be reasonable and useful. But, if sensitivity is low, then urine testing could make flying more rather than less dangerous; if specificity is less than 99%, pilots will rebel, refusing to risk becoming false-positive (and unemployed) test misses.

One recent development that is especially insidious is the use of computer scoring of lie detector tests. The computer can measure autonomic responses with high reliability, but improving the interscorer reliability of an invalid test is a specious advance. At least one practitioner has programmed his computer to print out what purports to be the "probability" that the examinee was truthful (or deceptive). This estimate is obtained by comparing that subject's score on the CQT with scores of college students who were given CQTs relating to mock crimes that some of these volunteers had been assigned to "commit." John Z. DeLorean was given such a CQT in relation to federal charges of drug trafficking and it was reported to the court that the computer-derived probability that DeLorean had been truthful was 1.0[1]! When the myth of the lie detector is mated with the myth of the computer, truth is unlikely to be among the offspring.

Years ago, I developed a method of polygraphic interrogation called the Guilty Knowledge Test or GKT (Lykken, 1959, 1960, 1981a) that detects, not lying, but whether the suspect possesses guilty knowledge. A GKT consists of a set of multiple-choice questions pertaining to facts of the crime known to the examiner and that would also be known to a guilty suspect, items like the following example:

The kidnapper always called his victim by a kind of "pet" name. If you are the man, you will know which of these names you used when you spoke to Mrs. Clarke. What name did the abductor use: Was it "Toots"? Was it "Lady"? Was it "Babe"? Was it "Sister"? Was it "Missy"? Was it "Girl"?

[1]*United States v. John Z. DeLorean*, No. CR 62-910-RMT, U.S. District Court for the Central District of California, Application *in Limine* to permit introduction of polygraph examination of John Z. DeLorean, Sept. 30, 1983.

A guilty suspect is likely to show a relatively larger autonomic response, a stronger "orienting reflex," to the GKT alternative that he recognizes as being correct. With a well-constructed item having five scored alternatives, an innocent suspect has only about one chance in five of giving his strongest response to the correct alternative. (Because people tend to react more strongly to the first of a set of stimuli, the first alternative in each GKT item should be incorrect and should not figure in the scoring.) With 10 GKT items like the example, we might classify as "having guilty knowledge" those who give their strongest response to the correct alternative on 5 or more of the 10 items. Those who hit on less than five items would be classified as "innocent." (Whether having guilty knowledge should be taken to imply actual guilt will depend upon the particulars of the case.) Assuming that the average probability of an innocent hit is .20 and that guilty suspects have an .80 probability of hitting on the average item, the sensitivity of this GKT will be 99.4%, and the specificity is about the same.

Thus, unlike lie detection methods, the GKT depends on reasonable assumptions, and research to date encourages the hope that it could be very useful in many cases of criminal investigation, useful not only in identifying the perpetrator but especially in protecting the innocent. I believe the present evidence (Lykken, 1988b) justifies my advocating careful, exploratory use of the GKT by police agencies in real-life settings. I would be among the first to oppose legislation or judicial actions leading to the routine admissibility of GKT results in courts of law. Until it has been used extensively as an investigative tool and its validity has been carefully assessed under real-life conditions, we cannot say with adequate confidence whether its psychometric properties will generalize from the laboratory to the real world.

A FRINGE BENEFIT OF ADVOCACY

Most academic psychologists justify their professional existence by reference to their research productivity. The truth is that most published psychological research is seldom cited by other investigators and, had it been printed in disappearing ink, would never have been missed (Lykken, in press). There is a friendly academic conspiracy to pretend that publication is a sufficient end in itself, but most of us know blue periods when our work does not seem to be getting anywhere and we are plagued by existential doubts. Though one may not have discovered it yet, most psychologists have—or could acquire—skills or special knowledge that could be of genuine use in the real world.

Since 1975, I have justified my existence (i.e., my position as a research professor at a large public university) by helping victims of polygraphy, either directly through advice or testimony or indirectly through public education or legislative lobbying. This activity does not demand great cleverness or creativity, yet there can be no doubt of its value to the individuals concerned nor any question that it is generally in the public interest. Winning the occasional battle is inherently gratifying. The recent passage by the U.S. Congress of legislation that will eliminate most polygraph testing of employees and job applicants in the private sector was very gratifying indeed (Molotsky, 1988). I have been inveighing against such abuses since 1974 and first testified in support of such legislation in 1977 (Lykken, 1977b).

There have been other encouraging recent developments. In Israel, a special

commission chaired by a Israeli Supreme Court justice reported in 1981 that polygraph findings are too unreliable to be admitted in evidence in Israeli courts
(Harnon, 1982). The Canadian Supreme Court has recently handed down a similar
ruling (*R. v Beland and Phillips*, October, 1987), although the Canadian federal
police (the Royal Canadian Mounted Police), like our FBI, use the polygraph
routinely in criminal investigation. A task force of the British Psychological Association, after long and careful study, reported (British Psychological Association,
1986) that the polygraph lie test is based on unlikely assumptions and that no
credible evidence in support of the industry's claims of accuracy has as yet been
adduced. The Council on Scientific Affairs of the American Medical Association
has taken a similar position (American Medical Association, 1986), and the American Psychological Association has laid it down that a psychologist who adminis-
ters such tests for a fee might be guilty of violation of the ethical canons of that
organization (American Psychological Association, 1986; Burnham, 1986).

   In the matter of admissibility at trial, the trend in recent years has been for state
appellate courts—in Colorado (*State v. Anderson*, 1981), North Carolina (*State v.
Grier*, 1983), Illinois (*State v. Baynes*, 1980), and Wisconsin (*State v. Dean*,
1981)—to join with the 20 other states that prohibit even stipulated polygraph
evidence (Lykken, 1984c). Three states once permitted criminal defendants to
introduce results of "friendly" polygraph tests. The California Legislature put a
stop to this practice in 1983, and the Supreme Judicial Court of Massachusetts
ended it in that state late in 1989, leaving New Mexico the last haven for
"friendly" polygraphers and their clients.

   I do not, of course, claim credit for all of this progress. Quite a number of other
scientific or legal scholars have joined in the chorus of critical comment (Abbell,
1977; Blinkhorn, 1988; Brett, Phillips, & Beary, 1986; Carroll, 1988; Cunningham, 1988; Furedy, 1986; Iacono & Patrick, 1987; Jones, 1988; Kleinmuntz
& Szucko, 1982, 1984; Orne, 1975; Saxe, 1984, 1985; Saxe, Dougherty, &
Cross, 1985). But it is a fact that few psychologists were aware in 1970 of the
growth of polygraphy or of its negative social consequences. Innocent citizens,
victimized by erroneous polygraph tests, had no way of knowing in 1970 that
respected scientists had serious doubts about the accuracy of supposedly scientific
lie detection. It is also a fact that lawyers, judges, and legislators require the
assistance, in matters of this kind, of scientifically sophisticated consultants. Once
one has mastered the issues, this consultative role is interesting, useful, and sometimes rewarding.

   Meanwhile, having invested a considerable portion of my professional endeavor
in this way, my own behavior genetics research does not have to be justified to
anyone (except periodically to funding agencies). It can be pursued for the best
possible reason, namely, because I find it interesting.

SUMMARY

   What are the reasons behind this continuing, often heated argument about polygraphy? With respect to the Guilty Knowledge Test, there does not seem to be a
controversy regarding either its theory or validity. The theory flows directly from
a large body of research on the orienting reflect (e.g., Lykken, 1968, pp. 435–
442), and the validity of a well-constructed GKT can be predicted from the number of items and alternatives, as shown earlier. There is disagreement, however,

about whether a skillful investigator would find it possible to use the GKT in a significant number of criminal cases. Many polygraphers contend that case facts potentially useful as GKT items nearly always will be revealed to potential suspects either through publicity or prior questioning.

With respect to polygraphic lie detection, however, there is controversy on all fronts. In the area of theory, claims for a specific lie response seem to have been abandoned (e.g., Raskin & Kircher, 1990). That leaves, as the main debating point, whether it is plausible to suppose that control questions will be more disturbing than relevant questions (e.g., "During the visit of May 15th, did you take Tommy's penis in your mouth?") for all criminal suspects who happen to be innocent of the charges.

Here is the proponent's position: "To avoid giving the impression of being the type of person who would have committed the crime, the subject chooses to answer control questions in the negative. Since innocent subjects are concerned about possible deception only when answering the control questions, it is expected that they will react more strongly to them than to the relevant questions" (Raskin & Kircher, 1990). I and others argue, on the contrary, that this expectation is psychologically naive, just as it is naive to assume that negative answers to control questions are invariably lies, that is, "that the subject is deceptive or is unsure of being truthful in answering the control questions" (Raskin & Kircher, 1990).

The major source of the current controversy is disagreement about the quality and generalizability of the existing research. Analog laboratory studies, using volunteer subjects in mock crime situations, are now relied on almost exclusively by one group of polygraphers because such studies permit a definite criterion against which to compare polygraph diagnoses. But most analog studies assign subjects to the guilty or innocent conditions and thus deprive them of both free choice and responsibility for their choices. Such circumstances may not adequately invoke the emotional concerns of real-life situation and, since autonomic responses are affected by the emotional state, the results of such analog studies may not generalize to the situation of actual criminal investigation. Moreover, control questions (e.g., "Have you ever committed an unusual sex act?") are just as real in the laboratory as in the police station, while in the laboratory, relevant questions refer to mock crimes and imaginary consequences. The reason why one sees so few false-positive errors in most analog studies is this reversal in verisimilitude and impact of the control and relevant questions.

Most field studies, on the other hand, suffer from the difficulty of obtaining a dependable criterion under real-life conditions. While a confession can usually be relied on, we have seen above that confessions elicited by polygraphers provide a highly selective criterion that overestimates the validity of the test. The quality of this literature is extremely variable, so that any meta-analysis must be correspondingly selective. In a recent issue of the journal of the American Polygraph Association, for example, a field study of 122 criminal suspects is reported that yielded perfect accuracy in detecting both lying and truthfulness (Matte & Reuss, 1989). In 70% of these cases, the lie detector tests were verified by confession. We have already seen how tests thus verified can appear to have perfect validity even though the tests overall have no more than random accuracy. We are told that 9% of the cases were verified by criminal convictions and the remaining 21% by "investigative results." We are not told, however, whether the 136 unverified cases were followed up in the same way as the 122 verified ones, nor do we know what "investigative results" were required before making a criterion decision. Therefore, because its criterion is tainted and unreplicable, I interpret this study as without scientific value. Many polygraph proponents will no doubt regard it as strong corroboration of their views.

Finally, there is a latent spectrum of opinion regarding just how accurate the polygraph test ought to be in order to justify its use in each potential application. [Because critics' and proponents' estimates of polygraph validity vary all the way from near chance to near perfect, this more interesting question of the minimum justifiable accuracy (MJA) has not yet been widely discussed.] The MJA will vary widely with different applications. As a bloodless method of inducing the guilty to confess, the MJA might be as low as 50% or chance since the polygraph is being used here merely as a stage prop. On the other hand, if the test results are to be the basis for testimony in a criminal trial, I would demand a very high MJA. Because of its scientific cachet combined with its clear and simple message—"In my professional opinion, the defendant lied in denying his guilt"—juries may be likely to give polygraph findings more credence than they deserve.

In the pre-employment screening application, psychologists are accustomed to making do with fairly low MJAs. For example, if one is selecting butter packers, then a selection process that improves productivity or annual supervisor ratings by only 10% over chance may seem worth using. Since applicants who do not achieve the cutting score merely fail to be hired for this particular job, we do not tend to worry about the MJA for selecting butter packers. A test that alleges to predict dishonesty, counterproductive behavior, disruptive personality, or the like, however, will defame and mislabel its inevitable test misses.

Even more disturbing is the prospect of such a test being shown to have sufficient validity to be highly cost-effective for employers and, therefore, its coming into general use. There will be a percentage of individuals unlucky enough to be consistent false-positive errors on this test and, since it is a psychological test after all, this percentage will not be trivial. As a result of its success and wide use, this perfectly respectable selection tool may condemn many honest and competent people to permanent technological unemployment. This is a problem that applied psychologists generally might ponder.

REFERENCES

Abbell, M. (1977). Polygraph evidence: The case against admissibility in federal criminal trials. *The American Criminal Law Review, 15*, 29–62.

American Medical Association. (1986). American Medical Association Council report: Polygraph. *Journal of the American Medical Association, 256*, 1172–1175.

American Psychological Association. (1986, February 1). APA resolution says reliability of polygraph test "unsatisfactory." Press release, American Psychological Association, Washington, DC.

Belt, J., & Holden, P. (1978). Polygraph usage among major U.S. corporations. *Personnel Journal, 12*, 80–86.

Bersh, P. J. (1969). A validation study of polygraph examiner judgments. *Journal of Applied Psychology, 53*, 399–403.

Blinkhorn, S. (1988). Lie detection as a psychometric procedure. In A. Gale (Ed.), *The polygraph test: Lies, truth, and science* (pp. 29–39). London: Sage.

British Psychological Association. (1986). Report of the working group on the use of the polygraph in criminal investigation and personnel screening. *Bulletin of the British Psychological Society, 49*, 81–94.

Brett, A. S., Phillips, N., & Beary, J. F. (1986, March 8). Predictive power of the polygraph: Can the "lie detector" detect liars? *The Lancet, ii*, 544–547.

Burnham, D. (1986, February 9). "Psychologists doubt polygraphs." *New York Times*, p. 19.

Carroll, D. (1988). How accurate is polygraph lie detection? In A. Gale (Ed.), *The polygraph test: Lies, truth, and science* (pp. 19–28). London: Sage.

Cunningham, C. (1988). Vetting, investigation, and interrogation. In A. Gale (Ed.), *The polygraph test: Lies, truth, and science*. London: Sage.

Einhorn, H. J., & Hogarth, R. M. (1978). Confidence in judgment: Persistence of the illusion of validity. *Psychological Review, 85*, 395–416.

Furedy, J. J. (1986). Lie detection as psychophysiological differentiation: Some fine lines. In G. H. Coles, E. Donchin, & S. W. Porges (Eds.), *Psychophysiology: Systems, processes, and applications* (pp. 638–701). New York: Guilford Press.

Harnon, E. (1982). Evidence obtained by polygraph: An Israeli perspective. *The Criminal Law Review*, pp. 340–348.

Horvath, F., & Reid, J. E. (1971). The reliability of polygraph examiner diagnosis of truth and deception. *Journal of Criminal Law, Criminology, and Police Science, 62*, 276–281.

Hunter, F., & Ash, P. (1973). The accuracy and consistency of polygraph examiner's diagnosis. *Journal of Police Science and Administration, 1*, 370–375.

Iacono, W. G., & Patrick, C. J. (1987). What psychologists should know about lie detection. In A. K. Hess & I. B. Weiner (Eds.), *Handbook of forensic psychology* (pp. 460–489). New York: Wiley.

Iacono, W. G., & Patrick, C. J. (1988). Polygraph techniques. In R. Rogers (Ed.), *Clinical assessment of malingering and deception* (pp. 205–233). New York: Guilford Press.

Jones, E. A., Jr. (1988). American individual rights and an abusive technology: The torts of polygraphing. In A. Gale (Ed.), *The polygraph test: Lies, truth, and science*. London: Sage.

Kleinmuntz, B., & Szucko, J. J. (1982). On the fallibility of lie detection. *Law & Society Review, 17*, 85–104.

Kleinmuntz, B., & Szucko, J. J. (1984). A field study of the fallibility of polygraphic lie detection. *Nature, 308*, 449–450.

Lykken, D. T. (1959). The GSR in the detection of guilt. *Journal of Applied Psychology, 43*, 385–388.

Lykken, D. T. (1960). The validity of the guilty knowledge technique: The effects of faking. *Journal of Applied Psychology, 44*, 258–262.

Lykken, D. T. (1968). Neuropsychology and psychophysiology in personality research. In E. Borgatta & W. Lambert (Eds.), *Handbook of personality theory and research* (pp. 413–509). Chicago: Rand McNally.

Lykken, D. T. (1974). Psychology and the lie detector industry. *American Psychologist, 29*, 725–739.

Lykken, D. T. (1975a). The right way to use a lie detector. *Psychology Today, 8*, 56–60.

Lykken, D. T. (1975b). The lie detector industry: Just nine years more to 1984. *Modern Medicine*, pp. 59–63.

Lykken, D. T. (1975c). Theory and validity of polygraphic interrogation. Testimony before the Royal Commission into Metropolitan Toronto Police Practices, Hon. Mr. Justice D. R. Morand, Commissioner.

Lykken, D. T. (1976). Polygraph tests in business: Unscientific, unAmerican, illegal. *Hennepin Lawyer*, pp. 4, 28–30.

Lykken, D. T. (1977a, December 7). Do lie detectors lie? *The Baltimore Sun*, p. A15.

Lykken, D. T. (1977b, November 15). Polygraphic interrogation of employees and prospective employees. Hearings of the Subcommittee on the Constitution, Committee on the Judiciary, United States Senate.

Lykken, D. T. (1978a). The psychopath and the lie detector. *Psychophysiology, 15*, 137–142.

Lykken, D. T. (1978b). Review of: "Truth and deception: The polygraph ('lie detector') technique, 2nd Ed." by Reid and Inbau. *Contemporary Psychology, 23*, 81–82.

Lykken, D. T. (1978c). Uses and abuses of the polygraph. In H. L. Pick, Jr., H. Leibowitz, J. Singer, H. Steinschneider, & H. Stevenson (Eds.), *Psychology: From research to practice*. New York: Plenum.

Lykken, D. T. (1979a). The detection of deception. *Psychological Bulletin, 86*, 47–53.

Lykken, D. T. (1979b, September 11). Polygraphic pre-employment screening in federal intelligence agencies. Hearings of the Subcommittee on Oversight, Permanent Select Committee on Intelligence, U.S. House of Representatives.

Lykken, D. T. (1980). Lie detector. *Encyclopedia of science and technology* (pp. 1–317). New York: McGraw-Hill.

Lykken, D. T. (1981a). *A tremor in the blood: Uses and abuses of the lie detector.* New York: McGraw-Hill.

Lykken, D. T. (1981b, February). To tell the truth. *Discover*, p. 10.

Lykken, D. T. (1981c, January/February). Impeaching the lie detector. *Hennepin Lawyer*, pp. 6–8, 20.
Lykken, D. T. (1981d). The law and the lie detector. *Criminal Defense, 8*, 19–27.
Lykken, D. T. (1981e). Review of: "The science and art of the polygraph technique" by A. Matte. *Contemporary Psychology, 26*, 479–481.
Lykken, D. T. (1981f). The polygraph: Truth or fiction? *Law Enforcement, 9*, 17, 19–20, 29.
Lykken, D. T. (1982a). Validity of "lie-detectors." *Physician and Patient, 1*, 50.
Lykken, D. T. (1982b, June). Polygraphic screening by federal intelligence agencies (testimony). The President's Foreign Intelligence Advisory Board, Washington, DC. Task Force on Counter-Intelligence, Washington, DC.
Lykken, D. T. (1982c, December 8). Polygraph vetting of security personnel: The American experience (lecture). Convocation of Senior Civil Servants and Members of Parliament, London.
Lykken, D. T. (1983a, February 17). Three big lies about the lie detector. Editorial. *USA Today*, p. 4.
Lykken, D. T. (1983b). Polygraphic interrogation: The applied psychophysiologist. In A. Gale & J. Edwards (Eds.), *Physiological correlates of human behavior* (pp. 241–254). London: Academic Press Ltd.
Lykken, D. T. (1984a). Lie detector. In R. J. Corsini (Ed.), *Encyclopedia of psychology*, (Vol. 2). New York: Wiley.
Lykken, D. T. (1984b). Polygraphic interrogation. *Nature, 307*, 681–684.
Lykken, D. T. (1984c). Trial by polygraph. *Behavioral Sciences and the Law, 2*, 75–82.
Lykken, D. T. (1984d). Detecting deception in 1984. *American Behavioral Scientist, 27*, 481–499.
Lykken, D. T. (1984e). The thought police: George Orwell and the polygraph test. *Minnesota Psychologist*, Summer, pp. 9–13.
Lykken, D. T. (1985a). The probity of the polygraph. In S. Kassin & L. Wrightsman (Eds.), *The psychology of evidence and courtroom procedure* (pp. 95–123). Beverly Hills, CA: Sage.
Lykken, D. T. (1985b). The scientific status of the lie detector (presented at the annual meeting of the AAAS, New York, May 29, 1984). *Society, 22*, 34–38.
Lykken, D. T. (1985c, July 30). The use of the polygraph in the private sector. Invited testimony at the Hearings of the Subcommittee on Employment Opportunities, Committee on Education and Labor, U.S. House of Representatives, Washington, DC.
Lykken, D. T. (1985d). . . . In a tumor in the brain. Review of: "Preemployment polygraphy" by R. Ferguson and C. Gugas, Sr. *Contemporary Psychology, 30*, 880–881.
Lykken, D. T. (1985e, August 7). Stop this 20th century witchcraft (editorial). *USA Today.* p. 4.
Lykken, D. T. (1985f). The case against the polygraph in employment screening. *Personnel Administrator, 30*, 59–65.
Lykken, D. T. (1985g, December 20). The polygraph and the Pentagon (editorial). *Los Angeles Times*, p. A12.
Lykken, D. T. (1986, May 21). Forensic and commercial applications of the polygraph: Implications for the bar. Invited address before the Bar Association of Puerto Rico. San Juan, Puerto Rico.
Lykken, D. T. (1987a). The validity of tests: Caveat emptor. *Jurimetrics, 27*, 263–270.
Lykken, D. T. (1987b). Reply to Raskin and Kircher. *Jurimetrics, 27*, 278–282.
Lykken, D. T. (1987c, December 15). Polygraphers are the last to know (editorial). *USA Today*, p. 4.
Lykken, D. T. (1988a). Forensic uses of polygraphic interrogation. In M. LeBlanc, P. Tremblay, & B. Blumstein (Eds.), *New technologies and penal justice*. Montreal: Centre International de Criminologie.
Lykken, D. T. (1988b). The case against polygraphy. In A. Gale (Ed.), *The polygraph test: Lies, truth, and science* (pp. 111–125). Beverly Hills, CA: Sage.
Lykken, D. T. (1988c). The detection of guilty knowledge: A comment on Forman and McCauley. *Journal of Applied Psychology, 73*, 303–304.
Lykken, D. T. (1988d, March 22). The role of polygraphy in military justice (lecture). Interservice Military Judges Seminar, Maxwell AFB, Montgomery, AL.
Lykken, D. T. (1990). The lie detector controversy: An alternative solution. In P. J. Ackles, J. R. Jennings, & M. G. H. Coles (Eds.), *Advances in psychophysiology: A research annual* (Vol. 4). Greenwich, CT: JAI Press.
Lykken, D. T. (in press). What's wrong with psychology anyway? In D. Ciccheti & W. Goves (Eds.), *Thinking clearly about psychology.* Minneapolis, MN: University of Minnesota Press.
Matte, J. A., & Reuss, R. M. (1989). A field validation study of the Quadri-Zone Comparison Technique. *Polygraph, 18*, 187–202.
Molotsky, I. (1988, March 3). Senate votes limit on polygraph use in private industry. *New York Times*, pp. 1, 14.
New Mexico v. James Archer. (1983, March). Carrizzozo, N.M.

Orne, M. (1975). Implications of laboratory research for the detection of deception. *Polygraph, 2,* 169–199.

R. v. Beland and Phillips (1987, October).

Raskin, D. (1982). The scientific basis of polygraph techniques and their uses in the judicial process. In Trankell (Ed.), *Reconstructing the past: The role of psychologists in criminal trials* (pp. 319–371). Stockholm: Norstedt & Soners.

Raskin, D. (1986). The polygraph in 1986: Scientific, professional, and legal issues surrounding application and acceptance of polygraph evidence. *Utah Law Review, 1,* 29–74.

Raskin, D. C., & Kircher, J. C. (1990). Comments on Furedy and Heslegrave: Misconceptions, misdescriptions, and misdirections. In P. Ackles, J. Jennings, & M. Coles (Eds.), *Advances in psychophysiology* (Vol. 4). Greenwich, CT: JAI Press.

Reid, J. E., & Inbau, F. E. (1977). *Truth and deception: The polygraph ("lie detector") technique* (2nd Ed., p. 423). Baltimore: Williams & Wilkins.

Saxe, L. (1984, March 7). *On the proposed use of polygraphs in the Department of Defense,* Presented at the request of the American Psychological Association. Statement before the Committee on Armed Services of the United States Senate, Washington, DC.

Saxe, L. (1985). On deceiving ourselves in detecting deceit: Espionage, science, and public policy. *Issues in Science and Technology, 11,* 15–16.

Saxe, L., Dougherty, D., & Cross, T. (1985). The validity of polygraph testing: Scientific analysis and public controversy. *American Psychologist, 40,* 355–366.

Slowick, S., & Buckley, J. (1975). Relative accuracy of polygraph examiner diagnosis of respiration, blood pressure, and GSR recordings. *Journal of Police Science and Administration, 3,* 305–309.

State v. Anderson. (1981). 637 P.2d 354 (Colo. 1981).

State v. Baynes. (1980). 88 Ill. 2d 225,430 N.E.2d 1070.

State v. Dean. (1981). 103 Wis.2d 228,307 N.W. 2d 628.

State v. Dorsey. (1975). 88 N.M. 184, 529 P.2d 204.

State v. Grier. (1983). 300 S.E. 3d 351 (N.C.).

United States v. John Z. DeLorean. (1983, September 30). CR 62-910-RMT, U.S. District Court for the Central District of California, application *in limine.*

Wicklander, D., & Hunter, F. (1975). The influence of auxiliary sources of information in polygraph diagnosis. *Journal of Police Science and Administration, 3,* 405–409.

22

The Effects of Prison Confinement

Paul B. Paulus and Mary T. Dzindolet

The issue of prison confinement has been a volatile one for a long time. Early prisons in the United States were promoted as humane alternatives to cruel and unusual punishment (Sommer, 1976). Ideally, such confinement would allow for a reassessment of lifestyle by the inmate and the opportunity for rehabilitation or reform.[1] This would involve various techniques designed to change the person in ways that make repetition of criminal behavior less likely. Rehabilitation could take the form of education, job or skill training, and attempts to change attitudes, values, or morals. Because of a high rate of recidivism (inmates returning to prison), severe doubts have been raised about the rehabilitative impact of prison, its specific programs, and alternatives to imprisonment (Brody, 1981; Martinson, 1974). This also raises the issue of the supposed deterrent effect of the threat of imprisonment.

Much has been written about the detrimental effects that imprisonment supposedly has on inmates while in prison and for their later adjustment to life in the free world (Goodstein, 1979; Walker, 1983). On the basis of these considerations, there would seem to be ample justification for arguments by prisoners' rights advocates for an end to long-term imprisonment (Sommer, 1976). However, with the increasing crime rates, public demands for severe prison penalties have also increased. This has resulted in a severe prison and jail overcrowding problem both in the United States and in other countries (Lacayo, 1989; Vita, 1989).

In this chapter, we critically evaluate the various perspectives on prison confinement. First, we briefly examine the major justifications for incarceration and the related empirical evidence. Next, we deal with the psychological effects of long-term prison confinement and examine the variables that influence reactions to prison confinement, such as the characteristics of inmates, the physical environment, and the type of institution. Finally, the theoretical and practical implications of this confinement literature will be developed.

We are grateful to Robert Sommer for his feedback on this chapter. However, we take the full responsibility for the views expressed in this chapter.
[1]The primary dictionary meaning of the term "rehabilitation" is one of restoring something to its former state or capacity. Therefore, some suggest that the term "reform" is better suited as a description of efforts to change criminals (cf. Sommer, 1976). However, since rehabilitation is the term primarily used in the criminal justice field, we will use it in this chapter as well.

UTILITY OF PRISONS

It seems that everyone has a fairly strong opinion about crime and punishment. Given the high levels of crime in the United States, many feel that stronger deterrents are needed. These typically involve increased use of incarceration rather than other approaches such as probation and community corrections (Foster, 1981; Wooldredge, 1988). As a result, the number of inmates in prison has doubled over the past 10 years while the total amount of crime has remained steady (U.S. Department of Justice, 1987, 1989; Lacayo, 1989). Of course, one could argue that this is evidence for a deterrent effect since one would have expected crime to increase with the increase in population. In fact, careful analyses of the deterrent impact of various sanctions suggest that sanctions do have an impact (Gottfredson & Hirschi, 1987). It appears that increasing the certainty of imprisonment for a large number of offenders at the expense of longer terms may be the most effective use of prison space as a deterrent (Blumstein, Cohen, & Nagin, 1978; McCord, 1985).

While there may be some deterrent effect of imprisonment, it is evidently limited in light of the high recidivism rates for offenders who have been incarcerated. Recidivism rates range from about 40% for first offenders to 60% for repeat offenders (Greenfeld, 1985). These figures are based on incarceration within the same state. Inclusion of those incarcerated in other states and those not caught for additional crimes could easily add 10–20% to these rates (Klein & Caggiano, 1986). These figures suggest that prisons are not very effective as agents of reform or rehabilitation. It is often suggested that the main factors stopping criminals from further crime are advancing age, death, or simply getting tired of the hassles of being incarcerated (Greenfeld & Langan, 1985).

One reason prisons do not have a better success record is that few have a set of strong programs designed to facilitate prisoner rehabilitation. Programs designed to deal with the educational and job-skill deficiencies of many inmates might increase their chances of successful adjustment to society upon release from prison. Other programs could focus on overcoming alcohol and drug dependency or on developing more positive social attitudes. Clinical programs could be designed for sex offenders and those suffering from various psychological problems. Unfortunately, it has been difficult to obtain a consensus about the utility of these various techniques. Some who have surveyed the literature conclude that rehabilitative efforts are not very successful (Brody, 1981; Martinson, 1974). Effective treatment of sex offenders seems to be particularly difficult (Furby, Weinrott, & Blackshaw, 1989).

Others come to a much more optimistic conclusion about the potential of rehabilitation (Gendreau & Ross, 1987; Palmer, 1983). Gendreau and Ross (1987) cite evidence for the efficacy of a wide variety of approaches both in the prison and outside, including education, job training, drug abuse programs, family intervention, and "get tough" programs. They note that whether these programs are effective depends on their quality, intensity, length, and degree of match with the particular characteristics of the offender. Certain techniques may work much better with first-time offenders than with repeat offenders, and violent offenders will require a different program than nonviolent offenders with drug abuse problems. Techniques that are based on sound psychological principles and are implemented in an appropriate manner with selected populations are likely to be quite effective. Obviously, one has to recognize that there are a broad variety of bases for offender behavior, including lack of education and job skills, drug and alcohol abuse, family and socialization deficits, and poor moral development. To be effective, rehabilitation should be designed to address the particular deficits.

One obvious benefit of incarceration is that it keeps inmates out of society so that they cannot commit crimes. Surveys indicate that for each conviction for crimes such as burglary, theft, or drugs, an inmate may have committed 10–20 more crimes, with rates as high as 600 crimes per year for some. At a cost of about $2,000 per crime, the savings involved in keeping a typical inmate in prison could easily compensate for the estimated $20,000 per year cost of incarceration (Zedlewski, 1987). These findings provide fairly strong justification for incarceration, but there may be serious drawbacks to using prisons as a primary means of controlling crime. Some have argued that prisons are inhumane environments in which inmates are brutalized both physically and psychologically (Cohen & Taylor, 1972; Sommer, 1976; Sykes, 1958). Others have argued that adjustment to the prison lifestyle, or prisonization, is counterproductive for the inmate's functioning after release, but solid evidence for this type of phenomenon is lacking (Homant & Dean, 1988; Wormith, 1984).

What then are the effects of prison confinement on the inmates? Is prison life really harmful for the physical and psychological well-being of inmates? In what ways do inmates change over the course of their prison sentence? What environmental, personal, and social factors influence the adjustment of inmates to prison confinement? These will be the primary issues we will address in the next section.

EFFECTS OF LENGTH OF CONFINEMENT

Psychological, Emotional, and Physiological Reactions

There are a wide variety of effects often attributed to long-term prison confinement. There are reports that the prison experience is traumatic and stressful for the inmates and is detrimental to their physical and mental well-being. Most of these conclusions are based on subjective reports or evaluations of prisons that rely on the interview technique. Not surprisingly, inmates describe their life in prison in fairly negative terms (Johnson, 1976; Toch, 1975, 1977). Yet a careful summary and evaluation of research studies using more objective and quantitive measures has revealed little evidence that long-term confinement has strong negative effects (Bukstel & Kilmann, 1980). The bulk of the evidence suggests that there is an elevated level of anxiety or stress during the initial time that the inmate is in prison. During the ensuing months, this level of stress is significantly reduced as inmates appear to adjust to the prison environment. Just prior to release, stress levels again become elevated as inmates become increasingly concerned about problems related to their release. Evidence for this type of pattern is found in both cross-sectional studies involving different groups of inmates at different points in their time in prison and in longitudinal studies in which the same inmates are tested over a period of time.

For example, in a study of Canadian prisons, Zamble and Porporino (1988) found that anxiety and depression were quite high in the first few weeks of imprisonment and declined to near normal levels after about 4 months. On the other hand, feelings of hostility and self-esteem each increased with time in prison. Ostfeld, Kasl, D'Atri, and Fitzgerald (1987) studied inmates in a medium security state prison and found a similar pattern of results. There was a decline in blood pressure, illness complaints, and anxiety over the period of 1.5 years, with anxiety rising again prior to release. Hostility and depression also increased somewhat prior to release. In a cross-sectional study of U.S. federal prisons, Paulus (1988) found decreases in blood pressure and illness complaints with increased length of time in prison for inmates housed in single cells. However, evaluation of the environment became more negative and feelings of choice lowered over time. A longitudinal study of male and female inmates in a co-correctional institution found a decline in blood pressure over a period of 4 months for both sexes (Paulus & Netherland, 1986). In contrast, ratings of the housing did not change, and the prison itself was evaluated more negatively at the end of 4 months than in the first few weeks. Total length of confinement, including time in other prisons, had similar relationships with various measures. Longer time in prison was related to negative evaluations of housing and the prison and to more reported concerns with family, finances, and life after release. However, overall mood state became more positive and feelings of control over other inmates grew with increased length of time in prison.

The research examined thus far seems to imply that prison confinement in itself does not act as a major stressor. The elevated indications of stress in the beginning of the prison term may reflect emotional reactions to the disruption of a prior lifestyle, family separation, and the uncertainties involved in being a resident in a new environment. Once these factors dissipate somewhat, there seems to be a reasonable degree of adjustment to prison life until new uncertainties and anxieties are produced by impending release. Furthermore, both Paulus (1988) and Ostfeld et al. (1987) report that stress level seems to be elevated whenever someone enters a new housing unit. This change in housing involves a temporary increase in uncertainty about relations with a new group of residents. Thus, the main source of stress seems to be change in status or environment. This notion is consistent with the ideas about the stressful impact of life changes (Gunderson & Rahe, 1974).

The major reported problems of prison inmates appear to be separation from family and friends, loss of freedom, and concern about life after release, the maintenance of self-esteem or self-identity, and time management (Flanagan, 1980; Johnson, 1976; Zamble & Porporino, 1988). While these follow naturally from the experience of long-term confinement, they are not responses to particular conditions of confinement (i.e., housing, fear of violence, treatment by guards). Furthermore, it is these very issues that are most likely to be salient at the beginning and end of the period of confinement.

Cognitive Functioning

One often presumed effect of prison confinement is a change in cognitive functioning due to the regimentation, boredom, and isolation from society that characterizes prison life (Rasch, 1981). There is some evidence that time perspective may be influenced by long-term prison confinement. For example, Flanagan (1981) reports that inmates have difficulty in thinking about the future beyond imprisonment. Yet most studies of cognitive processes have provided little evidence of basic changes in mental functioning or abilities (Bukstel & Kilmann, 1980). The idea of significant cognitive and emotional deterioration during imprisonment is also countered by evidence that coping styles stay fairly constant during the first 4 months of confinement. Inmates employ the same coping styles in prison as they do outside and these coping techniques seem to be related to somewhat lower indices of stress (Zamble & Porporino, 1988).

Social Behavior

There is evidence that inmates tend to become somewhat more isolated in their behavior patterns over the course of their sentence. Inmates show less involvement in social or recreational activities and tend to do their time with as little hassle as possible (Ostfeld et al., 1987; Sapsford, 1978; Zamble & Porporino, 1988). This social withdrawal does not appear to be an effective means of coping with prison stress since involvement in social activities is not related to lower levels of stress during confinement (Ostfeld et al., 1987; Paulus, 1984). It may also inhibit adjustment after release (Goodstein, 1979).

CONFINEMENT AND HEALTH

Some investigators have tried to compare the overall health status of residents in prison with comparable groups on the outside. One obvious problem with this approach is that it is difficult if not impossible to find an appropriate comparison group for prison inmates. Furthermore, prison inmates tend to have extremely high alcohol and drug abuse rates and to be in relatively poor health at the time of incarceration (Beck, Kline, & Greenfeld, 1988; Ostfeld et al., 1987). It is therefore not surprising that inmates appear to have higher rates of medical problems than do comparable populations outside of prison (Jones, 1976; Ostfeld et al., 1987). These rates may be inflated by the easy access to medical services in some prisons. In contrast, Greenfeld (1982) and Ruback and Innes (1988) find that prison inmates have lower mortality rates than comparison groups outside of prison. The limited availability of alcohol, drugs, weapons, and automobiles can be seen as major factors underlying these low mortality rates. Certainly, convincing evidence for poor inmate health due to prison confinement per se is lacking.

CONFINEMENT AND VIOLENCE

Violence is an aspect of prison life that has seen much attention by both scholars and the media (Sylvester, Reed, & Nelson, 1977). Sexual violence or threats are an ever-present problem in many jails and prisons (Ellis, 1984), and sexual violence appears to occur at a somewhat higher rate in prison than in the free world (Walker, 1983). This may be due in large part to the sexual deprivations that accompany prison confinement. Of course, violence level depends on the nature of the prison population and its management. In federal prisons, which are generally well-managed and have a low percentage of violent offenders, rates of sexual violence are lower than in state prisons (Nacci & Kane, 1984).

In state prisons, gangs may account for a high percentage of the violence (Ekland-Olson, 1986). Violence levels may also be elevated in jails where large numbers of inmates are housed together under conditions that limit monitoring of inmates by guards (Wener, Frazier, & Farbstein, 1987). Factors that disrupt prison routine rather than prison confinement in itself may be responsible for much of prison violence (Ellis, 1984). In the Texas prison system, changing from an inmate-based system of control to a guard-based one led to a temporary increase in violent incidents (Ekland-Olson, 1986). In Pontiac State Prison, Illinois, changing single cells to double cells led to a riot and destruction of prison buildings (Gibson & Smith, 1988).

CONFINEMENT AND SUICIDE

A number of studies suggest that suicide rates in prison may be higher than that in the free world (Hoff, 1973; Ruback & Innes, 1988; Topp, 1979). Suicides seem to be largely a reaction to the shock of being incarcerated since about 50% occur during the first 24 hours of incarceration (Anno, Harrison, & Rowan, 1983). Suicide rates are also higher for those who are awaiting trial than for those who are serving a sentence (Hankoff, 1980; Hoff, 1973), and suicides occur primarily among inmates housed in single cells (Anno, 1985; Gaston, 1979). It appears that prison suicide reflects a stress reaction to a major life change (incarceration) and an inmate's uncertain future (pretrial phase). In single cell housing, a prisoner is afforded a greater opportunity to carry out successful suicide than in housing where he or she can be more easily monitored by others. So far we have focused only on successful suicides. Rates of attempted suicides may be four or five times as high as suicide rates but they tend to follow the same pattern as suicides—much higher for pretrial than for posttrial inmates (Hoff, 1973).

CONFINEMENT AND CRIMINALIZATION

A common conception of prisons is that they serve as schools for crime (Walker, 1983). Demonstration of this idea would require the existence of higher rates of criminal activity by those sent to prison in comparison to comparable groups not sent to prison. Farrington (1977) found some evidence of this type, but it is quite possible that there were important differences between those sent to prison and those not sent that might account for these results (e.g., differences in family or job stability). Because of problems inherent in this type of comparison, there are simply no clear demonstrations of a crime-enhancing impact of imprisonment. There is some evidence that young inmates are somewhat more susceptible to social influence (Walker, 1983), and there might be more negative influence patterns with young populations. One study with young inmates did find that longer sentences were associated with more recidivism than shorter sentences (Wooldredge, 1988).

The idea that prisons strengthen the criminal orientation or attitude is consistent with much literature on polarization of attitudes in groups (Myers, 1982). This research has shown that groups of individuals who are similarly inclined in one direction on an issue tend to become more extreme in their feelings about the issue after group discussion. This type of strengthening of attitudes in groups has been found for a broad range of issues and has been related to the functioning of various groups (e.g., terrorist groups, McCauley & Segal, 1987). There appears to be no study that has directly examined the possible strengthening of the criminal attitude over the course of confinement. Of course, it could be argued that this attitude is already at an extreme level and little additional strengthening is possible with career criminals. It also would be difficult to get an accurate assessment of criminal attitudes because of self-presentational concerns. Criminal behavior is based to some extent on a value system that endorses such behavior. Therefore, it would seem important to evaluate the links between criminal attitudes and values and criminal behavior and to determine those factors in the prison environment that either reinforce or weaken these attitudes or values (Zastrow, 1988). It is interesting in this light that the movement to a bootcamp approach in corrections with some juveniles focuses on changing the attitudes of these young people toward themselves and toward criminal behavior (Gonzalez, 1989).

PERSONAL FACTORS IN REACTIONS TO CONFINEMENT

The general pattern of results on the impact of confinement suggests that prison confinement per se may not have particularly strong effects on inmate health and well-being. However, there appear to be certain individuals who are more affected by prison confinement than others (Ostfeld et al., 1987; Paulus, 1988). Higher education and socioeconomic levels are related to more negative reactions to prison environments. Inmates who have prior prison experience, who live in urban areas, and who come from large families react least negatively to prison confinement. Being in a numerical minority of some sort (racial, ethnic, or country of origin) is related to negative reactions (Ostfeld et al., 1987). In general, it appears that any characteristic that makes one prisoner somewhat different from the majority of the other inmates (e.g., education or racial/ethnic group) can result in elevated stress levels. These minority status inmates may find the social environment of the prison more uncertain or threatening and less supportive. Prior experience with living in crowded or modest environments (e.g., urban, large families, low socioeconomic level, prior prison history) may lead to an increased ability to tolerate or cope with prison crowding (Paulus, 1988).

Racial differences in adjustment to crowding have also been examined. Of course, racial/ethnic group is often confounded with the extent to which an inmate is in a numerical minority group in a particular prison. Clear assessments of the impact of racial/ethnic group independent of minority/majority status have not been done. Accordingly, it is not surprising that quantitative research on this issue has obtained quite varied results. Johnson (1976) found some evidence from interviews that urban Blacks adjust best and Hispanics most poorly to prison life. Urban Blacks may find prison life similar to the casual and unpredictable life in the urban ghetto. Hispanics place a strong premium on family ties and suffer much from the separation imposed by prison confinement. Hispanics tend to have relatively high rates of suicide in prisons (Johnson, 1976). Research in U.S. federal prisons has found little evidence for effects of race. However, in one prison near the Mexican border that held large numbers of Hispanic inmates, it was found that Mexican nationals reacted most positively, Anglo-Americans least positively, and Mexican-Americans in an intermediate fashion on measures of mood, environmental rating, illness, and blood pressure (Paulus, 1988).

Only a few studies have been done comparing male and female inmates. These indicate that women are somewhat more stressed than men in prisons in terms of illness, sleeping and headache problems, and blood pressure (Paulus, 1988).

Interpretation of these results on gender, race, and ethnic group is complicated by various factors. Without appropriate comparison with similar groups outside of prison, it is not known how much of the observed effect is due to differential reactions to confinement or to broad racial, ethnic, or gender differences across a wide variety of settings. Racial or ethnic group and gender may be confounded with numerical minority status or background differences. When such differences are controlled, observed effects may disappear or even be reversed. For example, in contrast to the studies suggesting high levels of stress for Hispanics in prison, when Hispanics are in a majority position in prison, they actually demonstrate low levels of stress (Paulus, 1988).

Although there has been some suggestion that prisons that house fairly homogeneous groups of prison inmates (along racial/ethnic lines) may yield less stress and conflict (Ostfeld et al., 1987), other research suggests that diversity along some dimensions may be positive. Prisons with mostly young inmates tend to be more violent than those that are designed to provide a mixture of younger and older inmates (Mabli, Holley, Patrick, & Walls, 1979). The older inmates may serve as stabilizing and controlling force for the younger inmates. Similarly, prisons in which both men and women are incarcerated may encourage more appropriate interpersonal and social behavior on the part of the inmates (Mabli et al., 1978).

ENVIRONMENTAL FACTORS IN CONFINEMENT

Security Level

One major fallacy in much of the work on prison confinement is the failure to relate findings clearly to the type of prison being studied. Horror stories about prisons are derived primarily from big maximum security prisons that hold large numbers of violent offenders (Jacobs, 1977; Sylvester et al., 1977) or over-crowded jails that provide little security (Wener et al., 1987). Yet there are many prisons that house inmates under much less onerous conditions. Some systems, such as those in Canada, The Netherlands, and New York, confine inmates only in single cells. Some prisons house primarily inmates who are of low risk to society and to others (minimum security). One would expect the stress-related effects of confinement to be more severe in highly crowded maximum security prisons than in uncrowded minimum security environments. From this perspective, it should be noted that none of the studies we have cited frequently as demonstrating few negative effects of long-term confinement were done in large, crowded maximum security state prisons that would be most stressful for the inmates. One study was limited to the relatively benign Canadian system in which inmates are provided single cells or rooms (Zamble & Porporino, 1988). The other studies were done in federal prisons (Paulus, 1988), a minimum security co-correctional facility (Paulus & Netherland, 1986), and a medium security state prison (Ostfeld et al., 1987).

Studies in U.S. prisons have found that higher security levels of prisons and of the inmates within a prison to be related to more negative environmental ratings and higher illness rates (Paulus, 1988). Similarly, inmates in jail cell-blocks that house mostly violent inmates appear to be more stressed than those in blocks that house nonviolent inmates (Paulus & McCain, 1983). Bukstel and Kilmann (1980), in their review of the confinement literature, note that with positive milieus and populations, the effects of confinement appear to be less negative. While some have argued that recidivism is relatively lower for inmates in such positive environments, inmates who qualify for such prisons should be somewhat more prone to change their ways.

Crowding

A major factor that has been shown to be associated with negative reactions to confinement is crowding. The problem of overcrowding in U.S. prisons and jails has reached crisis proportions. Forty-six states and territories are now involved in legal proceedings in regard to prison overcrowding (McConville, 1989). It is often argued in these cases that prison crowding violates constitutional protection from cruel and unusual punishment. Studies on the effects of crowding in prisons have generally supported arguments that it can indeed be harmful to the health and well-being of inmates (Cox, Paulus, & McCain, 1984; Ostfeld et al., 1987; Paulus, 1988). Paulus and his colleagues have found that overall crowding in prisons is related to elevations in disciplinary infractions, suicides, death rates, and psychiatric commitments.

Studies of inmates in particular housing units in prisons show that crowded prison housing is related to negative environmental ratings and mood states, as well as to elevated blood pressures, epinephrine and norepinephrine levels, and illness complaint rates. In particular, open dormitories with 20 or more inmates seem to be a source of stress. Double cells lead to negative ratings but not to negative physiological reactions. This research is based on an extensive 15-year effort involving visits to more than 60 prisons and jails, archival data from 5 different prison systems, and direct data from more than 4,000 inmates in jails and prisons across the full range of security levels. Other researchers have obtained similar results. In a detailed study of a medium security state prison, Ostfeld et al. (1987) found that dormitory living was related to elevated blood pressure and negative emotional reactions. Both Paulus (1988) and Ostfeld et al. (1987) found that inmates from urban residences showed less negative reactions to dormitory living and that movement to any new housing is associated with initial elevations in stress responses.

Once inmates are in a particular housing unit, various indices of stress, such as illness and blood pressure, decline over time. However, perception of housing remains unchanged (Paulus, 1988; Paulus & Netherland, 1986). Thus, while the environment continues to be perceived in a negative fashion, various health indices of stress decline.

THEORETICAL IMPLICATIONS

The data on prison confinement and crowding have presented an interesting puzzle. Why do inmates show adjustment or adaptation effects on some measures but not on others? Evaluation of the prison in general and feelings of hostility may become increasingly negative (or at least not decline) with increased time in prison, while a number of emotional and health dimensions indicate a lowering of stress level over time (Ostfeld et al., 1987; Paulus, 1988; Paulus & Netherland, 1986; Zamble & Porporino, 1988).

What accounts for this disparity in outcomes? Paulus and his colleagues have proposed a theoretical model that may be useful in understanding this state of affairs. They suggested that prison crowding involves three major elements: interference, cognitive load, and uncertainty. In crowded conditions, other inmates interfere with carrying out many activities in and outside of a prisoner's housing, and they increase competition for scarce resources (e.g., recreation, privacy, and lavatories). The presence of large numbers of inmates is a source of ever-present noise and social stimulation and interaction that has to be dealt with in some fashion (cognitive load). The basic unpredictability of these interactions and constant changes in housing, residents, and personnel provide for a high level of uncertainty. These three factors can combine to produce strong stress reactions.

Paulus (1988) has suggested that it is the uncertainty factor that is most likely to change over time and that this is the factor most strongly related to somatic stress reactions. He suggests that degree of cognitive load and interference play a predominant role in influencing perceptions of environments. Moreover, these perceptions are not likely to change over time because the degree of stimulation and interference is not likely to become more positive unless environmental conditions are improved. In other words, these are inevitable features of crowded prisons that are not easily changed by coping styles and that therefore are the basis for fairly consistent evaluations of environments. There may actually be increased sensitivity to these undesirable features of prison life with increasing length of confinement (Paulus, Cox, McCain, & Chandler, 1975), yielding increasingly negative reactions.

Uncertainty, on the other hand, is likely to change dramatically. Increased time in prison is characterized by increased familiarity with other inmates and with establishment of stable social contacts (Ostfeld et al., 1987; Zamble & Porporino, 1988). There is also presumably increased certainty about prison regulations and personnel. The strongly negative effects of living in large dormitories, moving to new housing, arriving in a prison, and getting ready to leave a prison can all be seen as reflecting high levels of uncertainty. As uncertainty is reduced and sense of control increases, stress levels and health related effects tend to decline (MacKenzie, Goodstein, & Blouin, 1987; Ostfeld et al., 1987; Paulus, 1988).

This perspective also explains the contradiction between conclusions drawn from interviewing inmates and those derived from more quantitative studies. Interviews focus on evaluations of problems of the prison environment. These evaluations are likely to be negative given the many deprivations of prison life that will not change much over time (Zamble & Porporino, 1988). The basic characteristics of the prison do not change. What does change is level of certainty, familiarity, and sense of control with increased time in prison (Figure 22.1). This level of certainty and control is of course disrupted by an impending release into the free world.

Herein lies the irony. It is probably true that prisons are basically unpleasant and adverse environments for most inmates. However, inmates may be able to learn to tolerate and cope with many of these negative features of the prison environment without changing their basic appraisal of the environment. There is much evidence in the crowding literature for such a process (Paulus & Nagar,

CONSTANT PRISON
CONDITIONS

Loss of freedom Potential for violence Limited facilities Limited programs Cognitive load Interference

→ STABLE NEGATIVE
EVALUATIONS

VARIABLE PRISON
CONDITIONS

Uncertainty Familiarity Predictability Perceived control

→ PHYSIOLOGICAL
CHANGES

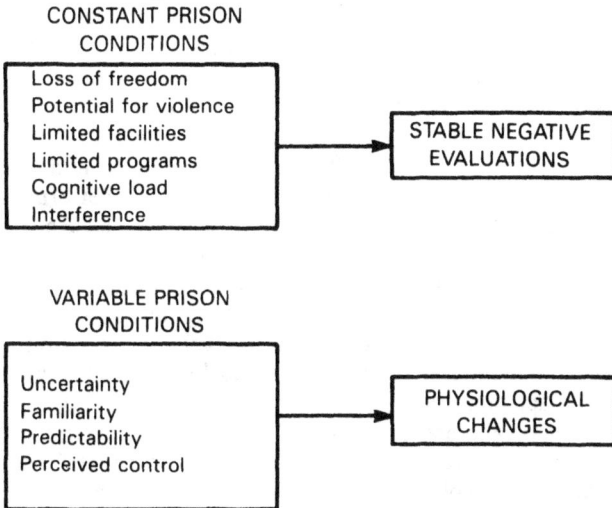

Figure 22.1   Some objectively negative prison conditions remain fairly constant over the period of typical incarceration. Therefore, subjective evaluations of these features of the environment are likely to remain fairly negative. In most cases, certainty, familiarity, predictability, and perceived control increase over the course of prison confinement but may decrease just prior to release. These changes may be responsible for the associated decrease and increase, respectively, of physiological indications of stress.

1987). However, while the evaluation of the environment remains a negative one, the increased familiarity, certainty, and sense of control over social interactions that typically accompany increased time in a prison and a prison housing unit are associated with reduction in stress-related indices. Furthermore, those individuals who are in a minority status and those who have little experience with prisons or crowded environments should have a more difficult time adjusting to the uncertainties of prison life.

It is therefore not surprising that considerable disparity exists between the subjective studies and writings and the more objective studies that use measures such as blood pressure and illness. We have found few people in prison and out who do not feel that imprisonment is an unpleasant condition. There are indeed significant pains and losses associated with prison confinement, no matter how pleasant the facility and its residents and personnel. Of course, these are exactly the costs that are intended by many of those who support imprisonment as a means of dealing with criminals. However, it appears that imprisonment has a negative impact on the health and emotional state of inmates primarily when there is a high level of uncertainty about the environment and its residents. This is particularly problematic in prisons where the potential for violent encounters is high. Also, to the extent that crowded and poorly managed prisons lead to high levels of violence, directly destructive effects of prison confinement are also observed.

POLICY IMPLICATIONS

What are the policy implications of this overview? We have found little to recommend prisons in terms of their impact on inmates. There is not much evidence for positive changes in prisoners, but there is also little evidence for negative changes. Short sentences may have some deterrent value, especially if they are given with some degree of certainty. The cost of incarcerating an inmate may be offset, to a large extent, by the savings of not having further crimes committed. Yet, in general, prisons do not seem to be effective change agents. Although prisons are perceived as rather unpleasant environments, they do not inevitably have detrimental effects on the health of inmates. It is primarily prisons that are crowded, filled with violent offenders, and poorly managed that appear to be related to various types of pathology and high levels of disruption and violence. There is a need for long-term studies of inmates living in such conditions to see whether strong adaptation effects still occur.

Those who support the use of prisons as a way for controlling crime will find comfort in the evidence that prisons may serve as a deterrent for some and may pay for themselves by keeping criminals off the street. We have not found strong objective evidence in support of those who oppose prisons on the basis of their presumed generally harmful effects. While it is possible that the balance of the evidence may change as a result of additional research that overcomes the limitations of some of the existing literature, there is considerable consistency in findings on a number of issues. Yet it would be shortsighted to focus on prisons as the primary solution to our crime problems. It represents a very costly solution and does not inhibit future criminal activity for most of its residents.

Few would quarrel with the need for incapacitation of violent or repeat offenders. The major issue is how to deal most effectively with juveniles, first offenders, and nonviolent repeat offenders. Since most of them return to society in less than 2 years only to commit further crimes, it would seem important to find ways to change the criminals' ways as well as taking them out of circulation for a short period of time. Many have argued that it is very difficult to encourage rehabilitation in a prison environment, but well-designed programs may be effective. Some evidence suggests that community-based corrections may be more effective in reducing recidivism than prison confinement (Wooldredge, 1988).

Much more definitive research is needed on various alternative programs in and out of prison. It also behooves us to address more seriously basic problems associated with crime—drug abuse, dysfunctional families, and lack of education and job skills. Yet, until we can convincingly demonstrate effective ways to change the criminal mind or attitudes, confining the criminal body for extended periods of time in humanely run uncrowded prisons can be justified on the basis of the evidence we have reviewed in this chapter.

REFERENCES

Anno, B. J. (1985). Patterns of suicide in the Texas Department of Corrections 1980–1985. *Journal of Prison and Jail Health, 5,* 82–93.
Anno, B. J., Harrison, B. P., & Rowan, J. R. (1983). *Recognizing and responding to medical emergencies and potential suicides.* Chicago, IL: National Commission on Correctional Health Care.

Beck, A. J., Kline, S. A., & Greenfeld, L. A. (1988). Survey of youths in custody, 1987. *The criminal justice archives and information network.* Washington, DC: U.S. Department of Justice, Bureau of Justice Statistics.

Blumstein, A., Cohen, J., & Nagin, D. (1978). *Deterrence and incapacitation: Estimating the effects of criminal sanctions on crime rates.* Washington, DC: National Academy of Sciences.

Brody, S. J. (1981). Review of effective correctional treatment. *British Journal of Criminology, 21,* 279–281.

Bukstel, L. H., & Kilmann, P. R. (1980). Psychological effects of imprisonment on confined individuals. *Psychological Bulletin, 88,* 469–493.

Cohen, S., & Taylor, L. (1972). *Psychological survival.* New York: Pantheon.

Cox, V. C., Paulus, P. B., & McCain, G. (1984). Prison crowding research: The relevance for prison housing standards and a general approach regarding crowding phenomena. *American Psychologist, 39,* 1148–1160.

Ekland-Olson, S. (1986). Crowding, social control, and prison violence: Evidence from the post-Ruiz years in Texas. *Law and Society Review, 20,* 389–421.

Ellis, D. (1984). Crowding and prison violence: Integration of research and theory. *Criminal Justice and Behavior, 11,* 277–308.

Farrington, D. P. (1977). The effects of public labelling. *British Journal of Criminology, 17,* 112–125.

Flanagan, T. J. (1980). The pains of long-term imprisonment. *British Journal of Criminology, 20,* 148–156.

Flanagan, T. J. (1981). Dealing with long-term confinement. *Criminal Justice and Behavior, 8,* 201–222.

Foster, R. W. (1981, November/December). New roads to justice: The alternatives to overcrowded prisons. *State Legislatures,* pp. 8–12.

Furby, L., Weinrott, M. R., & Blackshaw, L. (1989). Sex offender recidivism: A review. *Psychological Bulletin, 105,* 3–30.

Gaston, A. W. (1979). Prisoners. In L. D. Hankoff & B. Einsidler (Eds.), *Suicide: Theory and clinical aspects* (pp. 335–342). Littleton, MA: PSG.

Gendreau, P., & Ross, R. R. (1987). Revivification of rehabilitation: Evidence from the 1980's. *Justice Quarterly, 4,* 349–407.

Gibson, R., & Smith, W. (1988, July 18). Gangs lock Pontiac in a web of violence. *Chicago Tribune,* pp. 1–2.

Gonzalez, J. (1989, March 5). Life is hard, days are long in Texas' boot camp. *Fort Worth Star-Telegram,* pp. 1, 5.

Goodstein, L. (1979). Inmate adjustment to prison and the transition to community life. *Journal of Research in Crime and Delinquency, 16,* 246–272.

Gottfredson, M., & Hirschi, T. (1987). The methodological adequacy of longitudinal research on crime. *Criminology, 25,* 581–614.

Greenfeld, L. A. (1982). *Prison population and death rates.* Unpublished manuscript, National Institute of Justice, Washington, DC.

Greenfeld, L. A. (1985). *Examining recidivism* (Bureau of Justice statistics special report). Washington, DC: U.S. Department of Justice.

Greenfeld, L. A., & Langan, P. A. (1985). Characteristics of middle-aged prisoners. In D. P. Farrington & J. Gunn (Eds.), *Reactions to crime: The public, the police, courts, and prisons* (pp. 135–156). New York: Wiley.

Gunderson, E. K. E., & Rahe, R. H. (Eds.). (1974). *Life stress and illness.* Springfield, IL: Charles C Thomas.

Hankoff, L. D. (1980). Prisoner suicide. *International Journal of Offender Therapy and Comparative Criminology, 24,* 162–166.

Hoff, H. (1973). Prevention of suicide among prisoners. In B. L. Danto (Ed.). *Jail house blues: Studies of suicidal behavior in jail and prison* (pp. 203–214). Orchard Lake, MI: Epic Publications.

Homant, R. J., & Dean, D. G. (1988). The effect of prisonization and self-esteem on inmates' career maturity. *Journal of Offender Counseling, Services, & Rehabilitation, 12,* 19–40.

Jacobs, J. B. (1977). *Stateville: The penitentiary in mass society.* Chicago, IL: University of Chicago Press.

Johnson, R. (1976). *Culture and crisis in confinement.* Lexington, MA: Lexington Books.

Jones, D. A. (1976). *The health risks of imprisonment.* Lexington, MA: Lexington Books.

Klein, S. P., & Caggiano, M. N. (1986). *The prevalence, predictability, and policy implications of recidivism.* Santa Monica, CA: Rand.

Lacayo, R. (1989, May 29). Our bulging prisons. *Time,* pp. 28–31.

Mabli, J., Holley, C., Irons, D., Burkhead, J., Holley, P., & Turnball, C. (1978). Co-corrections evaluation: Preliminary data. *Offender Rehabilitation, 259,* 303–325.

Mabli, J., Holley, C., Patrick, J., & Walls, J. (1979). Age and prison violence: Increasing age heterogeneity as a violence-reducing strategy in prisons. *Criminal Justice and Behavior, 6,* 175–186.

Martinson, R. (1974). What works? Questions and answers about prison reform. *Public Interest, 35,* 22–54.

MacKenzie, D. L., Goodstein, L. I., & Blouin, D. C. (1987). Personal control and prisoner adjustment: An empirical test of a proposed model. *Journal of Research in Crime and Delinquency, 24,* 49–68.

McCauley, C. R., & Segal, M. E. (1987). Social psychology of terrorist groups. In C. Hendrick (Ed.), *Group processes and intergroup relations: Review of personality and social psychology* (vol. 9, pp. 231–256). Beverly Hills, CA: Sage.

McConville, S. (1989). Prisons held captive. *Contemporary Psychology, 34,* 928–929.

McCord, J. (1985). Deterrence and the light touch of the law. In D. P. Farrington & J. Gunn (Eds.), *Reactions to crime: The public, the police, courts, and prisons* (pp. 73–86). New York: Wiley.

Myers, D. G. (1982). Polarizing effects of social interaction. In H. Brandstatter, J. H. Davis, & G. Stocker-Kreichganer (Eds.), *Group decision making* (pp. 125–161). New York: Academic Press.

Nacci, P. L., & Kane, T. R. (1984). Inmate sexual aggression: Some evolving propositions, empirical findings, and mitigating counter-forces. *Journal of Offender Counseling, Services, & Rehabilitation, 9,* 1–20.

Ostfeld, A. M., & Kasl, S. V., D'Atri, D. A., & Fitzgerald, E. F. (1987). *Stress, crowding, and blood pressure in prison.* Hillsdale, NJ: Lawrence Erlbaum.

Palmer, T. (1983). The effectiveness issue today: An overview. *Federal Probation, 47,* 3–10.

Paulus, P. B. (1984). *Effects of crowding and confinement on inmates.* Washington, DC: National Institute of Justice.

Paulus, P. B. (1988). *Prison crowding: A psychological perspective.* New York: Springer-Verlag.

Paulus, P. B., Cox, V., McCain, G., & Chandler, J. (1975). Some effects of crowding in a prison environment. *Journal of Applied Social Psychology, 5,* 86–91.

Paulus, P. B., & McCain, G. (1983). Crowding in jails. *Basic and Applied Social Psychology, 4,* 89–107.

Paulus, P. B., & Nagar, D. (1987). Environmental influences on social interaction and group development. In C. Hendrick (Ed.), *Group processes and intergroup relations: Review of personality and social psychology* (vol. 9, pp. 68–90). Newbury Park, CA: Sage.

Paulus, P. B., & Netherland, N. (1986). *Stress of prison confinement in a co-correctional institution.* Unpublished research, University of Texas, Arlington, Texas.

Rasch, W. (1981). The effects of indeterminate detention: A study of men sentenced to life imprisonment. *International Journal of Law and Psychiatry, 4,* 417–431.

Ruback, R. B., & Innes, C. A. (1988). The relevance and irrelevance of psychological research. *American Psychologist, 43,* 683–693.

Sapsford, R. J. (1978). Life-sentence prisoners: Psychological changes during sentence. *British Journal of Criminology, 18,* 128–145.

Sommer, R. (1976). *The end of imprisonment.* New York: Oxford University Press.

Sykes, G. M. (1958). *The society of captives: A study of a maximum security prison.* Princeton, NJ: Princeton University Press.

Sylvester, S. F., Reed, J. H., & Nelson, D. O. (1977). *Prison homicide.* Jamaica, NY: Spectrum Publications.

Toch, H. (1975). *Men in crisis: Human breakdowns in prisons.* Chicago, IL: Aldine Publishing.

Toch, H. (1977). *Living in prison: The ecology of survival.* New York: Free Press.

Topp, D. O. (1979). Suicide in prison. *British Journal of Psychiatry, 134,* 24–27.

U.S. Department of Justice. (1987, October). Criminal victimization 1986. *Bureau of Justice Statistics Bulletin,* pp. 1–4.

U.S. Department of Justice. (1989, April). Prisoners in 1988. *Bureau of Justice Statistics Bulletin,* pp. 1–9.

Vita, M. (1989, May 7). Britain's aging prisons await help from modernization plan. *The Columbus Dispatch* (Columbus, OH), p. 12.

Walker, N. (1983). Side-effects of incarceration. *British Journal of Criminology, 23,* 61–71.

Wener, R., Frazier, W., & Farbstein, J. (1987). Building better jails. *Psychology Today, 21,* 40–49.

Wooldredge, J. D. (1988). Differentiating the effects of juvenile court sentences on eliminating recidivism. *Journal of Research in Crime & Delinquency, 25,* 264–300.

Wormith, J. S. (1984). The controversy over the effects of long-term incarceration. *Canadian Journal of Criminology, 26,* 423–439.

Zamble, E., & Porporino, F. J. (1988). *Coping, behavior, and adaptation in prison inmates.* New York: Springer-Verlag.

Zastrow, C. (1988). How to rehabilitate criminal offenders. *International Journal of Comparative and Applied Criminal Justice, 12,* 229–235.

Zedlewski, E. W. (1987). Making confinement decisions. In *National Institute of Justice.* Washington, DC: U.S. Department of Justice.

23

Coping with Prison

James Bonta and Paul Gendreau

During the past decade incarceration rates in the United States and Canada have increased dramatically. Particularly in the United States, where incarceration rates are three times greater than Canada and five times those of many other Western countries (Correctional Service of Canada, 1988), the increases have reached crisis proportions. Gibbons (1987) has observed that the number of inmates has outstripped available prison space to the point that prisons in the United States are operating at least at 110% of their optimal capacity. Furthermore, available prognostic indicators suggest no relief from these increases.

The high incarceration rates and the resulting prison overcrowding have produced considerable financial strains. Many states are also under court order to improve their prison facilities and/or build new prison beds. In 1989, President Bush requested more than one billion dollars from Congress in order to build an additional 24,000 prison beds (United States, 1989). Despite the allocation of large sums of money to build new prisons, it is unlikely that the additional beds will meet the existing demand.

Court interventions to reduce prison overcrowding and governmental requests to increase funding for prison construction have produced at least one benefit: Prisons have received more of the public's attention. Traditionally, prisons were closed environments largely ignored by the public. Now, because of the aforementioned costs and some sensational prison riots, prisons have come under public scrutiny. Along with this attention come the inevitable questions about what the role of prisons can and should be.

In this chapter, we examine the role of prisons within North America through consideration of three of the major expectations we have of prisons. They are:

1. Remove the dangerous from the community.
2. Deter the offender and others from continued criminal activity.
3. Provide rehabilitation under secure conditions.

We should note that prisons play roles other than those listed above. For example, prisons are intended to provide fair and just penalties for the crimes committed. Evaluating this function requires an extensive discussion of legal and ethical principles associated with punishment and the psychological effects of incarcera-

Authorship is alphabetical and the opinions expressed in this paper do not necessarily represent Solicitor General Canada policy.

tion. Reviews of these areas are available from other sources (Bonta & Gendreau, 1990; Rothman, 1980). Instead, we will turn our attention to the incapacitative, deterrent, and rehabilitative functions of prisons.

What we hope to demonstrate by examining these three functions is that, by and large, prisons have not been very successful in fulfilling their incapacitative and deterrent roles. That is, our burgeoning inmate populations are not simply a result of more criminals who require severe penalties to ensure that they conform or who are too dangerous to have freedom. This is not to say that all offenders pose a threat to the community; there certainly are many who do not.

Recent statistics (U.S. Department of Justice, 1987) indicate decreases in violent crimes and yet the prison population continues to grow. Much of the increase in the use of imprisonment is due to legislative and policy decisions of a conservative ideological bent that have not been based on empirical data (Currie, 1989). Our intent here is to bring research data into the forefront and link this to a more rational policy on imprisonment.

With respect to the third function of prisons, we hope to demonstrate that institutionally based programs can be viable when appropriate programming is provided. We will outline some general principles for effective treatment and discuss their implications for use within prisons.

PRISON VACANCY: ONLY THE MOST DANGEROUS NEED APPLY

Most penologists would agree that imprisonment should be reserved for those who commit the most serious crimes and, presumably, are the most likely to bring harm to the community. At time of sentencing, judges are guided by the principle of the least restrictive alternative to ensure that incarcerative sentences are used as the last resort. Theoretically at least, our prisons should house offenders who, if it were not for their confinement, would be committing offenses against the community. Are all inmates truly a threat to the community and do they therefore require physical control? Evidence related to the proportion of inmates who are dangerous comes from two areas: studies where the courts have released offenders and studies of offender classification research.

Court-ordered releases of prisoners provide estimates of the false positive error rates (i.e., predicted dangerous but, in fact, not dangerous). Many of these reports are of inmates judged by psychiatrists as dangerous and requiring incapacitation. Individual inmates and prisoner advocacy groups have challenged the state's decision to incarcerate individuals who *may* commit crimes and the successful challenges have resulted in court orders to release large numbers of prisoners.

For example, Johnnie Baxstrom was successful in his petition to the U.S. Supreme Court to overturn his placement in a hospital for the criminally insane. As a result, more than 900 other patients were transferred from hospitals for the criminally insane to regular psychiatric hospitals for eventual release. Steadman and Cocozza (1974) followed 98 of these offenders into the community (4 1/2 year follow-up). Only 14 were rearrested. That is, approximately four individuals were incarcerated in order to prevent one arrest.

The Steadman and Cocozza study is not alone in showing an unacceptably high rate of false positive errors. Thornberry and Jacoby (1979) found a 76.3% false positive rate for the "Dixon" patients and Steadman (1977) found a rate of 58.7% for the releasees of Patuxent Institution. Furthermore, these high rates are not restricted simply to the criminally insane. Kozol, Boucher, and Garofalo (1972) observed a 65% false positive rate for 435 sex offenders.

Perhaps the most convincing evidence pointing to our tendency to incarcerate offenders without much regard to the least restrictive alternative principle comes from classification research. Although overclassification (placement of offenders in custody settings beyond their needs) has long been suspected, strong evidence in support of this view has been lacking. Recently, two Canadian studies have provided the needed evidence. In the first study, Bonta and Motiuk (1987) reported that in a large detention center there were inmates who posed minimal risks to the community as assessed by an objective risk instrument but found that the existing subjective classification procedure identified just one-third of these inmates for halfway house placement. In a more recent study Bonta and Motiuk (1990) not only replicated the 1987 findings but also reported that the culprit in the overclassification of low-risk offenders appeared to be the correctional system's reliance on subjective risk assessments.

In light of these studies, we may conclude that the use of imprisonment is not reserved simply for the most dangerous offenders. Furthermore, reliance on subjective clinical assessments to make confinement decisions results in higher error rates. With objective risk assessments we may be able to minimize false positive errors and also place more inmates into the community. We can only speculate as to the costs saved by avoiding incarcerating those who pose little threat to the public.

PRISONS AS DETERRENTS

If prisons truly function as punishment, then imprisonment should suppress the reoccurrence of the offending behavior. It would seem to be a simple task to test the effectiveness of incarceration as a deterrent. However, testing this hypothesis is far from simple (Gendreau & Ross, 1981).

Assessing the effects of general incapacitation has been by two approaches. The first approach involves comparing the recidivism rates of incarcerated offenders to a matched group of offenders in a nonprison setting. The second approach examines the effect of imposing imprisonment and varied lengths of imprisonment upon recidivism. Using the first approach, a number of investigators have compared inmates to matched groups of probationers, parolees, and correctional halfway house residents. A sampling of the results, of these studies is shown in Table 23.1.

As shown in Table 23.1, there is little evidence that imprisonment has a deterrent effect when prisoners are compared to matched samples. In fact, a few studies (e.g., Bonta & Motiuk, 1987) even showed that incarceration was associated with an *increased* likelihood of recidivism.

The second approach is a reflection of the "get tough" political climate. The criminal justice system in North America appears to be relying more and more on mandatory incarceration policies and lengthier sentences to control recidivistic crime (Cullen & Gilbert, 1982). Once again, the empirical data seem to have had very little impact on correctional policy.

Although studies showing little or no relationship between the amount of inca-

Table 23.1 Imprisonment and Recidivism

		Recidivism rate (%)	
Study	Comparison sample	Prison	Comparison
Bonta & Motiuk (1987)	Halfway house residents		
	Sample 1	36.0	8.3*
	Sample 2	6.3	13.6
Bonta & Motiuk (1989)	Halfway house residents	12.7	10.7
Lamb & Goertzel (1974)	Halfway house residents	29.0	35.0
Vito & Allen (1981)	Probationers	17.0	12.0
Vito, Holmes, & Wilson (1985)	Probationers (first property offenders)	62.0	31.0*
Bohlander (1973)	Probationers	26.7	16.7*
Wheeler & Hissong (1988)	Probationers (first offenders)	8.0	14.0
	Probationers (prior convictions)	8.0	19.0
Dowell, Klein, & Krichmar (1985)	Female halfway house residents (mean # arrest)	1.8	0.9*

*$p = .001$.

pacitation and recidivism have long been available (e.g., Babst, Koval, & Neithercutt, 1972; Visher, 1987), it is disturbing that in 1987 an incapacitation policy was still advocated to control the crime rate (Zedlewski, 1987).

Many have recognized the problems inherent with general incapacitation and have argued that selective incapacitation may be more appropriate. Zedlewski (1987) has claimed, quite in error as it has turned out (Zimring & Hawkins, 1988), that approximately 10% of offenders each commit 600 crimes per year! The difficulty with selective incapacitation is identifying the offenders who are most likely to recidivate. As we have already noted, the present judicial and prison classification systems are not very precise in identifying minimum risk offenders, and there is no evidence to suggest they are any better with high risk offenders. Unfortunately, present selective incapacitation policies are largely based on the offense and these assessments produce poor results (Bonta & Motiuk, 1987).

LEARNING AND REHABILITATION IN PRISON

Thus far, our review has emphasized the failure of prisons to control crime through incapacitation. This does not mean that prisons do nothing. Prisons affect psychological and physiological functioning and fulfill a desire for justice (at least in the public's view). An often neglected yet important effect of incarceration is its influence on the learning of attitudes and behaviors. Certainly imprisonment forces intense associations with criminal others and exposure to antisocial attitudes and beliefs. Popular folklore holds that prisons are schools for crime. If so, there are important implications regarding recidivistic crime, and the crucial questions become: What aspect of criminality is learned in prison? and, What can be done to minimize such learning? The latter question addresses the issue of rehabilitation programs in prisons.

Attitudinal Learning

Clemmer (1940) introduced the concept of prisonization to describe a linear relationship between imprisonment and procriminal attitudinal development. The view was that prison, as a social system, fosters attitudes that both are unique to prison and are in opposition to staff expectations and beliefs (i.e., prosocial sentiments).

Wheeler (1961), however, argued for a U-shaped model, where there is a movement away from prisonization near the end of an inmate's sentence with the most marked deterioration of prosocial views in the middle of a sentence. He measured the degree of conformity to staff expectations among 237 inmates at different points in their sentences. Wheeler found that for inmates early and late in their sentences conformity to staff standards was relatively high, but it was low for inmates in the middle of their sentences. However, efforts to replicate these findings have yielded ambiguous findings (Akers, Hayner, & Gruninger, 1977; Atchley & McCabe, 1968; Troyer & Frease, 1975).

The independent variable in these studies, length of incarceration, was often viewed as sufficient to explain prisonization. The failure, however, to find consistency in the relationship between sentence served and prisonization indicated that prisonization is not a universal phenomenon, and sentence served is not a sufficient predictor of prisonization. What then are the other factors that may promote procriminal attitudinal changes? One of the most researched structural characteristics has been the custodial treatment typology of prisons.

Berk (1966) examined three minimum security settings differing with respect to their emphasis on treatment. He found that in the most custodial-oriented institution, 39% of the inmates expressed favorable attitudes toward the staff and the prison compared to 63% in the most treatment-oriented prison. Furthermore, these attitudes became more salient with increased lengths of time served.

Similar findings have been reported by Akers, Hayner, and Gruninger (1974, 1977) in a survey of more than 1,300 inmates in 22 prisons and 5 countries. Although prisonization effects varied as a function of the type of prison, it was the medium secure prisons and not the most repressive prisons that evidenced the clearest form of prisonization.

Another important variable is the individual. For example, Garabedian (1963) found that Wheeler's (1961) U-shaped model best fitted inmates described as "Square Johns," and the linear prisonization model best fitted "Outlaws." Since there appear to be individual variations in response to imprisonment, we need to consider individual characteristics present before incarceration.

Thomas and colleagues have examined individual attributes together with the fact of imprisonment. In a maximum security prison, prisonization was found to be mediated by post-prison expectations (Thomas, 1977; Thomas & Foster, 1972), community contact (Thomas & Foster, 1973), and social class (Thomas, 1973). Some of these results have been replicated with medium security felons (Thomas, 1975a) and young male offenders (Thomas & Zingraff, 1976).

Thomas' research supports the need to view prisons as partially open systems. The experiences and attributes of the offenders, the ongoing ties with the community, and expectations upon release all serve to moderate the prisonization experience. That is, factors outside the direct control of prison officials may play a more important role in prisonization than previously thought (Thomas, 1975b). This has important implications. For example, efforts to resocialize the offender may not be hampered so much by intraprison variables as by extraprison factors (Thomas, 1973).

Although studies have used sophisticated statistical analyses (e.g., path analysis, Thomas, 1977), they have been largely correlational. One study by Andrews (1980) did manipulate the membership composition and roles of groups experimentally within prison settings and found that variations in procriminal and prosocial attitudes followed. That is, inmates exposed to citizen volunteers discussing prosocial values showed decreases in procriminal attitudes and increases in prosocial attitudes. The Andrews (1980) study demonstrated the importance of attitudes and the feasibility of changing procriminal attitudes in a planned manner. That is, prison-based treatment programs focusing on attitudinal change are desirable. In fact, a study of such a treatment has been completed. Wormith (1984) evaluated a treatment program that in part focused on changing procriminal attitudes. He found not only reductions in these attitudes, but also reduced recidivism 3 years later.

Finally, before turning to rehabilitation programs in prisons, a comment on the role of self-esteem is necessary. Goffman (1961) and Sykes (1958) have described prisons as environments that strip away a man's self-concept and self-esteem. Incarceration deprives the offender of the material possessions and social support that serve to define the person's view of self that in turn affects self-esteem. To cope with threats to self-concept and self-esteem, it is hypothesized that inmates seek the company of each other, thereby forming a prison subculture with its own set of values. This collective response is thought not only to promote procriminal attitudes (i.e., prisonization) but also to facilitate the regaining of lost self-esteem through the establishment of a new and supportive social system.

Efforts to evaluate the role of self-concept and self-esteem have been plagued by unreliable measures (Eynon & Simpson, 1965), the phases of sentences have been unclearly defined (Hepburn & Stratton, 1977), and attrition has been a problem (Bennett, 1974). Furthermore, there has been little distinction between the terms self-concept (a personality construct consisting of attitudes, values, and beliefs about one's self) and self-esteem (the positive or negative evaluation of the self). Nevertheless, a number of tentative statements can be drawn from the studies completed.

First, not all inmates' self-esteem is equally affected by incarceration. Bennett (1974) tested 82 inmates at 6-month intervals over a period of 2 years and found that self-esteem increased for 36% of the inmates during the first 6 months and then leveled off. For 21% of the prisoners an inverted U-shape curve was found, and for the remainder of the sample there was a decreasing slope with respect to Self-Attitude Inventory scores or no change at all. Bennett's (1974) results, similar to the research on prisonization, indicated that individual differences are a potent determinant of self-esteem changes.

Culbertson (1975), employing a cross-sectional design, administered the Tennessee Self-Concept Scale to 222 male delinquents with varying lengths of incarceration (1 day to 550 days). In general, no change in self-concept was observed, but a more detailed analysis revealed different trends. First offenders showed a decrease while inmates with at least two previous incarcerations showed increasing self-concept scores. Hepburn and Stratton (1977) also found no general trends in self-esteem for 329 youthful prisoners. Unlike Culbertson (1975), however, prior incarceration was not related to self-esteem but did vary with the phase of an inmate's sentence.

Gendreau, Grant, and Lepciger (1979) conducted a 2-year follow-up of offenders serving their first prison sentence who were administered a self-esteem test at 6-month intervals. They found increases in self-esteem with offenders who expressed greater procriminal attitudes, and inmates in this category also had higher reincarceration rates 2 years after release from prison. Wormith (1984) reported an identical result with a 3-year post-prison follow-up.

In summary, the evidence does not support the conclusion that incarceration per se has negative consequences for self-concept and self-esteem. However, changes in attitudes along the attitudinal dimension (prosocial–procriminal) are likely. This is important since procriminal attitude formation may minimize the impact of rehabilitation programs (Zingraff, 1975). Thus, right from the start, efforts to rehabilitate inmates are hampered by the very fact of imprisonment.

Rehabilitation in Prison

In the preceding section, we asked the question, What is learned in prison? Briefly, the evidence suggest that for some offenders incarceration may continue the consolidation of procriminal attitudes and values that began prior to incarceration. In addition, for some, particularly those who may be considered low-risk or who have special needs (Bonta & Motiuk, 1987; Leschied, Austin, & Jaffe, 1988), the forced association with other inmates is likely to augment the formation of procriminal and antisocial attitudes. Indeed, the evidence is growing that the presence of procriminal attitudes and values is significantly associated with criminal behavior. Procriminal attitudes, values, and beliefs differentiate young offenders from nonoffenders (Shields & Ball, 1990), and these sentiments are predictive of future criminal conduct (Bonta, 1990). Also, knowledge of criminal sentiments provides information beyond that provided by criminal history information and personality (Andrews & Wormith, 1989).

The covariance of criminal sentiments with criminal behavior draws our attention to the importance of criminal sentiments as a target for treatment. Andrews, Bonta, and Hoge (1990) have described criminal sentiments as criminogenic, and therefore they are important treatment goals. Since incarceration may act to encourage the development of procriminal attitudes, prison-based treatment programs should offer interventions that counter this learning. Attitudes, however, need not be the only goals targeted by prison-based programs. Other worthy treatment targets are substance abuse, interpersonal problem-solving skills, and prosocial skill development. These are the typical treatment targets in many correctional programs, but we would like to emphasize the importance of prosocial and procriminal attitudes, especially in a prison setting.

Some researchers (Martinson, 1974, Whitehead & Lab, 1989) have lamented that correctional treatment programs are largely ineffective. In contrast, others (Gendreau & Ross, 1987; Palmer, 1975) have reached opposite conclusions after reviewing essentially the same literature. As Lipsey (1989) has pointed out, there is wide variability in the outcomes of treatment studies and, depending on where one looks, one may attend to different parts of the literature and reach different conclusions.

What is notably lacking in the evaluations of the treatment literature is a theoretical approach to correctional rehabilitation. Most reviewers simply code studies with respect to methodological rigor and perhaps setting factors. Rarely is there any questioning about why a treatment program is or is not effective (Cullen & Gendreau, 1989). A recent exception to this rule is the review by Andrews and colleagues (Andrews, Zinger, Hoge, Bonta, Gendreau, & Cullen, 1990).

The Andrews, Zinger, et al. (1990) review of the treatment literature carefully discriminated between appropriate and inappropriate correctional interventions. Appropriate correctional treatment was based on the principles of risk, need, and responsivity that were outlined in an earlier paper (Andrews, Bonta, & Hoge, 1990). An example of appropriate treatment might be providing intensive services to higher risk cases where these services target criminogenic needs and are delivered in a style and mode that is responsive to the individual characteristics of the clients.

Criminogenic needs include criminal attitudes, as already highlighted, along with substance abuse and lack of various prosocial skills. Examples of inappropriate treatments are services that fail to attend to the principles of risk, need, and responsivity. Many inappropriate treatments can be found in the criminal sanction literature (e.g., restitution, shock probation, and being "scared straight"), where sanctions are administered to offenders with little regard to their risk levels or needs.

Guided by this theoretical perspective on what constitutes appropriate correctional treatment, Andrews and colleagues found that, on average, appropriate treatment would reduce recidivism by 50%. Inappropriate treatment (e.g., criminal sanctions, mismatching of client to services) at best has negligible effects and at worst is associated with increases in recidivism.

The Andrews, Zinger, et al. (1990) review used the statistic phi to measure effects. For appropriate treatment, the average phi was .30. Of special interest to us in this chapter is their comparison of the effectiveness of treatment in the community and in institutional settings. Within community settings, the mean phi coefficient for appropriate treatment was .35. Within institutions, the mean phi was .20. Simply stated, the effectiveness of treatment programs within prisons is less than that of treatment programs carried out in the community. This is something we already expected from reviewing the attitudinal changes associated with imprisonment. It does not mean, however, that treatment within a prison setting is ineffective. After all, we must emphasize, $\phi = .20$ translates to approximately 30% reduction in recidivism.

Of considerable interest is the fact that inappropriate treatment programs carried out within institutions produced significantly more harmful effects than programs delivered in the community ($-.15$ versus $-.04$). Almost all of the treatment programs within prisons that produced reductions in recidivistic behavior were behavioral programs. The studies ranged from family counseling (Barton, Alexander, Waldron, Turner, & Warburton, 1985), the use of paraprofessionals (Ross & McKay, 1977), skill training (Sarason & Ganzer, 1973), individual programs (Jesness, 1975), token economies (Phillips, Phillips, Fixen, & Wolf, 1973), and group counseling (Grant & Grant, 1959).

It is of concern that only a few of the prison treatment studies (e.g., Ross, Fabiano, & Ewles, 1988) specifically targeted procriminal attitudes. Most of these interventions endeavored to alter ties to criminal others and to promote prosocial skills. Although it is likely that attitudes and beliefs change along with behaviors in these other areas, we as yet have no evidence of this. We are left without evidence as to how much we can increase our effectiveness with inmates if we also target their antisocial attitudes.

CONCLUSIONS

In North America, we have the highest incarceration rates in the Western world. Within the context of the present policies emphasizing incapacitation, the enormous prison population will not simply go away. Such extensive use of imprisonment may be justified if it is used to incarcerate chronic offenders, or if it deters offenders, or if it provides effective rehabilitation programs. However, courts for various reasons do not imprison only the worst offenders nor does incarceration per se appear to affect recidivism.

With respect to rehabilitation, the results justify cautious optimism. Treatment programs that carefully incorporate the principles of risk, need, and responsivity have been shown to be effective in reducing recidivism. Not all prison-based treatment programs, unfortunately, are so designed. In the Andrews, Zinger, et al. (1990) review, there were many inappropriate programs that produced, perhaps influenced by a prisonization process, results that were worse than anticipated.

In our opinion, it is very important for those who have knowledge of the empirical data to transmit this information to the legislators and policy makers. Effective correctional policy needs informed guidance. In fact, there is evidence to suggest that policy makers are misreading public opinion. Survey data (e.g., Cullen, Skovron, Scott, & Burton, 1990), even in conservative U.S. jurisdictions, discover that citizens still feel strongly that rehabilitation should be the main emphasis of prisons. Protecting society was ranked second. The onus is on us to inform.

REFERENCES

Akers, R. L., Hayner, N. S., & Gruninger, W. (1974). Homosexual and drug behavior in prison: A test of the functional and importation models of the inmate system. *Social Problems, 21,* 410–422.

Akers, R. L., Hayner, N. S., & Gruninger, W. (1977). Prisonization in five countries: Type of prison and inmate characteristics. *Criminology, 14,* 527–554.

Andrews, D. A. (1980). Some empirical investigations of the principles of differential association through deliberate manipulations of the structure of service systems. *American Sociological Review, 45,* 448–462.

Andrews, D. A., Bonta, J., & Hoge, R. D. (1990). Classification for effective rehabilitation: Rediscovering psychology. *Criminal Justice and Behavior, 17,* 19–52.

Andrews, D. A., & Wormith, J. S. (1989). Personality and crime: Knowledge destruction and construction in criminology. *Justice Quarterly, 6,* 289–309.

Andrews, D. A., Zinger, I., Hoge, R. D., Bonta, J., Gendreau, P., & Cullen, F. (1990). Does correctional treatment work? A clinically relevant and psychologically informed meta-analysis. *Criminology, 28,* 369–404.

Atchley, R. C., & McCabe, P. M. (1968). Socialization in correctional communities: A replication. *American Sociological Review, 33,* 774–785.

Babst, D. V., Koval, M., & Neithercutt, M. G. (1972). Relationship of time served to parole outcome for different classifications of burglars based on male paroles in fifty jurisdictions in 1968 and 1969. *Journal of Research in Crime and Delinquency, 9,* 99–116.

Barton, C., Alexander, J. F., Waldron, H., Turner, C. W., & Warburton, J. (1985). Generalizing treatment effects of functional family therapy: Three replications. *American Journal of Family Therapy, 13,* 16–26.

Bennett, L. A. (1974). The application of self-esteem measures in a correctional setting: II. Changes in self-esteem during incarceration. *Journal of Research in Crime and Delinquency, 11*, 9–15.

Berk, B. B. (1966). Organizational goals and inmate organization. *American Journal of Sociology, 71*, 522–534.

Bohlander, E. (1973). *Shock probation: The use of and effectiveness of an early release alternative.* Columbus, Ohio: Doctoral dissertation, Ohio State University.

Bonta, J. (1990, June). *Antisocial attitudes and recidivism.* Paper presented at the Annual Conference of the Canadian Psychological Association, Ottawa, Canada.

Bonta, J., & Gendreau, P. (1990). Re-examining the cruel and unusual punishment of prison life. *Law and Human Behavior, 14*, 347–372.

Bonta, J., & Motiuk, L. L. (1987). The diversion of incarcerated offenders to correctional halfway houses. *Journal of Research in Crime and Delinquency, 24*, 302–323.

Bonta, J. L., & Motiuk, L. L. (1989). *The LSI in institutions: Classification and one year recidivism.* Toronto: Ministry of Correctional Services.

Bonta, J., & Motiuk, L. L. (1990). Classification to halfway houses: A quasi-experimental evaluation. *Criminology, 28*, 497–506.

Clemmer, D. (1940). *The prison community.* New York: Rinehart.

Correctional Service of Canada. (1988). *Basic Facts About Corrections in Canada 1988* (Catalogue No. JS 12-17). Ottawa: Minister of Supply & Services, Canada.

Culbertson, R. G. (1975). The effect of institutionalization on the delinquent inmate's self-concept. *Journal of Criminal Law and Criminology, 66*, 88–93.

Cullen, F. T., & Gendreau, P. (1989). The effectiveness of correctional rehabilitation: Reconsidering the "nothing works" doctrine. In L. Goodstein & D. L. MacKenzie (Eds.), *The American prison: Issues in research policy* (pp. 23–44). New York: Plenum.

Cullen, F. T., & Gilbert, K. E. (1982). *Reaffirming rehabilitation.* Cincinnati, OH: Anderson.

Cullen, F. T., Skovron, S. E., Scott, J. E., & Burton, V. S. (1990). Public support for correctional treatment: The tenacity of rehabilitative ideology. *Criminal Justice and Behavior, 17*, 6–18.

Currie, E. (1989). Confronting crime: Looking toward the twenty-first century. *Justice Quarterly, 6*, 5–25.

Dowell, D. A., Klein, C., & Krichmar, C. (1985). Evaluation of a halfway house for women. *Journal of Criminal Justice, 13*, 217–226.

Eynon, T. G., & Simpson, J. E. (1965). The boy's perception of himself in a state training school for delinquents. *Social Service Review, 39*, 31–37.

Garabedian, P. G. (1963). Social roles and processes of socialization in the prison community. *Social Problems, 11*, 139–152.

Gendreau, P., Grant, B. A., & Lepciger, M. (1979). Self-esteem, incarceration, and recidivism. *Criminal Justice and Behavior, 6*, 67–75.

Gendreau, P., & Ross, R. R. (1981). Correctional potency: Treatment and deterrence on trial. In R. Roesch & R. R. Corrado (Eds.), *Evaluation and criminal justice policy* (pp. 29–57). Beverly Hills, CA: Sage.

Gendreau, P., & Ross, R. R. (1987). Revivification of rehabilitation: Evidence from the 1980s. *Justice Quarterly, 4*, 349–408.

Gibbons, D. C. (1987). *Society, crime, and criminal behavior.* Englewood Cliffs, NJ: Prentice–Hall.

Goffman, E. (1961). *Asylums: Essays on the social situation of mental patients and other inmates.* Garden City: NJ: Anchor.

Grant, J. D., & Grant, M. O. (1959). A group dynamics approach to the treatment of conformists in the navy. *Annals of the American Academy of Political and Social Science, 322*, 126–135.

Hepburn, J. R., & Stratton, J. F. (1977). Total institutions and inmate self-esteem. *British Journal of Criminology, 17*, 237–250.

Jesness, C. F. (1975). Comparative effectiveness of behavior modification and transactional analysis programs for delinquents. *Journal of Consulting and Clinical Psychology, 43*, 758–779.

Kozol, H., Boucher, R., & Garofalo, R. (1972). The diagnosis and treatment of dangerousness. *Crime and Delinquency, 18*, 371–392.

Lamb, R. H., & Goertzel, V. (1974). Ellsworth house: A community alternative to jail. *American Journal of Psychiatry, 131*, 64–68.

Leschied, A. W., Austin, G. A., & Jaffe, P. G. (1988). Impact of the Young Offenders Act on recidivism rates of special needs youth: Clinical and policy implications. *Canadian Journal of Behavioural Science, 20*, 322–331.

Lipsey, M. W. (1989). *Juvenile delinquency treatment: A meta-analytic inquiry into the variability of effects* (Research Synthesis Committee of the Russell Sage Foundation). Claremont Graduate School.

Martinson, R. (1974). What works? Questions and answers about prison reform. *The Public Interest, 35*, 22-54.

Palmer, T. (1975). Martinson revisited. *Journal of Research in Crime and Delinquency, 12*, 133-152.

Phillips, E. L., Phillips, E. A., Fixen, D. L., & Wolf, M. W. (1973). Achievement place: Behavior shaping works for delinquents. *Psychology Today, 6*, 75-79.

Ross, R. R., Fabiano, E. A., & Ewles, C. D. (1988). Reasoning and rehabilitation. *International Journal of Offender Therapy and Comparative Criminology, 32*, 29-35.

Ross, R. R., & McKay, H. B. (1977). A study of institutional treatment programs. *International Journal of Offender Therapy and Comparative Criminology, 21*, 165-173.

Rothman, D. J. (1980). *Conscience and convenience: The asylum and its alternatives in progressive America*. Boston: Little, Brown.

Sarason, I. G., & Ganzer, V. J. (1973). Modeling and group discussions in the rehabilitation of juvenile delinquents. *Journal of Counseling Psychology, 20*, 442-449.

Shields, I. W., & Ball, M. (1990, June). *Neutralization in a population of incarcerated young offenders*. Paper presented at the Annual Conference of the Canadian Psychological Association, Ottawa, Canada.

Steadman, H. (1977). A new look at recidivism among Patuxent inmates. *The Bulletin of the American Academy of Psychiatry and the Law, 5*, 200-209.

Steadman, H. J., & Cocozza, J. J. (1974). *Careers of the criminally insane: Excessive social control of deviance*. Lexington, MA: Lexington Books.

Sykes, G. (1958). *The society of captives: A study of a maximum security prison*. Princeton, NJ: Princeton University Press.

Thomas, C. W. (1973). Prisonization or socialization? A study of external factors associated with the impact of imprisonment. *Journal of Research in Crime and Delinquency, 10*, 13-21.

Thomas, C. W. (1975a). Theoretical perspectives on alienation in the prison society: An empirical test. *Pacific Sociological Review, 18*, 483-499.

Thomas, C. W. (1975b). *The importation and deprivation model perspectives on prisonization: A comparison of their relative importance*. Paper presented to the Society for the Study of Social Problems, San Francisco.

Thomas, C. W. (1977). Prisonization and its consequences: An examination of socialization in a coercive setting. *Sociological Focus, 10*, 53-68.

Thomas, C. W., & Foster, S. C. (1972). Prisonization in the inmate contraculture. *Social Problems, 20*, 229-239.

Thomas, C. W., & Foster, S. C. (1973). The importation model perspective on the inmate social roles: An empirical test. *The Sociological Quarterly, 14*, 226-234.

Thomas, C. W., & Zingraff, M. T. (1976). Organizational structure as a determinate of prisonization: An analysis of the consequence of alienation. *Pacific Sociological Review, 19*, 98-116.

Thornberry, T. P., & Jacoby, J. E. (1979). *The criminally insane: A community follow-up of mentally ill offenders*. Chicago, IL: University of Chicago Press.

Troyer, J. G., & Frease, D. E. (1975). Attitude change in a western Canadian penitentiary. *Canadian Journal of Criminology and Corrections, 17*, 250-262.

United States. (1989, July/August). President Bush proposes new anticrime measures. *National Institute of Justice Reports, 215*, 7.

U.S. Department of Justice. (1987, November). *Violent crime trends*. Washington, DC: Bureau of Justice Statistics.

Visher, C. A. (1987). Incapacitation and crime control: Does a "lock 'em up" strategy reduce crime? *Justice Quarterly, 4*, 514-543.

Vito, G. F., & Allen, H. E. (1981). Shock probation in Ohio: A comparison of outcomes. *International Journal of Offender Therapy and Comparative Criminology, 25*, 70-76.

Vito, G. F., Holmes, R. M., & Wilson, D. G. (1985). The effect of shock and regular probation upon recidivism: A comparative analysis. *American Journal of Criminal Justice, 9*, 152-162.

Wheeler, S. (1961). Socialization in correctional communities. *American Sociological Review, 26*, 697-712.

Wheeler, G. R., & Hissong, R. V. (1988). Effects of criminal sanctions on drunk drivers: Beyond incarceration. *Crime and Delinquency, 34*, 29-42.

Whitehead, J. T., & Lab, S. P. (1989). A meta-analysis of juvenile correctional treatment. *Journal of Research in Crime and Delinquency, 26*, 276-295.

Wormith, J. S. (1984). Attitude and behavior change of correctional clientele: A three year follow-up. *Criminology, 22,* 595–618.

Zedlewski, E. W. (1987). Research in brief: Making confinement decisions. *National Institute of Justice research in brief.* Washington, DC: National Institute of Justice.

Zimring, F. E., & Hawkins, G. (1988). The new mathematics of imprisonment. *Crime and Delinquency, 34,* 425–436.

Zingraff, M. T. (1975). Prisonization as an inhibitor of effective resocialization. *Criminology, 13,* 366–388.

Name Index

Subject Index

Advocacy, 3-10, 71-72, 99-100, 313-320
Affirmative action, 121-132, 137-146
Age, 95-97
Aggressive behavior:
  learning theory and, 181, 208-209
  measurement problems, 180, 192
  prison confinement and, 331-332
  scripts for, 209-210
  television and, 179-187, 191-199, 209, 210, 218
  war environment and, 215-216
  weapons availability and, 201-219
American Booksellers Association, 152, 155, 156
American Civil Liberties Union, 152, 155, 167
American Psychological Association (APA), 256, 263-264
Amnesia, stress-induced, 287-288
Anger, 72
Antisatellite weapons (ASAT), 74
Antisocial behavior, 165-169, 173-175, 212-213
Anxiety, 214, 215, 329
Appeasement, 76
Arms control negotiations, 75
Assault weapons, 238
Attitudinal changes, from exposure to pornography, 168, 174, 175
Attorney General's Commission on Pornography (1986), 153-155, 166-167, 170-172, 175-176
Availability, 63-64, 75

Behavioral change, 100, 101, 169, 172-175
Bias, 57-58, 64, 185, 193-196
Boose v. Digate, 277
Buffer territory, 77

Capital punishment, 243-254
Category distinctiveness, 127, 129
Censorship, 150, 158-159, 168
Child sexual abuse, 175
Civil rights, 152, 159
Cognitive complexity, 72, 78
Cognitive distortion, 96, 97, 99
Cognitive error, 59-60
Cognitive function, prison confinement and, 330-331
Cognitive priming effect, 160
Cognitive rules, 53
Collaboration, interdisciplinary, 71
Collective resistance, 97
Commission on Obscenity and Pornography (1970), 150, 151, 165-167
Complex decision rules, 33, 35-36, 48
Comprehensive test ban (CTB), 75
Confidence-building measures, 75
Confinement, 327-338
Conflict-resolution workshops, 72
Conservatives, 152-153, 167
Constitution, U.S., 250
Control question tests, 297-302
Controversy, 7-9, 283, 315-316
Conventional forces in Europe (CFE), 75
Cooperative workshops, 130, 132
Coping, in prison, 331, 333, 336
Criminalization, 332-333
Crises, 72-76
Crisis-induced stress, 87-88
Crowding in prison, 327, 333-338
Cuban Missile Crisis, 78
Cumulative developmental effects, 182, 196-197

Dangerousness, 344
Death penalty, 243-263

For Product Safety Concerns and Information please contact our EU
representative GPSR@taylorandfrancis.com
Taylor & Francis Verlag GmbH, Kaufingerstraße 24, 80331 München, Germany

www.ingramcontent.com/pod-product-compliance
Lightning Source LLC
Chambersburg PA
CBHW070542270326
41926CB00013B/2172

9 781138 984073